FROM EASTERN BLOC TO EUROPEAN UNION

Studies in Contemporary European History

Editors:

Konrad Jarausch, Lurcy Professor of European Civilization, University of North Carolina, Chapel Hill, and a Director of the Zentrum für Zeithistorische Studien, Potsdam, Germany

Henry Rousso, Senior Research Fellow at the Institut d'histoire du temps présent (Centre national de la recherche scientifique, Paris)

For a full volume listing, please see back matter

FROM EASTERN BLOC TO EUROPEAN UNION

Comparative Processes of Transformation since 1990

Edited by
Günther Heydemann and
Karel Vodička

berghahn
NEW YORK · OXFORD
www.berghahnbooks.com

Published in 2017 by
Berghahn Books
www.berghahnbooks.com

English-language edition © 2017, 2020 Berghahn Books
Original German-language edition © Vandenhoeck & Ruprecht GmbH & Co. KG,
Günther Heydemann and Karel Vodička (Eds.): *Vom Ostblock zur EU*, Göttingen, 2013
First paperback edition published in 2020

Library of Congress Cataloging-in-Publication Data
Names: Heydemann, Günther, 1950-, editor of compilation. | Vodička, Karel,
1949-, editor of compilation.
Title: From Eastern Bloc to European Union : comparative processes of
transformation since 1990 / edited by Günther Heydemann and Karel Vodička.
Other titles: Vom Ostblock zur EU. English
Description: New York : Berghahn Books, [2017] | Series: Contemporary
European history ; volume 22 | Originally published: Göttingen :
Vandenhoeck & Ruprecht, 2013. | Includes bibliographical references and
index.
Identifiers: LCCN 2017014722 (print) | LCCN 2017024966 (ebook) | ISBN
9781785333187 (e-book) | ISBN 9781785333170 (hardback : alk. paper)
Subjects: LCSH: Post-communism--Europe. | Europe, Eastern--Politics and
government--1989- | Europe, Central--Politics and government--1989- |
Europe, Eastern--Relations--European Union countries. | Europe,
Central--Relations--European Union countries. | European Union
countries--Relations--Europe, Eastern. | European Union
countries--Relations--Europe, Central. | Democracy--Europe, Eastern. |
Democracy--Europe, Central.
Classification: LCC DJK51 (ebook) | LCC DJK51 .V62513 2013 (print) | DDC
341.242/20947--dc23
LC record available at https://lccn.loc.gov/2017014722

British Library Cataloguing in Publication Data
A catalogue record for this book is available from the British Library

ISBN 978-1-78533-317-0 hardback
ISBN 978-1-78920-821-4 paperback
ISBN 978-1-78533-318-7 ebook

CONTENTS

FIGURES AND TABLES

Figures

Tables

PREFACE

Vladimír Špidla, former Prime Minister of the Czech Republic and former EU Commissioner

I read this volume on the transformation of the new, Eastern EU countries with fascination, for a number of reasons. First of all, as an active politician, I had had the opportunity to participate in the process of the Czech Republic becoming a member of the EU. I took part in dozens of fundamental decisions and experienced a lot of necessary, radical changes that worked deep changes in our society. I found it extremely interesting to look back at this process from a neutral, scientific point of view.

The transformation processes were connected to fundamental change in laws and institutions. Somewhat exaggeratedly, when setting our government's agenda we called that a 'legislative storm'. Reading this volume once again reminded me of how special and complex this transformation process has been and still is. The transformation was doubtless due to the enormous efforts of the government, that is, the subsequent governments and parliaments that changed the entire structure of society step by step. It is fascinating to realize how few people were actively involved in the transformation at the political level. Meanwhile, huge numbers of people had to adjust actively, as did enterprises and non-governmental organizations.

Quite confirming the results of this study, I see the crucial aspects of the entire development process after 1989 as awareness of moving towards the European Union and knowledge of EU structures and practices. In the political and social awareness of East Central and South Eastern European countries, however, the crucial moment was not the start of the accession talks but the fall of the Iron Curtain. From that moment, the direction was obvious. The actual start of the process of EU accession was just the formal confirmation of an almost continuous running development.

The constitutive power of the process of moving towards the EU – particularly the great eastward EU enlargement known as the Big Bang – held enormous significance for individual states' internal development and was also essential to stabilizing the entire region. Without the beacon of EU accession, further development of the systems would have been much more complicated, and we would have expected escalation to an inestimable extent. In my opinion, the systemic development would at best have been comparable to that in the Balkans. The outcome would have been completely open-ended, like the configurations of the newly developing political structures in the countries concerned. Although comparability is certainly limited, one might identify parallels to the 1930s that clearly show that no variant – not even an extremely radical one – could have been ruled out.

The move towards the EU that so clearly characterized the transformation of East Central and South Eastern European countries went smoothly. Even though only a relatively small group of actors actively contributed to the process, this move may be seen as based on a broad, if passive support from the majority of the populations. Therefore I affirm this study's conclusion that the process of integration into the EU has proved an essential part of system transformation in the region and offered the guarantee of a comparably quiet development.

In those countries joining the EU, of course, the European example exerted a valuable influence on the development of institutional structures and democratic cultures. In particular, these states had the opportunity to compare their components to functioning institutions and thus to assess the possible consequences of certain decisions – an important advantage in the hands of the politicians who shaped the transformation. At the same time, political responsibility was an extraordinary personal burden at that strategic level, precisely because those bearing responsibility were aware of not only the consequences of their actions but also the considerable risk of adverse outcomes of their decision-making. Their ability to refer to observations and comparisons was thus particularly significant. Sustainable support from both European institutions and individual member states was a critical element of the transformation processes. It enabled policy-makers to gain a deeper, more thorough understanding of how individual processes were functioning, to set the right priorities and, finally, to create a comparably extended network of personal and political relations.

In the end, the entire process of system change was frequently successful, as demonstrated by the new EU countries' smooth integration into the European legal system as well as the EU's decision-making and institutional systems. During my tenure as an EU Commissioner, I observed that when it came to the number of proceedings concerning violations of European law, there was no quantitative difference between new and old EU countries.

This collection makes another significant contribution by providing evidence that the transformation processes happened differently in each individual country, despite a number of commonalities. It documents a variety of differences that are mostly due to historical constellations and historically grown structures, and makes clear that the new members of the EU, far from showing the same structures, display certain differences that will also be there in the future. Differences between social traditions in individual countries are especially obvious. Although several social systems were much more similar than we expected, there remain significant divergences, particularly concerning traditions and the perception of certain concrete measures. As an EU Commissioner, I was somewhat surprised at how differently some decisions were perceived. For example, some countries or groups of countries regarded certain family-political decisions as just, whereas others saw them as unjust. This variety, so convincingly documented by the present study, is a phenomenon that no politician at the European level should ever forget.

Meanwhile, the transformation's trend towards homogenization of political structures and political cultures with the EU core countries seems obvious and probably irreversible. Yet we should not rely too heavily on this conclusion, because some developments in single countries indicate an awakening of political trends traceable to pre-communist times. It must be emphasized that in some countries, authoritative regimes were not connected to communist dictatorships alone but also referred to older traditions. This fact influenced the course and results of transformation.

Certainly, the road to fully working democracy will be neither direct nor easy, and we must expect a variety of setbacks. However, this volume's comparison of individual country reports shows convincingly that system transformation towards classical democracy is the predominant and crucial direction. We must expect occasional defeats and single setbacks, but on the whole the journey towards functioning democracy has begun. To be sure, the speed of transformation depends on factors such as historical traditions and historical memories. A country's geographic location matters too, as does its size – certainly Estonia requires other methods and approaches than the much larger Czech Republic, for example.

Another very important aspect of the present volume is that it deals with transformation processes as such, giving specific examples in specific fields to an extent sufficient to reach valid conclusions. One of its most important findings, in my view, is that the overall course of the deep social transformation will take many years, even if it happens relatively fast.

Probably a realistic period of time is one generation, which in the demographic context of Europe means about twenty-five to thirty years. This is particularly significant given that the modern society is one of deep, lasting change. Yet even if these changes are as radical as may be imagined, they will still likely take only about one generation.

Democratic politics thus faces the essential task of maintaining a long-term consensus – a challenge made all the more difficult by the absence of a master plan or blueprint for processes of social transformation. Instead of such a plan, one must assume that over the course of time, a great many components of the construction underway will have to be reassessed again and again. One example of this interesting and, in my opinion, fundamental transformation is the energy transition in the Federal Republic of Germany. There, too, it should be expected to take at least one generation and require reassessment of some partial aspects as well as some approaches. Achieving long-term consensus will be vital to successfully concluding the overall process.

In providing a comparative understanding of the transformation processes in East Central and South Eastern Europe, the present volume is doubtless not only a compelling intellectual work but also an important resource for political decision-makers across the European Union, both at EU institutions and in individual member states. Regardless of differences in the various EU countries' cultural and political substance, their similarities are nonetheless sufficient to offer insights that might serve the common good.

ABBREVIATIONS

AWS, Election Action Solidarity (Akcja Wyborcza Solidarność)
BKP, Bulgarian Communist Party (Balgarska kommuniticeska
   partija)
BSP, Bulgarian Socialist Party (Balgarska socialisticeska partija)
BTI, Bertelsmann Transformation Index
CDU, Christian Democratic Union (Christlich-Demokratische Union)
COMECON, Council for Mutual Economic Assistance
CPLit, Communist Party of Lithuania
ČSSD, Czech Social Democratic Party (Česká strana sociálně
   demokratická)
ČSSR, Czechoslovakian Socialist Republic (Československá socialistická
   republika)
CSU, Christian Social Union (Christlich Soziale Union)
DPS, Movement for Rights and Liberties (Dvizenie sa Prava i Svobodi)
FIDESZ, Alliance of Young Democrats (Fiatal Demokraták Szövetsége)
GDP, gross domestic product
GDR, German Democratic Republic
GERB, Citizens for European Development in Bulgaria (Grazdani za
   evropejsko razvitie na Balgarija)
GNP, gross national product
HAIT, Hannah-Arendt-Institut für Totalitarismusforschung
HZDS, Movement for a Democratic Slovakia (Hnutie za demokratické
   Slovensko)
IMF, International Monetary Fund
JL, New Era (Jaunais Laiks)
KDH, Christian Democratic Movement (Krest'anskodemokratické
   hnutie)
KDNP, Christian Democratic People's Party (Kereszténydemokrata
   Néppárt)

KNAB, anti-corruption bureau (Korupcijas novēršanas un apkarošanas birojs)

KOZ, Confederation of Trade Unions (Konfederácia odborových zväsov)

KPL, Communist Party of Latvia (Latvijas Komunistiskā Partija)

KRRiT, National Broadcasting Council (Krajowa Rada Radiofoni i Telewizji)

LC, the Latvian Way (Latvijas Ceļš)

LDDP, Lithuanian Democratic Workers' Party (Lietuvos demokratiné darbo partija)

LMP, Politics Can Be Different (Lehet más a politika)

LNNK, Latvian Movement for National Independence (Latvijas Nacionalas Neatkaribas Kustiba)

LPP, Latvia's First Party (Latvijas Pirmā Partija)

LSDP, Social Democratic Party of Lithuania (Lietuvos socialdemocratu partija)

MDF, Hungarian Democratic Forum (Magyar Demokrata Fórum)

MP, member of parliament

MSZMP, Hungarian Socialist Workers' Party (Magyar Szocialista Munkáspárt)

MSZP, Hungarian Socialist Party (Magyar Szocialista Párt)

NATO, North Atlantic Treaty Organization

NFI, National Investment Funds (Narodowe fundusze inwestycyjne)

NGO, non-governmental organization

NPD, National Democratic Party of Germany (Nationaldemokratische Partei Deutschlands)

NSF, National Salvation Front

ODS, Citizens' Democratic Party (Občanská demokratická strana)

OECD, Organisation for Economic Co-operation and Development

OKP, Citizens' Parliamentary Caucus (Obywatelski Klub Parlamentarny)

OPZZ, All-Poland Trade Union Alliance (Ogólnopolskie Porozuminienie Związków Zawodowych)

OSCE, Organization for Security and Co-operation in Europe

PID, authorized investment company (pooblaščene investicijske družbe)

PiS, the Law and Justice party (Prawo i Sprawiedliwość)

PO, the Citizens' Platform (Platforma Obywatelska)

PSL, Polish People's Party (Polskie Stronnictwo Ludowe)

PZPR, Polish United Workers' Party (Polska Zjednoczona Partia Robotnicza)

SaS, Freedom and Solidarity (Sloboda a Solidartita)

SC, Harmony Centre (Saskanas Centrs)

SD, Polish Democratic Party (Stronnictwo Demokratyczne)

SDK, Slovakian Democratic Coalition (Slovenská demokratická koalícia)

SDKÚ, Slovakian Democratic and Christian Union (Slovenská demokratická krest'anská únia)

SDL', Party of the Democratic Left (Strana demokratikej l'avice)

SDS, Union of Democratic Forces (Sajuz na democraticnite sili)

SED, Socialist Unity Party of Germany (Sozialistische Einheitspartei Deutschlands)

SED-PDS, Party of Democratic Socialism (Partei des Demokratischen Sozialismus)

SLD, Democratic Left Alliance (Sojusz Lewicy Demokratycznej)

Smer-SD, Towards Social Democracy (Smer-Sociálna demokracia)

SNS, Slovak National Party (Slovenská národná strana)

SPD, Social Democratic Party of Germany (Sozialdemokratische Partei Deutschlands)

SSR, Soviet Socialist Republic

TB, Fatherland and Freedom (Tēvzemei un Brīvībai)

TP, People's Party (Tautas Partija)

TS-LK, Fatherland Union-Lithuanian Conservatives (Tévynés Sajunga-Lietuvos Krikščionys Demokratai)

VPN, The Public against Violence (Verejnost' proti násiliu)

WTO, World Trade Organization

YPA, Yugoslav People's Army

ZSL, United People's Party (Zjednoczone Stronnictwo Ludowe)

ZZS, Union of Farmers and Greens (Zaļo un Zemnieku Savienība)

INTRODUCTION

~~~~~~~~~~~~~~~~~~

Günther Heydemann and Karel Vodička

Since the end of World War II, no event has changed Europe more fundamentally than the breakdown of the Eastern Bloc in the years 1989–1991. The domino effect of collapsing communist-authoritarian societies, economic systems and systems of rule in Eastern and South Eastern Europe, which finally reached even the Soviet Union itself, altered the map of Europe and launched extensive transformation processes that are still ongoing in individual countries, including the former German Democratic Republic (GDR) or so-called New Federal States of Germany. From the outset, overcoming and successively shaking off the straitjacket of Real Existing Socialism was a dual task. It was not enough to reconstruct the complex of state structures, legal system, administrative apparatus and media and – not least – establish a functioning democratic community; at the same time, it was also essential to undertake the fundamental regulatory task of transforming a centralized, state-directed planned economy into a liberal market economy.

Meanwhile, another quarter of a century has passed since this truly epochal break, and the great hopes and expectations from the early days have had to be revised. Indeed, 'the prediction that structures and cultural patterns in East and West would soon be adjusted, which was widespread among social scientists, has proven far from reality'.[1] The transformation process did not run as quickly and smoothly as expected in Germany or elsewhere. Furthermore, it is now obvious that the individual former Eastern Bloc countries have taken quite different paths of transformation that may be expected to continue. Two initial burdens were especially consequential. First, the length of a country's subjection to communist, fascist or other authoritarian dictatorships – including National Socialism – played a considerable role. Second, the state of its

---

Notes for this chapter begin on page 6.

socio-economic structures and social-mental conditions before the epochal break of 1989/90 was a decisive factor that remains influential today. Both transformation research and the analyses presented in this volume lead to the conclusion that the gradual change of mentalities is the core problem of transformation.

These are only the most important factors, however – they are far from all of them. Mental attitudes, behavioural stereotypes and the actual quality of a state's market economy and democracy are closely interconnected. The post-communist countries also still suffer from insufficient development of a committed civil society and a broad, economically efficient middle class, due especially to the burden of the past and the problems arising in the course of the transformation processes. Developing and consolidating an independent, active civil society and a business middle class will probably take decades longer. Independent thinking and acting cannot be simply created but must unfold and mature, and much points to the truth of Dahrendorf's 1990 prediction that 'the realisation of civil society' will take two generations or as long as sixty years.[2]

Even if the illusion of 'speedy recovery' was followed by commensurate disillusionment, one should not underestimate or overlook eastern EU countries' substantial turns towards democracy, rule of law, market economy and pluralist society, conditions that, back in the spring of 1989, seemed utopian. Given the still existing deficits and problems at various levels, some of which will endure for years to come, people sometimes lose sight of this basically positive development.

Furthermore, two decades of intensive research work have greatly increased knowledge about not only the national transformation paths of each country but also the transformation process as a whole. As early as 1990, political and social scientists, followed by economists, launched their initial investigations and analyses of the transformation processes that had begun in the countries of the then collapsed Eastern Bloc. Unsurprisingly, they generated extraordinary interest, as these countries were seen as large-scale experimental, state-run socio-economic laboratories where the post-communist transformation process was happening at various levels, often skipping over other levels. For a time, transformation research even dominated both disciplines. Meanwhile, politics urgently needed information to adequately control the process, in view of the frequent danger of social unrest and revolt in societies coping with momentous breaks and radical changes in a comparatively short span of time after decades of totalitarian or authoritarian rule. Overall, transformation research has seen its greatest progress in the field of political sciences, maybe most in Germany, where research conditions have been very favourable.[3]

Five years ago, the Hannah-Arendt-Institut für Totalitarismusforschung (HAIT) at the Technische Universität Dresden started to treat the transition process in the former Eastern Bloc states comparatively, as contemporary history.[4] Developments in the GDR were included from the outset, as researchers were aware that reunification with the Federal Republic in 1990 made it, and still makes it, a special case within the context of transformation. Indeed, the GDR was assisted by a 'big spender' that not only provided it with the capital needed for its regulatory restructuring from centralized planned economy to social market economy, including funding for its social systems and much more, but also, and most importantly, completely included it in a proven democratic constitution and federal structure. Unquestionably, therefore, the GDR or New Federal States have taken a special path. However, it would be premature to call any comparison between the GDR and other former Eastern Bloc states inappropriate.[5] On the contrary, the fact is and remains that for more than forty years, just like other Eastern and South Eastern European countries, the GDR and its population was deeply influenced by a one-party communist system that inculcated psychological reactions and habitual ways of behaving that are still very much in effect.

Thus, in what follows, the GDR or the East German federal states will again be consciously included in the overall context of post-communist system transformation, to allow common grounds and differences between the respective developments after 1989/90 to be worked out from a comparative point of view. Comparison of system change in the GDR, Hungary, Poland and the Czechoslovak Socialist Republic (CSSR) has already been undertaken,[6] so the present volume considerably extends the range of reference countries in respect of the transformation process to include all the former Eastern Bloc countries that became EU members in 2004 and 2007. These are the Baltic states of Estonia, Latvia and Lithuania, all formerly Soviet republics; the Central European states of Poland, the Czech Republic and Slovakia, followed by Slovenia and Hungary; and, finally, the South Eastern European countries of Romania and Bulgaria. From the beginning, we worked from both a contemporary-historical and a comparative political science point of view to pinpoint and clarify individual developments and phases of each national transformation process.

Conducted through political science comparison from the standpoint of transformation research, this comparative presentation and analysis of all former Eastern Bloc countries that have become part of the European Union – including the East German federal states – has proven abundantly fruitful. The structural comparability of the country reports, together with the comparative overall analysis of all countries in the post-communist area of the EU, brought to light a number of insights that were new to comparative political science or transformation research. The post-communist area was defined as consisting of the eastern German federal states and the eastern EU states. As proven by the comparative analysis in this volume's concluding chapter, the post-communist EU area is characterized by certain substantial common grounds and analogous trends of development that qualitatively distinguish it from the established EU democracies on the one hand and from the other former Eastern Bloc countries on the other.

The post-communist EU countries carry a deeply influential burden of history that differentiates them from established EU democracies like the Netherlands, Austria and the former West Germany, taken as points of reference. Besides being scarred by the trauma of forty years of violent communist rule, the post-communist EU societies are also characterized by the subsequent nearly thirty years of radical transformation. In 1990, Václav Havel, last president of the ČSSR and first president of Czech Republic, described the state of society after liberation from dictatorship as follows: 'We have become morally ill because we have become used to saying one thing while thinking the other. We have learned to believe in nothing, to behave indifferently towards each other, to care only about ourselves'.[7]

The nearly thirty years of transformation since the implosion of the communist regimes, with their distortions, injustice, insecurities and growing social disparities, have not been able to cure this illness. Even today, the social resources of ethos, trust and morality that are requisite for a vital civil society, efficient economy and uncorrupted politics are rare goods in the post-communist EU, where citizens combine distrust of political parties and state institutions with a basic scepticism of politics. Because they do not believe they are able to change actual politics through their behaviour, they are seldom committed; therefore, voter turnout is consistently much lower than in established democracies. The political parties are only superficially rooted among the population. They have few members and the share of swing voters is high, so the parties are unstable and, as a consequence, governments' average time in office is often too short. Political parties' limited recruiting potential works to benefit right-wing and left-wing extremist parties. Corruption is massive and widespread, in part because the sceptical-apolitical citizenry has insufficient control over decision-makers. Thus, in comparison to established EU democracies, the post-communist EU shows a variety of democracy deficits at the levels of representation (particularly in virulent party systems), actors (liability to corruption) and civil society (weak support for democracy and lack of readiness to participate).

On the other hand, the eastern German federal states and eastern EU countries also differ from former Eastern Bloc countries that have not been able to join the EU, in that the former are clearly amidst a sustainable consolidation process and rank at the top of transformation countries worldwide as the most consolidated market economy democracies. This becomes obvious when all former Eastern Bloc countries are compared. The European Union definitely earned its Nobel Peace Prize of 2012 for its successful democratization of the post-communist EU area, among other reasons. Whereas independent experts count all eastern EU countries among 'consolidating democracies', other former Eastern Bloc countries achieve at best Ukraine's rank of 'defective democracy', all others rating lower still as strongly defective democracies or even moderate or hardcore autocracies. In the post-communist EU area, on the other hand, the risk of radical de-democratization may currently be estimated as low (for South Eastern Europe) or very low (for East Central Europe). In this context, the external framework conditions, in particular EU and NATO membership, work as an essential stabilizing factor for young, still fragile eastern EU democracies.

To achieve the most analogous accounts possible and thus enable coherent comparison (see this volume's Conclusion), the individual country reports were structured according to the macro levels of politics/constitution, economy and society, a standardization that was imposed to make the contributions handbook-like. Accordingly, this volume attempts to satisfy a need for information at levels as disparate as policy-making and school-teaching.

The individual country reports in this volume were updated several times by their authors, and here we wish to express our deepest gratitude for their particular efforts. Many thanks to Mrs Kristin Luthardt and Mr Walter Heidenreich for their sometimes difficult editorial work and the layout. Special thanks go also to the Bundesstiftung zur Aufarbeitung der SED-Diktatur (Federal Foundation for the Reappraisal of the SED Dictatorship).

A comparative look at the transformation processes in former Eastern Bloc countries that today are EU member states will doubtless be a focal point of debate for national and international politics and the public, as well as a topic of work in political science, economics, social science and, not least, contemporary history.

After having completed his studies in history, German philology, social studies and Italian studies, as well as having earned his doctorate (1980), **Günther Heydemann** worked as a member of the scientific staffs of the Universities of Erlangen and Bayreuth as well as of the Deutsches Historisches Institut London. After his habilitation (1991) and interim professorships in Munich and Bonn, he was appointed to the Chair of More Recent and Contemporary History of the University of Leipzig. Since 2009 he has also been Director of the HAIT, and has held visiting professorships and fellowships in Italy, the USA, Russia and Tunisia. His research work focuses on the history of historical science, comparative European history, the dictatorships of the twentieth century as well as the postsocialist transformation processes.

Karel Vodička, Dr of Jurisprudence, born in Aussig, Czechoslovakia, in 1949, went into political exile in the Federal Republic of Germany together with his family. He has undertaken scientific work as a philologist at the HAIT (until 2014) and as a lecturer in the Faculty of Philosophy at Jan-Evangelista-Purkyne University (UJEP) in Ústí nad Labem, Czech Republic. He has published on the history and the political system of the Czech Republic as well as on system transformation in the post-communist EU area. He has authored 126 scientific articles and is the author of sixteen books, most recently *Zündfunke aus Prag: Wie 1989 der Mut zur Freiheit die Geschichte veränderte*, co-authored with Hans-Dietrich Genscher and Petr Pithart (Munich, 2014).

Notes

1. H. Best and E. Holtmann, 'Die langen Wege der deutschen Einigung: Aufbruch mit vielen Unbekannten', in H. Best and E. Holtmann (eds), *Aufbruch der entsicherten Gesellschaft: Deutschland nach der Wiedervereinigung* (Frankfurt a. M., 2012), 15.
2. R. Dahrendorf, *Betrachtungen über die Revolution in Europa* (Stuttgart, 1990), 101; see also W. Merkel, *Systemtransformation: Eine Einführung in die Theorie und Empirie der Transformationsforschung* (Opladen, 1999), 164; S. Kirelli, 'Vom Plan zum Markt: Der wirtschaftliche Transformationsprozess in Ostmitteleuropa', *Der Bürger im Staat* 97(3) (1997), 164–68, here 164–65.
3. In two decades of researching the transformation process in the New Federal States, psychological and anthropological issues have increasingly come to the fore, more so as changes in mental-habitual ways of behaviour are clearly what take the longest. Furthermore, the sometimes radical changes in living conditions and employment situations created much uncertainty at both the individual and the collective levels. See Best and Holtmann, 'Die langen Wege'.
4. See C. Vollnhals (ed.), *Jahre des Umbruchs: Friedliche Revolution in der DDR und Transition in Ostmitteleuropa* (Göttingen, 2011).
5. See A. Rödder, *Deutschland einig Vaterland: Die Geschichte der Wiedervereinigung* (Munich, 2009), 314, which is nevertheless currently the best and most balanced description of German reunification.
6. See Vollnhals, *Jahre des Umbruchs*.
7. Cf. K. Vodička, 'Wir sind moralisch krank geworden: Die Neujahransprache des tschechoslowakischen Staatspräsidenten', *Osteuropa* 40(4) (1990), 248–53, here 250.

Chapter 1

ESTONIA

Ralph Michael Wrobel

Introduction

With the dissolution of the Soviet Union in 1991, the Republic of Estonia once again became an independent European state. It took the new country only a few years to establish a functioning market economy and build an entire state apparatus. Estonia's economic transformation epitomized radical, consistent, successful market economy reform in Central and Eastern Europe. A crucial part of the transition – opening Estonian commodities and financial markets to foreign trade – resulted in high levels of foreign direct investment that in turn spurred impressive growth.

Like its southern neighbour, Latvia, Estonia traditionally oriented itself more to Western Europe, particularly Germany and Scandinavia, than to Russia. German nobility came to rule as Estonian farmers' feudal lords in the thirteenth century, when first Danes and then the Order of the Teutonic Knights conquered and Christianized Estonian lands. At this time, several Hansa cities such as Reval/Tallinn and Dorpat/Tartu were founded in Estonia and settled by German merchants and craftsmen. By the end of the Middle Ages, the Teutonic Order was gone, but the German nobility and Hansa cities retained their privileges under Swedish rule (c. 1560–1721). Even after the Nordic War (1700–1721), Estonia and wide parts of Latvia remained relatively autonomous within the Russian Empire as the 'German Baltic Provinces', and German was the official language well into the nineteenth century. The Estonian people, however, remained unassimilated.

Then, in the mid nineteenth century age of 'national awakening', Estonians developed strong national sentiment that fuelled a victorious fight for independence after World War I.[1] This freedom was short-lived:

the Soviet Union occupied Estonia in 1940, then annexed it after World War II.[2] The effects of the Soviet period – characterized by deportation, expropriation and a massive influx of Russian-speaking Soviet citizens – linger in society today. Estonians in the Estonian Socialist Soviet Republic were able to maintain a certain degree of cultural and linguistic autonomy, but most of the population considered the situation as an occupation. The emergence of a peaceful resistance movement during the late 1980s led to the country's second declaration of independence in 1991.[3]

Over the next twenty years, the fields of politics, economy and society changed radically in Estonia, as in other East European transformation states. The actual transformation process can be said to have ended in 2004, when Estonia joined the European Union. Analyses of the socio-economic transformation have always emphasized the economic aspect, as Estonia pursued a comparatively radical reform strategy that very soon developed in a positive direction.[4] Above all, the privatization process, introduction of a currency board system and development of the labour market attracted much interest.[5] Analyses of change in the political system, on the other hand, are few, probably because in Estonia this process was comparatively untroubled.[6] Rather, in the following years many studies were published on the question of how to adjust Estonia's economic system to meet the requirements of the European Union.[7] More recent publications include some overviews of Estonia's economic and political transformation, from the first steps up to becoming an EU member state.[8]

This chapter will first briefly sketch the changing system in the early 1990s and analyse the political, economic and social transformation leading up to EU accession. It will then describe the process of European integration and analyse how much Estonia has changed since joining the EU.

System Change

With the demise of the Soviet state's power in the late 1980s, its apparatus of suppression dissolved as well, making it increasingly possible to speak one's mind. As early as 1987, plans for phosphorite mining in north-eastern Estonia that would have catastrophically damaged the environment triggered growing demonstrations of the Estonian population's political dissatisfaction with the ruling system.[9] Like their neighbours in the two other Baltic states, Latvia and Lithuania, Estonians expressed their wish for change, and particularly for national autonomy and democracy, at musical events throughout the country. Thus, the Baltic road to independence earned the moniker of the 'Singing Revolution'.

As the 1980s ended, the extent of the economic crisis in the Estonian Socialist Soviet Republic became obvious. Infrastructure dilapidated by a lack of investment, pollution by industrial plants and the consequent deficit of capital were particularly serious problems. Estonia had always enjoyed greater prosperity than the rest of the Soviet Union, but now Mikhail Gorbachev's policies of glasnost and perestroika were making the advantages of democratic and market economy systems ever more obvious to everyone in the Soviet Union.[10] Against this background, and in a context of growing popular political resistance, the Estonian Communist Party more and more found itself questioning its own ideals.

In January 1990, many communist politicians who had turned themselves into various kinds of reformers united to form the democratic association Vaba Eesti (Free Estonia), as communists had minimal chances of success under democratic conditions. Their efforts – the beginnings of reform towards a market economy – were focused on detaching Estonia's economy from the Soviet economic system. The first attempt at such disentanglement was the Isemajandav Eesti (Economically Autonomous Estonia) project in 1987, through which the Estonians intended to take control of companies in Estonia that had previously been under Moscow's direct control.

The actual resistance movement, however, developed only in 1990, in the form of an elected popular assembly, the Congress of Estonia. Its debates no longer concerned whether Estonia should strive for renewed independence but only how independence was to be achieved. A third way between capitalism and socialism was no longer taken into consideration. When a military coup shook the Soviet Union in the summer of 1991, Estonia made its final decision. Its independence was formally declared on 21 August 1991 and internationally recognized soon thereafter.[11]

In the autumn of 1991, after a transition period characterized by initial, cautious attempts at reform, Estonians democratically elected a government for the first time since the loss of independence. The victors were radical reformers who set the basic course of the Estonian transformation process. The new government, led by the party Isamaaliit (Union of the Fatherland), set the goal of creating a free market economy in Estonia to prevent the emigration of its qualified workforce and to attract foreign investment. This government saw fundamental transformation of the Estonian economic system as both its main objective and a precondition for raising the population's living conditions.[12] The introduction of a free market economy was thus an expression of the primary goal of the Estonian transformation process. In the meantime, another key step in this context was to set up new state structures.

Establishment of the Democratic Constitutional State

Parliamentary System and Political Parties

In its first period of independence in the 1920s and 1930s, Estonia had had a democratic constitution and rule of law. In the fledgling independence movement at the end of the 1980s, democracy and rule of law were an overarching political goal, second only to the sovereignty of the national state.[13] In early September 1991, only a few days after Estonia had declared its renewed independence, the Congress of Estonia decided to establish a constitutional assembly, whose first constitutive meeting was held on 13 September.[14] According to the new constitution, approved by referendum on 28 June 1992, the Republic of Estonia is an independent, sovereign and democratic republic whose supreme sovereign is the people.[15]

The legislative power is exercised by the Riigikogu, a unicameral parliament elected every four years. Its 101 seats are distributed according to proportional representation.[16] Every Estonian citizen aged eighteen or over has active and passive electoral rights.[17] Like other transformation countries, Estonia's party system was strongly segmented and fluctuated for many years. For some time, anywhere from eight to eighteen parties competed for votes. Some parties vanished; others appeared out of the blue. However, as a party had to meet a 5 per cent threshold for inclusion, only six to nine parties shared the 101 parliamentary seats in each electoral period. Thus, excessive polarization of the political spectrum was avoided.

No extremely right- or left-wing party plays a crucial role in Estonian politics, and no parties are controlled by oligarchs. Rather, political parties represent the socio-economic interests of certain groups. This long caused voters' preferences to change radically from election to election when coalitions did not meet the people's expectations. Many governments did not survive their terms of office due to the comparatively frequent changing of coalitions and heads of government.[18] More recently, Estonian politics has been surprisingly quiet. Since 2005, the liberal politician Andrus Ansip has continuously governed the country.

Government and Administration

The writers of Estonia's new constitution took note of experiences from the more recent constitutional histories of Germany, Sweden and Finland, although none of these constitutions was copied. Rather, the new Estonian constitution was modelled on the old one from the early 1920s. Considering Estonia's bad experiences in the 1930s, when the amended constitution

TABLE 1.1. Result of the 2007 parliamentary elections

Party	Ideological orientation	%
Eesti Reformierakond (Estonian Reform Party)	liberal	27.8
Eesti Keskerakond (Estonian Centre Party)	populists, former communists	26.1
Isamaa ja Res Publica Liit (Fatherland and Res Publica Union)	right-liberal, conservative	17.9
Sotsiaaldemokraatlik Erakond (Social Democratic Party)	Social Democrats	10.6
Eestimaa Rohelised (Estonian Green Party)	environment	7.1
Eestimaa Rahvaliit (The People's Union of Estonia)	agricultural lobby	7.1

Source: Vabariigi Valimisko misjon Rigiko gu valimine, 4 March 2007 (http://www.vvk.ee/varasemad/?v=r07).

had allowed for a presidential democracy that progressively changed into a presidential dictatorship,[19] the new constitution had to create a parliamentary democracy without any authoritarian elements. Thus, the President of the State, who is elected every four years, is mostly restricted to representation.[20] The president can only indirectly influence the country's politics, by refusing to sign laws which he or she believes to be unconstitutional or, as a second step, appealing to the Constitutional Court.[21]

The executive power lies with the government, led by a prime minister.[22] It has the right of initiative and can pass decrees on the implementation of laws.[23] However, the parliament's ability to take control of the government is so far-reaching that the executive authority cannot be said to have superiority. Parliamentary committees may change any of the government's bills before a plenary session decides on them.[24] Furthermore, the government is not voted on as a collective; instead, both the prime minister and other ministers are individually elected by the parliament, which thereby influences the structure of the government. These competences give the parliament an efficient control over the government.[25]

The bodies of the executive authority were up and functioning quite early in the new Estonia, but for many years public administration lacked qualified staff, particularly where legal questions were concerned.[26] The flaws of the system of municipal self-administration must similarly be considered to have disadvantaged the entire process of democratization.[27]

Districts exist only at the municipal level, where the mayors of a total of 247 (since 2005 227) municipalities are democratically elected. This means a big city like Tallinn, with more than 400,000 inhabitants, is equal in rank to a small rural municipality like the island of Ruhnu, with fewer than fifty inhabitants. Reform of local self-administration has been debated for quite some time.[28]

Jurisdiction and Control of State Power

The judiciary acts as a check on the executive and legislative authorities, whose decisions' constitutionality is decided by a constitutional chamber of the Supreme Court. Only the President of the State and a 'Chancellor of Justice', an Estonian peculiarity concerning the control of authorities, have the right of action.[29] The parliament elects the latter for life, to secure his or her independence. The chancellor's task is to evaluate the constitutionality of every law. In case of doubt, he or she may immediately bring action. Furthermore, every citizen is entitled to petition the Chancellor of Justice with doubts and requests for action concerning laws. The members of the Supreme Court are also elected for life by the parliament and are thus independent of political directives. Other judges are appointed for life by the President of the State and can only be unseated if convicted of a criminal deed, so Estonia has an independent judiciary. In the early years of transformation, the judiciary's main problems were insecurity about which laws applied in numerous fields of law-making, and the insufficient experience of the members of the judicial authority.[30]

Another control on political decision-makers in Estonia is the free and independent press. Estonia's mass media were privatized at an early stage of the transformation process. Both formal constitutional regulations and the actually existing variety of media guarantee freedom of speech and the press. Estonia has several daily newspapers in the Estonian language (*Postimees, Eesti Päevaleht* and *Äripäev* should be mentioned) and some in Russian. There are several state and private radio channels, as well as commercial TV channels with public programmes. Some parties have tried to establish their own newspapers on the Estonian market. The big media organizations are serious economic players, but ownership is increasingly concentrated among certain foreigners from the neighbouring Scandinavian countries.[31] The available print media and radio/TV channels are increasingly complemented by the internet. In the context of worldwide comparison, Estonia is a pioneer of widespread public internet access (in state buildings, on buses etc.).[32] Furthermore, in 2010, almost 70 per cent of Estonian households were equipped with internet access (see Figure 1.1).

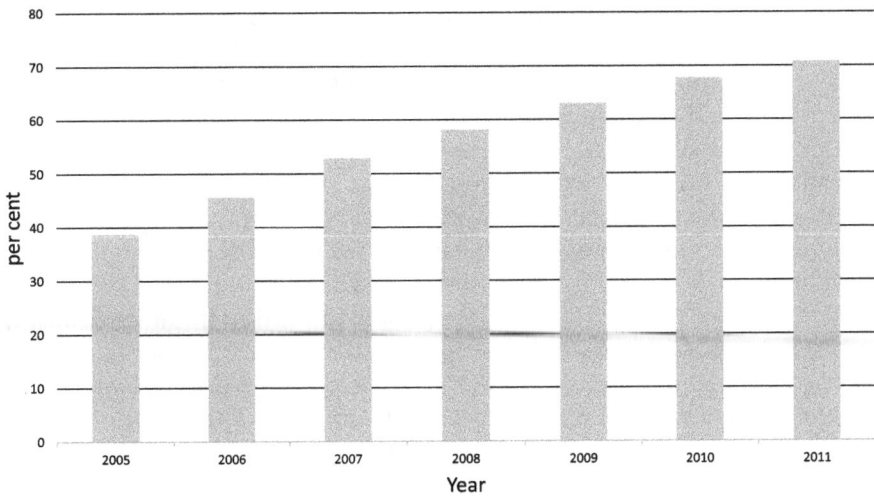

FIGURE 1.1. Households with an internet connection

Source: Statistics Estonia.

Democracy and Civil Society

On the whole, the process of political transformation has been a success. As early as June 1997, in a statement on Estonia's application for EU membership, the European Commission judged Estonia's political system favourably:

> Estonia's political institutions are running smoothly and are stable. The institutions respect the separation of powers and cooperate. In 1992 and 1995 there were free and just elections . . . .. The opposition plays its appropriate role within the institutional structure. The attempts at improving the judiciary as well as anti-corruption measures must be intensified. . . . The country shows every feature of a democracy and has stable institutions guaranteeing the rule of law and respect for human rights.[33]

Since then, there have been further improvements. For example, an expert report of 2003 published by the Bertelsmann Foundation points out that Estonia rightly has no reputation for extensive corruption. If necessary, it says, judicial authorities take decisive action against corrupt office-holders to guarantee the rule of law and prevent conflicts of interests.[34] In fact, Estonia leads the transformation countries of Central and Eastern Europe in this respect.[35]

Estonia very quickly developed a lively civil society and is accordingly characterized by a dense network of cooperatives, associations and interest groups linking politics and society. Estonians have the right to freely form associations and are not required to formally register them with state authorities. All groups supporting ethnic or religious matters are allowed, as long as they act within the framework of the democratic system. Thus, freedom of association is not illegally restricted, and freedom of assembly is even guaranteed by Article 47 of the Estonian constitution. Such restrictions are common in democracies and are handled with the utmost caution. Despite these freedoms countrywide, most organizations are located in the capital, Tallinn. Also, the population's participation in voluntary organizations is rather weak, due to the fact that it was obligatory in the Soviet period to participate in civil society organizations. Only about 40 per cent of the population participates in non-governmental organizations.[36] However, the Estonian state tries to orient its legal and fiscal framework to support conditions for civil society's development.

Transformation of the Economic System

Liberalization and Market Access

Estonia's process of economic transformation had begun before independence, but only in 1992 was the first democratically elected government, led by Isamaaliit, able to actually start comprehensive transformation of the economic system. The reform was characterized by rapid, universal introduction of the constituting principles of a market order, particularly a functional pricing structure, private property and macro-economic stabilization. In this context, the question of privatization proved the most difficult. Another characteristic of the Estonian transformation process was the gradual way in which it established a competitive framework.

By the end of the 1980s, Estonians had come to recognize the significance of a pricing mechanism to market functionality. In late 1989, therefore, two years before Estonia regained its independence, price liberalization was gradually introduced. Most prices of goods had been liberalized by 1992, but price controls were retained for fuel, energy, rents, staple foods, transport, water, telecommunications and pharmaceuticals. For a time during the period of radical change in 1992, fixed prices and rationing were reintroduced for essential goods, but by the year's end, prices had been liberalized again.[37] In parallel with price liberalization, market access and departure were legally regulated, as foreign entrepreneurs' entry into the market proved especially necessary for a market economy environment. Another new law required enterprises to be registered, which required much effort but was not at all prohibitive.

Regulations concerning the founding of joint ventures, private limited companies and public limited companies were also introduced at this time. Since then, the latter have become the most frequent kind of company. Special limitations exist only in fields that are subject to state price controls or reserved for the state's own economic activities, such as the fields of public utilities and infrastructure. Involuntary exit from the market was already regulated by a law of 6 June 1992, which provided that a debtor must go bankrupt if a court confirms his or her insolvency.[38] All these regulations were successfully implemented in the short term.

Privatization

The issue of privatization was characterized by a fundamental internal conflict between two approaches to property reform that often confronted each other in public debate in the early 1990s. The 'economic' approach considered property reform to be only a tool for the creation of more or less market economy structures. Pursued by the transition governments before the first democratic elections of 1992, this approach was politically consonant with their understanding of Estonia as a 'new' nation. The 'political' approach, on the other hand, emphasized restitution of the property of citizens of the 'old' Estonia who had been dispossessed by the Soviet Union after 1940. Supporters of this approach demanded the radical transfer of state property to private hands and either restitution or compensation paid to the original owners by way of vouchers. In this regard, foreign investors were to be treated equally, to initiate the urgently needed influx of capital. The first democratically elected government emphasized the 'political' approach. Its leadership under Isamaaliit attached particular significance to restitution of property originating from the first Republic, as it represented the political continuity of the Estonian state throughout the period of Soviet occupation. Indeed, it considered restitution of private property analogous to restitution of the entire Republic and thus politically indispensable.[39]

Privatization in Estonia began in 1990 with 'small' privatization. A law passed that December required privatization of all trade and services enterprises worth less than 500,000 roubles (or, after May 1992, 600,000 Estonian crowns), in all about 2,850 enterprises.[40] An exception was made for enterprises on which there were restitution claims. This small-scale privatization was implemented by the State Property Authority (Riigivaraamet), founded in 1990, or by municipal administrations if they were the current owners. The procedure was standardized. Claims by employees were preferentially treated until May 1992, and only Estonian citizens were entitled to participate in the auctions. These restrictions met with much political resistance, as employee takeovers of enterprises often prevented necessary structural changes. In response, the later existing preferential treatment of employees was restricted by an amendment of May 1992, which sped up the privatization process.[41]

Meanwhile, 'big' privatization, which concerned about three hundred enterprises in Estonia, began in April 1991 with the privatization of seven enterprises. Only in August 1992 was a law passed on privatizing another thirty enterprises. To implement this plan, the Estonian Privatization Enterprise (Erastamisettevötte) was founded in September, following the example of Germany's Treuhand. With the help of German advisers, the Privatization Enterprise was supposed to handle the privatization of enterprises worth more than 600,000 crowns and also, in this context, to attract foreign investment.[42] Accordingly, thirty-two enterprises went up for sale internationally in late 1992. This slowed privatization overall, however, as the concerned enterprises were partly subject to restitution claims.

The Law on the Basic Features of Property Reform stipulated that all natural and legal persons who had been expropriated between 1940 and June 1981, or their heirs, were to be given back their original property or be compensated for it. From the perspective of the new Estonian government, the progress of the privatization process was unsatisfactorily slow. On 17 June 1993, the government therefore passed a new privatization law that changed the organizational competences (as well as some less important provisions) by restructuring the two previously existing organizations in charge of privatization into a single, unitary institution, the Estonian Privatization Agency (Eesti Erastamisagentuur), which was controlled by the Finance Ministry.[43]

According to the new privatization law of 1993, the Privatization Agency could apply the following methods: (1) put enterprises or parts of them up for sale by tender after negotiations; (2) put enterprises up for sale at public or restricted auctions; (3) sell shares publicly; and (4) otherwise effect privatization to the best of the agency's judgement, if methods 1–3 were unsuccessful. Of these options, sale by tender was the most complicated and time-consuming,[44] but it also offered an advantage: the seller could purposely approach foreign investors, who then were supposed to provide new capital and modern management.[45] Thus, although the privatization process went no faster, it was possible to seek suitable investors for each enterprise. All the same, the restitution clause again and again proved a crucial obstacle to the entire privatization process in Estonia, clearly complicating and slowing privatization in many cases.

Macro-economic Stabilization

The breakdown of the Soviet Union's centrally administered economic system was accompanied by a decline in economic stability. After all, the Soviet – later Russian – central bank was hardly interested in monetary stability, its task being instead to provide sufficient funding for Russia's deficient state enterprises. The result was four-digit inflation rates. The Estonian economy suffered from this too, for even after independence in 1991 Estonia was, at least for the time being, a rouble zone member whose monetary policy was still determined by the Russian central bank in Moscow. This post-Soviet currency union made monetary stabilization unattainable in Estonia. In the first half of 1992, the situation worsened when a decline in cash supplies from Russia diminished the money supply in Estonia.[46]

The idea of introducing an independent Estonian currency was floated as early as 1989, but only in 1992 did growing inflation, along with the declining cash supplies from Russia, force the Estonian government to undertake an immediate currency reform. On 22 June 1992, the country left the rouble zone and introduced the Estonian crown as its national currency. The currency switch happened between 20 and 22 June 1992, making Estonia the first of the three Baltic countries to leave the rouble zone. From day one, the goal of the currency reform was to create a stable currency as a foundation for the Estonian economy – that is, to enable national enterprises and foreign investors alike to have confidence in the long-term stability of the Estonian crown.[47]

To this end, several stability-oriented measures were taken. First, legislators formulated the Law on the Central Bank of the Republic of Estonia,[48] guided by precepts of a central bank's independence. Additionally, they ratified rules for conducting Estonian monetary policy by way of a currency board system that pegs the national currency to a second, reserve currency. In Estonia, this was the German mark, with a currency rate of eight crowns to one mark (since 1999, the euro). The currency board is only in charge of organizing the buying and selling of foreign currency, so it does not allow for any monetary-political leeway.[49] The advantages of such a currency system lie in the 'credibility loan' from the external anchor and the reduced exchange rate risk. A devaluation of the Estonian crown, meanwhile, could not be decided by the central bank but only by passage of a law in the Estonian parliament, the Riigikogu.[50]

Another result of instituting a currency board was that the central bank had no general discretion to grant loans. A loan to a commercial bank can be no more than the sum total of the bank's excess cash. Thus, the Estonian Central Bank (Eesti Pank) was incapable of functioning as a 'lender of last

Total

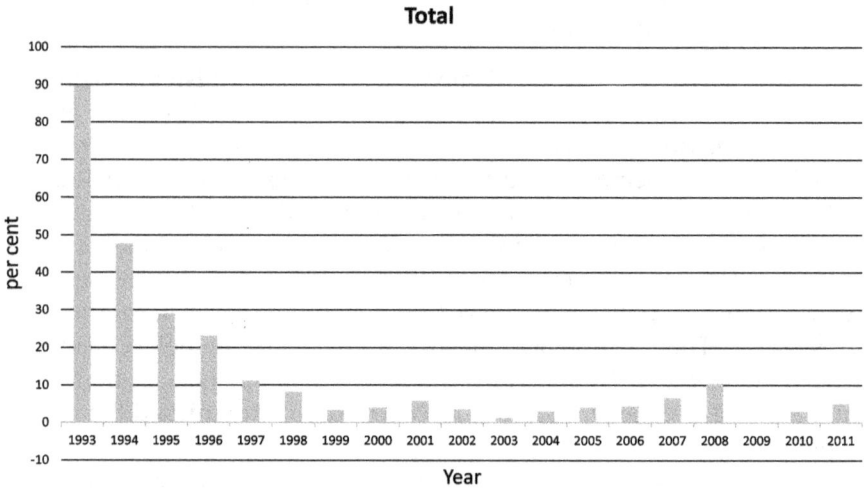

FIGURE 1.2. Consumer price index, change over previous year

Source: Statistics Estonia.

resort' that continuously offers refunding possibilities to commercial banks. Accordingly, Eesti Pank had only a limited set of monetary-political tools and could not influence the country's interest rates through either money market operations or administrative measures (see Figure 1.2). It was furthermore forbidden to extend loans to the state or the municipalities. In 2011, Estonia was the first of the Baltic states to introduce the euro. Also, the 1993 Law on the National Budget made the 'balanced budget' principle legally valid.[51] The Estonian government is therefore forced to orient its spending to its revenues. This means revenue shortfalls must be compensated by spending cuts. So far, Estonia has sometimes even managed to achieve a budget surplus (Figure 1.3). Since its introduction in 1992, the currency board system has provided exchange rate stability and continuously curbed inflation. Within just a few years, Estonia succeeded in reducing its inflation rate from more than 1,000 per cent in 1992 to less than 10 per cent. Between 1999 and 2006, it was even constantly below 5 per cent. Furthermore, the currency board and the balanced budget rule have fostered budgetary discipline in Estonia. With a few exceptions – particularly in years of crisis – the Estonian state has always spent less money than it took in.

Foreign-Political Opening

Early on, Estonian politicians recognized the need to ground Estonia's transformation process in a foreign-economic orientation, given the

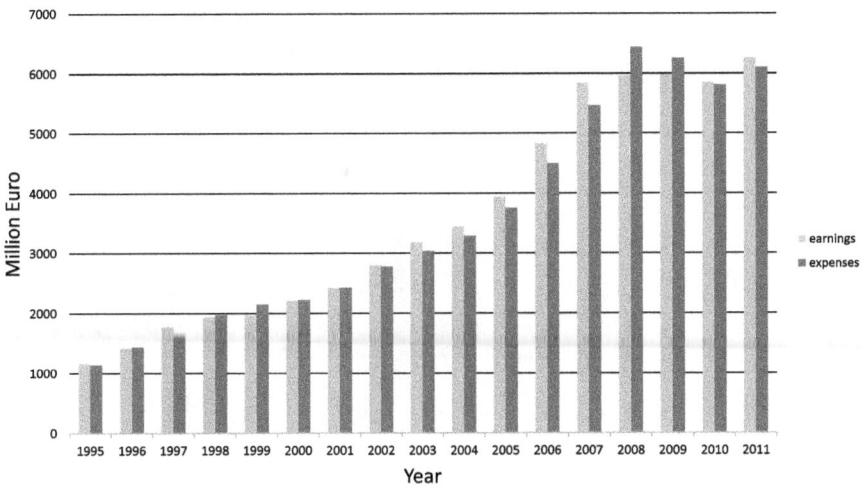

FIGURE 1.3. Revenue and expenditure of general government

Source: Statistics Estonia.

country's size and geographic location. Because Estonia has only a very small domestic market, its function as a pivot between East and West – due in particular to its harbours – had to be optimally integrated into the world economy.[52] Accordingly, before EU accession, the Republic of Estonia's foreign trade regime was not only the most liberal among the Baltic countries but one of the most liberal in the world. Its legal basis was provided by the Customs Act of 15 September 1993, according to which foreign trade faced minimal tariff obstacles. Meanwhile, quantity restrictions and import subsidies were largely abandoned.[53] Foreign trade increased considerably as a result. The country's constantly negative trade balance mainly reflects foreign direct investments and is thus only a minor problem (Figure 1.4).

Also at an early stage, Estonia opened its gates to foreign capital. The relevant legislation includes a law on foreign investment – passed on 10 September 1991, just a few days after independence – that allows foreign investors to sell their shares at any time and to transfer their gains without restriction.[54] As early as the first half of the 1990s, these very attractive framework conditions found expression in foreign companies' growing investment activities in Estonia.[55]

All other capital transactions between Estonia and foreign countries were likewise liberalized. In 1994, Estonia permitted all trade balance transactions in convertible currency between non-residents and

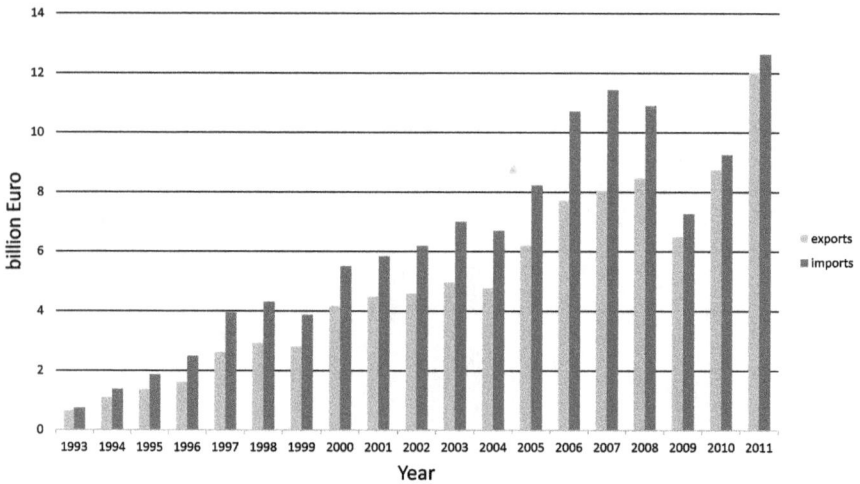

FIGURE 1.4. General exports and imports

Source: Statistics Estonia.

Estonians, according to Article VIII of its agreement with the International Monetary Fund.[56]

Tax- and Competition-Political Framework Conditions

Although Estonian tax reform had begun by the late 1980s, a comprehensive approach to reform was embraced only in March 1991. It put an end to the predominance of direct taxation by introducing a system of indirect taxation.[57] In doing so, however, it integrated several investment-supporting regulations, rendering taxation rather complicated.[58] Subsequently, an amendment of 16 December 1993 considerably simplified taxation in Estonia, fixing the proportional income tax rate at 26 per cent for natural persons and enterprises. Today it is only 20 per cent. Moreover, reinvested gains are exempted from taxation.[59] Enterprises pay 33 per cent social security and health insurance tax on gross wages. Most other Estonian taxes are insignificant, but it is worth mentioning the value-added tax, an 18 per cent net all-phase tax with input tax deduction.[60] Thus, the structure of the Estonian system of taxation resembles those of other Western market economies. Its hallmarks are its broad assessment basis and low tax rates, which make it simple and investment-supporting.[61]

With all the above-mentioned measures, Estonia introduced the constitutive principles of a market order quite quickly. However, establishing a regulatory framework took longer. In the first phase of transformation, Estonia's competition policy was based only on the potential existence of competitors. At the time this was a tidy solution to the problem, as Estonia has only a small national economy and it was highly unlikely that informal market obstacles would emerge during the transition period. Regardless, the consensus was that this could not be a long-term solution. Thus, legislators began developing a law on competition. The new government's Law on Competition was passed by parliament in 1993, only to be amended later that same year.[62] Its aim – to secure free competition – was initially supposed to be achieved through bans on restrictive agreements, abuse of dominant market positions and cartels.[63] In 1998, the Law on Competition was once more fundamentally revised, in view of Estonia's intention to join the European Union.[64]

Changes in the Social Structure and Social Conflicts

Social Security and Social Structure

Since Estonia's transformation process began, the population's wealth has grown constantly. Both per capita gross national product (GNP) and labour productivity grew from just under a third of the EU average in 1995 to about two thirds in 2007, a change of 30 per cent over roughly a decade (see Figure 1.5). This was possible because Estonia pursued strongly neoliberal economic and social policies.[65] On the other hand, it placed little value on social balance during the transformation process. According to the Isamaaliit-led government of the early 1990s, there was no other choice. Western industrial states too, it claimed, had had to become rich by way of a free market economy before they could afford their welfare state redistribution systems.[66] Thus, for quite some time the Estonian social security system offered nothing more than a minimum basic security. Strictly speaking, the Estonian system of social security even today consists only of a pension scheme and health insurance. Both work according to a pay-as-you-go system in which the entire field of social security is funded by a social tax of 33 per cent on wages, paid by employers in the form of a special tax,[67] of which 13 per cent goes to health insurance and 20 per cent to the social security and pension scheme.[68] There is also a child allowance – for minimum wage earners – and an accommodation allowance administered by the respective municipality. All legal residents of Estonia participate in this system.[69]

Until 1991, pensions in Estonia were paid according to the Soviet pension system. Since then, a number of laws have revised and extended the

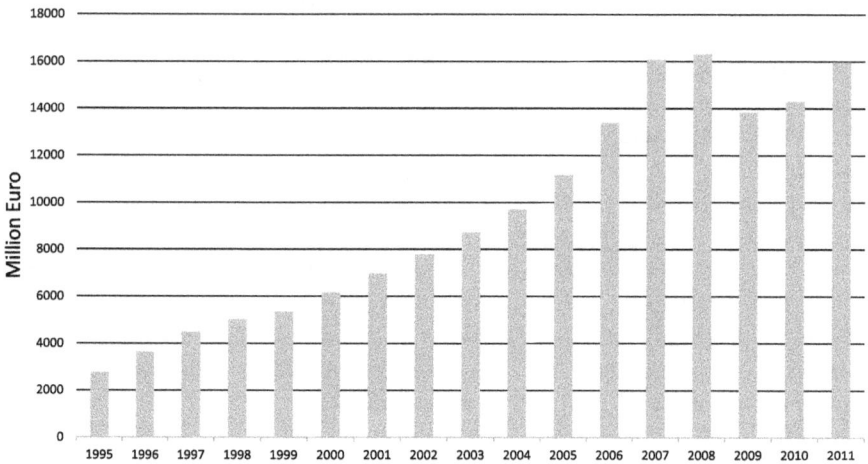

FIGURE 1.5. Gross domestic product by expenditure approach

Source: Statistics Estonia.

pension system. Today it rests on three pillars: (1) state pensions funded by a pay-as-you-go system; (2) obligatory privately purchased supplemental insurance; and (3) voluntary supplemental insurance. In 2003, state pensions in Estonia were only 40.5 per cent of the average income, which is the minimum standard in Europe.[70] Until 1992 the public health service was mostly run by the state, supported by payments from state enterprises and collective farms. All medical services were free to citizens. A new health insurance law passed in 1992 regulates the handling of the mandatory health insurance, payments for services and sickness allowances, as well as the costs of medical treatment.[71]

Estonia's consistent economic transformation, together with its modest social policy, resulted in a fundamental redistribution of income. Disparities grew constantly for many years due to increasingly divergent pay grades, unemployment and low pensions.[72] Since the start of the millennium, for example, financial sector employees earned 3.4 times as much as those working in agriculture.[73] Despite such income inequality, the basic consensus among the population on the need for further free market reform prevented a reversion to socialist traditions.[74] Since 2000, Estonia's Gini coefficient has clearly gone down again, though disparities in income distribution remain (Table 1.2). Estonia is still among those European countries that are ready to pay for their rapid economic development with a high degree of social inequality, but inequality there is nonetheless trending downwards.

TABLE 1.2. Development of the Gini Index

Year	1996	1997	1998	1999	2000	2001	2002	2003	2004	2005
Gini Index	37	38	37	37	36	35	35	34	37	34

Source: Eurostat.

Regional Disparities

A comparison of district-level population densities reveals a striking disparity between the Harju (Harjumaa) district, where the city of Tallinn is located, and the rest of Estonia. The population per square kilometre in Harjumaa is 120.3 people, whereas in the rest of the country it is less than 51.4 people. Thus, Estonia has only one densely populated centre – the capital Tallinn and its immediate vicinity in the Harju district. However, there are two other regional centres. One is the city of Tartu, which is renowned for its university and functions as the country's intellectual and cultural centre. The other, the Ida-Viru district in north-eastern Estonia, is a medium-sized economic centre where oil shale is mined to be processed into electricity.

The regional distribution of the GNP is all too clear. Whereas north Estonia, including Tallinn, produces 60 per cent of GNP, the rural regions of the country all lag far behind. The Ida-Viru district in the North-East of Estonia accounts for another 7.7 per cent of GNP, though it covers only a small area. Estonia's purely rural regions, on the other hand – that is, the entire rest of the country – are extremely thinly settled and produce only slightly more than 30 per cent of Estonia's economic output.[75] Tallinn, with its Harjumaa suburbs, and Tartu and its Tartumaa district are clearly far ahead of other regions in economic development (see also Figure 1.6). In 1994, Estonia developed a comprehensive catalogue of regional-political measures to create secure living conditions for all citizens of every region, but the country had no real regional policy until its accession to the EU in 2004.

Social Consensus and Conflict

In the past, Estonian society featured a high degree of consensus on the necessity of market economy reform. In this respect a kind of historically grown Estonian individualism and liberalism is salient, as is the political exclusion of most of the country's Russian-speaking people. The Soviet Union often banned religious services to speed up the secularization of the population, so today only about a quarter of the population is religious. Due to Estonia's historic connections to Germany and Sweden, most

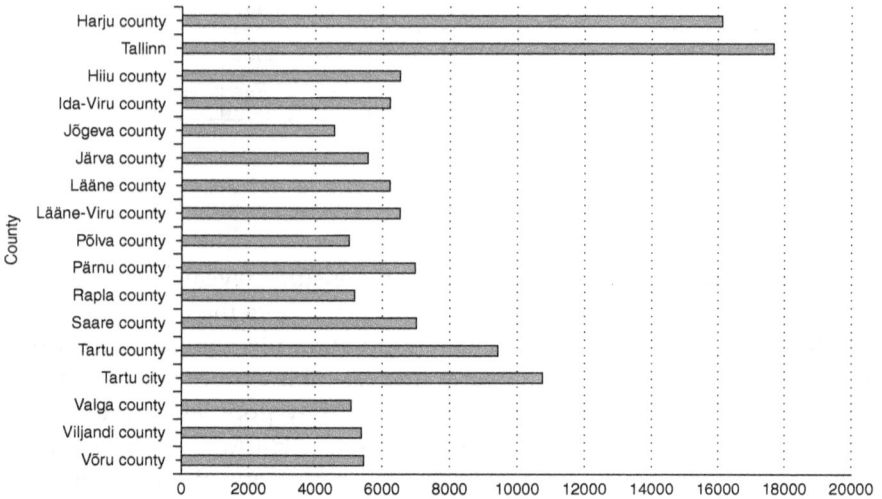

FIGURE 1.6. Gross domestic product, 2008

Source: Statistics Estonia.

religious ethnic Estonians belong to the Lutheran Church. The country's Russian-speaking inhabitants, on the other hand, are Russian Orthodox or – particularly around Lake Peipus in the east of the country – Old Believers. There is no state religion or ideology, and secularized Estonians coming from a Lutheran tradition are the primary religious demographic, so religious dogmas and church functionaries have zero influence in national politics or law-making processes. This is reinforced by a tradition of strict separation between church and state dating from the period between the two world wars.[76] Thus, Estonians' comparatively liberal, individualistic worldview can be attributed to Protestantism or the traditional distance between the Church and broad sectors of the population.[77]

This way of seeing things extends also to politics, in part because Estonia created its democratic structures for ethnic Estonians alone, and not for the considerable share of its society that immigrated after World War II to what was then the Estonian Soviet Republic. Defining the Estonian 'demos' is therefore the most difficult and intensively discussed problem of Estonia's democracy. Strictly speaking, the Estonian state is not conceptually based on ethnicity: it granted citizenship to all people who were Estonian citizens in 1940 when the Soviet occupation began, and their descendants. In practice, however, this excluded all Russian-speaking inhabitants and their descendants who immigrated to Estonia after 1940, which means one-third of Estonia's population.[78] It must be acknowledged that the institutions of the Estonian state work smoothly even in the Ida-Viru district, where Russians form a majority of 80 per cent. Nevertheless, in 2007, Estonia was shaken by a violent uprising of Russian-speaking youths when a monument to the Red Army, the so-called Bronze Soldier, was moved from the centre of Tallinn to a military cemetery on the outskirts. The division between the ethnically Estonian society and the Russian sub-society is one of the biggest social problems.

The Process of European Integration

Since the mid 1990s, Estonia's transformation process has been increasingly influenced by its integration into the European Union. Estonia had many reasons for wishing to become a full member of the EU, from the desire to become an integral part of European culture and the historic community of Europe again, to the prospect of receiving funding from the EU's Structural Funds and Common Agricultural Policy.[79]

The three Baltic states started their integration into the European Union together. For example, the free trade agreements between the three Baltic republics and the EU, which took effect on 1 January 1995, were an important step towards these countries' inclusion in the community of Western states. These agreements replaced agreements on trade-political and economic cooperation that had been signed on 11 May 1992. Furthermore, on 28 November 1994, the Council of the European Union gave its mandate for signing association agreements with the three Baltic states as prospective future members of the EU. The agreements with Estonia, Latvia and Lithuania were initialled on 12 April 1995 after only two days of negotiation, and signed on 12 June. The essential elements of the free trade agreements were integrated into the three association agreements, which were much more comprehensive and provided for establishing long-term close relations between the Baltic states and the EU. As potential future members, the three Baltic republics were thus included in the structured dialogue with the Central and Eastern European countries.[80]

Estonia was able to achieve an association agreement without undergoing the transition period that had previously been obligatory for associated states. This highlights the very different speeds at which the Baltic states' integration-related reform efforts proceeded. Like all other European agreements, the one between Estonia and the EU required the applicant state to adjust its legal regulations to European Community law. In early July 1997, the European Commission presented its convergence reports, which suggested that the first enlargement round should include the Central and Eastern European applicants Poland, Hungary, the Czech

Republic, Slovenia and indeed Estonia. Talks started in Brussels on 30 March 1998. Thus Estonia, as a candidate that had made great progress in the sphere of legal adjustment, was accepted as a member of the European Union in the course of the first round of eastern enlargement. This clearly changed the country's path of development.

Development since EU Accession in 2004

Estonia has always earned top scores in the freedom rankings of the Heritage Foundation. For the year 2007, the Heritage Foundation placed Estonia seventh in the world, with 1.75 points.[81] However, a downward trend since the country's accession to the EU is evident. For example, Estonia's free trade policy has been replaced by the EU's common trade policy and thus is subject to the latter's protectionism. Estonia's inclusion in the EU's regional and agricultural policies and its adoption of European social and environmental standards have also caused economic freedom to decline.[82]

Another result of Estonia's EU membership has been a regional-political turnaround since 2004, even though the EU had already been co-funding the country's regional-political programmes for some time prior. Besides the Cohesion Fund, it is Objective 1 funding in particular that covers the entire country. However, the years 2004–2006 were a 'phasing in' period for new member states during which – unlike in the older cohesion countries – financial transfers were still comparatively low.[83] Overall, Estonia received about 371 billion euros from the Structural Funds during this period, as well as another 309 million euros from the Cohesion Fund and smaller payments from the common initiatives Interreg and Equal. According to the standard procedure, a national development plan was drafted to allocate these EU funds to fields that were of significance for Estonia.[84] For the funding period 2007–2013, Estonia was supposed to receive a total of 3.45 billion euros.[85] Between 2000 and 2007, EU funding had the positive effect of reducing the gap between rural and average household income in Estonia: by 2007, rural households were earning 92 per cent of the average income, versus 86 per cent in 2000.[86]

Estonia has likewise benefited from European agricultural policy since 2004. At the same time, though, consumers have had to cope with several massive price increases for foods such as sugar.[87] Furthermore, once Estonia was included in European structures, its expenditures for social security rose, more than doubling between 2000 and 2007 (see Figure 1.7). For example, since the implementation of the European Social Fund,

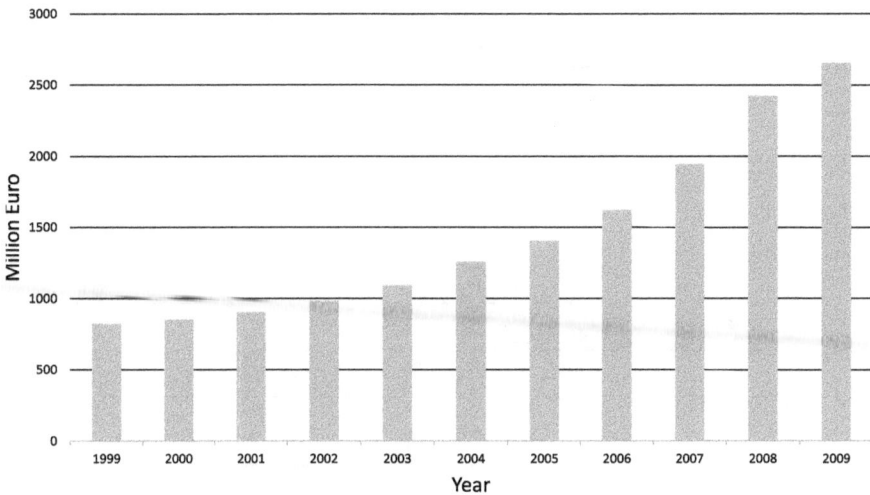

FIGURE 1.7. Expenditure on social protection

Source: Statistics Estonia.

spending on active labour market policy has risen sharply, as has spending on family policy matters and pensions.[88]

These measures, which unquestionably benefited people, triggered an economic boom in Estonia and fostered extremely positive expectations for further development of the economy. One result of this was a period of energetic construction financed by cheap loans. Like other countries, Estonia developed a real estate bubble whose subsequent burst triggered a financial and economic crisis. In the period 2007–2008, commercial banks' asset portfolios grew by some 40 to 50 per cent per year, as did the population's personal debt. As commercial banks borrowed ever more from foreign countries, the Estonian population's foreign debt rose too.[89]

With the bursting of the speculative bubble in the United States, the Estonian economy also met with hardship. Foreign trade declined rapidly, GNP sank by 14.4 per cent in 2009 (see Figure 1.5) and the unemployment rate rose from 5.5 per cent in 2008 to 13.8 per cent in 2009 (Figure 1.8). Since 2010, however, growth rates have become positive again, and unemployment has clearly declined (see Figures 1.5 and 1.8).

At any rate, 2011 was a successful year for Estonia because on 1 January the country was able to introduce the euro. Thus, Estonia became the seventeenth member of the eurozone and its third new member state, after Slovenia and Slovakia. Estonia, together with other new member states, had begun participation in Exchange Rate Mechanism II in 2004 in the

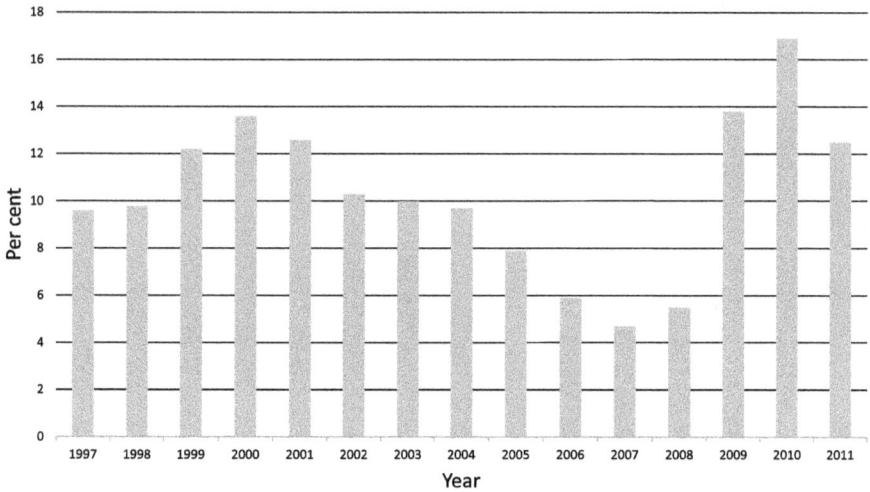

FIGURE 1.8. Unemployment rate of population aged 15–74

Source: Statistics Estonia.

context of the European Monetary System. Accordingly, Estonia fixed an exchange rate between its currency and the euro and committed itself to keeping the margin of fluctuation below +/- 15 per cent. The exchange rate of the Estonian crown was fixed at 15.6466 crowns to one euro, which followed from the crown having been pegged to the German mark in 1993 at an exchange rate of one mark to eight crowns.[90]

Conclusion

Since regaining independence, Estonia has enjoyed remarkable political stability and continuity. It successfully established democratic institutions and structures in a very short span of time, in parallel with a burgeoning of civil society. Integration into the European Union went smoothly: Estonia made it into the first round of enlargement and was able to introduce the euro in 2011. Estonia's process of political transformation can therefore be considered very successful. In this context, the country's foreign-political success is attributable to its economic-political strategy.

From the outset, Estonia's economic policy aimed at creating attractive conditions for investment in order to stabilize the political and economic framework conditions. In doing so, Estonia followed a radically liberal path that also enabled it to come out ahead in international competition for capital. For several years, Estonia had one of the highest per capita inflows of direct investment among Central and Eastern European countries. Thus, the development of Estonia's economy after 1991 must generally be judged favourably, as the country's transformation crisis of 1993 bottomed out comparatively soon. Though Estonia was hard hit by the Russian crisis of 1998 and the international financial and economic crisis of 2008, its economy has been in recovery since 2010.

One consequence of Estonia's combination of consistent economic transformation with a modest social security policy was a fundamental change in income distribution among both individuals and regions. The successive Estonian governments have basically accepted this so as not to endanger the economic upswing. In the meantime, society was splitting into Estonian and Russian-speaking parts. The two sub-societies are drifting ever further from each other, even though for some years the EU has increasingly helped to implement regional-political remedies. The EU has also forced further integration steps on the Russian-speaking part of the population, but Estonia's integration policy for this sector of the population remains unsatisfactory. All in all, however, Estonia's path of development deserves a very positive assessment.

Ralph Michael Wrobel is Professor of Economics, especially Economic Policy, at West Saxon University of Applied Sciences in Zwickau, Germany. Previously he worked as Lecturer in Economic Policy at the University of Tartu in Estonia and in the administration of the University of Erfurt, Germany. His research interests are varieties of capitalism, especially social market economy and transformation of economic systems. Additionally, he specializes in the analysis of emerging markets in Central and Eastern Europe as well as in East Asia.

Notes

1. On this, see e.g. the historic overview by Z. Kiaupa, A. Mäesalu et al., *Geschichte des Baltikums* (Tallinn, 1999).
2. On the history of the independent Baltic states, see especially the standard reference G. von Rauch, *Geschichte der baltischen Staaten*, 2nd ed. (Munich, 1986).
3. See, e.g., D. Feest, *Zwangskollektivierung im Baltikum: Die Sowjetisierung des estnischen Dorfes 1944–1953* (Cologne, 2007); O. Mertelsmann (ed.), *Der stalinistische Umbau in Estland: Von der Markt- zur Kommandowirtschaft* (Hamburg, 2006).
4. See, e.g., J. Reiljan, 'Die wirtschaftspolitischen Probleme des selbständigen Estland', *Deutsche Studien* 29(116) (1991), 371–89; K. Schrader, *Estland auf dem Weg zur Marktwirtschaft:*

Eine Zwischenbilanz (Kiel, 1994); B. Burger and M. Lenzner, *Estland: Die Entwicklung der Wirtschafts- und Sozialpolitik*, Studie 4, HWWA-Report No. 145 (Hamburg, 1994); O. Lugus, *Transforming the Estonian Economy*, International Center for Economic Growth (Tallinn, 1995); K. Schrader and C.-F. Laaser, *Der Transformationsprozess in den baltischen Staaten: Ordnungspolitische Fortschritte und strukturelle Anpassungsprozesse*, Kieler Arbeitspapiere No. 783 (Kiel, 1997); R. Wrobel, *Estland und Europa: Die Bedeutung des Systemwettbewerbs für die Evolution und Transformation von Wirtschaftssystemen* (Tartu, 2000); Ü. Ennuste and L. Wilder, *Essays in Estonian Transformation Economics* (Tallinn, 2003); R. Wrobel, 'Die ökonomische Transformation Estlands: Ein Beispiel endogenen Wandels', in M. Brunn, F. Ettrich et al. (eds), *Transformation und Europäisierung: Eigenarten und (Inter-)Dependenzen von postsozialistischem Wandel und Europäischer Integration* (Münster, 2010), 201–21.

5. On privatization, see e.g. A. Purju, 'Voucher Privatization in Estonia', *Communist Economies and Economic Transformation* 7(3) (1995), 385–408; H. Schmidt, 'Methodenfragen der Privatisierung, dargestellt am Beispiel Estland', in L.-E.-Stiftung (ed.), *Soziale Marktwirtschaft als historische Weichenstellung* (Bonn, 1996), 523–57. On the currency board, see e.g. M. Sõrg, 'Estonian Strategies in the Reconstruction of Its Monetary System', D.E. Fair and R. Raymond (eds), *The Competitiveness of Financial Institutions and Centres in Europe* (Dordrecht, 1994), 171–82. On the labour market, see R. Eamets, 'Labour Market and Employment Issues in Transition Economies: The Case of Estonia', *Communist Economies and Economic Transformation* 6(1) (1994), 55–73.

6. See, e.g., A. Hansson, 'Transforming an Economy while Building a Nation: The Case of Estonia', WIDER (World Institute for Development Economics Research), Working Paper No. 113 (1993); R. Winkelmann, *Politik und Wirtschaft im Baltikum: Stabilisierung von Demokratie und Marktwirtschaft in Estland, Lettland und Litauen* (Saarbrücken, 2007); H. Palang and A. Printsmann, 'From Totalitarian to Democratic Landscapes: The Transition in Estonia', in J. Primdahl and S. Swaffield (eds), *Globalization and Agricultural Landscapes* (Cambridge, 2010), 169–84.

7. See, e.g., K. Schrader and C.-F. Laaser, 'Die baltischen Staaten auf dem Weg nach Europa: Lehren aus der Süderweiterung der EG', in H. Siebert (ed.), *Kieler Studien*, Vol. 264 (Tübingen, 1994); K. Schrader, 'Integration of the Baltic States with Europe', in L. Orlowski and D. Salvatore (eds), *Trade and Payments in Central and Eastern Europe's Transforming Economies* (London, 1997), 330–45; B. Seliger, 'Integration of the Baltic States in the European Union in the Light of the Theory of Institutional Competition', *Communist Economies and Economic Transformation* 10(1) (1998), 95–109; R. Wrobel, 'Die Osterweiterung des europäischen Leviathan: Der Integrationsprozeß des marktwirtschaftlichen Musterknaben Estland in die wohlfahrtsstaatliche EU', *Liberal – Vierteljahreshefte für Politik und Kultur* 41(4) (1999), 66–70; P. Oberender, *Osterweiterung der EU und Transformation als Herausforderungen: Zur Situation in Rußland und Estland* (Bayreuth, 2001); C.-F. Laaser, 'Knocking on the Door: The Baltic Rim Transition Countries Ready for Europe?' in L. Hedegaard et al. (eds), *The NEBI Yearbook: North European and Baltic Sea Integration*, 5th ed. (Berlin, 2003), 21–45.

8. See, e.g., M. Laar, *Das estnische Wirtschaftswunder* (Tallinn, 2002); H. Hannula, S. Radosevic and N. von Tunzelmann (eds), *Estonia, the New EU Economy: Building a Baltic Miracle* (Aldershot, 2006); J. Sepp, 'Estland – eine ordnungspolitische Erfolgsgeschichte?' in B. Seliger, J. Sepp and R. Wrobel (eds), *Das Konzept der Sozialen Marktwirtschaft und seine Anwendung: Deutschland im internationalen Vergleich* (Frankfurt a. M., 2009), 143–61; M. Lauristin, *Estonia's Transition to the EU: Twenty Years On* (London, 2010).

9. See M. Butenschön, *Estland, Lettland, Litauen: Das Baltikum auf dem langen Weg in die Freiheit* (Munich, 1992), 29–36.

10. See A. Rothacher, 'Estland: Wirtschaft und Politik in der reinen Marktwirtschaft', *KAS-Auslandsinformation*, No. 01/97 (1997), 94–101, here 96–98.
11. See Wrobel, 'Die ökonomische Transformation Estlands', 205.
12. See T. Schumacher, *Transformation und wirtschaftliche Selbstverwaltung: Das Beispiel Estland* (Frankfurt a. M., 1997), 120.
13. See Butenschön, *Estland, Lettland, Litauen*, 37–40.
14. See ibid., 340f.
15. See §1 of the Estonian constitution, available in English translation on http://www.servat.unibe.ch/icl/en00000_.html.
16. On the Riigikogu, see §§59–76 of the Estonian constitution; on the electoral law, see also the law on parliamentary elections.
17. See §57 of the Estonian constitution.
18. See Bertelsmann Stiftung, *Ländergutachten Estland* (2003), 8 (http:// bti2003.bertelsmann-transformation-index.de/176.0.html).
19. See Schrader and Laaser, 'Die baltischen Staaten', 6.
20. See President of the Republic Election Act.
21. See §§77–85 of the Estonian constitution.
22. According to §3 of the Law on the Government, the government consists of a prime minister and fourteen ministers at most.
23. See §26 of the Law on the Government.
24. See §§86–101 of the Estonian constitution.
25. See Schrader and Laaser, 'Die baltischen Staaten', 22f.
26. See Kommission der Europäischen Gemeinschaften, *Stellungnahme der Kommission zum Antrag Estlands auf Beitritt zur Europäischen Union*, KOM (97) 2006 (Brussels, 1997), 14f.
27. See Bertelsmann Stiftung, *Ländergutachten Estland*, 4.
28. See R. Wrobel, 'Local Administration Reform in Estonia: Alternatives from an Economic Point of View', *Post-Communist Economies* 15(2) (2003), 277–95, here 278–83; J. Reiljan, 'Vergrößerung der regionalen Disparitäten der Wirtschaftsentwicklung Estlands', *Ordnungspolitischer Diskurs* No. 2010–3 (2010), 10 (http://www.ordnungspolitisches-portal.de/05_02_OPO_Diskurse_2010–03.pdf).
29. On this, see §§139–45 of the Estonian constitution.
30. See Kommission der Europäischen Gemeinschaften, *Stellungnahme*, 15.
31. See Bertelsmann Stiftung, *Ländergutachten Estland*, 6; for more details, see M. Lauristin and P. Vihalemm, 'The Transformation of Estonian Society and Media: 1987–2001', in P. Vihalemm (ed.), *Baltic Media in Transition* (Tartu, 2002), 17–63; A. Risberg and A. Ainamo, 'Expansion of the Nordic Business Press: Äripäev in Estonia as a Carrier of Western Discourses', in P. Kjaer and T. Slaatta (eds), *Mediating Business: The Expansion of Business Journalism* (Copenhagen, 2007), 101–28; D. Grundey, 'Media Business in the Baltic States: A Comparative Analysis of Lithuania, Latvia and Estonia', *Transformations in Business & Economics* 7(1) (2008), 104–36.
32. On this, see also R. Sommer, *Estlands Weg in die Informationsgesellschaft: ökonomische, soziale, politische und kulturelle Faktoren* (Saarbrücken, 2007).
33. Kommission der Europäischen Gemeinschaften, *Stellungnahme*, 21.
34. See Bertelsmann Stiftung, *Ländergutachten Estland*, 7.
35. According to Transparency International, Korruptionswahrnehmungsindex (2009, 2010), 5f. (http://www.transparency.de/uploads/media /09–11–17–CPI_2009_Pressemappe.pdf), no. 27 together with Slovenia.
36. See Bertelsmann Stiftung, *Ländergutachten Estland*, 5–9.
37. See Schrader and Laaser, *Transformationsprozess*, 26.

38. See Wrobel, 'Die ökonomische Transformation Estlands', 210 f.
39. See ibid., 207.
40. See A. Kein and V. Tali, 'The Process of Ownership Reform and Privatization', in Estonian Academy of Sciences and Institute of Economics (eds), *Transforming the Estonian Economy* (Tallinn, 1995), 140–68, here 146.
41. See Schrader and Laaser, 'Die baltischen Staaten', 37f.
42. 600,000 Estonian crowns is about 37,000 euros.
43. See Wrobel, 'Die ökonomische Transformation Estlands', 207–9.
44. See Eesti Erastamisagentuur (Estonian Privatization Agency), *Privatization in Estonia* (Tallinn, 1994), 8.
45. See V. Sarnet, 'Economic Transition in Estonia – 1996', in A. Böhm (ed.), *Economic Transition Report 1996* (Ljubljana, 1996), 113–131, here 114.
46. See Schrader and Laaser, *Transformationsprozess*, 33.
47. See Eesti Pank (Bank of Estonia), 'Estonian Kroon – Finance Economy' (June 1993), 5.
48. On this law, see Eesti Pank (Bank of Estonia), 'Law on the Central Bank of the Republic of Estonia', Version 18 (May 1993), English translation, manuscript with no year given.
49. See A. Freytag, 'Einige Anmerkungen zur Wahl der Reservewährung eines Currency Boards', *Zeitschrift für Wirtschaftspolitik* 47(1) (1998) 3–19, here 3f.
50. See Deutsche Bank Research, 'Währungsreformen in den baltischen Staaten', *Bulletin – Aktuelle Wirtschafts- und Währungsfragen* (11 April 1994), 14.
51. See Chapter VIII of the Estonian constitution.
52. See A. Kala, 'Foreign Trade', in Estonian Academy of Sciences and Institute of Economics, *Transforming the Estonian Economy*, 280–308, here 282.
53. See Kommission der Europäischen Gemeinschaften, *Stellungnahme*, 25.
54. See E. Vitsur, 'Investment Policy and Development of Foreign Investments', in Estonian Academy of Sciences and Institute of Economics, *Transforming the Estonian Economy*, 208–25, here 212f.
55. See Schrader and Laaser, *Transformationsprozess*, 44.
56. See S. Kallas, 'Estonia and the European Union', *European Business Journal* 8 (1996), 13–20, here 19.
57. See T. Paas, 'Estonia – A Small Open Economy', *EMERGO* 4(2) (1997), 37–53, here 47f.
58. See Osteuropa-Institut München, 'Den Transformationsschritt messen: Die staatliche Einflußnahme auf die Wirtschaftstätigkeit in ausgewählten Transformationsstaaten, Gutachten, erstellt im Auftrag des Bundesministeriums für Wirtschaft' (Munich, 1997), 142f.
59. On this see R. Wrobel, 'Umstrittene Standortpolitiken in Europa: Estland und Irland im Vergleich', in Tallinner Technische Universität and Tartuer Universität (eds), *Sammelband zur XIII. wirtschaftspolitischen Konferenz* (Tartu, 2005), 346–54.
60. See A.A. Pajuste, 'Entwicklung des Steuersystems in Estland', in W. Wacker (ed.), *Europäisierung des Steuerrechts und steuerliche Entwicklung in Osteuropa* (Göttingen, 1997), 75–83, here 79f.
61. See Osteuropa-Institut München, 'Transformationsschritt', 144f. On the Estonian tax law, see also J. Sepp and R. Wrobel, 'Das Steuersystem in Estland im Spannungsfeld zwischen Transformationserfordernissen und EU-Harmonisierung', in R. Hasse, K.-E. Schenk and A.W. von Czege (eds), *Europa zwischen Wettbewerb und Harmonisierung* (Baden-Baden, 2002), 69–75; and on the current situation, see Wrobel, *Umstrittene Standortpolitiken*.
62. See Osteuropa-Institut München, *Transformationsschritt*, 135.

63. See OECD, *Investitionsführer Estland*, ed. Zentrum für Zusammenarbeit mit den Reformländern der OECD (Paris, 1997), 83.
64. See J. Sepp and R. Wrobel, 'Besonderheiten der Wettbewerbspolitik in einem Transformationsland: Die Entwicklung der Wettbewerbsordnung in Estland als Beispiel', *Wirtschaft und Wettbewerb* 1 (2000), 26–44, here 32–44.
65. See Sepp, 'Estland', 143.
66. See K. Kilvits, *Industrial Restructuring in Estonia*, Estonian Academy of Science, Preprint 43 (Tallinn, 1995), 12.
67. See Kommission der Europäischen Gemeinschaften, *Stellungnahme*, 29.
68. See Osteuropa-Institut München, *Transformationsschritt*, 156.
69. See Burger and Lenzner, 'Estland', p. 51–57; for more details, see M. Leinsalu, *Troubled Transitions: Social Variation and Long-Term Trends in Health and Mortality in Estonia* (Stockholm, 2004). As demonstrated e.g. K. Leping, *Ethnic Wage Gap and Political Break-ups: Estonia During Political and Economic Transition* (Tartu, 2007); however, a clear pay gap exists between the Estonian and Russian-speaking parts of the population.
70. See D. Eerma and J. Sepp, 'Estonia in Transition under the Restrictions of European Institutional Competition', *Ordnungspolitische Diskurse* (2009),7, available at http://www.ordnungspolitisches-portal.com/Diskurse/Diskurse_2009-02.pdf; for more details, see L. Leppik and G. Männik, 'Transformation of Old-Age Security in Estonia', in W. Schmähl and S. Horstmann (eds), *Transformation of Pension Systems in Central and Eastern Europe* (Cheltenham, 2002), 89–124; or L. Leppik, *Transformation of the Estonian Pension System: Policy Choices and Policy Outcomes* (Tallinn, 2006).
71. See Wrobel, *Estland und Europa*, 217f.
72. See P. Cornelius and B. Weder, 'Economic Transformation and Income Distribution: Some Evidence from the Baltic Countries', *IMF Working Paper* 96/14 (1996), 17f.
73. See M. Raudjärv, 'Wirtschaftspolitsche Ziele und marktwirtschaftliche Transformation in Estland', *Wirtschaftswissenschaftliche Diskussionspapiere* 4 (2004), 8.
74. See Rothacher, 'Estland', 98f.
75. See Kommission der Europäischen Gemeinschaften, *Regional Policy – Info regio*, no year given (http://ec.europa.eu/regional_policy/country/gateway/estonia_en.cfm?gw_ide=1719&lg=en).
76. Bertelsmann Stiftung, *Ländergutachten Estland*, 5.
77. On this debate, see R. Wrobel, 'Culture and Economic Transformation: "Economic Style" in Europe, Russia and China', in M. Jovanovic, L. Dalgon and B. Seliger (eds), *System Transformation in Comparative Perspective: Affinity and Diversity in Institutional, Structural and Cultural Patterns* (Berlin, 2007), 163–85, where Estonia is compared to Russia and China.
78. Bertelsmann Stiftung, *Ländergutachten Estland*, 4f.; for more details, see Denis Gruber, *Zuhause in Estland? Eine Untersuchung zur sozialen Integration ethnischer Russen an der Außengrenze der Europäischen Union* (Berlin, 2008).
79. On this see Wrobel, *Estland und Europa*, 157–62.
80. See R. Wrobel, 'Die Bedeutung der Institutionen-Transformation für die EU-Integration der drei baltischen Staaten', in Tallinner Technische Universität and Tartuer Universität (eds), *Aktuaalsed Majanduspoliitika Küsimused Euroopa Liidu Riikides Ja Eesti Vabariigis*, Vol. 2 (Tallinn, 1996), 393–403, here 399.
81. See Heritage Foundation (ed.), *Index of Economic Freedom*, 2006 (http://www.heritage.org/research/features/index/downloads.cfm#scores).
82. See Sepp, 'Estland', 157.

83. See M. Kämpfe, 'EU-Strukturfonds: Aufstockung der Mittel nach jüngster Erweiterung zu erwarten', *Wirtschaft im Wandel* 7 (2004), 209–13, here 212.
84. See Eesti Riiklik Arengukava, *European Union – Structural Funds* (Tallinn, no year given), 2.
85. See Europäische Union, *Arbeiten für die Region: EU-Regionalpolitik 2007–2013* (2008), 5.
86. See Ministry of Social Affairs, *Health, Labour and Social Life in Estonia 2000–2008* (Tallinn, 2009), 29.
87. On this, see K. Toming, 'The Price Impact of Adopting the Common Agricultural Policy in Estonia: Estimated versus Actual Effects', *University of Tartu/Faculty of Economics and Business Administration Working Paper* No. 45/2006.
88. See Ministry of Social Affairs, *Health, Labour and Social Life*, 93–97; see also J. Aidukaite, 'The Transformation of Welfare Systems in the Baltic States: Estonia, Latvia and Lithuania', in A. Cerami (ed.), *Post-Communist Welfare Pathways* (Basingstoke, 2009), 96–111.
89. See Eerma and Sepp, *Estonia in Transition*, 7.
90. Auswärtiges Amt, *Estland – Wirtschaft*, 2010 (http:// www.auswaertiges-amt.de/diplo/ de/Laenderinformationen/Estland/Wirtschaft.html).

Chapter 2

LATVIA

Claudia-Yvette Matthes

Introduction

Like many other countries in Central and Eastern Europe, Latvia is a latecomer as a national state, having declared its independence only in the wake of World War I, on 18 November 1918. The 1922 constitution (*Satversme*) established a parliamentary system of rule oriented to the Weimar constitution of the German Reich and vested far-reaching competences in the parliament and president. As it provided citizens with extensive possibilities for participation and comprehensive minority rights, this constitution was considered one of the most modern in Europe.[1] Following the initial consolidation of society and economy, however, the economic crisis at the end of the 1920s led to political crises and frequent changes of government in Latvia. President Kārlis Ulmanis reacted to this with a coup, declaring a state of emergency on the night of 15–16 May 1934, dissolving parliament, banning political parties and 'Latviaizing' the economy.[2] Many Latvians nevertheless have positive memories of Ulmanis's authoritarian regime, not least in comparison to the invasion by Soviet troops in August 1940.

Latvia's reintegration into the Soviet Union – interrupted by German occupation from July 1941 to October 1944 – had dramatic consequences. In the course of the political and economic restructuring, the country's intellectual elite was almost eradicated by mass deportations to Siberia that removed 16,000 people in June 1941 alone. Furthermore, so many Latvians emigrated that the population is estimated to have shrunk by around 30 per cent by 1945.[3] Meanwhile, the country's industrialization and militarization, with Riga at the centre of the Baltic Military District, drew many Russian or Russian-speaking[4] immigrants to Latvia, drastically changing the proportions of nationalities: in 1935, 76 per cent of the inhabitants had been Latvians, but by 1989 they made up only 52 per cent.[5] The effects of these experiences linger today, influencing the country's foreign policy and fuelling conflicts over domestic policy and debates among the political parties.

The Road to Independence and Democracy

The Actors of the Radical Change

When Mikhail Gorbachev's perestroika began in the mid 1980s, a protest movement against the political situation developed and grew in Latvia. The population's discontent focused most of all on the 'national' question, that is, how to maintain or re-establish Latvian identity rather than welcome the efforts the political leadership in Moscow was making to re-educate the inhabitants of all Soviet republics as 'Homo sovieticus'. This desire for cultural autonomy lay behind the growing demand for political autonomy and more democracy.

Three groups among the opposition movement unfolding in the 1980s were particularly relevant: the folklore movement, organized around singing festivals that, as a mode of national self-assertion, inspired the name 'the Singing Revolution'; the ecology movement, which understood the protection of nature as defence of the Latvian territory against the consequences of Russian occupation and formed in 1987 around the planning of a dam on the Daugava River; and the human rights movement, which developed in 1986 as a reaction to the Helsinki Final Act. These movements first organized huge demonstrations in 1987, to commemorate the deportations to Siberia. The peak of the protests came on 23 August 1989 with the 'Baltic Way', a human chain stretching from Lithuania to Estonia. Its more than two million participants wanted to memorialize the signing of the Molotov-Ribbentrop Pact, the secret annex to the Hitler-Stalin Pact that had led to the loss of Baltic independence.[6]

In 1988, two larger political coalition movements emerged from this rather loosely organized opposition. In June, members of environmental and human rights groups founded the Latvian Movement for National Independence (Latvijas Nacionālās Neatkarības Kustība, LNNK). Its goals were to first achieve Latvian independence and then introduce democracy. The People's Front of Latvia (Latvijas Tautas Fronte), formed in October 1988, propagated the opposite way – democracy first, then an independent Latvia. About 20 per cent of its active members were not Latvian themselves. The People's Front soon grew to become the largest movement, with about 250,000 members versus the approximately 8,000 members of the LNNK.[7]

In addition, the Latvian Social Democratic Party (Latvijas Sociāldemocrātiskā Strādnieku Partija) was refounded in December 1989. Established in 1904, it had been active in Swedish exile after 1940. Then, in January 1990, the Latvian Green Party (Latvijas Zaļā Partija) was established. Its understanding of environmental protection extended beyond trees and animals to cover the Latvian nation as well.[8]

Lastly, in January 1989, those forces speaking out in favour of Latvia staying with the Soviet Union organized themselves as the International Front of the Working People of Latvia, also called Interfront (Latvijas Internationālā Darbaļaužu Fronte). Some 80 per cent of its members and supporters were Soviet soldiers and workers or functionaries of the Communist Party of Latvia (Latvijas Komunistiskā Partija, KPL). Its initial membership was around 10,000.[9]

Elections as a Catalyst for System Change

On 26 March 1989, citizens of the Soviet Union were allowed to participate in choosing the members of the Soviet Union's law-making body, the Congress of People's Deputies, for the first time. In these elections, the People's Front won thirty of the forty-one Latvian seats. It was victorious again in the municipal elections held on 10 December 1989 – even in Riga, where there were more Russians than Latvians. The success of the People's Front in elections for the Supreme Soviet on 8 March 1990 finally cleared the way to independence.

The People's Front formed an all-party coalition led by Prime Minister Ivars Godmanis, who in May 1990 declared the country independent and announced a transition period to complete sovereignty. This declaration was strongly opposed by the KPL, whose reactionary wing (the party had formally split in April 1990) called for violent action against independence. In early January 1991, the Special Purpose Mobile Unit of the Soviet Ministry of the Interior – the so-called OMON troops – occupied the press building in Riga, and on 20 January they stormed parliament. With the help of committed citizens, the Latvian government managed to successfully defend itself against this attempted coup.[10]

To underline the legitimacy of the movement for independence, the Godmanis government held a 'consultative referendum' on 3 March 1991. It was consultative insofar as the prevailing legal opinion was that the Soviet occupation had only interrupted independence. According to the Soviet constitution, a republic could leave the Federation only by way of a two-thirds majority vote. Latvia voted 73.7 to 24.7 per cent in favour of becoming independent of the Soviet Union, with a turnout of 87.6 per cent.[11] Only after the attempted coup against Gorbachev in Moscow on 19 August 1991 and Boris Yeltsin's seizure of power did the Soviet Union finally acknowledge Latvia's independence. Yet open questions remained: the withdrawal of the armed forces (the last Russian troops left Latvia in 1994); the military radar station at Skrunda, which Russia did not dismantle until 1998; some sectors of the border between the two countries; and the issue of citizenship.[12]

The Founding of the Independent State and First Reforms

Unlike its Estonian counterpart, Latvian legal opinion held that the institutions of the interwar period were still valid. Accordingly, the parts of the 1922 constitution that were considered relevant came into force again. The other sections were to be reactivated after the first really free parliamentary elections in the independent state, due in 1993 upon the elapse of the then current three-year legislative term.[13]

The electoral law of 1922 stipulated proportional representation with five electoral districts. It was augmented with a newly introduced threshold clause of initially 4 per cent and then, from 1995, 5 per cent. Latvia has multi-candidate constituencies with loosely connected tickets, and voters may vote preferentially for certain candidates.[14] The number of seats is determined using the Sainte-Laguë method.[15]

Besides setting the political-constitutive course, the Godmanis government also started to reform the economic system. The prevailing conditions in the early 1990s were favourable, insofar as Latvia had a highly skilled workforce and did not have to assume any of the Soviet Union's debts. The country had been a major car manufacturer, producer of agricultural goods and food processor. It also produced tobacco and paper, and processed wood and leather. However, as a former member of the Soviet system of work-share, Latvia had to make enormous restructuring efforts, particularly regarding the All-Union plants.[16]

Basically, the economic transformation happened in several steps. In this context, the government prioritized financial-political stabilization over privatization or liberalization of the national economy. The primary goal was to get away from the Russian rouble as soon as possible. The very strict monetary policy of Latvia's central bank proved essential to the country's transformation towards a market economy. Between 20 July 1992 and 5 March 1993, the central bank first replaced the Russian with the Latvian rouble, then the latter with lats. From 1994 to 2005, the lat was linked to the currency basket of the International Monetary Fund (IMF), but since 2005 it has been pegged to the euro (1 euro = 0.702804 lats).[17] In preparation for these measures, the government introduced a new tax system in 1991, abandoned price controls from 1991 and 1992, and pushed development of commercial banks, which ended in 1993.[18]

As for the privatization of state enterprises, parliament passed the necessary legal framework in March and September of 1992. It allowed for various ways of changing ownership structures: auctions, leasing, transformation into corporations, distribution of shares among the population by way of vouchers,[19] and also liquidation. At first, only smaller enterprises were privatized, and restitutions were carried out for both buildings and land. Large-scale privatization came later. In the course of liberalizing its economy, Latvia signed a free trade agreement with its Baltic neighbours in 1993.[20]

Politics

Institutional Structure, Administration, Judicial System and Media

With the first free elections on 5 and 6 June 1993, the country finally returned to its old constitution and the parliamentary system of rule from the interwar period. Once again, the parliament (Saeima), called the 5th Saeima in continuation of the old sequence, had one hundred members and consisted of one house. The Saeima's usual tasks are law-making, deciding about a government and controlling it. Its structure comprises factions, which are often very fragile, as well as standing, temporary and special committees, for example to investigate political scandals. The parliamentary leadership includes representatives of the opposition, although the latter are often at a disadvantage when it comes to designating committee chairs.[21]

The President of the State has the power to dissolve the Saeima on the basis of a referendum, but should the referendum fail, the president must step down him- or herself. So far, no president has had to resign. In cases of simple laws, law-making by the people is possible: if at least one tenth of eligible voters supports it, parliament must discuss a popular initiative. The president and parliament may initiate a referendum, which can be held to vote on amending the constitution and has been held regarding Latvia's accession to the EU. Another of the president's powers is the right of legislative initiative.[22]

Voter turnout in Latvia has been in decline. In 1992 it was 89 per cent; in later years 70 per cent. In 2006 and 2010, however, it was only about 62 per cent. Non-Latvians tend to vote rather left wing, which in Latvia means 'pro-Russian', whereas Latvian voters predominantly favour right-wing, that is, nationally oriented parties. Due to proportional representation, there are no close contacts between members of parliament (MPs) and voters. International organizations such as the Organization for Security and Co-operation in Europe (OSCE) regularly observe elections in Latvia and say they are free and fair. However, on the same regular basis, they criticize the high number of inhabitants who are ineligible to vote, even at the municipal level, because they are not citizens.[23] The number of non-citizens is declining, but they still made up 15.5 per cent of the population in 2010.

The first elections, held in June 1993, had resulted in the formation of a quite stable government coalition consisting of the Latvian Way (Latvijas Ceļš, LC) and the Latvian Farmers' Union (Latviešu Zemnieku Savienība) with Valdis Birkavs (LC) as prime minister, but after each of the following elections the weakness of the political parties made forming a government more difficult. The leading parties, following the first four elections, had all been founded less than one year before. Thus, governments either had very large majorities consisting of all Latvian parties aligned against representatives of the interests of the Russian-speaking population, or they were minority governments. Both types proved rather short-lived, and so far no government has survived a complete term of office, having been forced to step down in most cases. To date, only two heads of government have been re-elected (Aigars Kalvītis in 2006 and Valdis Dombrovskis in 2010 and 2011).[24] Thus, no constructive political dualism has yet developed between a governing majority and its opposition.[25]

The government is elected en bloc by the parliament, and its members need not be MPs. The parliament is entitled to withdraw its support from the government as a whole, or it may vote individual ministers out of their offices. The government must step down if parliament rejects the budget. The head of government cannot ask for a vote of confidence. The President of the State is involved in forming a government only insofar as he or she must choose a head of government who is capable of winning a majority. However, given the fragility of both the party system and the factions, the president has a certain steering function. If the third attempt to form a government should fail, new elections must be held.[26] By and large, the administration works satisfactorily, though it suffers from a blatant staff shortage. Furthermore, after elections too many positions are newly occupied by office holders who are not always sufficiently qualified.[27]

Initially parliament elected the President of the State for a three-year term, but since 4 December 1997, the term has been four years. The president may be elected for one more term, but he or she may also be voted out of office by a two-thirds majority. In the context of law-making, apart from the right of initiative, the president also has the power of veto and can initiate a referendum on a law. A candidate must be at least forty years old to be elected president. The current president is Latvia's fourth. The first, Guntis Ulmanis of the Farmers' Union, presented himself as the political successor of his uncle Kārlis Ulmanis, who was president during the interwar period. By the end of the 1990s, Guntis Ulmanis tended towards the more liberal end of the political spectrum, particularly regarding the question of citizenship, and supported attempts at reform.[28]

His successor in 1999 was Vaira Vīķe-Freiberga, a re-immigrated Canadian-Latvian professor of psychology. She gained much respect among the population, in part because in March 2007 she vetoed some democratically dubious laws on national security and saw to their revision. After her two terms of office, the parties in the then current government met in secret at the Riga Zoo and agreed on supporting a little-known physician, Valdis Zatlers. He achieved a clear majority of fifty-eight parliamentary votes, and despite the informal manner of his selection, he acted politically independently.[29] Zatlers also strove to keep this independence regarding his firm stand against Latvia's oligarchs. On 28 May 2011, after an investigation by the attorney general found sufficient evidence that they had interfered with politics, he dissolved parliament, which had been elected just nine months before. However, the old parliament was already scheduled to elect a new President of the State before new parliamentary elections were held. Zatlers was defeated by the entrepreneur and politician Andris Bērziņš from the Union of Farmers and Greens (Zaļo un Zemnieku Savienība, ZZS), which is headed by one of Latvia's most powerful oligarchs, Aivars Lembergs. Zatlers, however, succeeded in being voted into parliament with his own party, newly founded in September 2011.[30]

The Constitutional Court, newly introduced in 1996, consists of seven judges elected for ten years by a simple majority of the Saeima.[31] The government, the president or a group of at least twenty MPs may introduce a motion for an abstract review. Since 2001, individual citizens may file a constitutional complaint. For years, the EU and Latvian NGOs have demanded reform of the judicial system, criticizing judges' qualifications and the influence the Ministry of Justice exerts on both their selection and the funding of courts. Cases of corruption within the judicial system have been revealed repeatedly, as have legal cases in which lawyers had secret preliminary talks with judges. The reputation of the judicial system has suffered accordingly; Eurobarometer 2009 documented that 59 per cent of interviewees distrusted it.[32] Administrative courts, on the other hand, have done a good job since being introduced in 2004, and with their relatively uncorrupted, well-qualified staff have enhanced the reputation of the judicial system as a whole.[33] Further reform has clearly improved at least the staff situation, the level of judges' qualification and the reputation of the judicial system overall.[34]

Initially, from October 1996 to March 2007, the National Bureau of Human Rights had supervised the upholding of human rights. On 1 January 2007, the Kalvītis government, urged by the President of the State, introduced the office of ombudsman to receive complaints from the population and represent their interests, including minority issues, before the judicial system, government and parliament. By general agreement of the parties, the parliament elected former Minister of Justice Romāns Apsītis ombudsman in March 2007. Apsītis succeeded in extending the ombudsman's term of office to five years, making it independent of the parliamentary term. He considers himself the champion of the civil interests of all, including non-citizens. His recommendations to the government are not binding, however.[35]

After fifteen years of debate, the Godmanis government reformed the country's administrative structure in June 2009. For example, it abandoned the use of 500 districts as a second administrative level, restructuring them to form 109 bigger unities, the *novad*s. It also increased the number of independent cities, which have the same legal status as the *novad*s, from seven to nine. Despite Riga's particular role in social and economic terms, it has no special regulation. This reform met with some local-level protest, as the ZZS is particularly deeply rooted in rural regions and feared a loss of influence. Elections to the self-administrative bodies of the *novad*s and independent cities were held in June 2009.[36]

The freedom of the media is legally protected. Some media – above all the daily newspaper *Diena* – consider themselves supervisory institutions with the task of uncovering corruption scandals and protecting the state of law.[37] In some cases, the political class has tried to restrict the freedom of the media, but the journalists concerned were protected by Latvian or European courts of law.[38] Concerning language, the media landscape is divided. Almost all private media in the Latvian language are foreign-controlled, whereas those in Russian are mostly owned by Russian nationals and based in Riga. Many Russian-language channels also feature programmes broadcast directly from Russia.[39] Sometimes the Russian-language press presents a selective version of history, for example by denying that the Soviet Union occupied Latvia in 1940.[40] For some time in the 1990s, *Diena* also appeared in a Russian edition, but this ended due to lack of interest among readers.

Parties

At first, the founding of political parties was regulated by the Law on Social Organizations and Associations of 15 December 1992. Only a group of at least ten Latvian citizens were allowed to found a party; non-citizens could only start social organizations and associations. As of 26 June 2006, an additional law on political parties gave non-citizens with permanent resident status the right to join a party, as long as they do not form a majority of its members. Anti-constitutional, anti-democratic parties may be banned, or they were not permitted to register in the first place.[41] Organizationally, the structure of political parties in Latvia is still very fragmented, although sometimes certain concentration processes are discernible. The parties' ideological development has been influenced by personal animosities between politicians, programmatic-strategic considerations and most of all the ethno-political[42] division line. The general structuring process of the party system so far is roughly divisible into five partly overlapping periods.

First, as the divide solidified between the People's Front and the LNNK on the one hand and Interfront and the KPL on the other in the period before and after the elections of 1990, further parties were founded. Regarding their attitude towards independence and the question of citizenship, the majority of their members considered themselves 'right wing', that is, pro-Latvian. These parties included the Green Party, the Farmers' Union, the Christian Democratic Union (Kristīgi Demokrātiskā Savienība) and the very nationally oriented Fatherland and Freedom (Tēvzemei un Brīvībai, TB). The newly formed rather moderate or 'left-wing' (on the question of citizenship) parties were the Democratic Centre (Demokrātiskā Centra Partija), the National Harmony Party (Tautas Saskaņas Partija), which originated in the People's Front and is also left wing on the economy, and the refounded Social Democrats.[43]

In the second period – around and after the elections of 1993 – parties developed to focus mainly on transition-connected problems such as poverty, insufficient economic growth or corruption. One of them was the LC, which called itself a 'party of experts' and presented itself as economically liberal, socially-politically conservative and, concerning the question of citizenship, pragmatic. Several prime ministers have come from its ranks. The New Era party (Jaunais Laiks, JL), founded in 2002 by the head of the central bank, Einars Repše, centred on the fight against corruption.[44]

In the third period, some of the 'old' parties merged. Since 1997, the right-wing camp has been dominated by the merger of TB and the LNNK, resisting further privatization. In 2002, the Farmers' Union merged with the Green Party to become the ZZS, a move that secured their re-election to parliament. In 2004, Indulis Emsis became the first prime minister from their ranks. In 2007, the LC merged with the Christian-oriented Latvia's First Party (Latvijas Pirmā Partija, LPP).[45] Meanwhile, parties supporting the Russian-speaking population moved closer to each other. In 2005, Harmony for Latvia united with smaller parties to form the left-wing alliance Harmony Centre (Saskaņas Centrs, SC), which has since enjoyed great electoral success. In 1993, former members of the KPL formed the Equal Rights (Līdztiesība), which in 1998 united with other groups (including the SC, for a time) to form the alliance For Human Rights in a United Latvia (Par Cilvēka Tiesībām Vienotā Latvijā).[46] Despite these concentration processes, political parties are generally not very deeply rooted in society – few have more than a thousand members.

In the fourth period, so-called oligarchs took over existing parties or founded new ones, sometimes pursuing their thus-connected interests very much in the open. In some cases, they were clearly convicted of abuse of power or criminal actions yet remained active, influencing political decision-making and assuming political office with varying success. In 1998, for example, Andris Šķēle, the owner of a huge Latvian group of companies, founded the conservative-economically liberal People's Party (Tautas Partija, TP), chaired it, and was twice Latvia's prime minister. His terms of office were much debated due to his uncooperative way of administration, his appointment of ministers said to have contacts with organized crime, and quarrels over the issue of further privatization. In 2008, Šķēle came under suspicion of having illegally taken over state shares of Latvia's biggest mobile phone providers during the digitalization of the Latvian media system. He was also involved in the attempt by his successor, Aigars Kalvītis, to unseat the head of the anti-corruption bureau known as Korupcijas novēršanas un apkarošanas birojs (KNAB).[47] In July 2011, the TP was dissolved. The reason given officially was insufficient public support, and indeed in the most recent surveys the party had only 2 per cent of the electorate. However, the TP had also been trying for some time to avoid paying a penalty of one million lats (1.4 million euros) after being convicted of illegal fundraising and expenses in the context of the 2006 election campaign. As a result of its dissolution, the party evaded payment.[48]

In 2006, Ainārs Šlesers became chairman of the LPP/LC. From 2002 to 2006, he had been deputy prime minister and minister of transport but had had to step down from the latter position after being found guilty of attempting to bribe the mayor of Jurmala. In January 2006, Šlesers tried to push through a law that was supposed to ban foreign-funded NGOs from monitoring the activities of Latvian parties.[49] Once the LPP/LC and the TP both ran the danger of not reaching the 5 per cent threshold, they united to form the alliance For a Good Latvia (Par Labu Latviju, PLL). Former President of the State Guntis Ulmanis became its chairman.[50] However, with only 7.55 per cent of the vote, this alliance did not achieve the desired result, and in 2011 its parliamentary re-election bid failed.[51]

Aivars Lembergs, the mayor of Ventspils since 1988 and the owner of the Ventspils Nafta oil company, which also holds shares in the three big Latvian daily newspapers[52] and other media, financed and for some time chaired the ZZS.[53] Its ethno-politically motivated understanding of environmental protection fit Lembergs' political worldview well. As the party's top candidate in the 2006 elections, he based his success on anti-liberal and nationalist rhetoric. In March 2007, Lembergs was arrested on suspicion of having paid five million lats in bribes to various parties and politicians, and he spent some months in jail. At first his popularity remained intact, but by 2011 his party's share of votes had declined to just 12.2 per cent.[54]

These oligarchs' activities were facilitated by the Latvian law on political parties, which until 2008/2009 did not provide for restrictions on media campaigns, state financing of parties or compensation for election expenses. Neither were private donations to parties sufficiently regulated. Meanwhile, expenses for political campaigns could not exceed 474,000 lats. Since 2010, however, all parties achieving more than 2 per cent of the vote receive 50 santimi (75 eurocents) per vote as compensation for election expenses. Furthermore, parties must release their campaign budgets, and all campaigning must end at midnight before election day.[55]

In the fifth period, out of strategic and/or programmatic considerations, the parties tried to distinguish themselves differently, in ways not previously common in Latvia. In this context, the example of the Sabiedrība Citai Politikai (Society for a Different Kind of Politics) must be mentioned. It was founded in September 2008 by former ministers Aigars Štokenbergs and Artis Pabriks to address voters who were economically and socio-politically left wing.[56] In another such instance, the Citizens' Union (Pilsoniskā Savienība) developed from the JL in April 2008 to address the previously neglected topic of regional development. Members of TB/LNNK also joined this new party.[57] Before the 2010 election, the two new parties and JL united to form the Vienotība (Unity) alliance, which went on to win most of the vote. In 2011, Vienotība became only the third-strongest power, for although its stabilization policy was successful, it had been unable to curb the oligarchs' influence.[58]

In 2010, the LPP/LC, the TP and Vienotiba had publicly declared they were considering a coalition with the SC. At first, the idea reflected the SC's increasing power, but it also allowed for the assumption that should this occur, the ethno-political line of conflict might become less important in the medium run. The idea of a coalition was dropped, however, mostly because of differences over continuing the policy of cutbacks on social spending.[59] In 2011, with 28.5 per cent, the SC indeed became the strongest political power. In the meantime, the continuing importance of the ethno-political line of conflict became obvious when politicians, then of Vienotība and Valdis Zatler's new 'anti-oligarch' Zatler Reform Party (Zatlera reformu partija), were unable to persuade their parties to form a coalition with the SC. Instead, they invited the nationalist party All For Latvia (Visu Latvijai, VL-TB/LNNK)[60] to participate in the government.[61]

Socio-political Lines of Conflict

The predominant lines of conflict affecting the structure of the party system are still the ethno-political debate on citizenship and the law on languages. Also important, if to a lesser degree, is a related debate on history policy and national identity in Latvia as well as relations with Russia.[62] Latvia's accession to the EU as such is not a debated issue among the parties; rather, they argue over the reforms that are repeatedly demanded by the EU. This contention has involved the parties' different objectives on the one hand and those of the people on the other, regarding the further privatization of key industries, the restructuring of the social systems and the fight to overcome economic crisis.[63] In particular, however, the EU influences laws on fighting corruption and supporting the improved integration of non-Latvians. Accordingly, these topics are the most difficult aspects of the EU accession. Thus, the role of the EU will be a topic in the following sections, whereas the process and consequences of EU accession will be dealt with in a section of their own.

The question of citizenship

The relation between the nation proper and the Russian immigrants who arrived after 1940 – whom many Latvians refer to as 'occupiers' – initially concerned the basic understanding of what citizenship means. The identification cards that the citizens' committee of the LNNK distributed in the late 1980s to those who had been citizens before 1940 were considered a first step towards a historically and ethnically defined kind of citizenship.[64] The new citizenship law introduced by the Birkavs government in 1994 was grounded in this basic understanding. It provided automatic citizenship to all who lived in Latvia before 1940 and their descendants.

Some 200,000 of the 900,000 people of Russian origin in the country met this criterion, but the new law excluded about 40 per cent of Latvia's inhabitants from citizenship. They were allowed to apply for it, under certain conditions. As of 4 May 1990, they had to have lived in Latvia for at least five years. They had to speak Latvian, have legal income, and prove their knowledge of Latvian history and of the national anthem. They also had to renounce any other citizenship. Meanwhile, applications were supposed to be reserved for certain age cohorts according to a 'window system'.[65] Each window was supposed to last one year. This meant that elderly people would probably die before their cohort could request naturalization and this was one of the major critiques regarding this law and one of the reasons why the government finally amended it and gave in to the pressure from the EU and OSCE. Originally, the OSCE and the European Council had had to intervene to keep an even stricter variant from becoming law. Former members of the Russian military were in principle denied Latvian citizenship.[66]

In reality, this law placed considerable political, economic and social restrictions on non-citizens. They were only partially able to take part in privatization, they are not allowed to purchase land, real estate, businesses or certain licences, and they receive less in social benefits than do citizens.[67]

By 1996, about 60,000 inhabitants had obtained Russian passports, and a number of international observers, in particular the OSCE representative for national minorities and the human rights representative of the European Council, had criticized the law. Only after the EU announced in late 1997 that its accession talks with Latvia would not begin until this problem was resolved did the Guntars Krasts government (TB/LNNK) decide on reform.[68] By April 1997, Latvia had introduced a passport for stateless people.[69] It also scrapped 'immigration windows' in 1998, made the *ius soli* retroactively effective from 1991 for newborn children, reduced the language requirements for people over sixty-five, and established a working group to work out a programme for integrating non-Latvians into society.[70]

After this reform, the number of naturalizations jumped to more than 10,000 per year. The same happened after Latvia's EU accession. In 2004 in Latvia, non-Latvians with citizenship outnumbered those without it for the first time. In January 2010, 344,095 people, or 15.5 per cent of Latvia's inhabitants, were non-citizens. Of these, 65.9 per cent were of Russian origin, and most others were of Ukrainian or Belarusian origin. Only about 2 per cent of non-Latvians are Russian citizens, and 15 per cent are stateless.[71]

Taking reform a step further, in 2002 the government created the Ministry of Social Integration and appointed the renowned ethnic relations expert Nils Muižnieks minister.[72] Muižnieks introduced special programmes aimed at supporting tolerance and starting training projects. Since 2006, non-citizens have been allowed to work for certain state authorities, such as the court of auditors.[73] In August 2008, however, the Godmanis government eliminated the office of the integration minister in the course of slimming down the state administration. As of 2009, its tasks were transferred to the Ministry of Family, Children and Integration.[74]

On the whole, Latvia has taken some definitely successful steps to soften the initially very rigid citizenship policy. Together with other legal initiatives, these steps were also a reaction to the social effects of the original policy; thus it can be said that purposeful attempts have been made to integrate the Russian-speaking population of Latvia. Since EU accession, however, the state has clearly reduced its financial and political commitment to the integration of non-Latvians.[75]

Language policy
The second dimension of relations with the non-Latvian population concerns language policy. As early as 1989, Latvia's Supreme Soviet passed a language law that made Latvian an official language and was supposed to put it on an equal footing with Russian.[76] At the same time, this law restricted the free choice of language in the political, economic and to some degree the social realm, in reaction to the earlier practice of disadvantaging Latvians. Even in municipalities whose inhabitants were mostly non-Latvian, Latvian was the only official language.[77]

The language law's revised version of 5 May 1992 made a language certificate a prerequisite for practising any profession and defined the respective required skill levels. This law implied no general discrimination against people who did not speak Latvian; in fact, state-organized language classes were made available free of charge, or at least inexpensively. Still, concerned non-Latvians and international organizations criticized certain aspects of the language law's implementation: the difficulty of the language tests, the absent or short transition periods, the oversight of the language laws by special inspectors empowered to impose fines in cases of insufficient use of the Latvian language or illegal use of a foreign language, and the general validity of these laws even in regions densely settled by non-Latvians.[78]

The debate on language policy did not abate, so in 1999 the parliament passed a new language law regulating, in much detail, the use of Latvian in the public and the private realms. However, it did not include all the mitigations demanded by the EU; for instance, it still stipulated the use of Latvian in the private economy. After severe criticism of the law by the Council of the Baltic Sea, the OSCE and the EU endangered Latvia's presence in the first round of enlargement, then President Vīķe-Freiberga vetoed the law. Parliament took up a new debate and passed a somewhat modified version. Nevertheless, the topics of assistance with language acquisition and integration of non-Latvians remained on the agenda of EU progress reports written in the context of the accession negotiations, and the pressure to further liberalize the language law endured.[79]

In May 2002, the Bērziņš government neglected the regulation stipulating that candidates for public office had to meet the criteria for the highest level of language skill. It did so under pressure from the United States and the EU, which threatened to block the country's accession to NATO.[80] In June 2003, the Constitutional Court declared the 75 per cent quota for Latvian language in mass media null and void. According to the verdict, the language of the media should be determined by supply and demand.[81]

Mass protests erupted in 2004, when the government more firmly established the Latvian language as the language of education in schools for ethnic minorities. Since then, 60 per cent of classes are conducted in Latvian. Criticism, even by international organizations, addressed less the law as such than the insufficient inclusion of minority representatives in the working out of the law. Ultimately, though, many citizens were disgusted by the protest movement, which was co-financed by Moscow, and it gradually ebbed away.[82]

Basically, the state-organized language acquisition programmes have helped improve the language skills of non-Latvians: whereas 22 per cent of inhabitants stated that they did not speak Latvian in 1996, in 2003 only 12 per cent made such a statement.[83] However, problems persist in the labour market as well as in engaging with authorities. Furthermore, in 2007, the government increased the number of language inspectors from twelve to seventeen. Their purview extends not only to public institutions but also to private sector spaces such as shops and department stores.[84] The language issue's power to polarize and mobilize is obvious in the context of the referendum of February 2007, which was intended to raise Russian to the status of second official language. With nays at 75 per cent, it was a clear failure, but following the very emotional debate the turnout of 69 per cent was higher than that for the preceding parliamentary elections. Only in the aftermath did all parties call for restraint and a new dialogue between the Russian- and Latvian-speaking parts of the population.[85]

Corruption
In Latvia, the degree of corruption is most obvious in the political realm, where entrepreneurs try to influence politics. It is less virulent in the economy itself and the administration. As already described in the section on political parties, the insufficient regulation of party funding favours such a development. In 2001, years after the World Bank in particular, along with other internal and external actors, had in 1997 demanded

more commitment to the fight against corruption, the Bērziņš government passed some anti-corruption laws as well as plans for establishing an anti-corruption authority. But only the government under Einars Repše (JL), which quite explicitly promised to fight corruption, established an anti-corruption bureau. The KNAB has been fully operational since February 2003; however, it is directly controlled by the government.[86]

The KNAB is supported by the Latvian court of auditors, the attorney general and appropriate police units. It investigates cases of corruption, contributes to formulating and passing relevant laws and is tasked with controlling the budgets of political parties. In this latter capacity, it ordered the People's Party (TP) to refund more than one million lats (ca. 1,435,132 euros) received in compensation for electoral expenses.[87] In March 2007, the KNAB managed to prove the oligarch Aivars Lembergs guilty of money laundering, blackmail, abuse of power and the illegal funding of several parties and MPs.

By uncovering additional minor and major cases of corruption among judges, police, customs authorities and high-ranking politicians, as well as cases of illegal funding of parties, the KNAB, despite its modest financial and staff situation, managed to score some successes. Most of all, it has succeeded in increasing the population's sense of corruption as wrongdoing. Meanwhile it enjoys much confidence, made obvious not least by the reactions to the politically motivated dismissal in September 2007 of the head of the KNAB, Aleksejs Loskutovs, whom some politicians saw as having conducted somewhat overly detailed investigations of corruption by oligarchs. Not since the Singing Revolution had so many people taken to the streets.[88] Finally, Prime Minister Kalvītis yielded to the pressure from the street and reappointed Loskutovs. Later, Kalvītis himself had to step down due to this affair. The succeeding Godmanis government, which also had a critical attitude towards the KNAB, finally dismissed Loskutovs at the end of July 2008.[89] Due to the changed attitudes among those who are politically responsible, corruption remains a virulent problem provoking much debate among the political parties.

EU accession
For a long time, Latvian politicians prioritized accession to NATO over EU membership because the former, as a military alliance, offered more protection against Russia. Nevertheless, Latvia was the first Baltic state to submit its application for membership in Brussels. In 1997, when the EU declared that for the time being it could not start official negotiations, the much-criticized citizenship law was one of the reasons. After the relevant reform and the incorporation of explicitly formulated basic civil rights into the constitution, in March 2000 the EU, after its Helsinki session of

1999, started official accession negotiations by discussing the first eight chapters.[90]

In the course of these negotiations, Latvia took further steps of reform, reacting to criticism in the progress reports, which criticized the treatment of minorities, the handling of corruption, the judicial system and the insufficient support of regional development in particular. Not all political actors supported the appropriate measures, so sometimes only legal and institutional 'frames' were established and then left without substantial policy to fill them. Thus, again and again the EU complained about Latvia's slow implementation of its demands.[91]

On the whole, the EU's policy of conditionality has definitely had some effect. For example, reforms to better integrate the Russian-speaking population or fight corruption are to a considerable degree a result of international pressure. On the other hand, despite general assent to EU integration among wide parts of the population, the continuous monitoring has resulted in a kind of 'inferiority complex' and an ambivalent attitude towards the EU.[92] This became particularly obvious after Latvia's accession on 1 May 2004. Whereas about 50 per cent of the population supported accession at the time of the negotiations and about 67 per cent supported it in the referendum of 20 November 2003, by 2009 only 23 per cent expressed support for it.[93]

Economy: Reform Policy and Economic Trends

The struggles between the political parties and the respective government coalitions did not much influence the agenda of economic reform. All successor governments continued the economic-political course set by the People's Front government. Only some fields were negatively affected by the conflicts between political parties or the parties' weak social rootedness.

One project that was largely successful was privatization. In 1994, the Birkavs government established an agency for this purpose, which concentrated the coordination of privatization, previously organized by several ministries and municipalities, in one authority. Privatization of medium and small-scale enterprises was finished by 1998, but state enterprises' transformation proved lengthier due to political considerations. On 1 September 2006, the Kalvītis government officially terminated the distribution of vouchers, thus bringing privatization to an end. Nevertheless, the state did not completely withdraw from all strategic enterprises, and certain big enterprises, such as Lattelecom, remained state-owned. Land reform, conducted according to the 'restitution rather than compensation' principle, was also concluded in 2006.[94]

Just as in other transformation states, the initial phase of reform in the fields of monetary policy, privatization and foreign trade in Latvia at first caused the economy to deteriorate. The gross domestic product (GDP) fell by 50 per cent, and despite the opening up to the West, foreign trade suffered a massive breakdown at the beginning of the 1990s. The truck and bus manufacturer Rīgas Autobusu Fabrika (RAF) and the big electronics maker Valsts Elektrotehniskā Fabrika/State Electrotechnical Factory (VEF) went bankrupt. Unemployment skyrocketed, and the black market economy spread enormously. In 1995, despite the central bank's initially rigid monetary policy, the first great bank failure added to these woes. Banka Baltija, Latvia's biggest bank, collapsed because of weak banking supervision, and as a result many Latvians lost all their deposits. On top of that, Russia imposed punitive tariffs on several occasions and threatened economic boycotts.[95]

By the end of the 1990s, however, the first successes of macro-economic transformation were obvious. Almost 75 per cent of employees were working in the private sector, and at 6 per cent the unemployment rate was one of the lowest in Europe. Furthermore, precisely because of pressure from Russia, Latvia had successfully redirected its trade towards the Baltic Sea area and the EU in general, and exports were rising again in sectors such as wood, textiles, metal and foodstuffs. The economy had grown from 3.3 per cent (1996) to 8.0 per cent (2001), and the inflation rate dropped from 951 per cent (1992) to 2.5 per cent (2001).[96]

Further structural reforms were enacted during this period of economic recovery. A particular focus in this context, and from an economic-political point of view, was pension reform. Implemented in several steps (January 1996, July 1998 and July 2001), it made private contributions by employees obligatory and factually reduced the pension benefits paid by the state.[97] Having learned its lesson from the bank crisis, in 2001 the Bērziņš government (LC) established a commission for oversight of finance and capital markets, but its record is not particularly good, as loans are still granted comparatively easily.[98]

Lingering deficits in the reform of the health system concern the inadequate quality of medical services and the high degree of bribery, as well as the fight against poverty among the elderly. According to official figures, in 2008 Latvia's share of people suffering absolute or extreme poverty – about one third of the population – was the biggest in the EU.[99] The country's infrastructure is insufficiently developed, and energy dependency on Russia is very high, which allows the latter to exert political pressure on Latvia. The majority of energy companies active in Latvia are privately owned, but their privatization was a lengthy process and could not be realized in all cases. For example, privatization of Latvenergo in 2000[100] and of Lattelecom in 2007 failed because their respective employees rejected it. The judicial system is not efficient enough, and at 0.69 per cent of GDP, expenditures on education and research and development are too low for Latvia to keep pace with neighbouring states in the long run.

Despite privatization, agriculture did not develop into a self-sustainable economic branch. Even though a shift in focus towards service and consumption industries reduced agriculture's share of the GDP from 17 per cent in 1992 to 4.5 per cent in 2003, it still depends on state funding for survival. In general, the country's rural regions benefited little from the economic boom at the turn of the millennium, and change happens but slowly. Actual GDP in Riga is about 2.5 times that in the Latgale region in the east of the country, where unemployment is 3.5 times as high as in Riga.[101]

After 2006, Latvia's economy came under pressure again as its initially tremendous growth rate of 11.9 per cent (2006) was eaten away by rising inflation, which rose from 6.8 per cent (2006) to 14.1 per cent (2007) and later 17.9 per cent (May 2008).[102] This development was due partly to the global crisis in the world economy, which had also reached Latvia, but it was increased by several home-grown problems that led to an overheated national economy and an enormous state budget deficit (23 per cent in 2007).[103] First, after EU accession, the government had ramped up both its own expenses and public sector wages, and continued its pro-cyclical fiscal policy despite warnings from the Latvian central bank. Furthermore, it had not created financial reserves in the years of growth. Added to this was a serious shortage of skilled personnel, many of whom had left the country for the West after EU accession. At the same time, and despite this shortage, unemployment rose to 15 per cent (in March 2009), which again burdened the budget.[104]

Second, the banks – both Latvian and foreign-owned – had expanded enormously since 2005 by providing extremely cheap credit. Ultimately, the amount of loans reached 60 per cent a year,[105] the highest rate in the EU. At first, this credit boom triggered an upward spiral of consumption-based growth, as well as growth in the real estate market and the construction industry. But the situation then changed to a downward spiral. In certain sectors, the demand for labour caused wages to explode at growth rates of 35 per cent in 2006 and 2007. As productivity stagnated, enterprises compensated for rising unit labour costs by raising prices, thus driving the inflation rate up to 17.9 per cent in May 2008. Meanwhile, the crisis also hit Latvia's banks, up to 60 per cent of which were nationally owned, producing a crisis in the national economy.[106]

Finally, Latvia had to nationalize the country's second biggest bank, Parex Bank, after it collapsed. In December 2008, the country had to accept a bailout package of 7.5 billion euros from the EU and the IMF. Without this packet and the accompanying measures, the Latvian government would not have been able to meet its payment obligations or continue linking the lat to the euro to avoid external devaluation. The money was used to finance the recapitalization of Parex Bank (500 million lats) and keep the budget deficit at 4.9 per cent or less. Wages in the public sector were lowered by about 25 per cent, the private sector sustained a similar reduction, and further austerity measures were implemented.[107]

Society: Social Structure, Demography, Political Participation and Civil Society Activities

The Soviet occupation clearly affected Latvia's social structure. Russian-speaking inhabitants moved primarily to Latvia's cities but also to the eastern region of the country, and soon they were overrepresented in the economy, military, police force, shipping and aviation, as well as in municipal administration. Latvians worked most of all in the realms of culture, health and education. As a consequence of intensive training of the national workforce, Latvian experts moved up from the mid 1960s onwards, but they were still in the minority.[108]

The change of system meant Latvia's demographic structure changed once more. Whereas until 1989 the country had experienced continuous immigration, now it had to deal with population decline. Latvia had 2.66 million inhabitants in 1989, but only 2.27 million in 2007, a drop of 11 per cent. In the first years, the decreased numbers were due to the re-emigration of Russians who had come after 1940, who went from being 34 per cent of the population in 1989 to 28 per cent in 2004. Thus, and also because of the return of 'Latvians in exile', the share of Latvians in the population rose, from 52 per cent in 1989 to 57.8 per cent in 2007. At the same time, however, fewer Latvians had children, so the youngest age cohort today is considerably smaller than that of people over sixty. After the accession to the EU, several hundred thousand young, well-trained Latvians emigrated to EU states, resulting in a population loss similar to that of 1944/45. The consequences of this development – that is, the fastest-ageing population in Europe – are but little alleviated by changes in family policy and an increased childcare allowance.[109]

These changes in the country's demographic structure demonstrate that many Latvians have reacted to the difficulties of system change with individualized strategies, such as emigration or having fewer children. Moreover, from a political-cultural standpoint it is obvious that Latvians have little interest in the kind of political engagement that could press towards tackling social problems by way of collective action. According to figures from 2008, only 7 per cent of the population – and only 1–2 per cent according to other surveys – are members of a trade union or political party.[110]

This low degree of political participation is an expression of the grave legitimation crisis of Latvia's political system, attributable to unstable governments and parties, growing corruption and the economic problems of the past years. It is reflected in declining election turnouts (formerly 89 per cent, now 62 per cent) and increasing rejection of the political class. In a survey conducted in 2006, 85 per cent of interviewees stated that they did not trust political parties, and 71 per cent distrusted the parliament. A majority of interviewees stated their preference for a strong leader. Although a 2009 poll showed most interviewees supported democracy as a form of government, 76 per cent were dissatisfied with the way it worked in their country (versus 61.6 per cent at the time of EU accession); furthermore, only 4.5 per cent trusted the parliament.[111]

The functioning of NGOs that show strong commitment and understand their task as controlling the state must be seen as a partial corrective. In 2000, a total of around 10,000 people worked for NGOs. Political decision-makers, for their part, have an ambivalent attitude towards civil society. On the one hand, in 2003 and 2004 the government passed laws in support of NGOs, according to which, for example, donations to NGOs are tax deductible; moreover, a parliamentary resolution of June 2006 declared that NGOs should contribute more to government decisions. On the other hand, in most cases critical NGOs working against corruption or in the realms of human rights, women's rights and environmental protection are in especially dire circumstances financially, as they receive little in international donations and have only a few members. An amendment that took effect in July 2009 lowered the tax deduction for donations to non-profit NGOs from 85 per cent to just 15 per cent.[112] Also, political parties, particularly those connected to oligarchs, have repeatedly tried to obstruct or prevent the control function of NGOs.

Since 1993, a continuous dialogue between government and social partners has taken place in the context of the Tripartite Council, though to little effect. In the 1990s, this lack of impact was still due to the transformation process's effects on trade unions and employers, and to their insufficient organizational structures and lack of capabilities to assume responsibility. Since then, the trade unions have found a new structure under their umbrella organization, the Free Trade Union Confederation of Latvia (Latvijas Brīvo Arodbiedrību Savienība).[113] In 1993, employers united in the Employers' Confederation of Latvia (Latvijas Darba Devēju

Konfederāticija); according to its own data, this institution represents enterprises employing about 35 per cent of Latvia's workers.[114] The Free Trade Union Confederation's quite successful mobilization of its members and supporters has been most obvious during the protests against the pension reform and the privatization of Latvenergo in 2000. From 2007, a new wave of demonstrations and a number of people's initiatives expressed the dissatisfaction of many NGOs as well as the unorganized parts of the population. Thus, it seems that the population has begun to more actively oppose its perceived grievances.

Numbering among these demonstrations are the protests organized in September 2007 by NGOs such as Delna, the Latvian section of Transparency International, after the dismissal of the head of the anti-corruption authority, Aleksejs Loskutovs. More than 10,000 people gathered in Riga's old city to stage their protest. As a result, the government was forced to restore Loskutovs to office, at least temporarily.[115]

In August 2008, the trade unions mobilized the population for a referendum intended to empower voters to initiate a referendum for the premature dissolution of the parliament followed by elections, something only the President of the State had been entitled to do so far.[116] Despite mass protest and demonstrations, the initiative failed to achieve the necessary quorum, gaining only 42 per cent of votes versus the required 50 per cent; however, the votes cast were 97 per cent positive, demonstrating the population's dissatisfaction with the political class.[117] After President Zatlers expressed strong support for such a law, on 8 April 2009 the Saeima agreed to the project, with a majority of eighty-five votes.[118]

On 23 August 2008, a referendum was held in favour of increasing pension benefits. With a turnout of only 22.9 per cent, this initiative also did not achieve the required quorum. However, 96 per cent of participants voted in favour of an increase.[119] From January 2009, repeated protests agitated against the austerity package the government had agreed to with the IMF and EU. Sixty-four per cent of the citizens spoke out in favour of new elections. While these referenda and protests may be considered clear indications of a confidence crisis, they also demonstrate that the population definitely sticks to basic democratic values and demands the same from its politicians.[120]

However, particularly in the past two years, groups with little interest in democracy have also attracted public attention. They include the 'NoPride Movement', which demonstrated against parades of homosexuals; right-wing extremist movements that still present a positive image of the Latvian division of the Waffen SS; and extremely nationalistic Russian parties and movements.[121]

Conclusion and Prospects

In sum, the democratization process in Latvia may be judged positively, but some problematic developments are still observed. Above all, the political parties are organizationally fragile and shallowly rooted in society. Sometimes personal animosities prevent parties with similar programmes from cooperating, or a party's leadership is politically active only to achieve the power and influence needed to enforce its economic interests. The fact that oligarchs have taken over some political parties has clearly hindered the development of organized political interests and acceptance of democratic rules, thus preventing a democratic consolidation of the governmental system.

Because of the parties' weakness, the leading political personnel are still characterized by personal rivalries. No government has yet survived a full term in office. Furthermore, Latvia has given up on stable fiscal policy and, for populistic reasons, abandoned its careful old-age policies. Due to the economic and financial crisis that began in 2008, Latvia introduced the euro (originally scheduled for 2012) on 1 January 2014. The battles against poverty and urban–rural disparities have found insufficient political support; in the same vein, politics has clearly dialled back the fight against corruption. This mismanagement not only reduces the successes of previous reforms but also endangers the consolidation of democracy. Accordingly, the population's support for the political elite is extremely low, and a deep confidence crisis is obvious.

At the same time, however, some positive developments are worth to mention. Recently, for instance, Valdis Dombrovskis became the first prime minister to be appointed three times in a row. Furthermore, the oligarchs' parties were pushed back in the parliamentary elections of 2010 and 2011, it still being an open question how independent from these circles President Bērziņš will prove to be. It is unclear how far the conflict about Latvia's Russian-speaking inhabitants will subside. On the one hand, 70–80 per cent of Latvia's Russian-speaking people call Latvia their home, and the majority are Latvian citizens. They have gained more political influence, and the number of marriages between Russian- and Latvian-speaking partners is rising – they made up 40 per cent of marriages in 2004. Also, some Latvian parties debated a possible coalition with SC, indicating that in the future, cooperation between parties might be decided according to topical issues rather than ethno-political belongings.[122] On the other hand, the coalition did not come about after all, and the referendum on the official language demonstrates how tense relations still are.

Most of all, however, the institutional control authorities, foremost the Constitutional Court, work very effectively to protect human rights, civil rights and freedom rights. Civil society also sees itself as an authority that is supposed to control the government. Able to organize quickly, it has even managed to prevent (at least temporarily) the implementation of constitutionally harmful measures like the dismissal of Loskutovs, the head of the anti-corruption bureau. The possibility of law-making by the people has an invigorating effect on the development of civil society and political participation by the population. Whether this will make policy-making more efficient and reliable in the long run, however, and whether it will increase confidence in political institutions must be left to the future.

The influence of external actors and organizations such as the EU, OSCE and World Bank, and to some extent Russia, has been very significant, particularly in respect of integration policy before EU accession. Having influenced law-making in Latvia, such actors are important points of reference. Yet this has not increased the population's confidence in the EU or given it the impression that Latvia is benefiting from EU membership. About 60 per cent of the population reject the EU or are indifferent towards it. Nevertheless, at 40 per cent, confidence in European institutions is still higher than in national institutions, in which only 11 (parliament) and 15 per cent (government) have confidence.[123] Overcoming this legitimation crisis is one of the greatest challenges facing Latvia.

Claudia-Yvette Matthes is a member of the scientific staff of the Institute of Social Sciences of Humboldt-Universität zu Berlin and head of the office for the international Master's programmes. She earned a doctorate in Political Science at the Freie Universität Berlin in the field of comparative government and democracy studies. Her research work focuses on the analysis of political institutions on the one hand and on a variety of political fields such as reforms of systems of social security, transitional justice or constitutional politics on the other. She analyses these topics most of all concerning the new EU member states, with particular expertise in Poland, Hungary and Latvia.

Notes

1. Cf. G. von Rauch, *Geschichte der baltischen Staaten*, 3rd ed. (Munich, 1990), 82–85; A. Šilde, 'Die Entwicklung der Republik Lettland', in B. Meissner (ed.), *Die Baltischen Nationen Estland, Lettland, Litauen*, 2nd ed. (Cologne, 1991), 63–74, here 63–70.

2. Ulmanis issued decrees on the compulsory expropriation of German and Jewish companies and the establishment of big state-run enterprises. See von Rauch, *Geschichte der baltischen Staaten*, 150–51.
3. See A. Schmidt, *Geschichte des Baltikums: Von den alten Göttern bis zur Gegenwart* (Munich, 1992), 117; R. Misiunas and R. Taagepera, *The Baltic States: Years of Dependence 1940–80* (London, 1983), here 274f.
4. The literature often uses the term 'Russian-speaking' because immigrant Russian civil servants, workers and soldiers were not necessarily ethnic Russians but could be Ukrainians (1989: 3.5 per cent) or Belarusians (1989: 4.5 per cent), who frequently spoke Russian. The term 'Russian-speaking' is also used here in the knowledge that these groups' political interests are not necessarily and always homogenous. Cf. N. Muižnieks, *Russians in Latvia – History, Current Status and Prospects 2004* (www.mfa.gov. lv/en/policy/4641/Muiznieks/print=on; accessed 25 January 2011).
5. See N. Götz, G. Hanne and E.-C. Onken, 'Ethnopolitik', in H. Graf and M. Kerner (eds), *Handbuch Baltikum heute* (Berlin, 1998), 299–334, here 306.
6. See C.-Y. Matthes, 'Die Herausbildung des Parteiensystems in Lettland seit Beginn der Perestroika', in Freie Universität Berlin (ed.), *Berichte der Berliner Interuniversitären Arbeitsgruppe Baltische Staaten* (Berlin, 1996), 42; H. König, 'Das deutschsowjetische Vertragswerk von 1939 und seine geheimen Zusatzprotokolle: Eine Dokumentation', *Osteuropa* 39(5) (1989), 413–58, here 422.
7. See C.-Y. Matthes, 'Politisches und Rechtssystem Lettlands', in Graf and Kerner, *Handbuch Baltikum heute*, 49–88, here 53f.
8. Ibid., 73–75.
9. See Matthes, 'Die Herausbildung', 45.
10. See E. Levits, 'Lettland unter der Sowjetherrschaft und auf dem Wege zur Unabhängigkeit', in Meissner, *Die Baltischen Nationen*, 139–222, here 194–97; Matthes, 'Die Herausbildung', 49–58.
11. On 1 March 1991, 22.9 per cent of eligible Latvian voters had taken part in a Soviet referendum held at barracks and KPL institutions. Of these voters, 95.1 per cent voted for Latvia to stay with the Soviet Union. See Levits, 'Lettland', 198; Matthes, 'Politisches und Rechtssystem Lettlands', 57.
12. The treaty on borders with Russia was signed on 23 March 2007. See Bertelsmann Stiftung, 'BTI 2010 – Latvia Country Report' (Gütersloh, 2009), 20; A. Moshes, 'Overcoming Unfriendly Stability: Russian-Latvian Relations at the End of the 1990s', in *Programme of the Northern Dimension of the CSFP*, vol. 4 (Helsinki, 1999), here 16–23; A. Plakans, 'Latvia: Normality and Disappointment', *East European Politics and Society* 24(4) (2010), 518–25, here 520.
13. See Schmidt, *Geschichte des Baltikums*, 126.
14. Latvian voters indeed exercise this option. Several new MPs were elected to parliament this way in 2010. See D. Akule, 'Parliamentary Elections in Latvia: Victory Celebrations Will Be Short as Austerity Measures Should Be Introduced Quickly', Policy Brief 27 (October 2010).
15. See T. Schmidt, 'Das politische System Lettlands', in W. Ismayr (ed.), *Die politischen Systeme Osteuropas*, 3rd ed. (Wiesbaden, 2010), 123–70, here 148.
16. All-Union plants, established in the course of the Soviet industrialization process of the 1950s and 1960s, were large industrial plants directly managed by ministries in Moscow that produced goods mainly for distribution in other Soviet republics.
17. See Schmidt, 'Das politische System Lettlands', 124; C. Matthes and U. Wethkamp, 'Aufbruch zur Marktwirtschaft: Lettlands Wirtschaft im ersten Jahr nach der

Unabhängigkeit', *Materialien und Dokumente zur Friedens- und Konfliktforschung*, No. 17 (Berlin, 1993), 1f.; K. Schrader and C.F. Laaser, 'Wirtschaft Lettlands', in Graf and Kerner, *Handbuch Baltikum heute*, 181–210, here 181.

18. Cf. Matthes and Wethkamp, 'Aufbruch zur Marktwirtschaft', 2f.
19. These were allotted to citizens only, according to the length of their residence in the country. See Matthes and Wethkamp, 'Aufbruch zur Marktwirtschaft', 5.
20. See Schrader and Laaser, 'Wirtschaft Lettlands', 185–90; Matthes and Wethkamp, 'Aufbruch zur Marktwirtschaft', 5.
21. See T. Schmidt, 'Die lettische Saeima zwischen Kontinuität und Wandel', in S. Kraatz and S. von Steinsdorff (eds), *Parlamente und Systemtransformation im postsozialistischen Europa* (Opladen, 2002), 221–45, here 226–29.
22. See Schmidt, 'Das politische System Lettlands', 134–37.
23. See J. Dreifelds, *Nations in Transit – Latvia 2007*. (www.freedomhouse.org/inc/content/pubs/nit/inc_country_detail.cfm?page=47&nit=457&year=2008&pf, accessed 21 January 2011); Akule, 'Parliamentary Elections in Latvia', 1.
24. However, in 2011 Dombrovskis' party lost 18 per cent, becoming only the third-strongest power. See R. Wolff, 'Historischer Erfolg für Linksbündnis', *Die Tageszeitung*, 18 September 2011; J. Rozenvalds, 'Ethnos und Demos: Die Parlamentswahlen in Lettland 2011', *Osteuropa* 61(11) (2011), 43–54, here 43–44.
25. See Schmidt, 'Das politische System Lettlands', 142–45; on the political constellations of the respective government coalitions, see G. Tiemann and D. Jahn, 'Koalitionen in den baltischen Staaten: Lehrstücke für die Bedeutung funktionierender Parteien', in S. Kropp, S.S. Schüttemeyer and R. Sturm (eds), *Koalitionen in West- und Osteuropa* (Opladen, 2002), 271–300.
26. See Schmidt, 'Das politische System Lettlands', 130, 139–41; Matthes, 'Politisches und Rechtssystem Lettlands', 63f.
27. See Dreifelds, *Latvia 2007*, 5; Bertelsmann Stiftung, 'BTI 2010', 17.
28. See G. Pridham, 'Securing the Only Game in Town: The EU's Political Conditionality and Democratic Consolidation in Post-Soviet Latvia', *Europe-Asia Studies* 61(1) (2009), 51–84, here 71; Matthes, 'Politisches und Rechtssystem Lettlands', 62.
29. See J. Dreifelds, *Nations in Transit – Latvia 2008*, 4. (https://freedomhouse.org/report/nations-transit/2008/latvia, accessed 21 February 2011); Schmidt, 'Das politische System Lettlands', 132f.
30. See A.M. Klein, 'Lettlands Parlament wählt neues Staatsoberhaupt', *KAS-Länderbericht Lettland*, 6 March 2011; Rozenvalds, 'Ethnos und Demos', 43f. From 1993 to 2004, Bērziņš was the director of Unibanka and a board member of the Latvenergo energy trust. His close connections to Latvia's oligarchs prompted many people to demonstrate in Riga's inner city on the evening of his election. See U. Bongartz, 'Lettland: Saeima-Abgeordnete wählen Ex-Banker Andris Bērziņš zum neuen Staatspräsidenten', *Lettische Presseschau*, 2 June 2011 (http://www.lettische-presseschau.de/politik/lettland/445–lettland-saeima-abgeordnete-waehlen-ex-banker-andris-brzi-zum-neuen-staatspraesidenten; accessed 4 April 2012).
31. Three judges are appointed by the parliament, for which the support of at least ten MPs is required; two by the cabinet; and two by the plenum of the Supreme Court. See Dreifelds, *Latvia 2007*, 12.
32. See Bertelsmann Stiftung, 'BTI 2010', 7. Schmidt, 'Das politische System Lettlands', 163–164.
33. See Pridham, 'Securing the Only Game in Town', 74.

34. See J. Dreifelds, *Nations in Transit – Latvia 2009*, 307–325, here 320f. (https://freedom house.org/report/nations-transit/2009/latvia, accessed 21 January 2011)
35. See Bertelsmann Stiftung, 'BTI 2010', 7; Schmidt, 'Das politische System Lettlands', 139.
36. J. Ikstens, 'Latvia', *European Journal of Political Research* 48 (2009), 1015–21, here 1016, 1020f.; A.M. Klein, 'Kommunalwahl in Lettland', *KAS Länderbericht Lettland*, 7 June 2010, 3.
37. Pridham, 'Securing the Only Game in Town', 76. On the development of the media system as a whole, see also H. Graf, 'Massenmedien', in Graf and Kerner, *Handbuch Baltikum heute*, 335–67.
38. In 2007, a journalist was convicted because he refused to reveal his informers. However, he was cleared by the Supreme Court. Another reporter, who had written an article accusing the Minister of Economy of violating regulations in the context of a privatization procedure, found justice only at the European Court of Human Rights. See Dreifelds, *Latvia 2008*, 8.
39. See Dreifelds, *Latvia 2007*, 8f.
40. See Plakans, 'Latvia', 523.
41. This reform also demanded that all parties had to be newly registered. Some twenty smaller parties were not permitted to register again, as they could not provide the now necessary proof that they had more than two hundred members. See Ikstens, 'Latvia', 1019; Schmidt, 'Das politische System Lettlands', 153.
42. By highlighting the political dimension of the conflict between Russian-speaking immigrants and the nation proper, this term indicates that the conflict is politically and socially constructed and instrumentalized.
43. See Matthes, 'Politisches und Rechtssystem Lettlands', 69–75.
44. Rather populist answers to corruption and enrichment were offered by the Saimnieks (Landlord) Democratic Party as well as the People's Movement for Latvia (Tautas Kustība Latvijai), founded in 1995 by the German right-wing extremist and former LNNK member Joachim Siegerist. See M. Kerner and A. Reetz, 'Parteiensysteme in den baltischen Staaten', *Der Bürger im Staat: Die baltischen Staaten* 54(2) (2004), 120–25, here 122f.
45. This party is backed by the same financial groups that in 1998 had brought the Jaunā Partija (New Party) into parliament, as well as parts of the Latvian Christian Democratic Union. See Kerner and Reetz, 'Parteiensysteme', 123; Schmidt, 'Das politische System Lettlands', 155.
46. See Schmidt, 'Das politische System Lettlands', 156–57; Matthes, 'Politisches und Rechtssystem Lettlands', 72.
47. See Dreifelds, *Latvia 2008*, 3f.; Schmidt, 'Das politische System Lettlands', 143; A.M. Klein, 'Eine unheilige Allianz', *KAS Länderbericht Lettland*, 16 June 2010, 2.
48. A.M. Klein, 'Partei ohne Volk', *KAS Länderbericht Lettland*, 20 July 2011, 1f.
49. Dreifelds, *Latvia 2007*, 7. Delna, the Riga branch of Transparency International, and Providus, which receive funding from the Soros Foundation, had often criticized the behaviour of these oligarchs.
50. Klein, 'Eine unheilige Allianz', 3.
51. A.M. Klein, 'Lettland reloaded: die Parteien versuchen, den Geist von 1991 zu beleben', *KAS Auslandsinformationen* 1 (2011), 76–90, here 78; Rozenvalds, 'Ethnos und Demos', 47f.
52. These are *Neatkariga Rīta Avīze*, *Latvijas Avīze* and *Vakara Ziņas*. See Schmidt, 'Das politische System Lettlands', 161.

53. By the end of the 1990s, Lembergs was considered the backstage mastermind controlling Vilis Krištopāns (Latvian Way, 1998–99). See D.J. Galbreath and D. Auers, 'Green, Black and Brown: Uncovering Latvia's Environmental Politics', *Journal of Baltic Studies* 40(3) (2009), 333–48, here 342–45.

54. Dreifelds, *Latvia 2008*, 3; Rozenvalds, 'Ethnos und Demos', 47f.

55. For details, see Galbreath and Auers, 'Green, Black and Brown', 339–41; Schmidt, 'Das politische System Lettlands', 153; Dreifelds, *Latvia 2009*, 323.

56. See Ikstens, 'Latvia', 1019f.

57. See ibid., 1019.

58. See Klein, 'Lettland Reloaded', 78.

59. In the elections to the European Parliament, the SC, with 19.5 per cent of votes, had become the second-biggest party, and had also constantly gained ground in polls leading up to the elections. See Klein, 'Lettland Reloaded', 83f.

60. 'Visu Latvijai!' (VL) is a right-wing party founded as a nationalistic youth movement in 2011 and as a party in 2011 that ran for elections together with TB/LNNK as National Alliance (Nacionālā apvienība VL-TB/LNNK).

61. A.M. Klein, 'Saeima bestätigt Mitte-Rechts-Regierung', *KAS-Länderbericht Lettland*, 31 October 2011; Rozenvalds, 'Ethnos und Demos', 51–52.

62. See also E.-C. Onken, *Demokratisierung der Geschichte in Lettland: Staatsbürgerliches Bewusstsein und Geschichtspolitik im ersten Jahrzehnt der Unabhängigkeit* (Hamburg, 2003).

63. See T. Schmidt, *Die Außenpolitik der baltischen Staaten im Spannungsfeld zwischen Ost und West* (Opladen, 2003).

64. See Matthes, 'Die Herausbildung', 53.

65. Under this window system, inhabitants who were eligible under these regulations could apply only when it was the 'turn' of their age cohort. From 1 January 1996, stateless Latvian-born sixteen- to twenty-year-olds could apply for citizenship; one year later, it was twenty- to twenty-five-year-olds and so on. Until after 2003, non-Latvian-born immigrants were supposed to be allowed to apply for citizenship, again divided into three steps according to age. See Gotz, Hanne and Onken, 'Ethnopolitik', 312.

66. See ibid., 312; D.J. Galbreath, 'European Integration through Democratic Conditionality: Latvia in the Context of Minority Rights', *Journal of Contemporary European Studies* 14(1) (2006), 69–87.

67. See Gotz, Hanne and Onken, 'Ethnopolitik', 314–16.

68. Not even a referendum initiated by Guntars Krasts' party could prevent these changes. Krasts implemented the reform mostly because of international pressure and less out of his own conviction. The referendum result was 53 per cent to 45 per cent, to the disadvantage of the applicants. See Pridham, 'Securing the Only Game in Town', 65.

69. On their status and organizations, such as the League of the Stateless, see Gotz, Hanne and Onken, 'Ethnopolitik', 313.

70. See I. Dose, 'Nationale Minderheiten im Ostseeraum: Geschichte und Gegenwart, Identität und territoriale Anbindung' (PhD diss., Humboldt-Universität zu Berlin, 2010), 286.

71. Akule, 'Parliamentary Elections in Latvia', 1.

72. Previously, Muižnieks had directed the Latvian Centre for Human Rights and Ethnic Studies, one of Latvia's big NGOs. In April 2004, Minister Muižnieks was replaced by Aivars Aksenoks, who was succeeded by Katarina Pētersone in April 2006, followed by Oskars Kastens in November 2006. See Dose, 'Nationale Minderheiten im Ostseeraum', 287.

73. See Dreifelds, *Latvia 2007*, 5.

74. See Dose, 'Nationale Minderheiten im Ostseeraum', 287f., 292.
75. See Ikstens, 'Latvia', 1016; Pridham, 'Securing the Only Game in Town', 78; a detailed insight into the relation between Russians and Latvians is provided by N. Muižnieks (ed.), *Latvian-Russian Relations: Domestic and International Dimensions* (Riga, 2006) (http://szf.lu.lv/files/petnieciba/publikacijas/no_vescas_majaslapas/latvian-russian_relations_final%281%29.pdf; accessed 24 January 2011).
76. Although there was no official Soviet language, Latvian had been strongly discouraged in all fields of life since 1940.
77. See Gotz, Hanne and Onken, 'Ethnopolitik', 318–21.
78. See ibid., 322.
79. See Pridham, 'Securing the Only Game in Town', 66; Dose, 'Nationale Minderheiten im Ostseeraum', 299f.
80. See Schmidt, 'Das politische System Lettlands', 129.
81. See Dreifelds, *Latvia 2007*, 8.
82. See Dose, 'Nationale Minderheiten im Ostseeraum', 303f.; Schmidt, 'Das politische System Lettlands', 130.
83. On the other hand, 78 per cent of Latvians stated that they speak Russian. See Plakans, 'Latvia', 524; Dose, ''Nationale Minderheiten im Ostseeraum', 303.
84. See Dose, 'Nationale Minderheiten im Ostseeraum', 302.
85. See K. Schuller, 'Gegen Russisch als Staatssprache', *Frankfurter Allgemeine Zeitung*, 19 February 2012; for background, see also K. Pētersone, 'Latvia: The Hot Month of February', *Baltic Review*, 14 February 2012 (http://baltic-review.com /2012/02/latvia-the-hot-month-of-february/; accessed 2 April 2012).
86. See Pridham, 'Securing the Only Game in Town', 67f.
87. See Dreifelds, *Latvia 2009*, 323.
88. See Dreifelds, *Latvia 2008*, 11.
89. On the pretext that two staff members of the KNAB had misappropriated funds, Godmanis held Loskutovs responsible and dismissed him, although the latter himself had reported the incident. See Pridham, 'Securing the Only Game in Town', 76; Dreifelds, *Latvia 2009*, 322.
90. See Pridham, 'Securing the Only Game in Town', 65; W. van Meurs, 'Der Weg der baltischen Staaten in die EU', *Der Bürger im Staat: Die baltischen Staaten* 54(2) (2004), 134–40.
91. See Pridham, 'Securing the Only Game in Town', 69.
92. See Plakans, 'Latvia', 521.
93. In the parliament, however, ninety-one of a hundred MPs voted in favour of accession. See Pridham, 'Securing the Only Game in Town', 70f.; Schmidt, 'Das politische System Lettlands', 166.
94. See Schmidt, 'Das politische System Lettlands', 125; Dreifelds, *Latvia 2007*, 4; C.-F. Laaser and K. Schrader, 'Die baltischen Staaten in der europäischen Arbeitsteilung', *Der Bürger im Staat: Die baltischen Staaten* 54(2) (2004), 141–46, here 142.
95. See Bertelsmann Stiftung, 'BTI 2010', 11; Meurs, 'Der Weg der baltischen Staaten', 137.
96. See Laaser and Schrader, 'Die baltischen Staaten', 142; Meurs, 'Der Weg der baltischen Staaten', 137.
97. See C.-Y. Matthes, M. Kačinskienė, F. Rajevska and A. Toots, 'Rentenreform im Baltikum: Neue Modelle im Praxistest', *Osteuropa* 57(7) (2007), 47–56.
98. See Bertelsmann Stiftung, 'BTI 2010', 11.
99. See ibid., 9; F. Rajevska, 'Vom Sozialstaat zum Wohlfahrtsmix: Das lettische Wohlfahrtssystem nach Wiedererlangung der Unabhängigkeit', in K. Schubert,

S. Hegelich and U. Bazant (eds), *Europäische Wohlfahrtssysteme: Ein Handbuch* (Wiesbaden, 2007), 423–42, here 424.

100. Indeed, since 2000, Latvenergo has even gained legal protection from further privatization attempts. See Bertelsmann Stiftung, 'BTI 2010', 12.

101. See Plakans, 'Latvia', 522; Meurs, 'Der Weg der baltischen Staaten', 138; Rajevska, 'Vom Sozialstaat zum Wohlfahrtsmix', 424.

102. See Schmidt, 'Das politische System Lettlands', 125.

103. See Bertelsmann Stiftung, 'BTI 2010', 12.

104. Schmidt, 'Das politische System Lettlands', 125; M. Hansen, 'Eine spektakuläre Geschichte von Boom und Pleite: Ein Blick aus Riga', in M. Ehrke (ed.), *Die globale Krise an der europäischen Peripherie: Ein Blick aus Zentral- und Südosteuropa*, Internationale Politikanalyse der Friedrich Ebert Stiftung (Berlin, 2009), 7–9, here 7.

105. The growth of credit supply or loan volume reached 60 per cent per year (credit supply is an indicator for how easy it is to borrow money). If there is more money available through low interest rates, then the economy is growing. But it may also lead to increasing inflation, which is bad and causes problems when people cannot pay back their credits.

106. Apart from self-inflicted causes, foreign actors also contributed to intensifying the crisis in Latvia. For example, the Swedish government announced that it would guarantee deposits at Swedish banks in Latvia, making these more attractive than the Latvian Parex Bank. See Hansen, 'Eine spektakuläre Geschichte', 7f.

107. Hansen, 'Eine spektakuläre Geschichte', 8f.; Ikstens, 'Latvia', 1020.

108. Götz, Hanne and Onken, 'Ethnopolitik', 307f.; Muižnieks, *Russians in Latvia*, p. 4.

109. See Plakans, 'Latvia', 519f.; Meurs, 'Der Weg der baltischen Staaten', 137; Rajevska, 'Vom Sozialstaat zum Wohlfahrtsmix', 440; Muižnieks, *Russians in Latvia*, 3.

110. See Ikstens, 'Latvia', 1019.

111. See Pridham, 'Securing the Only Game in Town', 64; Klein, 'Lettland Reloaded', 80; Eurobarometer 72 (Autumn 2009)(http://ec.europa.eu/public_opinion/archives/eb/eb72/eb72_fact_lv_en.pdf; accessed 20 October 2011).

112. See Dreifelds, *Latvia 2009*, 315; J. Dreifelds, *Nations in Transit – Latvia 2010*, 5f. (https://freedomhouse.org/report/nations-transit/2010/latvia, accessed 21 January 2011)

113. See G. Hartung, *Neue Staaten – neue Gewerkschaften? Die Gewerkschaften in Litauen, Lettland und Estland Anfang der 90er Jahre* (Leipzig, 1994).

114. See E. Blasum, 'Tripartism and Industrial Relations in Latvia', in G. Casale (ed.), *Social Dialogue in Central and Eastern Europe* (Budapest, 1999), 202–27, here 211 (www.lddk.lv/index.php?lang=2; accessed 25 March 2012).

115. Dreifelds, *Latvia 2008*, 11.

116. The draft stipulated that the quorum for an appropriate referendum should be half of the turnout of the previous parliamentary elections. See Ikstens, 'Latvia', 1018.

117. Ibid., 1017f.

118. At least 10 per cent of eligible voters are needed to initiate a referendum on the dissolution of parliament. If more than two thirds of voters who participated in the previous parliamentary election take part and a majority support the referendum, parliament is dissolved. See Dreifelds, *Latvia 2010*, 7.

119. See Ikstens, 'Latvia', 1018.

120. Regarding political participation, Latvians and Russians differ from each other on several points, e.g. more Latvians than Russians are trade union members; more Latvians than Russians took part in the 'Umbrella Revolution' opposing Loskutovs' dismissal, in elections to the European Parliament and in political debates generally. See I.B. Kehris,

'Citizenship, Participation and Representation', in N. Muižnieks (ed.), *How Integrated Is Latvian Society? An Audit of Achievements, Failures and Challenges* (Riga, 2010), 93–122, here 115–18.

121. See Ikstens, 'Latvia', 1018; Dreifelds, *Latvia 2007*, 8; Bertelsmann Stiftung, 'BTI 2010', 8.

122. Muižnieks, *Russians in Latvia*, 3. Concerning the SC's assessment of the past and particularly the question of whether Latvia was 'occupied' by the Soviet Union, the SC has come closer to the Latvian understanding of history and now also tries to woo voters by fighting corruption and the oligarchs. See Wolff, 'Historischer Erfolg'; Gerhard Gnauck, '20 Jahre nach "Sowjet-Besatzung" siegt ein Russe', *Die Welt*, 19 September 2011.

123. Eurobarometer 75 (Spring 2011) (www.eu.europa.eu/public_opinion/archives/eb/eb75/eb75_fact_lv_en.pdf; accessed 25 March 2012).

Chapter 3

LITHUANIA

⟨ЗVГ⟩

Rolf Winkelmann

Introduction

Historical Introduction

Even today, Lithuanians still like to remember that as early as the fourteenth century, their country enjoyed a kind of statehood as a territorially expanding grand duchy under Gediminas.[1] However, by the sixteenth century this Lithuanian statehood had come to an end via its union with Poland, whereupon Polish influence prevailed and whatever was specifically Lithuanian disappeared.[2] As of 1795, the Lithuanian princedom no longer existed, having become part of the Russian Empire under the tsars.[3] Only upon tsarist Russia's collapse in the chaos of World War I did modern Lithuania achieve its independence as a state.[4] This status of nation state did not come unexpectedly, as a broad national movement had developed at the end of the nineteenth century in Lithuania, providing an ideological foundation for the independent state.[5]

A democratic system of rule was established in Lithuania, but it lasted only until 1926, when President Smetona capitalized on internal crises to establish an authoritarian system.[6] In the years that followed, Lithuania came under foreign political pressure. At first it faced problems with Poland about the region of Vilnius; later, from 1933, it increasingly differed with the 'German Reich' about the factually annexed Memelland, which actually was under international administration. In 1938, the Memelland had to be handed over to Germany. Then there was Stalin's Soviet Union. In 1940, after his pact with Hitler gave Stalin free rein to stage Lithuania's accession to the Soviet Union, Lithuania was incorporated into the USSR.

Notes for this chapter begin on page 84.

After World War II, Stalin decreed new borders. By finally making the Vilnius region a part of Lithuania, he thus established Lithuania's present borders.[7] However, the country's incorporation into the territorial and political structure of the totalitarian and later authoritarian Soviet empire did not destroy the memory of independence. Rather, the idea of independence stuck, becoming virulent among the population. With Mikhail Gorbachev's assumption of office, there came a sense of change. The reforms initiated by Gorbachev resulted in massive changes in society and political structures. On the whole, this kind of transition to a democratic system may be called a 'pacted transition', that is, ruler and opposition came to an understanding on system change.[8] The transformation process began in the wake of regaining independence.

State of Research

Lithuania is often seen in the company of the other two Baltic states Estonia and Latvia. Many historical overviews of the country start with its early history in the Middle Ages[9] and reach as far as the first years after regaining independence. The most recent overview is presented in Kasekamp's *History of the Baltic States*,[10] which deals with the development of the Baltic states up to the world economic crisis after 2007 from a primarily political point of view. Mart Laar also takes the development into account in a study covering the entire former Eastern Bloc and referring to the period after World War II.[11] Lane, on the other hand, presents a very detailed, descriptive overview of Lithuania's development.[12] He focuses in particular on political and economic development during the first post-communist decade. These works also contain very good analyses of the system change, its causes and the way in which it happened.

The country report on Lithuania by Tauber in the handbook-like compilation *Die politischen Systeme Osteuropas* (The Political Systems of Eastern Europe)[13] provides an overview of all important institutional aspects of the political systems of Eastern European states. This report also sketches development in Lithuania over the past twenty years, though without taking economic development into consideration. Analyses of the Lithuanian party system are found in a volume by Reetz,[14] who, like Winkelmann,[15] analyses all three Baltic states. A very good depiction of the Lithuanian party system is found in a work by Ramonaite.[16] Winkelmann,[17] for his part, focuses on party funding in particular. Lithuania's institutional structure is very well explained by Krupavicius,[18] who also discusses the reasons behind the institutional structure of Lithuania's system of government, especially regarding the office of President of the State. This list is completed by Taube's study on the constitutional structures of

Lithuania, Estonia and Latvia.[19] All these overview studies discuss elections to Lithuania's parliament, the Seimas. Harfst's dissertation thesis merits particular mention for its detailed analysis of changes in the Lithuanian election system.[20]

Lithuania's economic transformation has been very well depicted by Böllhoff.[21] In her study representing Lithuania's political economy, Verena Fritz deals with the complex of 'state-building' questions.[22] Eurostat is a very good source of data sets on individual branches of the economy and on Lithuania's social structures and political culture (Eurobarometer). As for Lithuania's accession to the European Union, chief negotiator Austrevicius's very detailed depiction may be mentioned as one example of a study on this process.[23] In fact, Lithuania's EU accession has been treated from various points of view, as in the work of Hanssen-Decker[24] or Dauchert.[25] Lithuanian civil society, on the other hand, remains less researched for the time being and is still developing. Civil society is explicitly considered by Uhlin,[26] for example, though he deals with Lithuania only in passing. Fritz[27] and Macków,[28] however, also address civil society.

In sum, distinguished research has been done on Lithuania, and there is an interdisciplinary subject-related journal, the *Journal for Baltic Studies*. But compared to Poland, Hungary, the Czech Republic and Russia, Lithuania has sparked little interest in research in German-speaking countries, probably because of its small size and geographic location.

System Change

After 1985, the home policy of the secretary general of the Communist Party of the Soviet Union, Mikhail Gorbachev, changed the climate in the Soviet Union. The new policy of glasnost and perestroika was felt also in Lithuania. There, however, the ruling Communist Party of Lithuania (CPLit) was very reserved towards his policy. Only in 1987 did an opposition movement start to form in the Lithuanian Soviet Socialist Republic (SSR). At first it was dedicated to supporting Moscow's reform policy, working for environmental protection, coming to terms with Stalinism and publishing the Hitler-Stalin (Molotov-Ribbentrop) pact. Later, though, it started working for Lithuanian independence. The latter found institutional expression only later, with the founding of the opposition citizens' movement Sajudis.[29] At first the CPLit closed itself off from this movement, but in the long run it could not ignore it, as a number of party members and functionaries joined Sajudis or were sympathetic to it, including the CPLit's later secretary general, then minister and President of State

Algirdas Brazauskas. His political rival, the national-conservatively oriented Vytautas Landsbergis, was elected chairman of Sajudis.[30]

Sajudis achieved an overwhelming victory in the semi-free elections to the Congress of the People's Deputies in 1989. After this, the Communist Party increasingly cooperated more closely with the opposition movement, striving to secure its own position. Also in 1989, parliament condemned Lithuania's incorporation into the USSR as illegal, inspiring the so-called Baltic Way, a human chain from Vilnius to Tallinn that, as the opposition's biggest, most visible action, attracted international attention.[31] Meanwhile, Interfront, a movement to counter Sajudis, attracted numerous members of the military-industrial complex, mainly Russians and Poles.[32]

Elections to the Supreme Soviet of the Lithuanian SSR became another success of the opposition movement. The ruling CPLit had to be satisfied with 23 out of 141 MPs, making it obvious that the Communists were no longer finding sufficient support. Yet Moscow did not recognize the newly elected parliament's unanimous vote in favour of independence. Instead, Moscow tried to prevent Lithuania's secession with an economic blockade and, as the 1991 Gulf War progressed, to reverse things violently so as to keep Lithuania within the structure of the USSR. However, the use of violence only increased Lithuanians' desire for independence and attracted international attention to the Soviet republic. Only in the aftermath of the failed putsch in Moscow in August 1991 was Lithuania able to re-establish its independence.[33]

The independence movement and the citizens' wholesale political participation were a peak of Lithuanian civil society. Maintaining this level proved impossible; participation was to decline in the years to follow.

The Establishment of the Democratic Constitutional State

Politics

The constitution
The institutionalization of democracy in Lithuania had begun before the process of secession from the USSR. At first the aim was to clarify the question of the constitution. In 1990, parliament declared the Soviet constitution invalid and Lithuania's 1938 constitution – as a symbol of the state's continuity – valid for one day, to then be replaced by a provisional constitution.[34] The reformed Communists and the opposition debated whether Lithuania should have a parliamentary or a presidential system.[35] The framers of the constitution instituted a semi-presidential, unicameral

system dominated by parliament. The President of the State is directly elected and has limited powers.[36] Regarding its content, the Lithuanian constitution accords with those of established Western democracies – that is, apart from the structure of the state and the political system, it also firmly establishes human rights, basic rights and minority rights.[37] The institutionalization of democracy in Lithuania concluded the system change and had to prove its worth in the future. In the meantime, an independent judiciary that formally meets Western norms was created along with the constitution.[38]

The President of the State, the government and the administration

The President of the State is directly elected by the people for a five-year term of office. Tenure is limited to two terms. However, despite the president's direct legitimation, his or her functions are limited. Under certain conditions, the president is entitled to dissolve parliament but must meanwhile face the possibility of being forced by the newly elected parliament to hold new presidential elections.[39]

In the first decade of independence, Lithuania's development was characterized by frequent change of prime ministers.[40] Since 1990, there have been sixteen prime ministers, who in some cases headed several coalitions.[41] In 1999, Lithuania's government system went through a deep crisis, which – at first during power struggles and later in taking economic-political decisions – put the functionality of the constitutional institutions of parliament and president to the test. Since 2001, however, the stability of governments has improved. Up to now, the parties have only twice resorted to the possibility of a minority cabinet. The 1990s were dominated by one-party governments. Later coalition governments became necessary. At the same time, the internal stability of governments increased because prime ministers changed less frequently.[42] Still, again and again governments failed for different reasons, such as personal misconduct, internal power struggles and other scandals.[43]

In the course of institutionalizing democracy and the new structure of the state, its administration also had to be changed. This restructuring is now complete, but problems remain; in fact, public administration has become a chronic hotbed of corruption. This phenomenon is widespread, despite a number of structural changes and anti-corruption programmes. Corruption is a problem particularly among the lower ranks of administration, for example in the context of granting permits and issuing ID cards. Estimates put citizens' expenditures on bribes at about 0.7 per cent of yearly income.[44] Although Lithuania has made some progress in fighting corruption since independence, it is currently stuck at the levels recorded in 2001.[45]

Political parties and party systems

Lithuania's party system has its roots in the so-called Singing Revolution. With the formation of the Sajudis people's front, the CPLit lost its monopoly. Sajudis was an umbrella organization that united very diverse groups in opposition to the Communists. However, Sajudis and the ruling CP often overlapped regarding demands for more political and economic independence. Once victory was achieved over the Communist *ancien regime*, Sajudis lost its common point of reference and dissolved as various parties went their own ways.[46] By 2000, Lithuania had developed a stable-looking, bipolar party system that then, however, gave way to a multipolar one.[47]

Electoral system, elections and voter behaviour

The electoral system was also reformed. Having abandoned the Soviet system of an absolute majority vote system, Lithuania introduced a parallel voting system in 1992.[48] As a compromise, the political actors integrated two classical elements of electoral systems.[49] Accordingly, the Lithuanian parliament consists of 141 MPs, 71 directly elected in one-seat constituencies and 70 elected on their party's ticket. The first result of the parallel voting system was a reduction in the disproportionality of seats – that is, in the overrepresentation of successful parties – incurred by the previous majority representation system.[50] To keep the parliament from being overly fragmented, further thresholds were introduced: parties must achieve at least 5 per cent of votes, and electoral alliances 7 per cent, to be considered for the distribution of seats on a ticket.[51] In 1996, this threshold became applicable even for parties of ethnic minorities, which up to then had been exempted from the threshold requirements. Since then, the Election Action of Poles in Lithuania's representation in parliament has been only by direct elected representatives.[52]

Electoral behaviour in Lithuania is characterized by a high degree of change. Despite an initially bipolar party system, highly volatile voter behaviour regularly resulted in new coalitions among various parties. On the whole, however, the conservative parties were able to mobilize their voters more successfully. In particular, older and religious people voted for the conservative Homeland Union-Lithuanian Christian Democrats (Tévynés Sajunga-Lietuvos Krikščionys Demokratai, TS-LKD). Followers of the Social Democratic Party of Lithuania (Lietuvos socialdemocratu partija, LSDP) are mostly male and among the Russian minority. The Lithuanian Democratic Workers Party (Lietuvos demokratiné darbo partija, LDDP) recruits its voters from the rural population and ethnic minorities and can rely on their loyalty. Liberal voters, on the other hand, come from the big cities.[53] Despite efforts to remedy imbalances, however, voter turnout has clearly declined since the first free elections.[54] Observers have noted that election behaviour seems to be determined by general tendencies towards personalization, whereas ideological aspects take a back seat.[55]

Parliament

Lithuania has held six parliamentary elections since its independence. In addition, there have been several by-elections to fill seats reserved for direct election. Surprisingly, the first free elections brought the reformed ex-Communists back to power – a unique result worldwide, so far.[56] Until the election year of 2000, election results showed a stable bipolar party system, with the conservative TS-LKD and the reform-communist LDDP dominating their respective ends of the party spectrum and appointing the prime ministers. However, this bipolar party system was dissolved by the 2000 elections to the Seimas, a trend that continued in the elections of 2004 and 2008. The reasons for this include general political dissatisfaction and the restructuring of the party system, beginning with the emergence of new parties. Despite the presence of two large ethnic minorities (Russians and Poles) in Lithuania, their participation in elections was hardly visible. The ethnic parties' poor showing resulted partly from low turnout, but another cause was the ethnic conflict integrated into the right-wing/left-wing scheme in Lithuania. Where this conflict occurs, ethnic minorities tend towards the left of the political spectrum.[57] Currently, the most important parties in Lithuania are the Homeland Union – Lithuanian Christian Democrats (Tévynés sajunga – Lietuvos krikščionys demokratai), the LSDP and the Labour Party (Darbo Partija).

Justice

The restructuring of the judicial system was completed in 1993 with the creation of a court system consisting of two authorities. In the context of adjusting to EU norms, another reform in 1995 resulted in a four-level court system as well as a court of cassation and an administrative jurisdiction. Only the appellate courts and not the citizens may appeal to the Constitutional Court. Constitutional cases are comparatively few. Most requests for constitutional cases come from supreme courts and the Seimas. Through its work, the Constitutional Court has gained much trust, likely because of its non-political nature. Nonetheless, even today the judicial system suffers from the quality of its personnel. Courts have problems recruiting qualified staff. A new centre for the training of judges will improve the education and quality of judges in Lithuania.[58] Apart from this, police and public prosecutors are still subject to reform processes.[59]

Media

The Lithuanian media were privatized at a very early stage – while Gorbachev was still in power – and thus became more varied. When privatization began, the number of media outlets exploded; it then underwent a consolidation process.[60] Freedom of opinion and speech is protected by Lithuania's constitution (Articles 25 and 44).[61]

Regions and municipalities

Lithuania is a central state. Notwithstanding contention over how municipal bodies are to be organized, the principle of local self-government is undebated. The municipal level is the only one below the national level to be legitimated by elections, and apart from their own affairs, municipalities also implement the laws passed by the national parliament. In this context, the mayor is a notable representative with extensive rights and competences. Apart from the municipalities, there are also districts and rural boroughs without legislative institutions. Only under certain conditions may the national government interfere in municipal affairs. For the time being, the distribution of responsibilities between the national and municipal levels remains incomplete.[62] Early on in the phase of consolidation, the Landsbergis government attempted to weaken regions where there was a Polish majority as well as the Vilnius region, and to secure more decision-making rights for the government.[63] These measures reflected insecurities and antipathies towards Poles and the Polish minority, which since then have clearly become less significant.

Economy

Economic constitution

A number of structural reforms were introduced to institutionalize Lithuania's market economy. At first, property rights and rights of disposal had to be guaranteed, most notably in the country's constitution. Prices were liberalized, and a new (central) bank system was established. Parallel to this, socialist economic structures had to be dismantled and a market economy supported by way of privatization. Lithuania decided on a gradual process of transformation in the economic system (gradualism).[64] Privatization started with the distribution of shares – so-called vouchers – which helped wide parts of the population acquire residential property and/or enterprises. On the whole, up to the conclusion of this phase, the processes of privatization happened at different speeds.[65] The privatization of industrial enterprises in particular took time. Land purchases by foreigners were still restricted until 1998, which meant foreign investors – urgently needed to fund the modernization of the Lithuanian economy

– were hesitant because they faced investment insecurity.[66] Agriculture was also supposed to be de-collectivized, through restitution of lands and their sale to investors. By 1993, 83 per cent of agricultural lands had been privatized. However, the land reform brought serious problems with it, most notably growing insecurity among the people and a radical decline in productivity because farms were too small. In total, some ten thousand hectares lay fallow.[67]

The fixed prices of 'real existing socialism' were another focus of the institutionalization of market economy. In this regard, Lithuania faced a dual problem: on the one hand, connecting prices to supply and demand is a basic and indispensable principle of market economy; on the other hand, however, liberalization of prices caused inflation to skyrocket in Lithuania. To guarantee some social support, the state stayed involved in pricing and intervened by way of regulations. To this day, the state retains a right to intervene in single sectors like public transport or the energy market.[68]

The transition to market economy was characterized by rapidly growing unemployment. Most of all, women left the labour market, particularly those who worked in the fields affected first by the transformation crisis.[69] Especially in times of economic crisis, it was mainly women who were dismissed. However, women remained disproportionally represented in the services sector, an economic branch in which wages were particularly high. In 2005, 58 per cent of employees in this sector were female.[70]

The central bank and currency

At the beginning of transition, the resurrected Republic of Lithuania was still integrated into the rouble zone and thus largely dependent on the Russian central bank; meanwhile, the economy was in rapid decline. Lithuania initiated currency reform in 1991. At first, in 1992, an intermediary currency, the talonas, was instituted until links to the Russian rouble were dissolved. The litas was introduced later, in 1993. The newly founded central bank initially oriented itself to a currency basket consisting of the US dollar, deutschmark, franc and pound sterling, but a year later Lithuania established a currency board regime, tying its currency to the US dollar and later the euro.[71] The central bank's primary objective was to create trust in the new currency by containing the galloping inflation that, in the early days of independence, showed all the hallmarks of hyperinflation.[72]

From an agrarian to a services society? Structural changes in the Lithuanian economy

Traditionally, Lithuania's economic structure was characterized by the prominence of agriculture. In the past twenty years, however, Lithuania's economic structures, measured by their share of GDP, have changed massively. When the transformation began, agriculture still made up 24 per cent of GDP (1992); industry 50 per cent (1993); and the services sector another 26 per cent (1991).[73] Between 1997 and 2007, the primary sector fell from 11.4 to 5.3 per cent of GDP. But in that same period, the secondary sector grew even bigger. The industrial sector was comparably stable, with a 23.3 per cent share of GDP in 2007, compared to 23.5 per cent in 1997. The construction industry grew significantly in those same years, its share rising from 7.6 to 10 per cent.[74] However, after 2007 it was hit hard by the current crisis, whereupon it dropped again, to 6 per cent in 2009.[75]

Meanwhile, the services sector has been growing. Splitting this tertiary sector into three shows that in that same twenty-year period, the field of 'commerce, banking and telecommunication' grew from 27.7 per cent in 1997 to 31.5 per cent in 2007 and 'business-related and financial services' grew from 11.5 to 14.7 per cent, whereas 'other services' receded from 18.3 to 15.1 per cent of GDP.[76] These developments reflect the modernization of Lithuania's economy since 1991. Still, the agricultural sector is comparatively strong, and with 3.4 per cent of GDP it was above the EU-27 average of 1.9 per cent in 2007.[77] The fields of 'financial and other services' made a below-average showing in 2007, whereas all other fields' figures were above average. The growing significance of construction was explained by the Lithuanian real estate boom – which, however, came to an end with the economic crisis after 2007, resulting in problems for this sector.

Society

Social structure and societal lines of conflict

In past decades, Lithuania's demographic development was subject to ups and downs. World War II and the deportations during the years of Soviet occupation made deep cuts in the population. In 1990, Lithuania had about 3.7 million inhabitants. Since then, population growth has been negative. Currently, some 3.3 million people live in Lithuania.[78] Thus, Lithuania's population has declined by around 400,000 in the past twenty years. This development reflects constant migration to other countries: from 2002 to 2007, the migration balance was -0.18 per cent a year. Declining birth rates in Lithuania have also contributed to this demographic development. Although some improvement was recorded in 2006, the ratio of 1.31 children per woman is still relatively low.[79]

Lithuania's urban population makes up 66 per cent of the total; 34 per cent of people live in the countryside. The biggest cities are Vilnius with 665,000 inhabitants, Kaunas with 479,000 and Klaipeda (formerly Memel) with 273,000.[80]

The gender ratio is balanced, with women holding a slight majority at about 53 per cent of the population. The population's life expectancy rose between 1996 and 2006, but the increases for both men (from 64.6 to 65.39) and women (from 75.9 to 77.0) were small enough that life expectancy remains quite stable overall.[81] Estimates indicate that it can be assumed the demographic decline will continue and that by 2060 the population will be only 2.5 million.[82] The natural population growth is negative and is currently more than 10,000 inhabitants a year.[83] This development will lead to an ageing society and even more burdened social systems, so reform will be needed.[84] Poverty is one of Lithuania's urgent problems. Almost 80 per cent of Lithuanians believe that poverty is widespread.[85] From the citizens' perspective, however, accession to the EU has, in the end, brought more benefit than harm.[86] Meriting mention here is the fact that in 2009 a majority of Lithuanians believed their children would improve their opportunities by emigrating.[87] Accordingly, Lithuanians express broad satisfaction with EU membership and the euro.[88]

Lithuania's society is comparatively free of ethnic strife, but the political-economic transformation has fuelled a number of other conflicts. Economic success is visible most of all in urban regions, giving rise to conflict between cities and rural regions. At the same time, not all citizens can be said to have profited from the system change. The elderly and pensioners were particularly hard hit by the economic transformation to a market economy.[89] Increasing poverty, unemployment and low incomes have produced a society divided into winners and losers. Thus, classical distributive conflicts characterize Lithuania's socio-economic sphere.[90]

In 2001, 6.74 per cent of the population were Poles, 6.31 per cent called themselves Russians and another 2.57 per cent considered themselves Romani. There are also Jewish and Belarusian communities, each making up a share of 1.2 per cent of the total population. In the south-east, the Polish minority is almost one third of the population; Poles are even in the majority in some individual regions. Lithuanians, though ethnically dominant, feel their existence is threatened.[91] In 1989, parts of the Polish minority spoke out against the introduction of Lithuanian as the official language, despite the state's support of minority languages.[92] This resulted in a short period of distrust towards the Polish minority.[93]

The most important framework conditions for minority policy in Lithuania had already been developed by the end of the Soviet occupation. First, in 1990, all inhabitants were offered Lithuanian citizenship. Additionally, minorities were supposed to be granted the opportunity to maintain their cultures and traditions, and to establish their own schools. This early implementation of a modern kind of minority protection was duly recognized by international organizations.[94] Since 1992, further amendments have been made to the nationality law. Some of the amendments were reactions to recommendations of international organizations and complaints from the Constitutional Court and representatives of minorities against single rules that tended to have a discriminating effect.

Interest groups

Intermediary organizations of social partners exist to different degrees in Lithuania. Industrial, agrarian and business associations are comparatively well organized, whereas trade unions suffered a massive loss of members and have only gradually become stronger.[95] Only 14 per cent of employees are members of a trade union.[96] The trade unions are not particularly related to any political party. Employers' associations, on the other hand, are very strong. However, they do not dominate the system of social partners because important issues are resolved in the context of tripartite consultations. Labour agreements and minimum wages are negotiated at the national and the local levels, with the state participating.[97]

Churches

The Catholic Church is the most important religious entity in Lithuania. It contributed considerably to maintenance of the Lithuanian identity and the development of a broad opposition alliance in Lithuania.[98] Today, however, the Catholic Church has no role of political importance; in fact, it has mostly withdrawn, apart from in certain topical fields. Nevertheless, it does have a role in public life.[99]

Civil society

Any judgement about the development of civil society must differentiate between the period of gaining independence and the post-communist period. In the declining USSR, civil society organizations from the inter-war period underwent a revival, as glasnost and perestroika gave them more freedom of action than before. Particularly in the environmental field, civil society organizations started to develop in parallel with the independence movement. But once independence was regained, these newly developed structures dissolved again because the goal that united them had been achieved.[100]

Nevertheless, along with its democratization, Lithuania succeeded in establishing a civil society.[101] Today a variety of civil society organizations exist, though with limited opportunities to influence processes of political decision-making. Despite formally favourable preconditions, the expert class is dominant.[102]

Consolidation

Constitutional Consolidation

Lithuania's constitution has proven its worth in the past twenty years. Its biggest challenge was removing an elected president, Rolandas Paksas, from office. Paksas had been involved in dubious transactions, and at the same time he was accused of corruption. The cases against him did not end as expected, but the constitutional procedures worked, and there was no destabilization of the political arena.[103] Thus, constitutional consolidation in Lithuania may be considered complete.[104]

Consolidation of Actors

The party system: fragmentation, volatility, polarization, extremism

Instead of the kind of strongly fragmented party system seen in many other post-communist states, in Lithuania a bipolar system of conservatives and reform communists developed over a decade. This stability dissolved with the elections of 2000, when two new parties entered the stage: New Union (Social Liberals) and the Liberal Union of Lithuania. This process of depolarization continued in subsequent elections, when more parties and electoral alliances climbed over the thresholds. The former Sajudis parties had lost their predominance.[105] This restructuring of the party system was shaped by the economic crisis of 1999, economic-political decisions and the popularity (or unpopularity) of new or old party leaders.[106] And not only were new parties being founded, but several parties fused after 2000, also contributing to the restructuring.[107]

For the time being, no party in Lithuania, left or right, that is hostile to the system has succeeded in being elected to the Seimas. Meanwhile, ecological parties are missing. Lithuania's party families are similar to those of Western Europe.[108] For years, membership numbers have been declining, so the Lithuanian party system cannot be considered a system of mass parties. The parties lack the financial resources to establish efficient organizational structures, so the focus has shifted to national party bureaus and those of MPs.[109] At the same time, however, the parties must also be present in wide areas to be able to accomplish their tasks.[110]

Informal actors

Important actors not legitimated by elections who either influence politics to exploit it for their own purposes or have anti-constitutional intentions do not exist in this sense in Lithuania. What is conspicuous, however, are the close relations between media enterprises and politicians.

Interest groups

Lithuanian non-state actors behave according to the appropriate norms. Currently there are still problems concerning work relations between trade unions and employers, who participate in tripartite bodies but have not yet entered into a real dialogue. This is due in part to an unequal distribution of power and information deficits on the employees' side.[111]

Civil society

In the case of Lithuania, it is still too early to speak of a well-functioning civil society. A certain distrust, born of experiences in the Soviet period, lingers towards participation in society.[112] Most people are not interested in confrontation with the state. Accordingly, the information collection and education sectors dominate civil society, and citizens use their participation rights only to a limited degree.[113]

Media

The media landscape in Lithuania is highly varied. Its development was considerably influenced by the period of political change.[114] Due to their position within the political system, the media play a particular role in transformation and the consolidation of democracy in Lithuania. In the past few years there have been concentration processes, and some market-dominating media enterprises have developed.[115] The *Lietuvos rytas* (Lithuanian Morning), Lithuania's most important daily newspaper, was privatized as early as 1989. The market for weeklies is dominated by TV magazines and a few newspapers counted as tabloids that suffer from constant crisis. Since 1989, the number of magazines in Lithuania has grown by more than 50 per cent. About 100 magazines sell between 1,000 and 75,000 copies a week.[116]

The broadcasting situation is somewhat different. Apart from one dominant public service broadcaster, a number of private stations have developed since 1990. There are nine national, private broadcasting stations in total and almost thirty local ones, besides the state-run station. Probably the biggest changes since independence have happened in the TV sector. After the state monopoly ended in 1993 (with the launch of the first private TV channel), several other channels developed, and foreign investors became active in this market.[117] The Lithuanian media operate within the framework of the constitution. No anti-constitutional tendencies against the democratic principle have been observed. What does give cause for concern, however, is the close connection between politics and media, which may result – and in a number of cases has indeed resulted – in a less critical kind of journalism.[118]

Political Culture

The political culture in Lithuania is divided. On the one hand, the great majority of citizens support democracy; on the other, the population has little confidence in the country's political institutions.[119] The audio-visual media inspire more confidence than do the print media. Not even half of the citizens trust the army. Also conspicuous is the bad reputation of the judicial system – almost 80 per cent have little confidence in it. Similar figures hold for the government, the parties and the parliament. The majority also express little confidence in public authorities.[120] This leads to tendencies of alienation from the state's political structure. Meanwhile, there is great dissatisfaction with the performance of democracy in Lithuania. Almost 82 per cent of those who were interviewed for Eurobarometer 72 expressed dissatisfaction or much dissatisfaction with the achievements of democracy, thus reflecting Lithuanians' attitude of distance from the existing political system.[121]

However, no real threat to the democratic system in Lithuania has been observed. Almost everybody in Lithuania emphasizes his or her positive attitude towards the democratic principle.[122] Even though a majority of citizens are currently dissatisfied with the achievements of their democracy because their own ideas of democracy differ from the reality, the people are not open to other systems of rule.[123] Since the institutionalization of democracy, support for the new system in Lithuania has grown markedly from 47 to 71 per cent[124] – an unexpected development under the circumstances, given that in the early 1990s more than one third of Lithuanians thought democracy would collapse. Currently, only about 10 per cent hold this opinion.[125]

Consolidation of the Economic System

Economic constitution

In general, the market economy in Lithuania works relatively smoothly. But even here the effects of the world economic and financial crisis have left their mark, specifically a sharp decline in GDP. Lithuania has mostly recovered from the economic and financial crisis of the past few years.[126] Lithuania joined the eurozone in 2015 after it met the criteria in 2014. The criterion of inflation is not currently at the fore, but budget overruns will be the country's only means of coping with the crisis.

Attitudes

As was to be expected, at first the population was somewhat afraid of what was coming. The radical changes in society, economy and politics at the beginning of the 1990s had to be learned and got used to.[127] Yet at the same time, despite an obvious decline in the quality of life, the situation was calm. The people hoped the prospects for the future would improve after some time.[128] This is indeed what happened. Just as they embraced democracy, the Lithuanian population have also shown appreciation for the market economy. This positive attitude is partly due to their negative perception of communism, but the comparatively significant approval of the market economy renders it undoubted as an organizing principle.[129]

EU Integration

Accession Talks and Accession

Lithuania approached the European Community at a very early stage. A first agreement was signed in 1992, and from 1994 the EU signalled its readiness to accept the country as a member. Lithuania also started actively preparing for its accession with several follow-up agreements, among other measures. In 1999, negotiations began with all candidates for the next round of enlargement.[130] In the course of the Swedish EU presidency, Lithuania's EU accession talks gathered momentum, and it became possible to solve a number of problems.[131] Some of the talks focused particularly on agriculture, the Ignalina nuclear power plant and transit from Kaliningrad to the Russian Federation. These issues were resolved to everybody's satisfaction.[132]

Contribution to EU Institutions

As an EU member, Lithuania faces one basic problem: being a small state, it lacks enough sufficiently qualified personnel for all tasks. Thus, it must focus on some self-defined problem fields to gain influence within the EU. The same holds for MPs and their staff, for whom really efficient participation is possible only in certain committees.[133] The most important fields of Lithuanian involvement are the European Neighbourhood Policy and the Northern Dimension policy, the latter having been initiated by Finland. Lithuania cooperates closely with its Baltic neighbours, but at the same time it guards its sovereignty closely and acts with appropriate restraint.[134]

Integration Problems

The Republic of Lithuania is mostly integrated into the EU. Nevertheless, it still has to catch up economically and socially with the older member states. This process will take many years, during which Lithuania will remain a net beneficiary. After its accession, the country still had some minor problems to solve, but this was accomplished by 2010, whereupon Lithuania became fully legally integrated into the EU. Lithuanian citizens have also enjoyed freedom of movement within the EU since 2011, after the elapse of transitional periods regarding Germany, Austria and Finland.[135]

Attitudes towards the EU

During the accession talks, citizens already strongly favoured EU membership.[136] Despite the economic and financial crisis, this attitude has not changed significantly. A large majority of Lithuanians (71 per cent) support membership of the European Union. Support for EU membership is especially strong among the generation under thirty years old (75.7 per cent). Ethnic Lithuanians and well-educated people in particular also clearly approve of membership. Another indicator of support for membership is the marked interest in relevant information about EU institutions among the majority of the population.[137]

State of the Consolidation of Democracy

Constitutional Consolidation

Lithuania's development from a post-Soviet state into a member of the European Union clearly demonstrates that developments in this small country have been positive overall.

A functioning democratic community and state have developed and may be considered consolidated, despite lingering shortcomings and problems. The landscape of political parties represents highly varied political interests, a context featuring an undeniable tendency towards populism. The institutions are stable and functional. Not even the many changes in the office of prime minister have affected the stability of coalitions. Surprisingly, the stability of governments has even increased since the dissolution of the bipolar system. In 2004, Lithuania successfully withstood a test of political endurance with the impeachment of Rolandas Paksas. This episode did not affect the country's democratic structures, making it obvious that democracy in Lithuania has established functional mechanisms.

Consolidation of Actors

Unlike other democratic structures in Lithuania, the party system is not very stable, even if a seemingly stable bipolar system developed in the first years. Things are still in motion – even more so given the comparatively high degree of volatility, low voter turnout and a political culture that, for the time being, is insufficiently distinct.[138] That said, the absence of anti-system parties on the left or right at the parliamentary level deserves positive emphasis.

Thus, there is no danger to democracy in Lithuania or risk of its replacement with an authoritarian regime of any kind, and this will not change in the foreseeable future. Lithuanians have recognized democracy as 'the only game in town'.[139] Freedom House and Polity IV surveys consider the country a stable, consolidated democracy.[140] The elites are mostly loyal to the democratic system.[141] There has always been consensus on two foreign policy goals – accession to the EU and to NATO. Both objectives were finally attained in 2004.[142] This basic concord on foreign policy is also reflected in the support for the market economy, although ideas of what it should look like differ.[143]

However, the personal connections between the media and politics are problematic, as they might lead to deficient control of political institutions. Relations between politics, administration and civil society must improve before greater participation in society can be achieved. Also, the trade unions must find ways to become a social partner strong enough to contain the predominance of employers. Corruption will continue to be a problem for Lithuania.

Consolidation of Attitudes

In the years to come, Lithuania will not be a tolerant society. Unfortunately, the strong focus on the necessary economic development suggests that social conflicts will likely be neglected. This might become especially obvious in regard to issues such as homophobia and Islamophobia, as long as the conservative parties and their representatives latently or offensively show such attitudes.[144] Anti-Semitism will also continue to be widespread.[145]

Rolf Winkelmann has been teaching political science at Carl-von-Ossietzky University Oldenburg since 2004. He earned a doctorate in Oldenburg on the consolidation of the Baltic states with a particular focus on party funding. In the context of his doctoral thesis, but also later, he made research trips to Estonia, among other places. His research interest is in the fields of political parties, party funding with a regional focus on Estonia, Latvia and Lithuania, but also on the Federal Republic of

Germany. In 2013, in the context of the ERASMUS Programme, he was a teacher at Mykolas-Romeris University in Vilnius (Lithuania).

Notes

1. See A. Kasekamp, *A History of the Baltic States* (Basingstoke, 2010), 20–24, 43–50.
2. T. Snyder, *The Reconstruction of Nations: Poland, Ukraine, Lithuania, Belarus 1569–1999* (New Haven, 2003), 17–20.
3. See Kasekamp, *Baltic States*, 64–67.
4. See C. Aston, *Makers of the Modern World: Antonius Piip, Zigfrids Meierovics and Augustinas Voldemaras. The Baltic States* (London, 2010), 27–44.
5. See M. Garleff, *Die baltischen Länder. Estland, Lettland, Litauen vom Mittelalter bis zur Gegenwart* (Regensburg, 2001), 82–86.
6. See Kasekamp, *Baltic States*, 108f.
7. See H. Dauchert, *'Anwalt der Balten' oder Anwalt in eigener Sache? Die deutsche Baltikumpolitik 1991–2004* (Berlin, 2008), 80–85.
8. W. Merkel, *Systemtransformation: Eine Einführung in die Theorie und Empirie der Transformationsforschung*, 2nd ed. (Wiesbaden, 2010), 361.
9. See T. Lane, 'Lithuania: Stepping Westwards', in D.J. Smith and A. Pabriks (eds), *The Baltic States Estonia, Latvia and Lithuania* (London, 2002); Garleff, *Baltischen Länder*.
10. Kasekamp, *Baltic States*.
11. See M. Laar, *The Power of Freedom: Central and Eastern Europe after 1945* (Brussels, 2010).
12. See Lane, 'Lithuania'.
13. See J. Tauber, 'Das politische System Litauens', in W. Ismayr (ed.), *Die politischen Systeme Osteuropas*, 3rd ed. (Wiesbaden, 2010), 171–208.
14. See A. Reetz, *Die Entwicklung der Parteiensysteme in den baltischen Staaten: Vom Beginn des Mehrparteiensystems 1988 bis zu den dritten Wahlen* (Wittenbach, 2004).
15. See R. Winkelmann, *Politik und Wirtschaft im Baltikum: Stabilisierung von Demokratie und Marktwirtschaft in Estland, Lettland und Litauen* (Saarbrücken, 2007).
16. See A. Ramonaite, 'The Development of the Lithuanian Party System: From Stability to Perturbation', in S. Jungerstam-Mulders (ed.), *Post-Communist EU Member States: Parties and Party Systems* (Aldershot, 2006), 69–90.
17. See Winkelmann, *Politik und Wirtschaft*.
18. See A. Krupavicius, 'Semi-presidentialism in Lithuania: Origins, Development, Challenges', in R. Elgie and S. Moestrup (eds), *Semi-presidentialism in Central and Eastern Europe* (Manchester, 2008), 65–84.
19. See C. Taube, *Constitutionalism in Estonia, Latvia and Lithuania: A Study in Comparative Constitutional Law* (Uppsala, 2001).
20. See P. Harfst, *Wahlsystemwandel in Mittelosteuropa: Strategisches Design einer politischen Institution* (Wiesbaden, 2007).
21. See U. Böllhoff, *10 Jahre Systemtransformation in den baltischen Staaten: Eine vergleichende empirische Analyse unter besonderer Berücksichtigung länderspezifischer Ausgangsbedingungen und Aspekten zur Integration in die Europäische Union* (Freiburg, 2002).
22. See V. Fritz, *State-Building: A Comparative Study of Ukraine, Lithuania, Belarus, and Russia* (Budapest, 2007).

23. See P. Austrevicius, 'The Accession of Lithuania to the EU', in G. Vassiliou (ed.), *The Accession Story: The EU from Fifteen to Twenty-Five Countries* (Oxford, 2007), 225–58.
24. See U. Hanssen-Decker, *Von Madrid nach Göteborg: Schweden und der EU-Beitritt Estlands, Lettlands und Litauens, 1995–2001* (Frankfurt a. M., 2008).
25. See Dauchert, *'Anwalt der Balten'*.
26. See A. Uhlin, *Post-Soviet Civil Society: Democratization in Russia and the Baltic States* (London, 2006).
27. See Fritz, *State-Building*.
28. See J. Maćków, *Am Rande Europas? Nation, Zivilgesellschaft und außenpolitische Integration in Belarus, Litauen, Polen, Russland und der Ukraine* (Freiburg, 2004).
29. See R. Misiunas and R. Taagepera, *The Baltic States: Years of Dependence 1940–1990*, 2nd ed. (London, 2006), 303–16.
30. See A. Lieven, *The Baltic Revolution: Estonia, Latvia, Lithuania and the Path to Independence* (New Haven, 1999), 224–28; V. Rimantas, 'Political Rebirth in Lithuania, 1990–1991: Events and Problems', *Journal of Baltic Studies* 25(2) (1994), 183–88, here 184.
31. See Laar, *Power of Freedom*, 143; Kasekamp, *Baltic States*, 165f.; Garleff, *Baltischen Länder*, 183.
32. See Kasekamp, *Baltic States*, 167f.
33. See M. Huber, *Moskau, 11. März 1985: Die Auflösung des sowjetischen Imperiums* (Munich, 2002), 153–72.
34. See A. Hollstein, 'Das Verhältnis von Parlament, Staatspräsident und Regierung in der Republik Litauen', in B. Meissner, D.A. Loeber and C. Hasselblatt (eds), *Der Aufbau einer freiheitlich-demokratischen Ordnung in den baltischen Staaten: Staat-Wirtschaft-Gesellschaft* (Hamburg, 1995), 105–15, here 108.
35. See Lane, 'Lithuania', 132.
36. See Taube, *Constitutionalism*, 152f.
37. See J. Tauber, 'Litauen', in W. Weidenfeld (ed.), *Den Wandel gestalten – Strategien der Transformation*, Vol. 2: Dokumentation der internationalen Recherche (Gütersloh, 2001), 110–38, here 114.
38. See Taube, *Constitutionalism*, 152f.
39. See Krupavicius, 'Semi-presidentialism in Lithuania', 70f.
40. See J. Lemke, 'Zwölf Jahre, zwölf Regierungen: Akteure, Ereignisse, Spezifika der litauischen Politik', *Osteuropa* 52(9/10) (2002), 1236–48.
41. See G. Tiemann and D. Jahn, 'Koalitionen in den baltischen Staaten: Lehrstücke für die Bedeutung funktionierender Parteien', in S. Kropp, S.S. Schüttemeyer and R. Sturm (eds), *Koalitionen in West- und Osteuropa* (Opladen, 2002), 271–300, here 299.
42. See Fritz, *State-Building*, 248.
43. See ibid., 261.
44. See Tauber, 'Das politische System Litauens', 183f.
45. See CPI 2000–2010, Corruptions Perceptions Index since 2000 (http://www.transparency.org/policy_research/surveys_indices/cpi/about).
46. See Winkelmann, *Politik und Wirtschaft*, 59.
47. See Reetz, *Entwicklung der Parteiensysteme*, 63.
48. In political science, this term designates a particular electoral system. A parallel voting system exists when an election features two different electoral systems operating in parallel – in most cases, a majority system and a representational system. A share of MPs are elected according to the majority system in one-seat constituencies. These direct seats do not count for the ticket seats (representational system).

49. See Harfst, *Wahlsystemwandel in Mittelosteuropa*, 126.
50. See D. Nohlen and M. Kasapovic, *Wahlsysteme und Systemwandel in Osteuropa* (Opladen, 1996), 54.
51. See Harfst, *Wahlsystemwandel in Mittelosteuropa*, 126.
52. See Ramonaite, 'Development of the Lithuanian Party System', 69–90, here 78.
53. See Tauber, 'Das politische System Litauens', 194.
54. See http://www.vrk.lt/en/pirmas-puslapis/previous-elections (accessed 20 November 2010).
55. See Tauber, 'Das politische System Litauens', 194; Reetz, *Entwicklung der Parteiensysteme*, 181–88.
56. See Kasekamp, *Baltic States*, 174.
57. See Ramonaite, 'Development of the Lithuanian Party System', 78.
58. See Tauber, 'Das politische System Litauens', 201–3.
59. See ibid.
60. See M. Lukosiunas and V. Bartasevicius, 'Lithuania: Reshaping the Media and Society', in S. Hoyer, E. Lauk and P. Vihalemm (eds), *Towards a Civic Society: The Baltic Media's Long Road to Freedom. Perspectives on History, Ethnicity and Journalism* (Tartu, 1993), 253–61, here 253–57.
61. Constitution of the Republic of Lithuania (http://www.lrkt.lt/Documents2_e.html; accessed 2 November 2010).
62. See Tauber, 'Das politische System Litauens', 203f.
63. See Snyder, *Reconstruction of Nations*, 269.
64. See S.V. Vardys and W.A. Slaven, 'Lithuania', in W.R. Iwaskiw (ed.), *Estonia, Latvia and Lithuania: Country Studies* (Washington, 1996), 167–242, here 208.
65. See Lane, 'Lithuania', 174–79.
66. See Winkelmann, *Politik und Wirtschaft*, 268.
67. See Vardys and Slaven, 'Lithuania', 208.
68. See Böllhoff, *10 Jahre Systemtransformation*, 61.
69. See A. Motiejunaite, 'Female Employment in Lithuania: Testing Three Popular Explanations', *Journal of Baltic Studies* 41(2) (2010), 237–58, here 253.
70. See ibid., 244.
71. See K. Schrader and C.-F. Laaser, 'Wirtschaft Litauens', in H. Graf and M. Kerner (eds), *Handbuch: Baltikum heute* (Berlin, 1998), 151–79, here 162–65.
72. See Böllhoff, *10 Jahre Systemtransformation*, 41.
73. Vardys and Slaven, 'Lithuania', 212f.
74. Statistisches Amt der Europäischen Gemeinschaften, *Europa in Zahlen: Eurostat Jahrbuch 2009* (Luxemburg, 2009), 77.
75. http://epp.eurostat.ec.europa.eu/guip/themeAction.do.
76. Statistisches Amt der Europäischen Gemeinschaften, *Europa in Zahlen*, 77.
77. Ibid., 77.
78. Ibid., 137.
79. Ibid., 154.
80. http://www.stat.gov.lt/en/pages/view?id=371; accessed 20 June 2010.
81. Statistisches Amt der Europäischen Gemeinschaften, *Europa in Zahlen*, 160.
82. Ibid., 137.
83. Ibid., 147.
84. See J. Aidukaite, 'Die Entwicklung in der post-sowjetischen Ära: Das litauische Wohlfahrtssystem', in K. Schubert, S. Hegelich and U. Bazanz (eds), *Europäische Wohlfahrtssysteme: Ein Handbuch* (Wiesbaden, 2008), 403–22, here 403.

85. Eurobarometer Survey on Poverty and Social Exclusion 2009, EB 72.1, 15.
86. See Standard-Eurobarometer 72, 149–52.
87. See ibid., 139.
88. See ibid., 148 and 238.
89. See Kasekamp, *Baltic States*, 182.
90. See Winkelmann, *Politik und Wirtschaft*, 73–80.
91. See D. Budryte and V. Pilinkaite-Sotirovic, 'Lithuania: Progressive Legislation without Popular Support', in B. Rechel (ed.), *Minority Rights in Central and Eastern Europe* (London, 2009), 151–65, here 151f.
92. See ibid., 153.
93. See Kasekamp, *Baltic States*, 186.
94. See Budryte and Pilinkaite-Sotirovic, 'Lithuania', 154f.
95. See Fritz, *State-Building*, 254.
96. S. Mau and R. Verwiebe, *Die Sozialstruktur Europas* (Konstanz, 2009), 82.
97. See Tauber, 'Das politische System Litauens', 196.
98. See Kasekamp, *Baltic States*, 153.
99. See ibid., 187.
100. See Uhlin, *Post-Soviet Civil Society*, 51f.
101. See Maćków, *Am Rande Europas*, 238.
102. See N. Mzavanadze, 'Sustainable Development in Lithuania: Between the Government Agenda and the Undiscovered Civil Society', *Journal of Baltic Studies* 40(3) (2009), 397–414, here 403.
103. See Fritz, *State-Building*, 247.
104. See W. Merkel, 'Gegen alle Theorie? Die Konsolidierung der Demokratie in Ostmitteleuropa', in K.H. Schrenk and M. Soldner (eds), *Analyse demokratischer Regierungssysteme* (Wiesbaden, 2010), 545–62, here 550.
105. See Ramonaite, 'Development of the Lithuanian Party System', 69f.
106. See ibid., 73.
107. See Fritz, *State-Building*, 246f.
108. See Ramonaite, 'Development of the Lithuanian Party System', 75.
109. See ibid., 82.
110. See Winkelmann, *Politik und Wirtschaft*, 89.
111. See Tauber, 'Das politische System Litauens', 196.
112. See Mzavanadze, 'Sustainable Development', 403.
113. See Uhlin, *Post-Soviet Civil Society*, 88f.
114. See Lukosiunas and Bartasevicius, 'Lithuania', 255f.
115. See A. Balcytiene, 'Lithuanian Media: A Question of Change', in P. Vihalemm (ed.), *Baltic Media in Transition* (Tartu, 2002), 103–34, here 113–17.
116. A. Nugaraite, 'Lithuania', in S. Huber (ed.), *Media Markets in Central and Eastern Europe: An Analysis on Media Ownership in Bulgaria, Czech Republic, Estonia, Hungary, Latvia, Lithuania, Poland, Romania, Slovakia and Slovenia* (Vienna, 2006), 55–58.
117. See ibid.
118. See M. Stegherr and K. Liesem, *Die Medien in Osteuropa: Mediensysteme im Transformationsprozess* (Wiesbaden, 2010), 298.
119. See Tauber, 'Litauen', 117.
120. See Standard-Eurobarometer 72, 149–52.
121. Ibid., 155; O.W. Gabriel, 'Politische Einstellungen und politische Kultur', in O.W. Gabriel and S. Kropp (eds), *Die EU-Staaten im Vergleich: Strukturen, Prozesse, Politikinhalte*, 3rd ed. (Wiesbaden, 2008), 207.

122. O.W. Gabriel, 'Politische Einstellungen und politische Kultur', in O.W. Gabriel and S. Kropp (eds), *Die EU-Staaten im Vergleich: Strukturen, Prozesse, Politikinhalte*, 3rd ed. (Wiesbaden, 2008), 207.
123. See ibid., 47–50.
124. Ibid., 52.
125. Ibid., 55.
126. 'Lithuania Revises its Q3 Economic Growth to 1.1 Per cent' (http://www.balticbusinessnews.com; accessed 26 November 2010).
127. See R. Rose, 'Learning to Support New Regimes in Eastern Europe', in L. Diamond and M.F. Plattner (eds), *How People View Democracy* (Baltimore, 2008), 45–58, here 45.
128. See ibid., 51.
129. See Winkelmann, *Politik und Wirtschaft*, 70–72.
130. See Austrevicius, 'Accession of Lithuania', 226.
131. See Hanssen-Decker, *Von Madrid nach Göteborg*, 196.
132. See Austrevicius, 'Accession of Lithuania', 238–55.
133. See T.-G. Danckworth, 'Estlands Außenpolitik nach dem Beitritt zur Europäischen Union: Handlungsoptionen eines Kleinstaates' (PhD diss., TU Chemnitz, 2007), 234.
134. See Kasekamp, *Baltic States*, 191f.
135. See Austrevicius, 'Accession of Lithuania', 232f.
136. Ibid., 257f.
137. See 'Lietuva in Brief', *The Baltic Times*, 12–18 August 2010, 4.
138. See Ramonaite, 'Development of the Lithuanian Party System', 83ff.
139. See Rose, 'Learning to Support New Regimes', 56.
140. See C.W. Haerpfer, 'Post-Communist Europe and Post-Soviet Russia', in C.W. Haerpfer et al. (eds), *Democratization* (Oxford, 2009), 309–20, here 314f.
141. See A. Steen, 'The Baltic Elites after the Challenge of the Regime', in H. Best and U. Becker (eds), *Elites in Transition: Elite Research in Central and Eastern Europe* (Opladen, 1997), 166.
142. See Fritz, *State-Building*, 250.
143. See ibid., 258.
144. See 'Litauen verbietet Unterricht über Homosexualität', Spiegel Online, 19 June 2009 (http://www.spiegel.de/schulspiegel/ausland/0,1518,631413,00.html).
145. L. Donskis, 'Another Word for Uncertainty: Anti-semitism in Modern Lithuania', *Nordeuropaforum* 1 (2006), 7–26, here 23.

Chapter 4

THE GDR

Günther Heydemann

Peaceful Revolution 1989/90, Politics and Constitutional Development

In terms of its basic political and economic structures, the German Democratic Republic (GDR) was undoubtedly a 'real socialist', Soviet-type system of rule, economy and society for more than forty years.[1] Nevertheless, the division of Germany and the existence of another German state in the West made the GDR an exceptional case among the states of the former Eastern Bloc from the outset. Thus, during the 'Peaceful Revolution' that overcame the dictatorship of the Socialist Unity Party of Germany (Sozialistische Einheitspartei Deutschlands, SED) and the subsequent transition to parliamentary democracy and market economy, the question of a possible unification with the Federal Republic of Germany was already necessarily a crucial influential factor in the further development of the GDR.

At the level of foreign policy and diplomacy, this issue had been an open question for quite some time but would be solved surprisingly soon – as early as 3 October 1990 – by way of the international '2 + 4' treaty. At the domestic and party-political level, the development towards (re)unification with the Federal Republic had started even earlier, in late 1989. It had not seemed realistic at the time, but once the 'Government of National Responsibility' was formed in the GDR on 5 February 1990, with members of opposition parties and groups contributing for the first time, it was decided that elections should be held in March 1990, rather than in May as originally scheduled. In its early stages, the election campaign was already under the growing influence of West German parties. Nevertheless, until the People's Chamber (Volkskammer) elections on 18

March 1990, the GDR formally remained a real socialist state whose constitution and structures differed little from those of any other Eastern Bloc state.

As a result of the (final) elections to the People's Chamber, the GDR became a parliamentary democracy. For the first time since its founding on 7 October 1949, the East German sub-state had a government legitimated by free, competitive elections. From this moment on, it once again differed from its neighbours, as they then existed in East Central Europe – states where democratic elections would not happen until a later stage. At this point, however, another intention behind these elections came to the fore: not only was the government now democratically elected, but the great majority of voters had also assigned the task of dissolving the SED-created state as soon as possible and making it part of the Federal Republic. This paradox was due not least to the desire for a political and socio-economic situation like that in the Federal Republic. This found expression in the overwhelming electoral victory of the Alliance for Germany (Allianz für Deutschland) under the leadership of Federal Chancellor Helmut Kohl, which received 48.1 per cent of the vote on 18 March 1990. It was also reflected in the marginalization of anti-SED regime opposition groups that had in fact constituted the democratic nucleus of the GDR's Peaceful Revolution. Although the majority of the civil rights activists in the GDR entered into an alliance with the West German Green Party (Alliance'90), they garnered only 2.9 per cent of the vote. The reason for this crushing defeat was doubtless their persistent pursuit of an independent yet still socialism-oriented GDR. Their leadership supported a confederation of the two states but rejected reunification. Quite obviously, these political and socio-economic ideas ran contrary to the wishes of the broad majority of GDR citizens, who were striving for rapid reunification. Also, the Social Democratic Party of Germany (Sozialdemokratische Partei Deutschlands, SPD) – the presumed victor until just before the elections – suffered an unexpectedly bad showing of only 24.3 per cent, whereas the former communist Party, the later named Party of Democratic Socialism (Partei des Demokratischen Sozialismus, SED-PDS) got 16.3 per cent after all, thus still becoming the third-strongest party. The Liberals won 5.3 per cent of the votes.

Despite fierce internal struggles, the grand coalition consisting of the Christian Democratic Union (Christlich-Demokratische Union, CDU), the German Social Union (Deutsche Soziale Union), Democratic Start (Demokratischer Aufbruch), the Alliance of Free Democrats (Bund Freier Demokraten) and the SPD was neither able nor willing to deny this wish. Finally the unification of the Federal Republic and the GDR was negotiated according to Article 23 of the Basic Law – that is, the East German federal states joined the area of application of the Basic Law. Meanwhile, lawmakers forbore to create a new constitution (according to Article 146 of the Basic Law) for a unified Germany.

The unexpectedly speedy unification of the two German states on 3 October 1990 created a new, though ultimately only extended, Federal Republic and mostly preserved the existing constitutional order. Thus, after the passage on 31 August 1990 of the unification treaty, which involved abrogating, reformulating or changing only a few articles of the Basic Law, there was no revision of the constitution, nor talk of a new one. In a realistic assessment of the difficult and complicated foreign and domestic political situation overall, taking the doubtless considerable time needed to debate, formulate and pass a new constitution would likely have endangered the still incomplete process of reunification. Thus, 'the attempt to understand and enforce the creation of a constitution as founding the Republic once again'[2] did not succeed. Rather, five new federal states (Mecklenburg-Vorpommern, Brandenburg including East Berlin, Saxony-Anhalt, Thuringia and Saxony) joined the Federal Republic and the federal basic structure was retained (in conformance with the Law on the Introduction of Federal States), a structure that is, one might say, the oldest element of political cohesion in all German history. This way, the 'process of revolution, state unification and democratic re-foundation in the federal states … became a crossed-over process which was eclipsed by the process of German reunification but then also shifted into the federal states'.[3] Regarding the two crucial parameters of establishing and consolidating democracy in the course of the revolutionary development in the GDR in that *annus mirabilis* 1989/90, we may conclude that it would 'probably have been much more complicated, had it not happened under such exceptional circumstances: in the form of joining the already existing and … properly functioning German constitutional state'.[4]

Thus, the process of German (re)unification unfolded between two democracies, whereas in the other (still) real socialist states the democratic process started with further differentiation.[5] Even though the nascent transformation process was happening under the leadership of Federal Republic elites, it must not be overlooked that 'the democratisation of the GDR … [was] the condition demanded by the international community of states for a unification' of the two German states and was thus a foreign policy necessity.[6] After all, a united and thus enlarged Germany was acceptable to its European neighbours only if, by a democratic vote, the majority of the Germans in the GDR declared their wish to be unified with the Federal Republic. With the internationally legal completion of the unification of the two German states on 3 October 1990, a democratic, mostly non-violent, peaceful revolution had brought an end to more than forty years of rule by the Kommunistische Partei Deutschlands (KPD)/ Sozialistische Einheitspartei Deutschlands (SED) and changed real social- ist dictatorship in the GDR into a parliamentary democracy under the rule of law.

Almost from the very beginning, German reunification came under much temporal pressure both internally and externally. On the one hand, it had to proceed quickly to exploit the existing foreign policy 'window of opportunity' and, given the favourable international situation (i.e. the weakness of Soviet hegemony and the dissolution of the other real social- ist states), actually be completed. On the other hand, there was the pres- sure of massive internal socio-economic and most of all demographic problems. Between the fall of the Berlin Wall on 9 November 1989, a date that has come to symbolize the collapse of the entire Eastern Bloc under Soviet hegemony, and March 1990, 360,000 GDR citizens migrated to the Federal Republic. Indeed, emigration from the GDR started on 11 September 1989 with the opening of Hungary's border to Austria, prior to which thousands of GDR citizens had stayed at the Federal Republic's embassies in Budapest, Prague and Warsaw. In this respect too, the GDR was special compared to other Eastern Bloc states.[7] After the Berlin Wall and the German-German border had been opened, a daily average of 2,000–3,000 inhabitants of the GDR left the country.[8]

To be sure, the GDR did not disappear without a trace in the Federal Republic. Its economic system had to undergo (and is still undergoing) an extraordinarily difficult regulatory transformation from a socialist, cen- trally administered economy into an efficient social market economy (see below). And at the level of party politics, a new political party, the Left Party or Die Linke (formerly the SED-PDS, then PDS), markedly changed the previous (traditional) party system of the Federal Republic. Born out of the GDR's former 'state party', which had been the monopolist within a formally multi-party but actually one-party system, its (further) exis- tence in reunified Germany lastingly changed the party system of the pre-unified Federal Republic. Initially the prevailing expectation was that the East German party system would grow more like that in the West over time. However, as early as the elections of 18 March 1990 – the first time the SED-PDS ever had to compete in a fair, democratic election cam- paign – the party managed to come in third.

Since then it has gone through three different phases of development. It won its initial fight for survival, implementing a massive clientelist policy in the years 1989–1993. Then, up to the year 2000, it consolidated itself as a regional political power in the East. Subsequently it overcame a deep internal crisis and began anew in 2005. As a result of an alliance between Die Linke and the Election Alternative for Labour and Social Justice

(Wahlalternative Arbeit und Soziale Gerechtigkeit, WASG), 'a much trade union influenced left-wing split from the SPD in the old federal states',[9] and the fusion of the two parties on 16 June 2007, Die Linke was 'enlarged towards the West' that had brought it back to the Bundestag in 2005. Only very recently, due to weak leadership at the national level and an unsolved fundamental conflict within the party, has it has come into question once again: its membership base is shrinking in the East and stagnating, at a moderate level, in the West.[10] Whether as a milieu or an anti-capitalist protest party, Die Linke does not propagate 'a return to the GDR's real-Socialism but has reluctantly turned towards the democratic constitutional state of the Federal Republic of Germany'.[11] Although these days the party may no longer be considered communist, 'there is agreement on rejecting any fundamental criticism of Communism'.[12] The wings and groups in this internally heterogeneous party include, for example, the Communist Platform and the Marxist Forum, which support clearly extremist political approaches.[13] Fusion with the WASG did nothing to change this, as the latter brought its own extremist groups (e.g. Trotskyists of various kinds) into the alliance. Currently the intra-party struggles are so fierce that the party has difficulty electing new chairpersons. Furthermore, its high share of ageing former SED 'comrades' has, for the time being, prevented any really (self-)critical debate about its (own) GDR past. Nevertheless, the presence of Die Linke, heir to the SED, has recast the party system of the Federal Republic.

Moreover, as Die Linke is the third-largest party in the eastern federal states, the party system there differs substantially from that in the western ones.[14] Consequently, electoral behaviour in the 'new' Federal Republic has become more regionalized. Election results in the eastern federal states differ significantly from outcomes in the western ones; in the period 2002–2009 this tendency grew even stronger. However, to speak so soon of an 'East-West conflict' is a questionable proposition.[15] As recently became obvious, the fierce infighting within Die Linke points to a decline in the party's attractiveness to voters on the whole and thus also a decline in its political significance in the new federal states. Clearly the sometimes dubious constitutional loyalty of Die Linke indicates a lack of identification with parliamentary democracy as well as a rejection of market economy.[16]

As a matter of fact, Die Linke's electoral success decided the elections to the Bundestag in 2002 and 2009. Without it there would have been a sufficient majority for a black-yellow (conservative-liberal) coalition in the old federal states.[17] However, the election results would also have been different if the declining appeal of two major parties – the CDU/CSU (the latter being the Christlich Soziale Union/Christian Social Union) and

SPD – had not previously been revealed by successive declines in votes. In this context, eastern German voters exhibit a much lower degree of party identification and a higher degree of readiness to change preferences.

As already noted, however, the clearest difference between western and eastern Germany is that in the East the two major parties are confronted with Die Linke. It is thus unsurprising that this party first became part of a federal state government in 1998. In Mecklenburg-Vorpommern, its coalition with the SPD (the so-called Schwerin model) lasted until 2006. Another red-red coalition followed in Berlin in 2002, and since 2009 there has been a coalition of the same colours in Brandenburg. Thus, after the fourth electoral term since reunification, the party became 'the second-strongest faction in four out of five federal states', that is, in the East German state parliaments.[18] Since then Die Linke has lost this strong position.

Overall, since 1990, 'voters in Germany . . . have become more flexible. The diversification of the party system is an important result'.[19] Significant factors in this outcome include growing volatility, expressed in changing shares of votes compared to previous elections, as well as increasing polarization 'as a result of the old socio-economic left-right controversy on the one hand and the new political-cultural libertarianism-authoritarianism controversy' on the other.[20] The election results of 2013 (CDU/CSU 41.5 per cent, SPD 25.7 per cent, Die Linke 8.6 per cent, Bündnis 90/Die Grünen 8.4 per cent, Freie Demokratische Partei Deutschlands (FDP) 4.8 per cent, Alternative für Deutschland (AfD) 4.7 per cent) confirm that 'the new complexity of the party system in Germany has a really camp-busting effect'.[21]

Aside from markedly changing the German party system overall, reunification has also contributed to one of the most comprehensive socio-political reforms in the history of the Federal Republic. In fact, the inevitable inclusion of the population of the new federal states into the social security systems 'had on the whole more effect on the side of entitled beneficiaries than on the side of contributors'.[22] The expansion led to the biggest labour market and social security reform in Germany's history since World War II. The most important element of the so-called Hartz IV reforms was the continuing of unemployment benefits to many elements of social security as of 1 January 2005. Since then, social security is paid only to beneficiaries who are unable to work; whoever is capable of working at least three hours a day receives Hartz IV benefits. The intention was, according to the 'demand and support' principle, to make the (long-term) unemployed take up employment again.

Initially this fundamental reform did not look like a success story, for when Hartz IV was introduced, the number of registered unemployed rose to more than five million, a yearly average of almost 12 per cent.

Since then, however, things have improved considerably; by May 2012, fewer than three million were unemployed. This strong decline is not solely attributable to the satisfactory economic situation and job market in unified Germany (which have gradually improved thanks to demographic developments in the past few years too), for once the period of receiving unemployment benefits was reduced to twelve months, many unemployed tried harder to find work. Also, as part of the 'Agenda 2010' introduced by the red-green coalition under Chancellor Schröder, a liberalization of temporary work and mini-jobs made it easier for long-term unemployed and people with few vocational qualifications to (re)join the labour market. Thus, given that even today the unemployment rate in the new federal states is still higher than that in the West, the specific economic and social situation in East Germany has contributed to this distinct social-political reform in reunified Germany.

Though nowadays this reform is perceived as a success all over Europe, politically it was very costly: the second cabinet of the red-green coalition was voted out of office on 18 October 2005. Whereas the first Merkel cabinet was still based on a grand coalition of CDU/CSU and SPD, in 2009 the second Merkel cabinet was drawn from a Christian-Liberal coalition of CDU/CSU and the Free Democratic Party (Freie Demokratische Partei), which has stayed in power until 2013.

Acceptance and Consolidation of Democracy

The continuing consequences of the population's socialization under real socialism are another influential factor in the actual consolidation of democracy at the intermediary level of the party system. Even today, the forty-plus years of SED dictatorship contribute to measurable differences between the political and mental attitudes of East and West Germans. These discrepancies are mainly located in the subjective-emotional field, in particular regarding the acceptance of institutions that some East Germans still consider to have been forced on them from the outside – from 'West Germany'.

Political participation in the form of party membership, party identification and participation in elections is therefore still significantly weaker among the population of the new federal states than in the West.[23] Low levels of party identification mean the parties lack secure social bases and have weak regional and local presence.[24] The recruitment capability number of party members has for years been falling in both East and West, but in the East it is clearly much lower than in the West, and this difference has not changed.[25] Furthermore, in the East the recruitment capability of the major democratic parties CDU/CSU and SPD is many times lower, and Die Linke's recruitment capability many times higher, than in the West.[26] The consequent increase in voter volatility and party system instability has again worked to the benefit of extremist parties, for the time being. The hardcore extremism of the National Democratic Party of Germany (Nationaldemokratische Partei Deutschlands, NPD) and the soft extremism of Die Linke are thus more developed in the East than in the federal states in the West.[27] However, the deficits of democracy consolidation in the East are far more visible in the number of votes for right-wing extremist parties in East Germany than in the situation on the left wing of the party system.[28]

Also, in terms of the development of civil society and basic political convictions (valuing freedom over equality, acceptance of and satisfaction with democracy, trust in democratic institutions, attitude towards 'socialism'), the East German population still is rather opposed to the West of the Federal Republic (see Figure 4.1). Thus, whether one comes from an eastern or a western federal state still matters for how far one has developed a positive attitude towards democracy, whether one's sense of belonging is to Germany as a whole or rather to regional or municipal entities, whether one has confidence in politicians and political and legal institutions, and whether one contributes actively to the political process.

Despite twenty years of reunification, the political cultures in the East and the West are still so different from each other[29] that one must speak of two political cultures.[30] Again, this is due to their different political socialization under a democratic system and a dictatorship respectively from 1945 to 1989; to unemployment, which over the years has been twice as high in the new federal states; and to the effects of the international financial crisis of 2007–2009, as well as mass emigration from the East to the West of the Federal Republic.[31]

A distinct economic upswing and resulting decline in unemployment have been observed in East Germany since the international financial crisis ended. It will bring about stronger cohesion of the political cultures in the East and the West and will remain relevant to the further development of political culture in the Federal Republic.

One of the insights gleaned by research on political culture is that values are what take longest to change. The value preferences of the citizens of the eastern federal states differ from those of people in the West of Germany.[32] When it comes to defining priorities concerning personal freedom and social equality, preferences in East and West contradict each other. In the East, the majority (63 per cent) prefers equality and the minority (27 per cent) favours freedom; in the West, the majority

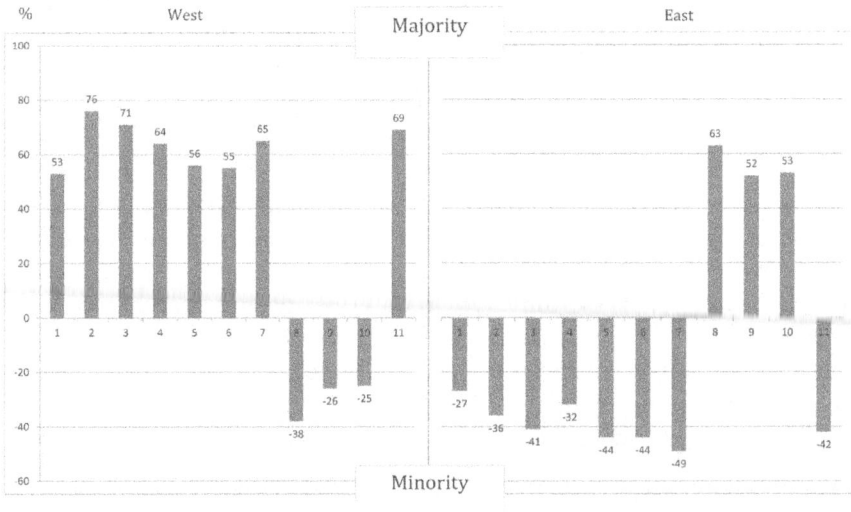

FIGURE 4.1. Majorities in the West and the East of the Federal Republic of Germany

1. *Valuing freedom more than equality*

2. *Democracy in the Federal Republic is the best system of government*

3. *Satisfaction with actual democracy*

4. *Strong democrats*

5. *Confidence in the Bundestag*

6. *Confidence in the federal government*

7. *Confidence in the state under the rule of law*

8. *Valuing equality more than freedom*

9. *Socialism is a good idea*

10. *Identity: being rather a West/East German than a German*

11. *Identity: being rather a German than a West/East German*

Sources: 1. Freiheit vor Gleichheit (Rudzio, *Das politische System der Bundesrepublik Deutschland*, 513); 2. Demokratie der Bundesrepublik beste Staatsform (Tuchscheerer, *20 Jahre vereinigtes Deutschland*, 166); 3. Zufrieden mit der realen Demokratie (ibid., 168; Heitmeyer, 'Leben wir noch immer in zwei Gesellschaften?', 32); 4. Starke Demokraten (Merkel, *Systemtransformation*, 424); 5. Vertrauen Bundestag (Beyme, *Das politische System der Bundesrepublik Deutschland*, 69); 6. Vertrauen Bundesregierung (ibid., 69); 7. Vertrauen Rechtsstaat (Merkel, *Systemtransformation*, 426); 8. Gleichheit vor Freiheit (Rudzio, *Das politische System der Bundesrepublik Deutschland*, 513; Noelle, 'Geteilte Freude'); 9. Sozialismus gute Idee (Tuchscheerer, *20 Jahre vereinigtes Deutschland*, 180); 10. Identitätsgefühl als West-/Ostdeutscher (ibid., 160); 11. Identitätsgefühl als Deutscher (ibid., 161).

(53 per cent) puts freedom first and a minority (38 per cent) opts for equality.[33] Thus, the priority of 'equality' versus 'freedom' represents significantly different value categories in post-reunification German-German society.[34]

On the whole, in reunified Germany the geographic-political East-West factor proves to be the most important criterion regarding acceptance of democracy.[35] A 2009 survey shows that more than two thirds of West Germans (76 per cent) consider 'democracy as we have it in the Federal Republic' the best system of rule; in the East this holds for only slightly more than one third of those interviewed (36 per cent).[36] In the old federal states, 65 per cent have confidence in the state under the rule of law, and 56 and 55 per cent have confidence in the Bundestag and the federal government respectively; in the East these figures are 49 per cent, 44 per cent and 44 per cent respectively – in other words, not even half of those interviewed have confidence in these institutions.[37]

Similarly, analysis of empirical data on democracy performance reveals substantial differences between East and West. According to a 2007 survey, more than two thirds of the citizens in the western part of the Federal Republic (71 per cent) are satisfied with the actual functioning of democracy. In the East, though, the majority of the population (59 per cent) is dissatisfied with democracy as it currently presents itself.[38]

A clear East-West contrast is also evident in citizens' judgements of socialism. A 2009 survey found that in the East, a majority (52 per cent) believes that socialism is a good idea that was only badly implemented, an opinion shared by only a minority in the West (26 per cent).[39] Accordingly, a considerable part of the East German population still considers the GDR to have been a 'more just kind of society' – not only in terms of social equality but also according to the criterion of distribution according to performance.[40] Less than one third (30 per cent) of citizens in the eastern federal states perceive the new society as just.[41] Furthermore, almost all eastern Germans (92 per cent) are convinced that social security in the GDR was superior to that in today's Federal Republic.[42] In this context it is seldom noted that the social transfers made available by the Federal Republic – and not least those for pensions – are far more extensive than those in the GDR.

Once again, however, it must be taken into consideration that the length of democratic experience – sixty years in western Germany, versus only twenty years in eastern Germany – naturally contributes to the different degrees of support for the political, that is, democratic system of the Federal Republic. Unsurprisingly, then, it has greater support in the West than in the East.[43] According to Ismayr, the scant support for the system in the eastern German federal states is most of all an 'expression of a political culture in the SED state which was characterized by obedience to authority, however it is partly also due to personal disappointment after accession to the Federal Republic'.[44] Such attitudes are found also in other post-communist countries.[45]

Forty years of living in contradictory systems during the period of division, however, affected not only Germans' ideas about democracy and market economy but also their national identity. Indeed, though overall German identity has increasingly developed in the eastern German federal states, still only 42 per cent of eastern Germans identify at all with the Federal Republic; 75 per cent, on the other hand, feel connected above all with 'East Germany'.[46] Only a minority (23 per cent) feel like 'real citizens of the Federal Republic'. Moreover, more than 60 per cent subjectively consider themselves 'second-class citizens'. Meanwhile, 46 per cent of Germany's eastern citizens perceive the social differences between East and West Germany as 'strong' or 'very strong'.[47] Even if these (self-)assessments are arrived at emotionally, they must be taken seriously and are highly relevant for both the further process of German-German integration and the attitude towards democracy in the Federal Republic.

In general, it must be said that a mature, vital civil society has not yet developed in East Germany. Also, the social market economy lacks broad support as a valid model for the eastern federal states.[48] More than in the West, in the new federal states confidence in democracy is characterized by materialist orientations, which also indicates a lower degree of democracy consolidation.[49] At the same time, the political parties are weakly rooted among the population.

Meanwhile dissatisfaction is reduced significantly, as it was due also to almost two decades of high unemployment in East Germany, which had considerably declined by the end of the international financial crisis of 2007–2009. On the contrary, skilled personnel are urgently needed in the East German labour market. Youth unemployment is thankfully at a record low; some branches in the new federal states cannot even fill all their apprenticeship positions. Of course, this much more positive situation is also due to the emigration of workforce after 1989/90 and the decline in the birth rate, the effects of which are now starting to be felt.[50] Usually, an improved socio-economic situation leads to growing approval of the political system – and thus, in this case, democracy.

If we go on to compare eastern Germany's doubtless existent democratic deficits to those in other transformation countries in East Central Europe, its results are once again relativized.[51] As measured by several consolidation criteria (see Figure 20 in the concluding chapter of this volume), eastern Germans definitely prove successful when seen in the broader context of the transformation process. For example, the reunified Germany's eastern federal states not only surpass all other post-communist countries but are also closest to Austria, the Netherlands and West Germany as reference countries that are, so to speak, genuine representatives of consolidated democracies.

Although it is certainly true for reunified Germany that 'still [we live] in two societies [and] that in East Germany the attitude towards the democratic system is significantly more negative',[52] it should not be overlooked that all findings are telling only in the medium term. To be sure, the labour and income situations in the East and West will differ over the long run, but the sense of German-German togetherness has become stronger than the former GDR's (declining) influence on state and society. This is shown by the most recent representative survey (in September 2012), according to which a total of 59 per cent of all Germans agree with the statement that in the past few years, eastern and western Germans have moved closer together (western Germans 62 per cent, eastern Germans 49 per cent).[53]

The Process of Economic Transformation and Consolidation

No matter how indispensable the precondition of the Peaceful Revolution of 1989/90 in the GDR was to the fall of the SED regime and thus reunification, the process of economic and social transformation that followed has in some respects been more consequential than the political revolution itself. In any case, it has been much longer and is basically ongoing even today.[54] Above all else, the core challenge has been to transform a state-organized, centrally planned economy into a social market economy.[55]

No less complicated and difficult were the transformation of the armed forces, the police, the judiciary, the health and traffic systems and the media, as well as the educational and other scientific institutions. Furthermore, apart from carrying out a near-comprehensive economic reform, it was necessary to renovate the run-down infrastructure of the GDR, replace its completely outmoded communications system and remedy grave environmental damage that had sometimes been wreaked for decades. Coping with these inevitable modernization measures also required enormous financial means.

Nevertheless, one should note that the Federal Republic of Germany was the first modern Western industrial state to confront such a fundamental transformation process at practically all levels, for worldwide there were no relevant experiences. Thus, no one could have been prepared – and certainly not in economic terms – to face a transformation process like the one that began in the context of German-German reunification after the Peaceful Revolution in the GDR.

Initially, but in subsequent years too, the most urgent problem was voluminous migration from East to West, particularly once the borders

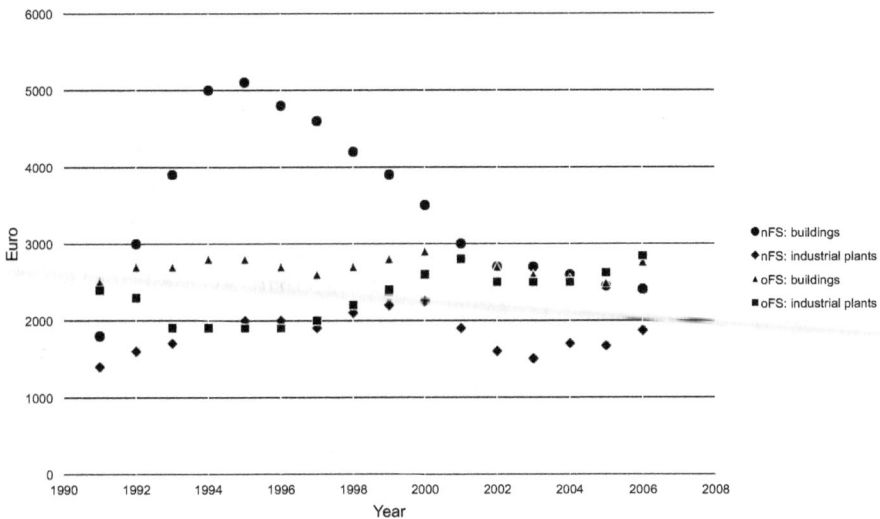

FIGURE 4.2. Investments in all fields of economy, per capita (East-West comparison; new and old federal states without Berlin; investments according to respective prices; inhabitants: average per year).

Source: Arbeitskreis, 'Volkswirtschaftliche Gesamtrechnungen der Länder' (August 2008).

were opened in early November 1989. It was imperative to create sustainable economic and social structures as soon as possible, so as to prevent the further exhaustion of the population and workforce of the still existing GDR – or the new federal states, as of 3 October 1990 – and thus avoid the potential for destabilization in the former East Germany. The Treaty on the Creation of a Currency, Economic and Social Union between the Federal Republic and the GDR, which took effect on 1 July 1990, provided that in the now joint currency area, 'all running payments (wages, pensions, rents and the likes) are to be switched 1:1 and savings as well as debts in a 1:1, 2:1 or 3:1 relation, each according to the amount, kind and time from which they date'.[56] Actually, however, switching the currency 1:1 for all running payments, including wages, meant a revaluation of 1:4 for the producers of trade goods.[57] Thus, socio-political considerations prevailed over criteria of economic and financial-political efficiency.

To resolve open ownership issues, expropriations carried out by the Soviet occupation power were confirmed; concerning the expropriations of real estate after 1949, however, the 'restitution instead of compensation' principle was applied (according to the Law on Compensation, effective as of 1994). It cannot be denied that these regulations came at the cost of 'unequal legal treatment'.[58] Another important precondition for the actual implementation of the treaty had already been created by the People's Chamber: the 'Treuhandgesetz' of 17 June 1990 was meant to guide the privatization of the GDR's nationalized companies (see below).[59]

The economic and social union resulted in the introduction of private property; free pricing; free movement of labour, capital and services; competition, including reorganization of the economy to suit a market-based approach; and an extensive social security system.[60] In this context, the adoption and integration of the GDR social security systems (i.e. health insurance, social insurance and pension schemes) proved particularly costly. Every year, the West to East social budget transfers totalled almost 30 billion euros (more precisely, 28.4 billion euros).[61] Furthermore, in the context of the currency union, it was necessary to exchange about 200 billion GDR marks that had become practically worthless after the reunification of 1990, which cost about 130 billion deutschmarks. Finally, there was the GDR's large foreign debt, which in the year of its collapse stood at about 14 billion US dollars.[62]

The diagnosis of the state of the GDR economy in 1989/90, and to some extent for years to come, was extraordinarily grim. 'After 40 years of existence, the Socialist planned economy had proven to be completely inefficient. The wrong goods were produced in the wrong amounts at wrong places.. . . The stock of capital was over-aged, the apparatus of state and administration was over-dimensioned, there was no productive middle class anymore'.[63] These inefficiencies had also led to an inadequate service economy. Additional system-specific problems in the planned economy of the GDR included shortages of raw materials, tools and spare parts, the need to repair run-down machinery, outmoded manufacturing facilities and, not least, the energy system's proneness to power outages. These factors alone had caused continuous decline in the GDR's productivity, which anyway was constantly lower than that of the Federal Republic. In 1989/90, the GDR, 'concerning production and employment, was at the same level as it had been found in the Federal Republic in the 1960s'.[64] Accordingly, at the time of reunification, the GDR's labour productivity was only 39 per cent of that in the Federal Republic. De facto, the GDR had only survived because it was artificially isolated within COMECON, the eastern economic bloc of those days. Measured against the demands of an increasingly globalized world economy, it had long since become unsustainable, especially as it made hardly any internationally marketable products. The situation was further worsened when the collapse of the Soviet Union after 1990/91 deprived it of its most important trade partner.

As continuing the centralized planned economy of the GDR was no longer a reasonable alternative, extensive privatization was inevitable.

Under the Law on the Privatization and Reorganization of Nationally Owned Property of 17 June 1990, from 1 July the Treuhand – the agency responsible for fundamentally transforming the GDR's economic system and adapting it to the social market economy of the Federal Republic – became the owner of all shares in former state enterprises that had been changed into corporations. The measure proved to be an immediately necessary, basic regulatory policy decision.[65] At the peak of its activities, the Treuhand was in charge of privatizing almost 15,000 enterprises with about six million employees.[66] Its various tasks included:

- quick privatization, purposeful reorganization and prudent shutdowns;
- the assessment and purchase of business concepts;
- the founding of job creation companies (meaning that in most cases the employees of dilapidated enterprises had to accept early retirement);
- ecologically minded waste disposal;
- mediation between the interests of the federal government and the federal states;
- the financing of its own business activities; and
- its own dissolution by the end of 1994.

About 70 per cent of enterprises could successfully continue in the form of privately or publicly owned companies, but the rest had to be liquidated. This allowed for creation of a business sector consisting mainly of small and medium-sized entities.[67] Even though some mistakes and deceptions could not be avoided in the course of the practical implementation of privatization, the Treuhand was undeniably very successful, and on 1 January 1995, its remaining tasks were transferred to the Federal Authority for Special Tasks Related to Reunification (Bundesanstalt für vereinigungsbedingte Sonderaufgaben) and other successor institutions. What was more, this regulatory turnaround had frequently happened under immense time pressure, because once the former GDR and then new federal states were opened to international markets after mid 1991, employment and production at companies in the East plummeted to about one quarter of their 1989 levels.

The comprehensive modernization process set in motion by the Treuhand's activities was indispensable to the further development of East Germany, especially as it overcame the decades-long stagnation and inefficiency of industrial production in the GDR and enabled a breakthrough towards a modern services economy. However, it must also be noted that this inevitable regulatory turnaround, which led at first to de-industrialization, cost much more than originally expected in 1990. Estimates then had assumed that privatizing East German enterprises would bring in about 600 billion deutschmarks, but the Treuhand ended its activities with a shortfall of about 230 billion deutschmarks, revealing a miscalculation on the order of 830 billion deutschmarks.[68]

A fatal consequence of the inevitable shutdown of inefficient and deficit-producing industrial plants was a similarly rapid decline in the number of jobs. By 1993, only 29 per cent of all employees had managed to keep the jobs they held in late 1989; more than two thirds had to seek other work.[69] In naked numbers – which hide human fates – the unemployed in the former GDR grew from about one million in 1991 to 1.614 million in 2005. However, in the following year the number of unemployed started declining again, and considerably at that, by an annual average of half a million (i.e. 511,000 people), or 32 per cent, between 2005 and 2009.[70]

High unemployment – for years twice as high as in the old federal states and sometimes even higher – caused significant social and social-psychological problems in eastern Germany. It was largely the reason why, after some time, the originally widespread approval of reunification and the Federal Republic's market economy system turned to deep frustration among broad parts of the eastern German population. On the whole, 'general dissatisfaction [was aimed at the] market economy which in the West was connected to the experience of upswing and 'Economic Wonder' but in the East primarily to an experience of collapse'.[71]

Another factor in the rapidly growing unemployment in eastern Germany during the first two decades after reunification was the timing of the comprehensive regulatory restructuring of the GDR, with its massive effects on its workers. When it took place, both former German states were already suffering a labour market crisis, if for completely different reasons and in different ways. The West was weathering a crisis of continuously growing unemployment due to progressing rationalization and constantly rising wages. The East, on the other hand, was facing a systemic employment crisis in the form of 'hidden unemployment' – too little work for too many employees. From mid 1991 onwards, job security – which the population of the GDR was accustomed to and had deeply internalized – ceased to exist, and its opposite prevailed: jobs were rationalized by the millions, and individual occupations were deeply changed.

Even though blue- and white-collar workers alike had often witnessed the decay and inefficiency in their companies in the days of the GDR and were themselves demanding extensive modernization,[72] they viewed the post-1990 intra-company and countrywide restructuring with mixed emotions when it meant they would lose their own jobs, or even worse attitudes if they had worked many years at the same company. What is more, decades of SED propaganda demonizing 'capitalism' (it had

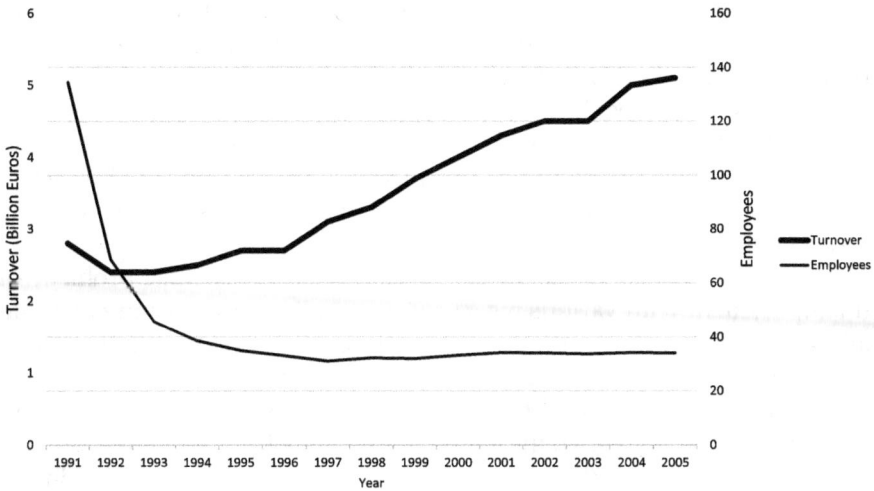

FIGURE 4.3. Saxony engineering: turnover (in billion euros)/number of employees

Source: Statistisches Landesamt Sachsen.

consciously never used the correct term, social market economy) was still having an effect, particularly among older employees in the East. Seemingly objectively, for many of the newly unemployed, the propagandistic prophecy of the SED – 'Once there is capitalism, there will be unemployment' – became subjectively true. Against this background, however, those affected tend(ed) to overlook that it was, after all, the SED – or else the centralized, planned economy it had created, which had existed for four decades – that had made this comprehensive transformation process absolutely inevitable.

Yet another problem of the now beginning socio-economic transformation process concerned the decision to quickly adjust wages in the former GDR – a country with the low wages typical of planned economies – to match those in the high-wage Federal Republic. This decision, which could not be avoided for socio-political reasons, inevitably caused production costs to rise in the new federal states, thus reducing their competitiveness at a stroke. Furthermore, unions and management in the new federal states – the metal industry being the forerunner – agreed that wages in eastern Germany should be adjusted to Western levels until 1994. Given the economic situation in the East, this excessive demand was not only unrealistic but also counterproductive in terms of overall economy, especially as companies had to shrink their workforces to adjust to the situation, thereby creating even more unemployed or simply abandoning the system of collective bargaining.[73]

Today, the income in eastern Germany has only reached 71 per cent of the West German level for full-time employees and 82 per cent for part-time employees,[74] but in comparison to Poland and the Czech Republic as reference countries, East Germany still has higher wages. In terms of competitiveness, then, those countries compare favourably to the new federal states. Overall, therefore, productivity has been ahead of wages in other former Eastern Bloc countries, whereas the reverse was true in the former East Germany.[75]

The state tried (and still tries) to counter the essential problem of unemployment with various measures, especially the short-time working allowance, measures promoting job creation and structural adjustment, early retirement severance payments and early retirement allowances.[76] The sustainable success of the previously applied labour market tools first became obvious when the effects of the financial and world economic crisis of 2008/2009 hit the labour market harder in the West than in the East. Despite the crisis, the number of unemployed in East Germany fell by just 2 per cent on average,[77] and between March 2006 and March 2011 the number of employees rose from 4.863 million to 5.298 million.[78]

However, the decade or so of mass unemployment that regulatory transformation had brought about in the new federal states had at the same time witnessed a clear explosion of wealth, which in a few years' time had fundamentally improved the living standards of eastern Germans. This was quite apart from the fact that the period of scarce resources had ended in the spring of 1990, when all kinds of goods, even high-quality goods, had become available. In 1989, private households in East Germany were mostly still at the level of West German households in the early 1960s, but by the mid 1990s they had reached the West's level from 1992, a welfare leap of three decades within just a few years.

The economic, currency and social union of 1 July 1990 also led to an average rise of 30 per cent in the legally fixed pensions for the elderly in eastern Germany, which put them at about 40 per cent of pensions in the West. After the introduction of the Pension Transformation Act on 1 January 1992, a common pension law became valid for the entire territory of the Federal Republic. Since then, the level of pensions in the East has more than doubled, going from 40.3 per cent of the western level as of 1990 to 88.7 per cent as of 2009.[79] Thus, most pensioners in the East number among the 'material profiteers' of reunification,[80] for the much more generous western German pensions not only allowed pensioners in the East to escape their often precarious economic and social situation after retirement, but frequently also left them financially better off than their counterparts in the West. This was particularly so for East German women, whose professional activities in the GDR often resulted in much longer periods of work than those of female employees in West Germany; therefore East German women could claim higher pension funds.[81]

To sum up, the economic structure in the new federal states has changed comprehensively. Thanks to the Treuhand's privatization measures and the founding of new companies in the context of the regulatory transformation process, there were many new small and medium-sized companies established. Continuous development since the mid 1990s has made the manufacturing sector a driving force of economic growth. Furthermore, the former East Germany has established a service sector that accounts for more than 71 per cent (in 2010) of the entire region's production and makes the East's contribution to German economic output nearly equal to that of the West.[82] Despite the rupture of 1991/92, just five years later (in 1996) per capita GDP in the new federal states was 68.3 per cent of the Western level, up from 42.9 per cent in 1991.[83] Today it is about around 80 per cent.[84] Indeed, 'in the past two decades [the new federal states] have developed into a powerful business location with a modern infrastructure'.[85] This eventually reduced the high unemployment that had so long prevailed in the new federal states, in particular after 2008/2009. The current unemployment rate in the new federal states is the lowest since 1989/90. Nevertheless, at 10.6 per cent compared to 5.7 per cent in the West (in May 2012), it was still almost double the rate in the old federal states but has since then been significantly reduced.[86]

At the same time, however, it must be acknowledged that the gradual adjustment to the level of the western German federal states has slowed in the past few years: in 2009, eastern Germany had reached almost 80 per cent of the western level of production, but since then things have only slowly improved.[87] Fundamental problems still prevent more rapid economic growth because the new federal states have 'primarily small-scale and supply-oriented industry as well as small branches of Germany's international enterprises'.[88] Precisely the latter is also a problem for tax revenues in the new federal states, the more so as not a single large enterprise is located there. Although such enterprises have established numerous plants and production sites in eastern Germany, the goods produced there contribute to taxes paid in the West, by western German or Western trusts.

Because international enterprises are located in the territory of the old Federal Republic, the East also lacks adequate research capacity; on average, therefore, it spends less on research and development than does western Germany. Measured as a share of GDP (as of December 2008), the eastern German economy's expenditures on research and development make up 0.9 per cent, compared to 1.9 per cent for the West.[89] This also leads to reduced export intensity. At the same time, the economic structure is still largely focused on the eastern German market. Enterprise-related and financial services are another weak spot in eastern economic growth.[90]

Finally, the development of the middle class in the former East Germany is still below average because Honecker, only half a year after seizing power in 1972, destroyed the last remnants of the middle class in the GDR via expropriations, among other measures. Only since reunification has profitable, job-creating industry allowed this social class to grow again in the new federal states.

For these reasons, the process of economic transformation has happened mostly in urban centres and their environments, and not across the whole territory of the former GDR. Meanwhile, 'flourishing landscapes', to quote Helmut Kohl's famous phrase, have developed in urban centres such as Leipzig/Halle and Dresden, and the cities of Thuringia, Berlin-Potsdam and Rostock, but much less in the rural regions. Development going forward may be expected to be different: peripheral regions, most of them structurally weak, will confront a few economically strong urban centres that will function as 'cores of economic growth'.

All in all, in the course of more than two decades, the former East Germany has gone through a process of overall economic adjustment to the situation in the West and thus changed to more closely resemble a modern, post-industrial services society. This change, though not yet complete, must still be considered very successful, as became obvious within only ten years: whereas between 1989 and 2004 the share of employees in the primary sector fields of agriculture and forestry declined from 9.0 per cent (1989) to 3.3 per cent (2004) and the share of those working in production (the secondary sector) fell from 46 per cent (1989) to 26.3 per cent (2004), employment in the tertiary sector, that is, services, rose from 45.1 per cent (1989) to 70.4 per cent (2004).[91]

Indeed, the process of catching up economically – needed after forty years of 'Socialist damage'[92] by the SED dictatorship – has meanwhile progressed so well that most recent national-economic and financial-political estimations recommend abandoning further funding of the new federal states when Solidarity Pact II runs out in 2019. In the future, it is 'less the inequality between East and West Germany [that] should be in the focus of interest but rather the convergence of (comparable) regions in the whole Federal territory', as recommended in an expert report issued by leading German economic research institutes in May 2011.[93] In fact, after 2019 all of Germany is supposed to come under a modified economic and financial policy that will be more 'overall-German', supporting structurally weak regions regardless of their geographic location.[94] Regarding the mid- and long-term economic development of the new federal states, a study ordered by the Ministry of Economy, Labour and

Technology stipulates implementation of four core measures: improving the financial situation of enterprises, supporting cores of innovation, supplying skilled labour and providing for the financial capability to act. Furthermore, future support programmes are to focus most of all on existing clear differences between the economic structures of the five new federal states.[95]

From an international point of view too, the socio-economic transformation process in the new federal states must be considered a success story. When development there is compared to that in some East European countries that, in regulatory terms, were also subject for decades to planned economy and moreover had to cope with the effects of this system without any 'big spender' by their sides, the differences are obvious. By one year of comparison, 2007, the new federal German states produced 72 per cent of the GDP per capita, whereas Slovenia, being the second-best country, reached only 58 per cent and the Czech Republic 42 per cent.[96] Taking work productivity as a parameter, East Germany has meanwhile achieved 79 per cent of the West German level and the Czech Republic only 32 per cent.[97] These figures make obvious that the path of 'revolutionary turnaround', as chosen by the new federal states, has definitely been a success.

Speaking generally, this process of a transformation from planned economy to social market economy – so far unique in the world – has only been possible by way of extraordinarily high, indeed gigantic, transfer payments, which furthermore have been continuously necessary for almost three decades and must still go on. The establishment of a German 'unity fund' on 25 June 1990 provided for financial transfers until 1994, by which date the fund was to be supplied with 160.7 billion deutschmarks. Up to 2004, the federal government contributed to the fund's further payments and the West German federal states contributed to its debt obligations. Since 2005, the fund's debts have been integrated into the federal government's general debt. By 2019, the fund is supposed to be finally dissolved, whereupon all liabilities as well as possible assets will be conclusively transferred to the federal government.

According to the Law on the Establishment of a Redemption Fund of 23 June 1993, the Treuhand debts and all other debts from 1995 onwards were to be combined under the regulations of Solidarity Pact I. In this context, a pioneering financial-political decision provided for funding the total costs of reunification not only through loans but also with a mixture of tax increases and state austerity measures. The Redemption Fund was to cover its liabilities by way of transfers from the federal budget as well as Bundesbank profits, a large share of the debts having been paid back meanwhile. Also contributing to this is a special tax, the 'Solidarity Tax', which is paid both in the old and new federal states and up to now has redeemed about 200 billion euros.[98] However, as further payments will have to come mainly from the federal budget, in financial terms this equates to debt refunding. Solidarity Pact I at the same time integrated the new federal states into the interstate fiscal adjustment system, thus benefiting them at two levels: on the one hand, due to their much worse financial situation, they received the biggest shares of horizontal balance payments between federal states; on the other hand, they received an additional share of vertical transfer payments from the federal budget by way of 'special needs federal completion transfers'.[99]

The Law on the Continuation of Solidarity Pact I via Solidarity Pact II, dated 20 December 2012, provided for restructuring the federal-level interstate fiscal adjustments and the further liquidation of the available German unity funds to continue the 'special needs federal completion transfers' that paid for 'special burdens due to the division of Germany'. Thus, the new federal states will receive further 'special needs federal completion transfers' until the end of 2019, at which point the transfer payments will probably reduced but not cancelled. Since 2005, the new federal states have received more yearly 'special needs federal completion transfers to balance special burdens due to structural unemployment'.[100] Therefore, by way of two Solidarity Pacts, they have received 45.4 billion euros in vertical and 127.2 billion euros in horizontal balance payments.

Finally, EU funding must also be mentioned, in particular funding for structural and agricultural policies. By the early 1990s, the new federal states already numbered among those regions receiving the highest EU funding, due to lacking socio-economic 'convergence' with Western European regions. Between 2000 and 2006, financial support from the EU's Structural Fund amounted to 18.3 billion euros, and in the period up to 2013, it received another 16.5 billion euros. Furthermore, the eastern German federal states received some 22.7 billion euros more from 1996 to 2008 to support agriculture, as well as an influx of about 7.4 billion euros from EU structural funds for rural development from 2000 to 2006.[101] By 2010, however, East German regions no longer qualified for the maximum EU regional aid funding because the average income per capita in the new federal states had risen to slightly more than 75 per cent of the EU average. Thus, EU funding has significantly diminished after 2013.[102]

From today's standpoint, looking back on more than two decades of German-German reunification, one must on the whole soberly state that despite the 'transformation shock',[103] the process of economic transformation from the GDR's socialist planned economy has taken much longer and has proven far more costly than originally expected in 1990. In retrospect, western German business and political elites frequently underestimated the actual, catastrophic state of the GDR economy, and thus also the extent of the transformation and modernization needed both at the macro and the micro levels. Obviously, the Federal Republic, as the export champion of the world economy and thus long internationally and globally oriented, simply overlooked the enormous economic problems of the second German state in its immediate vicinity. Also because of this misperception, 'it took some time to recognize that trust in market-economic adjustment processes alone was not enough to stop the developing downward spiral of the economic development'.[104]

This oversight contributed to bringing the former Federal Republic – the 'big spender' taking over the lion's share of the reunification costs – to the verge of its financial capability. As part of Germany's current total debt of about 2.042 trillion euros (as of 31 March 2012), reunification costs, including social transfer payments, are estimated to be between 1.3 and 1.6 trillion euros.[105] Accordingly, the total debt of Germany as a whole rose sharply after 1990, whereas the national income – in contrast to almost all other Western EU states – has declined by about 1,500 euros per capita since reunification.

At the same time, though, one must also recall that never before had there been any such experience in the world: no modern industrial state had ever confronted such a fundamental socio-economic transformation process without a blueprint. No one could have been prepared for the inevitable transformation shock that started after the Peaceful Revolution in the GDR, either economically or financially. Moreover, the intra-German migration of tens of thousands of GDR citizens that had begun even before the Berlin Wall fell on 9 November 1989 put the regulatory direction and control of this process under enormous time pressure from the very beginning. To boot, it was necessary to take over the GDR's social systems and much more. The fact that the transformation process in the new federal states, has shown great success is acknowledged worldwide as proof that the reunification, to which there was no real alternative, has also been an economic success story, despite the need for further measures. However, the extent to which economic convergence can be achieved between the old and the new federal states remains still a problem to be tackled.[106]

Society

Demographic Development

Besides having an unemployment rate twice as high as that in western Germany for nearly two decades, the former East Germany must unfortunately face another problem: demographic developments both as a whole and specifically in the new federal states. Indeed, birth rates in both German states have declined constantly since the mid 1970s, almost without exception. In the mid and long run, this problem is particularly momentous, because Germany, with 1.39 children per woman on average in 2011, already has one of the lowest birth rates in the world, although most recently there is a slight increase to note (1.50 in 2015). To maintain a stable population, Germany would need a birth rate of at least 2.1 children per woman, as is the case in France, for example.[107] The births-to-deaths ratio highlights this problem in Germany: the birth rate dropped suddenly when contraceptives were introduced in 1964, and natural population growth has been negative since then, for 'after the baby boom of the 1960s the two German societies readjusted to the secular worldwide trend of declining birth rates which accompanies the structural change towards modern society'.[108] After 1990, the birth rate in the new federal states even fell to 0.77 per cent for a short time owing to the effects of reunification, but it later rose again to 1.35 per cent.

There is no question that for decades Germany has been subject to a demographic change, as the population is both declining in numbers and ageing. In absolute numbers, the reunified Germany in 2008 was home to a total of about 82 million people, and the population of the new federal states was 16.2 million, that is, a share of about 20 per cent. Back in 1990, however, it had been 18.1 million; in other words, the eastern German population declined by about 9.5 per cent in the course of less than two decades. Only since 2014 the massive intra-German migration from East to West that started after 1989/90 came to an end when migration from western Germany eastwards began to prevail.

Despite that most recent development, the decline and ageing of the population are clearly happening faster in the eastern German federal states than in western Germany. Within a decade or so, the average age of the people living in eastern Germany rose from 38.6 (in 1991) to 42.1 (in 2002).[109] Rural regions are especially hard hit by the two above-mentioned demographic factors. In contrast to urban core regions such as Berlin, Potsdam, Leipzig and Dresden, as well as cities in Thuringia with stable or even growing populations, by 2020 the rural regions in the East of Germany will lose more than half of their inhabitants.[110]

The greatest contributor to this loss of population has been the emigration of young and in most cases well-educated people, which has altered the structure of the eastern German population with far-reaching consequences whose demographic 'echo effects' will be felt throughout the next two decades.[111] Of this young age cohort, women aged eighteen to thirty have left the new federal states more frequently than young men of the same age,[112] but 'being potential mothers [they] are a particularly critical group as regards the long-term demographic development of a region'.[113]

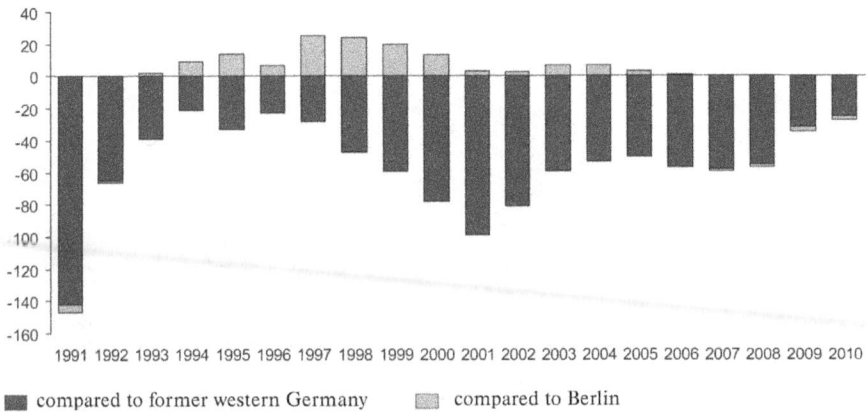

FIGURE 4.4. Migration balance for the New Federal States since 1991 (in thousands)

Source: Statistisches Bundesamt.

The absolute numbers are telling: about 364,000 men emigrated from the new federal states between 1991 and 2004, while women emigrants in the same period numbered 536,000.[114]

As intra-German migration reduces the fertile generation and affects the natural population balance – that is, the difference between numbers of births and deaths – as well as citizens' average age, the potential workforce in eastern Germany is getting smaller and older. Put more simply: 'In connection to a high share of emigrated young people, 20 years after reunification there is a lack of those people who might work against the rapid over-ageing and shrinking of society'.[115]

Although foreign immigration has risen rapidly in Germany most recently and cases of German re-migration from West to East are on the rise, eastern Germany – in terms of demography – has been 'emptied out' in the past two decades since reunification. Furthermore, '20 years after reunification [the] rapid decline in numbers of births resulting from transformation has reached the East German labour market'.[116] Reliable demographic estimates assume that the workforce (aged 15 to 64) in the former East Germany will drop from slightly less than 11 million in 2008 to 8.8 million in 2025.[117] Even now there is a shortage of young people, of apprentices and young employees. Thus, a lack of younger skilled employees will be unavoidable. Increasing the number of working women could help improve the labour market situation, as might the increased inclusion of older employees.

The definitely existing 'demographic crisis' in the new federal states has been paralleled by a rise in life expectancy since reunification. Men in the former East Germany now reach an age of 74.4 years on average

FIGURE 4.5. Regional polarization of the demographic development in East Germany 2003–2005

See Herfert, 'Regionale Polarisierung der demographischen Entwicklung in Ostdeutschland', 440.

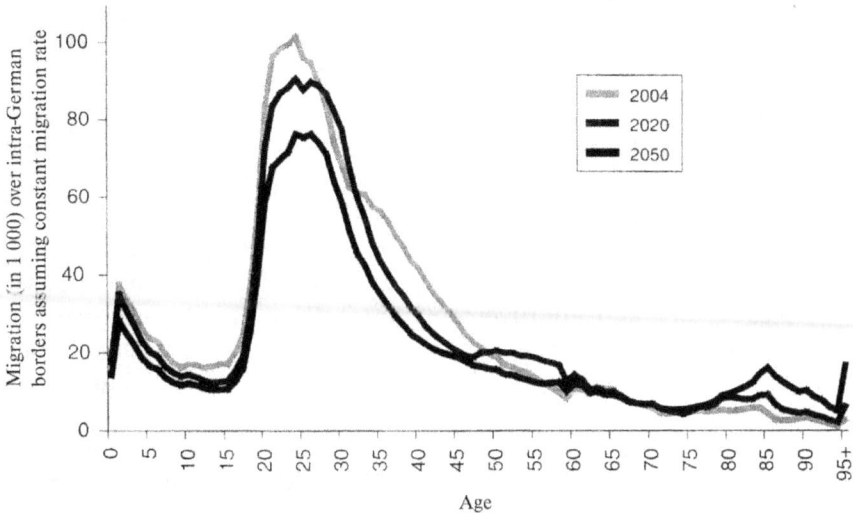

FIGURE 4.6. Present and future age-specific migration

See H.-H. Gatzweiler and C. Schlömer, 'Zur Bedeutung von Wanderungen für die Raum- und Stadtentwicklung', Informationen zur Raumentwicklung 3/4 (2008), 253.
Database: Statistisches Bundesamt: Sonderauswertung der Wanderungsstatistik 2004, 11. Koordinierte Bevölkerungsvorausberechnung (Variante 1 W2) © BBR Bonn 2008

(compared to 76.2 in western Germany), and women's life expectancy is 81.3 (81.6 in western Germany) – a gain of about 2.5 years in life expectancy for both sexes, though life expectancy in the former GDR has always lagged behind that of the Federal Republic.[118]

Changes in GDR Society since 1989/90

The radical change that reunification triggered in the social structure in eastern Germany may, according to Rainer Geißler, be called 'a catching-up modernisation combined with contradictions'.[119] He identified 'ten elements of radical change' from the former GDR society in the past twenty years:

1. Power was decentralized by way of 'catching-up differentiation'. The transformation of the system of political institutions decentralized and at the same time democratized the original power structure created by the SED. There developed pluralistic layers of services, the uppermost layer being 'superimposed by West Germans'.
2. Political system change was accompanied by far-reaching 'de-politicization' as politics withdrew from a number of functional fields.

Political loyalty's significance in both privilege and disadvantage was reduced to a Western 'ordinary measure' and pluralized at the same time.

3. Germany's reunification closed the 'West-East tertiarisation gap' at a stroke.[120] Within a short span of time, the collapse of East German industry, radical changes in agriculture and the associated labour market crisis changed an industrial society into a services society.

4. After 1989/90, the combination of a 'sudden wealth push' due to rising wages in East Germany, a 'quality push' in the consumption and services sectors, and improvements to (remaining) jobs, infrastructure and environment considerably diminished the previously existing wealth gap between the GDR and the Federal Republic within a brief time frame.

5. The reduction of the wealth gap, however, simultaneously increased differences in income, property ownership, quality of working conditions and the consequent living conditions and opportunities. At the higher socio-economic levels, there has been or is now a 'vertical upwards differentiation' creating new social inequalities.

6. By the mid 1970s, the 'old middle class' in the GDR had been almost completely destroyed as a social stratum, so currently it is undergoing a difficult period of reconstruction to become an important performer again, despite lingering qualitative and quantitative differences from the middle class in western Germany.

7. Since 1989/90, a levelled working and farming class has been restructured into a socially graduated services and middle class society. The society of the previous 'common people of the GDR' has successively changed into a 'differentiated industrial services and middle class society which is more socially graduated at a clearly higher level of wealth, however also exposed to greater risk'.[121]

8. The life expectancy of eastern Germans, which has risen throughout the past two decades thanks to the wealth push after reunification, is coming closer to the western German level.

9. In the past few years, the near closure of the East-West wealth gap has reduced the pressure of emigration significantly. Most recently, the number of eastern German 'emigrants' returning to their home regions has increased. At the same time, cores of growth in the new federal states are 'increasingly becoming more attractive for West German opportunity seekers',[122] chiefly from the upper-middle and upper classes.

10. Since reunification, the society of the former GDR, which is much more homogeneous than that of the Federal Republic, has experienced a 'catching-up pluralisation and individualisation'.[123] This is

manifested in an adjustment towards western German patterns of behaviour (e.g. marrying at a later age), an extension of individual freedoms and the rapid spread of alternative private ways of life.

Concluding his discussion of developments in the former East Germany, Rainer Geißler states that 'the catching-up modernisation of "objective structures" is accompanied by catching-up gratification; since reunification the East German social structure has increased its performance concerning the subjective well-being of the people'.[124] In the course of the transformation and integration processes taking place in eastern and western Germany for more than two decades now, it has furthermore become obvious that 'Germany's inner unity is a psycho-social long-term process which is most of all about breaking up and changing mental and emotional deep influences'.[125] Indeed, the different, sometimes contradictory socialization processes and life experiences of Germans across forty years in two German states, one a dictatorship and the other a democracy, have in some cases proven a 'burden for life' in the fullest sense and in any case have been extremely influential both collectively and subjectively. In all, the reunification process, which at the same time has been a German-German integration process, has primarily been a success. Fifteen years after the Peaceful Revolution, only small minorities in either the East (6 per cent) or West (6 per cent) of Germany wanted a rebuilding of the Berlin Wall.[126] Moreover, in the West, understanding of the 'Restructuring East' has grown; at any rate, 90 per cent are of the opinion that it must go forward, as it is an obligation of Germany as a whole. This clearly suggests more cohesion and a greater perception of Germany as a whole than the media sometimes convey.[127]

The primary goal must remain the greatest possible equality of living conditions between East and West (see Article 72, Section 2 of the Basic Law). However, after more than two decades of transformation in the new federal states, western Germany can no longer be the exclusive criterion for this. Rather, the further process of convergence will have to be more regionally oriented, especially considering that 'meanwhile highly productive East German regions [outperform] weak regions in the West. These overlaps also call for changing our ideas of the chosen reference system for the adjustment process'.[128]

From a present-day viewpoint, despite some persistent problems, we should not lose sight of the great task that has been fulfilled since the Peaceful Revolution in the GDR in 1989/90 – that is, to have mastered a 'double transformation process', going 'from dictatorship to democracy, and from a planned economy to a functioning and competitive market economy'.[129]

After having completed his studies in history, German philology, social studies and Italian studies, as well as having earned his doctorate (1980), **Günther Heydemann** worked as a member of the scientific staffs of the Universities of Erlangen and Bayreuth as well as of the German Historical Institute (Deutsches Historisches Institut) in London. After his habilitation (1991) and interim professorships in Munich and Bonn, he was appointed to the Chair of Modern and Contemporary History of the University of Leipzig. Since 2009 he has also been Director of the HAIT, and has held visiting professorships and fellowships in Italy, the USA, Russia and Tunisia. His research work focuses on the history of historical science, comparative European history, the dictatorships of the twentieth century as well as the post-socialist transformation processes.

Notes

1. Literature abounds on the post-1989/90 transformation processes in the former so-called 'real socialist' states. Here only the most important studies are given, in particular those focusing on the GDR or German-German developments: K.H. Oppenländer (ed.), *Wiedervereinigung nach sechs Jahren: Erfolge, Defizite, Zukunftsperspektiven im Transformationsprozess* (Berlin, 1997); K. Eckart and E. Jesse (eds), *Das wieder vereinigte Deutschland: Eine erweiterte oder eine neue Bundesrepublik?* (Berlin, 1999); K. Löw (ed.), *Zehn Jahre deutsche Einheit* (Berlin, 2001); O.W. Gabriel, J.W. Falter and H. Rattinger (eds), *Wächst zusammen, was zusammengehört? Stabilität und Wandel politischer Einstellungen im wiedervereinigten Deutschland* (Baden-Baden, 2005); E. Jesse and E. Klein (eds), *Das Parteienspektrum im wieder vereinigten Deutschland* (Berlin, 2007); E. Jesse and E. Sandschneider (eds), *Neues Deutschland: Eine Bilanz der deutschen Wiedervereinigung* (Baden-Baden, 2008); H. Best, R. Gebauer and A. Salheiser (eds), *Elites and Social Change: The Socialist and Post-Socialist Experience* (Hamburg, 2009); W. Heitmeyer (ed.), *Deutsch-deutsche Zustände: 20 Jahre nach dem Mauerfall* (Bonn, 2009); T. Großbölting, R. Kollmorgen, S. Möbius and R. Schmidt (eds), *Das Ende des Kommunismus: Die Überwindung der Diktaturen in Europa und ihre Folgen* (Essen, 2010); W. Merkel, *Systemtransformation: Eine Einführung in die Theorie und Empirie der Transformationsforschung*, 2nd ed. (Wiesbaden, 2010); G. Heydemann, 'Die Revolution nach der Revolution: Die wirtschaftliche und soziale Transformation in Sachsen im Kontext des vereinten Deutschlands seit 1989/90: Erfolge und Probleme', in K. Hermann (ed.), *Sachsen seit der Friedlichen Revolution: Tradition, Wandel, Perspektiven* (Dresden, 2010), 249–66; K. Bohr and A. Krause (eds), *20 Jahre Deutsche Einheit: Bilanz und Perspektiven*, 2nd ed. (Baden-Baden, 2011); E. Bakke and I. Peters (eds), *20 Years since the Fall of the Berlin Wall: Transitions, State Break-Up and Democratic Politics in Central Europe and Germany* (Cambridge/Berlin, 2011); A. Lorenz (ed.), *Ostdeutschland und die Sozialwissenschaften: Bilanz und Perspektiven 20 Jahre nach der Wiedervereinigung* (Opladen, 2011); C. Vollnhals (ed.), *Jahre des Umbruchs: Friedliche Revolution in der DDR und Transition in Ostmitteleuropa* (Göttingen, 2011); H. Vorländer (ed.), *Revolution und demokratische Neugründung* (Dresden, 2011).

2. H. Vorländer, 'Pathos und Ernüchterung: Über den Zusammenhang von Revolution und demokratischer Neugründung', in Vorländer, *Revolution und demokratische Neugründung*, 15–30, here 19.
3. Ibid., Introduction, 9.
4. See U. Backes, 'Strukturwandel realsozialistischer Autokratien: Vom Totalitarismus zur Transition', in Vollnhals, *Jahre des Umbruchs*, 141–58, here 158.
5. See M. Richter, 'Doppelte Demokratisierung und deutsche Einheit', *Aus Politik und Zeitgeschichte* 60(11) (2010), 20–26, here 20.
6. See ibid., 23.
7. See A.O. Hirschmann, 'Abwanderung, Widerspruch und das Schicksal der Deutschen Demokratischen Republik', *Leviathan* 20 (1992), 330–58.
8. See Bundesministerium des Innern (ed.), 'Jahresbericht der Bundesregierung zum Stand der Deutschen Einheit 2010' (Berlin, 2010), 11.
9. See F. Hartleb, 'Parteien in den alten Bundesländern seit 1990', in Jesse and Klein, *Das Parteienspektrum*, 65–83, here 76.
10. See U. Backes, 'Die Linke in der Zerreißprobe: Das "Superwahljahr" 2011 und seine Folgen', in E. Jesse (ed.), *Neue Herausforderungen des politischen Extremismus in Deutschland* (Baden-Baden, 2013).
11. E. Jesse and J.P. Lang, *DIE LINKE: der smarte Extremismus einer deutschen Partei* (Munich, 2008), 261.
12. Ibid., 262.
13. See ibid., 269.
14. Die Linke is represented in every parliament in the eastern federal states and has become a major party at the regional level. The party achieved its best results to date in the 2009 elections to the Bundestag. In Saxony-Anhalt and Brandenburg, it was the party with the most votes, 32 per cent and 29 per cent respectively. At the national level, it won almost 12 per cent of the vote and became the fourth-strongest party in the Bundestag (Backes, 'Die Linke in der Zerreißprobe').
15. See K. Beyme, *Das politische System der Bundesrepublik Deutschland: Eine Einführung* (Wiesbaden, 2010), 107.
16. See U. Backes, 'Probleme der Demokratiekonsolidierung im östlichen Deutschland', in G. Besier and K. Stoklosa (eds), *15 Jahre deutsche Einheit: Was ist geworden?* (Berlin, 2007), 41–56, here 49.
17. See U. Backes, 'Polarisierung aus dem Osten? Linke und rechte Flügelparteien bei der Bundestagswahl 2005', in E. Jesse and R. Sturm (eds), *Bilanz der Bundestagswahl 2005: Voraussetzungen, Ergebnisse, Folgen* (Wiesbaden, 2006), 157–76; E. Jesse, 'Parteien und Parteiensystem in den neuen Bundesländern', in V. Kronenberg and T. Mayer (eds), *Volksparteien: Konzepte, Konkurrenzen und Konstellationen, Erfolgsmodell für die Zukunft?* (Freiburg, 2009), 291–303, here esp. 301f.
18. E. Jesse, 'Bundestags-, Landtags- und Europawahlen in den neuen Bundesländern seit 1990', *Deutschland Archiv* 42(6) (2009), 965–72, here 969.
19. Ibid.
20. See E. Jesse, 'Parteiensystem im Wandel? Das deutsche Parteiensystem vor und nach der Bundestagswahl 2005', in U. Backes, A. Gallus and E. Jesse (eds), *Demokratie in Deutschland: Diagnosen und Analysen* (Cologne, 2008), 294–316, here 304.
21. See E. Jesse and R. Sturm, 'An den Grenzen des traditionellen Parteienwettbewerbs? Ein Ausblick auf das Wahljahr 2013', in E. Jesse and R. Sturm (eds), *'Superwahljahr' 2011 und die Folgen* (Baden-Baden, 2012), 435–51, here 448.

22. A. Rödder, *Deutschland einig Vaterland: Die Geschichte der Wiedervereinigung* (Munich, 2009), 324.
23. See W. Rudzio, *Das politische System der Bundesrepublik Deutschland* (Wiesbaden, 2011), 513.
24. See Beyme, *Das politische System*, 77, 82.
25. See O. Niedermayer, *Parteimitglieder in Deutschland: Version 2011* (Berlin, 2011), 32.
26. See Backes, 'Probleme der Demokratiekonsolidierung', 49.
27. See ibid., 43f.; E. Jesse, 'Die demokratische Konsolidierung der neuen Bundesländer', in C. Vollnhals (ed.), *Die friedliche Revolution in der DDR 1989/90: Transition im ostmitteleuropäischen Vergleich* (Göttingen, 2011), 359.
28. See Backes, 'Probleme der Demokratiekonsolidierung', 47. In the East of the Federal Republic – despite its much lower share of foreigners – xenophobic attitudes are more widespread than in the West. The results of the 2005 elections to the Bundestag showed disproportionate support for right-wing extremist parties in the eastern federal states. The NPD won 1.6 per cent of the second votes in the West and about twice that in the East (3.6 per cent) (ibid., 47). Likewise, in the 2009 Bundestag elections the NPD's share of votes in the eastern federal states was about double its share in the West (see http://endstation-rechts.de/index.php?option=com_ k2& view=item& id=3809:bundestagswahl-npd-mit-15–prozent-st%C3%A4rkste-recht-sextreme-partei/-dvu-bundeswei-bei-01–prozent&Itemid=384; accessed 31 October 2011).
29. See Backes, 'Probleme der Demokratiekonsolidierung'; O.W. Gabriel, 'Politische Einstellungen und politische Kultur', in O.W. Gabriel and E. Holtmann (eds), *Handbuch politisches System der Bundesrepublik Deutschland*, 3rd ed. (Munich, 2005), 459–522; O.W. Gabriel, 'Bürger und Demokratie im vereinigten Deutschland', *Politische Vierteljahreszeitschrift* 48(3) (2007), 540–52; W. Ismayr, 'Das politische System Deutschlands', in W. Ismayr (ed.), *Die politischen Systeme Westeuropas* (Wiesbaden, 2009), 515–65; K. Völkl, 'Fest verankert oder ohne Halt? Die Unterstützung der Demokratie im vereinigten Deutschland', in Gabriel, Falter and Rattinger, *Wächst zusammen, was zusammengehört?*, 249–84; B. Weßels and A. Wagner, 'Regionale Differenzierung des Wahlverhaltens', in H. Rattinger et al. (eds), *Zwischen Langeweile und Extremen: Die Bundestagswahl 2009, Wahlen in Deutschland*, Vol. 1 (Baden-Baden, 2011), 119–30; W. Heitmeyer, 'Leben wir noch immer in zwei Gesellschaften? 20 Jahre Vereinigungsprozess und die Situation Gruppenbezogener Menschenfeindlichkeit', in Heitmeyer, *Deutsch-deutsche Zustände*, 13–49.
30. See Weßels and Wagner, 'Regionale Differenzierung des Wahlverhaltens'; H. Tuchscheerer, *20 Jahre vereinigtes Deutschland: Eine 'neue' oder 'erweiterte' Bundesrepublik'?* (Baden-Baden, 2010), 306; Beyme, *Das politische System*, 81; O.W. Gabriel, 'Wächst zusammen, was zusammen gehört?', in Gabriel, Falter and Rattinger, *Wächst zusammen, was zusammen gehört?*, 385–420; Gabriel, 'Bürger und Demokratie'; Völkl, 'Fest verankert oder ohne Halt?'; Backes, 'Probleme der Demokratiekonsolidierung'; Besier, 'Das Ost-West-Verhältnis in Deutschland'.
31. According to Heitmeyer (*Deutsch-deutsche Zustände*, 265), twenty years after reunification 'the objective social split between East and West Germany is dramatically increasing'. This estimate may be exaggerated, but it is at least partially connected to the Federal Republic's division into booming regions and regions of economic decline, the eastern federal states numbering among the latter almost without exception; see Heydemann, 'Die Revolution nach der Revolution', 265. In the period 1991–2002, almost one million more people moved to the West than to the East; see ibid.,

262. Between 2010 and 2050, the population of the eastern federal states is likely to drop further to nine million, thus halving the workforce from eight million to four million.
32. See Rudzio, *Das politische System*, 513.
33. A. Kießling, *Politische Kultur und Parteien im vereinten Deutschland* (Munich, 1999), 105; E. Noelle, 'Geteilte Freude', *FAZ*, 27 November 2002.
34. See Rudzio, *Das politische System*, 512.
35. See Gabriel, 'Politische Einstellungen und politische Kultur', 522.
36. From 41 per cent to 36 per cent (see Tuchscheerer, *20 Jahre vereinigtes Deutschland*, 166).
37. See Merkel, *Systemtransformation*, 426 (state under the rule of law); Beyme, *Das politische System*, 69 (Bundestag, federal government).
38. Between 1990 and 2010, the share of those who were satisfied fell from 49 per cent to 41 per cent (figures in Tuchscheerer, *20 Jahre vereinigtes Deutschland*, 168).
39. See ibid., 180.
40. See Rudzio, *Das politische System*, 513.
41. See Forsa opinion poll 2009 passim.
42. See Besier, 'Das Ost-West-Verhältnis in Deutschland', 26.
43. See Rudzio, *Das politische System*, 503.
44. Ismayr, 'Das politische System Deutschlands', 432.
45. Rudzio, *Das politische System*, 514.
46. Figures in Beyme, *Das politische System*, 82; similar figures in Tuchscheerer, *20 Jahre vereinigtes Deutschland*, 160.
47. Figures in Sozialwissenschaftliches Forschungszentrum (ed.), *Sozialreport 2008* (Berlin, 2008); Heitmeyer, 'Leben wir noch immer in zwei Gesellschaften?', 45; Rudzio, *Das politische System*, 512.
48. The majority view 'socialism' as a good idea (see Tuchscheerer, *20 Jahre vereinigtes Deutschland*, 180).
49. Satisfaction with democracy that depends significantly on economic output is considered an indication that part of the citizenry does not yet sufficiently identify with democracy. In economically difficult times, democracy as a system may be questioned. As long as satisfaction with democracy depends on economic output, one must assume a low degree of democracy consolidation (Backes, 'Probleme der Demokratiekonsolidierung', 51).
50. 'Jugendarbeitslosigkeit erreicht Tiefstand', *FAZ*, 1 June 2012, 13. The unemployed population in reunified Germany is at a historic low (as of May 2012) of a total of 2.885 million (6.7 per cent). The unemployed number 1.964 million (5.7 per cent) in the old federal states and 0.891 million (10.6 per cent) in the new federal states. In this context, however, one must take into account that the drop in unemployment in the East is double that in the West (0.7 per cent vs. 0.3 per cent).
51. See W. Ismayr, 'Die politischen Systeme Osteuropas im Vergleich', in W. Ismayr (ed.), *Die politischen Systeme Osteuropas*, 3rd ed. (Wiesbaden, 2010), 9–78, here 68; Merkel, *Systemtransformation*, 425; J. Maćków, *Totalitarismus und danach: Einführung in den Kommunismus und die postkommunistische Systemtransformation* (Baden-Baden, 2005), 116; M. Brusis, 'Ostmittel- und Südeuropa', in Bertelsmann Stiftung (ed.), *Transformation Index 2010* (Gütersloh, 2009), 128; K. Vodička and L. Cabada, *Politický systém České republiky: Historie a sou čas nost*, 3rd ed. (Praha, 2011), 324; G. Pickel, 'Die subjektive Verankerung der Demokratie in Osteuropa: Die Legitimität der Demokratie in der Bevölkerung als Faktor demokratischer Stabilität und Qualität', in U. Backes, T. Jaskułowski and A. Polese (eds), *Totalitarismus und Transformation:*

Defizite der Demokratiekonsolidierung in Mittel- und Osteuropa (Göttingen, 2009), 261–83, here 268.

52. Heitmeyer, 'Leben wir immer noch in zwei Gesellschaften?', 45.
53. See survey by the Leipziger Institut für Marktforschung (IM) by order of Leipziger Volkszeitung, in *Leipziger Volkszeitung*, 2 October 2012, 1.
54. For the first well-grounded overview in terms of contemporary history, see Rödder, *Deutschland einig Vaterland*, 279–365.
55. From the abundant scientific literature, see most of all K.-H. Paqué, *Die Bilanz: Eine wirtschaftliche Analyse der Deutschen Einheit* (Munich, 2009); G.A. Ritter, *Wir sind das Volk! Wir sind ein Volk! Geschichte der deutschen Einigung* (Munich, 2009); H. Schmidt, *Auf dem Weg zur deutschen Einheit: Bilanz und Ausblick* (Reinbek b. Hamburg, 2005), and for sub-fields see K. von Delhaes, W. Quaisser and K. Ziemer (eds), *Vom Sozialismus zur Marktwirtschaft: Wandlungsprozesse, Ergebnisse und Perspektiven* (Munich, 2009).
56. Bundesministerium des Innern, 'Jahresbericht der Bundesregierung zum Stand der Deutschen Einheit 2010', 11.
57. See 'Wirtschaftlicher Stand und Perspektiven für Ostdeutschland', Studie im Auftrag des Bundesministeriums des Innern, Halle/Saale, 23 May 2011, 14.
58. Rödder, *Deutschland einig Vaterland*, 327.
59. See B. Breuel and M.C. Burda (eds), *Ohne historisches Vorbild: Die Treuhandanstalt 1990 bis 1994. Eine kritische Würdigung* (Berlin, 2005).
60. See Bundesministerium des Innern, 'Jahresbericht der Bundesregierung zum Stand der deutschen Einheit 2010', 11.
61. See M. Oppong, 'Was kostet die Deutsche Einheit?', *Freiraum* 7 (2005), 14.
62. See A. Volze, 'Zur Devisenverschuldung der DDR: Entstehung, Bewältigung und Folgen', in E. Kuhrt (ed.), *Die Endzeit der DDR-Wirtschaft: Analysen zur Wirtschafts-, Sozial- und Umweltpolitik* (Opladen, 1999), 151–83.
63. Bundesministerium des Innern, 'Jahresbericht der Bundesregierung zum Stand der deutschen Einheit 2010', 14.
64. U. Ludwig, 'Licht und Schatten nach 15 Jahren wirtschaftlicher Transformation in Ostdeutschland', *Deutschland Archiv* 38(3) (2005), 410–16, here 412.
65. Cf. Breuel and Burda, *Ohne Historisches Vorbild*.
66. See Bundesministerium des Innern, 'Jahresbericht der Bundesregierung zum Stand der deutschen Einheit 2010', 74.
67. See 'Wirtschaftlicher Stand und Perspektiven für Ostdeutschland', 14.
68. See G.A. Ritter, 'Die deutsche Wiedervereinigung', *Historische Zeitschrift* 286 (2008), 289–339, here 311.
69. See Rödder, *Deutschland einig Vaterland*, 343.
70. See Bundesministerium des Innern, 'Jahresbericht der Bundesregierung zum Stand der Deutschen Einheit 2010', 97.
71. Rödder, *Deutschland einig Vaterland*, 350.
72. On this see, among others, an oral history-based comparative study of two companies in Leipzig that clearly reveals that by the mid 1980s, employees there were convinced that fundamental restructuring of the production system was unavoidable (F. Weil, *Herrschaftsanspruch und soziale Wirklichkeit: Zwei sächsische Betriebe in der DDR während der Honecker-Ära* [Cologne, 2000]).
73. See 'Wirtschaftlicher Stand und Perspektiven für Ostdeutschland', 14.
74. See ibid., 38.

75. W. Hinrichs and R. Nauenburg, 'Unterschiedliche Demokratiezufriedenheit in West- und Ostdeutschland', *Deutschland Archiv* 38(3) (2005), 393–401, here 398.
76. Bundesministerium des Innern, 'Jahresbericht der Bundesregierung zum Stand der Deutschen Einheit 2010', 95f.
77. See ibid., 99.
78. Bundesministerium des Innern (ed.), 'Jahresbericht der Bundesregierung zum Stand der Deutschen Einheit 2011' (Berlin, 2011), 25.
79. Bundesministerium des Innern, 'Jahresbericht der Bundesregierung zum Stand der Deutschen Einheit 2010', 104f.
80. See R. Geißler, *Die Sozialstruktur Deutschlands: Zur gesellschaftlichen Entwicklung mit einer Bilanz zur Vereinigung*, 6th ed. (Wiesbaden, 2011), 87.
81. See ibid., 225.
82. See Bundesministerium des Innern, 'Jahresbericht der Bundesregierung zum Stand der Deutschen Einheit 2011', 25.
83. See Bundesministerium des Innern, 'Jahresbericht der Bundesregierung zum Stand der Deutschen Einheit 2010', 74.
84. See Bundesministerium des Innern, 'Jahresbericht der Bundesregierung zum Stand der Deutschen Einheit 2011', 24.
85. 'Wirtschaftlicher Stand und Perspektiven für Ostdeutschland', 58.
86. 'Jugendarbeitslosigkeit erreicht Tiefstand', *FAZ*, 1 June 2012, 13.
87. See 'Wirtschaftlicher Stand und Perspektiven für Ostdeutschland', 58.
88. 'Westdeutschland verdient heute an der Einheit', *FAZ*, 29 March 2012, 4.
89. See Bundesministerium des Innern, 'Jahresbericht der Bundesregierung zum Stand der Deutschen Einheit 2011', 31.
90. See 'Wirtschaftlicher Stand und Perspektiven für Ostdeutschland', 59.
91. See Ludwig, 'Licht und Schatten'.
92. See Paqué, *Die Bilanz*, 208.
93. See 'Wirtschaftlicher Stand und Perspektiven für Ostdeutschland', 59.
94. See 'Wirtschaftsforscher wollen Osten nicht länger subventionieren', *FAZ*, 27 February 2012, 11.
95. See Thüringischen Ministerium für Wirtschaft (ed.), 'Arbeit und Technologie, Zukunft Ost. Analysen, Trends, Handlungsempfehlungen', Studie der Roland Berger Strategy Consultants GmbH, August 2012 (http://www.thueringen.de/imperia/md/content/tmwta/zukunft_ost.pdf; accessed 8 October 2012).
96. See Paqué, *Die Bilanz*, 205.
97. Ibid., 199.
98. See 'Der Soli hat fast 200 Milliarden Euro gebracht', *FAZ*, 29 November 2011, 11.
99. On this see Paqué, *Die Bilanz*, 181–207.
100. See §11 Sect. 3a Finanzausgleichsgesetze (FAG) from 20 December 2001, which was amended by Art. 11 from 22 December 2009.
101. See Bundesministerium des Innern, 'Jahresbericht der Bundesregierung zum Stand der Deutschen Einheit 2010', 24f.
102. See 'Wirtschaftlicher Stand und Perspektiven für Ostdeutschland', 91 as well as Bundesministerium des Innern, 'Jahresbericht der Bundesregierung zum Stand der Deutschen Einheit 2011', 39f.
103. See J. Ragnitz, 'Wohl und Wehe von 20 Jahren Wirtschaftspolitik: Ostdeutschland als Beispiel für die Grenzen wirtschaftspolitischer Interventionen', in Lorenz, *Ostdeutschland und die Sozialwissenschaften*, 153–68, here 155.
104. Ibid.

105. On this in detail, see F. Zinsmeister, 'Die Finanzierung der deutschen Einheit: Zum Umgang mit den Schuldlasten der Wiedervereinigung', *Vierteljahrshefte zur Wirtschaftsforschung* 78(2) (2009), 146–60.
106. On this see critically U. Beck, 'Vereinigt und doch zweigeteilt: Zum Stand der deutsch-deutschen Konvergenz auf wirtschaftlichem Gebiet', in Bohr and Krause, *20 Jahre Deutsche Einheit*, 63–98.
107. See the overview by S. Kröhnert, F. Medicus and R. Klingholz, *Die demografische Lage der Nation: Wie zukunftsfähig sind Deutschlands Regionen? Daten, Fakten, Analysen* (Munich, 2006).
108. Geißler, *Die Sozialstruktur Deutschlands*, 45.
109. See J. Ragnitz and L. Schneider, 'Demographische Entwicklung und ihre ökonomischen Folgen', *Wirtschaft im Wandel* 13(6) (2007), 195–202, here 195. Accordingly, also 'the size of the age cohorts of 15–20-year-olds and 20–40-year-olds will decline dramatically, by -46% and -28% resp.' (ibid.).
110. See Bundesministerium des Innern, 'Jahresbericht der Bundesregierung zum Stand der Deutschen Einheit 2010', 59f.
111. See Bundesministerium des Innern, 'Jahresbericht der Bundesregierung zum Stand der deutschen Einheit 2011', 8.
112. One reason for this is that young women leave their home regions once they have graduated from school, whereas young men leave only after finishing their vocational training; furthermore, young women find it particularly difficult to find apprenticeships and are thus more ready to migrate. See G. Herfert, 'Regionale Polarisierung der demographischen Entwicklung in Ostdeutschland: Gleichwertigkeit der Lebensverhältnisse?' *Raumforschung und Raumordnung* 5 (2007), 435–55, here 449.
113. See A. Kubis and L. Schneider, '"Sag mir, wo die Mädchen sind. . .": Regionale Analyse des Wanderungsverhaltens junger Frauen', *Wirtschaft im Wandel* 13(8) (2007), 298–307, here 298.
114. See R. Mai, 'Die altersselektive Abwanderung aus Ostdeutschland', *Raumforschung und Raumordnung* 5 (2006), 355–69, here 360. According to Mai, emigration from eastern German regions happened in three phases: 1991–1993, 1994–1997 and 1998–2001. On the whole it continues, if to a lesser extent; see ibid., 364f.
115. 'Wirtschaftlicher Stand und Perspektiven für Ostdeutschland', 77.
116. Ibid., 78.
117. See ibid., 79.
118. See Geißler, *Die Sozialstruktur Deutschlands*, 51.
119. The following is based on Rainer Geißler's compendium on the social structure of Germany, which covers the current state of sociology research on the development of society overall up to 2010; see ibid., 367–70.
120. See ibid., 183.
121. Ibid., 369.
122. Ibid., 370.
123. Ibid.
124. Ibid.
125. W. Szalai, 'Sieben Anmerkungen', in C. John and K. Schimmel (eds), *GrenzFall Einheit: Zwischenberichte aus Sachsen* (Leipzig, 2005), 35–41, here 39. This collection relates quite different ways of subjectively experiencing the post-1989/90 process of transformation and integration.

126. 'Kaum einer möchte die Mauer wieder haben: Aktuelle Umfrage zu Stimmungen und Erwartungen in Deutschland: 15 Jahre nach dem Fall der Mauer', *Leipziger Volkszeitung*, 8 November 2004.

127. See ibid.

128. 'Wirtschaftlicher Stand und Perspektiven für Ostdeutschland', 53.

129. Bundesministerium des Innern, 'Jahresbericht der Bundesregierung zum Stand der Deutschen Einheit 2010', 25.

Chapter 5

POLAND

꒰ᘓᘏᘊ꒱

Klaus Ziemer

Introduction

In 1989, Poland became the first state under Soviet hegemony to have a government led by non-communists. Indeed, communist rule had shallower roots in Poland than in any other country in the Soviet sphere of power, as had already been proven by several serious system crises that ultimately resulted in the founding of the legal, party-independent trade union Solidarność in 1980/81. Not even after imposing martial law on 13 December 1981 and banning Solidarność did the ruling Polish United Workers' Party (Polska Zjednoczona Partia Robotnicza, PZPR) recover from this blow. In 1986, the PZPR leader General Wojciech Jaruzelski granted amnesty to all political prisoners and tried to integrate parts of the opposition. Considering Poland's dramatic weakening due to the political leadership's lasting loss of its own followers' confidence and the government's inability to stop ongoing economic decline, the historian Jerzy Holzer compared the country's situation to that at the end of the eighteenth century, when Poland was partitioned and disappeared from the map of Europe for 123 years. In a letter of 13 December 1987 addressed to Jaruzelski as well as to Solidarność chairman Lech Wałęsa – whom the ruling power considered *persona non grata* and prohibited mention of in official media – Holzer explained that only cooperation between Jaruzelski and Wałęsa could lead Poland out of this crisis. After renewed strikes in May and August 1988 (which the government managed to end only with help from leading members of the officially banned Solidarność) and intractable internal struggles on both sides, and thanks not least to mediation by representatives of the Catholic Church, a roundtable was established on 6 February 1989. There, the reform-oriented elites of the ancien régime and the moderate parts of the opposition started negotiations. The transition course they plotted from the authoritarian communist system under Jaruzelski to democracy was mostly in accordance with one of the classical scenarios developed in the political sciences following the wave of democratization in Latin America and Southern Europe (Spain, Portugal, Greece) since the 1970s.[1]

Until 5 April 1989, negotiators at the 'main' and several 'sub-tables' evaluated the foundations of the existing political and socio-economic system. The establishment of the roundtable had basically decided the crucial political question of re-legalizing the Solidarność trade union, but the details of the future system of institutions in Poland were fiercely debated. The opposition accepted that the elections held after the roundtable talks would not yet decide about political power, that is, that only the subsequent elections would be genuinely competitive. Yet it also wanted to acquire as many competences and positions as possible, so as to gain practical political experience during the coming electoral term.

In the given foreign relations international situation in spring 1989, Poland was surrounded by the Soviet Union, Husák's ČSSR and Honecker's GDR. All participants were aware that Jaruzelski personified Poland's credibility towards its allies, in particular loyalty to the Soviet Union, and would thus be indispensable to the future political system too. They also basically agreed that power would be transferred from party authorities to state authorities, as in Gorbachev's Soviet Union. Jaruzelski was interested in keeping as much power as possible by becoming the future President of the State, but for the time being he held such power only as the leader of the PZPR.

In the end, they decided on a semi-presidential system, borrowing heavily from the constitution of the French Fifth Republic. One of the strategic political goals of establishing a roundtable was to become able to form a government that would be both legitimated in the citizens' eyes and capable of enforcing even unpopular economic reforms, something the governments of the prior fifteen years had proven incapable of. To increase the legitimacy of the parliament, the Senate, which in Polish constitutional reality had possessed a centuries-long tradition but had been disbanded in 1947, was reintroduced. The elections to this upper chamber were free, even by Western standards. The Senate had fewer competences than the Sejm, the lower house of parliament whose election results were politically fixed in advance. The PZPR and its previous formal 'alliance partners', the United People's Party (Zjednoczone Stronnictwo Ludowe, ZSL) and the Democratic Party (Stronnictwo Demokratyczne, SD), were allotted a total of 60 per cent of the seats, and three Christian groups that cooperated with them (without the permission of the Episcopate) received

5 per cent. The other 35 per cent of seats were open to candidates without party affiliation and thus to members of Solidarność. As Solidarność was expected to achieve the majority in the Senate, the opposition at the roundtable was finally able to push through its demand that the Sejm would need a two-thirds majority (and not the 65 per cent majority that the government demanded for obvious reasons) to overrule a negative vote by the Senate.

In compensation for this expected relative strength of the opposition in parliament, the President of the State was given much authority. He could veto any law, and the Sejm needed a two-thirds majority to overrule him. His term of office was six years, whereas that of the parliament was only four years. After the parliament's electoral term ended (in 1993, according to the timetable established at the roundtable), the president, who would be in office until 1995, would be able to strongly influence the then happening formation of a government, due to his large competences. As Jaruzelski obviously had no chance of prevailing in a direct presidential election, the president was to be elected by the National Assembly, the joint assembly of Sejm and Senate, following the model of the Second Republic.[2] The president could veto the appointments of the minister for home affairs, the foreign minister and the minister of defence, something the opposition agreed to, given the foreign policy situation.

The negotiated measures seemed to secure the power of the PZPR for at least another four years after the termination of the roundtable. What was more, election dates were fixed already for early June 1989, leaving the opposition only two months in which to prepare once the roundtable negotiations ended. Yet the result of the semi-free elections of 4 June (as well as the second vote two weeks later) clearly revealed the strength of Solidarność and the concurrent weakness of the PZPR and its partners at a stroke, fundamentally changing the political situation. Solidarność won 99 of the 100 seats in the Senate and all 161 Sejm seats open to non-party members. Despite the extremely complicated electoral system, analysis of the results showed that Solidarność representatives in the Sejm had received four to five times as many votes as the new MPs from the previous government camp.[3] As agreed to at the roundtable, in the elections to the Sejm the representatives of the ancien régime gained a share of 65 per cent of the seats. However, for the first time the PZPR leaders did not have the power to nominate candidates – not even in respect of their own party – and thus could not be sure how 'reliable' individual MPs from their camp would be. Also, the PZPR was decisively weakened in the parliament by the electoral losses of thirty-three of the thirty-five candidates on the 'national list' – among them almost the entire PZPR elite, topped by Prime Minister Mieczysław Rakowski, who got less than 50 per cent of votes. The national list had been meant to spare the previous system's top politicians from competition from opposition candidates.

Representatives of the ancien régime had 299 seats in the National Assembly, and Solidarność had only 259 members, after one senator had died. However, Jaruzelski barely won the presidential election, receiving only one vote more than necessary. Thus, Jaruzelski's political position was significantly weakened, despite the president's large constitutional competences.

Jaruzelski appointed General Czesław Kiszczak (PZPR) prime minister, but Kiszczak was not able to form a government because the PZPR's previous 'alliance partners' the ZSL and SD refused approval, fearing that future competitive elections would punish them as the PZPR had been punished in 1989. The PZPR was now paying the price for its failure, in the 1989 elections to the Sejm, to insist for the first time that at least 50 per cent of Sejm members be members of the PZPR. Surprisingly, Wałęsa's demand that the slogan of 'Socialist parliamentarism' proclaimed by the PZPR in the previous months be taken seriously led to a coalition government of the Citizens' Parliamentary Caucus (Obywatelski Klub Parlamentarny, OKP), formed by Solidarność Sejm and Senate members, together with the ZSL and the SD under OKP leadership. Jaruzelski accepted the Catholic publicist Tadeusz Mazowiecki, a member of the inner leadership circle of Solidarność, as prime minister.

Mazowiecki, for his part, accepted Generals Kiszczak and Florian Siwicki (both PZPR members) as minister for home affairs and minister of defence. During their hearings in the Sejm committees tasked with confirming them, both promised to accept the parliament's primacy over the militia and the secret police as well as the armed forces, which up to then had, in practice, been among the PZPR's crucial pillars of power. The following weeks saw the demise of further informal structures that for decades had supported the communist ruling system, such as the nomenklatura system and the PZPR's control of the media, which the PZPR representatives at the roundtable had defended most stubbornly. In his government policy statement, Mazowiecki named the establishment of rule of law as his most urgent goal, calling it the precondition for implementation of fundamental economic reform. By the end of 1989, constitutional changes had rid Poland of the remaining key pillars of communist rule, such as the PZPR's power monopoly, and party pluralism had taken root. On a symbolic level, the state's name of 'People's Republic of Poland' was replaced by the traditional 'Rzeczpospolita Polska' (Republic of Poland), the eagle in the coat of arms received the crown back as a symbol of regained sovereignty, the national holiday of the People's

Republic was abolished and the national holidays of the Second Republic were reintroduced.

One deep break was the overnight introduction of a market economy on 1 January 1990. It abolished several subsidies and price fixing, lifted the state monopoly on foreign trade and made the zloty freely convertible. Real incomes consequently declined by about a quarter, even given the very low base level. Nevertheless, in its first months the Mazowiecki government had an approval rating higher than 80 per cent. Thus, though in a different way than expected, one of the goals that had prompted the establishment of the roundtable became reality. The architect of the Polish economic reform, Leszek Balcerowicz, assumed that a window of opportunity in which painful economic reform could be implemented would open only at the beginning of system transformation, and that later such draconic reforms would be politically impossible to carry out.[4] In the short run, Balcerowicz's 'shock treatment' caused the national economic growth figures to collapse, but by the end of 1992 Poland was the first transformation country to operate in the black with regard to its economic growth. By 1995, the inflation rate, which in 1989/90 had sometimes run into four figures, had fallen to 27.8 per cent. Meanwhile, new social security systems had to be established because unemployment, which before then had been unknown, had started growing dramatically upon the introduction of market economy.

Working out a new constitution took more time than expected. As had also happened after World Wars I and II, in 1992 a 'small' constitution was introduced, valid until passage of the 'actual' constitution, which above all was supposed to organize a more precise distribution of competences among president, government and parliament, an aim that ultimately enjoyed only partial success. The new constitution was not passed until 1997.

In the foreign policy sphere, Poland decided for complete reorientation towards integration into Western cooperation structures. Achieving this became fully possible only after the dissolution of the Soviet Union (at the end of 1991) and the Red Army's complete withdrawal from Polish territory (in 1992). With the neighbourhood treaty of 17 June 1991, the reunited Germany became the first state to support Poland's attempts at accession to the European Community.

Politics

The process of passing a new constitution lasted until 1997. In 1992, the parliament charged a committee of the National Assembly (Sejm and

Senate) with the task of hammering it out. In the 1993 Sejm election, several right-wing groups had failed to meet the newly introduced 5 per cent threshold, which meant the Democratic Left Alliance (Sojusz Lewicy Demokratycznej, SLD), together with its also 'turned-around' coalition partner, the Polish People's (Farmers') Party (Polskie Stronnictwo Ludowe, PSL), was clearly overrepresented in the parliament. Large sections of conservatives denied this parliament any legitimation to work out a constitution, although some of them were eventually co-opted onto the constitutional committee. Topical debates concerned such questions as whether the future constitutional body should be parliamentary or instead presidentially oriented. Ideological debates revolved mostly around the preamble, in particular the question of an *invocatio dei*, a feature of the constitution of 3 May 1791 as well as that of 1921. Finally, former Prime Minister Mazowiecki presented a compromise that satisfied both believers and atheists.[5]

On the way from the roundtable to the 1997 constitution via the small constitution, the distribution of competences changed: a presidential-parliamentary system became a parliamentary-presidential one dominated by the prime minister. Of the earlier competences, the president retains above all the right to veto laws passed by the parliament; however, the Sejm can now overrule a presidential veto with only a three-fifths, instead of the original two-thirds, majority. If the president comes from a different camp than the parliamentary majority and the government has a majority of less than 60 per cent of the seats, as was the case from 2007 to 2010 under President Lech Kaczyński of the Law and Justice party (Prawo i Sprawiedliwość, PiS) and Prime Minister Donald Tusk of the Citizens' Platform (Platforma Obywatelska, PO), the president's veto can indeed make the government's everyday work very difficult. Furthermore, the president has the right of legislative initiative, which holders of that office have made use of to different extents.

Of the two chambers of parliament, the Sejm is clearly predominant. Unlike the Sejm, whose political structure was fixed during the roundtable negotiations, the Senate was reintroduced in 1989 primarily to express the authentic will of society. As early as the first free Sejm election of 1991, the Senate's existence came into question, as the same voters elect both it and the Sejm and its electoral term is linked to that of the Sejm. In a case of premature dissolution of the Sejm, which the Sejm can itself decide by a two-thirds majority (as happened in 2007), the Senate is also newly elected. For the election of the 460 members of the Sejm, the constitution stipulates proportional representation, though without saying which kind exactly. Before the 2001 elections, in order to prevent an absolute majority of seats of the SLD, the successor party of the PZPR, the conservative majority of the Sejm reduced the number of constituencies from fifty-two to forty-one and replaced d'Hondt's equalization system by a modified Sainte-Laguë method (first factor 1.4, then 3, 5, 7. . .). The national list that had previously determined the distribution of 15 per cent of the seats was abandoned. Only parties that had received at least 5 per cent of valid votes nationwide were considered for the distribution of mandates in the constituencies. Parties of national minorities are exempted from this threshold, however, making it possible for the German minority concentrated in the Opole constituency to be represented in most cases by two seats in the Sejm, although nationwide they receive only about 0.2 per cent of the vote.

In practice, the Senate's main task is to work as a corrective to the Sejm's law-making, which is often criticized as technically insufficient. The Senate changes about half of the laws passed by the Sejm, which accepts the overwhelming majority of these alterations[6] but may also reject them by an absolute majority vote. Senators were elected in forty multi-representative constituencies according to relative majority representation (two or three seats; only in Warsaw is it four). Since the new electoral code of 2011, the senators are elected in 100 single member constituencies according to the FPTP system. This element of direct election makes it possible for a candidate with a strong regional background to become a senator even without a party's support. For example, former Prime Minister and Minister of Foreign Affairs Włodzimierz Cimoszewicz, who had stepped down as a presidential candidate just before the 2005 elections due to a quarrel with his party (the SLD), returned to the political stage as an independent senator.

Examples of institutional learning are found in both the constitution and Poland's law-making. For example, after the country went through eight prime ministers between 1989 and 1997, the new constitution introduced the constructive vote of no confidence as the only way to bring down a head of government. This allowed the head of government Jerzy Buzek (1997–2001) to function as the first prime minister over the entire term of office, although he headed only a minority cabinet after 2000. Meanwhile, the parliament may still dismiss individual ministers and indeed has tried to do so several times, though so far without success.

The role of the Constitutional Court has been enhanced. Created by Jaruzelski in the mid 1980s, the court met with fierce opposition from the GDR leadership, as it tended to put the PZPR's absolute power monopoly in question. Then, under the small constitution of 1992, the Constitutional Court had to accept as before that the Sejm could overrule its verdicts by a two-thirds majority, which indeed was still happening in the 1990s. Only since October 1999 – two years after the new constitution came into force – have verdicts of the Constitutional Court been immediately legally binding. The court's powers are modelled on those of the German Constitutional Court, and it may also decide individual actions.

Another example of institutional learning is the Law on Political Parties, whose first version of 1990 still expressed an unbounded belief in democracy and was restricted to a total of eight articles. Meanwhile it allowed for legal grey areas, particularly concerning the funding of parties, which was conducive to political parties being influenced by business actors. With sixty-four articles, the Law on Political Parties of 1997 was not only much more extensive but also more articulate.[7] It made democratic internal structures a precondition for political parties. Likewise, it upheld the principle of 'democracy capable of defending itself' insofar as the Constitutional Court may ban parties whose goals do not accord with constitutional principles – a power that has not been exercised, to date.

After the experience of the communist period, the offices of minister of justice and attorney general had been integrated so as to make prosecution independent of the influence of any political party (i.e. the PZPR). This integration later came into question when, in several cases, Minister of Justice Zbigniew Ziobro (2005–2007, PiS) was accused of abusing the authority of the attorney general to get rid of opponents. By a simple amendment, the two offices were separated on 31 March 2010.[8]

Even today, Poland is still influenced by the centralist traditions of the interwar period and, even more strongly, the Polish People's Republic. Nevertheless, the constitution introduced the subsidiarity principle, expressed in, for example, the administrative reform of 1 January 1999, which reduced to sixteen the forty-nine provinces or voivodeships that had existed since 1975. Because it also expanded the competences of both voivodeships and municipal self-administration, one may speak of a decentralization of administration. According to opinion polls, this decentralization has revitalized self-administration, whose results are perceived more positively than is national-level political life.[9]

The constitution introduced plebiscitary elements insofar as now there can be referendums; however, they require a minimum national turnout of 50 per cent of eligible voters to be valid. Constitutional referenda are exempt from this provision, a decision that turned out to be prudent: despite a high degree of emotional polarization before the vote on the 1997 constitution, only 42.9 per cent of those eligible to vote participated in the referendum. By 2003, the referendum on Poland's accession to the EU did reach the quorum, not least because the referendum took place on two days (Saturday and Sunday).[10] For referendums at the local or district level, a turnout of 30 per cent is required. If their topic is the dismissal of the respective executive body or the whole parliament – which has happened – the turnout must be at least 60 per cent of the election that brought the politicians in question into office.[11]

One remarkably grass-roots democratic element of the 1997 constitution is the regulation stipulating that parliament must debate a legislative initiative that is supported by 100,000 signatures collected within a three-month period. Several such projects – concerning, for instance, the tax deductibility of expenses – have been successful, thus supporting 'bottom-up' initiatives. Most of these initiatives – even when gathering the 100,000 signatures – fail, however.

Whereas the institutionalization of the constitutional system may be considered a success, the consolidation of democracy still has one weak spot: the party system, as in other states in East Central Europe. Since the first free election to the Sejm in 1991, only two parties have been represented in the parliament without interruption. Both are 'successors' to parties from the People's Republic: the SLD and the 'turned over' farmers' party, the PSL. Most other parties developed from the groups that emerged from the political wing of Solidarność after its rapid post-1989 dissolution. Having learned a lesson from the right wing's fragmentation in the 1993 elections to the Sejm, Election Action Solidarity (Akcja Wyborcza Solidarność, AWS) formed in 1996. With its victory in the 1997 elections, the country seemed to be on its way towards a bipolar party system with a 'moderate' centre. However, the AWS soon dissolved, and in 2001 four new parties were elected to the Sejm, three of which had been founded just months before, whereas AWS and the Freedom Union (Unia Wolności, a union of the intellectual elites of Solidarność), which in 1997 had started as government factions, were no longer in the Sejm.

In the 2001 elections, the SLD and its election coalition partner Labour Union (Unia Pracy, UP, a small party of left-wing Solidarność members and reformed communists) reached their political peak with 41 per cent of votes in the Sejm elections and 75 per cent of seats in the Senate. However, a number of political scandals and corruption affairs so discredited the government of Leszek Miller, the head of the SLD, that Miller stepped down immediately after Poland's accession to the EU in May 2004, and support for the SLD fell to 11.3 per cent in the 2005 elections. The SLD has been at that level ever since, having enduringly alienated most of its voters. The pro-European and anti-clerically inclined SLD, which like its junior partner, the UP, is a member of the Socialist International, represents entrepreneurs who enriched themselves via insider privatization in the late 1980s as well as members of the All-Poland Trade Union Alliance (Ogólnopolskie Porozuminienie Związków Zawodowych, OPZZ). Since Miller's fall, the comparatively young party leaders – Wojciech Olejniczak (born in 1973) as of 2004 and Grzegorz Napieralski, who is the same age, as of 2008 – have tried to create distance from the still influential former PZPR cadres, but intra-party quarrels make it difficult to formulate a programme that could appeal to potential centre-left voters, all the more because Miller who had left the party in 2007 returned in 2009 and became leader of the SLD again in 2011.

Since the parliamentary elections of 2005, the main division line of the Polish party system runs between the two parties PiS and PO, which both sprang from Solidarność. In the 2005 parliamentary elections, the national-conservative PiS, founded by the twin brothers Jarosław and Lech Kaczyński, achieved a relative majority of 27.0 per cent of valid votes, with a turnout of 40.57 per cent. Immediately thereafter, Lech Kaczyński won the presidential election. The PiS under Kazimierz Marcinkiewicz began as a minority government that was tolerated by the charismatic but unpredictable Andrzej Lepper with his left-wing populist Samoobrona (Self-Defence) party and the national-clerical League of Polish Families (Liga Polskich Rodzin, LPR), founded in 2001 with the young lawyer Roman Giertych at its head. In May 2006, Samoobrona and the LPR, which up to then had both been considered unfit for a coalition, became official coalition partners, and their leaders both rose to the position of vice prime minister. In July 2006, Jarosław Kaczynski replaced the popular Kazimierz Marcinkiewicz, but his efforts to establish a 'Fourth Republic' ended in failure (see the 'Prospects' section below). In the early elections to the Sejm in October 2007, the PiS made gains, but at the expense of its previous coalition partners, who have since disappeared from the political stage. With a considerable turnout – for Poland – of 53.99 per cent, the PiS won 32.11 per cent of the vote, but the previous opposition party, the PO, garnered 41.51 per cent and formed a coalition government with the PSL that lasted until the end of the electoral term (and even the next electoral term). Moreover, several prominent PiS MPs left the party because of Jarosław Kaczyński's authoritarian leadership style. After the previous Sejm Marshal Bronisław Komorowski (PO) beat Kaczyński in the presidential elections of July 2010 – made necessary by the death of Kaczyński's brother Lech in the Smolensk air crash of 10 April 2010 – the erosion in the PiS became obvious, but Kaczyński managed to hold his ground as party leader.

Since the 2007 parliamentary elections, the PO, founded in 2001, has undeniably been the strongest party. Prime Minister Donald Tusk came from the ranks of this EU-oriented, economically liberal party. The PO is also a member of the European People's Party, and every opinion poll until 2014 put it clearly ahead of the PiS, sometimes with the support of more than 50 per cent of respondents. Admittedly, this was due less to the performance of the government, which avoids making decisions about difficult problems, than to a lack of alternatives offered by other parties.

The fourth party represented in the Sejm, the PSL, claimed to have 140,000 members in 2010, which would make it the Polish party with by far the largest membership. An inquiry made in 2012 on the basis of membership fees declared by all parties represented in the Sejm showed that they could have all together 80,000 members and the PSL 3,000 at best.[12] It is particularly strongly rooted in rural regions of Central Poland as well as the south and south-east of the country. At the national level, it is the top choice of between 3 and 8 per cent of registered voters, according to opinion polls. Particularly when it was represented in the government, the PSL worked to preserve the vested rights of its clientele while contributing little to the urgently needed restructuring of the rural regions. As a 'successor party', it was twice represented in the government together with the SLD, and since 2007 it has been part of the government with the PO.

Parties that are not presently represented in the Sejm do not play any role at all. Yet this is not to say that the current party system will be forever unaltered. Opinion polls across society show that ties to parties are not very strong, and many voters state that no party actually represents their interests.[13] The high rate of Sejm MPs changing from one faction to another (2001–2005: 109 or 23.7 per cent; 2007–1 February 2011: 77 or 16.7 per cent; 2011–2015: at least 57 or 12.4 per cent)[14] confirms the thesis that the party system is still fluent. Nevertheless, since 1993 a relatively constant geographic distribution of the voting behaviour has been obvious. The north-west, north and south-west vote mostly 'left wing' (SLD) or liberal (PO), whereas the south-eastern half of the country votes predominantly conservative (AWS, PiS). The division line runs somewhat along the Vistula, which accords with the country's division into 'Poland A' and 'Poland B', as it is known from the interwar period.

In his government statement of 12 September 1989, the newly appointed Prime Minister Mazowiecki had emphasized that his government's top priority was to establish a state under the rule of law. Even the successful restructuring of the economic system depended on that. To increase judges' independence, the principle of their irremovability was introduced into the constitution. For the same purpose, a National Council of Justice was founded, on which there sat representatives of the legislative, the executive and the judiciary. Its duties include vetting candidates for judicial appointments, which are made by the President of the State. Poland has a tripartite judiciary consisting of general jurisdiction courts, military courts and administrative courts. It also has bodies for the control of state administration under parliamentary supervision, including the Supreme Control Chamber, which is comparable to Germany's Bundesrechnungshof (Federal Audit Office), and the Office of the Ombudsman, founded back in 1987, which annually receives tens of thousands of citizens' complaints about decisions by the state administration.[15]

Concerning Poland's print media, the Ruch trust was disbanded in 1990 by parliament. It had had a near monopoly on the distribution of newspapers and magazines, and its receipts had been a major revenue stream for the PZPR. Some of the papers were handed over to their editorial staffs; most others were sold to foreign investors. Nowadays, after several changes, German capital predominates in the print media market. The few papers with nationwide circulation for many years were characterized by a strong ideological polarization (e.g. between the liberal *Gazeta Wyborcza* and the conservative *Rzeczpospolita*).

As for the electronic media, a dual system had been set up by 1992. In the private sector in this field, foreign capital was strictly limited. The most important supervisory body for the field under public law, which meanwhile also grants licences to private broadcasters, was the National Broadcasting Council (Krajowa Rada Radiofoni i Telewizji, KRRiT). The KRRiT was supposed to ensure that political parties influenced the radio and television as little as possible. However, given that its originally nine, today five, members were from the outset appointees of the President of the State, the Sejm and the Senate, this body was selected according to party-political criteria and thus was highly politicized in practice – increasingly so after the PiS took the reins of government in 2005.[16] At that time, private television channels at least partly began to function as an alternative source of political information. A bill introduced by the Tusk government as early as 2007 was vetoed by President Lech Kaczyński, originating from PiS, once right-wing PiS and left-wing opposition party SLD had reached agreement on the distribution of the leading positions of the public TV channels.

The situation changed after the tragic death of Lech Kaczyński in 2010, when not only both parliamentary chambers but also Bronisław Komorowski, then still acting president, rejected the KRRiT's accounting, thus paving the way for the replacement of its members. Two were drawn from both the PO and the SLD and one from the PSL.

Economy

Poland was the first country in the then Council for Mutual Economic Assistance to launch a market economy. Indeed, in October 1989 it was the main goal of Finance Minister Balcerowicz's economic policy to contain inflation and restructure the economy. Private sector development in the 1980s had extended not only to agriculture – 75 per cent of land used for agriculture was privately owned – but also to the manufacturing sector, so that by 1989, the private sector already accounted for 27 per cent of the GDP. On 1 January 1990, in a kind of 'shock treatment', the new policy lifted most state regulations on the economy, introduced free business activity, liberalized prices, ended most subsidies, abolished the state monopoly on foreign trade and currencies, and made the zloty freely convertible. These extremely painful measures led to a collapse in economic growth, which plunged 11.6 per cent in 1990, and to an almost 25 per cent decline in real incomes, whose basic level had already been extremely low.

A reorientation to different economic models was part of the privatization of Poland's economy. Small and medium-sized enterprises could either be directly sold, changed into cooperatives or let to cooperatives for payment-based utilization for a maximum of fifteen years. Bigger enterprises were changed into wholly owned companies of the Treasury that were then sold to private, often foreign capital owners, or dissolved or partly liquidated for economic reasons. In 1995, 512 such companies wholly owned by the Treasury became part of the newly founded National Investment Funds (Narodowe fundusze inwestycyjne, NFI). Every Polish citizen was entitled to acquire shares that could be sold or exchanged for shares in one of these NFI companies.

The initial expansion of the private sector was mostly due to the founding of new enterprises, as the transformation of state enterprises progressed slowly by comparison. From 1 August 1990 to the end of 2009, 7,512 former state enterprises – that is, 86 per cent of state enterprises registered in mid 1990 – were subject to restructuring. Among them were 1,654 agricultural state domains that were transferred to the State Agency for Agricultural Estates, which was in charge of their privatization; and 1,933 companies subject to dissolution procedures, 1,094 of which were liquidated.[17] However, some privatization – and the attendant reduction of workplaces – was delayed, particularly in still subsidized sectors like mining, the steel industry and shipbuilding, which had been strongholds of Solidarność in the 1980s and now were threatened by mass dismissals.

Creating a government-independent central bank with a leadership elected by the parliament helped stabilize the currency. During some months of the year 1990, hyperinflation ran into four figures, but after this it declined. In 1993, the zloty was nominally devaluated: 10,000 zloty became one zloty, and new banknotes and coins were issued. The exchange rate of two zloty to one deutschmark stayed about the same for years. It was possible to reduce the horrendous foreign debt considerably by way of agreements with the London and Paris Clubs.

In 1992, Poland became the first former communist country to show positive GDP growth, which continued in the following years. At first, real incomes continued to decline. Taking the real wages of 1990 as 100,

TABLE 5.1. Basic data on economic development 1989–2009

	1989	1990	1995	2000	2005	2008	2009
GDP (billion Zł.) current prices	22	124	289	742	965	1,246	1,344
GDP real growth in per cent	0.2	–11.6	7.0	4.1	3.6	5.1	1.8
Inflation in per cent	351.1	685.8	27.8	10.1	2.0	4.0	3.3
Real income in per cent	9.0	–24.4	3.0		1.8	5.9	2.1
Foreign Direct Investment (million euro)			2,831	10,334	8,330	10,206	8,942
Import (million USD)	10,277.4	9,527.7	29,049.7	48,940.2	101,538.8	210,478.5	149,569.8
Export (million USD)	13,466.1	14,321.6	22,894.9	31,651.3	89,378.1	171,859.9	136,641.3

Sources: Own compilation, based on Mały Rocznik Statystyczny, several years; PAiIZ, Inwestycje zagraniczne w Polsce 1994–2010; Rocznik Statystyczny Handlu Zagranicznego 2010.

in 1980 they had been 138.9. This figure (139.0) was not reached again until 2005. In 2009, it was 165.0.[18] The frequent changes of government initially made foreign investors hesitate, but by the mid 1990s it was obvious that repeatedly replacing the head of government had not fundamentally changed the economic policy. The consequent boom of foreign direct investment contributed considerably to the modernization of the economy.

The direction of foreign trade, for its part, changed drastically. In the 1980s, the old Federal Republic and the GDR had typically been Poland's second and third most important foreign trade partners, and reunited Germany ranked first by 1990 and continues to be far ahead. After the 1940s, the Soviet Union was Poland's biggest trade partner, but it is now the states of the European Union, including Germany, which annually absorbs between one third and one quarter of Poland's exports. Meanwhile, about 75–80 per cent of Poland's exports go to the EU as a whole. And not only has the structure of trade partners changed; that of goods has changed too. Machinery and other high-tech products make up a considerable share of Polish exports today, so as a supplier it is becoming ever more complementary to the economies of the old EU members.

Despite its declining workforce, agriculture still plays an important role. It suffers from much-too-small landholdings, most of all in the former Habsburg partition region in the south-east. There is much subsistence farming; only if there is a surplus is there anything to sell on the market. In 2007, for example, only 'slightly more than half of the production was meant for sale'.[19] In 2009, a total of 1,766 farms worked 38.6 per cent of the agricultural lands. Whereas about 80 per cent of them were smaller than 10 ha, fewer than 2 per cent were bigger than 50 ha, yet they made up 18.6 per cent of the agricultural lands. Despite their small size, these farms are highly competitive, even in the EU. Between 2000 and 2009, the average size of a farm grew slightly, from 7.2 to 8.0 ha.[20]

Poland thus has the smallest farms among the EU-27. Almost 15 per cent of the population works in agriculture, but the sector contributed only 3 per cent of the GDP, indicating a high degree of inefficiency. This in part reflects the fact that many of the post-1990 unemployed took refuge in agriculture and tried to make a living out of subsistence farming.

EU accession allowed farmers in the new member countries to receive direct subsidies whose amounts are incrementally raised from 25 per cent of the amount of the EU-15 in 2004 to 100 per cent in 2013. Between 2003 and 2008, Poland's now completely liberalized agricultural export to EU countries tripled from 2.6 to 8.5 billion euros. Its imports grew too, but Poland is an agricultural net export country (0.7 billion euros in 2008).[21] Polish agriculture uses few artificial fertilizers and pesticides, and

TABLE 5.2. Poland's most important trade partners (import and export) 1985–2009

IMPORT

Year	1985	1990	1995	2000	2005	2008	2009
Total volume (in million USD)	10,836.4	9,527.7	29,049.7	48,940.2	101,538.8	210,478.5	149,569.8
1st partner (in per cent)	USSR (34.4)	Germany (20.1)	Germany (26.6)	Germany (23.9)	Germany (24.7)	Germany (23.0)	Germany (22.4)
2nd partner (in per cent)	FRG (6.7)	USSR (19.8)	Italy (8.5)	Russia (9.4)	Russia (8.9)	Russia (9.7)	China (9.3)
3rd partner (in per cent)	GDR (6.6)	Italy (7.5)	Russia (6.7)	Italy (8.3)	Italy (7.1)	China (8.1)	Russia (8.5)

EXPORT

Year	1985	1990	1995	2000	2005	2008	2009
Total (in million USD)	11,489.4	14,321.6	22,894.9	31,651.3	89,378.1	171,859.9	136,641.3
1st partner in per cent	USSR (28.4)	Germany (25.1)	Germany (38.3)	Germany (34.9)	Germany (28.2)	Germany (25.0)	Germany (26.2)
2nd partner in per cent	FRG (8.7)	USSR (15.3)	Netherlands (5.6)	Italy (6.3)	France (6.2)	France (6.2)	France (6.9)
3rd partner in per cent	ČSSR (6.2)	Great Britain (7.1)	Russia (5.6)	France (5.2)	Italy (6.1)	Italy (6.0)	Italy (6.9)

Sources: Own compilation, based on GUS, Rocznik Statystyczny 2010, p. 37

ecologically its products are of high quality. Improved marketing would make greatly increased exports possible.

Meanwhile, the funds Poland receives from the European Union are a key factor in its economic growth. The country is the biggest net beneficiary in the EU. Between 1 May 2004 and 31 December 2010, Poland received a net total of 27.791 billion euros, 7.738 billion in 2010 alone.[22] Nearly all this money goes towards infrastructure. Like other post-socialist countries, Poland suffers from insufficient infrastructure. Its road system, which lacks good highways, is a primary concern. In 2000 it had only 358 km of motorways. Although this figure rose to 552 km in 2005, 765 km in 2008[23] and almost 900 km by the end of 2010, it is nonetheless wholly insufficient for the rapidly increasing car and truck traffic on its interior and transit routes. Poland's railroad network and air infrastructure are also in urgent need of renovation. Furthermore, both are completely oriented to Warsaw. For example, to go from Gdańsk to Szczecin by air, one must go via Warsaw. It was hoped that the UEFA European Championship, which Poland and Ukraine organized together in 2012, would result in a mighty push for improved infrastructure, but not all planned motorways were completed in time.

Society

In the ongoing restructuring of Poland's economy, its employment structure has shifted towards a more services-oriented society. In the past two decades, the share of workers employed in industry and agriculture has declined by slightly more than 20 per cent. On the other hand, the fields of trade and several smaller services sectors have grown. The rise in numbers of private sector employees, which comes at the expense of those employed in the public sector, has not been uninterrupted. This seems to be due mostly to swaying unemployment. In international comparison, the employment rate is very low.[24] At the end of 2009 it was 50.4 per cent (males 58.3 per cent, females 43.3 per cent).

Another factor in the low employment rate is the legal retirement age, which is sixty-five for men but only sixty for women, although both actually leave the workforce well before legal retirement age. Against considerable resistance, in spring 2012 the Tusk government pushed its demand through parliament to gradually raise both men's and women's legal retirement age to sixty-seven. Furthermore, today a high percentage of Poland's workers still retire early due to occupational disability. This figure was high in international comparison even in the socialist period, and in the 1990s it was even considered a way to ease the labour market situation, so for years people retiring because of occupational disability outnumbered

TABLE 5.3. Urbanization and occupational structure 1950–2009

Parameters	1950	1960	1970	1980	1985	1990	1995	2000	2005	2008	2009
Total population (in thousands)	25,035	29,795	32,658	35,735	37,341	38,183	38,609	38,254	38,157	38,136	38,167
Urban population (in per cent)	36.0	48.3	52.3	58.8	60.2	61.8	61.8	61.9	61.4	61.1	61.0
Rural population (in per cent)	63.2	51.7	47.7	41.2	39.8	38.2	38.2	38.2	38.6	38.9	39.0
Total workforce (in thousands)	10,186	12,401	15,175	17,325	17,135	16,485	15,486	15,480	14,116	15,800	15,885
Employees in state enterprises and in public service (in per cent)	47.4	58.0	68.0	73.4	71.5	51.1	37.6	27.3		27.5	26.1
Employees in the private sector (in per cent)	52.6	42.0	32.0	26.6	28.5	48.9	62.4	72.7		72.5	73.9
Percentage of women in state enterprises	30.6	33.1	39.4	43.5	44.2	46.0	47.7	48.7			
Employees according to branches (in per cent)											
Industry	20.7	25.5	29.3	30.3	29.2	28.0	24.9	21.5	22.1	21.8	20.8
Construction	5.0	6.5	7.1	7.7	7.5	7.5	5.5	5.8	5.1	6.3	6.3
Agriculture, forestry and fishing	54.5	44.5	35.5	30.6	29.9	27.6	26.9	26.2	16.2	15.2	15.3
Transport and traffic	4.5	5.6	6.2	6.5	6.2	5.6	5.6	5.4	4.9	5.2	5.1
Trade	4.8	6.0	6.9	7.5	7.8	8.4	12.7	14.0	16.0	16.3	16.1

TABLE 5.3. (Continued)

Parameters	1950	1960	1970	1980	1985	1990	1995	2000	2005	2008	2009
Real estate activities	0.9	2.0	2.6	3.5	3.8	3.8	3.5		1.4	1.4	1.4
Professional, scientific and technical activities	0.2	0.3	0.5	0.8	0.6	0.6			3.2	3.4	3.4
Education	1.9	3.0	3.9	4.3	5.3	6.7	6.0	6.1	8.1	7.5	7.8
Arts, entertainment and recreation	0.3	0.5	0.6	0.5	0.5	0.7			1.0	1.0	1.1
Human health and social work activities			2.8	3.5	4.2	5.5	6.7	6.2	5.3	5.2	5.3
Sports and tourism		0.2	0.6	0.7	0.7	0.4					
State administration and justice	2.9	1.6	1.6	1.3	1.6	1.6	2.6	3.4			
Finance and insurance	0.5	0.5	0.9	0.9	0.9	1.1	1.8	1.9	2.3	2.5	2.5
Accommodation and catering									1.7	2.0	2.0
Information and communication									1.4	1.7	1.7
Administrative and support service activities									2.5	2.7	2.7
Public administration and defence; compulsory social security									6.8	6.5	7.0
Without indication		2.4		1.9		1.8			2.0	1.4	1.4

Source: based on K. Ziemer, 'Nachbar Polen heute: Bevölkerung, Sozialstruktur, Politik', in W. Keim (ed.), *Vom Erinnern zum Verstehen: Pädagogische Perspektiven deutsch-polnischer Verständigung* (Berlin, 2003), 127–44; Mały Rocznik Statystyczny 2010.

those simply taking their pensions. Radical reforms at the end of the 1990s drastically reduced the number of early pensioners.[25]

Up to the 1960s, the dynamic post-World War II development of Poland's population was able to compensate for the enormous losses during the war, and by 1990 the population had grown to more than 38 million people. Since then it has stayed at that level. In 1980, the birth rate was still 19.5 per 1,000 inhabitants, but it was only 9.3 in 2004, when for the first time the number of deaths exceeded that of births by 40,000. Thereafter the birth rate rose somewhat, reaching 11.0 in 2009. However, demographers assume that by 2035 Poland will have only 36 million inhabitants. Life expectancy, which rose by about four years between 1990 and 2007, is currently seventy-one years for men and eighty for women. By 2035 it is expected to rise to seventy-seven and eighty-three years respectively, due in part to a decline in the infant mortality rate from 19.3 per 1,000 live births in 1990 to 5.9 in 2005. Since the population's share of people over sixty-four is expected to rise to 24.2 per cent by 2035,[26] in the medium term both Poland and other European states are likely to face considerable problems in guaranteeing social security standards for the elderly.

The Buzek government was the first to attempt a solution, with the pension scheme reform of 1 January 1999. In the long run, it was intended to provide a new basis for the pension scheme by combining a pay-as-you-go pension scheme, funded pensions and private pension provision. As of 2009, however, the worldwide financial crisis massively affected the profits of private pension funds. In early 2011, it also prompted the Tusk government (or rather, its parliamentary majority) to declare that in the future, instead of 7.3 per cent of gross wages, only 2.3 per cent should be transferred to private pension funds and the difference of 5 per cent to the Social Security Board (Zakład Ubezpieczeń Społecznych) so as to minimize the budget deficit. This controversial decision triggered a renewed debate on the pension scheme.

An even more grave problem that concerns the majority of the population is the situation of the public health system, which relies on obligatory deductions from gross wages to maintain the National Health Fund (Narodowy Fundusz Zdrowia). Established in 2003 under the SLD government, the fund settles all payments to doctors, hospitals and so on. It is considered a voracious giant allowing for no competition, a scenario that, in a context of poorly paid doctors and bad service in hospitals, favours corruption. Hospitals are usually highly indebted, and almost all of them are under the supervision of cities or districts. Private health providers working at the level of Western standards do exist, but they are much too expensive for the vast majority of Polish patients. Hence, the Polish health system suffers from extreme differences in service and growing tension.

TABLE 5.4. Percentage of unemployment in Poland 1990–2010 (percentage of the population economically active in the civil sector, in January of each year)

1990	1991	1992	1993	1994	1995	1996	1997	1998	1999	2000
0.3	6.6	12.1	14.2	16.7	16.1	15.4	13.1	10.7	11.1	13.7

2001	2002a*	2002b	2003a	2003b	2004	2005	2006	2007	2008	2009	2010
15.7	18.1	20.1	18.6	20.6	20.6	19.4	18.0	15.1	11.5	10.4	12.9

*Data basis variant a: Agriculture Census 1996; data basis variant b: National Census of Population and Housing 2002; from 2004 data basis: National Census of Population and Housing.

Source: Own compilation on the basis of data from the Central Statistical Office (http://www.stat.gov.pl./gus/5840_677_ENG_HTML.htm; accessed 3 February 2011).

In the 2000s, no field occasioned more strikes and protests than did the health sector.[27]

The growing unemployment caused by the privatization of the economy and competitive pressure on companies was a new phenomenon, as under the socialist system there had formally been full employment. Now social security systems had to be built from scratch. Given the quickly rising number of jobless, the initially generous – for a post-socialist country – unemployment compensation had to be reduced drastically. By the end of 2010, a worker was entitled to unemployment benefits for only a six-month period. Only in districts with an unemployment rate more than 150 per cent above the national average were benefits paid for six more months. The percentage of registered unemployed receiving financial benefits dropped from 80 per cent in 1990 to 52.3 per cent in 1995, 20.3 per cent in 2000 and 13.2 per cent by the end of 2006.[28] In the first three months, the benefit was 742 zloty (c. 185 euros); it was then reduced to 582 zloty (c. 145 euros). After this, any necessary social benefits were paid according to available funds and individual situations.

The nationwide average unemployment figures hid enormous regional differences. In the former German parts of the country in the north and west, regions with relatively large numbers of former state-owned agricultural estates were particularly hard hit by unemployment. Upon their privatization, disproportionately high numbers of employees were reduced. Those who were dismissed typically had few qualifications and little mobility, and thus had hardly any chance of finding new jobs.

Similarly problematic was the collapse of companies that in their regions had had near monopolies on jobs – for example, the textile industry in Lodz, a city temporarily declared a deprived area. On the other hand, there was almost full employment in centres of economic growth such as Warsaw, Wrocław or Poznań. After Poland's accession to the EU, Great

Britain, Ireland and the Scandinavian states opened their labour markets to Polish citizens, and hundreds of thousands of young Poles seized the opportunity to make more money abroad than at home. This undoubtedly relieved the labour market, as is clearly obvious from the statistics, but the consequences were ambivalent. Along with an influx of foreign currency saved by these economic emigrants and their gains in know-how came negative socio-economic effects, as well as further consequences for the already problematic demographic development. Moreover, economic migration affected the cohesion of many families (producing so-called euro orphans). Since the end of the economic boom in the British Isles, however, many Poles have returned, contributing capital and know-how to their country's economic growth.

Another unwanted legacy of real socialism is the low pay in public sectors such as health care or education – that is, sectors that mainly employ white-collar workers. In the socialist period, the working class had been said to be the 'ruling class', a relation that was also supposed to be reflected in the wage structure. At the top were miners, whom the party leadership had repeatedly proclaimed as a kind of working class aristocracy of crucial significance for the country's economy. In the 1990s, however, a crisis in coal mining not only put their jobs in danger but also affected their self-esteem. In response, they transferred patterns of behaviour and experiences from the socialist period to the new system, for example by striking to enforce political demands and pay rises. In several cases, governments and the parliament, faced with sometimes violent demonstrations by miners in Warsaw, gave in and acceded to their demands.

Meanwhile, the number of those with a university degree has risen considerably. The number of university students went from 400,000 in 1990 to 1,954,000 in 2005 (when about half were students attending fee-based evening and weekend classes). This growth was connected to an expansion of the university system that pushed the number of state universities from ten in 1990 to seventeen in 2010. Additionally, there are twenty-three specialized universities (for medicine, economics, agriculture, etc.) as well as two universities supervised by the Catholic Church. Between 1991/92 and 2005/2006, the number of private universities exploded from twelve to 315.[29] The quality of the education they offer ranges from excellent to below average, however, and the demographic low is finding expression in declining numbers of students; hence, the economic existence of not only some private universities but also some faculties at renowned state universities is at risk.

As in almost all post-communist states, the system of social partnership is weakly developed, for the time being. This seems surprising, given Solidarność's political significance during the system change, but in fact it has never regained the importance it had as a trade union in 1980/81. Remarkably, the number of trade union members in Poland has almost constantly declined over the two decades since the system change. Today as before, the biggest trade union association is the OPZZ, an ally of the PZPR in the past and the SLD today. In the mid 1990s it still had 4.5 million members, but by the end of 2007 they numbered only 700,000. Solidarność, which in 1981 claimed to have almost ten million members, reported only 1.1 million in 2001 and 720,000 in 2005. A third big trade union, the Forum Federation, was established in 2002 after it split from the OPZZ. In 2011 it had more than 400,000 members, according to its own figures.[30]

The OPZZ and Solidarność once were very much involved in everyday politics. In 1991, Solidarność was even elected to the Sejm and the Senate as a trade union. Since a 1997 amendment to the Law on Political Parties stipulated a clear separation of political parties and other organizations, however, both have primarily concentrated on their trade union activities. The OPZZ clearly is still close to the SLD, whereas Solidarność is close to the PiS. Contrasting with the declining membership in trade unions – whose strongholds are at state enterprises and whose chances of gaining a foothold in new private enterprises are quite low – is the growing significance of entrepreneurs' associations.

The Catholic Church is still an important societal power, as more than 90 per cent of the population are its nominal members. As the main opponent of the PZPR's attempts to force not only a new political and economic order but also new values on Polish society, and as an organization that in the 1980s had outspokenly supported the opposition and contributed to making the roundtable a success, the Church was at the peak of its popularity in 1989. However, its leadership initially failed to recognize that its role was changing within a now pluralist society. The massive public presence of Church representatives intervening in political matters, endorsing certain political parties and so on caused its approval rate to drop from 88 per cent in 1989 to 38 per cent in 1993. Since then, by taking great care to control its public appearance, the Church has stabilized its approval ratings at 60–70 per cent.[31]

To be sure, indications of secularization are also obvious in Poland. Yet in European comparison, the Church is almost uniquely rooted in Polish society. About 40 per cent regularly attend Sunday services, including among the young generation, though with strong regional differences. Most recently, however, some cracks have appeared in this image of strength. Since the death of Pope John Paul II, the Church has lacked a leader. The Episcopate is obviously split, and the division extends to clerics and believers as well. The Episcopate lacks the necessary will to discipline the clerical-nationalist radio channel *Radio Maryja*, which is under control of the Redemptorist Order and propagates anti-Semitic, anti-European and xenophobic rhetoric with the overt backing of several bishops. So far, priests have only half-heartedly been investigated for possible cooperation with the communist secret service, despite the Archbishop of Warsaw's spectacular resignation in early 2007 after only two days in office, following the appearance on the internet of documents demonstrating his readiness to cooperate with the secret service. Compared to the rest of Europe, Poland will have a large number of clerics and nuns for a long time to come, but in recent years the number of vocations has clearly gone down.[32]

Prospects

Poland was the first 'real socialist' country to launch a transformation of its political and economic system, and with Balcerowicz's 'shock treatment' it embarked on a courageous – and, for society, initially very painful – path towards reform. When the individual factors of system transformation are considered in the overall context, the resultant balance differs according to each field of investigation but is positive on the whole.

The system of political institutions, which developed from a presidential-parliamentary to a parliamentary-presidential system between 1989 and 1997, has mainly proven its worth (if one overlooks the unclear distribution of competences regarding the formulation of foreign policy). Nevertheless, in 2009 three former presidents of the Constitutional Court declared that the President of the State's role as an 'arbiter' between the political powers had actually proven inappropriate and demanded the introduction of either a clearly parliamentary or clearly presidential system.[33] The new President Komorowski wanted to introduce constitutional provisions that would take Poland's EU membership into account in spheres such as law-making, and further Poland's goal of membership in the eurozone.[34]

A deep cut in the history of the Third Republic after 1989/90 was the attempt by PiS governments in the period 2005–2007 – and chiefly by Jarosław Kaczyński from May 2006 to August 2007 – to establish a 'Fourth Republic'. Correctly discerning that after 1989 the state apparatus had not been thoroughly checked for former cooperation with the communist secret service, that parts of the old nomenclature now were economically better off than they had ever been in the communist period, and that corruption is a fundamental evil of state and society,[35] they confronted these ills with a therapy that sometimes greatly overshot the mark and moreover did not accord with the principles of the rule of law. Its basic approach, albeit ideologically in reverse, sometimes betrayed its authors' socialization in the People's Republic. For example, it preserved both the conviction that the state needed strict top-down rule and the distrust of 'bottom-up' initiatives by civil society. The lack of basic consensus on undebated democratic values among the parties represented in the parliament is at least as serious a problem. Nonetheless, the PiS leadership under Jarosław Kaczyński, with its slogan of the 'Fourth Republic', maintains that the basic structures of the People's Republic are only partly removed, that values such as freedom and democracy or social justice are still far from being realized, and that 'actual' system change is yet to come.[36]

Opinion polls reveal remnants of authoritarian attitudes among the population. The general tendency is towards slight or clear dissatisfaction with the actual functioning of democracy, at least at the national level. On the other hand, there is growing satisfaction with politics at the municipal level.[37]

The low organizational capacity of civil society and low degree of social capital count as weak spots in Poland's development over the past two decades and find expression in, for example, low trust within society. Yet a number of studies have emphasized precisely the dominance of informal structures within Polish society as the factor that made victory possible for Solidarność. The comparably strong economy did not develop over the course of a long process but resulted from a market economy model introduced at the outset of transformation and at high social cost. The activity of the state, though, must be considered rather weak.[38]

Economic development has differed in each individual sector, but on the whole it is satisfactory, not counting the considerable regional disparities. This holds also for income levels. In 2009, the average gross wage in the Masovian Voivodeship, which includes Warsaw, was 4,180 zloty (c. 1,060 euros), whereas in the Carpathian foothills it was only 2,741 zloty (c. 685 euros).[39] Other drawbacks are the high unemployment rate and the poverty of low-income groups such as the unemployed or families with many children. These are hardly balanced by state social security measures, for although the state spends quite a high share of its budget on social security measures, the comparatively low GDP, in absolute numbers, means that individual payments are very modest. In terms of per capita GDP, measured by purchasing power parity, Poland pulled ahead of Latvia and Lithuania in 2009, but at 61 per cent of the EU-27 average, it was still fifth from the bottom in the EU.[40]

Concerning the standard of living, considerable discrepancies remain between urban and rural areas. They concern the health system, educational opportunities and cultural offerings, among other things. The urbanization process, which was observed over decades, came to a standstill in the 1990s (see Table 5.4). Today, 39 per cent of the population live in the countryside. Many of them must be considered losers of the transformation. Since 1999, the Ministry of Agriculture has in its name the completion 'Ministry of Agriculture and of Rural Development'. However, to date no one has come up with a coherent formulation to make country life more attractive to, say, doctors or teachers.

Employment patterns of the past two decades show a clear decrease in employees in the primary and secondary sectors. Yet no new social class, such as a middle class, has developed. Furthermore, the old structures of social stratification are mostly preserved. 'The privileged remain privileged, the disadvantaged stay disadvantaged.'[41]

Poland's accession to the EU has met with growing support thanks to the subsidies that have benefited even EU-sceptical groups, such as farmers. In April 2010, the approval rating of Poland's EU membership was 86 per cent, compared to only 9 per cent disapproving. Since 2001, the share of those who agreed the system change has been worth the effort has also grown significantly (from 56 per cent in 2001 to 65 per cent in 2004 and 83 per cent in 2010), whereas during the same period the share of those disagreeing fell from 30 to 9 per cent. As for the question of whether the change has brought more gains than losses to people in Poland, negative responses prevailed for a long time,[42] but now this relation has been reversed.[43]

Notwithstanding its specific problems, Poland boasts a stable political system and a comparatively robust economic system. In 2009, Poland coped better with the world economic crisis than did all other EU countries. Poland has become a bastion of stability in Eastern Europe and serves as an attractive model of successful transformation for the societies of its eastern neighbours Ukraine and Belarus, and beyond. At the same time, it shows signs of developing informal structures among the new EU member countries, thus becoming, in a way, their 'natural' representative not only because of its demographic and economic weight but also for political reasons.

Klaus Ziemer is Professor of Political Science at the Cardinal Stefan Wyszynski University in Warsaw (until 2011 at the University of Trier). From 1998 to 2008 he directed the German Historical Institute in Warsaw. His main fields of research are processes of political and socio-economic transformation in East Central and Eastern Europe, Polish contemporary history, German–Polish relations after World War II, and history policy. He has authored, among others, *Das politische System Polens* (VS Springer, 2013) and was co-editor with Jerzy Borejsza of *Totalitarian and*

Authoritarian Regimes in Europe: Legacies and Lessons from the Twentieth Century (Berghahn, 2006).

Notes

1. See, e.g., A. Przeworski, 'Some Problems in the Study of the Transition to Democracy', in G. O'Donnell, P.C. Schmitter and L. Whitehead (eds), *Transitions from Authoritarian Rule: Comparative Perspectives* (Baltimore, 1986), 47–63, here 54. The diary entries of the Episcopate's then press spokesman (and later bishop of Łowicz), Alojzy Orszulik, who was an important mediator between Solidarność and the PZPR leadership, sometimes read as an illustration of Przeworski's theses on cooperation between compromise-ready parts of the old and new political elites; see A. Orszulik, *Czas przełomu: Notatki z rozmów z władzami PRL w latach 1981–1989* [Time of Turnaround: Notes from the Talks to Those in Charge of the PPR 1981–1989)] (Warsaw/Ząbki), 2006.
2. The First Republic refers to the Polish-Lithuanian Commonwealth (until the third Polish partition in 1795); the Second Republic to the interwar period (1918–1939); and the Third Republic to the Polish state since 1989/90.
3. For details on the electoral system and the results, see among others K. Ziemer, 'Auf dem Weg zum Systemwandel in Polen (II)', *Osteuropa* 39(11/12) (1989), 957–80, here 965ff. The *Gazeta Wyborcza* (26 June 1989, 4) even demonstrated that the result of the elections did not reflect the negotiated ratio of 65:35 but a 37:63 proportion.
4. See L. Balcerowicz, *Socialism, Capitalism and Transformation* (New York, 1995).
5. '. . . [W]e, . . . the Polish people – every citizen of the Republic, both those believing in God as the source of Truth, Justice, the Good, and the Beautiful, and those not sharing this belief but deriving these universal values from other sources – hereby establish the Constitution . . .'.
6. See figures in K. Ziemer, *Das politische System Polens: Eine Einführung* (Wiesbaden, 2013), 55.
7. See the first Law on Political Parties of 28 July 1990 (Dz. U. 1990, No. 54, Pos. 312) and the currently valid one from 27 June 1997 (Dz. U. 1997, No. 98, Pos. 604) and its subsequent amendments.
8. Law from 9 October 2009 on amending the Law on Prosecution as well as some other laws (Dz. U. 2009, No. 178, Pos. 1375).
9. See CBOS, 'Opinie o działalności Parlamentu, Prezydenta i władz samorządowych' [Opinions on the Activity of the Parliament, the President and Self-Administration], *Komunikat z badań* 155/2014, Warsaw, November 2014 (www.cbos.pl/SPISKOM. POL/2014/K_155_14.PDF; accessed 13 August 2015); CBOS, 'Samorządność w Polsce: bilans dwudziestolecia' [Self-Administration in Poland: An Account of the Past 20 Years], *BS* 144, Warsaw, October 2010 (www.cbos.pl/SPISKOM.POL/2010/K_144_10. PDF; accessed 3 February 2011).
10. On 7 and 8 June 2003, 58.8 per cent of those eligible to vote participated in the referendum. Of valid votes, 77.5 per cent were in favour of Poland's accession to the EU; 22.5 per cent were against it.
11. For a detailed list of these regional and local referendums, see the homepage of the State Electoral Commission (www.pkw.gov.pl; accessed 3 February 2011).

12. T. Skory, 'Polskie partie to fikcja' [Polish Parties Are a Fiction], *RMF*24, Fakty, 11 December 2012 (http://www.rmf24.pl/fakty/polska/news-polskie-partie-to-fikcja,nId,72 4993; accessed 24 April 2015).

13. See, among others, CBOS, 'Partie bliższe i dalsze: Identyfikacje partyjne Polaków' [The Far-Away and the Close Parties: Identification with Political Parties in Poland], *BS* 73, Warsaw, May 2007 (www.cbos.pl/SPISKOM.POL/2007/K_073_07.PDF; accessed 3 February 2011). As a matter of fact, in the 2001 elections a party founded by previous PO MP Janusz Palikot ('Palikot Movement') received 10 per cent of votes.

14. See Ziemer, *Das politische System Polens*, 52 and the composition of the Sejm parliamentary clubs and circles at the end of the term (http://www.sejm.gov.pl/Sejm7.nsf/kluby. xsp; accessed 14 August 2015) as compared to the electoral result of 2011.

15. See, e.g., the Report on the Activity of the Ombudsman on the occasion of the 20th anniversary of the office in May 2008 (http://www.rpo.gov.pl/pliki/12108653290.pdf; accessed 3 February 2011) as well as the annual account (https://www.rpo.gov.pl/pl/content/informacje-roczne-o-dzialalnosci-rpo; accessed 14 August 2015).

16. See, among others, M. Maliszewski, 'Fernsehen und Rundfunk in Polen: Marktentwicklung und politische Einbettung', *Polen-Analysen* 6 (6 February 2007) (http://www.laender-analysen.de/polen/pdf/PolenAnalysen06.pdf; accessed 3 February 2011).

17. Mały Rocznik Statystyczny, Concise Statistical Yearbook (2010), 484.

18. Ibid., 610f.

19. M. Kwasowski and S. Zaleski, 'Die Landwirtschaft in Polen fünf Jahre nach dem Beitritt zur Europäischen Union', *Polen-Analysen* 51 (5 May 2009), 5 (http://www.laender-analy sen.de/polen/pdf/PolenAnalysen51.pdf; accessed 3 February 2011).

20. Mały Rocznik Statystyczny, *Concise Statistical Yearbook*, 312ff.

21. Kwasowski and Zaleski, 'Die Landwirtschaft', 3.

22. Information from Poland's Ministry of Finance (http://www.mf.gov.pl/files_/unia_europejska/programy_i_fundusze_ue/przeplywy_finansowe/2008/transfery_grud zien_2010.pdf; accessed 3 February 2011).

23. Mały Rocznik Statystyczny, *Concise Statistical Yearbook*, 368.

24. The employment rate is defined as the number of working people aged 15–64 in relation to the entire population of this age cohort.

25. See figures given in S. Golinowska, 'The National Model of the Welfare State in Poland: Tradition and Changes', in S. Golinowska, P. Hengstenberg and M. Żukowski (eds), *Diversity and Commonality in European Social Policies: The Forging of a European Social Model* (Warsaw, 2009), 213–60, here 235f.

26. See ibid., 243.

27. Ibid., 230.

28. See M. Szylko-Skoczny, 'Arbeitsmarktlage und Arbeitsmarktpolitik', in D. Bingen and K. Ruchniewicz (eds), *Länderbericht Polen* (Bonn, 2009), 294–308, here 304.

29. S. Steier, 'Bildungspolitik und Bildungssystem', in Bingen and Ruchniewicz, *Länderbericht Polen*, 477–95, here 479.

30. C. Rode, 'Die aktuelle Situation der Gewerkschaften in Polen', *Polen-Analysen* 36 (1 July 2008), 2–12 (http://www.laender-analysen.de/polen/pdf/PolenAnalysen36.pdf; accessed 3 February 2011).

31. See the table on trust in institutions in Ziemer, *Das politische Systems Polens*, 304.

32. For an account of religious ties in Poland, see e.g. the contribution by the head of the Catholic press agency KAI, Marcin Przeciszewski, 'Kościół, 20 lat wolności: religijność Polaków' [The Church, 20 Years of Freedom: Religiosity among the Poles], published

on 7 September 2009 (http://ekai.pl/wydarzenia/raport/x21292/kosciol-lat-wolnosci-religijnosc-polakow/?print=1; accessed 3 February 2011).

33. A. Zoll, M. Safjan and J. Stępień, 'Oświadczenie byłych Prezesów Trybunału Konstytucyjnego' [Declaration by Former Chairmen of the Constitutional Court], *Gazeta Wyborcza*, 5 February 2009 (http://wyborcza.pl/1,76842,6237771,Oswiadczenie_bylych_Prezesow_Trybunalu_Konstytucyjnego.html; accessed 3 February 2011).

34. Poland's current constitution stipulates that the zloty is the country's currency. On Komorowski's intentions, see e.g. 'Konstytucja Komorowskiego ukłonem w stronę PiS', *Wprost* 24 (15 November 2010) (http://www.wprost.pl/ar/217789/Konstytucja-Komorowskiego-uklonem-w-strone-PiS; accessed 3 February 2011).

35. The corruption index of Transparency International (yearly report 2009) presents Poland as no. 49 of a total of 180 states, together with Bhutan and Jordan (http://www.transparency.org/publications/annual_ report; accessed 3 February 2011).

36. On this, see e.g. S. Kowalski, 'Konstrukcja i dekonstrukcja III RP: Symetrie i asymetrie' [Construction and Deconstruction of the III Polish Republic: Symmetries and Asymmetries], in M. Czyżewski, S. Kowalski and T. Tabako (eds), *Retoryka i polityka: Dwudziestolecie polskiej transformacji* [Rhetorics and Politics: The 20th Anniversary of Polish Transformation] (Warsaw, 2010), 47–81.

37. In October 2010, 52 per cent of interviewees stated that people like themselves were able to influence municipal affairs; see CBOS, 'Samorządność w Polsce'.

38. See J. Wilkin, 'Rozpad i instytucjonalizacja ładu społeczno-ekonomicznego w Polsce: przypadek transformacji postsocjalistycznej' [Decay and Institutionalization of the Socio-economic Order in Poland: An Example of Post-Socialist Transformation], in *Więzi społeczne i przemiany gospodarcze: Polska i inne kraje europejskie. Zbiór esejów na jubileusz profesor Zofii Moreckiej* [Social Ties and Economic Restructuring: Poland and Other European Countries. Compilation of Essays in Honour of Prof. Zofia Morecka] (Warsaw, 2009), 64–74, here 68. See also Poland's comparatively weak position in the management index of the Bertelsmann Transformation Index, where it nevertheless moved from no. 53 (2008) to no. 19 (2010) because it had coped well with the world economic crisis (http://www.bertelsmann-transformation-index.de/bti/ranking/management-index; accessed 3 February 2011).

39. Mały Rocznik Statystyczny, *Concise Statistical Yearbook*, 658.

40. See the Eurostat press release of 15 December 2010 (http://epp.eurostat.ec.europa.eu/cache/ITY_PUBLIC/2–15122010–BP/DE/2–15122010–BP-DE.PDF; accessed 3 February 2011).

41. J. Wasilewski, 'Formowanie się nowej struktury społecznej' [Shaping a New Social Structure], in J. Wasilewskiego (ed.), *Współczesne społeczeństwo polskie: Dynamika zmian* [Today's Society in Poland: Dynamics of Change] (Warsaw, 2006), 47–102, here 99.

42. In 2001: 15 as compared to 55 per cent; all others: 'both . . . and' or 'difficult to decide'; see CBOS, 'Postawy wobec transformacji ustrojowej i oceny jej skutków' [Attitudes towards System Transformation and Assessment of Its Results], *BS* 94, Warsaw, July 2010 (http://www.cbos.pl/SPISKOM.POL/2010/K_094_10.PDF; accessed 3 February 2011).

43. In 2010: 47 as compared to 16 per cent; CBOS, 'Postawy wobec transformacji ustrojowej i oceny jej skutków'.

Chapter 6

THE CZECH REPUBLIC

❦

Karel Vodička

Introduction

Historical Introduction

After Warsaw Pact troops invaded Czechoslovakia in 1968, the originally democratic but now occupied country endured the most massive political repression in Europe. The Communist Party leadership, which the Russian occupation powers installed as governor in 1969, organized mass purges to intimidate and discipline the population. Several hundred thousand citizens who had sympathized with the reforms of the 'Prague Spring' or condemned the military occupation of Czechoslovakia were punished by employment bans.[1] A total of 400,000 Czechoslovakian citizens fled into exile.[2]

Ruling by way of the hierarchically structured party and state apparatus as well as massive indoctrination, the Communist Party leadership secured its monopoly of power through a complicated system of institutional and personal relationships. The most powerful tool for securing power was cadre policy, a job monopoly that made it possible to withdraw anybody's material basis of existence. This disciplining mechanism was ruthlessly employed during the period of so-called consolidation after the suppression of the Prague Spring. Half a million reform-oriented members were expelled from the Communist Party and forced to resign from their leading positions. Forty per cent of economic managers and 40 per cent of journalists lost their jobs this way.[3] The party's campaign of vengeance extended even to party expellees' children, who were not allowed to attend secondary schools or study at universities.[4] Punishing children was the most effective disciplining tool of all, as parents opted to dutifully sacrifice themselves by acting loyal to the regime, rather than put their children's future at risk.

Notes for this chapter begin on page 178.

State of Research

Research on the division of Czechoslovakia has clearly shown that the break-up of the Czech and Slovak Federal Republic did not reflect the will of the population and must be counted as a cost of transformation.[5] The Czech Republic is considered to have made much progress towards democratic consolidation, enough to make de-democratization most improbable.[6] The Bertelsmann Transformation Index (BTI)[7] lists it as the transformation country with the highest level of development in terms of democracy and market economy.[8] Analyses of the political system affirm that the Czech Republic is a parliamentary democracy that has free and fair elections and is mostly stabilized institutionally. However, democracy deficits are evident in the behaviour of formal and informal political actors and at the level of civil society, according to the BTI 2010 Country Report on the Czech Republic.[9]

The Structure of this Study

This chapter first sketches Czechoslovakia's 'Velvet Revolution' and briefly outlines the causes and consequences of its split. It moves on to describe the establishment of the democratic constitutional state and the relevant political institutions at the central, regional and municipal levels, as well as their function in the political process. At the same time, it discusses the party system, the electoral system, elections and voter behaviour. A section on the economy explains the economic constitution and development of the fields of industry, commerce and trade. The following section, on society, documents the current social structure, lines of social conflicts and the current situation of trade unions, churches and civil society. The focus then turns to a thorough analysis of the state of consolidation of the political system and the market economy, from various points of view. The study closes with an overview and a glimpse at the future.

System Change

Masses and Elites

Ten years of political dead silence followed the Warsaw Pact troops' occupation of Czechoslovakia in 1968. Those citizens who stayed in the country suffered from depression and social apathy, expressing their fear by retreating to the private sphere. A kind of social schizophrenia spread: publicly, the population behaved loyally towards the hated regime and paid homage to the Communist Party, whereas in private people were bold enough to express their true thoughts. Lies and hypocrisy were therefore part of everyday life.

Only with the emergence of the dissident movement Charta 77 was this silence broken. However, Charta 77 remained restricted to a small, elite circle that was completely isolated by state security. The masses continued their passive resistance. At last the launch of perestroika in the Soviet Union offered good reason to hope for an end to communist dictatorship, and by the end of the 1980s, a broad opposition movement had developed.

The Peaceful Revolution

Triggered by a student demonstration, the peaceful revolution of 1989 led to a quick implosion of the already undermined communist dictatorship. The brutality of the police suppression of the students' demonstration on 17 November 1989 mobilized the population – it was rumoured that one student had been killed – and consequently sparked a series of mass demonstrations with up to 800,000 participants, an unrestricted strike of university students and a nationwide general strike lasting two hours.

After ten days of peaceful demonstrations, the communist rulers gave in to the pressure exerted by the people. Communist Party leader Miloš Jakeš stepped down on 24 November 1989. The handover of power was negotiated between the Citizens' Forum, consisting of twelve opposition groups, and Prime Minister Ladislav Adamec. On 10 December 1989, as his last official act, President Husák appointed the Marián Čalfa government, which had a non-communist majority. In December 1989, the members of the Communist Federal Assembly, who up to then had been used to agreeing unconditionally to everything, elected Václav Havel, the protagonist of the anti-communist movement, president of Czechoslovakia, and Alexander Dubček, the emblematic figure of the 'Prague Spring', president of the Federal Assembly.

The Split of Czechoslovakia

On 1 January 1993, Czechoslovakia, the 'lucky child of the Versailles Treaty', dissolved itself by dismemberment.[10] From its estate there developed two new subjects of international law, the Czech Republic and the Slovak Republic. The split of the Czech and Slovak Federal Republic was part of a process of dissolving federal multinational states in Central and Eastern Europe after the breakdown of the communist dictatorships that had held these states together through violence, assisted by centralized Communist Party structures. However, in Czechoslovakia – in contrast to other countries – the split did not accord with the will of the majority of the people. Rather, the main causes of the division were the two peoples' different political cultures, divergent voting behaviour and lack of appropriate constitutional mechanisms for solving conflicts.

The Czech and Slovak peoples, though linguistically related, differed culturally. Their different attitudes towards market economics and privatization were particularly significant.[11] In the 1992 parliamentary elections, Czechs voted mainly for radical reforms that Slovaks opposed, so the Czech and Slovak winners of the elections supported respectively contradictory concepts. Moreover, the post-election coalition negotiations were marred by reluctance to compromise – neither side was willing to share power, positions or influence in the context of the future mass privatization of state property. The election results gave the Czech-Slovak controversies explosive momentum, which over the next few weeks led to the political decision to dissolve the common state.[12]

The actors in this division had prevented a referendum on the issue, leaving both Slovaks and Czechs feeling betrayed. Opinion polls showed that they would have voted against separation.[13] The most wholehearted supporters of the common state were Hungarians in Slovakia who believed a Czechoslovakian state would be the better protector of their minority rights. Subsequent developments proved they were right: the Slovak-Hungarian national conflict, which had been hardly perceptible in the Czechoslovakian state, was re-radicalized in independent Slovakia.[14] The dissolution of Czechoslovakia was a loss for both peoples that must figure as part of the price paid for transformation. Both successor states had to bear the political and economic consequences.[15]

The Establishment of the Democratic Constitutional State

Politics

The constitution
The currently valid constitution[16] takes the constitutional document of the first Czechoslovakian state as its historic model. This constitutional tradition supplied a constitutional structure, a parliamentary governmental system with two chambers, and proportional representation for the Chamber of Deputies. Certain regulations in the Czech constitution (e.g. immutability of its core provisions, regulations on the Constitutional Court) appear somewhat influenced by the German Basic Law, but unfortunately the Czech Republic did not adopt the constructive vote of no

confidence that a German government can be subject to. The constitution provides for just one immediate, democratic legitimation of a central constitutional body, namely, parliamentary elections. All other central constitutional bodies, including the President of the State, derive from the parliament and are correspondingly less legitimated.

President of the State, government, administration

PRESIDENT OF THE STATE   The President of the State is elected by both chambers of the parliament. The president is not accountable to anyone for his or her exercise of the office's authority and cannot be relieved of office during his or her term. Since the founding of the Czech Republic in 1993, there have been two Presidents of the State, Václav Havel and Václav Klaus.

The domestic and foreign political merits of Václav Havel, the first head of state of the Czech Republic, are immense. The most important figure of the anti-communist resistance, in 1989 he became the head of the Citizens' Forum (Občanské fórum), which organized the Velvet Revolution. As president after 1990, he supported democratically oriented forces and spoke out energetically in favour of keeping the parliamentary rules.[17]

Václav Klaus, for his part, is known for his remarkable ability to gain majorities and has been a key protagonist of transformation, in both the positive and the negative sense. He founded the Citizens' Democratic Party (Občanská demokratická strana, ODS), enforced his own ideas of radical economic reform and was a major player in the split of Czechoslovakia. His marked Euro-scepticism is often criticized both at home and abroad.

GOVERNMENT   The strong parliamentary faction of the politically isolated Communist Party, which is always in the opposition, has persistently hindered the formation of government coalitions. Stalemate is the norm following parliamentary elections, as no party has been able to assemble a convincing majority in the parliament: either the respective government has an extremely narrow majority, or it is tolerated by only one opposition party. Yet despite difficult majority situations in the Chamber of Deputies, Czech governments have been more stable than most in the post-communist area. In the 1989–2008 period, governments in many Eastern European states changed almost every year,[18] whereas 'only' four times (in 1998, 2004, 2005 and 2009) did a Czech government have to resign before the end of its term of office.

The first government coalition with a convincing majority emerged after the parliamentary elections of 2010. With 118 out of a total 200 MPs, the centre-right coalition consisted of the ODS and two newly founded parties, TOP 09 and the Public Affairs party (Věci veřejné). However, the populist Public Affairs, which lacks both a clear profile and experienced politicians, might prove an element of uncertainty in this coalition.

ADMINISTRATION   The Czech Republic is a centralized state. The central administrative bodies, which can be founded only through passage of an appropriate law, are in charge of the whole territory of the state. Act 2/1969 is the basis of two different kinds of central bodies of state administration: those headed by a member of the government (ministries), and those that are not. The central bodies of state administration are hierarchically organized and entitled by law to pass generally binding legal regulations within the scope of the law. Constitutional responsibility lies with the respective minister. Deputy ministers have no constitutional status.

Political parties and party system
The Czech Republic's first free parliamentary elections in 1990 were tantamount to a referendum in which the revolutionary movements convincingly prevailed against communism. This short period of negative consensus among the population came to an end as the main goal of politics shifted from overcoming the communist dictatorship to participating in power and upholding one's own ideas of democracy and market economics. A turbulent process of differentiation and polarization convulsed the entire party system. In 1990, MPs from nine parties were elected to the Federal Assembly, but factions dissolved so quickly that by the end of the 1990–1992 parliamentary term, a total of twenty-seven different political groups had been represented in the Federal Assembly.[19] After the parliamentary elections of 1992, however, a bipolar party system was firmly established, so that two strong parties (the ODP and the Social Democrats) take turns forming the government with smaller coalition partners.

Electoral system, elections and voting behaviour
Elections are based on the secret ballot and direct, universal and equal suffrage. Senate elections are conducted by a majoritarian method; elections to the Chamber of Deputies go by proportional representation. Czech citizens aged eighteen or over are eligible to vote; Amendment 204/2000 to the electoral law extended this right to those living in a foreign country. There is no compulsory voting.

Elections to the Chamber of Deputies are held every four years. According to Amendment 121/2002 to the electoral law, there exist fourteen constituencies that are identical to autonomous districts (*kraje*). Each party prepares lists of candidates for each constituency. The seats are distributed at constituency level according to the D'Hondt highest average method. Modifications to the proportional system include a percentage clause (5 per cent per party, including cases of election coalitions) and so-called preferential votes. Preferential votes give the voter the option to mark four names on a party's list of candidates. If at least 5 per cent of voters in a constituency use this option, the seats are distributed according to preferential votes. In the 2010 elections to the Chamber of Deputies, voters happily used their preferential votes, submitting 3.7 million of them. This radically changed the sequence of candidates on the party lists, and some (unpopular) high-ranking party functionaries withdrew from politics as a result. Though the possibility of preferential voting makes the democratic principle stronger, such a vote can have the problematic side effect of political newcomers making up two-thirds of a newly elected parliament.

Voting behaviour is particularly influenced by citizens' social status, values, faith and education. About a third of the population votes according to its economic position. Higher-income voters vote above all for right-wing parties, while those with low incomes tend towards Social Democrats or Communists. Social Democrats are elected mainly by workers – primarily those in the traditionally industrial regions of Northern Moravia and Northern Bohemia who, due to growing social disparities, are dissatisfied with their situation. However, Social Democratic voters identify only little with the party. Academics and entrepreneurs prefer the ODS. The highly disciplined base voters of the Communist Party of Bohemia and Moravia are mostly pensioners, often former party cadres who are disappointed with developments since 1989/90; young protest voters also choose these parties.[20]

Parliament
The legislative power lies exclusively with the bicameral parliament, consisting of the 200 representatives in the Chamber of Deputies (Poslanecká sněmovna) and the 81 senators in the Senate (Senát). The Chamber of Deputies dominates the legislative procedure. If the Senate rejects a bill, its veto may be overruled by an absolute majority of all representatives. Only 2 per cent – a very small number – of laws derive from a Senate initiative.[21] Nevertheless, the Senate has proven its worth as an institutional safeguard against manipulation of electoral law and the constitution by the big parties.

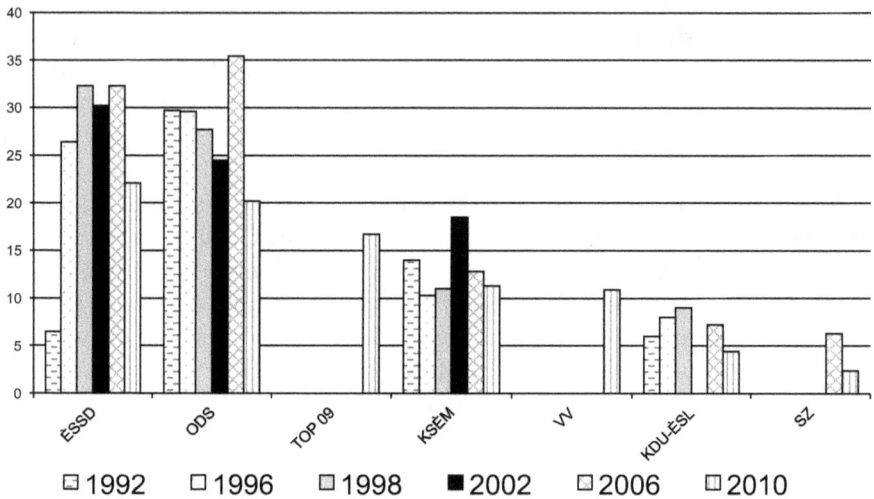

FIGURE 6.1. Results of the Chamber of Deputies 1992–2010

Sources: www.volby.cz; KDU-ČSL (Křest'ansko-demokratická unie-Československá strana lidová/ Christian Democratic Union-Czechoslovakian People's Party), SZ (Strana zelených/The Green Party).

Justice

The base level of the judicial system is composed of eighty-six district courts (Okresní soud) – which in Prague are called municipal district courts (Obvodní soud). The second level consists of eight regional courts (Krajskí soud), and the third of two high courts in Prague and Olomouc. Atop the system is the Supreme Court (Nejvyšší soud), which sits in Brno.

The judicial system is basically unitary, that is, the constitution does not provide for specialized branches such as labour, fiscal or social courts. One exception is the administrative jurisdiction exercised by specialized courts of the district courts and by the Supreme Administrative Court.[22] Military courts existed formerly but were disbanded in 1993.

Judges are appointed for life by the President of the State (and confirmed by the minister of justice) and are independent. No judge may be relieved from office or transferred to another court against his or her will. Exceptions, in particular those resulting from disciplinary proceedings, are regulated by the law.

After the turnaround of 1989, Czech justice was highly overburdened. Both the Czech public and representatives of the EU Commission criticized court proceedings as taking much too long, and only 26 per cent of citizens had confidence in the courts.[23] Since then (as of 2010), the courts have been provided with sufficient funding, and judges' salaries are two to five times the average wage. Generally, the efficiency of the judicial system is improving, but considerable regional differences still exist.[24]

Constitutional jurisdiction in Central and Eastern Europe triumphed upon the collapse of the communist regimes. The Czech model of Constitutional Court relies on a concept of specialized, centralized constitutional jurisdiction. The Constitutional Court consists of fifteen judges who are appointed for ten years by the President of the State, by agreement of the Senate. The judges of the Constitutional Court are independent: in taking their decisions, they need obey only constitutional regulations and international treaties on human rights. The Constitutional Court is entitled to invalidate laws and other legal regulations or individual legal decisions if they contradict the constitutional order. Decisions by the Constitutional Court must be respected by the institutions concerned.

Mass media and political slant
With the breaking of the communist monopoly on information, the Czech mass media underwent a stormy transition. From 1989 to 1999, the total number of periodicals grew from 772 to 3,894 (daily newspapers from 30 to 208), the number of registered publishing houses from 45 to 1,484, and that of published books from 4,000 to 13,000 per year.[25] Many of the published books had been banned in the communist period. Electronic media also experienced a spectacular upswing.

Electronic media activities are supervised and regulated by several institutions. The Council for Radio and TV Broadcasting, which is appointed by the Chamber of Deputies, distributes fixed-term licences among private radio and TV channels. The Council of Czech Radio and the Council of Czech TV are responsible for regular control of radio and TV channels under public law. Each of these institutions consists of nine members, also appointed by the Chamber of Deputies. The majority of private TV and radio channels are foreign-owned. Private TV channels achieve high profit rates, but the public service Czech TV increasingly operates at a loss.[26]

Most of the print media too are owned by foreign publishers. The tabloid *Blesk* (circulation 380,000, owned by the Ringier media company) shows no affinity to any political party and avoids political topics. The daily newspaper *Mladá fronta dnes* (311,000, Rheinisch-Bergische Druckerei und Verlagsgesellschaft) often supports positions of the ODS, whereas the newspaper *Právo* (184,000, Borgis) is rather close to the Social Democrats. The daily *Lidové noviny* (73,000, Mafra) has a right-wing liberal orientation. The Bavarian publishing house Passauer Neue Presse owns a majority of regional newspapers.[27]

Regions (districts)

The territory of the Czech Republic is divided into fourteen autonomous districts consisting of thirteen territorial districts and the capital, Prague. In the tradition of its formerly Austrian administration, Bohemia has bigger administrative territories called *kraje* and smaller ones called *okresy*, both names derived from the German language. These fourteen districts are divided into a total of seventy-six sub-districts, which themselves consist of 6,292 municipalities.

The districts were established as bodies of regional self-administration, according to Decision 347/1997 which came into force with the district elections of 2000. The creation of this regional level of self-administration has promoted stability in the political system, which now is less influenced by power shifts at the centre. Moreover, politicians who have proven themselves through experience in regional parliaments form a recruitment pool for the party centres. Various coalitions have formed in the districts, independently of the centre, reducing the polarity of parties.

The districts have both rights to self-administration (their own sphere of influence) and competences of state administration (transferred sphere of influence). Their comprehensive competences particularly concern the fields of traffic, health and schooling, monument protection and land use planning.

A district parliament (Krajské zastupitestvo), which the citizens elect for a four-year term, serves as the regional parliament. The district elections of 2008 were won by the Social Democratic Party (Česká strana sociálně demokratická, ČSSD), which received 36 per cent of the votes.[28] The district parliament elects the district-level executive bodies, consisting of a district council (Rada kraje), a district governor (Krajský hejtman) and his or her deputy.

Municipalities

Municipalities (*obce*) are the cornerstone of the system of self-administration. Municipal representative bodies are elected for four-year terms according to proportional representation. In municipal elections, the independent candidates are regularly the most successful; in 2006 they attained 58 per cent of the seats.[29] Municipalities are independent legal subjects and may own property. They administer their funds independently. They have both self-administrative competences (primary, independent competence) and the authority of the state administration (competences of state administration transferred by the state). Thus, the municipalities act as an executive body of central state administration. All Eastern European countries' municipal constitutions refer to the transferred sphere of influence, but in the Czech Republic, where district boards have been dissolved as bodies of state administration, this transfer has been particularly comprehensive.[30]

Self-administration has primary significance: all things are subject to self-administration, as long as no law rules otherwise. When exercising their competences of self-administration, municipalities must only obey the law. They may pass generally binding announcements that must fully accord with the laws and the constitution. Municipalities decide about their budgets and may establish various funds. Their intakes consist mainly of municipal taxes, dues and fees, and shares of state taxes as well as revenues from their own business activities. Furthermore, they receive subsidies from the state budget and EU regional programmes.

Economy

General information

The first Czechoslovakian state, which lasted from 1918 to 1939, ranked tenth in a worldwide survey of economic performance. In the communist period, however, its ranking fell drastically. After the peaceful revolution, foreign direct investment was crucial to the swift privatization and modernization of the state economy. As one of the most popular countries to invest in, the Czech Republic enjoyed not only modernized sites and structures but also rapid growth in both productivity and international competitiveness. More than 80 per cent of direct investments come from EU-15 countries. This investment mainly benefited the financial sector, trade, gastronomy, mechanical engineering and the automotive industry as well as transport and telecommunication.[31] According to a survey by the German Chamber of Foreign Trade, German investors consider the Czech Republic the most attractive country in Central and Eastern Europe. German enterprises invested more than 20 billion euros more in the Czech Republic than in the growing markets of China, Brazil, Russia and India.[32] However, the Czech Republic does have the disadvantage of comparably great fluctuations in the Czech crown.

Economic system

Free choice of both profession and entrepreneurial activities is guaranteed by the Czech constitution and indeed in reality. The state obliges itself to materially support, to an appropriate extent, those who through no fault of their own are unable to exercise their right to the free choice of profession. Concerning foreigners, a law may stipulate special regulations. The right to strike and the right of association with others to defend economic and social interests are guaranteed; however, people in certain professions (judges, state prosecutors, members of the armed forces and policemen) have no right to strike.

Industry

Industry's share of the Czech GNP is 32 per cent. At the turn of the millennium, foreign per capita investments were at a record high and positively impacting on economic development, the restructuring of companies and employment.[33] From 2002 to 2008, industrial growth was between 4 and 10 per cent annually.[34] Alongside mechanical engineering and the automotive industry, the chemical, petrochemical and pharmaceutical industries also merit mention. Despite all expectations, the predominance of the automotive sector in the export business turned out not to be a disadvantage during the crisis of 2009, when that sector recorded record sales. The constant growth in Czech industry's international competitiveness is due to per capita GNP rising faster than actual wages.

Commerce, trade, services

In the years 2000–2008, turnover in the services branch rose by 30 per cent (its share of GNP was 60 per cent), but in the crisis years 2009 and 2010, it went down again. Important segments of the services sector include tourism, foreign trade and financial services. Opening the borders in 1990 led to an unprecedented boom in foreign tourism. The population's annual outlays on travel rose by up to 200 per cent, and a similar dynamic applied to profits from incoming tourism.

Since 1989 the Czech Republic has become an export country. Its foreign trade turnover has grown rapidly, and its foreign trade surplus, in particular with EU countries, grows ever larger. Meanwhile, the structure of export goods has also improved with the continual expansion of the share of high-quality goods such as machinery, electronics and vehicles. Germany is the Czech Republic's most important foreign trade partner. In the years 1991 to 2004, imports from Germany rose threefold while Czech exports to Germany increased fivefold.[35]

Since the debt relief, restructuring and privatization of the banking sector in the 1990s, practically all large banks in the Czech Republic have been foreign-owned. Czech banks weathered the financial crisis of 2009 well, as their share of toxic assets proved manageable; most of them made profits in 2009.

Society

Social structure, social lines of conflict

In the 1970s, the Communist Party triggered a real baby boom by radically increasing child benefits. Most members of the baby boom generation ('Husák's children', as journalists call them) reached adulthood soon after the turnaround of 1989, which helped prevent population decline during the crisis of adapting to the market economy. In fact, a slight rise was recorded, from 10.3 million (1989) to 10.4 million (2008). In the years 1989 to 2008, the birth rate was constant at about 100,000 per year. In the same period the immigration/emigration balance was constantly positive, with a rising tendency. Whereas in 1989 men and women married at an age of twenty-two and twenty-five years on average, respectively, newlyweds in 2008 were clearly older, with an average age of twenty-nine and thirty-one. Within a historically short period, old traditions had been changed by the opportunities and risks that accompany freedom and a market economy, and by the influence of Western lifestyles – though, to be sure, these changes happened faster in Prague than in the countryside. In the years 1989–2008, life expectancy clearly rose, from seventy-five and sixty-eight (for women and men respectively) to eighty and seventy-four.[36] Today, problems connected to the ageing of society are becoming obvious.

The Czech Republic has a nationally homogeneous population, with only small minorities: 2 per cent Slovaks, 0.5 per cent Germans and 0.1 per cent Roma.[37] However, other estimates claim the actual share of Roma – the only big, socially excluded ethnic minority – is much higher than that stated in censuses: the country's 275,000 Roma make up almost 3 per cent of the total population.[38] Meanwhile, as the country's wealth increases, the share of resident foreigners (e.g. Slovaks, Ukrainians, Vietnamese, Poles, Russians, Germans) is constantly on the rise: in 2004, there were 256,000 foreigners; by 2008, they numbered 438,000[39] – about 4 per cent of the total population.

The period following the turnaround was characterized by radical change in the social structure, rapidly increasing social disparities and a weak middle class. The income gap between the metropolis of Prague and the rural areas became bigger.[40] In the 1990s, the share of employees in the private sector rose rapidly. Of the 4.7 million working people in 2001, 4 million were employees, 0.5 million were self-employed and 0.2 million were employers. Fifty-four per cent of Czech people have basic or vocational education, and 35 per cent have secondary education. Only 12 per cent have completed university education, but in general the share of university graduates is growing – in 1993 it was only 8 per cent.[41]

The first line of social conflict, developing in 1990, was between continuing the controversial debate on keeping the communist regime, represented by the Communist Party, and initiating a transformation process towards democracy and market economy, represented by all other parties.[42] Some more refined splits became obvious, reflecting debates on the direction, speed and depth of democratic and market economy reforms, and on various societal interests. Regarding the most important division line, economic policy, different forces approached from different positions, favouring (1) radical economic reform, liberalization of prices and privatization (the ODS and Citizens' Democratic Alliance, and since 2010, TOP 09); (2) those supporting a socially cushioned transformation (the ČSSD and the People's Party); and (3) general rejection of the reform process (the Communist Party). These elements of conflict were obvious even in 1992 and basically remain unchanged.

Since the split of Czechoslovakia, ethnic lines of conflict no longer play a role in the nationally homogeneous Czech Republic. Still extant is the line of conflict over the market economy, which is opposed by the Communist Party and supported by all others. Even though all other parties consider the Communist Party unfit for a coalition, it attracts many protest voters from low-income backgrounds.

Trade unions, entrepreneurs' associations, labour relations
The right to associate and form coalitions is guaranteed. Everyone is entitled to freely form associations to serve his or her own economic and social interests. Accordingly, trade unions and associations have developed independently of the state. The right to strike is guaranteed (except in certain professions).

With their several million members, the trade unions are the biggest intermediary organizations. They succeeded in shaking off the burden of the communist past and stopped the process of decay and fragmentation early on. On the other hand, privatization and the founding of small enterprises has led to constant decline in the number of employees represented by trade unions.

As the private sector developed, a rising need for unified representation of the interests of private entrepreneurs was answered by a spate of newly founded employers' and entrepreneurs' associations. Their purpose, as stated in the statutes of the Confederation of Employers' and Entrepreneurs' Associations of the Czech Republic, is to articulate and enforce their members' interests, participate in law-making processes relevant to entrepreneurial activities, and lobby.

Churches, religious communities, ideologies
Churches play only a moderate role in Czech society, as the Czech Republic is one of the most secularized countries in Europe. Only 32 per cent of its

citizens call themselves believers, and only 7 per cent describe their ties to a church as being strong. Most believers (83 per cent) belong to the Roman Catholic faith.[43] Trust in the church is higher than average in rural regions and among the older population. The middle-aged population, on the other hand, was socialized in the communist period and tends to take a dismissive attitude towards religion. The secularization process started in the communist period and continued during the 1990s, when the number of believers continually declined.[44] Besides the traditional distance towards religion, this development is also thought to relate to negative perceptions of the church's media presence in the context of the controversy over the restitution of church property.[45]

Citizens' initiatives, civil society
The most common type of association is the citizens' association, several thousand of which were founded every year in the 1990s. Whereas only a few hundred so-called voluntary associations had existed before the turnaround, by 1998 more than 37,000 citizens' associations were registered.[46] Cultural associations and sports clubs showed the most dynamic growth in numbers. This proliferation of citizens' associations was due on the one hand to the dissolution of the former, centrally controlled organizations, and on the other hand to citizens' increased will to participate.

The Consolidation of the Democratic Constitutional State

Consolidation of the Constitution, Constitutional Conflicts between Institutions

Constitutionally and institutionally, the political system of the Czech Republic has mostly been consolidated and is sufficiently efficient. The system of separation of powers works well, and the constitutional principles have successively made their way into political practice; hence, the gap between the text of the constitution and its reality has narrowed since the start of transformation. Political actors respect the decisions of the Constitutional Court. In the period of the ČSSD/ODS power cartel from 1998 to 2002, the Constitutional Court clearly fulfilled its function within the system of the separation of powers. When constitutional conflict arose between President Havel and the ČSSD/ODS parliamentary majority, the Constitutional Court presented itself as a powerful obstacle to the two big parties' efforts to marginalize smaller parties via unconstitutional manipulations of electoral law. And its ruling that the EU Treaty of Lisbon accorded with the Czech constitution was of Europe-wide significance, for thus did the Constitutional Court pave the way towards the treaty's ratification by the Czech Republic.

Consolidation of Actors

The party system: fragmentation, volatility, polarization, extremism
The party system was soon consolidated. After the 1992 parliamentary elections, a relatively stable, bipolar party system crystallized, and from 1998 to 2010 two big parties – the ČSSD and the ODS – took turns forming the government with smaller coalition partners. The dividing lines are clear, but polarization, extremism and factionalism are limited, leaving the party system only moderately fragmented. Voter volatility has tended to decline. Although voters' preferences change more dramatically than they do in established democracies, they are still more predictable than those in most other post-communist countries.[47]

However, the parliamentary elections of 2010 severely shook the thus far relatively stable party system. Both big parties, the ČSSD (with 22 per cent of votes) and the ODS (20 per cent) lost one third of their voters, and two newly founded groups were elected to parliament, the liberal TOP 09 (17 per cent) and the Public Affairs party (11 per cent) which declared itself a 'party of the centre'. During their election campaigns, both new parties had denounced corrupt practices and spoken out in favour of more transparency. Meanwhile, the traditional People's Party, which had been part of every coalition government since the founding of the Czech Republic, did not reach the 5 per cent threshold required for parliamentary representation; nor did the Green Party. However, the left-wing extremist Communist Party of Bohemia and Moravia (11 per cent) is still represented in the parliament.[48]

Informal and formal actors
The crucial question is whether informal actors (armed forces, financial capital, entrepreneurs) will pursue their interests within or outside the legitimate political system. In Czech tradition, the army is loyal. Some entrepreneurs, on the other hand, have tried to enforce their interests by way of machinations such as bribery, clientelism and fraud. All the while, influential interest groups have acted to maintain the currently non-transparent situation as long as possible in the Czech Republic. The extent of their activities can only be estimated according to various indicators (corruption analyses, polls, exorbitant prices in cases of public tendering, insider reports of a standard 'kickback' of 10 per cent). For years, no one has succeeded in passing an efficient anti-corruption law or taxing hazardous business activities. Some analysts emphasize the role of these

dubious interest groups as 'probably the most important obstacles for the transformation process'.[49]

Deficits are also clear in the behaviour of formal political actors, which are prone to corruption and clientelism. Bribery, which is strongly associated with pre-revolutionary networks, may be considered an integral part of society in the Czech Republic.[50] Yet the public is sharply critical of corruption, and the political elites' inability or unwillingness to solve this problem weakens the legitimacy of the political system and its institutions.[51] Thus, the factor of endemic corruption undermines the democratic system.

Interest groups
After the chaos of the early days of transformation receded, a structured intermediary system became discernible in the Czech Republic. Increasingly the intermediary institutions have come to fulfil the function of organized representation of interests.[52]

Civil society
The process of developing a mature civil society is not yet over. Compared to other post-communist countries, the Czech Republic often achieves the best poll ratings on a variety of indicators of support for democracy. Nevertheless, in comparison to Western EU countries, several democratic deficits are obvious: general support of democracy, satisfaction with democracy and trust in institutions are all lower than in established democracies; anti-democratic alternatives to the system are not vehemently rejected; and there is little readiness to participate.[53]

The media
Article 17 of the Charter guarantees freedom of expression and the right to information. Anybody has the right to express his or her opinion vocally, via printed information, in images or in any other way, and also to freely choose, receive and spread thoughts and information, independent of the state's borders. Censorship is illegal. By actually functioning, the media basically accomplish this constitutional task. Basically, the duality of privately owned TV and radio channels and those under public law has positively affected the plurality of opinions. However, some editorial staffs' affinity to certain political parties affects the objectivity of reporting.

Consolidation of Attitudes

Empirical studies have found that Czechs are characterized by a marked preference for democracy – at least, in comparison with other post-communist countries: 84 per cent agree with the statement that although democracy is not a perfect kind of governance, it is nevertheless the best one.[54] Almost 90 per cent reject any leader or any kind of dictatorship as an alternative to democracy.[55] General support for democracy is higher in Western European democracies but lower in other Eastern European countries.[56] The Czechs express less satisfaction with the actual functioning of democracy, however, and consider the current system, in comparison to the communist system, to have about as many advantages as disadvantages for them. They appreciate democratic freedoms but criticize the loss of social security. Nevertheless, 80 per cent do not want to return to the situation before the turnaround.[57]

The Czechs are deeply sceptical when it comes to assessing their possibilities of political participation. They are of the opinion that their opportunities to influence political life are the same as they were under communism.[58] Only 6 per cent believe themselves able to influence matters at the level of state.[59] The population sees decision-making by politicians as decisively influenced by corruption; citizens' interests and opinions are said to be secondary.[60] This high degree of scepticism is probably a factor in the low readiness to participate and low degree of satisfaction with democracy.

Stabilization of the Economic System

Economic System

The Czech Republic has a modern, transformed economic system. The constitution and the entire legal system provide a basis for a free, open market economy as well as economic competition.[61] The Czech Republic was the first East Central European country to become a member of the Organisation for Economic Co-operation and Development. Furthermore, it is a member of the World Trade Organization, the International Monetary Fund, the International Bank for Reconstruction and Development and the European Bank for Reconstruction and Development. In the context of the Czech Republic's EU accession in 2004, the entire legal system, especially laws concerning the market economy, was adjusted to the *Aquis Communautaire*. Commercial law, accounting law and bankruptcy law conform to Western standards. However, international companies have criticized legal certainty and tax predictability as insufficient.[62]

Actors

Private enterprises are the most important economic actors. In 2010, a total of 2.6 million companies were registered in the Czech Republic.[63] Early in the introduction of the market economy, many Czech citizens tried their luck and founded companies. Given the initial lack of competition, many succeeded, but most of them soon had to give up. Thus, the transformation period was a learning process. In the second phase of transformation, many companies were sold to foreign investors, so a large share of the biggest companies, which are also the most important economic actors in the Czech Republic, are Western European, and in particular German, enterprises.[64]

Attitudes

After their first practical experiences with its actual way of working, the Czechs' initial enthusiasm[65] for Klaus's 'market economy without adjectives' gave way to a more sceptical, differentiated view of things. In 1990, 87 per cent of interviewees were convinced that entrepreneurial activities needed unrestricted freedom, whereas by 1998 only 49 per cent agreed with this. The population also responded negatively to rapidly growing social disparities. In 1990, 89 per cent were of the opinion that wage differences should be bigger, but in 1998 only 39 per cent shared this opinion. An overwhelming majority of 80 per cent of the Czech people believe that 'these days people become rich in dishonest ways' – a conviction that certainly does not motivate correct behaviour. Enterprises' poor payment habits are considered a difficult problem – bills are paid after seventy-two days, on average.[66]

All in all, the public characterizes the economic transition as 'partly or completely successful', an assessment with which the following percentages agreed in the years after the transition: 68 per cent in 1993, 35 per cent in 1999, 55 per cent in 2005, and 57 per cent in 2007.[67] These percentages reflect the course of the transformation, wherein the 'Vale of Tears' was left behind in 1997–1999.

EU Integration

Accession Talks and EU Accession

Immediately after the turnaround of 1989, feverish diplomatic activity began to promote the goal of normalizing the now liberated Czechoslovakia's relations with Western democracies. The revolutionary movement Citizens' Forum titled its 1990 election programme 'Back to Europe' in accordance with the deepest desires of the population. Czechoslovakian politicians contributed actively to the dissolution of the Warsaw Pact and the Council for Mutual Economic Assistance (known as

COMECON). The prospect of joining the EU and the subsequent accession talks, critical progress reports and comprehensive process of legal adjustment were essential factors in developing the legal and economic culture of the Czech Republic.

Participation in EU Institutions

The Czech Republic's participation in EU institutions was of particular significance in the first half of 2009, when it presided over the EU Council. At first, the Czech presidency succeeded in mediating the gas conflict between Russia and Ukraine, thus securing further gas supplies for EU countries. However, in the midst of its presidency the Czech government was toppled by a parliamentary vote of no confidence and replaced by an interim government – at the very time when the EU sought ways to cope with the economic crisis. This, along with certain diplomatic lapses, damaged the image of the Czechs in Europe.

Integration Problems

The Czech Republic's European policy has not been consistent. The Social Democrats, who were in power from 1998 to 2006 and mostly identified with the European idea of the social state, staunchly supported the Czech Republic's integration into the EU. The government coalition led by the ODS after 2007 also had a more or less positive attitude towards EU integration. However, an extremely Euro-sceptical strand within this party, represented by a circle around President Václav Klaus, criticizes the EU's economic and social policies from a neoliberal standpoint, trying to undermine the process of EU integration. In the Constitutional Court of the Czech Republic, President Klaus defended a constitutional challenge brought by this ODS faction in the Senate, which contended that the Lisbon treaty violated the Czech Republic's constitutional order. The Constitutional Court's unanimous rejection of the challenge paved the way towards ratification of the Treaty of Lisbon. The signature of the Czech head of state was the last one in the whole European ratification process.

Attitudes of the Population towards the EU

Whereas enthusiasm for the Czech Republic's accession to NATO in 1999 was limited, approval of EU integration is high. This is largely due to Czechs' feeling that they have always belonged to Europe and that the communist interlude was merely a temporary interruption of this tradition. The other motivation for EU accession – the interest in security – not only refers to a general gain in political stability at home and abroad but is also, according to Czech belief, an effective means to contain and control Germany's 'supremacy' through the mechanism of EU regulations.[68] In a 2003 referendum, 77 per cent of participants voted in favour of EU accession. In the following years, approval of the EU was volatile, falling to a nadir of 45 per cent in 2007 and peaking at 69 per cent during the Czech presidency of the EU Council in 2009.[69]

Conclusion, Prospects

Favourable Factors

The transformation process in the Czech Republic has relied on a number of factors:

- Both the level of economic, social and cultural modernization achieved in pre-communist times and Czech educational traditions survived the communist period and supported democratic change.
- Society retained remnants of the pre-communist democratic political culture, and the Czechs saw no alternatives to democracy or a market economy – an extraordinarily important opinion during the disorientation and chaos of the early transition period, when 'new shores were visible'.
- The Czech Republic is nationally homogeneous, and its society is only moderately polarized.
- The statehood of the Czech Republic is solid and unquestioned by any relevant foreign or domestic political power.
- Anti-system parties have hardly any influence, and the strongest of them, the Communist Party, remains isolated.
- The prospect and then the process of EU accession, and subsequently EU membership, resulted in an additional consolidation push.

Consolidation Trends and the State of Consolidation in 2010

Concerning the level of consolidation, one may cite a consolidation trend on which analysts agree: in the course of transformation from 1990 to 2010, the Czech political and economic systems became considerably more stable and efficient. Although the level of consolidation has been volatile in the short run, seen against the historical background of these twenty years it has risen constantly.

Consolidation of the political system has progressed well at the constitutional and institutional levels. The system of the separation of powers is working, and institutional efficiency, transparency and inclusion are guaranteed. The intermediary system is also getting more stable. Freedom House's 2009 report characterized the Czech Republic as a free electoral democracy where human rights are upheld.[70] German Chancellor Angela Merkel calls the Czech Republic a consolidated democracy.[71] In the Bertelsmann Transformation Index,[72] which is a comparative analysis of 128 countries, the Czech Republic ranks first for the state of its development of democracy and market economy (Status Index) and ninth when it comes to political steering (Management Index). On the other hand, neither the behaviour of formal and informal actors nor the level of maturity of civil society can yet be called satisfactory.

The economic system is productive and reliable. Economic analysts call the Czech Republic a functioning, free, modern market economy, and the 2010 BTI ranks its market economy first among all transformation countries' economies.[73] Overall, economic efficiency has not yet reached the level of Western industrial nations, but a catch-up process is ongoing. The Czech Republic coped well with the financial crisis of 2009, proving its economy is sufficiently robust. The national deficit is 35 per cent of GNP, so the country's debts are moderate. Barclay's rating agency counts the Czech Republic as one of the world's most economically stable countries, listing it as eighth in the world and second in Europe, behind Germany.[74] In the 1990–2010 period, actual wages rose by 40 per cent (in euros, this increase is nominally more than fivefold). By 2010, Czech industry had recovered from the crisis and was reporting growing turnover and profits. As mentioned above, enduring deficits include insufficient legal security and tax predictability, clientelism and corruption, as well as enterprises' poor payment practices.

Mentality Change: The Key Problem of Transformation?

Changing people's mentality – along with the necessarily connected consolidation of behaviour, attitudes and development of civil society – has proven difficult and time-consuming. Yet changing thinking and behavioural stereotypes is obviously the key problem of transformation. Considering the high degree of proneness to corruption and pronounced clientelism, the behaviour of both formal and informal political actors cannot be considered satisfactory. The conviction among the population that bribery decisively influences political decision-making, and that in most cases people who become rich do so in dishonest ways, weakens the legitimacy of the system and is a cause of both citizens' low degree of readiness to participate and their dissatisfaction with democracy. The development of a mature, responsible, active civil society will clearly take some time. The same is true for the consolidation of the behaviour of the political and economic elites.

Prospects

Given the attitudes among the population, the constellation of political forces and the institutional configuration, the risk of radical de-democratization in the Czech Republic can be said to be extremely slight. The external framework conditions and the country's NATO and EU memberships have the effect of stabilizing democracy. However, it cannot be ruled out that the transformation process will come to a halt at the current level of consolidation, where the quality of democracy is still insufficient. Such a possibility lurks in the following sets of problems:

- Massively widespread corruption;
- Domination of politics by 'godfathers' – business bosses who finance political parties and, often directly, party functionaries, and thereby benefit from custom-made laws and well-paid public service contracts;
- Minimal public participation and a low degree of trust among disappointed citizens;
- Continuing inefficiency in public administration and justice, and lack of law enforcement;
- Low levels of such public services as the security, educational and health systems, sciences and basic research, traffic control and environmental protection.

Currently it is difficult to predict whether the parliamentary elections of 2010 will overcome the current standstill and revive the trend towards further consolidation of the system, or whether the solidified structures of dubious enterprises and the political elites will continue to dominate politics at not only the central but also the regional and municipal levels. Developments following the parliamentary and municipal elections of 2010, increased political commitment among citizens, and the launch of a number of citizens' initiatives give reason for some degree of optimism, in the sense of re-establishing the process of gradual consolidation of the system. This would correspond to the basic historical trend since the year 1990.

Karel Vodička, Dr of Jurisprudence, born in Aussig, Czechoslovakia, in 1949, went into political exile in the Federal Republic of Germany together with his family. He has undertaken scientific work as a philologist at the HAIT (until 2014) and as a lecturer in the Faculty of Philosophy at Jan-Evangelista-Purkyne University (UJEP) in Ústí nad Labem, Czech Republic. He has published on the history and the political system of the Czech Republic as well as on system transformation in the post-communist EU area. He has authored 126 scientific articles and is the author of sixteen books, most recently *Zündfunke aus Prag: Wie 1989 der Mut zur Freiheit die Geschichte veränderte*, co-authored with Hans-Dietrich Genscher (Munich, 2014).

Notes

1. See M. Mauritz, *Tschechien* (Regensburg, 2002), 198.
2. See K. Bartošek, 'Střední a jihovýchodní Evropa' [Central and Southeast Europe], in S. Courtois (ed.), *Černá kniha komunismu* [The Black Book on Communism] (Prague, 1999), 350–407, here 392.
3. See Mauritz, *Tschechien*, 198.
4. See K. Vodička, *Politisches System Tschechiens* (Münster, 1996), 33.
5. See P. Pithart, 'Konec dobrý, všechno dobré?' [All's Well That Ends Well?], in K. Vodička (ed.), *Dělení Československa: Deset let poté* [The Split of Czechoslovakia: Ten Years Later] (Prague, 2003), 317–21, here 320; E. Stein, *Česko-Slovensko: Konflikt – roztržka – rozpad* [Czechoslovakia: Conflict – Turnaround – Dissolution] (Prague, 2000), 229; I. Šujan, 'Hospodár ske a sociálne dosledky česko-slo venského rozchodu' [Economic and Social Consequences of the Czech-Slovak Split], in Vodička, *Dělení Československa*, 119–28, here 119; F. Gál, 'Roz pad Československa v politickej perspektíve' [The Split of Czechoslovakia from a Political Point of View], in Vodička, *Dělení Československa*, 105–18, here 105; K. Vodička, 'Příčiny rozdělení: shrnující analýza po deseti letech' [The Causes of the Division: A Summarizing Analysis Ten Years Later], in Vodička, *Dělení Československa*, 205–64, here 257.
6. See W. Ismayr, 'Die politischen Systeme Osteuropas im Vergleich', in W. Ismayr (ed.), *Die politischen Systeme Osteuropas*, 3rd ed. (Wiesbaden, 2010), 9–78, here 67; W. Merkel, 'Gegen alle Theorie? Die Konsolidierung der Demokratie in Ostmitteleuropa', *Politische Vierteljahresschrift* 48 (2007), 413–33, here 430; K. Vodička, *Das politische System Tschechiens* (Wiesbaden, 2005), 266.
7. See BTI Transformation Index 2010, *Politische Gestaltung im internationalen Vergleich* (Gütersloh, 2010).
8. See M. Brusis, 'Ostmittel- und Südosteuropa', in Bertelsmann Stiftung (ed.), *Transformation Index 2010* (Gütersloh, 2010), 125–43, here 128.
9. See BTI Transformation Index 2010 – 'Länderbericht Tschechien'; K. Vodička and L. Cabada, *Politický systém České republiky* [The Political System of the Czech Republic] (Prague, 2007), 342; Vodička, *Das politische System Tschechiens*, 270; Freedom House, 'Freedom in the World 2009' (http://www.freedomhouse.org/template.cfm?page=363& year=2009&country=7594; accessed 24 August 2010).

10. See I. von Münch and G. Hoog, 'Zánik československého státu z mezinárodněprávního hlediska' [The Dissolution of the Czechoslovakian State from the Point of View of International Law], in Vodička, *Dělení Československa*, 131–53, here 133; I. von Münch and G. Hoog, 'Auflösung des tschechoslowakischen Staates aus völkerrechtlicher Sicht', in R. Kipke and K. Vodička (eds), *Abschied von der Tschechoslowakei* (Cologne, 1993), 163–79, here 164.

11. See V. Krivý and I. Radičová, 'Atmosféra dovery a atmosféra nedovery?' [An Atmosphere of Trust and an Atmosphere of Distrust?], *Sociologické aktuality* [Current Matters of Sociology] 2 (1992), 1–5, here 2.

12. See K. Vodička, 'Koalitionsabsprache: Wir teilen den Staat!', in Kipke and Vodička, *Abschied von der Tschechoslowakei*, 77–106, here 79.

13. See M. Bútora and Z. Bútorová, 'Neznesiteľná ľahkost' rozchodu' [The Unbearable Lightness of Separation], in Vodička, *Dělení Československa*, 69–104, here 85.

14. See K. Vodička, 'Risikofaktoren im Konsolidierungsprozess der Slowakei', *Europäische Rundschau* 29(4) (2001), 43–52, here 47.

15. See Pithart, 'Konec dobrý', 320; Stein, *Česko-Slovensko*, 229; Šujan, 'Hospodár ske', 119; Gál, 'Roz pad Československa', 105; Vodička, *Das politische System Tschechiens*, 53.

16. See Constitution of the Czech Republic, Constitutional Law 1/1993.

17. See Vodička, *Das politische System Tschechiens*, 210.

18. See W. Ismayr, 'Die politischen Systeme Osteuropas im Vergleich', in W. Ismayr (ed.), *Die politischen Systeme Osteuropas*, 3rd ed. (Wiesbaden, 2010), 9–78, here 33; W. Ismayr, 'Die politischen Systeme Osteuropas im Vergleich', in W. Ismayr (ed.), *Die politischen Systeme Osteuropas* (Opladen, 2004), 9–69, here 31.

19. See Vodička, *Politisches System Tschechiens*, 258.

20. See Vodička, *Das politische System Tschechiens*, 196.

21. See Z. Mansfeldová, 'Das tschechische Parlament in Zeichen allmählicher Stabilisierung', in S. Kraatz and S. von Steinsdorff (eds), *Parlamente und Systemtransformation im postsozialistischen Europa* (Opladen, 2002), 111–25, here 119.

22. See M. Polián, 'Die Verwaltungsgerichtsbarkeit in Tschechien', in B. Wieser and A. Stolz (eds), *Vergleichen des Verwaltungsrecht in Ostmitteleuropa* (Vienna, 2004), 459–89, here 461.

23. See P. Holländer, 'Die Gerichtsbarkeit in der Tschechischen Republik', in M. Joseph et al. (eds), *Revolution und Recht: Systemtransformation und Verfassungsentwicklung in der Tschechischen und Slowakischen Republik* (Frankfurt a. M., 2000), 87–115, here 103f.; Vodička, *Das politische System Tschechiens*, 228f.

24. See Vodička and Cabada, *Politický systém*, 293.

25. See I. Možný, *Česká společnost: Nejdůležitější fakta o kvalitě našeho života* [Czech Society: The Most Important Facts Concerning the Quality of Our Lives] (Prague, 2002), 150.

26. See L. Tvarůžková, 'Jak zachránit Kavčí hory', *Týden* 16 (2003), 40–44, here 44.

27. See *Ekonom* 42 (2004), 7; Vodička and Cabada, *Politický systém*, 245.

28. See website about the elections in the Czech Republic (http://www.volby.cz/pls/ps2010/ps?xjazyk=CZ; accessed 13 August 2010).

29. See ibid.

30. See A. Stolz, 'Die Verwaltungsorganisation im Vergleich', in Wieser and Stolz, *Vergleichen des Verwaltungsrecht in Ostmitteleuropa*, 159–95, here 188.

31. See See website of Raiffeisenbank Austria (www.raiffeisen.at/eBusiness/rai_⁰template1/18 4143574777874146–1864886712102259381878702675102755880–123682842415716912–NA-1–NA-NA-NA.html) (accessed 5 October 2010).

32. See AHK Poll, Tschechien Online, 29 June 2010 (http://www.tschechien-online.org/news/17096–tschechien-deutschen-investoren-favorisiert; accessed 5 October 2010).
33. See F. Eckert, *Vom Plan zum Markt: Parteipolitik und Privatisierungsprozesse in Osteuropa* (Wiesbaden, 2008), 227.
34. See magazine E15–3 (http://www.e15.cz/financni-data/makroekonomika/?utm_medi um=cpc&utm_source=seznam&utm_campaign=prum-mzda; accessed 23 September 2010).
35. Figures: Český statistický úřad (http://www.czso.cz); 'Innovations-Report: Tschechien wichtigster Handelspartner in Mittel- und Osteuropa' (http://www.innovations-report. de/html/berichte/statistiken/bericht-9702.html; accessed 23 September 2010).
36. Figures: Český statistický úřad (http://www.czso.cz; accessed 4 October 2010).
37. See ibid.
38. See United Nations Development Programme, 'UNDP-Bericht: 'Únik z pasce závislosti. Rómovia v strednej a východnej Európe' [UNDP Report: Ways out of the Dependency Trap. Roma in Central and East Europe] (Bratislava, 2003).
39. Figures: Český statistický úřad (http://www.czso.cz; accessed 4 October 2010).
40. See P. Machonin and M. Tuček, *Česká společnost v transformaci* [Czech Society in Transformation] (Prague, 1996), 333; P. Machonin and M. Tuček, 'Proměnysociálních nerov ností' [Changes of Social Inequities], in M. Tuček et al. (eds), *Dynamika české společnosti* [The Dynamics of Czech Society] (Prague, 2003), 197–223, here 205; P. Machonin and K. Müller, 'Problémy a perspektivy modernizace a sociální soudržnosti', in Tuček et al., *Dynamika české společnosti*, 392–413, here 401.
41. Figures: Český statistický úřad (http://www.czso.cz).
42. See Vodička, *Das politische System Tschechiens*, 146.
43. See Český statistický úřad [Czech Statistics Authority], *Statistická ročenka* [Statistics Yearbook] (Prague, 2002) (www.czso.cz/cisla1/10/2002/index; accessed 4 October 2010).
44. See ibid.
45. See U. Widmaier, A. Gawrich and U. Becker, *Regierungssysteme Zentral- und Osteuropas: Ein einführendes Lehrbuch* (Opladen, 1999), 68.
46. See Možný, *Česká společnost*, 123.
47. See K. Vodička, 'Das politische System Tschechiens', in W. Ismayr (ed.), *Die politischen Systeme Osteuropas* (Wiesbaden, 2010), 275–315, here 295.
48. Figures: Election results on the website Volby, 2010 (http://www.volby.cz/pls/ps2010/ ps?xjazyk=CZ; accessed 13 August 2010).
49. See V. Krivý, 'Súvislosti hodno tenia činnosti vlády SR verejnosťou' [Public Judgement on the Government's Activities], in G. Mesežnikov (ed.), *Povolebné Slovensko* [Slovakia after the Elections] (Bratislava, 2003), 21–41, here 34; J. Sopóci, 'Ekonomické záujmové skupiny v slovenskej politike v 90 rokoch' [Economic Interest Groups in Slovakian Politics in the Nineties], *Politologický časopis* [Journal of Political Sciences] 2 (2001) 166–76, here 174; M. Klíma, 'Klientelistická strana' [Clientelist Party], *Mladá fronta dnes*, 7 April 2003, 8; J. Pehe, 'Vítězství politického šíbrovství' [The Victory of Political Profiteering] (http://www.pehe.cz/zapisnik/2003/vitezstvi-politickeho-sibrovstvi; accessed 2 October 2010); K. Vodička, 'Political Systems of the Czech and Slovak Republics: A Comparison of Risks and the Consolidation Process', in G. Mesežnikov and O. Gyárfášová (eds), *Slovakia: Ten Years of Independence and a Year of Reforms* (Bratislava, 2004), 27–48, here 41.
50. See V. Lopourová, 'Koncept korupce v českém transformačním kontextu' [The Concept of Corruption during the Czech Transformation Process], *Politologický Časopis* 11(4) (2004), 354–69, here 366.

51. See K. Vodička, 'Na nebezpečné české stezce: Demokracie v Česku' [The Dangerous Czech Path: Democracy in the Czech Republic], *Ekonom* 1 (2010), 36f., here 37.
52. See Vodička, *Das politische System Tschechiens*, 270.
53. See ibid., 273.
54. See J. Červenka, 'Demokracie, lidská práva a korupce mezi politiky' [Democracy, Human Rights and Corruption among Politicians], CVVM Company Report 2002, 3 (http://www.cvvm.cas.cz/upl/zpravy/100110s_ pd21004.pdf; accessed 15 September 2010).
55. See G. Pickel and J. Jacobs, 'Einstellungen zur Demokratie und zur Gewährleistung von Rechten und Freiheiten in den jungen Demokratien Mittel- und Osteuropas', Frankfurter Institut für Transformationsstudien, *Studie No. 9/01* (Frankfurt (Oder), 2001), 6.
56. See ibid., 6; F. Plasser, P. Ulram and H. Waldrauch, *Politischer Kulturwandel in Ost- und Mitteleuropa: Theorie und Empirie demokratischer Konsolidierung* (Opladen, 1997), 122–25.
57. See Vodička, *Das politische System Tschechiens*, 93f.
58. See F. Kalvas and T. Kostelecký, 'Hodnocení současného vývoje v České republice veřejností' [Public Judgement on the Current Development in the Czech Republic], in Mesežnikov, *Povolebné Slovensko*, 43–54, here 52.
59. See N. Horáková, 'Uplatňování demokratických práv občanů a hodnocení politického systému u nás' [The Implementation of Democratic Civil Rights and How Our Political System Is Judged], CVVM Company Report 2004 (http://www.cvvm.cas.cz/upl/zpravy/100322s_pd40216.pdf; accessed 6 September 2010).
60. See A. Seidlová, 'Zájem občanů o politiku' [The Citizens' Interest in Politics], CVVM Report 02–01, PD 20322, 2002, 3.
61. See T. Borič and J. Pokorná, 'Die Wirtschaftsverfassung der Tschechischen Republik', in Marko et al., *Revolution und Recht*, 117–47, here 147; Vodička, *Das politische System Tschechiens*, 78.
62. See magazine E15–1 (www.e15.cz/domaci/ekonomika/danova-jistota-v-cesku-pokul hava-tvrdi-firmy; accessed 31 August 2010).
63. See web portal of the business directory of the Czech Republic, Databaze, 2010 (http://www.databaze-firem.net; accessed 30 August 2010).
64. See list of the biggest companies in the Czech Republic 'Liste der größten Unternehmen in Tschechien', as of 2008 (http://de.wikipedia.org/wiki/Liste_der_größten_Unterneh men_in_Tschechien; accessed 30 August 2010).
65. See Krivý and Radičová, 'Atmosféra dovery', 2.
66. See opinion poll, RadioCz: 'Zahlungsmoral der Unternehmen in Tschechien verschlechtert sich' (http://www.radio.cz/de/nachrichten/131050#5; accessed 1 September 2010).
67. See J. Kubátová, 'Názory české veřejnosti na ekonomickou transformaci a její sociální důsledky v období 1989–1998' [Opinions among the Czech Public Concerning Economic Change and Its Social Consequences in the Period 1989–1998], 2001, 39–55, here 42 (http://publib.upol.cz/~obd/fulltext/Politologica1/Politologica4.pdf); CVVM, 'Veřejnost o úspěšnosti ekonomické transformace' [The Public on the Success of Economic Transformation] (http://www.cvvm.cas.cz/upl/zpravy/100497s_ev50622.pdf; accessed 18.9.2010); M. Škodová, 'Hodnocení ekonomické transformace po roce 1989' [Judgement on the Economic Transformation after 1989], 3 (http://www.cvvm.cas.cz/upl/zpravy/100702s_ev70626.pdf).

68. See A. Hudalla, *Der Beitritt der Tschechischen Republik zur Europäischen Union* (Münster, 1996), 114.
69. See Sociological agency STEM Report, 29 January 2010 (http://zpravy.ihned.cz/cesko/c1–40246650–pruz-kum-s-clenstvim-ceska-v-eu-jsou-spokojeny-skoro-dve-tretiny-lidi; accessed 28 September 2010).
70. See Freedom House, 'Freedom in the World 2009'.
71. See Merkel, 'Gegen alle Theorie?', 430.
72. See BTI Transformation Index 2010 Transformation Index 2010.
73. See ibid.; Eckert, *Vom Plan zum Markt*, 378; Borič and Pokorná, 'Die Wirtschaftsverfassung', 147.
74. See *Ekonom* 39 (2010), 40.

Chapter 7

The Slovak Republic

⟨❦⟩

Rüdiger Kipke

Introduction

Today's Slovak Republic is one of Europe's most recent states. After the demise of the Greater Moravian Empire in the tenth century, the region became part of the Kingdom of Hungary and remained an integral part of the latter for 1,000 years, though without any special political-administrative status. In the aftermath of World War I, Czechs and Slovaks seized the unexpected historical opportunity to form a common state from the debris of the Austro-Hungarian Monarchy and founded the Czechoslovakian Republic in October 1918. In March 1939, in the course of breaking up Czechoslovakia under the Munich Agreement, Slovakia gained independent statehood for a few years, though it remained politically dependent on Germany. Once Czechoslovakia was resurrected after World War II, the Communist Party managed to seize power in February 1948 and establish a political regime following the Soviet model. Both at the level of the whole state and in Slovakia – formally an autonomous region and, after 1969, a federal state within the federalized Czechoslovakian Socialist Republic (ČSSR) – there still existed some party blocs, which nonetheless were subject to the communists' claim of leadership and had no independent political profile. The so-called Prague Spring of 1968, an attempt by reform-minded communist elites to liberalize the political system, came to an end after a few months with the country's military occupation by Soviet troops.

Like the other European 'people's democracies', the ČSSR experienced a severe crisis as of the mid 1980s. No steps had been taken to democratize the country. The *prestavba*, a Czechoslovakian economic reform modelled after Soviet perestroika, was not a success. The political

Notes for this chapter begin on page 201.

actors had completely lost credibility among the population. By the end of the decade, the Czechoslovakian political opposition was growing, stimulated by Mikhail Gorbachev's reforms in the Soviet Union and public resistance to the regimes in neighbouring communist countries. Opposition organizations and groups with different political orientations mushroomed. The most important of them was the civil rights movement Charta 77, which had been founded back in 1977. Political demonstrations filled the streets of the capital Prague, peaking on 17 November 1989 in a huge demonstration that prompted massive police intervention, in the course of which many people were injured. This watershed event signalled a political change. Leading representatives of Charta 77 constituted the Citizens' Forum (Občanské fórum), which became the opposition's central organization. There were mass protests against the regime all over the country as well as a general strike lasting several hours.

In the Slovakian capital of Bratislava, events were less spectacular than in Prague. Bratislava had no distinguished milieu of dissidents.[1] Only on 19 November 1989 was the opposition alliance The Public against Violence (Verejnost' proti násiliu, VPN) founded. It soon developed into the central coordinating institution for Slovakia's growing political opposition and the partner organization of the Czech Citizens' Forum. Except in Poland, the Communist Party's ultimate relinquishment of power was not due primarily to the work of national reform-oriented counter-elites but to mass revolt by the people – though this is not to belittle the particular significance of Charta 77 and its representatives as the intellectual and organizational leaders of the Czechoslovakian opposition before and during the change.

In both the Czech and the Slovakian autonomous republics, the first national democratic elections of the post-communist era were held in June 1990. They were more a plebiscite on the previous communist regime than a vote based on parties' political programmes. Only two years later there were new parliamentary elections, and this time voters were deciding about the direction to take politically. The election results made it extremely difficult to form a government. The victors in the respective autonomous republics had very different basic political ideas, yet at the national level they were expected to form a coalition government. Fruitful cooperation between Czech and Slovakian politicians was obviously impossible. As a last resort, however, both sides were ready to divide the state. On 1 January 1993, the Czech Republic and the Slovak Republic therefore became completely sovereign, independent states.

Establishment of a Democratic Constitutional State in Slovakia

Transformation of the Political System

The Constitution of the Slovak Republic (Slovenská republika) was already in effect on 1 October 1992, that is, even before the country became formally independent. It is not oriented to specific constitutional traditions of the First Czechoslovakian Republic (1918–1939); rather, it is a declaration in favour of Western constitutional culture. It lays out the principles of sovereignty, democracy and rule of law as the foundation of the republic. It extensively catalogues human rights and basic rights, including general liberty and political rights, minority rights for the ethnicities living in the country, and economic, social, cultural and environmental rights. The self-administration of the territories is guaranteed, and the economy must be run according to the principles of a socially and ecologically oriented market economy. A law of March 1996 explicitly repudiated the communist system, declaring it immoral and criminal.

The political order is based on a system of parliamentary government. The parliament, called the National Council (Národná rada), consists of one chamber of 150 members who are elected for a legislative term of four years. The House can be prematurely dissolved by a qualified majority of its members. Its major tasks are law-making and the political control of the government. The institution of the parliamentary vote of no confidence is the strongest guarantee of the government's responsibility towards the MPs, as it allows an absolute majority of National Council members to force the resignation of a cabinet or one of its members.

The electoral system for the National Council stipulates proportional representation. All citizens have the active right to vote from the age of eighteen and to stand for election from the age of twenty-one. A party must achieve at least 5 per cent of all valid votes to be elected to parliament. For electoral alliances, there is a threshold of 7 per cent; if it consists of four or more parties, it is 10 per cent. The distribution of seats is calculated using the Hagenbach-Bischoff procedure.

Shortly before the 1998 election, electoral law was tightened up so that from then on, any party, regardless of any electoral alliance, needed at least 5 per cent of the votes to sit in parliament. Behind this lay the then government's obvious intention to at least hinder the fragmented opposition's access to the National Council in the upcoming elections. In response, several smaller parties of various political orientations formed an alliance for the sake of their sheer political survival. Once it was finally elected, the previous opposition was able to form a government and revoke the electoral law reform.

A number of parties and political movements developed at the time of the turnaround and in the following years. The strongest political power of the 1990s was the Movement for a Democratic Slovakia (Hnutie za demokratické Slovensko, HZDS), led by its charismatic chairman, Vladimír Mečiar. It had developed from the opposition movement VPN and considered itself a party of the democratic, national-emancipatory centre. Next to follow – at a considerable distance – was the Party of the Democratic Left (Strana demokratickej l'avice, SDL'), which had split from its predecessor, the Communist Party. Furthermore, some smaller parties with quite diverse orientations – Christian-conservative, national-liberal, nationalist or left-wing-socialist – were elected to the National Council. This party system was unstable from the outset: fragmentation processes began at a very early stage and were continuous throughout the country's political development. Party schisms due to personal or programmatic conflicts, the founding of new parties and alliances, and the dissolution of parties frequently changed the party landscape.

Along with representative democracy, the constitution also provides for plebiscitary democracy. A referendum may be initiated by a petition of at least 350,000 citizens or, if it concerns important questions of public interest, by a decision of parliament. Its result is binding if a majority of voters take part and a majority of them votes in favour. Experiences with direct democracy thus far are not encouraging; in most cases referendums have failed due to a lack of participation.

The head of state is the President of the Republic (Prezident Slovenskej republiky), elected to a five-year term. His or her functions include representing the state to citizens and the outside world, promulgation and appointing the prime minister, ministers and other high-ranking officials. Under certain conditions, he or she may prematurely dissolve the National Council. Furthermore, the president may reject any law passed by the parliament as long as he or she gives a reason; his or her suspensive veto may be overruled by members of parliament after renewed consultations and by renewed decision-making.

The government (*vláda*) consists of the prime minister, his or her deputies, and the ministers. Within thirty days of its members' appointment by the President of the Republic, it must present its political programme and ask for the parliament's vote of confidence. If a majority of MPs withhold their vote of confidence, the President of the State must dismiss the government. The prime minister has no formal advisory competency but may politically exploit his or her nominating power in the context of ministerial appointments, as a constitutional amendment of 1999 compels the

President of the State to follow his or her recommendation. The government decides as a college about the government programme, basic questions of home and foreign policy, bills and other issues.

Having already led the country towards independence, Mečiar (HZDS) was elected the first Prime Minister of the Slovak Republic and became the dominant political figure of the early years. With one short interruption, and in the context of various coalitions in which he did not disdain to cooperate with extremist forces, he was head of the government until mid 1998. It was a time of fierce struggles. A constant struggle for power between the prime minister and President Michal Kováč found expression in, for example, the president's repeated refusal to appoint ministers nominated by Mečiar or withholding, with reference to constitutional arguments, the necessary approval of a referendum initiated by the government. Meanwhile, Prime Minister Mečiar made several attempts to politically isolate the head of state and force his premature resignation. One highlight of this campaign was ordering staff members of the state administration, under threat of sanctions, to sign a petition by the minister of cultural affairs demanding the dismissal of the President of the State.[2]

Furthermore, Mečiar ignored a verdict of the Constitutional Court by revoking the mandate of a 'renegade' member of the National Council. This was not the only time the executive power ignored a decision by the Constitutional Court. Under Mečiar's leadership, clientele structures and nepotism flourished in politics. The situation in those years made foreign countries, particularly Western ones, fear that political elites using authoritarian and illegal practices under the guise of formal democracy might establish themselves in this young state.[3]

Municipalities and districts have the right to self-administration, as guaranteed by the constitution. In the context of self-administration, the municipalities take over tasks such as those connected to public order, public services and environmental protection. The competences of the larger unit of self-administration, the district, include implementation of development programmes, supra-local environmental protection and solving problems concerning several municipalities within one district, among other powers. District bodies are also tasked with implementation of state administrative measures. The population's democratic participation in self-administration is ensured by municipal councils and referendums at the municipal and district level, as well as bodies of self-administration, municipal and district parliaments, and mayors or district chairpersons, each of which is directly elected by local citizens (including citizens of member states of the EU) with permanent address for four years.

Justice has two levels: a supreme court, and district courts that also function as appellate courts. Both levels hear civil and criminal cases as well as cases of a public nature. Initially, the parliament elected professional judges nominated by the government to a four-year term, after which re-election was to an unlimited term. This way of proceeding obviously compromised judges' independence from politics, as many a judge could be supposed to have avoided issuing verdicts that might alienate political decision-makers during the 'probationary period'. Since 2001, all judicial appointments are for life, and by nomination of an independent council of judges.

The Constitutional Court (*ústavný súd*), created to ensure that the state acts in accordance with the constitution, is characterized by a remarkable degree of independence from political influence.[4] Initially, the President of the State appointed the judges for seven years, by nomination of the parliament, but since then their term of office has been changed to twelve years and reappointment is no longer possible. This reform increased the judges' independence. The Constitutional Court has extensive competences. For example, it is in charge of judicial review of law-making (including review of international treaties and ordinary laws to ensure conformance with the constitution), handles power struggles between central bodies of state administration, and in cases of dispute decides how the constitution must be interpreted. Finally, the court has the decision-making competence regarding the protection of citizens' basic rights.

After the turnaround, foreign capital played a considerable role in the founding of a number of privately owned national newspapers. The government-critical tabloid *Nový čas* has by far the widest circulation. The large circulation of weeklies without political news (concerning, say, family matters or TV programmes) also merits mention. Also, private radio and TV channels have been established alongside the radio and TV under public law. The privately owned channel *TV Markíza* very soon gained tremendous significance by way of an aggressive marketing strategy and a simple entertainment programme, achieving a market share of more than 70 per cent.

Under the Mečiar government, critical media and journalists were under considerable pressure. For example, political satire programmes on public TV were cancelled, and several members of broadcasting and TV councils were dismissed because of their government-critical stance. Privately owned channels also were not spared, as ultimately they were no longer allowed to report on election campaigns. Early in 1995, a proposal to raise the value-added tax on newspapers by up to 50 per cent failed because the government coalition had qualms about silencing critical papers in this way.[5] At the time, neither national nor international criticism of these actions had much effect on the government.[6]

Consolidation of the Political System

The parliamentary elections of 1998 brought fundamental political change. The former opposition was victorious in elections that were generally considered a vote on the politics and the figure of then Prime Minister Mečiar and his party, the HZDS. Prior to the elections, several smaller parties had allied to form the Slovakian Democratic Coalition (Slovenská demokratická koalícia, SDK) in reaction to the electoral law reform discussed above. Now the SDK became the leading force in a new government coalition, and its chairman, Mikuláš Dzurinda, became prime minister. The other members of the new government alliance were the left-wing SDL', the Christian-conservative party of the Hungarian minority Party of the Hungarian Coalition (Strana mad'arskej koalície, SMK) and the socially oriented, pro-market-economy Party of Civic Understanding (Strana občianskeho porozumenia, SOP). Given this structure, it was hardly surprising that the first government crisis emerged after only a few months.

At first, the government had the support of a considerable majority in the National Council, but coalition conflicts led to its rapid meltdown. Nevertheless, the Dzurinda cabinet survived the full term of office by displaying a surprising capacity for action. His government amended the constitution several times. For instance, a measure introduced in 1999 provided that the President of the State was to be elected by the people – a step made necessary by the parliament's inability to elect a new president with the requisite majority of three-fifths of its members – and an extensive constitutional amendment followed in 2001. It also enabled the country to join the European Union, as it recognized the transfer of sovereignty rights to the EU as well as the priority of EU law over national law. Furthermore, the Dzurinda government initiated far-reaching social and economic reforms as well as changes in the realm of administration. Its declared objective was the country's integration into Western structures, which was finally achieved. At the end of 2002, Slovakia was invited to join NATO, and a few months later its treaty of accession to the European Union was signed. Dzurinda also initiated a change in media policy. Slovakia was now in the international public eye, and in the interest of the country's foreign policy goals it was necessary to stake out a clear distance from the repressive practices of the Mečiar period.[7]

The second coalition government headed by Dzurinda was in office as of mid 2002. Now Dzurinda was chairman of the Slovakian Democratic and Christian Union (Slovenská demokratická a kresťanská únia, SDKÚ), which developed out of the SDK and styles itself as the home of Christians of all denominations, modern conservatives and liberals. Besides the SDKÚ, the party of the Hungarian minority SMK and the Catholic, conservative

Christian Democratic Movement (Krest'anskodemokratické hnutie, KDH) were members of the government coalition. Dzurinda's party had not achieved very strong results in the previous election, so his coalition started the legislative term with quite a tight majority in parliament. Nevertheless, he continued the course of social and market economy reforms. This caused a considerable conflict within both his party and the government, and again the government lost its parliamentary majority in the course of the legislative term. Next the prime minister tried individual agreements with opposition MPs and accepted changing majorities – skilful tactics that allowed for a surprisingly assertive government capable of implementing important projects like health and pension reform. The coalition fell apart in February 2006, just a few months before the new elections.

After a convincing victory in the elections of June 2006, the party Towards Social Democracy (Smer-Sociálna demokracia, Smer-SD) was able to form a coalition government with the HZDS and the national-ist Slovak National Party (Slovenská národná strana, SNS); its chairman, Robert Fico, was elected prime minister. The alliance with the SNS led mainly to much international criticism of the Social Democrats and to con-flict with the European Social Democrats. But in Slovakia itself, consider-able economic growth boosted the popularity of the head of government and his party, which only the international financial and economic crisis brought to a halt. Fico scrapped his predecessors' privatization policy and slightly revised their social and tax policies. The announced campaign to further develop the knowledge society – an urgent task, given the inadequate state of the country's education and vocational training – did not actually happen. Against the background of the great crisis, heated debates divided the National Council, the line of conflict sometimes run-ning between coalition partners rather than between them and the largely ineffective opposition. The prime minister's power was underlined by his dismissal, against the will of the coalition partner HZDS, of an HZDS minister responsible for a dubious real estate deal.

The right-wing potential of Slovak society cannot be overlooked. Violent attacks against Roma and a hostile attitude towards the Hungarian minority have attracted public attention. The SNS, long represented in the parliament and a member of government coalitions, may be considered a political forum for right-wing extremists; it makes a name for itself chiefly by behaving aggressively towards these two minority groups and the Republic of Hungary. Left-wing extremism is of less significance. Some of its adherents are close to the Communist Party of Slovakia (Komunistická strana Slovenska), which was represented in the National Council for one electoral term after the 2002 elections. A positive attitude towards Joseph Stalin's role in history is found among the ranks of this party.

Before the political change of 1998, the people had a mostly nega-tive assessment of the country's social and economic development. In the years since, the basic mood has become even worse. In a representative poll taken in June 2002, 52 per cent of interviewees stated that the over-all situation in Slovakia had worsened since the change in 1998, while only 9 per cent spoke of improvement. The major problems were fear of unemployment and concerns about living standards and social security. The intended accession to the European Union was generally judged posi-tively: in autumn 2002, 74 per cent of interviewees supported this policy. NATO membership, on the other hand, was a debated idea; at the time, 52 per cent voted in favour. The attitude towards the constitutional bodies increasingly soured, though initially, after independence, a majority had had confidence in them. After September 2001, widespread distrust of the President of the State lasted until then President Rudolf Schuster's term of office ended. Even before then, though, a majority had been distrustful towards parliament and government, and their number only increased. In March 2000, only 34 or 35 per cent had trusted these two institutions, but by November 2005, only 24 or 21 per cent of interviewees did.[8] These results suggest that the parliamentary system is not well rooted in society.

The Slovak Republic's Integration into Europe

All Slovakian governments have expressed interest in membership of the European Union in their programmatic statements, though some forces in the initially ruling HZDS adhered to the idea of the country functioning as a bridge between East and West. The association agreement between the Slovak Republic and the EU became effective in February 1995, but Slovakia had to wait longer than its post-socialist neighbours to be invited to accession talks. The reasons were obvious: the EU and other Western actors were critical of the domestic political situation administered by Prime Minister Mečiar and his coalition government. In 1997, the European Commission expressed its reservations with unusual candour: 'Even if in several countries wishing to join there must still be progress towards effective democracy and the protection of minorities, only one state which has applied for accession – Slovakia – does not meet the political criteria as defined by the European Council in Copenhagen'.[9] After the change of leadership in 1998, overall relations with the EU and the West changed fundamentally. The Dzurinda governments made every political effort for quick success in questions of Western integration. The prime minister saw his course confirmed in May 1999, when the Slovakian foreign minister, newly appointed the United Nations' special representative on the Kosovo issue, was entrusted with an important international function.

At the EU summit in Helsinki in December 1999, Slovakia was accepted as a 'second round' country with which the EU was ready to start accession talks in the context of the coming eastward enlargement. The negotiations were sometimes difficult. All accession candidates had expended great effort, having basically adopted the complete body of EU legal regulations and adjusted their respective legal systems accordingly. Special regulations and temporary arrangements were agreed on with each individual country to facilitate its adjustment process. The treaty on the accession of ten Eastern European states, including the Slovak Republic, to the European Union was signed in April 2003.

Today Slovakia is closely connected to the EU. Free and fair competition within the Union has become indispensable to its economy. Regarding issues of energy policy, the Fico government has openly supported nuclear energy in Brussels. Remarkably, the prime minister expressed reservations towards the Charter of Fundamental Rights of the European Union in October 2009, despite having ratified the Lisbon Treaties months before the parliament in Bratislava. Obviously fearing the charter might cast doubt on the validity of the Beneš Decrees, he wanted a special regulation for his country – a stance in line with that of Czech President Václav Klaus. However, Fico's public declaration had no effect, and the government has not yet made contact with the EU regarding this issue.[10]

In polls, the population has always stated a positive attitude towards European integration. The country's EU membership is met with much approval, and confidence in European institutions is high. A majority have spoken out in favour of an enlargement of the Union and consolidation of integration. Meanwhile, the political public allots European issues only a minor role. Low turnout in the elections to the European Parliament confirms this: only 17 per cent of voters in Slovakia participated, and no other country has ever recorded such a low turnout in European elections. In 2009, this figure was only slightly higher, at 19.6 per cent.[11]

Structural Elements of Post-Communist Society

Slovakia, located on an area of 49,000 square km in the geographical heart of Europe, had about 5.3 million inhabitants in 1993. Since then, the population has risen slightly and is now more than 5.4 million. The average life expectancy has increased continuously, and not only since the turn-around; currently it is 79.5 years for women and 71.5 years for men. About 520,000 or 9.7 per cent of citizens are ethnic Hungarians, most of them living in a Hungarian settlement area in the southern regions bordering the Republic of Hungary. Statistics put the Roma minority at about 90,000 or 1.7 per cent of the total number of inhabitants, but the actual number of Roma is estimated to be considerably higher. The share of foreigners is low; some thousand Czechs are the strongest national group.[12]

Households of one and non-marital partnerships as ways of life differing from classical family structures are more rare. Inequality in household incomes may be called comparatively moderate: in 2006, the uppermost fifth of the population had four times the income of the lowest fifth.[13] What is remarkable is the growing divorce rate: in 2004, 33 per cent of couples were divorced – quite a high figure, for a mostly rural country where a middle class Catholic idea of family is widespread. The fertility rate has declined considerably in the past decades, dropping almost 50 per cent since 1980. In 2004, at 1.24 children per woman, it was clearly below the rate of reproduction.[14] Likely causes of this development include transformation problems, pessimism about the future and tendencies of social disintegration.[15]

A number of social lines of conflict are currently relevant. Among them, socio-economic divisions stand out: the inherent contradictions of capitalism have obviously become the dominant theme. So far, Slovakian society is moving towards the Western European situation,[16] and there has been no indication that social peace is endangered. Among OECD countries, Slovakia has one of the lowest numbers of strike days per year.

The national-ethnic division between Slovaks and Hungarians appears deeply rooted. Without doubt, history has created fertile ground for mutual prejudice and hostile stereotypes.[17] Immediately after the turnaround, Slovakian Hungarians demanded autonomous status for their settlement region, something that had no chance of realization. Since then, many a political decision has exacerbated the difficulties of the two ethnic groups' coexistence within a single state and society. During the Mečiar period, for example, the restriction of minority rights led to renewed conflict. The foremost aim was to suppress public use of the Hungarian language, so in the Hungarian region Slovakian became the public authorities' only official language and the only language allowed in written exams at school. After taking office in 1998, Prime Minister Dzurinda acknowledged the obligation to quickly raise the minority rights of the Hungarians to the international standard. However, his policy did not fundamentally improve the interethnic situation.

Another division line separates the ethnic minority of the Roma from the rest of the population. The Roma are not integrated into society. Many of them live in great poverty and endure brutal living conditions. They generally have little education; accordingly, their rate of unemployment is high. For the time being, measures to improve their social situation and integration into society have had little effect. Only some years ago in East

Slovakia, violent struggles erupted between Roma and security forces after shops were looted.[18] The number of Roma in Slovakia is uncertain because many of them do not publicly state their ethnic belonging, for fear of discrimination and racism. In the 1990s, a number of members of this ethnic group emigrated to Western countries, some of them successfully applying for political asylum.

A final significant contrast is that between the centre and the marginalized rural regions. A comparatively small country, Slovakia traditionally experienced great disparity of development that has only increased, given the unequal dynamics of modernization since the downfall of the communist regime. The capital Bratislava and its environs on the south-western tip of Slovakia show the highest settlement density and comparatively high productivity, along with commensurately high per capita income. The eastern part of the country, by contrast, is rather poor and underdeveloped. These socio-economic disparities could engender not only threats to social peace but also political and cultural confrontations.[19] State programmes have been initiated to develop infrastructure in the eastern part of the country, and their implementation is a crucial precondition for more foreign investment in these underdeveloped regions.

The constitution guarantees freedom of religion and stipulates that churches are independent of the state. Churches and religious communities have a right to run schools and social institutions. On the whole, the number of people with religious ties has increased since the communist period ended. Almost 70 per cent of citizens are Roman Catholic; Slovakia has two archdioceses and four dioceses. About 7 per cent are Lutheran (Augsburg Confession), about 4 per cent are Greek Catholic, and some 2 per cent of the population belong to the Reformed Church (Calvinist). Furthermore, about a dozen other religious communities are officially registered, and around 13 per cent of inhabitants are unaffiliated with any religion. The Catholic Church has a strong position in both state and society and has sometimes managed to exert considerable influence on political decision-making processes. The conservative Catholic orientation finds political expression in the party KDH. These days, dividing lines between denominations, or between atheists and people indifferent to religion on the one hand and active Christians on the other, have little social relevance.[20]

Various citizens' initiatives and NGOs emerged after the communist regime fell, but they have not meaningfully stimulated the development of civil society. To date, only one case of civil society commitment is worth mentioning here: the campaign for free and fair elections in the run-up to the 1998 parliamentary elections, which succeeded in mobilizing a substantial share of the population. Obviously, Mečiar's authoritarian governance had sparked a rebellious mood among society.[21] Today, individual adjustment to new ways of life, and above all concerns about securing one's own sustenance, have inevitably eclipsed any interest in civil society activities. Furthermore, the young republic still lacks the traditional recruitment base for such activities – namely, a home-grown middle class – as communism in Czechoslovakia deprived this class of its economic basis of existence.[22]

Establishment of the Market Economy

Transformation of the Economic System

Until the end of World War II, Slovakia's primary economic bases were agriculture and forestry. During the communist period, an expansive industrial sector was established, with a focus on the energy- and raw-material-intensive sectors of metallurgy, armaments and chemicals. Today, the country's formerly rich deposits of raw materials are exhausted or of little economic relevance; worth mentioning are only its brown coal and lignite deposits, which are still exploited thanks to state funding. Dependence on foreign countries for raw material supplies has intensified accordingly.

The constitution documents the turning away from socialist economy. It supports free enterprise, a social and ecological market economy, and economic competition. The right to private property is guaranteed; expropriation is possible only in cases of imperative public interest and must be appropriately compensated. The constitution safeguards the freedom of association as well as the freedom to strike, and it grants all citizens the right to work. Furthermore, it charges the government with the task of elaborating the right of employees to just and satisfying working conditions: laws must regulate, for example, payment, dismissal and health protections as well as the maximum duration of working hours. Such regulations can have the paradoxical effect of restricting the free collective bargaining that the constitution also safeguards.

After the turnaround, the national economy had to undergo a process of radical change to be competitive as a market economy. The essential element of this development was the privatization policy, whose foundations had already been laid in post-communist Czechoslovakia. At first, restitution measures were carried out: nationalized property was returned to the original owners, or they were financially compensated. The sale of small businesses at public auction followed, most of all in the service sector. This 'minor privatization' came to an end in 1993. As for 'major privatization', which started in 1991, most state enterprises in every economic field were sold. The various methods of privatization included direct sale, public auctions and the selling of shares that the people could pay for with investment vouchers. In 1995, privatization by way of vouchers was stopped and replaced by direct sales. The private sector share of the GNP rose constantly, and by early 1998 it was 82.6 per cent.[23]

In the early years, foreign investors showed little interest in the Slovak Republic, above all because of the bad image its politics under the Mečiar governments conveyed to Western countries and the related fact that initially the country had no clear prospect of joining the EU. Finally, at the beginning of 1992, a big automobile producer set an example for the future by starting production in Bratislava.

After the turnaround, heavy industry production rapidly declined at first. Industrial production's overall contribution to the GNP was more than halved within a short span of time. There was no capital for the requisite modernization and structural changes. The services sector, on the other hand, contributed more and more to the GNP, crucially aided by the founding of numerous small private businesses. By this time, agriculture and forestry had long since lost their earlier significance.

Though this economic decline was inevitable, given the lack of competitiveness, it stopped surprisingly soon. The GNP may have shrunk by 3.7 per cent in 1993, but by 1994 the growth rate was 4.9 per cent, and it was more than 6 per cent every year from then until 1997, whereupon annual rates clearly began falling. The weak economic growth at the end of the decade was partly a result of the austerity programme of the Dzurinda government in office since 1996, which had taken over the preceding government's considerable budget deficit and high foreign debt. Rising unemployment was a major concern: at first, the rate gradually declined to 12.5 per cent in 1997, but then it peaked in 1999 at 19.2 per cent.[24]

The Consolidation of the Economic System

The modern economy that developed in the course of Slovakia's transformation has shown considerable growth in the twenty plus years since the turnaround. This successful development was perhaps most strikingly manifest on 1 January 2009, when Slovakia became the first former Soviet bloc country to introduce the euro. Today, the services sector and industrial production form the backbone of its economy. Together with the structural change, the structure of vocations changed as well. The services sector has marked an increase in skilled jobs, which meanwhile have decreased in industry, construction and agriculture. Likewise, the number of unskilled employees has also declined.[25]

From the start of its term, the first Dzurinda government tried to improve the investment climate in Slovakia. To this end, in 1999 it secured the passage of a whole bundle of measures to provide more favourable framework conditions for foreign investment, mostly through changes in customs and tax legislation. Foreign direct investments (including reinvestments) increased greatly in the decade up to 2010: 2008 saw in inflow of about 2.2 billion US dollars. In the crisis year of 2009, capital inflows were only a third of the 2008 number, but the economy can be expected to improve rapidly.[26] Improvement in locational quality was also supported by the introduction of a simplified 19 per cent flat tax on personal income, value added tax and corporate income tax. Finally, comparatively low wages also number among the favourable conditions for investment. Official statistics state the average monthly wage in 2009 as 754.50 euros.[27]

The Dzurinda governments carried on apace with the privatization of state enterprises. In those years, Slovakian Telekom, the Transpetrol oil company, the energy producer Slovenské elektrárne and other energy suppliers as well as banks were among the (partly) privatized companies. The government of Social Democratic Prime Minister Fico, who came to power in 2006, brought an end to further privatization and instead attempted to regain political influence by buying back (shares of) enterprises.[28]

After the turnaround, the communist trade union's successor, named the Confederation of Trade Unions (Konfederácia odborových zväzov, KOZ), and the Association of Entrepreneurs (Asociácia zamestnávateľských zväzov a združení), an alliance of several individual associations, gained crucial significance. Because of its role in the communist period, the KOZ permanently lost standing: more than two thirds of the 2.4 million members it had in 1990 left the confederation in just a few years. During the system transformation, the range of social interests has become ever more extensive and is represented by a huge number of trade union and entrepreneurs' associations, chambers of commerce and other social and business organizations.

As a forum for social dialogue, at first a Council for Economic and Social Agreements (Rada hospodárskej a sociálnej dohody) was established. On it, employees, employers and the state were equally represented. This tripartite body passed a yearly general contract setting benchmark data for the country's economic and social development, which was not legally binding but politically effective. In case of conflict with the government, both the trade unions and entrepreneurs at times exerted political pressure by refusing to cooperate within the Council. In 2004, the Dzurinda government had this kind of corporatist cooperation phased out and established a new body, the Council for Social and Economic Partnership (Rada sociálneho a hospodárskeho partnerstva), whose functions regarding social and economic-political issues are only advisory. This does not, however, mean that the position of organized interests is weakened. Rather, the associations have generally managed to increase their influence on politics. They work through direct connections, contacting political decision-makers and ministries to remind them of their interests. Apart from this, widespread clientelism also maintains specific structures of influence.[29]

Today, Slovakia's manufacturing field is dominated by automotive production. Several international automobile producers have built production sites there, and a strong industrial branch has developed concurrently to produce components and accessories for automobiles. Another important segment is electronics production, which was untouched by the economic crisis due to high demand for consumer electronics and TV sets on export markets.[30] Foreign trade is very much dependent on the two branches of automobile and electronics production. Engineering and metallurgy are also highly significant, as are the chemical, plastics, food, alcohol and tobacco industries. The wood and paper industries also deserve mention.

The country still depends heavily on Russia for its energy supply. Its supplies of gas and oil come almost exclusively from there. The January 2009 natural gas supply conflict between Russia and Ukraine dealt a painful blow to Slovakia, and diversification of supply sources has not yet become part of solving this problem. Regenerative energy is of minor political significance, even though the preconditions for its use (water, geothermics, biomass) are comparatively favourable. Renewable energy currently makes up 4 per cent of energy supplies. Increasing this share to about 14 per cent by 2020 is currently being debated, but its realization is unlikely; potential investors show little interest because of the lack of political support.[31] The political weight is instead behind expanding nuclear energy. Two reactors of the Jaslovské Bohunice nuclear power station were switched off more than a decade ago for reasons of security, two others are still running and another two are under construction. Moreover, it seems to have been decided that new sites will be constructed at Jaslovské Bohunice and Kecerovce.

Tourism holds considerable potential, though its development is still hindered by insufficient infrastructure. One of the most important centres of tourism is the mountain chain of the High Tatras, which offer recreation and winter sports. Added to this are several national parks and nature reserves as well as many spas and bathing resorts, among them the internationally renowned thermal spa of Piešťany.

In 2008, immediately before the worldwide financial and economic crisis hit with full force, Slovakia's GNP was 67.2 billion euros, that is, about 12,400 euros per citizen – the second highest among the post-communist countries of East Central and Eastern Europe, behind the Czech Republic.

During the phase of economic weakness in 1999, the economic growth had been close to 0 per cent; in 2007 it was a remarkable 10.4 per cent and in 2008 it was still 6.4 per cent. In 2009, due to the crisis, the economy declined, but for 2010, growth of 2.0 per cent was predicted. The unemployment rate remains high: in 2007 it was about 11.1 per cent, and in 2009 it grew moderately to an estimated 12.3 per cent. The downside is that the economy increasingly lacks qualified workers.[32] Over time, the orientation towards gainful employment has grown, particularly among men, but in the EU comparison it is still below average. In 2006, almost 60 per cent of the working-age population was integrated into the labour market.[33]

Today, the population hardly questions free enterprise and the market economy, perceiving no alternative to the existing economic system. On the other hand, Slovaks' widespread dissatisfaction with the socio-economic conditions of life cannot be overlooked. In a representative poll in October 2009, only 48 per cent of interviewees said their living standard was better than twenty years ago, and 61 per cent complained that it was harder to find a job. Only 31 per cent were of the opinion that honest work would improve their chances of achieving an appropriate social status.[34]

Current State of Democratic Consolidation

The Slovak Republic has developed into an institutionally consolidated democracy. Its constitutional bodies have proven their functionality for implementing far-reaching reforms in the social and economic fields as well as the country's integration into Western structures. In the context of exerting political power, however, repeated deficiencies have contradicted the demands of modern democracy. The existing problems include deficiencies in both political control and the separation of powers; recently, political and administrative pressure on independent judges has also attracted attention.[35]

All former prime ministers and other leading figures across the political spectrum have been accused of corruption and nepotism, and rightly so. In early 2012, a corruption scandal that was never completely proven, the so-called 'Gorilla' affair, provoked great outrage among the population. The scandal referred to matters from 2005 and 2006 – the period of the second Dzurinda government – that pointed to a well-organized network of corruption and corruptibility: a group of investors was said to have promised considerable percentages to several politicians from both the government and the opposition camp, if upcoming privatizations were decided in their favour.

A striking problem in Slovakian society that also burdens relations between the governments in Bratislava and Budapest is the already mentioned interethnic conflict between Slovakians and Hungarians. These struggles were pushed onto the back burner during the years of EU accession talks, lest they endanger their successful completion. Now that accession is achieved, tensions are rising again, and for reasons that sometimes appear trivial.[36] The media air reports of ethnic Slovaks singing hate songs in football stadiums and violently attacking their Hungarian fellow countrymen. Meanwhile, the fact that many among the Hungarian minority call Slovakia 'Upper Hungary' (alluding to 1,000 years of history) does not calm the situation.

So far, the party system cannot be characterized as consolidated. Its fragility is strikingly demonstrated by the fact that sixteen out of 150 MPs defected from their factions in the 2006–2010 legislative term alone. Two of the newest parties deserve emphasis; founded in 2009, they soon drew a strong response from the population and by June 2010 had managed to clear the 5 per cent threshold. They are the market-liberal Freedom and Solidarity (Sloboda a Solidartita, SaS) and the Most-Híd party (the Slovakian and Hungarian words for 'bridge'). Overcoming the rift between Slovaks and ethnic Hungarians is the latter's stated primary objective.

An important step on the way to consolidation of the party system concerns the Social Democratic Smer-SD and the SDKÙ-DS – 'DS' standing for Demokratická strana (Democratic Party), the leading party of the conservative Christian Democrat camp – both founded around the turn of the millennium: in recent years, both have developed into consolidated political organizations with leadership skills. As large parties receive considerable funding from the state,[37] they may easily come to depend on it and thereby lose their rootedness in society.

Smer-SD was the strongest political force in the 2010 elections but was unable to put together a government coalition. Instead, the SDKÚ-DS, KDH and the two new parties SaS and Most-Híd formed a coalition. Iveta Radičová, vice-chairwoman of the SDKÚ-DS, was elected prime minister. But no sooner was the coalition established than some MPs threatened to withdraw their support, believing their positions to be insufficiently represented by the common government programme. The Radičová government declared its primary objectives to be reducing the budget deficit and creating new jobs. In its very first weeks in office, it was already sending the EU clear signals that met with much annoyance in Brussels, where they were seen as expressing a lack of solidarity. The new government high-handedly cancelled the Fico government's promise to contribute to assistance loans for Greece. In October 2011, the coalition fell apart after the prime minister connected the parliamentary vote on extending the so-called Euro

Rescue Package to a vote of confidence. Due to the related financial risks for Slovakia, the coalition partner SaS was unwilling to support the decision and did not take part in the vote. In a second vote, Smer-SD voted in favour, creating a majority for the extension. The Social Democrats had connected their vote to an agreement on new elections in March 2012, in which Smer-SD attained an absolute majority in the parliament. Now, with Robert Fico, the prime minister comes from its ranks again.

Twenty years after the end of the communist system, 57 per cent of interviewees in a representative poll called the 'Velvet Revolution' one of the greatest events in Slovakia's modern history, and 59 per cent judged the establishment of a democratic order a success. Nevertheless, many people were sceptical about society's development. At the beginning of 2010, only 46 per cent had a positive opinion of it; 45 per cent viewed it negatively. At the same time, a majority of interviewees distrusted both the parliament and the government. The President of the State, on the other hand, met with the trust of the majority. The political parties fared extremely poorly, with only 19 per cent expressing trust in them. These sobering results are explained by the many unsolved problems of Slovakian society, of which unemployment and corruption/nepotism are perceived as the gravest.[38] Furthermore, the people's general mood is increasingly characterized by weariness of reform: since communism ended, and particularly in the context of joining the EU, they have endured a process of constant reform in which the concomitant expectations of wealth have not been met.[39]

Rüdiger Kipke is a retired Professor of Political Systems and Public Law at the University of Siegen. He studied juridical science, political science and Slavic Studies in Göttingen, Berlin (West) and Prague, and earned his doctorate in juridical science in Göttingen. After having worked as a lawyer in Brunswick for a short time, he worked as a research consultant for a faction of the Deutscher Bundestag in Bonn. In 1977, he started teaching at the University of Siegen. He has been a visiting fellow at several universities in Germany and abroad. One focus of his research work is regional studies.

Notes

1. See W. Merkel, H.-J. Puhle et al., *Defekte Demokratie, Band 2: Regionalanalysen* (Wiesbaden, 2006), 400.
2. See Europäische Kommission, 'Stellungnahme der Kommission zum Antrag der Slowakei auf Beitritt zur Europäischen Union', *Bulletin der Europäischen Union*, Beilage 9/97 (Luxemburg, 1997), 17.

3. See R. Kipke, 'Das politische System der Slowakei', in W. Ismayr (ed.), *Die politischen Systeme Osteuropas*, 3rd ed. (Wiesbaden, 2010), 317–56, here 327f.
4. See K. Schmid, 'Die Slowakische Republik seit dem 1. Januar 1993: Verfassung und Verfassungsleben', in M. Hofmann and H. Küpper (eds), *Kontinuität und Neubeginn: Staat und Recht in Europa zu Beginn des 21. Jahrhunderts* (Baden-Baden, 2001), 368–83, here 376f.
5. See Kipke, 'Das politische System der Slowakei', 344.
6. See K. Cramer-Langer, *Demokratisierung in der Slowakischen Republik: Entstehung und Entwicklung des Parteiensystems seit 1989*, special edition (Cologne, 1998), 31.
7. See Kipke, 'Das politische System der Slowakei', 344.
8. See O. Gyárfášová and M. Velšic, 'Public Opinion', in G. Mesežnikov, M. Kollár, and T. Nicholson (eds), *Slovakia 2002: A Global Report on the State of Society* (Bratislava, 2003), 219–46, here 220–26; Kipke, 'Das politische System der Slowakei', 342f.
9. Europäische Kommission, 'Agenda 2000: Eine stärkere und erweiterte Union', *Bulletin der Europäischen Union*, Beilage 5/97 (Luxemburg, 1997), 46.
10. See M. Bútora et al., 'Foreign Policy: The Year of Anniversaries and Challenges', in M. Bútora, G. Mesežnikov and M. Kollár (eds), *Trends in Quality of Democracy: Slovakia 2009* (Bratislava, 2010), 105–23, here 114.
11. See Z. Bútorová and O. Gyárfášová, 'Contemporary Slovakia in Public Opinion', in Bútora, Mesežnikov and Kollár, *Trends in Quality of Democracy*, 125–55, here 147f.
12. http://www.lexas.net/laender/europa/Slowakei/bevoelkerung.asp.
13. See S. Mau and R. Verwiebe, *Die Sozialstruktur Europas* (Konstanz, 2009), 187.
14. See ibid., 107, 94.
15. See S. Hradil, *Die Sozialstruktur Deutschlands im internationalen Vergleich* (Wiesbaden, 2006), 53.
16. See R. Štefančík, *Christlich-demokratische Parteien in der Slowakei* (Trnava, 2008), 84.
17. See Kipke, 'Das politische System der Slowakei', 346f.
18. See ibid., 347f.
19. See S. Kämpfer, 'Regionale Ungleichheiten in der Tschechischen und Slowakischen Republik im Zuge des Erweiterungsprozesses der Europäischen Union: Eine empirische Untersuchung im Zeitraum von 1998 bis 2003', *Soziale Welt* 59 (2008), 351–71, here 352, 370.
20. See Kipke, 'Das politische System der Slowakei', 332f.
21. See Merkel, Puhle et al., *Defekte Demokratie*, 404.
22. See Z. Mansfeldová, 'Zivilgesellschaft in der Tschechischen und Slowakischen Republik', *Aus Politik und Zeitgeschichte* 48(6–7) (1998), 13–19, here 18.
23. See G. Mesežnikov, 'Die Slowakei', in A.U. Gabanyi and K. Schroeder (eds), *Vom Baltikum zum Schwarzen Meer: Transformation im östlichen Europa* (Munich, 2002), 339–66, here 350–52.
24. See Bundesstelle für Außenhandelsinformation, 'Wirtschaftsdaten aktuell: Slowakische Republik' (Cologne, November 1999); Bundesstelle für Außenhandelsinformation, 'Ostmittel- und Osteuropa im Aufholprozess: Transformation und Wirtschaftslage in Ostmitteleuropa und der GUS 2000/2001' (Berlin, 2001), 24.
25. See Mau and Verwiebe, *Die Sozialstruktur Europas*, 149.
26. See Germany Trade & Invest, 'Wirtschaftstrends Slowakische Republik: Jahreswechsel 2009/10' (Cologne, 2009), 7.
27. http://portal.statistics.sk/showdoc.do?docid=16415.
28. See Germany Trade & Invest, 'Energiewirtschaft 2008/09: Slowakische Republik' (Cologne, 2010), 2.

29. See V. Krivý, 'Citizens' Value Orientations', in Z. Bútorová (ed.), *Democracy and Discontent in Slovakia: A Public Opinion Profile of a Country in Transition* (Bratislava, 1998), 37–49, here 42.
30. See Germany Trade & Invest, 'Wirtschaftstrends Slowakische Republik', 14.
31. See Germany Trade & Invest, 'Energiewirtschaft', 3.
32. See Germany Trade & Invest, 'Wirtschaftsdaten kompakt: Slowakische Republik' (Cologne, November 2009); Germany Trade & Invest, 'Wirtschaftstrends Slowakische Republik', 1–3.
33. See Mau and Verwiebe, *Die Sozialstruktur Europas*, 135.
34. See Bútorová and Gyárfášová, 'Contemporary Slovakia in Public Opinion', 152.
35. See G. Mesežnikov, P. Učeň and S. Szomolányi, 'Democratic Institutions and the Rule of Law', in Bútora, Mesežnikov and Kollár, *Trends in Quality of Democracy*, 15–39, here 38.
36. See J. Pänke and I. Samson, 'Zwischen Wirtschaftswunder und Extremismus: Schatten auf der slowakischen Euro-Euphorie?', *DGAPanalyse* 2 (2009), 9f.
37. See H. Gehring and A. Pešková, *Wahlhandbuch Slowakei 2010* (Bratislava, 2010), 8.
38. See Bútorová and Gyárfášová, 'Contemporary Slovakia in Public Opinion', 151, 126, 134.
39. See K.-O. Lang, 'Populism in "Old" and "New" Europe: Trends and Implications', in M. Bútora, O. Gyárfášová, G. Mesežnikov and T.W. Skladony (eds), *Democracy and Populism in Central Europa: The Visegrad Elections and Their Aftermath* (Bratislava, 2007), 125–40, here 125.

Chapter 8

SLOVENIA

❧

Božo Repe

Introduction: Parting with Yugoslavia

Slovenia was one of the six former Yugoslav republics and the first to opt for independence as a result of the unbearable conditions in the state of Yugoslavia. The decision to become a completely independent state matured in the second half of the 1980s. The first multi-party elections since World War II were held in the spring of 1990, and the wish for independence was confirmed by a plebiscite that December. Among the reasons for deciding on an independent status were Yugoslavia's inability to democratize itself, its failure to overcome the severe economic crisis caused by its economically and politically ineffective socialist system, and its desire to join the European Economic Community, which later became the European Community and, finally, the European Union. Moreover, although Slovenia had been part of Yugoslavia for seventy years, the fears Slovenes had harboured since their fateful experience with Germany and Italy in World War II were now slowly abating in view of changed conditions in Europe, particularly after the Helsinki Conference of 1975, and the strengthening of European integration.

After lengthy political conflicts between Slovenia and the still existing federation, Slovenian independence was finally attained through an armed revolt that led to a ten-day war against the Yugoslav army. Thanks to an intervention by the European Community, a truce was declared, and Slovenia subsequently suspended its decision to pursue independence for three months.[1] The continuation of the war in other parts of the former state, along with the Badinter Commission's conclusions that Yugoslavia had disintegrated and that only the republics fulfilling the conditions for independence would be permitted to apply for international recognition,

---

Notes for this chapter begin on page 225.

brought the European Community to recognize Slovenia in January 1992, followed by the Great Powers and other countries. However, the European Community and Great Powers did not favour Yugoslavia's disintegration or Slovenia's pursuit of independence. Hence, the struggle for international recognition was difficult and at first highly uncertain, as it depended on various international circumstances following the end of the Cold War and the events taking place at the EU summit, particularly the signing of the Maastricht Treaty. At that time in international politics, Germany played the decisive role in recognizing Slovenia (and Croatia) as independent states.

Throughout nearly thirty years now, Slovenia has taken an ambivalent stance towards other republics of the former Yugoslav state. The same attitude prevails towards citizens who moved to Slovenia during the time of the former common state. Upon the plebiscite decision for independence in December 1990, Slovenia guaranteed all its rights to citizens of other republics of former Yugoslavia who had permanent residence in Slovenia in December 1990. However, it only partially adhered to this promise. The majority of those citizens (close to 100,000) who applied for citizenship status received it, but over 24,000 people who had not applied for it, or whose applications were denied for various reasons, were simply 'erased' from the Permanent Population Register. This treatment caused great harm to them and their families. Their documents were destroyed, leaving them unable to find employment, obtain health insurance or attend schools and universities. This injustice has been corrected in the past few years by the overturning of the previous decisions on an individual basis, but the state has not made any efforts to compensate the people thus erased – not even symbolic gestures (e.g. an official apology by the national authorities). The first multi-party government had decided on erasure as a measure of collective judgement exclusively against citizens of other former Yugoslav republics, thus exempting other foreign nationals. A number of politicians (and probably also the majority of the population) did not care for the *izbrisani* (the erased), as propaganda depicted them as opposing Slovenia's quest for independence and neglecting to clarify their status, even though they could have. Likewise, the government has not treated workers who arrived in Slovenia following independence with much leniency: to this day they have not been granted their rights, even as their brutal exploitation is tolerated.

So far, no group of Slovenian residents who came from other states in the territory of the former Yugoslavia has achieved minority status. They have finally been permitted to found cultural societies, and new legislation on national radio and television (which was rejected in a referendum) has at last opened up the possibility of cultural programmes. In the 1990s, Slovenia's foreign policy followed the principle of turning 'away from the Balkans', deliberately creating the impression that the country had never had anything to do with the former Yugoslavia. Lately this policy has changed; however, the trust that was lost due to unprincipled politics in the years after the disintegration will be difficult to regain. Meanwhile, other countries (particularly Austria) have expertly entered the political and economic arena.

Legal System

The constitution, adopted by the National Assembly of the Republic of Slovenia on 23 December 1991 to ensure the standard political, economic and social rights of its citizens, was a milestone between the old and the new in terms of the social order and the state itself. Slovenia signed the European Convention on Human Rights and Freedoms in 1993 and ratified it a year later. Since then, the constitution has been altered several times. In July 1997, foreign nationals were permitted to purchase real estate in Slovenia, which was a condition (particularly urged by Italy) of Slovenia's convergence with the West. In July 2000, a proportional voting system was introduced, and in March 2007, constitutional provisions were adopted to enable Slovenia's accession to the EU and NATO. An amendment of June 2007 provided the option to organize Slovenia by regions, but this did not materialize as it ran counter to parties' political interests and some heavy lobbying by a number of mayors (many of them deputies in the National Assembly).

As was the case elsewhere, the legal transition happened gradually. In its history as a Yugoslav republic, Slovenia had received its first constitution in 1947 (a federal constitution had been adopted in 1946). This constitution granted the right of self-determination, including the right to secession. The postwar decades saw dynamic changes in the Yugoslav and Slovenian constitutional orders. Later on, the last Yugoslav constitution (of 1974) was the subject of harsh polemics between advocates of centralism and confederalism. The federal constitution was partially amended in 1988 in an attempt to introduce a market economy. Then, in March 1989, Serbia interfered with the Yugoslav legal order by arbitrarily amending its constitution (to abolish its autonomous regions). Under threat of a coup d'état, Slovenia followed suit that same year, legally securing its sovereignty with several amendments (to prohibit the declaration of a state of emergency without a decision by the Slovenian parliament, among other measures).

The complex structure of the Slovenian parliament is based on the principle of representation and, in part, on corporately elected representatives (i.e. the Socio-political Chamber, Chamber of Communes, and Chamber of Associated Labour). The first multi-party, democratic elections were held in April 1990. Prior to this, following the Polish example, there had been an attempt to reach agreement on the electoral law and the eventual division of authority between representatives of the opposition and representatives of the elites (i.e. socio-political organizations) under the Socialist Alliance of Working People, but it had not succeeded. Hence, the multi-party electoral law was adopted without the prior political agreement of the Socialist Assembly, a manoeuvre in which the Constitutional Commission played an important role. Even before the 1990 elections, Dr Janez Drnovšek, one of several Slovenian candidates, had been elected a member of the federal presidency by direct vote in the spring of 1988, defeating a favourite of the elites, among others, and the Socialist Assembly, authorized to decide the legitimacy of the election, had simply confirmed it. Such elections reflected democratic changes in the second half of the 1980s that also encompassed many other factors: the powerful ascent of civil society; the drawing up of an alternative constitution that later became the basis of the new Slovenian constitution; the liberation of the media; and reform processes in the League of Communists after Milan Kučan took over its leadership in 1986.[2]

The presence of constitutional courts is considered one of the greatest differences between communist and post-communist constitutional systems. Yugoslavia's communist constitutional system was established in 1963, mainly to ensure the distribution of power among the different federal levels and preserve the legality of the system, not to protect individual changes and freedoms. In the transitional 1980s, however, this system began to change. Until today, the issue of Slovenia's break with Yugoslavia and the old legal system generated ambivalence and differing explanations in both the international situation (e.g. the succession of certain agreements) and domestic law. In the case of domestic law, the conflict between right and left revolved mostly around interpretations of the so-called AVNOJ resolutions (i.e. whether or not they represented the foundation of Slovenian statehood).[3]

The criminal law system in Yugoslavia and Slovenia became more moderate from the 1950s onwards, though with important differences between the two entities. In Slovenia, political judicial proceedings were the exception from the 1960s on; the last two took place in 1974. In 1988, the military court of the Yugoslav People's Army (YPA) took on a special role when its proceedings against four Slovenes accused of high treason triggered a mass movement in Slovenia. At the time, conflict between Slovenia and the YPA was at a peak; the YPA was staging various scenarios so that a state of emergency could be declared and the Slovenian leadership and most critical emerging opposition eliminated.

The Slovenian peace movement and other alternative movements had been demanding the abolition of the death penalty in Yugoslavia since the mid 1980s. Slovenia abolished it in 1989, when it was still part of Yugoslavia (though the death penalty had not actually been used since the early 1950s). In the first five years of independence, the relative per-missiveness of the former legislation allowed the old penal code to stand, with minor corrections, but in 1995, Slovenia drew up a new, modern code that retained twenty years of imprisonment as the maximum penalty. Later changes increased the severity of the maximum sentence, raising it to thirty years of imprisonment in 1998 and then, in a quickly passed new law of 2008, to life imprisonment.[4]

Media

In Yugoslavia, the Slovenian media were common social property man-aged by socio-political organizations (the Socialist Alliance of the Working People, which was a successor to the Liberation Front of World War II; the Alliance of Socialist Youth; the Alliance of Socialist Trade Unions; the League of Communists). Throughout the 1980s, however, they were allowed more room. As of the 1970s, foreign journalists, both accredited and unaccredited, had free access to individuals and institutions. The Socialist Alliance controlled the federation's leading daily newspapers and television channels and appointed the editors as well. The complex censorship system was subject to editors' judgement as well as so-called public social criticism in the form of, for instance, discussion of individual articles and journalists at various meetings of socio-political organiza-tions. Technically, a law prohibiting verbal offence was in force, but it did not apply in Slovenia in the 1980s; however, prosecutors had the option of confiscating individual articles. The most provocative newspaper – *Mladina*, a gazette of the Alliance of Socialist Youth – was the first to evade control.

By the end of the 1980s – even before the change in authority – most of the Slovenian media (except the national RTV) had shaken off their depen-dence on the state. For example, the leading newspaper, *Delo*, replaced the slogan 'The gazette of the Socialist Alliance of the Working People' with the motto 'An independent newspaper for an independent Slovenia'. But they were not at all prepared to replace their dependence on the state with dependence on the market, advertisers, and the new owners and their economic interests. The new authorities' political conviction was that the media had remained predominantly left wing; therefore, the opposition leader, Janez Janša, spoke of a 'swan song' as the change of power began. Meanwhile, the new authorities found it unbearable that they had only one, newly founded paper, *Demokracija*, and set up a special media pluralization fund to enable the creation of right-wing newspapers as early as 1991. All of them – *Slovenec* and *Jutranjik*, in addition to *Demokracija* – failed, as did *Republika* on the left, but this did not jeopardize the primacy of the three leading newspapers *Delo*, *Dnevnik* and *Večer*, and any other, related publications. The notion that the left controlled the media persisted: for instance, six times in 2003, Janša demanded his media contacts be changed, and some 10,000 of his supporters signed a petition asserting *Nekaj je treba storiti* (Something must be done).

The media act adopted in 1994 replaced the designation 'founder' with 'publisher', which could apply to anyone, be it an individual, company or commercial organization. This concept did not apply to RTV, a public service founded by the Republic of Slovenia. Polemics in parliament focused on whether there was a need for a special law and whether privatization should indeed take place following the general privatization act. In practice, the media were privatized by transferring portions of the value of the ordinary shares to special funds (10 per cent to the pension fund, 10 per cent to the compensation fund and 20 per cent to the development fund of the Republic of Slovenia, which distributed it among authorized investment companies later). A second stage of the privatization process consisted of internal buyouts. This way, journalists had substantial (perhaps even a major) opportunity to influence the independence of the media; however, they generally sold their shares when the prices rose, and to a large extent the state did too. This was most obvious in the case of *Delo*, which was first listed on the stock exchange in 1995. Its ownership division followed the rule of 20 per cent of the capital for internal distribution, 40 per cent for internal buyout, 10 per cent each for the pension and the compensation fund, and 20 per cent for the development fund. Within a few years, internal ownership had dropped from 60 per cent to 5 per cent;[5] similar trends could be observed elsewhere. The situation that set in during the decade following the adoption of the law and largely exists today is:

> most of the Slovenian print media do not have strategic owners, meaning owners whose basic concern are the media. The newspaper *Delo*, which is also the majority owner of the most popular daily newspaper *Slovenske novice*, is owned by a brewery, quasi-government funds, and an investment company. The newspaper *Dnevnik* is controlled by a company that formally dealt with

publishing, yet invests all its money in purchasing shares of the marina, spas, an insurance company, and a distribution company; the owners holding the majority of the newspaper *Večer* are a bank and an investment company connected to it.

Owners sell and buy media shares so quickly that even media experts can barely keep up with the changes.[6] The first political attempt at a media takeover happened in 2000 under a right-wing government that lasted only a few months; the second took place in the years 2004 to 2008, when Janša's likewise right-wing government was in power and tried to gain control over *Delo* with an agreement to sell the largest commercial enterprise, Mercator, to the Pivovarna Laško brewery, while in exchange the brewery would leave the management of *Delo* to individuals favoured by the government. This did in fact happen: *Delo* underwent changes and its editorial policy was altered. However, a subsequent dispute between Janša and the other protagonists prevented final implementation of the decision. In 2005, the ruling group pursued the political option of forming (and controlling) the RTV Slovenija Council through passage of the Radotelevizija Slovenija Act, which received majority support in the National Assembly.[7] In 2010 the new, left-wing liberal power tried to change this, but its proposal was rejected in a referendum with a very small turnout.

Politics

Slovenia's political system operates through proportionality; a party must clear a 4 per cent threshold to sit in the National Assembly (the election of the National Council, which has limited jurisdiction, is based on the proportional principle). No attempts to change it into a majority system have yet succeeded (a referendum was held on the question in 1996, and its results were so close it had to be decided by the Constitutional Court). The parliament is the linchpin of the political system in Slovenia, and the central executive power is held by the government. Lawyers who participated in drawing up the Slovenian constitution in 1992 admitted openly that this power distribution was intended to limit the authority of President Milan Kučan as much as possible. Kučan, a reformed communist and the person most responsible for the peaceful transformation, exerted great influence on the public and by all indicators was the most popular Slovenian politician from the end of the 1980s to the termination of his mandate in 2002 and beyond. The political right tried to reduce his influence with systematic public attacks (accusations ranged from hiding weapons to organize a coup d'état to running an organized association of the former secret police and the mafia, the so-called *udbo* mafia), and the political left did not welcome his influence.

Slovenia's most pronounced political crisis to date has been attributed to a 'post-independence syndrome' in 1993/94, when, unsatisfied by the brief skirmishes with the YPA during the ten-day war for independence, Military Intelligence and the paramilitary organizations connected to it intruded into the civil sphere with bugging devices and tracking. In the end, Military Intelligence arrested and manhandled a civilian (said by some to be a police collaborator). Meanwhile, still unrevealed affairs were ongoing; they involved the sale of weapons to Croatia, Bosnia, Herzegovina, and indeed to anyone who profited from the war. These affairs continue to generate political conflict to this day. In February 1994, the Special Brigade Moris, a kind of 'praetorian guard' under the minister of defence, even carried out an unannounced training session in which a helicopter dropped onto the headquarters of the Ministry of Defence in the capital and motorized units participated on the ground.[8] After some hesitation, and prodded by protests in front of the parliament building and the supportive cheers of RTV journalists who broadcast the events live, President Janez Drnovšek had the minister of defence, Janez Janša, removed from office.

Many of the decisions adopted by parliament during the transition were not then in effect, as they could not simply be transferred from one sphere to another. Having been adopted during a political turning point, they were very difficult or impossible to retroactively amend. Denationalization and privatization, the looting of nationalized property, dealings with the Catholic Church (which were handled in an old-fashioned manner by returning feudal property and quietly letting it adopt the status of an established church) and the attitude towards the media count among the fundamental errors of the Slovenian parliament's since its foundation. Today's Slovenian parliament must be seen from two angles. On the one hand, its nearly thirty years of existence and operation have ensured the normal functioning of the entire political structure and the balance of power among the three separate branches of government. On the other hand, there are obvious conflicts in which parliamentary instruments and procedures are blocked or abused to divert attention from actual problems, affairs and criminal activities, with the troubling result of an air of hysteria spread throughout society.

The upshot for Slovenia is that the latter excesses obstruct the inherently understood function of parliament as a forum in which to air problems and sincerely discuss any issues that arise, in order to avoid escalation into social conflict. Many deputies have understood and still interpret the immunity of freedom of speech as the right to launch primitive attacks, to say anything that comes to mind about anything to anyone and to cause problems rather than try to solve them by consensus. Confidence in the Slovenian parliament (and in politics in general) has been severely lacking in the past. Regarding levels of confidence, the political parties rank lowest, the parliament (National Assembly) somewhat higher, and the Catholic Church highest. Though society is highly politicized, only around 5 per cent of the electorate are active members of parties. Since 1968, public opinion polls have shown Slovenes' confidence in their own institutions to be far behind the European average, even during socialist times.[9] Polls conducted by newspapers indicate that the current level of confidence in politics (under a left-wing government in a permanent state of crisis) is probably at its lowest point in the entire period. The present situation strongly resembles the Hungarian one: the left has deeply disappointed the electorate, whereas the right attempts to incite a right-wing revolution by radically amending the constitution but cannot muster the two-thirds major-ity needed to do so. Numerous inquiry commissions aiming at uncovering affairs, various obstructions of parliamentary work and the turning over of decision-making to referendums (even on such topics as protection of human rights) signal a decided return to a 'people's democracy'.

Slovenian parties have developed from two political sources, according to which they are divided into the springtime of democracy in Slovenia and parties of 'political continuity' (successors to previous socio-political organizations). This division primarily indicates who was for indepen-dence and who against, and who is for democratic change and who rejects it. In fact, the majority of the parties are home to former communists, many of whom, including leading politicians, had attempted a political or some other public career under the former system. On both left and right, the parties themselves have undergone a number of mergers and separa-tions. Since 1992, the parliament has comprised seven or eight parties. Due to the proportional voting system, all the governments so far have been politically mixed but typically contain a leading liberal party, with the exception of the six-month government of Andrej Bajuk in 2000 and the government of Janez Janša in 2004 to 2008. The relative winners in the 2008 elections, the Social Democrats (successors to the former League of Communists), formed a government; they also held the relative majority in the first multi-party elections in 1990. The only party that has never been part of a coalition is the Slovenian National Party, a populist party with controversial stances that nonetheless had no difficulty making its way into parliament. Slovenia has not had a green party in parliament since 1992, but it does have a pensioners' party, and for a time there was also a Youth Party. The Hungarian and Italian minorities, which the constitution deems autochthonous, each have one representative in parliament.

TABLE 8.1. Parliamentary election results (1990–2011)

Party	1990 %	1990 seats	1992 %	1992 seats	1996 %	1996 seats	2000 %	2000 seats	2004 %	2004 seats	2008 %	2008 seats	2011 %	2011 seats
LDS	14.5	39	23.4	22	27.0	25	36.3	34	22.90	23	5.21	5	1.48	–
SLS	12.6	32	8.6	10	19.3	19	–	–	6.82	7	5.21	5	6.83	6
SLS+SKD	–	–	–	–	–	–	9.5	9	–	–	–	–		
SDS	7.1	17	3.3	4	16.1	16	15.8	14	29.08	29	29.26	28	26.19	26
SKD	13.0	23	14.5	15	9.6	10	–	–	–	–	–	–		
NSi	–	–	–	–	–	–	8.7	8	9.09	9	–	–	4.88	4
ZLSD/SD	17.3	36	13.5	14	9.0	9	12.1	11	10.17	10	30.45	29	10.52	10
DESUS	–	–	–	–	4.3	5	5.2	4	4.04	4	7.45	7	6.97	6
SNS	–	–	10.2	12	3.2	4	4.4	4	6.27	6	5.40	5	1.80	–
Party for Real (Zares)					–	–	–	–	–	–	9.37	9	0.65	–
LZJ-PS	–	–	–	–	–	–	–	–	–	–	–	–	28.51	28
LGV	–	–	–	–	–	–	–	–	–	–	–	–	8.37	8
DS	9.5	30	5.1	6	–	–	–	–	–	–	–	–	–	–
LS	2.5	4	–	–	–	–	–	–	–	–	–	–	–	–
ZS	8.8	17	3.7	5	–	–	–	–	–	–	–	–	0.36	–

TABLE 8.1. (Continued)

Party	1990 %	1990 seats	1992 %	1992 seats	1996 %	1996 seats	2000 %	2000 seats	2004 %	2004 seats	2008 %	2008 seats	2011 %	2011 seats
SSS	5.3	14	–	–	–	–			–	–	–	–	–	–
SMS	–	–	–	–	–	–	4.3	4	–	–	–	–	–	–
Independent deputies	–	22	–	–	–	–	–	–	–	–	–	–	–	–
Representatives of national minorities	2.5	6	2.2	2	2.2	2	2.2	2		2		2		2
Other parties	9.4	–	17.9	–	11.5	–	3.8	–	11.72		7.65	–	3.44	
Total		240		90		90		90		90		90		90
Turnout (in %)		80		85.6		73.7		70.14		60.64		63.10		65.60

Only one of the three chambers between 1990 and 2011 was elected by proportional representation. The percentages refer to this chamber, while the number of seats is a total of all three chambers with eighty respective seats.

Parties: DeSUS (Democratic Party of Pensioners of Slovenia); DS (Democratic Party); LDS (Liberal Democracy of Slovenia); LS (Liberal Party); NSi (New Slovenia-Christian People's Party); SDS(S) (Social Democratic Party of Slovenia); SDS (Slovenian Democratic Party) since 2004; SKD (Slovenian Christian Democrats); SLS (Slovene People's Party); SMS (Youth Party of Slovenia); SNS (Slovenian National Party); SSS (Socialist Party of Slovenia); ZLSD (United List of Social Democrats); SD (Social Democrats) since 2005; ZS (Greens of Slovenia)

Sources: Summarized after http://www.dvk.gov.si; http://de.wikipedia.org/wiki/Parlamentswahl_in_Slowenien_2011. For an interpretation of the elections and of conditions in Slovenia in general, see also D. Fink-Hafner, 'Slovenia since 1989', in S.P. Ramet (ed.), Central and Southeast European Politics since 1989 (Cambridge, 2010), 246–57. See also R.M. Rizman, Uncertain Path: Democratic Transition and Consolidation in Slovenia (Texas, 2006).

Government's Coalitions

28 June 1990: The government of Alojz Peterle (Executive Council of the Assembly of the Republic of Slovenia) consisted of the Slovenian Democratic Union (SDZ), SDS(S), SKD, Slovenian Farmers' Union, Slovenian Craftsmen's Party and Greens of Slovenia joined in the Demos coalition.

14 May 1992: The first government of Dr Janez Drnovšek was formed after a constructive vote of no confidence in the Demos government was passed. Dr Drnovšek became a new mandatary. The government consisted of the parties SDS, DS, ZS, LDS, ZLSD and SSS.

25 January 1993: The second government of Dr Janez Drnovšek consisted of the LDS, SKD, ZLSD and SDS(S). In 1994, the SDS(S) left the coalition when an SDS(S) minister was replaced; in 1996, the ZLSD did the same.

27 February 1997: The third coalition government of Dr Janez Drnovšek consisted of the LDS, SLS and DeSUS.

7 June 2000: The government of Dr Andrej Bajuk came to power after parliament passed a vote of no confidence in the third Drnovšek government on 8 April 2000 and appointed the government of Dr Bajuk. The coalition consisted of the SDS and SLS+SKD.

30 November 2000: The fourth coalition government of Dr Janez Drnovšek consisted of the LDS, ZLSD, SLS and DeSUS.

19 December 2002: The government of Anton Rop was formed upon the resignation of Dr Janez Drnovšek, who stood as a candidate for the presidency of the Republic of Slovenia and won in the second ballot. The Rop government was appointed; Dr Drnovšek himself chose Rop as his party successor and prime minister, while the coalition consisted of the same parties: LDS, ZLSD, SLS and DeSUS.

3 December 2004: The coalition government of Janez Janša consisted of the SDS, NSi, SLS and DeSUS.

21 November 2008: The coalition government of Borut Pahor consisted of SD, LDS, Zares and DeSUS.

Economy

From the standpoint of economic history, the development in the first twenty years in Slovenia can be divided into a period of recession due to the transformation process (1990–1992), the transformation process itself (1993–1995), a period of balanced economic development (1996–1999) and, at the turn of the millennium, a period of inflation shock and declining economic growth (2000–2003).[10] The years 2004–2008 were a time of relatively high growth (and the reappearance of inflation) along with an overheated economy and high debt due to developments on the stock market. Since then Slovenia has been experiencing an economic crisis it was not at all prepared for. This became evident in 2009, the first year of the economic crisis, when numerous companies that had not modernized themselves during the transformation process went bankrupt.

The first practical shock to the Slovenian economy was the market's drastic shrinking from 22 million consumers in Yugoslavia to two million consumers in Slovenia.[11] The ratio between Slovenia's volume of trade with foreign countries and that with Yugoslav republics favoured the republics by over 60 per cent as late as 1989. In the following years, this share dropped to 10 per cent. Slovenian companies, particularly those in processing industries that had formerly sold most of their products on the Yugoslav market, found themselves in deep crisis. With the disintegration of Yugoslavia and its rather protected market, and the opening of the domestic market to foreign imports, demand for many domestic products faltered. These circumstances were further aggravated by the fall of the Berlin Wall and disintegration of the Soviet Union, which had been an important market for Slovenian products, as well as by the depth of the transitional crisis in the former socialist countries of Central and Eastern Europe. In 1989, Slovenia was still the origin of almost one quarter of the goods exported from Yugoslavia to those socialist markets. By 1991, Slovenian industrial production had dropped by one quarter since the start of the Yugoslav market's disintegration in the second half of the 1980s. In 1992, the country's industrial production barely reached two thirds of its 1988 output before the onset of Yugoslavia's economic collapse.

During this crisis, many industrial companies started reducing costs by closing down research and development departments and making cuts in employees and services, an approach that had harmful long-term consequences. The budgetary share allocated to the Slovenian Department for Science and Technology – compared to both the budget and the GDP – was reduced in the first years of Slovenian independence, and numerous small service and production companies subcontracted by large-scale industry also found themselves in difficulty. The drop in activities that had formerly generated much of their income through international exchange of services was particularly steep. Foreign tourism, which had been hardest hit by the ten-day war for independence, had fallen to only one quarter of its 1989 income by 1991. Large banks were also in deep crisis.

By 1993, the number of unemployed people registered in Slovenia had risen from 28,000 in 1989 to almost 130,000. In comparison, during the last years of the Yugoslavian socialist economy there were estimated to be at least 40,000 unemployed people in Slovenia, whereas from 1988 to 1992 the number of employed people in Slovenia dropped by 162,000 (from 819,000 to 657,000). Only after the first half of 1994 did the unemployment rate stabilize at 14 per cent (9 per cent, according to the International Labour Organisation). Meanwhile, the average standard of living of the population dropped visibly, whereas social differences increased. Workers organized numerous strikes to protest unpaid wages and impoverishment. The strike wave reached its peak in 1992, which saw around 200 large-scale strikes with an average participation of 400 workers and an average duration of two to three days.

Public finances were heavily burdened by the doubling of the number of pensioners through mass early retirement, payments to the unemployed workforce and other social benefits. As a share of Slovenia's public expenditure between 1991 and 1993, pension funds and disability insurance increased from 11.1 to 14.1 per cent of GDP, and health insurance went from 5 to 7.4 per cent of GDP. The share for public consumption on the national level jumped from 16.6 to 22.8 per cent of GDP, whereas the share for consumption at the municipal level dropped. Only after 1989 did the GDP drop, for the most part in the years 1991 and 1992. Meanwhile, a very high inflation rate prevailed in the now independent state of Slovenia. In January 1992, prices were 262 per cent higher than they had been a year before.

The first period of the independent state thus came at great economic cost, despite the political discourse's idealized, ecstatic portrayal of the promise and expected results of the market economy and independence from Belgrade. The transitional crisis that hit the Slovenian state and economy was due particularly to the transformation from a socialist to a market economy, and from a regional economy in a former federal state to a national Slovenian economy, as well as to the massive structural economic changes involved in adapting to foreign markets and the challenges of globalization. The economy's transformation from socialism to capitalism, as originally designed by the vice-president of the Demos government, Dr Jože Mencinger, struck a balance between social and economic goals. Privatization was not to be an end to itself or a mere political act by which Demos would simply mix political power with economic power. The point was to bring about a more effective economy, with the burden of the transition borne by the affluent.

However, many politicians in the Demos coalition did not agree with this. In June 1990, Mencinger submitted the first proposal of a privatization model to the Assembly. According to the proposal, a company would be managed by those who held at least one tenth of its shares; at the same time, he opposed the free distribution of property. Mencinger continued to entrust the companies' management to their existing management, the so-called red directors. For this, he was criticized particularly among the ranks of Demos; it was said that he was protecting the red directors and that his ideas concerning the economic method of transitioning and gaining independence showed insufficient enthusiasm for gaining independence. The president of the government, Peterle, particularly disagreed with Mencinger, believing his method would leave the economy in the hands of the former communist directors or managers. Hence, Peterle sought another method, especially one that would dispense with the current directors. In his view, privatization was a way of eliminating so-called directorial socialism, which had been introduced by Ante Marković in a reform of enterprises. Following a model created by the American economist Dr Jeffrey Sachs, it had allowed many people to found a company, often becoming directors of themselves alone as they lacked the capital needed to run the company.[12] According to Mencinger, the transformation of a socialist economy to a market economy began under the illusion that the introduction of a market would immediately, or at least quickly, transform the former socialist economies into welfare states – an illusion shared by the new political elites on the one hand, and by international financial institutions and Western experts on the other. Mencinger resigned, and Demos dissolved at the end of 1991, mostly due to the differing views on denationalization and privatization.

Thereafter, the liberal new government of Dr Janez Drnovšek passed the Ownership Transformation of Companies Act, which was a kind of intermediate model between Mencinger's and Sachs', and a highly generous return of assets in kind (including feudal church property) began in accordance with the Demos act. During this process of privatization, citizens received non-transferable stock warrants, later to be exchanged for shares. Some managed to invest them in successful companies, but the majority ended up in so-called authorized investment companies (*pooblaščene investicijske družbe*, PIDs) without any great value, even though the leaders of the PIDs and their successors (various brokerage firms) for the most part became very wealthy (this was 'tycoon privatization'). The value of a stock warrant depended on how long it was held. By 1993, the initial transitional recession was over, and economic growth began again. Only in the second half of the 1990s did conditions begin to settle down and Western European markets replace the former Yugoslav ones: in 1997, for example, 64 per cent of exports went to markets in EU countries, and almost 17 per cent once again went to countries of the former Yugoslavia, particularly Croatia, Macedonia and Bosnia and Herzegovina.[13]

The tolar, introduced in 1992, became convertible in 1995. Slovenia's biggest investment went towards infrastructure improvement, specifically the building of a road network. After gaining independence, the country had virtually no foreign reserves left, but by the end of 1997 it had accumulated 4,424 billion US dollars. It succeeded in reaching agreement with foreign creditors about the federal debt of the former Yugoslavia and gaining access to the main international financial institutions. At the end of 1997, its external debt amounted to 4,176 million dollars, 4,041 million dollars of which was long-term debt. In 1996, the GDP reached 18.5 billion dollars; in 1997 it was about 18 billion dollars (i.e. 12,165 dollars per capita). Within five years, Slovenia had managed to reduce inflation, which in 1997 dropped to 9.1 per cent. Of course, the formally favourable indicators of economic change did not reveal the various consequences of the transformation process as experienced by the people, particularly those of the lower and middle classes, who bore the brunt. In connection with this, the official data are particularly striking: they stated that positive trends in employment were still being observed as late as 1999 (even though unemployment was still over 12 per cent in 2000). That is, despite an average annual economic growth rate of more than 4 per cent, employment was already declining or at least stagnating by the end of the 1990s, for the most part due to the economic restructuring process.[14]

Slovenian politics thus opted for a gradual approach based on pragmatism and avoidance of political or other shocks. Dr Janez Drnovšek symbolized political gradualism. Until 2004, his politics were considered a 'success story', for Slovenia attained far better results than the other transitional countries; still, the crisis between 2005 and 2011 raises some doubts. Aleksander Lorenčič's comparison of the Slovenian transition with those in the Czech Republic, Hungary and Poland – with which Slovenia, despite its much more gradual policy, had a great deal in common – shows that 'everywhere, technical solutions were the result of a combination of political power and randomly selected western privatizers. . . . As for privatization, glorious administrative operations were being effected everywhere, which would be the envy of any central planner. The idea was that the market economy could also be decreed, as had been the case during socialist times'.[15] As the comparative analysis demonstrates, the transition had indeed accelerated economic development in the countries in question, but they still lagged behind the more developed Western European countries. Slovenia and the Czech Republic were among the countries whose per capita GDP was about 10–20 per cent lower than the EU average. Hungary and Poland ranked much lower; their per capita GDP was around 30–50 per cent lower than the European average.

In the years since EU accession, Slovenia has boasted significant advantages, particularly with respect to the greater openness of the Slovenian economy and unemployment. However, the unparalleled edge Slovenia enjoyed in the start-up phase of transition has rather melted away. In 1990, at 8,000 dollars per capita, its GDP was substantially closer to the EU bottom (Portugal, Greece) than to that in the Eastern European countries, over which it still held a significant advantage.[16] Nevertheless, differences from comparable Western regions or countries, such as Carinthia in Austria or Friuli-Venezia Giulia in Italy, which Slovenia had already aspired and tried to catch up with during socialist times, remained. Mencinger still saw advantages in gradualism, as Slovenia could afford it. The reforms in Yugoslavia had endowed it with elements of a market economy and a decentralization of property through self-management and nationalization of property – which had preserved high levels of social cohesion during the transitional years – comparable to those of Scandinavia. However, in his opinion, the myth of Slovenia as the winner of the transition had perished in the 'gambling' years of 2005 to 2008, when banks and tycoons as well as ordinary citizens believed in returns as high as 30 per cent on securities and real estate while the net foreign debt rose from zero to ten billion euros.[17]

Conclusion

After gaining independence and its initial international recognition in late 1991 and early 1992, Slovenia became a member of the UN in May 1992, a member of the International Monetary Fund in 1993, and a full member of the Council of Europe. In 1998, it became a non-permanent member of the UN Security Council and presided over it. It became a member of the EU and NATO in 2004; in 2007, it became a member of the euro area and adopted the euro, also becoming a member of the Schengen Area by the year's end. In 2008, as the first eastern member, it successfully presided over the EU without significant complications. Slovenia also became a member of the OECD in 2010. Its GDP exceeds the European average; it has surpassed several older members and, to some degree, managed to preserve the social state. It is now a modern state with a diversified school system, well-developed information technologies accessible to the majority of the population, and excellent infrastructure with a road network of about 650 kilometres of motorways (however, its railway system is superannuated). Furthermore, it is among the ecologically more developed countries and boasts a low crime rate and a comfortable standard of living.

Nevertheless, the difficulties experienced during the creation of the Slovenian state were complex and multi-layered, for it had been a double process: in addition to gaining independence, it entailed the establishment of a multi-party democracy and a market system. The country's small size meant its elites were weak, which soon became evident everywhere. Whereas politicians and the people had expected the West to offer a climate of understanding for the young Slovenian state and its historical traumas, various impediments to its accession to the EU and NATO proved frustrating. This again led Slovenes to a kind of defensive attitude marked by a sense that the country and its people possessed the capacity to be self-sufficient, without any outside help. Uncritical imitation of Western countries and the acceptance of all demands from there, in exchange for the coveted EU membership and distance from anything connected with the former Yugoslavia, were the hallmarks of Slovenian politics in the first decade after independence. It is still obvious today that, when given the historical chance to seize the moment and create a state, Slovenia subordinated democracy to national goals.

Thus, the transformation 'in the Slovenian way', which long appeared to have been a 'success story', today shows a rather troubled side as well. The current crisis has revealed many formerly hidden weaknesses. In the past two decades, local state institutions' authority was reduced to insignificance as they fell prey to different political parties or political options, which remains the case to date. The logic of non-compliance with what are in fact often poorly written laws has dragged on since the time of Yugoslavia, when non-recognition of the state institutions' authority and manipulation of legislation were considered virtues. The once excessive egalitarianism has been replaced by radical individualism, and the main criteria of success are political power and affluence. The means to end this situation are negligible. Politics controls all social segments, while civil society is poorly developed. Other notable characteristics are a small elite with rapidly acquired wealth; the bankruptcy of numerous once-successful companies as a result of internal depletion caused by their managers' unsuccessful attempts at privatization; a rather high percentage of people living at or below the poverty threshold; and an accelerated shrinking of the middle classes – despite which, certain international comparisons show, the social cohesiveness of Slovenian society has been preserved.[18]

The regional division of Slovenia has given way to fragmentation into small municipalities without regions. With 20,273 square kilometres of surface and two million inhabitants, there are 210 municipalities, with incentives for further new municipalities in the offing. The government is unable to pass a law on the regions that would connect them better than before 1989/90. Therefore, Slovenia's internal structure does not differ significantly from that of the former Yugoslav republics, even though, so far, it is the only one to have gained membership in the EU and the majority of the most important international organizations. In making such an assessment, one must also add that the Slovenians have reason to feel content with all they have achieved – although, to their own detriment, they have an overly developed sense of injustice, both genuine and alleged, that they have (supposedly) suffered, that is conditioned in part by history and in part by mentality.

Nowadays, Slovenia is home to a dire cultural and political struggle between left and right deriving mainly from the past and the way the past is interpreted. History is the pawn of constant political struggles to help or hinder programmes for further development. The ideological struggle between Catholicism and liberalism began back in the nineteenth century with the thesis that 'only a Catholic could be a true Slovene', which received new impetus in the 1930s and peaked during World War II. During the hardships of that time, and under the leadership of the Communist Party, the Liberation Front organized armed resistance to the German, Italian and Hungarian military occupation forces that had condemned the Slovenian nation to extinction. However, the collaboration between the communist nature of the resistance on the one hand, and the bourgeois parties together with a segment of the Catholic Church on the other, led to simultaneous conflict among the Slovenes themselves. The victory of Josip Broz Tito's Yugoslav Army (with the participation of Slovenian partisan units) at the end of the war and in its aftermath led to the secret elimination of some 13,500 Slovenian members of the Home Guard (German collaborationist units) repatriated from Carinthia, Austria, by the British Allies.[19] The secret killings became known to the broader public only in the mid 1970s; public polemics on the topic emerged in the 1980s and intensified upon the introduction of a multi-party system in the 1990s. The Catholic Church, which had a dominant role in Slovenian society anyway, gained power once more. The political elites prevented a referendum on the controversial return of assets (including land), which strengthened the country's economic power even though the majority of the population opposed it.

Politically, the country has achieved a large number of its goals with the so-called Vatican Agreement,[20] advocating the principle that the state and the Catholic Church, both within their own organizations, are independent and autonomous and that therefore the Catholic Church in the Republic of Slovenia is free to act upon canon law in accordance with the legal order of the Republic of Slovenia. The Constitutional Court confirmed the agreement; nevertheless, some of its articles remain unspecified or provide the option to draw up additional special agreements with respect to certain realms. Despite the constitutional separation of church and state, the Catholic Church in particular is trying to establish denominational lessons in state schools and to introduce a Catholic military diocese. It also has great influence on the public media and the national administration (a former minister of justice, for instance, is a Knight of Malta who, under the Religious Freedom Act and by other methods, helped strengthen the Catholic Church's influence within society and stepped up employment of Catholic theologians and clerks at various ministries). The Catholic Church pays special attention to the (re)interpretation of history, attempting to reduce and relativize its collaborationist actions during World War II (in 2007 its successes included convincing a court to annul a 1946 final verdict under which Dr Gregorij Rožman, a former Ljubljana bishop who had managed to escape after the war, was sentenced to eighteen years in prison for collaboration). According to the population census of 2002, 57.8 per cent of Slovenes declare themselves to be Catholic (1,135,626), 1 per cent Evangelical or otherwise Protestant (15,500), 2.3 per cent Orthodox Christian (45,908), 2.4 per cent Muslim (47,488) and 10 per cent atheist (199,264).[21] Nevertheless, religiosity or identification especially with the Catholic Church (but not with other Christian churches) has clearly declined: in the 1991 census, 71.6 per cent identified as Catholic. The extent of the decline in the last decade is unknown, but in a 2001 census in urban settlements Catholics were already less than one half of the entire population.[22]

History, as a central issue in the political conflict, is also reflected in other arenas. Once a multi-party system had been established, new holidays were adopted; streets and squares, schools, certain institutes and the University of Ljubljana were renamed; and some statues were removed, the one of Tito that once stood in front of the parliament building prompting the most discussion. These symbolic changes sparked public and parliamentary debates and, in the case of partisan and socialist monuments, vandalism as well. Some towns have so far preserved the names of streets and squares named after Tito and other leading communists (as well as those of leading organizers of the resistance during World War II); in Ljubljana, by contrast, the right-wing municipal authorities changed them in 1991. At present, the most topical subjects of biting polemic are the questions of naming a new street in Ljubljana after Tito and depicting the legendary commander of the Slovenian partisan army Franc Rozman-Stane on the two-euro coin. The past, and the anniversaries and celebrations related to it, have triggered polemics and conflicts not only in reference to World War II but also about various aspects of Slovenia's gaining of independence. The latter question has incited a struggle to argue merits but also to establish an ideological construct to do justice to the historic complexity the different camps aim to express.

This construct pits advocates for independence – that is, the then new oppositional political forces – against opponents of independence, namely, the former political elites who had nevertheless succeeded in preventing Slovenia's subordination to Yugoslav centralism until 1990. Its leading representative, Milan Kučan, had, as the directly elected president, prioritized decisive, consensual enforcement of the project of gaining independence. Later on, the thus established division is still said to be the basis for informal lustration under present conditions and in anticipation of future elections. The right-wing (currently oppositional) forces generally follow the example of the right-wing revolution in Hungary, including its demand for a constitutional amendment that would establish a so-called second republic in Slovenia.

After Slovenia became a member of the EU, the ideological struggle spread to the nature of the former socialist system in Yugoslavia and Slovenia, a topic that has inspired polemics ever since the end of the 1980s and the country's transformation into a multi-party system. In international relations in the first few years, right-wing politicians still emphasized the specificities of the former Yugoslav and Slovenian version of socialism: a semi-market economy with social property and limited private entrepreneurship, open borders, the westward orientation of part of the economy, and a workforce of over 70,000 carrying out so-called temporary work in Western countries. Later, as Slovenia's international position grew stronger and became institutionalized, this need for distinction faded. Early on, though, connections to European right-wing parties reinforced the impression that Slovenia was no different from other Eastern European countries, and that the totalitarian regime in Slovenia had also lasted until 1990. Within the European realm, this ideological divide gave a segment of Slovenian politicians the status of Eastern European dissidents, although Slovenia had not seen classical dissidence since at least the 1980s; altogether, most of the cultural opposition had come from civil servants (university professors, researchers, established writers and editors, among others).

The 'Movement for Justice and Development' founded by the late Dr Janez Drnovšek deserves to be listed among movements surviving the division of the last few years. It follows the principle of 'making the world a better place', transcends ethnocentrism, opposes any instance of discrimination, emphasizes the ecology and a decent life for everyone, and stands against all forms of violence. Criticized for blending his presidential function with a spiritual one, Drnovšek resigned as the leader of the movement, which has continued to exist since his death. However, it has lost its impetus, and in the general civil society's attempts to overcome politics, it does not stand much of a chance in Slovenia.[23]

Božo Repe has been Professor of Modern History at the Faculty of Philosophy of the University of Ljubljana since 2002. After having earned his doctorate in 1992, on the topic of 'Liberalism in Slovenia', he was a teacher at the Faculty of Educational Sciences in Maribor. Apart from his activities as a university teacher, he dedicated himself to curricula for the teaching of history, and in 1996–1998 he headed the commission in charge of this. Currently he publishes in several scientific journals and is a columnist of *Mladina*, an independent Slovenian weekly magazine on political issues. His publications on the history of Slovenia include *Slowenien und der Zerfall Jugoslawiens* (Ljubljana, 2002); *Quellen der Demokratisierung und Unabhängigkeit Sloweniens* (3 vols, Ljubljana, 2002–2004); *Zwischen Mythos und Ideologie: Einige Ansichten über slowenische Zeitgeschichtsschreibung* (Ljubljana, 2010). He has also participated in a compilation on the history of Slovenia, entitled *Umrisse der modernen allgemeinen und slowenischen Geschichte* (Ljubljana, 2003).

Notes

1. B. Repe, *Jutri je nov dan: Slovenci in razpad Jugoslavije* [Tomorrow is a New Day: Slovenes and the Disintegration of Yugoslavia] (Ljubljana, 2004).
2. For more on this topic, see L.P. Pregelj, A. Gabrič and B. Repe, *The Repluralization of Slovenia in the 1980s: New Revelations from Archival Records* (with an Introduction by Dennison Rusinow) (Seattle, 2000).
3. The Anti-Fascist Council for the National Liberation of Yugoslavia (AVNOJ) was a Yugoslav partisan parliament founded in November 1942. In November 1943, it founded a new, federative Yugoslavia, thus recognizing the statehood of the future republics, to which Slovenia also referred when declaring independence. Before World War II ended, the dualism of power with the royal government in exile was abolished, a common government under Tito's leadership was appointed and pre-war deputies and newly elected representatives of federal units swelled AVNOJ's ranks. In November 1944, the AVNOJ presidency adopted a resolution to confiscate the property of the so-called Volksdeutsche (a German minority). In 1992, in an Austrian government memorandum, Austria appointed itself 'protector' of the Austrian or German-speaking ethnic

group in Slovenia known as Old Austrians (Altösterreicher), demanding that Slovenia renounce AVNOJ and thus enable the return of property.

4. Interview: Dragan Petrovec (Ranka Ivelja, Miča Vipotnik), *Dnevnik*, Objektiv, 23 April 2011, 10–14.
5. S.B. Hrvatin, 'Media Liberalism', in Ramet and Fink-Hafner, *Democratic Transition in Slovenia*, 168–84.
6. S.B. Hrvatin, L.J. Kućić and B. Petković, 'Medijsko lastništvo: Vpliv lastništva na neodvisnost in pluralizem medijev v Sloveniji in drugih post-socialističnih evropskih državah' [Media Ownership: Impact on Media Independence and Pluralism in Slovenia and Other Post-Socialist European Countries], The Peace Institute, Ljubljana, 2004 (http://mediawatch.mirovni-institut.si/edicija/seznam/15/mediawatch15.pdf).
7. http://www.uradni-list.si/1/objava.jsp?urlid=200596&stevilka=4191.
8. B. Zgaga, 'Good Evening and Good Night', in M. Drčar-Murko et al. (eds), *Five Minutes of Democracy: The Image of Slovenia after 2004* (Ljubljana, 2004), 213–46.
9. V. Rus and N. Toš, *Vrednote Slovencev in Evropejcev: Analiza vrednostnih orientacij Slovencev ob koncu stoletja. Dokument Slovenskega javnega mnenja* [Values of Slovenes and Europeans: Analysis of Value Orientations of Slovenes at the End of the Century. A Document of the Slovenian Public Opinion Survey] (Ljubljana, 2005), 333–68. See also N. Toš and K.H. Müller (eds), *Political Faces of Slovenia: Political Orientation and Values at the End of the Century* (Vienna, 2005).
10. A. Lorenčič, 'Tranzicija slovenskega gospodarstva v letih 1990–2004' [Transition of the Slovenian Economy in the Years 1990–2004' (PhD diss., Department of History, Faculty of Arts in Ljubljana, 2010).
11. Summarized after T. Krašovec, 'Deset let gospodarskega razvoja v samostojni Sloveniji' [Ten Years of Economic Development in Independent Slovenia], The Managers' Association of Slovenia, Ljubljana, 2001 (http://www.uradni-list.si/1/objava.jsp?urlid=200596&stevilka=4191). This note covers all following statistics.
12. http://sl.wikipedia.org/wiki/DEMOS.
13. Data from the Government Public Relations and Media Office from 1998 (http://expo98.literal.si/slo/paviljon/ureditev/informativno-jedro/gospodarstvo.html-l2).
14. Republic of Slovenia, Ministry of the Economy, National Development Programme 2001–2006.
15. Lorenčič, 'Tranzicija slovenskega gospodarstva', 292.
16. B. Hren, 'Konec mita o Sloveniji kot zmagovalki tranzicije' [The End of the Myth of Slovenia as the Winner of Transition], *Dnevnik*, Objektiv, 23 April 2011, 4.
17. Ibid., 6.
18. According to the Gini coefficient, a measure of income inequality, Slovenia is the country with the most evenly distributed household income in the European Union (Eurostat data for 2008). The share of employees whose wages are higher than three average wages has for years remained at a level slightly over 2 per cent; the share of those whose wages are higher than eight average wages is slightly under 0.01 per cent; and, like tax redistribution, social transfers are also strong. What stands out is the narrow circle of those who were enriched by the transition or who, as managers, paid themselves high bonuses, even ones worth millions: the top 1 per cent of employees distributes among itself a share of income roughly the same as that of the bottom 10 per cent. Other data also show great social differences: a steep rise in the materially deprived; increased risk to some social groups that are already the most at risk, i.e. the unemployed (in this regard Slovenia is still below the euro area average), families with three or more children, households with dependent children that lack a wage earner;

and poverty risks that differ greatly between individual categories of the population (e.g. homeowners and renters). B. Hren, 'Slovenija je po dohodkovni (ne)enakosti še v socializmu' [Judging by Income (In)Equality Slovenia is Still in Socialism], *Dnevnik*, 12 March 2011, digital version (http://www.najdipredogled.si/trident/quickpreview.jsp?q= socialne+razlike+po+Ginijejevem+koli%C4%8Dniku&qpts=2158&rn=25633121).

19. J. Golob et al., *Žrtve vojne in revolucije* (zbornik) [Victims of the War and the Revolution (Journal)] (Ljubljana, 2005). For data on the victims, see p. 21. Slovenia's dead numbered around 98,000 or 6 per cent of the population, most of them civilians (over 35,700, killed mainly by violence perpetrated by the occupier), followed by members of partisan units (over 27,000)

20. An agreement between the Republic of Slovenia and the Holy See on legal issues, adopted by the National Assembly of the Republic of Slovenia at a session on 28 January 2004 (http://www.uradni-list.si/1/content?id=47165).

21. http://www.stat.si/popis2002/gradivo/si-92.pdf.

22. S. Dragoš, 'The Religious Picture of Slovenia – Who Is to Blame?', in M. Drčar-Murko et al., *Five minutes of Democracy*, 309–27.

23. D. Fink-Hafner, 'Slovenia since 1989', in S.P. Ramet (ed.), *Central and Southeast European Politics since 1989* (Cambridge, 2010), 247.

Chapter 9

HUNGARY

❦

Jürgen Dieringer

Background

Hungary is a successful transition country that has made its way into the Western European and transatlantic community of states. Despite its current difficulties, in the two decades leading up to 2010 Hungary has in many fields outperformed the so-called PIGS states (Portugal, Italy, Greece and Spain) in efficiency, sustainability and success. Yet in the group of Central and Southern European states, Hungary's position is rather declining. This is surprising, as at the time of the turnaround in 1989/1990, Hungary was considered a pioneer in the process of democratization and market-economic reorganization. Particularly in the past few years, the quality of democracy and reliability of economic policy in Hungary have increasingly come into question.

The Hungarian transformation is part of the third global wave of democratization,[1] which, after washing over Latin America, Southeast Asia and parts of Africa, finally also reached the socialist states of Central and Eastern Europe. But even the Prague-Vladivostok thesis[2] is too narrow to explain the specific course of this transformation. Instead, the keys to the success or failure of a transformation to democracy and market economy are the state or nation's individual constitution, traditional patterns, windows of opportunity and constellations of elites. Here, structure and actor work hand in hand, and alternative development scenarios are indeed imaginable.

The development of Hungary's liberal democratic political system under the constitution of 1990 has been determined by three framework conditions:[3] (1) the political culture, particularly problems relating to elements and larger parts of depoliticization attempts in the Kádár period, a revanchist nationalism rooted in the Trianon trauma, and general cultural

---

pessimism; (2) path dependency-creating decisions by the framers of the constitution; and (3) Hungary's Europeanization, understood here as an extensive modernization process leading to the country's westward orientation to the institutions of the European Union. Starting from these three structuring basic facts – problematic political culture, path dependency of political processes and inclusion in a European modernization process – what follows will describe the determinants of Hungary's society, governmental system and economic development.

What were Hungary's particularities? The Kádár regime, so called after party chief János Kádár,[4] developed after the Stalinist terror and the violent suppression of a popular uprising in 1956. After an initial period of repression towards participants in the uprising, the party eventually came to accept that the only way of coping with the situation was an 'unwritten social contract'. The latter proceeded as follows: the communist regime granted freedoms (e.g. the freedom to travel) and provided the people with a sufficient supply of consumer goods (e.g. refrigerators and cars), earning the desired result of society's depoliticization. Stalin's dictum 'Whoever is not with us is against us' was replaced by 'Whoever is not against us is with us'. In this way, the regime generated mass loyalty until the late 1980s, when economic crisis made the pact obsolete. Once Mikhail Gorbachev's glasnost and perestroika loosened the grip of foreign policy, the communist regime was doomed, and the 'happiest shack in the Eastern Bloc' (as the regime was also called, though only in the West) revealed the sad reality: its mixture of counterproductive ordering principles typical of socialist systems (i.e. patterns of distance, hierarchy and secrecy) made efficient government impossible.[5]

Under the specific conditions of the Kádár system, a counter-elite was able to develop from the mid 1980s onwards, under relatively little pressure from the ruling system. Only seldom was this counter-elite actually a mass movement, as was the case on 15 March 1989, or on the occasion of the ceremonial reburial of Imre Nagy that same year. Rather, it consisted of somewhat nationalist-minded cast-offs from the Communist Party – called the Hungarian Socialist Workers' Party (Magyar Szocialista Munkáspárt, MSZMP) – that is, members of the nomenclature who had allegedly received unfair treatment, the Budapest samizdat and an uncompromising youth movement.

By the mid 1980s, the state party had finally arrived at the insight that crisis was inherent in the system. Basically, the communist elite had an interest in a 'socialist kind of market economy', in the sense that their power was supposed to depend on the connection to a social market economy. Economic policy reforms at the end of the decade – laws on competition, privatization, deregulation, world market orientation – pointed in that direction. However, the momentum of world political events did not allow for this sub-systemic division between state and market. The freedoms provided under the Kádár system were germ cells and hotbeds of the opposition, which had become independent by the time political parties were founded in 1987. With the fall of the Iron Curtain at the latest – as a matter of fact, Hungary was the place where it started falling – the growing pressure broke the system.[6]

Without question, the transformation of the system centred strongly around the elites in Hungary, compared to other states in the region. Thus, the unavoidable system change happened by way of an elite pact negotiated by a roundtable that administered an orderly handover of power. In return for the state party's acceptance of the creation of a liberal democratic system, the opposition refrained from 'settling the score' with the old elites who, thereby comparatively unhindered, were able to use privatization to transform their power to govern into economic power. Thus, the nomenclature survived in the formerly state-run enterprises. Meanwhile, ways of dealing with 'state security files' and the events of 1956 as well as the restitution of confiscated property were discussed in the 1990s but hardly grasped as legal categories, at least in comparison to the handling of such matters in other states in the region. Rather, 'settling the score' was left to voters, whose memory is generally short.

It should be noted that the development of ideologically differentiated political opposition to the system was a consequence of the system transformation. In Hungary, no organized opposition alliance – like the Solidarność trade union in Poland, the Citizens' Forum in the Czech Republic or the Public against Violence in Slovakia – was needed. Splits in the party landscape were limited, so the party system was relatively stable until it collapsed in the spring of 2010. That the belated transformation crisis caused the current power shifts indicates a widespread opinion that the system change was incomplete. Hungary has finished a historical period, but only now is it opening its heavy load of historical baggage. This load interferes with democratic principles not yet deep enough rooted in political culture. 'Power' as a narrative supersedes 'democracy and rule of law' in this context.

The second and third Viktor Orbán governments offered a demonstration of this type of political behaviour. Many measures – the new constitution (called basic law, *alaptörvény*), the introduction of the right to fire public officials, the reformulation of the media law, the curtailment of the Constitutional Court's competences, the retroactive implementation of certain laws, the misuse of public funds – point into this direction. Criticism is extensive, and given the government's systematic way of proceeding, many consider democracy in Hungary to be at risk these days.

The genesis of the political system during the period of system change relied on certain purposeful structural decisions, coincidence and also, repeatedly, exploitation of small *kiskapuk* – minor regulatory loopholes whose frequent use means that reality in Hungary often differs greatly from what is written on paper. That is why the President of the State is constitutionally commander-in-chief of the armed forces yet can give no orders, or why the Constitutional Court, according to the constitution, has its seat in Esztergom, whereas physically it convenes in Budapest – just two examples from among a remarkable number of strange things.

The roundtable negotiations during the phase of systemic change tended towards a semi-presidential system. Just a small majority of some thousand votes in a referendum that actually asked the citizens to decide about something completely different gave the parliament the right to elect the President of the State. Since then, the constitution has retained bits and pieces of this concept, even though the voters have rejected it. Though the text of the constitution is semi-presidential in tone, the constitutional practice is clearly parliamentary. This is clear from an overview of Constitutional Court verdicts – for example on the supreme commander of the armed forces, on what media actors the President of the State is entitled to appoint, or on the institution of the referendum – which the court skilfully combined to fit the patterns of parliamentary democracy.

In the end, a parliamentary system that, in contrast to a semi-presidential or indeed presidential system, is not grouped around leading figures is well positioned to reflect social heterogeneity and the various societal powers – or, in other words, the plurality of a nation tending towards individualization or maybe even, gradually, towards post-materialism. In Hungary, however, it seems that a dichotomous pattern of urban cosmopolitan progressiveness and national-conservative forces with rather rural ties is being restored. This pattern is familiar from the interwar period and even from the Dual Monarchy. These groups succeed only when appropriate leading figures reach the top of the respective political movement. It will be interesting indeed to see whether society is modernizing itself despite government's backward lending rhetoric, or the governing forces will try to shape their particular 'realities' within the polity of a more and more presidential and autocratic political system.[7]

The Political System and the Field of Political Forces

Hungary is a republic. According to its constitution, the country consists of the national level, the counties, the county-free cities and the municipalities. Apart from this, regions and so-called small districts[8] exist for statistical purposes only. The hierarchy of competences favours the central state and municipal levels. The municipalities have their own responsibilities and the central state has also devolved administrative tasks to them. The counties have their own, directly elected assemblies, but they still have few competences and hardly any financial means. Cities and municipalities have lost some competences and their funding has been reduced over the years. Numbering about 3,200, the local self-administered entities were organized so dysfunctionally that reform is was urgently needed. A centralization took place. Thus, Hungary suffers in a straitjacket made of an over-dimensioned central state bound to a sub-sidiarity-oriented reform that, in 1990,[9] went 'in the right direction, but too far'.[10] The self-administered entities have no representation at the level of the central state. However, since 1994 a growing number of mayors had become national MPs. With the parliamentary reform before the elections 2014 this *cumul des mandats* was stopped. As a consequence, the local level became politically less influential.

The political range of Hungary's party system goes back to the period before the turnaround. The structure of the former cadres of nomenclature who made up the old elite and those of the new elite of the democratic opposition did not culminate in bipolarity. Rather, the negotiated transition left room for the opposition to become differentiated between the nationally minded and the liberal. Thus, democratic Hungary started with a tripolar party system. The Hungarian Socialist Party (Magyar Szocialista Párt, MSZP), as the reformed state party, represented the left wing. The liberal camp consisted of the Alliance of Free Democrats (Szabad Demokraták Szövetsége), which is mostly a party of the urban intelligentsia, and the Alliance of Young Democrats (Fiatal Demokraták Szövetsége, FIDESZ), which was actually a movement countering the Communist Youth Alliance (Kommunista Ifjúsági Szövetség). In the bourgeois-national camp, the broadly positioned Hungarian Democratic Forum (Magyar Demokrata Fórum, MDF) was the leading force, while the Independent Smallholder's Party (Független Kisdazdapárt) and the Christian Democratic People Party (Kereszténydemokrata Néppárt, KDNP) occupied the edges, serving as clientele parties for the countryside and for Hungarians of the Catholic faith.

However, the appearance of a functional equivalence to the traditional Western European party system featuring conservatives, liberals and social democrats is deceiving. For years, the structurally conservative electoral system prevented any changes to the party system, in terms of adjustments to socio-demographic determinants. Only since 2010 has the reality of society broken through these barriers to foster a new party system reflecting the specific political culture, with all its democratic shortcomings such as nationalism, euro-scepticism and disrespect for all sorts of minorities.

The changes in electoral law after 2014 did not substantially change this picture. Hungary has developed an electoral system that reflects the consensus between the old and new elites at the roundtable talks. The mixed electoral system, with its compensatory elements,[11] is a system that divides majority elements (direct candidates) from proportional elements (voting on county lists) and partly rebalances. It grants smaller parties access to parliament, but at the same time it provides for disproportionate distribution of MPs to the victorious party in an election – as was clearly demonstrated in the 1994 elections, when the MSZP, with one third of the votes, achieved an absolute majority of MPs; and in the 2010 election, when FIDESZ won two thirds of MPs with a narrow majority of votes (see Table 9.1).

Blocs began to form as soon as the new electoral system's effects on the distribution of seats became clear (in 1994 at the latest). The tripolar structure changed into a bipolar one with a national-conservative side and a liberal-progressive side. The liberal camp, for its part, was divided into a national-liberal and a left-wing liberal party. Quite obviously, smaller parties were unlikely to survive this polarization. In the end, FIDESZ managed to become a magnet for the right-wing camp, while the left-wing camp was pulled towards the MSZP. The smaller satellite parties were at first marginalized, then pulverized. Since 2010, only two of the originally six parties have been represented in parliament.[12] However, the two core parties were, as of 2010, complemented by two newcomers: the green-liberal Politics Can Be Different (Lehet más a politika, LMP) and the right-wing, radical Jobbik (a play on words meaning 'better' and 'more right-wing').

Here, the idea of cleavage[13] is useful for revealing how the parties work as a mechanism of social selection. Of course, in Central and Eastern Europe, the classical lines of conflict – labour vs. capital, state vs. church, centre vs. periphery, city vs. countryside – are not directly applicable. First, just as there had been no industrial proletariat in socialist states since the postwar period, there had also been no classical industrialist or employer. The classical left-wing/right-wing pattern thus has little relevance for the region. Next, the opposition between the clerical and the secular must be approached in a country-specific way: it is strong in Poland and weak in the Czech Republic, for example. Hungary is closer to the Czech Republic than to Poland. Hungarian Catholicism is rather a kind of 'folklore' or 'cultural Catholicism' that cannot be transformed into political power. Given this societal reality,

TABLE 9.1. Election results 1990–2014*

Year / Party	2014		2010		2006		2002		1998		1994		1990	
	Seats	CE %	Seats	CE %	Seats	CE %	Seats	CE %	Seats	CE %	Seats	CE %	Seats	CE %
FIDESZ in %	133 / 66.86	43.55 ***	263 / 67.88	52.73 ***	164 / 42.49	42.03 ***	188 / 48.70	41.06 **	165 / 42.74	41.06 **	–	29.48	20 / 5.18	7.01
MSZP in %	38 / 19.10	26.21	59 / 15.28	19.30	190 / 49.22	43.21	178 / 46.11	42.05	134 / 34.72	–	–	32.92	209 / 54.14	32.99
Jobbik in %	23 / 11.56	20.69	47 / 12.18	16.67	–	–	–	–	–	–	–	–	–	–
LMP in %	5 / 2.51	5.47	16 / 4.15	7.48	–	–	–	–	–	–	–	–	–	–
SZDSZ in %	–	–	–	–	20 / 5.18	6,50	20 / 5.18	5.57	24 / 6.22	–	–	7.57	69 / 17.88	19.73
MDF in %	–	–	–	2.67	11 / 2.85	5.04	–	**	–	****	–	–	38 / 9.84	11.73
FKGP in %	–	–	–	–	–	–	–	0.75	48 / 12.44	–	–	13.15	26 / 6.74	8.82
MIÉP in %	–	–	–	–	–	2.20	–	4.37	14 / 3.36	–	–	5.45	–	–
KDNP in %	–	***	–	–	–	***	–	–	–	–	–	2.31	22 / 5.70	7.03

Key: CE = votes for county elections. 1990 parties above the 4 and 5 (after 1994) per cent threshold which is mandatory for county elections. *1990–2000 386 deputies each, independent candidates are not included; 2014 199 seats; **joint list of MDF and FIDESZ; ***joint list of KDNP and FIDESZ; ****two MDF seats included into FIDESZ.

Source: valasztas.hu.

the national-conservative camp's rhetorical use of Catholic terms and concepts often looks hypocritical.

As for the divide between centre and periphery in Hungary, it is very much a structural question. Budapest, the capital, with its 1.7 million inhabitants (almost three million with agglomeration, in a total Hungarian population of about ten million) dominates political and cultural life. The urban–rural contrast, by comparison, is less dominating, but still significant.[14] Meanwhile, in Hungary these four cleavages must certainly be augmented by the line of conflict between the old and new systems, which characterized the first parliamentary elections but became less significant after 1994. In terms of voter volatility and coalition options, the old stigmatization no longer played a dominant role, the MSZP was able to find coalition partners. If the lines of conflict presented above are applied to the party system, a national-conservative camp and a cosmopolitan-liberal camp become obvious. The cosmopolitan camp consists of the MSZP, LMP and smaller groups descending from the MSZP. The LMP is a new, green, grass-roots, rather urban party whose rather post-materialistic programme appeals to both non-voters and the collapsing liberal camp. Strikingly, in this context, the classical social democratic camp seems to lack a political home. Although the MSZP is a platform party giving a home to many political strands, its political direction is rather liberal. This also explains why the orientation of social protest in Hungary is not left wing but right wing. Concerning this, the right-wing FIDESZ has a new rival that must be taken seriously: Jobbik, which has a broad base in society. It attracts voters of all ages from all over the country, both the educated and the less educated, people with higher incomes and those receiving social benefits.

Hungary has a parliamentary system of rule. This has resulted less from planned action than from unforeseeable political and social processes, as originally the system of rule – as described above – was supposed to be semi-presidential. Certainly, the originally intended direct election of the President of the State, who was supposed to have quite considerable powers, pointed in that direction. It reflected a compromise between the former state party MSZMP, which was able to field a popular candidate, the reformer Imre Pozsgay, and the most important opposition actor, the national-conservative MDF, which had reason to hope to appoint the President from its ranks after the parliamentary election. However, this combination was not to be. The concept developed by the roundtable has been relativized by the Constitutional Court and by referendums. By way of a referendum, the liberals succeeded in postponing the presidential election to a date after the parliamentary elections. Direct election of the President of the State was changed to election by the parliament, and

TABLE 9.2. Governments in Hungary

Period of time	Prime Minister	Coalition
1990–1993	József Antall (†1993, MDF)	MDF-KDNP-(FKGP); oversized*
1993–1994	Péter Boross (MDF)	MDF-KDNP; minimum-winning**
1994–1998	Gyula Horn (MSZP)	MSZP-SZDSZ; oversized
1998–2002	Viktor Orbán I (FIDESZ)	FIDESZ-MDF-FKGP; oversized
2002–2004	Péter Medgyessy	MSZP-SZDSZ; minimum-winning
2004–2006	(independent)	MSZP-SZDSZ; minimum-winning
2006–2008	Ferenc Gyurcsány I (MSZP)	MSZP-SZDSZ; minimum-winning
2008–2009	Ferenc Gyurcsány II(MSZP)	MSZP; minority government
2009–2010	Ferenc Gyurcsány III (MSZP) Gordon Bajnai (independent)	Government of experts, supported by MSZP and SZDSZ
2010–2014	Viktor Orbán II (FIDESZ)	FIDESZ-KDNP; two-thirds majority
2014–	Viktor Orbán III (FIDESZ)	FIDESZ-KDNP: first two-thirds, then majority

*Oversized: the coalition consists of more parties than actually needed for establishing a government majority; **Minimum-winning: minimum number of parties and seats needed for establishing a majority in parliament.

Source: Author's own data.

the liberal Árpád Göncz became president. The Constitutional Court, oriented to the model of a parliamentary system, subsequently curtailed the president's competences,[15] successively reducing presidential elements in the constitution. Ever since, the parliament has been the centre of the political system, and the prime minister the essential actor.

Hungary's government adheres to the departmental principle and the cabinet principle. The constitution states that the prime minister lacks any advisory competency. Formally, the prime minister appears as a *primus inter pares*; nevertheless, as the leader of the majority party, he or she is the most important actor. The strong prime ministers József Antall, Gyula Horn, Viktor Orbán and Ferenc Gyurcsány retained this status even when the chairmanship of the party was given to a 'deputy' for a time.[16]

As of 1990, the Hungarian parliament consisted of 386 MPs in a unicameral system. From 2014, however, the number of MPs was reduced to about 199.[17] Formally, the parliament is the centre of the political system. Nevertheless, only gradually has the Országgyülés (National Assembly) managed to achieve a strong independent position. Given the executive power's instability, there were ample possibilities for establishing a strong parliament; however, the opportunity was not taken. In this context, the system-typical East Central European 'opportunity-capacity problem' deserves mention.[18] In the initial, troubled period after the system change,

MPs were mostly inexperienced and standing orders were unproven. Before opportunities could be seized, parliamentary work first had to be practised. 'Party tourists' – MPs moving from faction to faction – were common. In the course of time, a rationalized kind of parliamentarianism developed, based on growing party discipline, a better organized committee system and ever more consolidated lines of interaction and communication with the government.

The parliament is Hungary's chief law-maker. The president's veto is only suspensive and can be overruled by a simple majority. To control the government, MPs have the right of interpellation. More important than these formal rights are the networks of MPs, which extend into the executive branch of government. Often these networks owe their high functionality not just to use of party channels but also to the considerable crossover of powers. The frequent changes of government (2006 being an exception) explain why many MPs, from both from majority and opposition party groups, have personal executive experience. The control function is exercised by the committees, which are structured alongside the ministries of the government.

Hungarian MPs are elected via either a party ticket or a direct mandate. The understanding of the mandate or its related duties can vary according to how the MP was elected: directly elected MPs have stronger connections with their constituencies and often see their main task as representing their constituency within the political system, whereas those elected on tickets are more concerned with international issues and have a greater sense of obligation to their parties. MPs enjoy immunity and indemnity.

Apart from the President of the State (suspensive veto, right to appeal to the Constitutional Court, promulgation), the Constitutional Court, direct democracy and the European Union are also veto players in the political system. In European comparison, Hungary's Constitutional Court is considered quite powerful. Accordingly, it has repeatedly issued verdicts restricting the government's ability to act towards other actors. The term under the Constitutional Court's first president (and later also President of the State), László Sólyom, from 1990 to 1998 is considered the chief period of the court's activism. Sólyom himself, in explaining his minority opinion that the death penalty was unconstitutional, referred to an 'invisible constitution' (*láthatatlan alkotmány*) that, during the nascence of legal certainty in Hungary, declared norms of international law applicable even if Hungary's constitution did not explicitly postulate them. The term was never used again, but it nevertheless demonstrates that the members of the court intended to be active in further developing the constitution. Meanwhile, the powers of the Constitutional Court have been cut back by way of individual measures and constitutional amendment. The court has lost its jurisdiction over certain fields (budget matters), the *actio popularis* has been restricted and judges can no longer be re-elected, though their term of office has been extended from nine to twelve years.

Thus, just as the Constitutional Court restricted the originally quite significant powers of the President of the State, the court's own power was restricted by a two-thirds majority in the parliament. Meanwhile, direct democracy has increasingly proven to be another veto player in the past years. It is used as a legitimating tool in cases of transference of sovereignty to international organizations, as well as in home policy controversies. In fact, this originally rather secondary, supporting tool has developed into a means of mobilization for both the parliamentary opposition and independent citizens' movements. For example, via referendum the parliamentary opposition succeeded in stopping the privatization of hospitals and the government favoured Budapest candidacy for Olympic Games. Direct democracy may also have a pre-emptive effect, as in the case of party funding, when an impending referendum urged the parliament to action.

The process of European integration has heavily influenced Hungary's political system and politics. Adjustments to political institutions have included establishment of European departments at the ministries and a European Committee in the parliament, passage of a scrutiny law[19] and the founding of regional institutions to implement European cohesion and regional policy. By and large, these institutions, which often look very strong on paper, work quite satisfactorily. Nevertheless, strong words on paper sometimes turn out to be a paper tiger, for example in regard to how the parliament handles European matters.[20] The extent to which EU membership restricts political actors' scope of action was evident in the reforms the second Orbán government (since 2010) was forced to implement during the economic crisis. Instead of passing a higher budget deficit, Brussels urged the government to adopt a policy of consolidation and austerity. More and more, the rhetoric between Budapest and Brussels became hostile. Meanwhile, Hungary is considered the enfant terrible in the club, and several measures were adopted against undemocratic behaviour of the Orbán government. Orbán, on the other side, frequently uses EU-bashing to stabilize his diminishing popularity.

The Europeanization of Hungary's political system culminated in the first half of 2011 with Hungary's presidency,[21] as the third successive part of the tripartite presidency of Spain, Belgium and Hungary. During the preparatory period, the presidency started quite ambitiously, but in the course of time its focus shrank to a few essential points, such as Balkans policy, the European strategy for the Danube region[22] and preparations for the European framework budget after 2013.

Economic Development

The economic crisis of the 1980s terminated Hungary's own way in economy policy. The country's 'Goulash Communism' collapsed when Gorbachev's perestroika dissolved essential foreign policy ties and the debt crisis – another consequence of the import of consumer goods – revealed that the economy's macro-steering was moribund. The solution was to promote market economy, a new path trodden most enthusiastically under Prime Minister Miklós Németh at the end of the 1980s. Even before the turnaround, Hungary had devised a modern law on competition, made it easier to found enterprises and launched spontaneous privatization. Taking the sum of all these measures as a criterion, one may indeed state that in Europe's East, Hungary was the best-prepared transformation country in terms of economy policy. Clearly these reforms showed the spirit of the Washington Consensus on liberalization, privatization and deregulation.

However, Hungary has not been able to maintain its advantage. At first, the conservative Antall government attempted a course of moderate modernization as of 1990, pushing socio-political motivations to the fore. Its successor government, that of Gyula Horn, also made attempts to go in that direction. Only when even basic macro-economic stability could not be assured did the government, led by Finance Minister Lajos Bokros, change course and steer towards the shock therapy propagated by the World Bank and IMF, implementing the so-called Bokros package in 1995. Since then, Hungary's economy policy has proceeded in the following pattern: left-wing governments (Horn from 1995, Péter Medgyessy, Ferenc Gyurscány, Gordon Bajnai) pursued a neoliberal economic course based on the Washington Consensus, with a market-allocative, supply-oriented focus; whereas right-leaning governments (Antall, Orbán's first, second and third) instead relied on state-allocative, demand-oriented economic policy. This pattern, which is untypical of Western Europe, resulted from the respective oppositions' tactical-political reactions to the government policy (they had to present an alternative) and, structurally, the start of the socialist nomenclature's 'march towards business' after 1989/90, whereby it became the group benefiting most from privatization, deregulation and liberalization. In contrast, the democratic opposition made efforts to occupy state institutions.

The economic and political organization of Hungary's transition from a socialist planned economy to a market economy oriented to the Western model can be structured into three phases. The initiation phase included the period of immediate turnaround and passage of fundamental legislation on competition, privatization, deregulation and business groups, as

TABLE 9.3. Economic status quo

	EU-28	Hungary	Czech Republic	Austria	Portugal
GDP 2005 (per capita in Euro)	23,400	9,000	10,700	30,800	15,100
GDP 2010	25,500	9,800	14,900	35,200	17,000
GDP 2016	29,000	11,500	16,500	40,000	17,900
Inflation (%, 2015)	0.0	0.1	0.3	0.8	0.5
Unemployment rate (%, 2015)	9.4	6.8	5.1	5.7	12.6
General government debt 2016	83.5	74.1	37.2	84.6	130.4
Public balance (%, 2016)	−1.7	−1.8	0.6	−1.6	−2.0
Old age dependency ratio 2016	29.3	27.2	27.6	27.5	31.8

Source: Eurostat

well as the legal determination of property rights. These measures were tantamount to a market-economic basic law. Next, the modernization phase involved the introduction of modern governance, along with definition and implementation of essential redistributive and regulative policies like environmental policy and regional policy, as well as a complete restructuring of agricultural policy. The third, ongoing phase includes the Europeanization of Hungarian economic policy in the context of the country's EU accession and the challenge of coping with competition on the domestic market. In this third phase, however, Hungary applies a so-called 'unorthodox' economic policy, partly directed against principles of the European Single Market and provoking conflicts with trade partners and international institutions.

Privatization, an essential field whose structuring effect on politics, the national economy and societal development can hardly be overestimated, also happened in three phases in Hungary. At first, a kind of 'spontaneous privatization' arose even before the formal system change and was steered in an orderly institutional direction by the first post-turnaround government. Then, when the economic crisis of 1995 made accelerated proceedings necessary, privatization increased as the so-called Bokros package was carried out. Finally, there was a new wave of privatization between 2002 and 2010. These privatization waves have in common that they were mainly driven forward by socialist governments. Unlike Czechoslovakia, Hungary did not opt for the method of voucher privatization; instead it organized tenders that, in the context of EU accession, were clearly organized according to European rules of competition. In this way, it quickly succeeded in privatizing the big network providers in the energy and telecommunication branches. However, the railroad system of the Hungarian State Railway was not privatized at all, and air traffic privatization was unprofitable.[23] Further privatization in the field of public services was likewise unsuccessful. Numerous scandals and conflicts attended the privatization of hospitals and individual water suppliers. After the second Orbán government came into office in 2010, privatization in these branches came to a standstill.

Trends in agricultural policy were contradictory. After the turnaround, the significance of agriculture declined constantly at first: the number of farms went down to about one third, indicating a high degree of concentration. The number of employees in agriculture declined from 700,000 in the years of the turnaround to about 170,000 in 2008. Of late, their numbers have stabilized at about 2 per cent of all employees. Against the background of the Common Agricultural Policy after Hungary's EU accession, farmers may have a future again, since they benefit from direct income subsidies paid by the EU, and the government fosters investments into the sector.

Social security reform is a never-ending story. Despite a number of attempts, politicians have not been able to relieve the strain that demographic development has caused to the pension scheme originally (a three-pillar system, under Orbán being transformed back into a one-pillar system) and the healthcare system (fee-for-service system). The labour market and social benefit system, for their part, suffer from too much bureaucracy; some programmes' administrative expenses exceed the volume of allocation. Structural reform in this field is indispensable. Hungary has been more successful in the fields of classical economy policy, with a high share of foreign investment; competition policy, having established strong, independent, efficient oversight of competition; and, despite problems such as the red sludge disaster, environmental policy, with a strongly rising share of renewable energies.

From 1960 to the year of the turnaround, 1989, Hungary's gross domestic product[24] grew gradually but steadily (in 1960, GDP was US$100 billion). The turnaround both caused and was caused by a break in this trend in which GDP fell between 1990 (317) and 1993 (259). Growth then resumed until the year of crisis, 2009 (when it hit 414), whereupon domestic production dropped again to its 2004 level (386). In other words, the onset of crisis in 2009 pushed Hungary back five years. Until 2012 it had not yet managed to achieve growth again, it is only recently that Hungary's growth rates are promising again.

TABLE 9.4. Economic development 1991–2016

	1991	1995	1997	2000	2004	2008	2012	2016
GDP per head in US dollars	8,213	9,032	11,260	13,562	16,952	19,732	22,011	27,596
Development of trade volume	1960	1970	1980	1990	2000	2008	2012	2015
– import	100	274	473	505	1,535	2,508	3,080	3,739
– export (1960 = 100%)	100	266	588	800	1,978	4,035	5,215	6,265
National debt in per cent of yearly GDP	2002	2003	2004	2005	2007	2009	2010	2016
	53.5	56.2	55.7	58.1	61.6	72.8	73.9	74.1

Sources: KSH, OECD.

A rosier picture emerges of Hungary's foreign trade, which has shown dynamic development due to steadily improving access to the European domestic and world markets. Hungary has become an export nation with a considerable trade surplus. By far, its most important economic partner is Germany; Hungarian economic cycles are therefore closely connected to those in Germany. More than half of Hungary's imports come from the EU, while three quarters of Hungary's exports go to the EU. Even export rates to the new EU members are at surprisingly high levels, approximating those of exports to non-EU states. Thus, the country's trade-policy integration into the European domestic market has been very successful, with the trade volume doubling over the past ten years. Few countries are as dependent on exports as Hungary. In 1991, Hungary's foreign trade accounted for a 33 per cent share of the GDP, whereas in 2012 the figure was 81 per cent – that is, four fifths of the economy depended already on foreign trade.

At the beginning of its transformation, Hungary was a highly attractive location for foreign direct investment, initially attracting almost half of all foreign direct investments in the region. Since then, the figures have become more balanced. Compared to similarly populated states, Hungary lags far behind Austria (with one half its level) and slightly behind the Czech Republic (about two thirds), but is clearly ahead of Portugal (about double). Certainly, the next step will be to create investment conditions that will increasingly offer technological skills, good education and efficient administration, along with the traditional competitive wage cost advantages. The most recent investments in the automobile branch (by Daimler, GM/Opel, Audi) confirm both the attractiveness of such conditions and, once again, the close interrelation with Germany.

On the whole, the Hungarian national economy is well integrated into the international division of labour, with a growing tendency towards high technology, a small but stable agricultural sector, a strong industrial sector and a developing services sector. Risks and shortcomings are identifiable in the quality of the administration, the rickety fiscal policy (reflected in the repeated postponement of the euro's introduction and in excessive tax burdens on enterprises and citizens), the blocked reform of the social system and the internally comparatively immobile labour market with strong brain drain towards the West.

Societal Developments

After World War II, Hungary's population grew steadily to the maximum of 10.7 million in 1980 and then entered a decline still ongoing today. In the

TABLE 9.5. Social parameters

	1989	1998	2004	2009	2015
Population (in millions)	10.42	10.14	10.12	10.03	9.86
Life expectancy for men	65.44	66.14	68.59	70.05	72.09
Life expectancy for women	73.79	75.18	76.91	77.89	78.61
Suicides	4.133 (1990)	3.247	2.742	2.461	1.870
Number of reported legal offences	216.800	593.900	414.400	394.000	280.113
Books published (Mio)	108.4	47.0	32.0	36.0	28.1

Source: I. Harcsa, G. Papp and G. Vukovich, 'Magyarország a társadalmi jelzőszámok tükrében', in T. Kolosi, I. Tóth and G. Vukovich (eds), *Társadalmi Riport 2006* (Budapest, 2006), 435–66, updated with data of the Hungarian Statistical Office (KSH).

summer of 2010, the number of inhabitants fell back below ten million for the first time due to the combination of a negative migration balance and a very low birth rate, compared to the European average. The causes of the latter are well known. Hungarian children are expected to support their elderly parents, but the younger generation's different ideas of life are leading to later marriage and economic insecurity. One striking difference from Western countries is that after 1990, women were temporarily but strongly pushed out of work life. Nevertheless, the birth rate did not rise.

Hungary is a rapidly ageing society. The generation of the turnaround period in particular has to cope with specific problems such as exclusion, due to lack of knowledge of modern technologies and Western languages, or for political reasons. One might venture to call them a 'lost generation' without prospects of employment. These people hardly appear in statistics any longer. Of course, this is a transition phenomenon. The same holds for the Roma, whose integration into the labour market worsened appreciably after 1990. Reforms to the political system have been blocked and the population is unprepared to accept cuts to the social safety net, so socio-political and demographic problems have piled up ever since. Various statistical averages put the official poverty rate in Hungary at 12 to 16 per cent of the population, but the statistics do not reflect the actual rate, which is more like 20 per cent. The suicide rate, on the other hand, which in the 1980s was still one of the world's highest, has clearly fallen since the system change and is now almost half the original rate. This suggests the originally high rate was attributable to socialist narrowness and hopelessness.

TABLE 9.6. Turnout in per cent

Election year	1990	1994	1998	2002	2006	2010	2014
1st round of elections	65.11	68.92	56.26	70.53	67.83	64.38	61,73
2nd round of elections	45.54	55.12	57.01	73.51	64.39	46.66	X*

* Only one round

Source: www.valasztas.hu.

Hungarian political culture is characterized by a mixture of artefacts of perceived traumata and unsolved conflicts. Patterns resulting from the interwar period should be distinguished from the relics of the Kádár regime. First of all, there was the Trianon trauma,[25] which created fertile ground for cultivating a nationalist-revanchist-xenophobic right-wing societal fringe. Anti-Semitism and hostility towards Roma are also widespread. Hungarian passivity, on the other hand, is a relic of the Kádár period that is observable in, for instance, voting behaviour. Particularly during the system change, turnout in Hungary was much lower than in the surrounding formerly socialist countries – an after-effect of the unwritten social contract and its politicization taboo. These days the figures have stabilized at a comparatively low level well under 70 per cent, declining since 2006.

Alongside the Trianon trauma, the resulting irrational conspiracy theories, sense of being doomed ('we are always on the wrong side') and other severe social distortions contribute to what sociologists have called 'Hungarian pessimism'. Hungarian society's most serious problems include, among others, a flash-in-the-pan mentality, conflicts between the political parties, indifference[26] and melancholia attended by flightiness.

Only 24 per cent of the Hungarians surveyed for a recent special Eurobarometer report[27] stated that they had felt 'alive' in the past four weeks – the lowest percentage among the EU-28. The European average was 59 per cent, for Germany it was 67 per cent, for Finland 91 per cent. This snapshot is hardly a suitable point of reference for a long-term assessment of the emotional situation, but for four years these data remained more or less stable, unlike those for some other states, such as Spain, and moreover the figure corresponds well to the overall image. One may well hypothesize that the emotional situation in Hungary is a mixture of frustration at the crisis (apart from Greece and the non-EU country Iceland, Hungary has been hit hardest by the global economic crisis of 2009) and long-term situations of political and cultural conflict.

This low emotional situation of the Hungarian people contrasts with the impressive developments in the structures of civil society, notwithstanding day-to-day political problems. The population is much more inclined to mobilize than it was during the transition period, when out of all Central Europeans the Hungarians were least willing to be mobilized, especially once the transition turned out to be a pact negotiated among elites. Today, demonstrations and referendums feature in the Hungarian citizen's protest repertoire. Much happened in the time between the taxi drivers' blockade in 1990 and the protests against the Gyurcsány government in 2006 to 2009; most recently, Hungarians mobilized to oppose measures supported by the Orbán government.

Furthermore, there has been a quick, comprehensive build-up of social capital. Helpful in this context was a regulation stipulating that donations to non-governmental organizations were income tax deductible by initially 1, then 2 per cent. In 1983 the number of civil society associations was at a low of just 3,500, a result of purposeful destruction by the socialist regime. But just ten years after the system change, modern laws of associations and assembly had already prompted 60,000 organizations to register as such. Meanwhile, internationalization and Europeanization have also expanded civil society's basic knowledge, allowing cross-border actors to develop.

Another problematic field is that of the media. The 'second public' – that is, the democratic opposition – was originally active in the samizdat context. The system change was ultimately effected through temporary cooperation of various subcultures,[28] without linkages between official, semi-official or oppositional sub-milieus, and absent any central umbrella organization. These loose coalitions dissolved immediately after the 'turnaround'. Since then, the respective governments and oppositions have struggled for access to and control over the state media. Private media are often foreign-owned, which basically ensures a plurality of opinions; nevertheless, the political parties have successfully established their own media empires, which dominate at least the national press.

At the end of 2010, the second Orbán government passed a new law on media that reinforces state control over Hungary's media. The law has since met with bitter political resistance at the national level as well as from international organizations, most of all the EU and its member states. The primary criticism is that the new media authority is entitled to impose fines large enough to threaten media's very existence, on grounds of 'squishy' categories of offence (e.g. 'imbalanced political reporting'). Also, there is the accusation that positions at the media authority have been filled according to political loyalty. During the last years, tycoons close to Orbán have gained control of many national and regional media,[29] thus establishing a strong imbalance between the political right and left camps.

Prospects

In the first twenty years after systemic change, Hungary has certainly been developing into a modern, liberal democratic political system structured around a market economy. Via membership of the United Nations, OECD, OSCE, NATO and the EU, the country is fully integrated into the global and regional North Atlantic and continental system of institutions. Thus, the transformation process basically ended with EU accession in 2004. The first task in assessing Hungary's prospects is therefore a statement comparing its situation to that of fellow travellers in Central and South East Europe that have gone through the same process of transformation.

A look at the Bertelsmann Transformation Index (survey period 2008 to 2016) supports the image of Hungary's completed political and economic transformation. However, the country has regressed in the areas of the steering function of the political system and the quality of democracy. Though it hovered near the top for years, Hungary has currently fallen considerably. The Freedom House Index, which is based on a one-year survey period, asks about the quality of democracy. In international comparison, Hungary features among the middle ranks. The extent of

TABLE 9.7. Bertelsmann Transformation Index (BTI) 2016

Status index	Management index
(Level of political and economic transformation; over 8.5: much progressed)	(Policy-making on the road to democracy and market economy; over 7: successful)
1 Taiwan (9.53)	1 Uruguay (7.56)
2 Estonia (9.49)	2 Chile (7.51)
3 Czech Republic (9.40)	3 Taiwan (7.48)
4 Uruguay (9.26)	4 Estonia (7.40)
5 Poland (9.23)	5 Poland (7.28)
6 Lithuania (9.15)	6 Lithuania (7.19)
7 Slovenia (9.01)	7 Latvia (6.97)
8 Chile (8.77)	8 Slovakia (6.96)
9 Slovakia (8.75)	9 Botswana (6.95)
10 Latvia (8.75)	10 South Korea (6.89)
18 Hungary (7.69)	76 Hungary (4.67)

Source: www.bertelsmann-transformation-index.de

TABLE 9.8. Freedom House Index

Country	Elections	Civil society	Independent media	National democratic governance	Local democratic governance	Justice	Corruption	Democracy score	Status
Czech Republic	1.25	2.00	2.75	2.75	1.75	1.75	3.50	2.25	Consolidated democracy
Poland	1.50	1.75	3.00	3.25	1.75	3.25	3.50	2.57	Consolidated democracy
Hungary	3.00	2.75	4.25	4.25	3.00	3.00	4.50	3.54	Semi-consolidated democracy
Slovakia	1.50	2.00	2.75	2.50	2.50	2.75	3.75	2.61	Consolidated democracy
Romania	3.00	2.25	4.25	3.50	3.25	3.75	3.75	3.39	Semi-consolidated democracy

Key: 1 = best score, 7 = worst score, data from 2017.

Source: www.freedomhouse.org.

corruption and the situation of the media come in for the greatest criticism. Like the BTI, Freedom House additionally identifies more and more steering deficits in the field of governance.

In the long run Hungary's negative trend is quite clear: it has suffered decline since the mid 2000s. Hungary is not alone in this respect; other countries in the region have shown similar trends. Nevertheless, in Hungary the Gyurcsány crisis can be identified as a point of culmination that generated numerous instabilities, and the Orbán governments added to it by posing power issues over the rule of law and democracies, proposing a 'illiberal democracy', actually a contradiction in terms. Other explanations, more on the meta level, refer to the declining interest in reform after accession to the European Union in 2004, which led to the so-called post-accession crisis.[30] Certainly the two explanations may be combined.

Until 2010, state institutions suffered from the inflexibility of the constitution of 1990. However, it is not just the steering function and consequent institutional design that are problematic in Hungary: considering its path dependency, the obstruction of reform may also serve to explain current problems. Yet the political culture is no less fundamentally important. Hungary's intermediary institutions suffer from anaemic participation by the long-depoliticized society, so state institutions have only fragmentary, imbalanced means of shaping public opinion. The society – and as a functional consequence, the party system too – is also polarized by the dominant line of conflict between Western-liberal, pro-market modernizers and nationally oriented believers in the state. Hungarians have not yet come to terms with several pathologies stemming from the troubled history of Central Europe. In the socialist system, lack of mobility and scarce distribution of information supported a culture of enemy stereotypes. Since then, one's own culture – or at least reference to it – has been regarded as a means of social cohesion. But constant reference to 'others' tends to result in needless overemphasis on one's own culture. This can only be remedied by encounters and comparisons, which are easily experienced among the Schengen countries in the context of Erasmus programmes and European basic liberties. Thus, the 'cultural question' is also a question of the generations.

Change is also due in the fields of constitutional law and the governance system. In the years 1990 to 2010, the system was outmoded but not completely dysfunctional; it reflected a minimal consensus, negotiated by the political camps in 1990, that was only unilaterally changed by the Constitutional Court.[31] In 2010 the Hungarian people gave political carte blanche to one party, so in the sixth legislative period the FIDESZ had a two-thirds majority. This was enough to change the constitution, and indeed, FIDESZ used this majority to create a new constitution to suit its own taste. This marks a final end to the system transformation. The provisional constitution, which was never more than that, has become history.

The new constitution, the Basic Law, makes fundamental statements about the values of the nation, as in the 'national confession' in the Preamble. On the whole, it is more national and more conservative (e.g. 'marriage is a relationship between a man and a woman'). It changes the structure of the state very little and generally leaves relations among state institutions untouched. Unfortunately, however, its framers were unable to remedy the law on two-thirds majorities, so the problem of legislative obstruction remains virulent.

The most important changes concern the reduction of the parliament from 386 to 199 MPs and consequent changes to the electoral law, as well as the centralization of the territorial self-administrating bodies. The 'reforms' were finalized in 2012.

Meanwhile, criticism was levelled less at the constitutional revision and these two essential reform projects than at individual measures. International critics – the EU among them – are mainly concerned that the competences of the Constitutional Court were summarily curtailed after its judges issued a verdict that was not in the government's favour. The debate on the new law on media also raises questions, as do the retroactive effect of some laws and the newly established possibility of arbitrarily firing public officials. Thus, debates on fundamental questions of democratic responsibility, division of powers and the system of checks and balances have recently been revived. Besides the democratic debate on correct decisions in certain fields of politics, a Hungarian macro-debate revolves around topics of general suspicion, being possessed by history and absolute claims to power. Twentyfive years late, so to speak, the Hungarians have begun an open discourse about the past, and about which political system will represent the majority that was – in the course of an elite-controlled transformation process, whether consciously or only owing to haste – neglected at the roundtable.

Jürgen Dieringer is Honorary Professor for Political Science at Andrássy University Budapest, Hungary, and Visiting Professor at KU Leuven, Belgium. He has published numerous articles on transition countries of East and Central Europe, with special emphasis on Hungary. Other research areas are European integration, regionalism/decentralization and economic policies.

Notes

1. See S.P. Huntington, *The Third Wave: Democratization in the Late Twentieth Century* (London, 1990).
2. The thesis holds that transformation everywhere, from the Czech Republic to all of Russia, has happened in the same way.
3. See in detail J. Dieringer, *Das politische System der Republik Ungarn: Entstehung – Entwicklung – Europäisierung* (Opladen, 2009).
4. Kádár came to power in the wake of the suppression of the people's uprising in 1956. He was Hungary's chief political figure until the end of the 1980s, occupying several crucial positions. On Kádárism, see A. Schmidt-Schweizer, 'Der Kádárismus – das "lange Nachspiel" des ungarischen Volksaufstandes', in R. Kipke (ed.), *Ungarn 1956: Zur Geschichte einer gescheiterten Volkserhebung* (Wiesbaden, 2006), 161–87. On Kádár as a person, see in English R. Gough, *A Good Comrade* (London, 2006).
5. For Hungary, see M. Bihari, *Magyar Politika 1944–2004* [Hungarian Politics 1944–2004] (Budapest, 2005), 255.
6. A good overview of events during the turnaround is provided by A. Oplatka, *Der eiserne Vorhang reißt* (Zürich, 1990).
7. Accordingly, e.g. Körösényi does identify presidentialization tendencies in this sense. See A. Körösényi, 'Gyurcsány-vezér: A magyar politika "prezidencializálódása"' [Gyurcsány – Leader: The 'Presidentialization' of Hungarian Politics], in P. Sándor, L. Vass and A. Tolnai (eds), *Magyarország politikai évkönyve 2006* (Budapest, 2006), 141–49.
8. These were created mainly to facilitate implementation of European policies.
9. This is based on Gesetz 1990: LXV Law on local self-administration.
10. I. Verebélyi, 'A magyar közigazgatás modernizációja' [The Modernization of Hungarian Administration], in S. Kurtán, P. Sándor and L. Vass (eds), *Magyarország politikai évkönyve* (Budapest, 1993), 80–86, here 80.
11. About one half of the seats are elected in one-seat constituencies (two rounds, the first with an absolute majority, then a relative majority). The other half are filled by way of county tickets and a nationwide compensatory ticket.
12. Here the KDNP can no longer be considered an independent party, as only with the help of FIDESZ (same candidates, joint tickets) was it able to be elected to parliament.
13. See S. Lipset and S. Rokkan, 'Cleavages Structures, Party Systems and Voter Alignments: Introduction', in S. Lipset and S. Rokkan (eds), *Party Systems and Voter Alignments: Cross-National Perspectives* (New York, 1967), 1–64.
14. Hungary's second-biggest city, Debrecen, has only about 200,000 inhabitants.
15. See, e.g., the decisions on the supreme commander of the armed forces and on appointing members of broadcasting councils.
16. As for the other prime ministers, Boross and Bajnai were just transitional figures, whereas Medgyessy failed precisely because of his insufficient control of his party.
17. Hungary's level of representation is thus congruent with the regional average: in the bicameral parliament of the Czech Republic, a country about the size of Hungary, the Chamber of Deputies has 200 MPs; the smaller Slovakia has a one-chamber parliament with 150 MPs.
18. A. Ágh, 'The Role of ECE Parliaments in the EU Integration', in A. Ágh (ed.), *Post-Accession in East-Central Europe: The Emergence of the EU 25* (Budapest, 2004), 69–92, here 84f.
19. Under this law, the parliament controls the activities of the government at the European level and, if necessary, confers binding mandates on the government regarding voting in the Council of Ministers.

20. On this, see J. Dieringer, 'Zwischen Parlamentsvorbehalt und Regierungsdominanz: die wachsende Bedeutung des ungarischen Parlaments im europäischen Integrationsprozess', *Zeitschrift für Parlamentsfragen* 38(4) (2007), 764–75.
21. On the preparations, see in detail Z. Horváth and B. Ódor (eds), *Magyar EU-elnökség 2011* [Hungarian EU Chairmanship 2011] (Budapest, 2010).
22. On this, see J. Dieringer, P. Laukó and G. Schneider, 'Towards a European Strategy for the Danube Area', in A. Ágh, T. Kaiser and B. Koller (eds), *Europeanization of the Danube Region: The Blue Ribbon Project* (Budapest, 2010), 64–91.
23. For more detail on network-connected industries during the crucial period of reorganization, see J. Dieringer, *Staatlichkeit im Wandel? Die Regulierung der Sektoren Verkehr, Telekommunikation und Energie im ungarischen Transformationsprozess* (Opladen, 2001).
24. For figures, see Hungarian Statistics Authority KSH (www.ksh.hu).
25. The Treaty of Trianon (one of the post-World War I Paris treaties – 'Hungary's Versailles') of 1920 deprived Hungary of two thirds of its territory (mainly regions that actually were not much populated by Hungarians). This treaty was negotiated when Hungary's domestic situation was destabilized by a communist coup d'etat under Béla Kun. Today Hungarians consider the treaty a peace dictate, victor's justice and a great moral wrong. 'As a people who were suppressed by the Habsburgs', Hungarians do not feel responsible for World War I.
26. A. Körösényi, C. Tóth and G. Török, *A Magyar politikai rendszer* [The Hungarian Political System] (Budapest, 2003), 27.
27. See Special Eurobarometer 345, 'Mental Health', October 2010, 15. Note that the fieldwork was done before the parliamentary elections (May/June).
28. See M. Szabó, 'Die Zivilgesellschaft in Ungarn: Zwischen EU-Beitritt und globalen Herausforderungen', in J. Dieringer and S. Okruch (eds), *Von der Idee zum Konvent: Eine interdisziplinäre Betrachtung des europäischen Integrationsprozesses* (Budapest, 2004), 81–98, here 82.
29. For example the daily newspapers *Magyar Hírlap, Népszabadság, Napló*, as well as several TV channels.
30. See A. Ágh, 'Bumpy Road Ahead in East Central Europe: Post-Accession Crisis and Social Challenge in ECE', in A. Ágh and A. Ferencz (eds), *Overcoming the EU Crisis: EU Perspectives after the Eastern Enlargement* (Budapest, 2007), 7–35. The economic crisis of 2009 has prompted Europe to dramatically increase pressure towards reform.
31. These changes occurred primarily during the term of the Constitutional Court's first president, László Sólyom (1990–2000), who maintained an activist approach. The Horn government of 1994–1998 attempted to write a new constitution but failed.

Chapter 10

Romania

Bogdan Murgescu

Introduction

In Romania, the decline of communism differed significantly from the prevailing pattern in East Central European socialist countries. In most other countries in the region, the communist elites accepted the inevitability of change and, at best, negotiated a peaceful transition of power. Romania, however, experienced a violent revolution that left more than 1,100 dead[1] – a development caused by the specificities of the Romanian political system before 1989. Having emancipated itself from complete subordination to the Soviet Union in the early 1960s, the Romanian communist leadership gradually evolved into a family-run version of national communism, in which almost no one in the system dared to openly challenge decisions made by party leader Nicolae Ceaușescu. In other Eastern European socialist countries, the Soviet leadership exerted a moderating influence on the national communist leaders, effectively blocking any attempts at massive repression, but this control mechanism had no influence on the national communist leadership of Romania. Hence, the very moment Ceaușescu refused to accept change and began massive repression of local demonstrations, his yes-men – who had been appointed to the political decision-making bodies of the Romanian Communist Party to reward and further secure their obedience – unquestioningly accepted these decisions while the regime's power structures, namely the Securitate and the army, willingly executed the orders. At the same time, though, various individuals within the system realized the inevitability of political change and abandoned both Ceaușescu and the regime to save their own skins. Consequently, on 22 December 1989, the regime collapsed much more rapidly than anyone had expected.

Notes for this chapter begin on page 275.

As the population felt entitled to a better life, this collapse created genuine enthusiasm and high expectations. Having vented all their hatred and frustrations on Nicolae Ceauşescu and his spouse, Romanians felt that the couple's removal alone would be the key to the country's swift recovery. Yet as Daniel Dăianu pointed out, Romania was, poorly prepared for the post-communist transformation:

> In the late 1980s the Romanian economy, the country, and the people offered a desolate picture. After more than four decades of forced industrialization, the competitiveness of the economy was at the lowest level in the 'communist league', the imbalances between the different sectors and the shortages were on the rise, and the suffering of the people was unimaginable; Romania lagged behind the neighboring countries with respect to the institutional prerequisites required for the post-communist transition, the psychological preparation of the population for social change, and the social basis for reforms towards the market economy.[2]

This desolation was thus experienced both objectively and subjectively. The Romanian economy had been in deep crisis throughout most of the 1980s as Ceauşescu pursued his course of increased economic autarchy, curbing imports in order to pay off foreign debt and become less vulnerable to economic and political pressures from abroad, especially Western demands for alleviation of his oppressive internal policy. Ceauşescu's policies deepened the imbalances specific to the communist system,[3] especially the overcapacities of heavy industry and relative underdevelopment of the services sector. They also burdened every sector of the economy with inefficiencies. Productivity stagnated, technological progress almost completely stalled, and resources were allocated or denied arbitrarily. Falsified reports and random decisions exacerbated the poor management of the economy, leading to shortages and disruptions in economic flows and processes. Most companies were unable to compete on foreign markets – or defend their positions on the internal market, had it been opened to competition. The population had the lowest living standard in Eastern Europe (with perhaps the exception of Albania), which reinforced the demands to increase consumption after the demise of communism.

The repressive characteristics of the Ceauşescu regime effectively prevented any open deliberation about political, economic and social alternatives to the official line of the communist leadership. Romanian society thus found itself poorly equipped for pluralistic public debate, a significant handicap after the demise of communism. Likewise, the regime had blocked the formation of significant opposition groups that might otherwise have been able to assume and effectively handle power after Ceauşescu's fall. As a matter of fact, the rapid collapse of the Ceauşescu regime fuelled suspicions that a group of conspirators within the communist system had staged a palace coup to secure the seizure of political power by the council of the National Salvation Front (NSF), led by Ion Iliescu. Yet upon examination, the course of events reveals striking heterogeneity in the group that coalesced around Ion Iliescu and its difficult relationship with the existing military command structures.[4] Meanwhile, although the NSF was clearly heterogeneous and unprepared to lead the country, despite the communist backgrounds of some of their representatives, the forces emerging from civil society and dissident groups were even less capable of competing for political power or taking over. Therefore, the most prominent political alternatives to the NSF were groups of veterans of pre-communist political parties who had survived the communist prisons and were already in their seventies in 1989.[5] Taking advantage of their tried and tested solidarity, the National Peasant Party (which also defined itself as a Christian Democratic party), the Liberal National Party and the Social Democratic Party were resurrected and embarked on a course of fundamental political opposition to Ion Iliescu and the National Salvation Front, whom they condemned as 'neo-communists'. Thus, a radical divide between Iliescu's NSF and the 'historic' parties soon defined the political field, and the consequent polarization distorted the development of a pluralistic political culture.

Politics

Generally, all the political forces agreed to a pluralistic political system based on free elections.[6] On the evening of 22 December 1989, the NSF issued a proclamation announcing free elections in April 1990. A decree of 31 December 1989 regulated the founding and functioning of political parties on a very liberal basis. Requiring a minimum of 251 members, the presentation of statutes and a political programme to the authorities who registered the party as a legal entity, this decree set the stage for the immediate registration of numerous parties: thirty in January 1990 alone, about eighty by the first free election season in May 1990, and almost two hundred by 1991.[7] Political parties diminished in number only after more restrictive laws took effect, increasing the number of members a political party needed to renew its registration to 10,000 in 1996, and then to 25,000 in 2003; additionally, at least 700 members had to be from each of least eighteen counties. The Provisional Council of National Unity had drawn up the general features of the political system by March 1990, basing the Election Law 92/1990 on a semi-presidential system in which both the President of the State and the president of the bicameral parliament were to be elected by universal suffrage.[8]

This semi-presidential political system, confirmed by the 1991 constitution and retained in the amended constitution of 2003, created significant confusion and several conflicts in the triangle formed by president, government and parliament. Although the majority of the population considered the president the most powerful state actor, in fact the constitution limited his prerogatives and reserved most of the executive powers for the government. This arrangement strengthened the position of the prime minister, who, once invested, could only be dismissed by a parliamentary vote of no confidence. Romania experienced such a dismissal only once in its first twenty-one years after communism, when the dissolution of a grand coalition between the Liberal Democrats and the Social Democrats led the parliament to dismiss the government on 13 October 2009. Moreover, even in this case the vote of no confidence did not result in an actual change of government: all the prime ministerial candidates nominated by President Traian Băsescu were unacceptable to the existing parliamentary majority, so the then Prime Minister Emil Boc continued to lead the government until the presidential elections of 22 November and 6 December 2009. After the elections, the re-elected President Băsescu reappointed Boc as prime minister, and the new government, supported by a new majority, was confirmed by parliament.

In such circumstances, it seems obvious that any president would have a marked interest in nominating only individuals of proven loyalty for the position of prime minister. Sometimes, when the prime minister accepted the president's political dominance, this kind of hierarchical relationship worked reasonably well.[9] At other times, the prime minister resisted the president and pursued an independent policy – as was particularly evident from 2005 to 2008, when Prime Minister Călin Popescu-Tăriceanu, backed by most of the government coalition and the opposition, rejected President Băsescu's request to step down in order to allow for early parliamentary elections. Moreover, Popescu-Tăriceanu even ousted the Democratic Party, which had remained loyal to the president. On 19 April 2007, the parliament voted to suspend the president, but in a subsequent referendum the population voted the president back into office, thereby wresting a concession from parliament and prolonging the antagonistic cooperation until parliamentary elections in November 2008. The conflict of 2005 to 2008 is perhaps an extreme in the history of post-communist Romania, but it is not an isolated incident, as indicated by the diverging opinions of Prime Minister Petre Roman and President Iliescu in 1991 or the strained relationship between President Emil Constantinescu and Prime Minister Radu Vasile in 1998 and 1999, which ultimately led to the prime minister's dismissal by the president.

Although this confirms that the government is able to maintain its position even when its opinions diverge substantially from those of the President of the State, the open conflict of 2005 to 2008 was atypical, because in most such cases these two branches of the executive power have managed to work out some reasonable cooperation. On the other hand, overly close cooperation between the president and the prime minister has proven detrimental to the role of parliament. As recent experience has shown, the government is able to push legislation through parliament through a procedural assumption of responsibility. Hence, many members of parliament – even those who object to major components of new legislation – have refrained from challenging the government, aware that the president might renominate the prime minister and that an escalation of institutional conflict could lead to early elections.

Another major quirk of the Romanian political system is that except for the NSF in 1990, no political party has managed to achieve an absolute majority in parliament. Since 1991, therefore, every government has depended on either coalitions or the support of parties that, for one reason or another, were not participating in government directly. Most governing coalitions have included several parties theoretically espousing different political ideologies. This variety within coalitions indicates that the roles of political ideology and ideological affiliation are negligible. Romanian political parties have demonstrated a remarkable facility for shifting from one ideology to another. The Democratic Party is one of the best examples. Upon its origin in the 1990s, it defined itself as centre-left and struggled for acceptance as a member of the Socialist International. In 2004, however, it allied with the National Liberals to advocate the introduction of a flat tax, and in 2005 – without any actual internal debate or dissent – it decided at a party congress to become a centre-right party, shifting its allegiance to the European People's Party from then on.

It was not only parties that changed their names and official ideologies: individual politicians proved even more flexible, at both the local and national levels. For example, during the legislature of 2004 to 2008, almost one fifth of the MPs changed their political affiliation, a trend that continued even after 2008. Considering these circumstances, it comes as no surprise that the population assumes politicians represent not political ideas (or still less, ideals) but mostly their own personal interests. This is why the state and the politicians are generally perceived as corrupt. According to a recent survey by Transparency International, Romania, with a corruption perception index of 3.7, ranked 69th out of 178 countries and 25th out of the (at the time) 27 EU countries.[10]

On the whole, the structure of the political field is based less on the political options offered by doctrines and ideologies, and more on the pros and cons of the leading politicians' relative positions on the national stage. This was especially noticeable in the 1990s and early 2000s, when the political field was divided between President Iliescu's followers and enemies until a major rift gradually separated followers and allies of President Băsescu from his opponents, resulting in a major realignment after 2005. This political pattern was consistent with both the popular perception of the president as the most important politician in Romania and the genuine capabilities of Ion Iliescu (in the 1990s) and Traian Băsescu (in the 2000s) as party powerhouses in the struggle for political power. Iliescu was the major factor in the electoral successes of the NSF in 1990, the Democratic NSF in 1992, and to a lesser extent the Party of Social Democracy in Romania in 2000, each time achieving (despite losses in the elections of 1996) significantly better results than the party supporting him. Traian Băsescu, for his part, managed to turn the tide in 2004 by winning the presidential election and establishing his government, even though the coalition that had supported him (DA Alliance, Alliance for Justice and Truth) lost the parliamentary elections. He was re-elected in 2009 with an even closer margin of less than 0.67 per cent, a result basically determined by the votes of Romanians abroad. He subsequently managed to persuade the Democratic Union of Hungarians in Romania, the deputies of the national minorities and several dissident MPs to support the Democratic Liberal Party and establish a new coalition government under Prime Minister Emil Boc.

This personalized pattern of the political field had several consequences. The parties' economic and political programmes were seldom well thought out, and even more rarely did parties negotiate policy compromises for the public good. In fact, in terms of energy spent, policymaking was eclipsed by personal issues and efforts to gain privileged access to public resources. Most parties developed a culture of political discrimination regarding the distribution of resources, which only reinforced the inclination towards political flexibility among both local and central public administrators, who often shifted their allegiance to the ruling party or made false compromises with people influential in government.

The media[11] contributed heavily to the polarized, personalized pattern of the Romanian political field. The early 1990s were dominated by state-owned (and state-controlled) audio-visual media, especially the public television service, while at the same time newspapers flourished and took very clear sides in the political turmoil. Gradually, this situation changed. Private capital expanded its interest, founding new media and taking over existing outlets, especially those of the print media. New private television channels emerged in the mid 1990s, several of them gradually outstripping public television in terms of audience share and influence. Commercial interests gradually prevailed over political affiliations, although some emerging media empires attempted to use their influence to gain political leverage for their owners. In a context of media saturation and declining professional standards,[12] the combination of media influence with political leverage and patronage led to oligopolistic concentration and distorted competition, prompting foreign investors to either retreat entirely (as, for example, with the German WAZ Medien Gruppe's withdrawal from the Romanian media[13]) or limit themselves to marginal shares of the Romanian media market (e.g. Ringier or the SBS Broadcasting Group).

The personalization of politics and its interference with vested economic interests might lead one to conclude that the political system will develop towards oligarchy or tyranny. Nonetheless – at least from the perspective of competitive elections – the democratic system has functioned rather well. Despite rumours and accusations that elections were rigged or at least plagued by various irregularities (except for the presidential elections of 2009 and 2012), in fact since 1992 all the governments that had organized and supervised the electoral process lost power.[14]

Meanwhile, the number of parties represented in parliament has declined significantly because of restrictive changes in the legal prerequisites for organizing political parties and the threshold for gaining parliamentary seats (3 per cent in 1992 and 1996, 5 per cent since 2000). Only five parties (and legally recognized organizations of national minorities that benefit from a special constitutional provision) managed to obtain parliamentary representation in 2008: the Democratic Liberal Party, the Social Democratic Party, the National Liberal Party, the Democratic Union of Hungarians in Romania, and the Conservative Party (the latter only in alliance with the Social Democrats). In 2010, these parties were joined by the National Union for the Progress of Romania, founded by dissident social democratic and liberal MPs. Although the Greater Romania Party passed the threshold in the European Parliament elections of 2009, and despite various opinion polls showing that other parties might also gain significant shares of the vote in future elections (e.g. the People's Party created by television star Dan Diaconescu), it is safe to say that the Romanian political scene is currently dominated by three major parties that each represent popular social democratic and liberal political trends, along with the Democratic Union of Hungarians in Romania. All other parties are struggling to meet the threshold and survive politically.

Today, the post-communist Romanian political system can boast of several political successes. The two most important are Romania's accession to NATO and its EU membership. Romania first approached NATO in

1992, applying for membership in 1993 and joining the Partnership for Peace in 1994. NATO did not grant Romania membership in its first effort to expand towards East Central Europe in 1997, but cooperation intensified. After the 1999 Kosovo War and the terrorist attack on the United States of America on 11 September 2001, additional expansion was seen as beneficial. NATO invited Romania to join at the Prague Summit in 2002, and the country finally became a full NATO member in 2004.

The EU became Romania's main economic partner in the early 1990s. Romania first applied for EU membership in 1995, but only after several years on the waiting list was it invited to begin its accession talks in 1999. These negotiations were finalized in late 2004, and Romania signed the accession treaty in 2005 and became a full-fledged member of the EU on 1 January 2007 (at the same time as Bulgaria). To be sure, these successes were less attributable to Romanian politicians than to the strategic expansion decisions of the leaders of NATO and the EU member states. Nonetheless, EU membership and NATO are essential to Romania, not only symbolically – in recognition of its democratic credentials after 1989 – but even more so as guarantees of security, spurs to internal reform and opportunities for economic and political development. Another important political success was the normalization of the interethnic relationship with the Hungarian minority, which was further strengthened by the Romanian-Hungarian treaty of 1996, the two nations' common membership in NATO and the EU, and partial administrative decentralization in the early 2000s.

Nevertheless, the Romanian political field was meanwhile still plagued by some persistent structural problems. After 2007, the government's ability to forge a minimal consensus on a few basic issues[15] was limited and apparently even declining. Obtaining membership of NATO and the EU had been a common goal for all major political forces and a broad majority of Romanian society, but after this objective was met, internecine political conflicts escalated and were fought with increasing embitterment. Back in the 1990s, almost all the significant political parties had begun evolving into oligarchic groups striving to monopolize access to administrative positions and public resources. To achieve this, all the ruling parties, whether on the national or the county level, systematically distorted the distribution of resources to the advantage of their members so as to pressure various people in the administration and local notables to join the party that controlled the resources. Simultaneously, politicians, new post-communist capitalists, leading journalists, media tycoons and influential members of the justice system, police, secret services and military engaged in massive networking and exploitation. Besides draining public resources and often misrepresenting the functioning of vital state institutions, these extractive elites tended to isolate themselves from the larger segments of society. The polarization, along with the contrast between the political parties' rhetoric and various politicians' non-partisan dealings, undermined the credibility of most political actors and engendered public cynicism about politics. Participation in elections declined dramatically, particularly in urban areas.[16]

Of course, one might argue that discouraging voters from voting serves the interests of incumbent politicians and existing parties, in that it may reduce costs and allow a limited number of voters mobilized by party machinery to make a difference, especially in rural areas. Yet this is also a risky approach, as voters may decide to rebel, rejecting existing parties and their nominees in favour of new parties or populist outsiders. The media usually support politicians in their desire to control access to the public agenda and to circumvent unpredictable newcomers; sometimes, however, mobilized voters can generate unwelcome surprises at the voting polls. A glaring example was the elections of the year 2000, when the nationalist Greater Romania Party surged to become the second political power in parliament while its candidate, Corneliu Vadim Tudor, succeeded in reaching the second round of the presidential elections. Still, as shown by the subsequent inefficiency and gradual decline of the Greater Romania Party, as well as the limited success of later populist outsiders, the existing political system appears to have managed to control the damage without ever addressing the roots of public dissatisfaction with its performance.

Another major structural problem of the Romanian political system was and still is its weak control institutions, exemplified by the Romanian Court of Accounts.[17] Re-established in 1993, the Court of Accounts was responsible for controlling public spending, investigating financial irregularities, and bringing to justice those individuals and institutions that misappropriated public resources. The Court of Accounts soon became feared for its controls, whereupon it was gradually stripped of its powers and relegated to the role of a harmless audit institution. In 1999, for instance, the government backed a law accelerating economic reform that annulled the court's rights to control the privatization process and transferred pre-emptive financial control from the Court of Accounts to the Finance Ministry. In 2003, in the context of revising the constitution in order to allow EU accession, the Court of Accounts was stripped of its jurisdiction with the provisional promise that the financial irregularities unveiled by the court's comptrollers would be brought to justice in future, specially founded courts of law. These special courts were still non-existent in 2011.

The justice system as a whole also illustrates the weakness and dysfunctionality of Romanian control institutions. The constitution recognizes the importance of the judicial system as a major public authority, stating that judges 'shall be independent and subject only to the law' (Article 124). In fact, however, severe shortcomings have plagued the functioning of the judiciary. Most of the judges and prosecutors inherited from the communist system were unprepared for the multitude of litigations and judicial issues in the post-communist period and reluctant to deal with felonies committed by members of the political and economic elite. Legal loopholes, procedural shortcomings and contradictory rulings slowed the administration of justice, almost paralysing the system. Not just slow but also expensive for common people seeking justice, the system proved ineffective at fighting corruption.

Efforts to reform the system met with only limited success, as they generally aimed at strengthening the judicial system's independence. Judges could not be removed from their positions, so the 2003 revision of the constitution shifted a large portion of the prerogatives of control of the justice system from the minister of justice to the Superior Council of Magistracy, supposedly to guarantee the independence of justice (Articles 133–134). But as it was the magistrates who elected most of its members, the Superior Council often condoned the wrongdoings of its constituency and hence was more a defender of their privileges than a vector of reform. Under these circumstances, the EU provided the main stimulus for improving the functioning of the justice system by establishing a cooperation and verification mechanism and closely monitoring the progress of judicial reform in Romania (and Bulgaria).[18] Under pressure from the EU, several specialized institutions were founded to fight corruption (including the National Anticorruption Directorate of the Public Ministry and the National Integrity Agency) and some progress was made in bringing wrongdoers to justice. In 2011, the government also began to streamline judicial procedures, but it is still too early to assess the impact of these efforts. Clearly, given the politicization of the debates about the functioning of the judicial system, future improvements will require a great deal of internal effort and external support.

John Keane described the rise of monitory democracy as a major achievement of the twentieth century.[19] Several civil society organizations emerged in Romania after the decline of communism, many of them heavily politicized. Overall, participation remained low.[20] Nevertheless, some NGOs specialized in maintaining and protecting democracy by monitoring elections (e.g. the Pro-Democracy Association), overseeing the general activities of the political field (e.g. the Institute for Public Policy) or fighting corruption (e.g. Alliance for a Clean Romania). Though foreign assistance was and remains crucial to such organizations' operation, they are gradually making their mark by gaining internal support and becoming major references in public debates.

Economy

At the beginning of 1990, the Romanian economy was completely unprepared for the post-communist transformation. Its sole, debatable asset was that the foreign debt had been paid off due to tremendous efforts in the 1980s. These, however, had succeeded at the cost of restricted consumption, almost complete cessation of technological imports and the sheltering of large parts of the economy from the outside world. Therefore, after an initial compensatory consumption boom in the first months of 1990, the Romanian economy faced a severe crisis triggered by the collapse of the structures of the socialist command economy, both domestically and abroad. The subsequent development of the Romanian post-communist economy[21] is chronologically divisible into phases:

- 1990–1992: collapse of production and partial disintegration of the structures of the command economy; initial elements of transformation (foreign trade and price liberalization, dissolution of agricultural cooperatives) upset by plummeting GDP (which in 1992 was only 71 per cent of the 1989 level), inflation (210 per cent in 1992) and unemployment (8.4 per cent in 1992);
- 1993–1996: partial recovery within a framework combining cautious gradual reforms with the revival of economic command structures, tax reform (introduction of VAT), limited foreign investment, privatization favouring locals (voucher privatization, management employee buyouts, etc.), avoidance of major restructuring and subsidization of various companies via credits from state-owned banks;
- 1997–1999: transformation crisis involving political decisions to restructure large parts of the economy and close down deficit-creating companies; severe drop in output (industrial output declined by more than 20 per cent), which in combination with the unfavourable effects of the Asian and Russian financial crisis of 1997–1998 unleashed a crisis; privatization of several large companies with strategic foreign direct investments;
- 2000–2008: economic restructuring and growth in the context of EU accession; major privatizations (industry, banking system, energy sector, etc.); economic takeovers by transnational corporations that boosted output, especially in the manufacturing and service industries; significant temporary labour migration to Western Europe; and

TABLE 10.1. Structural change of the Romanian economy by sector

		1990	1995	2000	2005	2010
Agriculture	% of labour force	29.0	34.4	41.4	31.9	29.1
	% of GDP	21.8	19.8	11.1	8.9	6.0
Industry and constructions	% of labour force	43.5	30.4	27.3	29.0	30.0
	% of GDP	45.9	39.5	30.9	30.9	35.2
Services	% of labour force	27.5	32.0	31.3	39.1	40.9
	% of GDP	34.6	43.8	57.8	60.2	58.8

Sources: Murgescu, *România și Europa*, 470, 475; Institutul Național de Statistică (labour force data for 2009 and estimates of GDP for 2010).

overheating of the economy after 2005, due especially to increased internal consumption and public expenditure;
- 2008–2010: economic crisis caused by a combination of declining foreign demand for Romanian exports, collapse of a real estate bubble and the need to adjust the public sector;
- 2011: belated slow recovery fuelled by the export sector.

As in other post-communist countries, the structural transformation of the economy in Romania entailed a decline in agriculture and industry combined with growth in the services sector, which had remained underdeveloped during communism.

De-collectivization was the main factor shaping Romanian agriculture after 1989. This generally refers to agrarian reform via the parcellization and cultivation of land, as well as the dismantling of the existing production and distribution systems. Thereupon a dual agricultural structure emerged, consisting of approximately four million small cultivated parcels of land and approximately 20,000 modern farms producing the lion's share of commercial crops and animal products. Since approximately 75 per cent of the farmland was used for subsistence only, the agricultural sector as a whole suffered from low productivity and structural impediments adapting to EU standards. Temporary labour migration to the West provided a certain relief to some rural areas with a surplus of young labour, but a sustainable solution would require schemes encouraging the creation of alternative jobs and supplementary sources of income for the rural population.

Under socialism, Romanian industry had been excessive, overly diversified and economically inefficient. These structural problems had been exacerbated by Ceaușescu's autarchic policies of the 1980s. The subsequent collapse of the communist system triggered a severe crisis, with many companies unable to find a market for their products. This predicament was intensified by the liberalization of foreign trade and prices, the opening of the internal market to imports, legal uncertainty and mismanagement (i.e. managers' inability to resist the temptation to use the resources of the companies under their control to accumulate their own economic capital). Some industries managed to survive and even to consolidate their position, but most companies suffered a severe drop in output and revenues, and thus were forced to either downsize or close down completely. Early retirement schemes mitigated unemployment, but overall, the industrial labour force declined from more than four million in 1989 to about two million in 2000.

Eventually, foreign direct investments in the context of EU accession enabled a revival of industrial activity in Romania. The most spectacular example is that of the Dacia automotive manufacturer, which Renault took over in 1999. Over the next five years, it restructured the company and designed the new Dacia Logan, which was unveiled in 2004 and became a major success in the years 2005 to 2010. Capitalizing on the intrinsic features of this model (durability, reliability and affordability), the rising demand for low-priced cars in Western Europe and the marketing know-how of Renault Nissan, the company managed to acquire significant market shares worldwide. In fact, Dacia fared well even during the financial crisis of 2008–2010: while most car dealerships experienced serious difficulties, overall sales of the Dacia Logan rose to more than 300,000 annually, most sold within the EU. In the meantime, Dacia moved the production of its new models to Romania, opening an industrial engineering centre there, and began preparing for the challenges of the 2010s. Dacia Renault has become the showcase for industrial success, but other transnational corporations too have taken advantage of relatively low-cost Romanian labour and easy access to the EU market to develop profitable manufacturing companies, especially in the areas of textiles, electric and electronic devices, pharmaceuticals and various other industrial goods.

Following a slump in the early 1990s, the performance of the construction sector was determined by the housing requirements of those segments of the population that managed to prosper economically and by the real estate bubble of 2005 to 2008. Although the subsequent crisis affected the sector severely, it managed to survive on EU-funded energy-saving rehabilitation programmes for old urban apartment housing blocks.

The services sector experienced the most spectacular post-communist dynamics, but development varied markedly across its subsectors. Commercial trade was one of the first to profit from opportunities opened up by the transition to a market economy. By the early 1990s, the large number of emerging small commercial companies had proved critical to the first phase of capital accumulation by the new class of local entrepreneurs. Starting in the mid 1990s, international retail chains entered the market and soon controlled significant shares.

The banking system diversified (businessman Ion Țiriac founded the first private Romanian bank in 1991) but grew only slowly during most of the 1990s. Its expansion gained momentum when major European banks began to penetrate the Romanian market with takeovers of Romania's most important banks (e.g. Banca Română de Dezvoltare by Société Générale in 1998; Banca Agricolă by Raiffeisen in 2001; Banca Comercială Română by Erste Bank in 2005; Țiriac Bank by HypoVereinsbank and, subsequently, Unicredit in 2005). Insurance companies and other financial services also made gains but remained underdeveloped in comparison to those in other EU countries. The dynamics of the telecommunications sector proved particularly dynamic, whereas Romania's infrastructure and traditional transportation systems, like most public services (education, healthcare, urban utilities) still lagged behind EU standards.

The post-communist transition also triggered a boom of temporary labour migration to foreign countries. In the 1990s, most Western European countries shielded themselves from labour migration by enforcing restrictive visa and labour permit regulations. Many Romanian migrant workers thus were forced to seek employment in the somewhat less controlled construction sector, or in countries outside the EU (e.g. Israel, Turkey, Hungary). This situation changed in 2002, when the EU granted Romanian citizens visa-free entry to the Schengen area for brief stays. Some countries, especially Italy and Spain, also offered easy legal (and illegal) employment. By 2006, the number of Romanian labour migrants had increased significantly to more than two million, most of them working in construction, agriculture and domestic services. This helped ease social tensions in regions strongly affected by post-communist deindustrialization. Meanwhile, remittances (estimated at about six billion euros in 2008) became a major factor in balancing Romania's foreign trade deficit. Official accession to the EU did not entail major changes in the labour market, as most migrants had begun working abroad in the pre-accession phase; furthermore, the labour market restrictions introduced by several EU countries applied to citizens of Romania (and Bulgaria) until 2014. In any case, the economic crisis of 2008 to 2010 reduced employment opportunities in Western Europe, especially in the severely affected Spanish construction sector.

EU accession was an indispensable opportunity for economic development in Romania. The accession negotiations were decisive for the pace of the economic reforms and establishment of a functional market economy. At the same time, the prospective EU membership was crucial to capital inflow from foreign direct investments. From 2000 to 2008, the Romanian economy experienced not only economic growth but also a considerable convergence with EU standards. This marked a turning point in Romania's economic history. The crises of late communism and the first decade of post-communist transition had increased the country's development lag, leaving its per capita GDP in 2000 at about 26 per cent of the EU average. The EU accession process halted and reversed this divergent trend, and by 2008 Romania's per capita GDP had climbed to almost 47 per cent of the EU average.

The severity of the economic crisis of 2008 to 2010 in Romania was above average for the EU, and the divergent trend picked up again slightly: according to Eurostat, Romania slid to about 45 per cent of the EU-28 average. The prospects for economic development have become better since 2011/12, given the successful completion of the critical phase of adjusting public-sector spending. Macro-economic equilibrium has been restored, EU funding is supporting investments in infrastructure, and rising exports are expected to advance the entire economy.

Society

One of the first changes triggered by the revolution in December 1989 was the repeal of the ban on abortions. Ceauşescu's anti-abortion policies had forced birth rates up and delayed the completion of the demographic transition from traditional demographics – high birth rate, high mortality, low life expectancy – to late modern demographics – low birth rate, low mortality, high life expectancy. Liberalization caused a severe drop in the birth rate, which subsequently stabilized at slightly more than 10 per cent, annually. Consequently, Romania shifted towards a pattern of natural demographic reduction that, combined with net emigration, caused the population to diminish from about 23 million in 1990 to about 21.4 million in 2010.[22]

Ethnic Romanians make up about 89 per cent of the total population of Romania. Eighteen legally recognized national minorities are represented in the parliament and receive state support to preserve their cultural specificity. Hungarians, numerically the greatest minority, constituted about 6.6 per cent of the total population in the 2002 census. With lower birth rates and higher emigration rates than the national average, the total number of Hungarians in Romania declined from almost 1.7 million in 1990 to about 1.4 million in 2010. Transylvania is home to the largest segment of the Hungarian minority, which constitutes an absolute majority of the population in the Harghita and Covasna counties and a significant minority in several others, particularly Mureş, Bihor, Satu Mare, Cluj and Sălaj. In the context of the post-communist revival of nationalism, strained interethnic relationships in the early 1990s culminated in massive street fighting in Târgu Mureş on 19–20 March 1990. Such clashes were avoided thereafter, but nationalist resentment continued to poison interethnic relationships and influence politics, not only at the local and county levels (e.g. the nationalist Gheorghe Funar was elected mayor of Cluj in 1992 and re-elected in 1996 and 2000) but also nationally. Nevertheless, the situation gradually normalized as politicians on both sides strove to avoid confrontation and find compromises to resolve disputes. An important element was the finalization of a Romanian-Hungarian treaty of understanding, cooperation and good neighbourliness in September 1996, as both countries attempted to clear the way for admission to NATO. The treaty put an end to any Hungarian territorial claims concerning Transylvania, recognized the Hungarian state's right to support Hungarians in Romania and laid a foundation for fruitful cooperation between the two states. Moreover, after the elections of November 1996, the Democratic Union of Hungarians in Romania became part of the government coalition and proved crucial to gaining the majority in every subsequent Romanian government, except the grand coalition of 2008/2009. Hungarians were thus able to exert political pressure to influence decentralization decisions, improvements to minorities' legal status at the national level and the distribution of resources at the local and county levels.

According to the 2002 census, Roma represent about 2.5 per cent of Romania's total population; however, their ever-rising birth rate has led some independent observers to presume the actual number is much higher than the official data indicate. The Roma population is distributed across the entire country, with notable concentrations in Central Transylvania and Southern Walachia. Generally poor, less educated than the national average and resident in secluded traditional communities, many Roma have had difficulty integrating and are subject to various forms of discrimination. Simultaneously, many Roma engage in criminal activities, thereby reinforcing already widespread prejudices among other population groups. Stereotypical biases are further supported by incidents involving Romanian Roma in Italy and France, which Romanian media have covered widely. The Romanian state has developed various positive action schemes to offer better education to Roma and encourage social inclusion, but the results are meagre; most problems persist.

From the twelfth to the late twentieth century, Germans formed another significant population group in Romania. In the late socialist period, their numbers dwindled as they increasingly emigrated to the Federal Republic of Germany. In the 1980s, the communist authorities' restrictions and chicaneries caused the annual number of emigrating Germans to fluctuate between 10,000 and 15,000, but this number surged to about 60,000 in 1990 and diminished only after the pool of potential emigrants had been exhausted.[23] The 2002 census recorded about 60,000 Germans still living in Romania at that time, most of them senior citizens. Given the negligible birth rate, the trend pointed towards accelerated reduction of the German minority – a severe loss to Romanian society as a whole, since on average the German population traditionally was more educated and productive than the Romanian population. Germans' potential was also confirmed in Sibiu, where despite representing only 1.6 per cent of the population, the representative of the German Democratic Forum was elected mayor in 2000 (then re-elected in 2004 and 2008) while its faction managed to gain majorities in the local and the county councils.

The Ukrainian, Russian, Turkish, Tatar, Serbian, Slovakian and Bulgarian minorities of Romania are unevenly distributed, regionally, and live mostly in rural areas. In contrast, Greek, Jewish and Armenian minorities live in urban areas and are better off than the average population but demographically are experiencing a declining trend due to assimilation and low birth rate (as well as appreciable emigration during communism, in the case of the Jewish population).

The post-communist transformation triggered a process of selective pauperization. Inflation eroded revenues and accumulated resources. Many people became unemployed; many were unable to adapt to the new challenges. The free distribution of land after the dissolution of agricultural cooperatives and the sale of state-owned apartments at low prices provided some relief but also locked beneficiaries into inflexible low-revenue activities and arrangements. Some people successfully took advantage of new economic opportunities and became an emerging class of capitalist entrepreneurs, but most Romanians experienced a severe decline in living standards throughout most of the 1990s. A certain recovery followed during the economic growth period of 2000 to 2008, but overall it failed to stop the process of social polarization. As a result, the Gini index for Romania rose from about 20 in 1991 to about 36 in 2008.

Early retirement schemes, designed to prevent social resistance to deindustrialization and avoid unemployment, increasingly strained the social systems. From 1990 to 2008, the number of employees fell from about 8.1 million to 4.8 million, while the number of pensioners grew from roughly 2.8 million to 5.7 million. Thereafter, the economic crisis pushed the number of employees ever lower, making the entire social security system less and less sustainable. Further worsening the situation was the multitude of special pensions paid to army and police personnel, members of the judiciary and various other categories opting for early retirement. To counteract this, a new law adopted in 2010 tried (without much success) to bring more order to the system by reducing the number of special pensions and, above all, implementing a gradual shift towards later retirement (at age sixty-five by 2030), finally also bringing women in line with men (women had previously been entitled to retire five years earlier than men).

The healthcare system also had to confront severe problems. Under communism, healthcare had been free for everyone and centrally controlled by the Health Ministry, but now the changing age structure of the population and the state's financial difficulties began to cause extreme pressure. In the 1990s, a first reform, implemented with the assistance of the World Bank, established a Health Insurance Agency in charge of collecting contributions and distributing available resources to public and private healthcare institutions alike. But even though funding increased, most resources for medical supplies were drained. Reacting to the prevailing conditions, underpaid medical personnel either shifted to private institutions or emigrated to other EU countries, leaving public hospitals increasingly understaffed. The need for a major healthcare reform appeared on the public agenda in 2011, being also requested by the International Monetary Fund.

Most changes in the education system during the 1990s were reactions to the involutions of the last decade of communism. Ceaușescu had enforced a standard of ten years of compulsory education and promoted the dominance of industrial profiles in the secondary school system (71 per cent of students had industrial profiles in 1989; fewer than 5 per cent had theoretical profiles), meanwhile diminishing the number of study places to be allocated in higher education. His demise prompted immediate changes: grades nine and ten were no longer compulsory, some secondary schools shifted to theoretical profiles and universities were granted significant academic autonomy and permitted to enrol higher numbers of students.

The scarcity of study places in the 1980s had heightened social pressure to obtain degrees in higher education. As public universities proved unable or slow to meet demand, several private universities were founded. At the same time, local elites lobbied in favour of founding public universities in various cities, leading – despite the frequent insufficiency of available resources – to considerable expansion of the university system during the 1990s. The Ministry of Education's efforts to establish order by instituting an accreditation procedure were only nominally successful. In response to the chronic underfunding of the public education system, a change implemented in the late 1990s based the financing of public universities mainly on the number of enrolled students. It also granted public universities increased financial autonomy and permitted them also to enrol paying students. This move led to the massification of higher education, pushing public and private universities to compete for tuition fees and undermining the quality of education. Altogether, the number of students attending university skyrocketed from about 8 per cent of the student-age cohort in 1989 to more than 40 per cent in 2010 – and this percentage only partially accommodated the number of adults wishing to participate in higher education programmes.

Primary and secondary education also experienced several waves of change. Curricula and syllabi were changed, and as of 1995, alternative textbooks were introduced. Yet these reforms failed to improve educational quality, as the system's administrative capacity to implement the new norms was limited. Moreover, teachers were underpaid, demoralized and unwilling to change old habits, and the social turmoil of post-communism disoriented most pupils. Accordingly, the Pisa Study of 2006 and 2009 placed Romania in the bottom quarter of the country rankings. At the same time, more and more people began to question the value of university studies and the actual functioning of most Romanian institutions of higher education. Outside pressure to implement more decisive changes to the system, increase accountability and open the universities to competition met with staunch resistance from entrenched elites. After bitter controversy, the government finally managed to push a new education law through parliament, to be enforced as of 2011. Its goals were to partially decentralize the management of primary and secondary education by increasing local communities' involvement, streamline the universities and classify them according to quality standards, strengthen quality control throughout the entire education system and more closely link education to the labour market by implementing a national qualifications framework and encouraging lifelong learning.

In general, the post-communist decades diversified people's experience of life and living. Social and economic change was all-pervasive in Romania, and contacts with the world at large intensified. Many Romanians travelled abroad for business, work, education or leisure. Exposure to various media increased exponentially. Media saturation came hand in hand with increased social flexibility but also with normative laxity, as various crimes and moral transgressions became more visible than ever before. There was less job security than in the past, and trade unions proved ineffective at protecting employees from arbitrary decisions by employers and managers. Uncertainty increased as both family ties and the public safety net began to unravel. People reacted to these challenges in diverse ways. Some adapted by focusing on individual performance, often at the cost of traditional values and social ties. Others, reluctant to change, resented the post-communist transformation and its profiteers. But although public opinion polls pointed to a certain amount of nostalgia for the communist period, perceived as more stable, and to the preference among large segments of the population for authoritarian patterns and a strong, paternalist state, these attitudes were less profound than generally assumed and did not actually endanger Romania's overall evolution into a so-called Western-type society based on political democracy and a market economy. Yet the Romanian society clearly did not entirely conform to the EU model either. The social state was much weaker than those of most EU countries, and like most post-communist countries, Romania experienced a wilder type of capitalism than that found in the social market economies of continental Europe.[24]

Another major variance concerned the role of religion. In most European countries religion is in a secular decline, but it still plays an important role in post-communist Romania. Eastern Orthodoxy, by far the largest religious denomination, is professed by about 86.7 per cent of the population, according to the 2002 census. Catholicism, Calvinism and various neo-Protestant denominations are the next largest, followed by rather small numbers of Muslims, Lutherans and Jews. Although the Romanian Orthodox Church was challenged due to its previous compliance with the communist regime and many high-ranking clerics' cooperation with the Securitate, it avoided radical renewal, focusing instead on institutional expansion and capitalizing on the general disorientation induced by the post-communist transformation. The Orthodox Church had to accept in the wake of the revolution the restoration of the Greek Catholic Church (which it had absorbed in 1948), but managed to limit its losses and to maintain its grip on most of the Romanian population.

Having somewhat reluctantly accepted that, legally, Romania is a secular state and all officially recognized denominations are theoretically equal, the Romanian Orthodox Church used its social influence to establish close relationships with state officials of various political affiliations. Of course, such proximity came at a price. Notwithstanding its conservative rhetoric, the Orthodox Church had to accept and sometimes support Romania's opening towards the West. In 1999, Patriarch Teoctist's invitation to Pope John Paul II to visit Romania resulted in the first visit by a pope to a predominantly Eastern Orthodox country since the schism of 1054. The church also had to accept the adaptation of Romanian legislation to EU standards, including provisions to prevent discrimination against sexual minorities. In exchange, the state extensively supported the church's efforts to strengthen its own economic and institutional power. In the two decades after the fall of communism, about 4,000 new churches were erected, with the Orthodox Church pushing forward the project of a large cathedral in Bucharest. Religion became part of the school curriculum, and the Orthodox Church established a media network with its own television channel and a multitude of publications promoting conservative values.

Concluding Remarks

Romania's post-communist transformation came about through a combination of internal and external determinants. The initial impulse sprang from the large majority of Romanian society that wished to end communist rule, perceived as having provided incompetent leadership that frustrated the economic needs of the people. Lacking a clear vision of the future at hand, those who took to the streets in December 1989 hoped to bring their society closer to the Western model, democratic and affluent. This primary impulse lost its momentum under the strain of economic hardship and social turmoil, but the basic orientation towards the Western model persisted. Nevertheless, the burden of existing social, economic and cultural structures heavily influenced the actual elements of the post-communist transformation and, in combination with various policy mistakes by the politicians in power, caused Romania to partially diverge from the group of more successful East Central European transition countries in the 1990s.[25] However, the ultimate determiners of the basic outcome of the post-communist transformation were globalization pressure and the Western political decision to incorporate even the least successful countries of the region, including Romania. Thus, Romania became an open market economy dominated by transnational companies as well as a disciplined member of NATO and the EU.

The transformation of various spheres was closely interrelated, even though extensive resistance led at times to setbacks in one sector or another (e.g. the conservative governance of education from 2001 to 2003). To avoid paralysing resistance, leading politicians often had to buy off specific segments of society. These informal trade-offs generated privileges, distorted competition, added to the moral hazards of post-communism and elicited resentment from societal segments that lacked the leverage needed to obtain such benefits. All in all, those privileges obstructed Romania's transition towards an open access society.[26]

As already indicated, the burden of historically accumulated underdevelopment also marred Romania's post-communist transformation. Romania's EU accession and membership present a chance to overcome this constraint at least partially, but they are no guarantee. Between 2000 and 2008, Romania experienced some convergence due to the basic advantage of a comparatively cheap labour force, and the country will probably rely on this again going forward. Although the difference in average wages has diminished since the 1990s, it is still large enough to attract outside capital, and to induce Romanians to seek employment abroad. But this difference will eventually disappear, and at some point (possibly by 2020, barring a major depression before then) relatively low wages will no longer be an engine for economic growth and convergence. Then the country will either enter a new phase of development based on diversified economic activity providing more added value, stagnate or even regress due to low productivity (as Portugal did as of 2001 after fifteen years of post-accession convergence). Furthermore, as in some other EU countries, a demographic bomb is ticking in Romania. Currently, the society's ageing is still slowed by the relatively numerous generations born in the last two decades of communism, and the pension law's gradual raising of the retirement age ensures a certain equilibrium. After 2030, however, this balance will be increasingly difficult to maintain as the overall population aged twenty to sixty-four will shrink dramatically while the economically dependent segment of the population will likely increase.[27] Therefore, it is crucial that Romania succeed in consolidating an economic structure based on high value-added activities before 2030. To achieve this, the country needs to upgrade its human capital and establish strong institutions that can offer incentives attractive to foreign investors.

Hence, the quality of institutions is the basic variable in Romania's future. In spite of multiple reforms and EU support, there is great variance in the functioning of its institutions. Some have significantly improved their performance. The best example is the National Bank of Romania, which has kept its monetary policy in line with both macro-economic constraints and International Monetary Fund requirements, managing also to keep the financial sector relatively secure and functional in the midst of global financial crisis. Meanwhile, many other Romanian institutions are either dysfunctional or captive to various interest groups. This problem is attributable to the quantitative expansion of the public sector and unsustainable growth of public expenditures from 2005 to 2008. In 2009, with the supervision and support of the IMF and EU, Romania had to begin implementing a major adjustment that was still underway in 2011. Budgetary cuts and administrative downsizing are certainly required in Romania, but these alone will not suffice to successfully improve the quality of its institutions; rather, implementing change will call for vision, persistence, and at times also resources.

After more than two decades of post-communist transition, one may ask whether Romania is a consolidated democracy. In 1996, Linz and

Stepan still voiced serious reservations concerning this question.[28] Yet by 2011, democracy could be said to be 'the only game in town', even though many citizens were unhappy with its actual functioning. Elections are free, and progress has been made in such areas as establishing a market economy and a functioning civil society, including minorities and even adapting the rule of law. However, serious issues remain to be resolved. Besides a dearth of functioning institutions and a general need to upgrade state capacities, Romania must cope with the risk of becoming locked into a political culture that favours informal arrangements to the detriment of formal rules and procedures.[29] Therefore, the single most crucial elements of Romania's consolidation of democracy will be strong law enforcement with respect to the elites (doorstep condition 1 in the transition model elaborated by North, Wallis and Weingast) and, beyond that, establishment of impersonal means of incentivizing expanded access to political and economic organizations and resources, so that the non-elite population may benefit from them as well.[30]

Bogdan Murgescu is Professor of Economic History and director of the Council for Doctoral Studies, University of Bucharest. He has been Roman Herzog Fellow of the Alexander von Humboldt Foundation in Berlin (1998–2000; recurring 2006) and Visiting Professor at the University of Pittsburgh (2002) and Central European University, Budapest (2004). Currently president of the Romanian Society for Historical Sciences, he participated in various international research projects and is a member of several academic boards. His main fields of interest are economic and social history, the history of communism and of the post-communist transformation, and the development of human capital.

Notes

1. The best overview of the Romanian revolution of 1989 is P. Siani-Davies, *The Romanian Revolution of December 1989* (Ithaca, 2005).
2. D. Dăianu, *Transformarea ca proces real: De la comandă la piață* (Bucharest, 1999), 106.
3. For the general problems of communist economies, see J. Kornai, *The Socialist System: The Political Economy of Communism* (Oxford, 1992). The specific elements of the economic crisis in Romania are outlined in C. Ionete, *Criza de sistem a economiei de comandă și etapa sa explozivă* (Bucharest, 1993), and in B. Murgescu, *România și Europa: Acumularea decalajelor economice (1500–2010)* (Iași, 2010), 369–407.
4. In fact, just a few days after 22 December, the top leaders of the Securitate were arrested under suspicion of plotting against the new power, and the chief of the general staff was removed from his position while the vacant post of defence minister was

filled by the retired general Nicolae Militaru, whose relations with most of the commanding generals inherited from Ceauşescu were strained. For a more general discussion of the conspiracy theories, see Siani-Davies, *The Romanian Revolution*, 165–90, 267–75.

5. M. Fischer, 'The New Leaders and the Opposition', in D. Nelson (ed.), *Romania after Tyranny* (Boulder, CO, 1992), 45–65.

6. For the party system and the functioning of the political field in post-communist Romania, see C. Preda and S. Soare, *Regimul: partidele şi sistem ul politic din România* (Bucharest, 2008). For the elaboration of the constitution and the genesis of political institutions, see M. Enache and M. Constantinescu, *Renaşterea parlamentarismului în România* (Iaşi, 2001). For the political culture, see A. Mungiu-Pippidi, *Politica după comunism: Structură, cultură şi psihologie politică* (Bucharest, 2002). A more sociological approach to Romanian politics in the early 1990s can be found in V. Pasti, *The Challenges of Transition: Romania in Transition* (Boulder, CO, 1997).

7. Preda and Soare, *Regimul*, 76–78.

8. Enache and Constantinescu, *Renaşterea parlamentarismului*, 91–101.

9. This type of hierarchical cooperation existed in the periods 1992–1996 (between Prime Minister Nicolae Văcăroiu and President Ion Iliescu), 1996–1998 (Prime Minister Victor Ciorbea and President Emil Constantinescu) and after December 2008 (Prime Minister Emil Boc and President Traian Băsescu). More balanced, but ultimately avoiding major conflicts, was the relation between Prime Minister Adrian Năstase and President Ion Iliescu in the years 2000–2004.

10. See Transparency International's Corruption Perceptions Index 2010 (http:\\www.tra nsparency.org/policy_research/surveys_indices/cpi/2010/results).

11. For an informative overview of the Romanian media, see P. Bajomi-Lázár, *Romania: A Country Report for the ERC-Funded Project on Media and Democracy in Central and Eastern Europe* (Oxford, 2011).

12. See, e.g., the recent analysis by Ştefan Cândea (http://www.nieman.harvard.edu/rep orts/article/102575/Abandoning-a-Broken-Model-of-Journalism.aspx).

13. C. Simion, A. Gheorghe and I. Comănescu, *Cartea albă a presei III: Probleme economice ale presei* (Bucharest, 2007), 36–37.

14. This was even true of the parliamentary elections of 1992, which were considered rigged by both the opposition and some Western scholars (H. Carey [ed.], *Romania since 1989: Politics, Economics, and Society* [Lanham, MD, 2004], 561–65); however, the NSF, led by Petre Roman, which controlled the Interior and the Justice Ministries, won only slightly more than 10 per cent of the vote and was relegated to the opposition for the next four years.

15. For the importance of this ability, see A. Lijphart, *Modele ale democraţiei* (Iaşi, 2000), 49–73.

16. V. Alexandru, A. Moraru and L. Ercuş, *Declinul participării la vot în România: Doar jumătate din participanţii la vot din'90 mai sunt astăzi interesaţi să voteze* (Bucharest, 2009), 16–18.

17. B. Murgescu (ed.), *History of the Romanian Court of Accounts (1864–2004)* (Bucharest, 2005), 302–414.

18. See the reports at http://ec.europa.eu/dgs/secretariat_general/cvm/progress_reports_ en.htm.

19. J. Keane, *The Life and Death of Democracy* (London, 2009), 686–736.

20. P. Sum and G. Bădescu, 'An Evaluation of Six Forms of Political Participation', in Carey, *Romania since 1989*, 189–91.

21. In this paragraph, where I provide no specific references, I rely mainly on Dăianu, *Transformarea*; S. Gardó, 'Rumänien: Wirtschaft in Transformation', in T. Kahl, M. Metzeltin and M. Ungureanu (eds), *Rumänien* (Vienna, 2006), 655–92; and Murgescu, *România și Europa*, 465–80. For the general features of the post-communist economies, see also L. Csaba, *The New Political Economy of Emerging Europe* (Budapest, 2005), and I.T. Berend, *From the Soviet Bloc to the European Union: The Economic and Social Transformation of Central and Eastern Europe since 1973* (Cambridge, 2009).

22. Unless otherwise indicated, the data in this section are taken from publications of the National Institute for Statistics. For minorities, see also P. Jordan and T. Kahl, 'Ethnische Struktur', in Kahl, Metzeltin and Ungureanu, *Rumänien*, 63–87. For social polarization, see also C. Zamfir (ed.), *Raport social al ICCV 2010. România: răspunsuri la criză* (Bucharest, 2011). For religion, see L. Stan and L. Turcescu, *Religion and Politics in Post-Communist Romania* (Oxford, 2007).

23. R. Poledna, *Sint ut sunt: Aut non sunt? Transformări sociale la sașii ardeleni după 1945: O analiză sociologică din perspectivă sistemică* (Cluj-Napoca, 2001), 227.

24. M. Albert, *Capitalisme contre capitalisme* (Paris, 1991).

25. For an unfavourable assessment of Romania's situation in the late 1990s, see G. Ekiert and S.E. Hanson (eds), *Capitalism and Democracy in Central and Eastern Europe: Assessing the Legacy of Communist Rule* (Cambridge, 2003).

26. D. North, J. Wallis and B. Weingast, *Violence and Social Orders: A Conceptual Framework for Interpreting Recorded Human History* (Cambridge, 2009), 21–27.

27. V. Ghețău, 'Impactul evoluțiilor demografice asupra structurii profesionale', in S. României (ed.), *Reprofesionalizarea României II: Raport al Institutului de Proiecte pentru Inovație și Dezvoltare (IPID)* (Bucharest, 2009), 63–66.

28. J.J. Linz and A. Stepan, *Problems of Democratic Transition and Consolidation: Southern Europe, South America, and Post-Communist Europe* (Baltimore, 1996), 344–65.

29. Mungiu-Pippidi, *Politica după communism*, 212–14.

30. North, Wallis and Weingast, *Violence and Social Orders*, 26.

Chapter 11

Bulgaria

❦

Karel Vodička

Introduction

Historical Introduction

Bulgaria's road to national statehood was long: only after 500 years of Ottoman rule did it succeed in gaining independence around 1800. The Bulgarian monarchies that followed did not create democratic structures or start any democratic traditions.[1] After World War II, the country became a vassal state of the Soviet Union, and a ruthless one-party communist dictatorship was installed. During the four decades of this one-party rule, the Bulgarian people clearly resisted communist dictatorship less than did the peoples of the Central European states of the Eastern Bloc, such as Poland, Hungary and Czechoslovakia, which had had pre-totalitarian experiences with democracy. In the communist period, Bulgaria was the most loyal and stable of all the Soviet Union's bloc partners. Correspondingly, the anti-communist dissident movement had only a low profile.[2]

State of Research

In the post-communist EU context, country reports and comparative studies characterize Bulgaria as a less consolidated democracy.[3] At the same time, however, Bulgaria is counted as a consolidating democracy and meets essential criteria for democratic institutions and political stability.[4]

Notes for this chapter begin on page 300.

System Change

The Palace Coup

Change in the Bulgarian political system started with the demission of state and party leader Todor Zhivkov on 10 November 1989, enforced by the reform-oriented leadership of the Bulgarian Communist Party (Balgarska kommuniticeska partija, BKP). This event also launched the process of system transformation, which would prove particularly difficult in this country.[5] Zhivkov's fall had not been planned and initiated by mass demonstrations or a strong counter-public of intellectual dissidents or citizens' movements; rather, a 'palace coup' within the BKP had put an end to the communist regime. Some leading members of the BKP, recognizing that the strictly authoritarian policy of earlier days was no longer tolerable, demanded not only adjustment to the new domestic and foreign policy line initiated in the Soviet Union by Mikhail Gorbachev's perestroika, but also radical change in the BKP leadership. On 17 November 1989, reformer and then foreign minister Petar Mladenov was appointed the new chairman of the state's highest decision-making body, the State Council, and by mid December 1989, the BKP had ceded its constitutionally fixed claim to leadership and declared its readiness for roundtable negotiations with representatives of the opposition. On 1 April 1990, the BKP was renamed the Bulgarian Socialist Party (Balgarska socialisticheska partija, BSP), and in Aleksandar Lilov, who had been dismissed from the Politburo in 1983 for criticizing Zhivkov, it got a new chairman who was also accepted by the public.[6]

Masses and Elites

Before the turnaround, there had been almost no organized resistance to the Communist Party's leadership in Bulgaria.[7] Only after Zhivkov's resignation did the country's political life become pluralized, which came as something of a shock. New political parties and groups mushroomed over the course of the following weeks and months. At a meeting of eighteen opposition groups in Sofia in December 1989, ten of them united to form the Union of Democratic Forces (Sajuz na democraticnite sili, SDS). However, unlike the BSP, which was well equipped with staff and infrastructural and organizational resources, the SDS, as an alliance of heterogeneous interests, was disadvantaged not only in its decision-making processes but also in structural and financial terms. These unfavourable programmatic and organizational start-up conditions hampered the middle class opposition considerably until 1997, influencing the political power balance between the BSP and SDS – and thus also the process of system transformation. Perhaps most dire, in this period of radical change, was the lack of political leaders who possessed both experience as dissidents engaged in underground activities before the turnaround that could have earned them repute among the population, and the capability to critically analyse the system and take political action.[8]

Transformation Process 1989–2012

Politics

Constitution

Bulgaria was the first post-communist country in Europe to have a new constitution. Immediately after the collapse of the communist regime, the current Bulgarian constitution (ConstL 56/1991)[9] made it through the Grand National Assembly[10] with 309 out of 400 votes. The BSP strove to expedite the writing of the new constitution because at the time it had a parliamentary majority sufficient to push through its intentions (e.g. a regulation prohibiting foreigners from acquiring real estate).[11] This constitution, inspired by the French, German and Spanish constitutions, provides the basis for the transition to parliamentary democracy and includes binding statements on democracy, separation of powers and rule of law. The country's constitutionally established system of government is a parliamentary democracy, with the government being accountable to the parliament. The constitution states that the Bulgarian Republic is a uniformly structured state with municipal self-administration; it makes no provision for autonomous regional institutions of self-administration (Art. 2 ConstL 56/1991). According to the constitution, basic human and civil rights are irrevocable and defended against violation (Art. 57). In contrast to many other states' constitutions, Bulgaria's does not mention national minorities. Learning the Bulgarian language is the right and obligation of every Bulgarian citizen (Art. 36, Para. 1), and citizens whose native tongue is not Bulgarian have a constitutional right to also 'learn and use their own language' (Art. 36, Para. 2). Furthermore, the constitution explicitly guarantees religious freedom and bans any violent assimilation (Art. 13 and Art. 37, Para. 1).

The President of the State

The President of the Bulgarian State embodies national unity and represents Bulgaria to foreign countries (Art. 92 ConstL 56/1991). The constitution provides the president with the usual domestic and foreign policy competences. He or she is directly elected by the people for a term of five years. The direct election of the president is only valid if a quorum of at least 50 per cent of eligible voters participates in the first round (Art. 93). If no candidate achieves the necessary majority in the first round, a run-off vote between the two most successful candidates of the first round must be held within one week. According to the constitution, a president may be re-elected only once, so ten years is the maximum term of office of the Bulgarian president. As in all Eastern EU states (except Slovenia), the president may veto a law passed by the parliament (Art. 101, Para. 1). In Bulgaria, this is a suspensive veto that may be overruled by an absolute majority of the parliament. The again-passed law must then be promulgated.[12]

Parliament
The Bulgarian Grand National Assembly consists of 240 MPs who are elected every four years (Art. 63 ConstL 56/1991). The parliament has no second chamber. One of its most important tasks is the election of the prime minister and Council of Ministers. One fifth of all MPs is sufficient to initiate a vote of no confidence against the prime minister and Council of Ministers; the vote is considered valid if an absolute majority of all MPs support it. The Bulgarian National Assembly has resorted frequently to the option of the vote of no confidence. A substantial share of parliamentary work is done in committees, which, according to Art. 17 of the standing orders of the Bulgarian parliament, are either permanent committees or ad hoc committees.[13]

With almost 40 per cent of the vote and 116 seats, Bojko Borissov's Citizens for European Development in Bulgaria (Grazdani za evropejsko razvitie na Balgarija, GERB) party was the victor in the 2009 elections. The BSP, on the other hand, suffered a clear defeat, with less than 18 per cent of the vote and only forty seats for the entire Coalition for Bulgaria under its leadership. Meanwhile, the Movement for Rights and Liberties (Dvizenie sa Prava i Svobodi, DPS), sometimes called the 'Turkish Party', achieved the best result in its history, becoming the third-strongest party in parliament. It was able to draw more than 100,000 votes from foreign countries, above all from the Turkish-Bulgarian community in Turkey. The liberal National Movement for Stability and Progress (Nacialno dviženie za stabilnost i važhod) of former tsar Simeon Sakskoburggotski, which had been part of the government in the previous term, failed to meet the 4 per cent threshold; Sakskoburggotski immediately stepped down as party leader.[14]

Government
The Council of Ministers (Ministerski savet) consists of the prime minister, his or her deputies and the ministers (Art. 108 ConstL 56/1999). Having

TABLE 11.1. Results of the 2009 parliamentary elections

Party/Coalition	Votes	Per cent	Seats
Citizens for European Development in Bulgaria (GERB)	1,678,641	39.72%	(90 + 26) 116
Coalition for Bulgaria*	748,147	17.70%	40
Movement for Rights and Liberties (DPS)	610,521	14.45%	(33 + 5) 38
Ataka	395,733	9.36%	21
Blue Coalition	285,662	6.76%	15
Order, Security and Justice	174,582	4.13%	10
Total	4,226,194		240

* The coalition for Bulgaria is a leftist coalition of the following parties: Bulgarian Socialist Party, Bulgarian Communist Party, Party Bulgarian Social Democrats, Political Movement Social Democrats and Party of the Roma. See http://de.wikipedia.org/wiki/Koalition_f%C3%_BCr_Bulgarien (accessed 20 February 2013).

Source: R. Schmitt, Kleines Handbuch Bulgarien (Rostock, 2012), 53.

won the 2009 parliamentary elections, GERB started coalition talks with other conservative forces in the National Assembly, particularly the Blue Coalition and the Order, Security and Justice party. During the election campaign, the fight against corruption and regaining the confidence of the European Union were the main issues of all three parties. When coalition talks produced no results, GERB (with 116 out of 240 seats) formed a minority government that was tolerated by the conservative parties as well as the nationalist Ataka party.[15] On 2 February 2013, the government under GERB chairman Bojko Borissov resigned in response to enduring, sometimes bloody mass protests.[16] In contrast to other post-communist EU countries, though, Bulgaria has only an average frequency of premature resignations by governments (see Figure 12.2 in the concluding chapter of this volume).

Administration

Austerity measures, made necessary by economic crises and conditions set by international institutions, have affected public administration. Given the black market's immense share in the economy – about 50 per cent of annual GDP – consolidation of an effective financial administration is urgently needed. Yet instead of reinforcing this field, decision-makers have continuously cut personnel. Another permanently debated issue is the low pay in the public sector, especially for police and educators.[17] The wages the state pays to citizens are no longer 'enough to make a living'.[18]

Major political parties

The conservative Citizens for European Development in Bulgaria – GERB – emerged as the winner of the 2009 elections. This party became the leading political power in Bulgaria soon after its founding in 2006 and has been a member of the European People's Party since 2007. It enjoyed victories in the May 2007 elections to the European Parliament and the October 2007 municipal elections. In the run-up to the 2009 parliamentary elections, GERB held talks with the Blue Coalition about a joint ticket, but nothing came of them. GERB thus ran on its own and, with 40 per cent of the vote, was the clear winner. In the 2009 elections, when for the first time thirty-one (out of a total of 240) MPs were elected by majority vote, GERB gained twenty-six of these seats. The party states its primary goals as fighting corruption and the Mafia, and regaining the confidence of the country's European partners.[19]

The longstanding BSP was founded in 1891 as the Bulgarian Social Democratic Workers' Party. From 1948 to 1990, it was called the Bulgarian Communist Party; then, upon abandoning Marxist-Leninist doctrine in April 1990, it renamed itself the Bulgarian Socialist Party. During the period of the turnaround, the BSP leadership's primary concern was to maintain the property and positions of the old nomenclature, a goal best achieved by way of quick privatization of state property. The party has never distanced itself from its communist past or the crimes committed in this context.[20] In 1996 and 1997, the socialist government under Žan Videnov, which served the interests of the 'red millionaires', caused a dramatic economic crisis. Thus incurring heavy losses in the 1997 parliamentary elections, the BSP and its Faction of the Democratic Left lost more than half of their seats. Later, in the 2009 parliamentary elections, the BSP suffered another historic defeat that halved the number of its seats to the forty it now holds.[21]

The DPS was founded in 1990 to represent the interests of the Turkish minority, which had endured the traumatic experience of forced Bulgarization under the Zhivkov regime and was now organizing to protect itself from future attempted repression. Together with other Muslim minorities such as the Pomaks, the Turkish minority forms the party's base. Since its founding, the DPS has consistently garnered about 7 per cent of votes and twenty of the 240 parliamentary seats. Thus, it is the third-biggest faction behind the BSP and the SDS. After the 2001 elections, the DPS became a government party, joining in a government coalition with Simeon II's National Movement under former tsar Simeon Sakskoburggotski. In the 2009 parliamentary elections, the DPS received 14 per cent of the vote and gained five additional seats by majority vote for a total of thirty-eight parliamentary seats – the best result in its history.

However, the party was also accused of having manipulated the elections in the regions it dominated.[22]

Ataka (Bulgarian for attack) is a nationalist, xenophobic, right-wing extremist party. It publishes the newspaper *Ataka* and also runs its own TV channel, Alfa. The Ataka party's founding in 2005 was inspired not least by the growing participation of the Turkish-Muslim minority, in particular the DPS, in the political life of the country. Due to its nationalist orientation, the party is able to instrumentalize not only the dividing line of ethnicity but also the socio-economic gulf between the winners and losers of system change. The party's goal is to unite Bulgarian nationalists in the fight against EU and NATO integration. Ataka won 9 per cent of the vote in the 2009 parliamentary elections, and with twenty-one MPs it is the fourth-strongest faction in parliament.[23]

Electoral system and elections

Both elections and referendums are conducted by secret ballot on the basis of universal, equal and direct suffrage (Art. 10 ConstL 56/1991). Bulgarian citizens older than eighteen (including those living abroad) are eligible to vote (Art. 42). Citizens must be twenty-one or older to exercise the passive right to vote (Art. 65). There is no compulsory suffrage. Bulgarian citizens responded enthusiastically to the first free elections, in which turnout was 91 per cent. However, the voters' commitment has radically declined over the course of transition, and after many disappointments. The turnout in 2009 was only 61 per cent.[24] In the post-communist EU context, the Bulgarian rate of participation in elections is about average (see Figure 12.3 in the concluding chapter of this volume).

The Bulgarian National Assembly is elected according to proportional representation. Votes from thirty-one multi-seat constituencies are counted according to the d'Hondt procedure (Art. 6 Election law 2001); there is a 4 per cent threshold. A rule change before the 2009 parliamentary elections introduced a mixed system, so that in addition to proportional representation there were thirty-one constituencies with majority vote. The government parties expected elements of majority vote in the electoral law to be to their advantage, but as is often the case, changes to the electoral law worked against their originators: the then opposition party GERB succeeded in winning twenty-six of the thirty-one majority-vote constituencies.[25]

According to the Bertelsmann Transformation Index (BTI) Transformation Report 2012, Country Report Bulgaria, there are no legal restrictions on free and fair elections in Bulgaria. Apart from legal regulations, however, irregularities do happen, including vote buying, influencing the vote and granting immunity to legally persecuted people.[26] Bulgaria's pluralist media landscape provides voters with a broad variety of political opinions, but the independence of politically and economically influential media is dubious.[27] According to Transparency International, canvassing, agitation on election day, bribery, vote buying and the manipulation of votes violate the constitutional principle of free elections. A poll of voters found that about 12 per cent of interviewees had been paid to vote for a certain party, whereas 14 per cent had taken money but still voted for their preferred party.[28]

Voting behaviour

Voting behaviour correlates most strongly with citizens' social status, values, faith and education. Younger and more educated voters from big cities tend to support the liberal, market economy-oriented SDS and, later, GERB. The post-communist BSP, on the other hand, found its greatest support among the parts of the population that were hit hardest by the political and (especially) economic system change and at the same time benefited least from it – that is, the older age cohorts and the inhabitants of smaller provincial towns and villages. In the 1990s, about 60 per cent of eligible voters were loyal to the two big parties at the time, the BSP and the anti-communist SDS, or to the 'Turkish' DPS party. About one third of eligible voters, however, had no party affiliation. This group of swing voters was often crucial to an election's outcome. Eventually, in the summer of 2001, the fast-growing category of protest voters catapulted former tsar Simeon II to the top of the Bulgarian government.[29]

Justice

The judiciary is still a weakness of Bulgaria's political system. According to opinion polls – and in contrast to other post-communist EU countries – the judiciary has the lowest reputation of all three powers; confidence in the judiciary is at 14 per cent (i.e. 86 per cent distrust), the lowest level in the entire EU (see Figure 12.12 in the concluding chapter of this volume). Bulgarians are disappointed at the lack of prosecution of those responsible for the bankruptcy of banks and devious 'loan millionaires'. The predominant opinion is that corruption is everywhere, even around the government itself, and that nowhere near enough is done to expose it.[30]

This popular opinion is indeed confirmed by the EU report on Bulgaria's progress, issued in the context of the cooperation and control procedure in 2011. The fight against upper-echelon corruption has not produced decisive results, and the fight against organized crime wants considerable improvement overall. To date, the leading figures of the judiciary have shown no serious commitment to legal reform. Concrete progress in the fight against corruption and organized crime will require substantially improved accountability and professional practice among the judiciary and the investigative authorities. In the short term, improvements in the appointment, assessment and skills of judiciary staff are essential, as is the development of structures capable of tackling organized crime. The passage of new legislation on the confiscation of property is the key to improving safeguards against organized crime and corruption.[31]

The Constitutional Court (Konstitucionen săd) consists of twelve judges. One third of them are appointed by the parliament, another third by the president and the final third by the judges of the Supreme Court of Cassation and Supreme Administrative Court (Art. 147 ConstL 56/1991). The Constitutional Court has the task of issuing binding interpretations of the constitution and, when required by third parties, deciding whether laws and presidential acts accord with the constitution. Furthermore, it is entitled to decide quarrels about the legality of parliamentary and presidential elections, and also hears appeals against outcomes when there are serious indications of electoral fraud.[32] The Constitutional Court tends to contribute to the juridification of political conflicts.

Districts

The constitution stipulates the state structures of municipalities and regional administrative districts (Art. 135 ConstL 56/1991). Bulgaria is mostly a centralized state with regional autonomous areas of self-administration (Art. 2). These regional units, the *Oblasti*, are not guided by elected bodies of self-administration but by the centre, as part of the state administration. An *Oblast* is an administrative-territorial unit controlled by a district administrator appointed by the Council of Ministers and serving the interests of the state's central administration. The district administrator ensures implementation of state policies in his or her region and is responsible for preserving the national interest, law and public order (Art. 143).

Municipalities

The municipalities are the foundation of the system of self-administration. The municipality (*Obshtina*) is the basic administrative-territorial unit in which municipal bodies of self-administration represent and politically organize the interests of the respective municipality. Citizens may participate in the administrations of their municipalities both immediately, by way of referendums, or at plenary assemblies of the members of the respective municipality. Elections to the local bodies of self-administration, the Municipal Councils (*obstinski savet*), are held every four years. The mayor, as the municipality's chief executive, is directly elected by the citizens. Obedience to the law is the only constraint on citizens' use of their powers of self-administration. The municipalities are independent legal subjects and may own property. They administer their money independently, decide their budgets and may establish funds.[33]

Economy

From plan to market: the Bulgarian drama

In Bulgaria, where practically the entire economy was state-owned, transforming the system from a planned to a free market economy required a radical process of adjustment and reform. Part of this was a kind of 'shock treatment' that was extremely painful from a social perspective. It involved liberalizing prices, abandoning the tools of central planning and extensively privatizing state property while also founding institutions intended to ensure fair competition in the context of the developing market economy. Since then, the interdependencies between the still immature subsystems of the economic, legal and political systems in *statu nascendi* have further impeded the overall transition even more. In addition, the process of economic transformation has been burdened by Bulgaria's high foreign debt, a legacy of the communist period. Economic dependence on the Soviet Union was yet another obstacle on the road to economic transformation: until 1989, about 60 per cent of Bulgaria's foreign trade was with the Soviet Union, and 20 per cent was with the other COMECON countries.[34]

Bulgaria was an almost purely agrarian state until the communist period, when it experienced a push towards industrialization and modernization. This consisted especially of the development of energy- and raw material-consuming heavy industry, some branches of which (pharmaceutics, engineering, electronics) were definitely successful on the COMECON markets of those days. After the system change and loss of the Soviet market, the Bulgarian economy fell into a deep crisis. In the 1990s, the industrial gross product declined almost continuously, and by 1998 it was only 47 per cent of its level in 1989.[35] The once well-developed computer hardware industry disappeared completely. The period 1989–95 saw dramatic decline in the population's real incomes and standard of living. Social systems, in particular health insurance and pension schemes, collapsed. The BSP-led government under Žan Videnov did nothing to remedy the situation, instead primarily supporting the interests of the former nomenclature. In the spring of 1996, high public debt made the economic crisis even worse. Banks collapsed, and the state had trouble paying its debts to foreign creditors. In the hope of obtaining World Bank and International Monetary Fund support, the government passed a structural programme oriented to the recommendations of these international institutions, pegging the Bulgarian lewa to the deutschmark, liquidating a number of unprofitable state enterprises, and making intensive efforts to attract foreign investors with tax incentives.[36]

After the economic crisis of 1996/97, the introduction of new currency board regulations in 1997 and the pegging of the lewa to the deutschmark did much to stabilize the economy. The economic policies of 1998 set Bulgaria on a path of solid yearly growth rates averaging about 5 per cent until 2008.[37] Budgetary discipline between 1998 and 2012 resulted in a budget deficit of less than 1 per cent of GDP, which allowed public debt to gradually diminish as well. The private economy's slowly rising share of GDP and a sizeable influx of foreign investments betokened an improving economic environment. However, another result of the structural reforms, and sometimes also of their belated implementation, was rising unemployment. Since peaking in 2001, it has declined only slowly (a phenomenon found in all post-communist EU countries). Bulgaria was also not spared the worldwide recession of 2009 (with GDP at -6 per cent). However, as early as 2010 the country had managed to reverse the situation (GDP at +0.4 per cent). An annual growth rate of about 1 per cent was projected for 2012 and 2013. Bulgaria's GDP in 2012 was 39 billion euros (1.5 per cent of the German GDP).[38] From 1999 to 2010, Bulgaria's per capita GDP, measured as a per cent of the EU average, grew significantly (see Figure 12.15 in the concluding chapter of this volume).[39]

The framework conditions for business have gradually improved in the context of the country's efforts to join the EU and its subsequent EU membership. Still, considerable efforts are needed to increase the efficiency of the public administration and legal system, and to improve them in respect of corruption, bureaucracy and tax and customs procedures, as well as bankruptcy frameworks. The banking sector, which is mostly in foreign hands, is characterized by rising numbers of loans and growing savings, but the capital market as a whole remains underdeveloped.[40]

Liberalization of prices
Liberalization of previously centrally regulated prices was an indispensable step in the transition from planned to market economy. To initiate the market-economic process of free formation of prices, prices that had been set for reasons of social policy had to be abandoned. As the centrally set prices in Bulgaria were frequently far below the actual value of goods and services, price liberalization led to dramatic inflation and even, in 1997, hyperinflation at the incredible rate of more than 1,000 per cent[41] – a negative record for transformation processes in the post-communist EU area. Recipients of fixed transfer payments, most of them pensioners, were hardest hit by this explosive process and often fought for sheer survival during the 'winter of starvation 1996/97'.[42]

Privatization

Privatization is central to regulatory change from a planned to a market economy and alters the very structure of economy, society and politics. That said, the privatization process in Bulgaria was compromised by irregularities, corruption and misappropriation. Before the process began, almost all Bulgarian enterprises were state-owned. The privatization law was not passed until April 1992,[43] making Bulgaria the last of the Central and Eastern European transformation countries to take concrete steps towards privatization of state property. This belated start was due in part to fear, in those days, that entire economic sectors would be taken over by the financially relatively powerful Turkish minority.[44] The privatization law provided a legal basis for both major and minor privatization. For state-owned enterprises, a state-run privatization agency organized and supervised the process. Municipally owned enterprises were privatized by institutions run by the respective municipality, whereas smaller enterprises were sold by the Ministry of Trade. The board of the state privatization agency was appointed jointly by the Council of Ministers and the parliament for a period of four years.[45]

In the first phase of transformation, most Bulgarian enterprises were changed into corporations with the Bulgarian state as the sole shareholder, which was not really privatization but just a change of legal status. The denationalization process actually started with the launch of mass privatization.[46] Insiders from the old nomenclature often organized the privatization procedures to suit their own interests. For example, managers of state enterprises took out cheap loans from state-owned banks and then immediately redirected them to their own private companies, often causing the state company to go bankrupt.[47] The old communist nomenclature, who at first remained in power, knew how to maintain their influence over state enterprises while restructuring the enterprises to benefit themselves. Transfers of property frequently took place without any control, resulting in shadowy concentrations of power and the development of influential business groups.[48]

On the whole, Bulgaria's privatization proceeded rather slowly. In the year 2000, the private sector's share of GDP was still only 61 per cent.[49] In April 2002, law-makers introduced a new privatization procedure that had clearer regulations and provided for more transparency regarding the remaining 2,000 or so companies in which the state was the majority shareholder. A strategy for liberalizing the electricity sector that went into effect in 2002 involved substantially higher increases and the privatization of public utilities.

Property ownership in Bulgaria is legally and constitutionally regulated (Art. 17 ConstL 56/1991). The real estate sector still lacks a nationwide land register system. Foreigners still cannot legally buy real estate.

To do so, they must, under Bulgarian law, create a legal person in the form of a trade company, whose capital may be 100 per cent foreign-owned. Such a legal person, according to Bulgarian law, is entitled to buy real estate.[50]

Society

Social structure, emigration

The time after the turnaround was characterized by radical change in the social structure, growing social disparities and a weak middle class. Income-related differences between the metropolitan region of Sofia and the provinces became bigger. Indeed, the capital Sofia experienced an upswing that is also observable, though weaker, in other big cities in the country. But the provinces became desolate, and even in Sofia wages are still the lowest in the EU, clearly behind those in the Baltic states and Romania.[51]

Poverty and lack of opportunity led to a mass emigration of Bulgarians seeking a better life elsewhere. The figures reveal dramatic population decline: whereas Bulgaria still had 8.1 million inhabitants in 2001, one decade later it had only 7.3 million – almost one million fewer.[52] A declining birth rate contributed to this drop, as was the case almost everywhere in Europe, but the precipitousness of Bulgaria's decline is due primarily to massive labour emigration.[53] As in the rest of the post-communist EU area, it is mostly the young, well-educated workforce – above all doctors, engineers and skilled labourers – who leave the country for the West, because in Western EU states they earn about ten times as much as they do at home. This emigration began many years before Bulgaria's accession to the EU, and it dealt the country a double blow: first, Bulgarian tax revenues paid for the emigrants' school education, university studies and vocational training, and then Bulgaria lost the benefits of the emigrant workforce's labour to other states.[54] In fact, the systematic emigration of highly qualified and motivated people has proved a lasting impediment to Bulgaria's economic competitiveness. On the other hand, remittances from the migrants help balance the trade deficit and also, as an important source of income for family members back home, stimulate consumption.[55]

Lines of social conflict

After the demise of the communist regime, Bulgaria's first and deepest line of conflict, developing in 1990, was the controversy over whether to keep a changed, perestroika-like but still communist-dominated regime, represented by the BSP, or introduce a transformation process towards democracy and a market economy, represented by the SDS. Unlike in other post-communist countries in East Central Europe, the system conflict between communism and liberal democracy was not decided by the foundational elections of 1990 but lasted into the 1990s. Subsequent elections reproduced the prevailing lines of social conflict, though slightly less stridently.

The conflict pitting (post-)communism against anti-communism revealed Bulgarian society's most important fault line, embodied in the party system by the two big parties of the time, the BSP and SDS. The extreme polarization and bitter struggle between the two blocs were comparable to a 'cold civil war'. This conflict was particularly fierce between 1991 and 1994, when only three parties were represented in the National Assembly. The electoral victory of Simeon II's National Movement at least temporarily ended the split of the electorate between supporters of the BSP and those of the SDS.[56]

A second line of conflict runs between ethnicities and finds organizational expression in the existence of the predominantly Turkish DPS. Bulgaria was on the verge of violent ethnic confrontation several times between 1990 and 1992. Since the mid 1990s, however, nationalist parties and ethnically motivated policies have steadily lost significance. Tensions between the majority population and minorities have been contained and embedded in a democratic system of conflict solving. Ethnic Turks from the DPS served as ministers in the government of Simeon Sakskoburggotski.[57]

Minorities
Bulgaria is a multinational state. Minorities make up 15 per cent of its population, Turks being 9 per cent and Roma another 4 per cent.[58] Relations between Bulgarians and their Turkish fellow citizens are heavily burdened by a history of forcible Bulgarization of Turks during the period of communist dictatorship.[59] Meanwhile, the situation of the Roma minority has proven increasingly complicated. Several studies have estimated the Roma minority at much more than the 4 per cent of total population recorded in censuses, for which only a fraction of Roma admit their ethnic belonging.[60] As in other post-communist states during the period of system change, in Bulgaria the Roma were particularly vulnerable to unemployment and dependence on social transfer, due to their mostly low level of education, illiteracy, lack of vocational qualification and social exclusion. The BTI Transformation Report 2003 describes the Roma as a particularly problematic group who live in slums on the outskirts of Bulgarian cities and are completely marginalized in society, the educational system and the labour market.[61] The immigration of Bulgarian

Roma – by far the poorest population in by far the poorest EU member state – to developed Western EU countries is problematic.[62] In German cities, for instance, there is growing discontent with the rising number of 'poverty immigrants' from Bulgaria.[63] This emigration of very poor people endangers social peace in Western Europe; one will soon have to admit that the social integration of Bulgarian (and other) Roma is an overall European task.[64]

Trade unions and entrepreneurs' associations

Freedom of association is guaranteed in Bulgaria. All have the right to freely associate to defend their economic and social interests. Accordingly, trade unions and associations developed independent of the state. The freedom of strike is guaranteed (except in certain professional groups). The trade unions are Bulgaria's biggest intermediary organizations. The Confederation of Independent Trade Unions (Konfederacija na nezavisimite sindikati), which in the past was loyal to the regime, has about 600,000 members; the new Podkrepa (Solidarity) trade union has about 154,000; others have fewer than 10,000 members altogether.[65] The privatizations and closures of unprofitable enterprises, along with the previously unknown phenomenon of unemployment, confronted Bulgarian trade unions with unprecedented challenges. Their first reaction was only protest, but in the following months and years the unions had to accept that unprofitable enterprises could not be subsidized forever.[66]

As the private sector developed, businesspeople perceived a need for common representation of their interests. The most important entrepreneurs' and employers' association is the Bulgarian Economic Association. Furthermore, the Bulgarian Chamber of Commerce and Industry (with which all Bulgarian companies are obliged to register) and two smaller entrepreneurs' associations are invited to tripartite negotiations. The Bulgarian Economic Association functions as both an entrepreneurs' association and an economic think tank. It is structured into individual branch associations.[67]

Churches and religious communities

The main church in Bulgaria, the Bulgarian Orthodox Church, is an autocephalous church of Christian, Byzantine Orthodoxy guided by its Holy Synod, with a patriarch at the top. The debate on the Church's role in the communist period soon culminated in a schism lasting from 1992 until 2001, which contributed to a decline in the Church's public reputation.[68] The split within the Orthodox Church demonstrated the extent of the rupture and suffering caused by the burden of the communist past.[69] In January 2012, the commission investigating the personal files of the

Bulgarian State Security reported that high-ranking clerics of the Bulgarian Orthodox Church had been involved in the activities of State Security under the communist regime. According to the report, eleven of the fifteen members of the Holy Synod had collaborated with State Security.[70] To improve its prospects in future, the Church will need to raise the educational level of parish priests and encourage the participation of active, educated members in the Church's decision-making processes.[71]

Citizens' initiatives and civil society
Civil society was almost completely extinct under the communist dictatorship, so building an active civil society, as part of the transformation from authoritarian one-party state to democratic state under the rule of law, has been a particular challenge. Accordingly, civil society in Bulgaria has developed only slowly. On the whole, it seems that the citizens' support of democracy is not yet sufficiently sustainable and active. Apart from the trauma of dictatorship, a highly likely cause of these insufficiencies is the deep wounds that system transformation cut into most citizens' professional and private lives, from alarming economic crises such as the 'winter of starvation 1996/97'; to unemployment, previously unknown; to the growth in social disparities after the turnaround. On the other hand, there has also been success, proving that Bulgaria's EU accession has positively influenced the development of civil society (see Figure 11.1).[72]

Without active, broad-based support, a democracy cannot be considered truly consolidated.[73] Some citizens have yet to identify with this acceptance of democratic values, institutions and processes.[74] Civil society has developed more readily in the transformation countries where remnants of civic culture survive from the pre-totalitarian period.

Bulgaria is not such a country. As its Freedom House ranking makes obvious, Bulgaria features the lowest level of consolidation of civil society of all the post-communist states – though at the same time it must be stressed that Bulgaria has also made the most progress (see Figure 11.1).

Mass media and coverage of politics
The system change in 1989 prompted an immediate explosion in numbers of publications as well as state and private radio and TV channels. Despite a comprehensive trend towards concentration in the course of the transformation from 1990 to 2013, Bulgaria's media landscape has on the whole been multifaceted and plural since the turnaround of 1989. In the field of electronic media, Bulgaria has a TV channel and a broadcasting service under public law, respectively known as BNT (Balgarska nacionalna televizija, Bulgarian National Television) and BNR (Balgasko nacionalno radio, Bulgarian National Radio), as well as various private

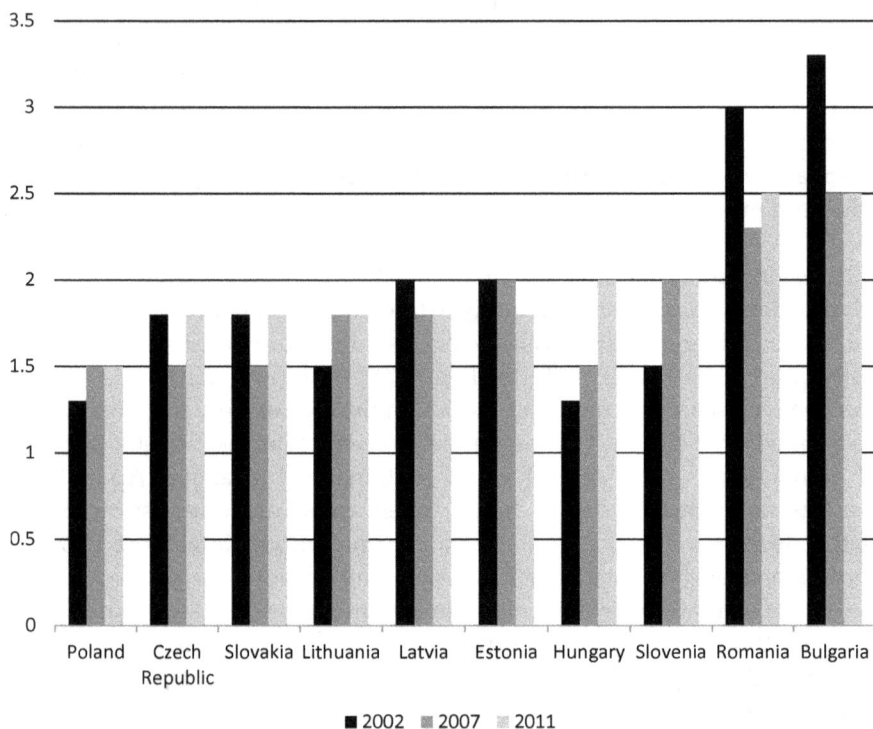

FIGURE 11.1. Bulgarian civil society 2002–2012 in the post-communist EU context (Freedom House scale: 1 = maximum achievement, 7 = minimum achievement)

The indicators for evaluating 'civil society' are the growth of non-governmental organizations, their organizational capacities and financial sustainability, the legal and political environment within which they work, the development of free trade unions and the participation of interest groups in the political process.

Source: Freedom House, Nations in Transit, Years 2002/2007/2011 (http://www.freedomhouse.org/sites/default/files/inline_images/NIT-2011-Tables.pdf, accessed 27 February 2012), sequence of countries according to 2011 figures.

radio and TV channels. The main private TV channels are bTV, Nova televizija, SKAT and TV Evropa. Among radio stations, the private channel Darik Radio predominates. The broadcasting sector is regulated by a (nominally) independent institution, the Council for Electronic Media (Savet za elektronni medii), which registers and grants licences and has a supervisory function.[75]

The process of concentration was especially far-reaching in the print media. Of the more than 1,000 newspapers and magazines published in Bulgaria between the end of 1989 and 1995, about 500 magazines and 300 newspapers still existed at the end of 1995. Ten years later, this initial variety was reduced to about 200 newspapers and magazines. Nevertheless, press outlets may still be called numerous. Until the end of 2010, the WAZ group owned the country's biggest daily newspapers – *Trud, 24 Casa* and *168 Casa* – as well as the business-oriented Economedia publishing house; they are now owned by BG Printinvest.[76] Other foreign investors are also active in this field. Additional major daily newspapers include *Dnevnik, Standart, Sega* and *Duma*.[77]

In 2004, most Bulgarian media adopted a code of ethics requiring the media to actively contribute to democratization by enabling their audiences to form their own opinions.[78] Journalism in Bulgaria had to withstand difficult conditions. The general continuity of elites has meant some media are still controlled by the old nomenclature, which makes critical, investigative research difficult. In situations involving strong economic and political pressure, media personnel often find themselves in positions that are incompatible with their responsibility to civil society.[79] Even after Bulgaria's EU accession, journalists there still face political pressure and death threats from organized crime for exposing criminal practices.[80] Alarmingly, the most recent report by Reporters without Borders appears to indicate that the standards of media liberty in Bulgaria might be revoked. In the worldwide index of the freedom of press, Bulgaria's ranking has plunged from 36 in 2003 to 87 in 2013, a number unworthy of an EU member. Indeed, Bulgaria not only comes last among EU countries in the Reporters without Borders ranking of the freedom of press, but it also comes after countries such as Sierra Leone, Tanzania, Kenya and Lesotho[81] – results that correspond to Freedom House's ranking,[82] which also shows deterioration of the media freedom in Bulgaria in the 2002–11 period. The Konrad-Adenauer-Stiftung (KAS) report 'On the Situation of the Media in Bulgaria'[83] also finds considerable need for improvement in Bulgaria's media landscape. Analyses of the actual freedom of information and media in Bulgaria reveal frequent violations of the constitutionally guaranteed freedom of the press and media. Meanwhile, on a positive note, the KAS report, the Freedom House assessment and the expert report of the BTI index all emphatically commend the development of online media and blogs, underlining their importance to the free flow of information.[84]

Corruption
Corruption is a grave and persistent problem in Bulgaria. The European Anti-Fraud Office has complained several times about corruption and the misappropriation of EU funds in Bulgaria. In November 2008, the EU reduced its financial support for the country by 220 million euros in response to the lack of progress in the fight against corruption. Corruption is considered the most serious obstacle to institutional stability.[85] Bulgaria's rank of 86 on Transparency International's worldwide

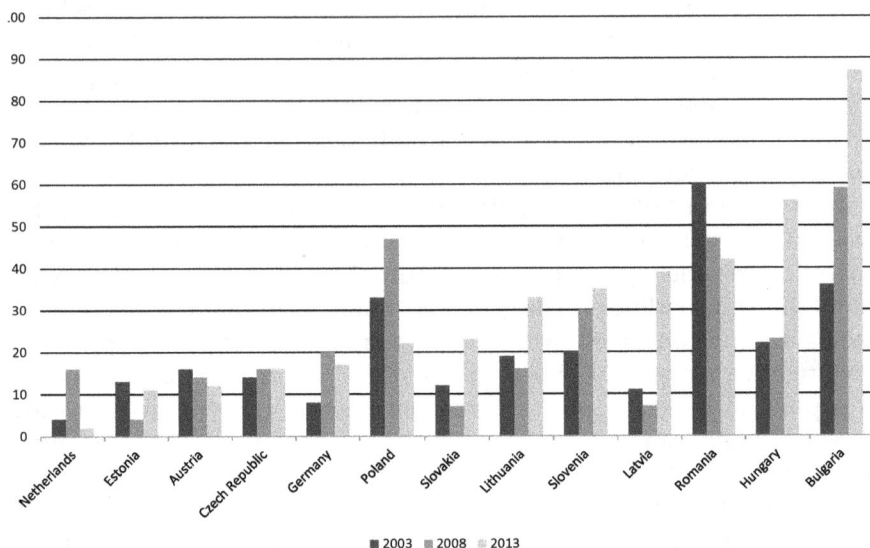

FIGURE 11.2. Bulgaria's position in freedom of press rankings 2003–2013

Source: 'Reporter ohne Grenzen, Ranglisten der Pressefreiheit', respective yearly reports (http://www. reporter-ohne-grenzen.de/pressearchiv/ranglisten-pressefreiheit/2003;/2008;/2013; accessed 13 February 2013); S. Riedel, 'Das politische System Bulgariens', in W. Ismayr (ed.), *Die politischen Systeme Osteuropas* (Wiesbaden, 2010), 677–728, here 714–16; BTI-Transformationsbericht 2012 (http://www.bti-project. de/fileadmin/Inhalte/reports/2012/pdf/BTI%202012%20Bulgaria.pdf). The Netherlands, Austria and Germany are reference countries

Corruption Perception Index 2011 was the lowest among all EU countries. A setback between 2005 and 2011 is cause for much concern: Bulgaria's ranking fell from 55 in 2005 to 86 in 2011 (see Figure 12.7 in the concluding chapter of this volume), behind countries such as El Salvador, Columbia, Lesotho and Ghana.[86]

State of Consolidation in 2012

Politics

The structural conditions in Bulgaria are particularly unfavourable to the process of democratic consolidation. Pre-totalitarian democratic traditions are almost entirely absent. The population identifies modernization mainly with the communist regime. At the time of the 1989 revolution, there was no civil society – not even a nascent one – or distinct dissident movement that could have presented a credible non-communist alternative. As a result, after 1989/90 the (post-)communists remained continuously in power and were able to advance their interests by occupying influential positions in political and economic fields. In the 1990s, a time of extreme polarization, a 'cold civil war' raged between (post-) communist and anti-communist parties and forces,[87] limiting Bulgaria's democratic and market-economic transformation to only slow, unsteady progress.[88]

Under such circumstances, Bulgaria's remarkable improvement of a situation plagued by such low indicators at the outset has been all the more impressive over the past decade, as evidenced by both the BTI Transformation Index (see Figure in the concluding chapter of this volume) and the Freedom House evaluation. The clearest improvement in the figures for Bulgaria's consolidation was in the 2003 to 2008 period, suggesting a positive influence from the process of EU accession and a consequent mobilization of democratic, pro-European forces.

In Bulgaria, as in the other post-communist EU countries, the consolidation of the political system has made good progress, particularly at the institutional level. A constitution based on the rule of law and guaranteeing human rights has been passed. The constitutional judiciary has contributed to the juridification of political conflicts. According to the Freedom House Report 2011, Bulgaria is a free electoral democracy where human rights are respected.[89] The BTI Status Index, a comparative analysis of 129 transformation countries worldwide, assigned Bulgaria the lofty rank of 14 for the development of its market economy and democracy, thus placing it in the small, successful group of twenty-three transformation countries classed as 'consolidating democracies' in the BTI ranking.[90]

At the same time, in the post-communist EU context, Bulgaria is still seen as a country with various democratic deficits. Both the change of mentality with the subsequent consolidation of behaviour and attitudes, and the development of a civil society have proven difficult and lengthy. Changing stereotypes of thinking and behaviour is obviously the key problem of transformation. In view of the high susceptibility to corruption and distinct clientelism in Bulgaria, the behaviour of formal and informal political actors cannot be considered satisfactory. The development of a mature, responsible, active civil society will take more time, as will the consolidation of democratic behaviour among the political and economic elites.

Economy

In contrast to most states in (particularly Southern) Europe, Bulgaria is able to present a solid state budget. A policy of austerity halved the budget deficit to 2 per cent of the GDP in the course of three years (2008 to 2011), and the trend has continued. By the end of 2011 the national debt was only 17 per cent, rising in 2012 to a moderate 19 per cent of GDP. As the poorest EU country, with only 44 per cent of the average European per capita GDP and almost half of its population at risk of poverty (according to definition), Bulgaria still has a long way to go to catch up economically with the other EU countries. At current growth rates, this cannot happen in the foreseeable future, even though the absorption of EU funds, which was very low for a long time, has risen significantly since Tomislav Donchev, the minister in charge of managing funds from the EU, took office in 2009. The main hindrance to faster absorption is the insufficient capacity of an administration that is not always oriented to the common good. Bulgaria still has a lower absorption quota than do most other EU states.[91] In the budget period from 2007 until February 2013, Bulgaria drew only a quarter of available EU funds.[92]

Bulgaria's progress as an international business location is owed above all to macro-economic stability (i.e. competitiveness of the state's budget and improved infrastructure thanks to EU-funded investments in the fields of water supply, e-government, waste disposal etc.). Persistent consolidation deficits include insufficient legal and tax security, clientelism, corruption and enterprises' poor payment habits. Further complaints concern the absence of progress in the inefficient justice system, which often does not offer effective legal protection; obstructive and non-transparent economic regulation; and organized crime. Finally, the pension scheme and the health and educational systems also suffer from great deficits.[93]

Society

Forty years of violent communist rule followed by more than twenty years of radical change and the insecurity caused by transformation have deformed the moral and ethical values of Bulgarian society. Distrust towards political parties is extremely high, affecting a striking 88 per cent of citizens: only 12 per cent trust the parties.[94] Citizens' low level of readiness to participate is connected to this distrust of political parties—and, in this context, of democratic institutions as a whole. The people do not believe they are able to influence the government's policy. Election turnouts in Bulgaria are therefore permanently lower than in established democracies: turnout of eligible voters was 56 per cent in the 2005 parliamentary elections and at least 61 per cent in 2009.[95]

The shock treatment part of the system change from planned to market economy hit much of the Bulgarian population with great force. Corruption, which was already extremely widespread under the communist regime, has since consolidated further and reached quite new dimensions. The abandonment of old legal norms and the temporary absence of new ones after the turnaround enabled the old Communist Party cadres to enrich themselves free of normative restrictions, inflicting high unemployment and mass poverty on wide parts of the population. These negative transformation phenomena have caused widespread distrust towards democracy and market economy as such: More than twenty years after the turnaround, support for the system is significantly lower in Bulgaria than in established democracies.[96] On the other hand, there is still much trust in EU institutions, and enthusiasm for an integrated Europe runs high among Bulgarians.[97] This may have a positive effect on the consolidation of democratic values among society: in one survey, more than 60 per cent of respondents expressed confidence in the EU.[98]

Civil society is the foundation both of democracy and of market economy. However, the communist regime prevented civil society from developing in Bulgaria. Having been mostly depoliticized in the period of dictatorship, the citizenry must now shake off the passive stereotypes of behaviour they are used to and learn how to organize and become politically committed. Development of a lively, well-organized civil society is the linchpin of the democratic consolidation.[99] The field of business is likewise undergoing a learning process in which people must nurture entrepreneurial skills such as readiness to be proactive and take risks.

Prospects

As the poorest of all EU states, Bulgaria faces huge hurdles posed by its consolidation deficits in the fields of politics, economy and society. One challenge is paramount: tackling the close connection of politics and business and the resultant endemic corruption. Given the corruption and disappointment with real democracy and market economics, another pressing need is to win a citizenry disenchanted with politics over to political commitment. Improving the investment climate in Bulgaria will require increased efficiency in public administration and justice as well as better law enforcement. And minority policy faces the long-term task of promoting the social integration of the Roma minority, particularly by ensuring that their children receive better education and providing the Roma ethnicity as a whole with means to improve vocational qualifications.

Conversely, Bulgaria stands out for its remarkable consolidation progress in the period 1990 to 2012: though it started from a particularly low level of consolidation in the EU context, it chalked up greater progress than any other country in the post-communist EU area (see Figure 12.19 in the concluding chapter of this volume). If this trend continues (and by all indications it will), mostly positive development can be expected in the fields of society, economy and politics. The stability and efficiency of the economic and political systems increased during the transformation process from 1990 to 2012, and institutional consolidation has made particularly good progress. The constitutionally based rule of law and the system of the separation of powers prevail in the political practice. In this context, the constitutional judiciary has proven its worth as a vital factor in the successive juridification of political conflicts and a tool for making political processes more constitutional.

Despite the severe crises and social ruptures after the system change of 1990, Bulgarian citizens remain enthusiastic supporters of integrated Europe and its institutions. Thus, given the current state of institutional configuration and constellation of political powers, Bulgaria's risk of radical de-democratization in the event of a deep socio-economic and political crisis may be estimated as comparatively low. External framework conditions, especially EU and NATO membership, are an essential stabilization factor that Bulgaria's young and still fragile democracy will need for quite some time.

Karel Vodička, Dr of Jurisprudence, born in Aussig, Czechoslovakia, in 1949, went into political exile in the Federal Republic of Germany together with his family. He has undertaken scientific work as a philologist at the HAIT (until 2014) and as a lecturer in the Faculty of Philosophy at Jan-Evangelista-Purkyne University (UJEP) in Ústí nad Labem, Czech Republic. He has published on the history and the political system of the Czech Republic as well as on system transformation in the post-communist EU area. He has authored 126 scientific articles and is the author of sixteen books, most recently *Zündfunke aus Prag: Wie 1989 der Mut zur Freiheit die Geschichte veränderte*, co-authored with Hans-Dietrich Genscher (Munich, 2014).

Notes

1. See U.K. Paschke (ed.), *Holle Universalgeschichte* (Erlangen, 1991), 383f.; R. Schmitt, *Kleines Handbuch Bulgarien* (Rostock, 2012), 12; W. Höpken, 'Bulgarien', in W. Weidenfeld (ed.), *Demokratie und Marktwirtschaft in Osteuropa* (Gütersloh, 1995), 195–212, here 195f.
2. See H. Brahm and J. Deimel, 'Bulgarien', in A. Gabanyi and K. Schroeder (eds), *Vom Baltikum zum Schwarzen Meer* (Munich, 2002), 197–220, here 197–98; Höpken, 'Bulgarien', 195f.; Paschke, *Holle Universalgeschichte*, 632f.; Schmitt, *Kleines Handbuch Bulgarien*, 12f.

3. S. Riedel, 'Das politische System Bulgariens', in W. Ismayr (ed.), *Die politischen Systeme Osteuropas* (Wiesbaden, 2010), 677–728, here 677.
4. See W. Ismayr, 'Die politischen Systeme Osteuropas im Vergleich', in Ismayr (ed.), *Die politischen Systeme Osteuropas*, 9–78, here 68; 'Transformationsindex BTI 2012: Politische Gestaltung im internationalen Vergleich' (Gütersloh, 2012), W. Merkel, 'Gegen alle Theorie? Die Konsolidierung der Demokratie in Ostmitteleuropa', *Politische Vierteljahresschrift* 48 (2007), 413–33, here 430; Brahm and Deimel, 'Bulgarien', 197–98; Schmitt, *Kleines Handbuch Bulgarien*, 60–63.
5. See Paschke, *Holle Universalgeschichte*, 632f.; Schmitt, *Kleines Handbuch Bulgarien*, 12f.; Brahm and Deimel, 'Bulgarien', 197–98; Höpken, 'Bulgarien', 195f.
6. See Brahm and Deimel, 'Bulgarien', 197–98; Höpken, 'Bulgarien', 195f.; Paschke, *Holle Universalgeschichte*, 632f.; Schmitt, *Kleines Handbuch Bulgarien*, 12f.
7. See Brahm and Deimel, 'Bulgarien', 197–98; Höpken, 'Bulgarien', 195f.; Paschke, *Holle Universalgeschichte*, 632f.; Schmitt, *Kleines Handbuch Bulgarien*, 12f.
8. See Brahm and Deimel, 'Bulgarien', 197–98; Höpken, 'Bulgarien', 195f.; Paschke, *Holle Universalgeschichte*, 632f.; Schmitt, *Kleines Handbuch Bulgarien*, 12f.
9. 'Verfassung der Republik Bulgarien', *Dăržaven vestnik*, 56/1991; 'Verfassungsänderungen', *Dăržaven vestnik*, 85/2003; *Dăržaven vestnik*, 18/2005; *Dăržaven vestnik*, 27/2006; 'Urteil des Verfassungsgerichts Nr. 7/2006', *Dăržaven vestnik*, 78/2006; *Dăržaven vestnik*, 12/2007.
10. Riedel, 'Das politische System Bulgariens', 678–79.
11. See Brahm and Deimel, 'Bulgarien', 206.
12. Riedel, 'Das politische System Bulgariens', 684f.; Schmitt, *Kleines Handbuch Bulgarien*, 53f.; P. Rosůlek, 'Bulharsko: Monokameralismus se silným postavením premiéra', in L. Cabada (ed.), *Nové demokracie střední a východní Evropy* (Prague, 2008), 181–98, here 188.
13. Riedel, 'Das politische System Bulgariens', 684f.; Schmitt, *Kleines Handbuch Bulgarien*, 53.
14. Riedel, 'Das politische System Bulgariens', 684f.; Schmitt, *Kleines Handbuch Bulgarien*, 53f.; Rosůlek, 'Bulharsko', 188.
15. Riedel, 'Das politische System Bulgariens', 684f.; Rosůlek, 'Bulharsko', 188; Schmitt, *Kleines Handbuch Bulgarien*, 53f.
16. 'Reaktion auf Proteste: Bulgarische Regierung tritt zurück', *Frankfurter Allgemeine Zeitung*, 20 February 2013 (http://www.faz.net/aktuell/politik/ausland/europa/reaktion-auf-proteste-bulgarische-regierung-tritt-zurueck-12087068.html; accessed 20 February 2013).
17. Riedel, 'Das politische System Bulgariens', 687f.
18. S. Mihai, 'Rumänien und Bulgarien: Hoffen auf Europa', *Aus Politik und Zeitgeschichte* 63(6–7) (2013), 42–46, here 45.
19. Schmitt, *Kleines Handbuch Bulgarien*, 53f.; Rosůlek, 'Bulharsko', 194.
20. Brahm and Deimel, 'Bulgarien', 203f.; Schmitt, *Kleines Handbuch Bulgarien*, 53.
21. Riedel, 'Das politische System Bulgariens', 700f.; Schmitt, *Kleines Handbuch Bulgarien*, 53.
22. Riedel, 'Das politische System Bulgariens', 700f.; Brahm and Deimel, 'Bulgarien', 203f.; Schmitt, *Kleines Handbuch Bulgarien*, 53.
23. Riedel, 'Das politische System Bulgariens', 700f.; Brahm and Deimel, 'Bulgarien', 203f.; Schmitt, *Kleines Handbuch Bulgarien*, 53.
24. Figures: European Election Database (http://www.nsd.uib.no/european_election_data base/country; accessed 28 February 2012).

25. 'BTI-Ländergutachten Bulgarien 2012', 2. Political Participation (http://www.bti-proj ect.de/laendergutachten/ecse/bgr/2012/#chap2; accessed 2 February 2013); Rosůlek, 'Bulharsko', 188; Riedel, 'Das politische System Bulgariens', 700f.
26. 'BTI-Ländergutachten Bulgarien 2012', 2. Political Participation; Riedel, 'Das politische System Bulgariens', 695f.; Brahm and Deimel, 'Bulgarien', 203f.; I. Georgiev, 'Wahlen im postsozialistischen Bulgarien: Mittel für politisches Krisenmanagement?, in K. Ziemer (ed.), *Wahlen in postsozialistischen Staaten* (Opladen, 2003), 57–78, here 69f.
27. 'BTI-Ländergutachten Bulgarien 2012', 2. Political Participation.
28. Transparency International 2009, quoted after Riedel, 'Das politische System Bulgariens', 699–700; 'BTI-Ländergutachten Bulgarien 2012', 2. Political Participation; Rosůlek, 'Bulharsko', 188; Brahm and Deimel, 'Bulgarien', 203f.; Georgiev, 'Wahlen im postsozialistischen Bulgarien', 69f.
29. Georgiev, 'Wahlen im postsozialistischen Bulgarien', 69f.
30. Brahm and Deimel, 'Bulgarien', 206.
31. 'EU-Bericht 2011 über Bulgariens Fortschritte im Rahmen des Kooperations- und Kontrollverfahrens' (http://europa.eu/rapid/press-release_MEMO-11–525. de.htm?locale=en; accessed 13 February 2013); see also Rosůlek, 'Bulharsko', 188; Riedel, 'Das politische System Bulgariens', 716f.
32. Riedel, 'Das politische System Bulgariens', 718f.
33. Constitutional Law No. 56/1991; Riedel, 'Das politische System Bulgariens', 720f.; Rosůlek, 'Bulharsko', 192; Schmitt, *Kleines Handbuch Bulgarien*, 53.
34. Brahm and Deimel, 'Bulgarien', 208–209; Schmitt, *Kleines Handbuch Bulgarien*, 60–63.
35. Brahm and Deimel, 'Bulgarien', 208–209; Schmitt, *Kleines Handbuch Bulgarien*, 60–63.
36. Schmitt, *Kleines Handbuch Bulgarien*, 60–63; Brahm and Deimel, 'Bulgarien', 208–209; Commission report (2002) on the accession of Bulgaria (http://www.fifoost.org/bulgar ien/EU_Bulgarien_ 2002/node28.php; accessed 2 February 2013).
37. See Commission report (2002) on the accession of Bulgaria; see also Auswärtiges Amt, 'Wirtschaftsbericht Bulgarien', 12/2012 (http://www.auswaertiges-amt.de/sid_6A4FBE 74679C8D61CFCFFB0F953C90B2/DE/Aussenpolitik/Laender/Laenderinfos/Bulgarien/ Wirtschaft_node.html#doc360620bodyText1; accessed 13 February 2013).
38. See Auswärtiges Amt, 'Wirtschaftsbericht Bulgarien'.
39. Source: Eurostat (http://epp.eurostat.ec.europa.eu/tgm/table.do?Tab=table&init=1&plu gin=1&language=de&pcode=tec00114; accessed 30 June 2012).
40. See 'BTI-Ländergutachten Bulgarien 2012', Teil Wirtschaft; Auswärtiges Amt, 'Wirtschaftsbericht Bulgarien'.
41. Commission report (2002) on the accession of Bulgaria.
42. See M. Dauderstädt, 'Transformation und Integration der Wirtschaft der postkommu- nistischen Beitrittsländer', *Aus Politik und Zeitgeschichte* 43(5–6) (2004), 15–24, here 15; Brahm and Deimel, 'Bulgarien', 208–209; Schmitt, *Kleines Handbuch Bulgarien*, 60–63; Commission report (2002) on the accession of Bulgaria.
43. R. Bakardjieva, 'Der Privatizierungsprozess in Bulgarien: Strategien, Widersprüche und Schlussfolgerungen', Universität Potsdam (http://opus.kobv.de/ubp/volltexte/2011/48 80/pdf/fiwi-disk_s05.pdf; accessed 13 February 2013).
44. H.H. Glismann and K. Schrader, 'Privatisierung staatlichen Eigentums in den mittel- und osteuropäischen Ländern: Eine kritische Analyse', *Kiel Working Paper No. 573* (Kiel Institute for the World Economy, 1993), 28 (http://www.econstor.eu/ bitstream/10419/640/1/04301237X.pdf; accessed 13 February 2013).
45. Glismann and Schrader, 'Privatisierung staatlichen Eigentums', 29.

46. Bakardjieva, 'Der Privatisierungsprozess in Bulgarien'; BTI 2003, 'Ländergutachten Bulgarien' (http:/bti2003.bertelsmann-transformation-index.de/182.0.html; accessed 13 February 2013).

47. B. Chichkova, *Der Transformationsprozess in Bulgarien: Politische, ökonomische und soziokulturelle Aspekte* (Frankfurt a. M., 2006), 66.

48. Glismann and Schrader, 'Privatisierung staatlichen Eigentums'; Bakardjieva, 'Der Privatisierungsprozess in Bulgarien'; Chichkova, *Der Transformationsprozess in Bulgarien*, 66.

49. Glismann and Schrader, 'Privatisierung staatlichen Eigentums'; Bakardjieva, 'Der Privatisierungsprozess in Bulgarien'; Chichkova, *Der Transformationsprozess in Bulgarien*, 66; BTI 2003, 'Ländergutachten Bulgarien'.

50. Bakardjieva, 'Der Privatisierungsprozess in Bulgarien'; BTI 2003, 'Ländergutachten Bulgarien'.

51. M. Martens, 'Armut und Abwanderung: Exodus aus Bulgarien', *Frankfurter Allgemeine Zeitung*, 18 February 2013 (http:/www.faz.net/aktuell/politik/ausland/europa/armut-und-abwanderung-exodus-aus-bulgarien-12085240.html; accessed 18 February 2013).

52. Figures: Martens, 'Armut und Abwanderung'.

53. Ibid.: Riedel, 'Das politische System Bulgariens', 699.

54. See Martens, 'Armut und Abwanderung'; Brahm and Deimel, 'Bulgarien', 206–207.

55. Mihai, 'Rumänien und Bulgarien', 45.

56. Georgiev, 'Wahlen im postsozialistischen Bulgarien', 69f.

57. Brahm and Deimel, 'Bulgarien', 206–207; Georgiev, 'Wahlen im postsozialistischen Bulgarien', 69f.

58. B. Gjuzelev, 'Die Minderheiten in Bulgarien unter Berücksichtigung der letzten Volksbefragung vom Dezember 1992', *Südosteuropa* 43(6–7) (1994), 361–73.

59. See Brahm and Deimel, 'Bulgarien', 206–207.

60. See K. Vodička, 'Die Roma in der Slowakei: Stolperstein auf dem Weg in die EU?', *Osteuropa* 51(7) (2001), 832–46; K. Vodička, 'Einmal Verlierer, immer Verlierer? Zur Situation der Roma in der Slowakei', *Blätter für deutsche und internationale Politik* 48(6) (2003), 724–30.

61. BTI 2003, 'Ländergutachten Bulgarien'.

62. See Martens, 'Armut und Abwanderung'; Brahm and Deimel, 'Bulgarien', 206–207.

63. See R. Soldt, 'Städtetag besorgt über Armutseinwanderung', *Frankfurter Allgemeine Zeitung*, 14 February 2013 (http://www.faz.net/aktuell/politik/inland/appell-an-bund-laender-und-eu-staedtetag-besorgt-ueber-armutseinwanderung-12080995.html; accessed 18 February 2013).

64. See ibid.

65. See 'Entwicklung der Gewerkschaften und Arbeitgeberverbände in Bulgarien' (http://www.set-online.de/Info_Wirtschaft/Metallindustrie/Metallindustrie_Inhalt/Metallindustrie%2009/Bulgarien.PDF; accessed 5 February 2013).

66. See Brahm and Deimel, 'Bulgarien', 206–207.

67. See 'Entwicklung der Gewerkschaften und Arbeitgeberverbände in Bulgarien'.

68. Brahm and Deimel, 'Bulgarien', 207; M. Arndt, 'Nach den Stasi-Enthüllungen – die bulgarisch orthodoxe Kirche in Staat und Gesellschaft', Konrad-Adenauer-Stiftung (http://www.kas.de/wf/doc/kas_6329–1442–1–30.pdf?120329113718; accessed 13 February 2013).

69. See Brahm and Deimel, 'Bulgarien', 207.

70. Arndt, 'Nach den Stasi-Enthüllungen'.

71. Ibid.
72. S.R. Roos, 'EU-Erweiterung: Wachhund und Kooperationspartner', Entwicklung und Zusammenarbeit, 24 February 2010 (http://www.dandc.eu/de/article/zivilgesellschaftli che-organisationen-kaempfen-rumaenien-und-bulgarien-fuer; accessed 2 February 2013).
73. W. Merkel, *Systemtransformation: Eine Einführung in die Theorie und Empirie der Transformationsforschung* (Opladen, 1999), 164; G. Pickel, 'Die subjektive Verankerung der Demokratie in Osteuropa: Die Legitimität der Demokratie in der Bevölkerung als Faktor demokratischer Stabilität und Qualität', in U. Backes, T. Jaskułowski and A. Polese (eds), *Totalitarismus und Transformation: Defizite der Demokratiekonsolidierung in Mittel- und Osteuropa* (Göttingen, 2009), 261–83, here 283.
74. J. Jakobs, *Tücken der Demokratie: Antisystemeinstellungen und ihre Determinanten in sieben postkommunistischen Transformationsländern* (Wiesbaden, 2004); W. Merkel, *Systemtransformation: Eine Einführung in die Theorie und Empirie der Transformationsforschung*, 2nd ed. (Wiesbaden, 2010), 423; Pickel, 'Die subjektive Verankerung', 283.
75. Commission report (2002) on the accession of Bulgaria, Chapter 20: 'Culture and audio-visual media'; C. Christova and D. Förger, 'On the situation of the media in Bulgaria', Konrad-Adenauer-Stiftung (http://www.kas.de/wf/doc/kas_30139–1522–1–30.pdf?120 213153734; accessed 15 February 2013); Riedel, 'Das politische System Bulgariens', 714–16.
76. See Riedel, 'Das politische System Bulgariens', 715–16.
77. See ibid., 715–16; Schmitt, *Kleines Handbuch Bulgarien*, 94–95; Christova and Förger, 'Zur Situation der Medien in Bulgarien', 12.
78. See Christova and Förger, 'Zur Situation der Medien in Bulgarien', 12.
79. See ibid., 6.
80. See Riedel, 'Das politische System Bulgariens', 716; Christova and Förger, 'Zur Situation der Medien in Bulgarien', 16f.
81. See 'Reporter ohne Grenzen, Ranglisten der Pressefreiheit', respective yearly reports (http://www.reporter-ohne-grenzen.de/pressearchiv/ranglisten-pressefreiheit/2003; /2008;/2013; accessed 13 February 2013).
82. See Freedom House, Nations in Transit 2011 (http://www.freedomhouse.org/sites/de fault/files/inline_images/NIT-2011-Tables.pdf; accessed 27 February 2012).
83. See Christova and Förger, 'Zur Situation der Medien in Bulgarien', 6.
84. See 'Reporter ohne Grenzen, Ranglisten der Pressefreiheit', respective yearly reports.
85. Riedel, 'Das politische System Bulgariens', 677; BTI-Transformationsbericht 2012 (http://www.bti-project.de/fileadmin/Inhalte/reports/2012/pdf/BTI%202012%20Bulgaria.pdf); Brahm and Deimel, 'Bulgarien', 206; 'Korruption in Bulgarien: Der überschattete Schatten', *Frankfurter Allgemeine Zeitung*, 16 July 2012 (http://www.faz.net/aktuell/poli tik/europaeische-union/korruption-in-bulgarien-der-ueberschattete-schatte-11822513. html; accessed 9 February 2013).
86. Source: Transparency International, Corruption Perceptions Index for the respective years; 6 March 2012.
87. Georgiev, 'Wahlen im postsozialistischen Bulgarien', 69f.
88. Riedel, 'Das politische System Bulgariens', 677; 'BTI-Ländergutachten Bulgarien 2012'; Brahm and Deimel, 'Bulgarien', 197–98; Höpken, 'Bulgarien', 195f.
89. Freedom House, 'Freedom in the World 2011' (http://www.freedomhouse.org/template. cfm?page=363&year=2011&country=7594; accessed 24 February 2012).
90. See Transformationsindex BTI 2012, appendix.
91. See Auswärtiges Amt, 'Wirtschaftsbericht Bulgarien'.
92. Mihai, 'Rumänien und Bulgarien', 46.

93. See Riedel, 'Das politische System Bulgariens', 716f., 'BTI-Ländergutachten Bulgarien 2012'; Brahm and Deimel, 'Bulgarien', 205–206; Auswärtiges Amt, 'Wirtschaftsbericht Bulgarien'.

94. Source: Democracy Index based on Eurobarometer Survey 2009 (http://ec.europa.eu/ employment_social/2010againstpoverty/extranet/Eurobarometre_150DPI_091113.pdf; accessed on 28. February 2012).

95. Source: European Election Database (http://www.nsd.uib.no/european_election_data base/country; accessed 28 February 2012).

96. See M. Ehrke, 'Die Europäische Union und der postkommunistische Raum', in *Kompass 2020* (2007), 6 (http://www.fes.de/kompass2020/pdf/postkommunismus.pdf; accessed 7 May 2012); Pickel, 'Die subjektive Verankerung', 267, based on WVS 1999/2000; G. Pickel and J. Jacobs, 'Der soziokulturelle Unterbau der neuen Demokratien Osteuropas', in G. Pickel, D. Pollack, J. Jacobs and O. Müller (eds), *Osteuropas Bevölkerung auf dem Weg in die Demokratie: Repräsentative Untersuchungen in Ostdeutschland und zehn osteuropäischen Transformationsstaaten* (Wiesbaden, 2006), 31–52.

97. Mihai, 'Rumänien und Bulgarien', 43.

98. Ibid., 46.

99. See Pickel, 'Die subjektive Verankerung'; W. Merkel, *Systemtransformation: Eine Einführung in die Theorie und Empirie der Transformationsforschung*, 2nd ed. (Wiesbaden, 2010), 423; Pickel and Jacobs, 'Der soziokulturelle Unterbau'.

POST-COMMUNIST SPACE
State of Consolidation and Prospects: Politics, Economy, Society

❦

Günther Heydemann and Karel Vodička

Post-Communist EU Region: Definition and Shape

The post-communist EU region consists of the East German federal states and the eastern EU states.[1] It is characterized by certain substantial common grounds and analogous trends of development that significantly distinguish it from both the established EU democracies and the other countries of the former Eastern Bloc.

Two groups of countries looking back to two different histories have united under the umbrella of the EU. What makes the post-communist EU countries different from the established Central European EU democracies[2] is the traumatic experience of violent communist rule, which devastated the moral values of the pre-totalitarian period, lastingly distorted the population's political culture and extinguished civil society. These distortions could not be revised in the course of the transformation process of 1990–2012, a time of uncertainty and radical social change. As a consequence, various democratic deficits are still identifiable at the representative level (highly virulent party systems), the actors level (liability to corruption) and the level of civil society (weak support for democracy and lack of readiness to participate).

On the other hand, the East German federal states and eastern EU states differ from the other former Eastern Bloc states in that they are clearly in the midst of a sustainable consolidation process and – worldwide – occupy top positions among transformation countries as the most consolidated market economy democracies.[3] Whereas independent experts count the post-communist EU countries without exception among 'democracies in consolidation', other former Eastern Bloc countries reach at best the status of 'defective democracy' (Ukraine); all others rank even lower, among strongly defective democracies or even moderate or hardcore autocracies.[4] In the post-communist EU region, by contrast, the risk of radical de-democratization is currently estimated as low (in South East Europe) or very low (in East Central Europe).

Politics

The Hard Road towards Democracy

Risks during the transition to democracy
The mainly non-violent (except in Romania) revolutions of 1989 marked only the beginning of a long road. The transition from dictatorship to democracy concerns a number of risks and is typically beset by conflicts and setbacks.[5] One sticking point in post-communist system change is the necessity of transforming the political, economic and social systems all at the same time.[6] Countries with pre-dictatorial democratic experience have a greater chance of re-establishing democracy, as relics of a democratic political culture have survived there. Majorities of these countries' populations support democracy – not only as a model but as a real system – and reject anti-democratic alternatives more clearly.

Four levels of consolidation within the political system
The consolidation model developed by Wolfgang Merkel[7] seems suited to a comparative analysis of the success of the consolidation, as it allows for evaluation of individual segments of a political system. Merkel distinguishes four levels of consolidation: constitutional consolidation, representative consolidation, consolidation of behaviour,[8] and consolidation of civil society (Figure 12.1). At all levels the consolidation process runs parallel, but usually it is completed first at the constitutional level and last at the level of civil society. A young democracy may be considered crisis-proof only after all four levels have been consolidated.[9]

Constitutional or Institutional Consolidation

Institutionalization as a precondition for power control
After the communist regimes had been replaced, revolutionary elites or actors promoting radical-reformist system change seized power. The next decisive steps towards the consolidation of a democratic system were to institutionalize political rule, introduce political competition and bindingly norm the processes of political decision-making.[10] With the passage

Constitutional Consolidation
constitution, electoral law, constitutional body,
acceptance through players

Representative Consolidation political parties
pres. groups, chambers, churches, citizens associations

Behavioural Consolidation formal and informal political players

Consolidation of the civil society   political culture supporting democracy,
civil society structures, participation

FIGURE 12.1. Levels of consolidation within a political system

of a constitution, an electoral law and further institutional regulation mechanisms, the unrestricted political power that revolutionary elites held after the collapse of the authoritarian or totalitarian system was shifted from an individual or a social group to institutionalized procedures. These mechanisms were intended to restrict the executive power, allow for continuous control of power and enable substantial corrections to decision-making and to the system itself.

Constitution of the state

More than 80 per cent of Eastern European citizens are of the opinion that a democratic constitution is an essential foundation of society.[11] In the 1990–1993 period (1997 in Poland), most eastern EU states installed completely new constitutions drawing on the experience of Western democracies and adopted extensive elements of their constitutional regulations.[12] Some of those countries (Estonia, Poland, the Czech Republic) were able to reach back to democratic traditions and link their modern constitutions to constitutional regulations from the pre-totalitarian period. Latvia, for example, adopted the same constitution it had had in the pre-dictatorship period (of 1922) and ratified it in 1993, having completed it with an extensive charter of fundamental rights and some modernizing modifications. The East German federal states joined the Basic Law of the Federal Republic of Germany. The reunification of the two German states, which happened surprisingly quickly on 3 October 1990, created a new, merely extended Federal Republic of Germany: reunification has hardly touched the institutional order.[13]

Only one country treated here did not abandon its constitution from the early communist period (that of 1949): Hungary, which was adhering to specific conditions of a negotiated system change. After subsequent extensive modifications and completions, Hungary can also be considered to have a democratic constitution and be a state under the rule of law.[14] Nevertheless, its constitution is still somewhat provisional in nature, which twenty-two years later turned out to be a serious disadvantage. On 1 January 2012, the constitutional majority of FIDESZ (Alliance of Young Democrats) passed a new Hungarian constitution that some experts consider highly problematic[15] and that was sharply criticized by the EU Commission.[16] Its dubious passages include in particular its ethno-nationally determined emphasis on a 'unitarian Hungarian nation' as a constitutional subject, the undermining of the inviolability of the fundamental rights, the restriction of the Constitutional Court's controlling competences and the restriction of the constitutional independence of the central bank and the data protection authority. The EU Commission resolved to initiate a procedure against Hungary for violation of the EU Treaties.[17] In 2012, the Hungarian Constitutional Court declared some of the regulations of this constitution invalid, as they contradicted the spirit of a democratic constitution.[18]

Basically, however, all constitutional charters of the eastern EU countries are rooted in the principles of sovereignty, democracy and rule of law, as the foundations of these new democratic states. They all include extensive charters of human and fundamental rights, especially general liberties, political rights and minority rights as well as economic, social, cultural and environmental rights. Territorial self-rule is constitutionally guaranteed in all of these countries, and their economies are obliged to uphold the principles of a social and ecological market economy. Overcoming the dichotomy of the text of the constitution and the reality of its application, which is bigger than in established democracies, has proven the main problem in the consolidation process at the constitutional level.

Parliamentary systems of government
In the eastern EU, parliamentary systems of government were rooted by the countries' respective constitutions (except in Poland). The parliaments independently control the executives (in contrast to presidential or semi-presidential systems of government), and all eastern EU countries know the fundamental right to dismiss the prime minister or government with a vote of no confidence, a right that generally characterizes parliamentary systems of government.[19] Transformation research suggests that parliamentary systems of government are advantageous when it comes to solving political conflicts because they become constitutional conflicts less often than they do in presidential systems.[20]

Poland's constitutional system differs fundamentally from those of all other eastern EU countries. In view of the president's strong position and extensive veto rights in the context of the parliamentarian process, the Polish governmental system may be called parliamentary-presidential.[21]

The President of the State

According to their constitutions, each eastern EU country is a republic headed by a President of the State. In Bulgaria and Romania, attempts to connect to historical traditions and establish monarchies have failed. In Lithuania, Poland, Romania, Slovenia and Slovakia, the people elect their presidents directly; in the other eastern EU countries they are chosen by parliaments. Although direct election increases a head of state's legitimacy, no correlation is identifiable between the electoral procedure and the respective constitutional competences. The most elementary competences of all presidents include representing the state to the inside and the outside world, proclaiming laws to be effective, nominating prime ministers and ministers (who must seek their majorities in the parliaments) and appointing other high-ranking officials.

In all eastern EU countries (except Slovenia), the president may reject a law passed by the parliament.[22] However, this is a suspensive veto that may be overruled by a majority in the parliament, usually a qualified majority of all MPs (absolute majority), though in Estonia, Latvia, Hungary and Romania a simple majority is sufficient. Having once again been passed, a law must then be promulgated. Early on in the transformation, presidents' veto power was applied more frequently, and to great effect in many cases. Later in the transition period, the presidential veto power was used more seldom and lost significance (except in Bulgaria).[23]

Poland's President of the State has the strongest veto power: his or her veto can only be rejected by a three-fifths majority of the Sejm. If the president and the parliamentary majority belong to different political camps, and if the government's majority is less than 60 per cent of the seats (which is very often the case), the president's veto may significantly obstruct the government's everyday work. As a constitutional element, such a strong veto power vested in the President of the State is generally alien to the system of parliamentary rule.[24]

Government

In every eastern EU state, the head of government is nominated by the president and confirmed by a vote of confidence in the first chamber of the parliament (the second chamber too, in Romania). In most countries, not only the prime minister but the entire government as well must ask for the parliament's vote of confidence. Usually the vote of confidence comes

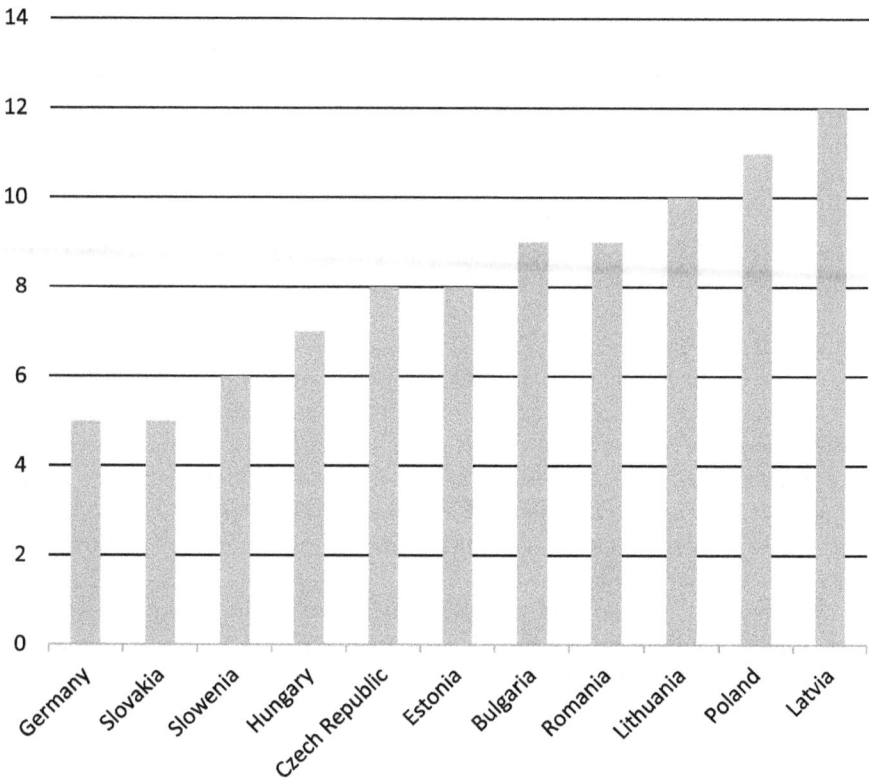

FIGURE 12.2. Number of changes of government 1990–2008 (stable to unstable)

Source: F. Grotz and F. Müller-Rommel (eds), *Regierungssysteme in Mittel- und Osteuropa* (Wiesbaden, 2011), appendix, 321–79, here 370–72.

with approval of a government programme presented to the parliament before the vote of confidence.[25] Most eastern EU states have undergone frequent changes in governments (see also Figure 12.2).[26] This indicates that consolidation of the democratic political systems is still incomplete, and that the systems are still characterized by instabilities in the party systems and the consequent turbulence in the parliamentary process. Only a few times has a vote of no confidence by the parliament been the actual reason for a change of government. In most cases, either programmatic or personal confrontations among a coalition's partners led to its break-up or intra-party controversies caused a split in a party or faction, thus prompting a change of head of government or ministers.[27]

The average time government members spend in office is considered an indication of the effectiveness of a government's policy implementation.

Cabinet members are said to need at least three years in office to substantially influence the process of political decision-making and introduce new policies.[28] In the eastern EU countries, though, government members surviving more than three years in office have rather been the exception. From 1990 to 2008, heads of government were in office for an average of only 2.4 years. Slightly more than one quarter of prime ministers (28 per cent) did not survive a year in office. Over time, governments tend to become more stable and stay in office longer, which indicates a successful consolidation of the political system.[29]

Parliament

In all post-communist countries, the legislative power lies with the respective parliament. Concerning parliaments, institutional consolidation appears on the whole to be completed. Most of the countries have unicameral parliaments. Germany, Poland, Romania, Slovenia and the Czech Republic further involve a second chamber in the legislative process, but in all these countries (except Germany) the second chamber's right to exist has often been debated.[30]

The eastern EU countries' parliaments have clearly proven more stable than their governments. In the early phase of transformation in most of these countries, a new government had to be formed almost every year, but only in single cases were parliamentary elections held early. The parliaments of East Central European countries were characterized by quite a high degree of the institutional and political independence that favours parliamentary work. However, turbulence within party systems and voter volatility led to low numbers of re-elected MPs – significantly lower than in Western Europe – which proved disadvantageous and also slowed the professionalization of parliamentary work.[31]

The parliaments developed cooperative structures to allow for a more efficient division of work and competences. In the parliaments of the eastern EU countries, changes in standing orders in the 2002–2010 period (except in Poland and Bulgaria) resulted in expanded minority rights, particularly clearly in the Czech Republic and Slovakia. The position of permanent committees relative to parliamentary plenaries was institutionally strengthened, allowing not only for improved inclusion of opposition MPs but also overall re-evaluation of the position of the legislative regarding the executive.[32] In the context of juridification of political decision-making processes in the consolidation period of 1990–2012, parliamentary committees' significance for legislative work tended to increase.[33]

In the course of the transformation process, the parliaments of the eastern EU countries have proven capable of decision-making and acting, and thus of considerably influencing the process of transformation and consolidation. Despite virulent majority situations, in the transformation phase 1990–2012 an enormous number of laws necessary for transition – from state economy to private market economy, from dictatorship to democracy, from a strictly central state administration to regional and local self-administration, and from a controlled society to an open, structured civil society – were successfully passed. A second, extreme legislative effort concerned the process of joining the EU; in this context, hundreds of legal norms of the *Acquis communautaire* had to be adopted and included in each country's legal system.

Electoral systems, elections and voting behaviour
GENERAL STATEMENTS ON ELECTORAL SYSTEMS IN THE CONTEXT OF THE CONSOLIDATION PROCESS   From the perspective of consolidation, elections may well have an ambivalent effect: without them the consolidation process would not be possible, but at the same time, elections may result in political constellations that negatively affect the consolidation process. In this sense, both relative and absolute majority systems may obstruct democratic consolidation. Against all expectations, majority representation did not, in countries where it had been introduced, have any stabilizing effect on the governments because the party systems were highly fragmented and parties showed only a low degree of cohesion. Meanwhile, systems of purely proportional representation without thresholds made it harder to form stable parliamentary majorities and affected the governments' stability as well, in that representation of too many political groups in parliament led to heterogeneous coalitions and short-lived cabinets. Systems of proportional representation with thresholds proved the best solution, contributing to the consolidation of party systems and a relatively high degree of government stability.[34]

ELECTORAL SYSTEMS IN THE EASTERN EU REGION   In both eastern EU countries and the Federal Republic of Germany, elections are based on general, equal, direct suffrage and the secret ballot. Accordingly, they may be called free and mostly fair. None of these countries has compulsory suffrage. In most, all citizens aged eighteen and older are eligible to vote; however, voting age is twenty-three in Romania and twenty-five in Lithuania. In all eastern EU countries, the regular legislative term is four years. In Estonia and Latvia in the 1990s, the legitimacy of elected institutions was partly limited because strong Russian minorities were denied citizenship rights and thus also suffrage.[35] Latvia still refuses to grant citizenship rights to some of its Russian-speaking minority and thus excludes about 15 per cent of the population from elections.[36]

The constitutional rootedness of an electoral system encourages stability in the political system, thus reducing the risk that a temporary simple majority will manipulate electoral law for reasons of political power. However, only in Estonia, Latvia and the Czech Republic is the electoral system constitutionally fixed. In the other states it was decided by passing an ordinary law, though in several countries any change to the electoral law requires a qualified parliamentary majority.[37] No post-communist country (other than the East German federal states) simply imported a proven electoral system, and in all cases considerations of political power weighed more heavily in deciding on a certain electoral system than did the possibility of adopting proven patterns. The respective groups of actors always preferred the foreign or national model that they expected to best suit their own electoral results. In Hungary, some changes made to the electoral law to serve the interests of the FIDESZ leadership were rooted in the 2012 constitution; however, the Hungarian Constitutional Court declared important elements of these regulations null and void, as they contradicted the constitution.[38]

During the 1990–2012 transformation process, the tendency was towards systems of proportional representation that, typologically speaking, resemble each other more than they do those in Western Europe. Those countries that had initially introduced systems of majority representation or mixed systems when the transformation began later adopted systems of proportional representation.[39] In the interests of making government coalitions more stable, reducing the high degree of fragmentation in the parliaments and stabilizing the party systems, these systems of proportional representation were modified by thresholds (in most countries 5 per cent, in Bulgaria 4 per cent and in Slovenia 3 per cent). In Slovakia, Latvia and the Czech Republic, thresholds are even higher for electoral alliances, to prevent the thresholds' circumvention. In most eastern EU countries, the existence of multi-seat constituencies forms a natural obstacle to party fragmentation. At constituency level, 'loose' tickets often allow changes in the sequence of candidates on the ticket.[40]

ELECTIONS In the first free elections, the populations of Central East and South East Europe turned out enthusiastically in high numbers to welcome their newly gained freedom of suffrage after the long period of communist dictatorship. But the voters were soon disappointed by institutionalized democracy as well as the social problems caused by the transition from state to market economy. Thus, turnout declined significantly in subsequent elections. In earlier parliamentary elections in the post-communist area, turnout was generally about 60 per cent, though Lithuania (46 per cent) and Romania (39 per cent) achieved negative records. In Poland,

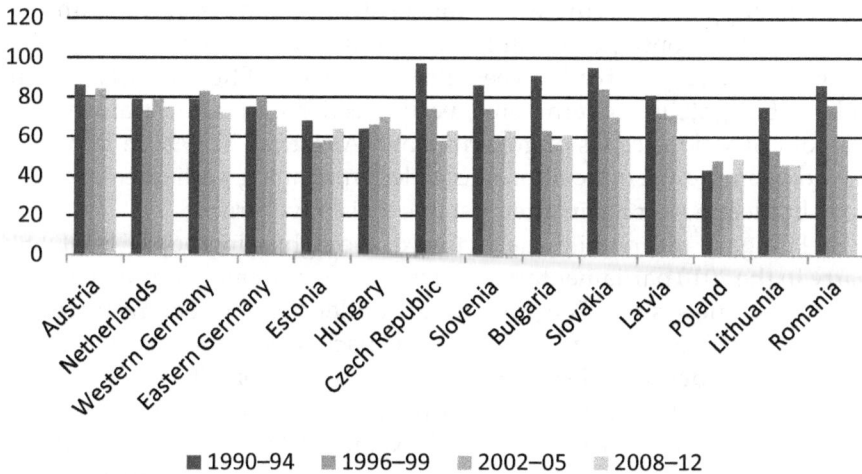

1990–94   **1996–99**   **2002–05**   **2008–12**

FIGURE 12.3. Parliamentary election voter turnout in percentages

Sequence of countries according to latest turnout; Austria, the Netherlands and western Germany are reference countries.

Source: European Election Database (http://www.nsd.uib.no/european_election_database/country; accessed 28 February 2012); for FRG-West und FRG-East: Deutscher Bundestag, 'Entwicklung der Wahlbeteiligung in der Bundesrepublik Deutschland 2009' (Berlin, 2009).

too, citizens' participation in parliamentary elections – always below 50 per cent – must be considered low. For the 2009 European elections, turnout in the eastern EU states was only 32 per cent on average; in Slovakia and Lithuania, only one fifth of eligible voters (20–21 per cent) took part.[41] In the eastern EU states and the East of Germany, voter turnout is permanently lower than in the established democracies of the reference countries of Austria, the Netherlands and the West of Germany (Figure 12.3). This is attributable to the rudimentary state of civil society as well as scepticism among populations that, having been disappointed several times, are convinced their own (voting) behaviour is unlikely to influence their governments' policies.[42] Bulgaria and Romania even recorded a clear decline in the turnout for parliamentary elections.[43]

VOTING BEHAVIOUR   As regards voting behaviour, different political-cultural regions can be identified. In the East Central European states, the regime issue was decided by the founding elections.[44] In the two South Eastern European countries Bulgaria and Romania, on the other hand, the so far authoritarian Communist Party managed, by shuffling its top personnel and taking advantage of its existing party structures, to mobilize enough electoral support to secure a win for (post-)communists in the founding elections. As a consequence, Bulgaria has had extremely frequent parliamentary elections – five between 1990 and 2001. When a party system fails to form stable governments, early elections are almost always the way out of serious crises of government.[45] As late as in 1996 in Romania, the non-communist opposition succeeded in winning parliamentary elections but lost power again after just one legislative term.

In Hungary, meanwhile, the victory of the right-wing populist FIDESZ party in the 2010 parliamentary elections seems extremely problematic for the democratic system. The government under Victor Orbán restructured Hungary's political system, thus stepping back from principles of a democratic state under the rule of law. By way of a new constitution, as well as further organizational and staff measures, it has weakened the separation of powers, centralized the state and expanded the power of the prime minister. As for the assessment of Hungary's democracy in the long run, a clearly negative trend is clear.[46] Some authors do not completely rule out the possibility that democracy in Hungary will morph into a hybrid regime, melting elements of democracy and elements of authoritarian rule into one.[47]

Judicial system and judiciary
CONSTITUTIONAL COURTS   After the collapse of the communist regimes in Central and Eastern Europe, independent constitutional jurisdiction triumphed. In reaction to the totalitarian arbitrariness of parliamentary majorities organized by the communist parties and to instrumentalization of the law in abuses of power, the nascent democracies established legal institutions for the protection of constitutional and human rights. In the post-communist EU region, constitutional jurisdiction has proven to be a key factor in the juridification of previously erratic political conflicts. The constitutional courts of the eastern EU countries (except Estonia) are modelled on the concept of specialized, concentrated constitutional jurisdiction. In the eastern EU countries, constitutional judges have more extensive competences than in Western Europe.[48]

Besides actual judicial review in the context of an ordinary legal proceeding, all these eastern states introduced abstract judicial review, which may proceed independently of any actual legal case. The right of petition is always accorded to the President of the State and usually also to the government. In most eastern EU countries, a parliamentary minority or a certain parliamentary quorum may ask that a law or other legal norm be reviewed for its constitutionality, a right that can also be used as a political tool by the opposition. The basic possibility that the opposition may bring a constitutional action against a constitutionally dubious law passed by the government majority also has the pre-emptive effect of forcing the government to act constitutionally.[49]

In all eastern EU countries and in the Federal Republic, verdicts of the constitutional courts are definitive and accepted as a matter of principle. On the whole, these courts have been able to maintain their independence and play an indispensable role in the process of democratic consolidation by juridifying political processes and successively overcoming dichotomies between constitutional law and constitutional reality.[50] Yet despite the frequently positive account of independent constitutional jurisdiction, a number of institutional conflicts have arisen between constitutional courts and other state authorities, in particular the executive. The FIDESZ-led government in Hungary caused a considerable stir when, helped by its constitutional parliamentary majority, it changed the personnel of the Constitutional Court to suit its own intentions and restricted the court's competences.[51] And Hungary's head of government, Orbán, enforced compulsory early retirement of judges until the European Court of Justice put a stop to the practice, calling unfounded compulsory retirement an act of discrimination.[52]

In 2012, the Romanian Constitutional Court played a crucial role in a conflict that caused quite a commotion, even internationally, when Romania's Prime Minister Victor Ponta and his cabinet attempted illegally to remove President Traian Băsescu from office. At first, the parliamentary majority of the government coalition suspended the president from office. To finally relieve him of office, however, the constitution demanded that a quorum of 50 per cent of eligible voters participate in a referendum on the topic. This quorum was not attained, though the overwhelming majority of voters who did vote favoured removing the president from office. The Romanian Constitutional Court, which had to determine the constitutionality of the referendum, declared it null and void because the quorum requirement had not been met. The judges revealed that before the decision, the government and Interim President Crin Antonescu had subjected them to enormous pressure, including threats to their families. After the court announced its verdict, leading representatives of the government camp defamed the judges as '*politruci* [political officers] of the illegitimate President Băsescu'.[53] The behaviour of the Ponta government drew fierce criticism both nationally and internationally. In particular, the EU and western EU states criticized Romania sharply, showing their determination to defend the independence of its judiciary.[54] Only the insistent reaction of the EU and the United States kept the government coalition under Ponta from realizing its intentions through massive violation of valid legal norms.[55] The Romanian and Hungarian examples demonstrate that whether a country is an EU member state is of the utmost significance for democracy and rule of law in the post-communist region.

ORDINARY JURISDICTION   The independence of the courts is constitutionally guaranteed in all eastern EU countries. However, ordinary jurisdiction still suffers from considerable deficits concerning the way the judicial system works as well as legal certainty and law enforcement. After the turnaround, the judicial systems of Central and South Eastern European countries were enormously overburdened and, due to a number of factors, inefficient. As entire societal and economic systems were transformed, legislation also changed fundamentally, and at breath-taking speed. Judges had to work according to new laws and new principles that they had first to learn. Inundated with numerous complicated trials about property restitution and commercial disputes between newly created enterprises, the courts found themselves wholly unprepared due to a lack of capacity and judges' insufficient education. Often the material equipment of the judiciary was also insufficient. Sometimes the weakness of state mechanisms of regulation and enforcement allowed a shadow judiciary of non-state, private and sometimes criminal self-help to develop.[56]

State of institutional consolidation 2012
The constitutional or institutional consolidation of systems in the post-communist region has progressed relatively well. The systems proved sufficiently capable of institutional learning, and during the transformation from 1990 to 2012 they cleared away the major potential obstructions to their functioning. Comparatively stable institutional configurations developed, demonstrating adequate institutional efficiency, transparency and inclusion. The texts of the eastern EU countries' constitutions envision these states as developing under the rule of law and pluralist democracy, and emphasize the maxim of the people's sovereignty. All these constitutions explicitly guarantee human rights – which, in contrast to the previous situation under communist regimes, are generally indeed respected.

In Germany, the new federal states were surprisingly rapidly integrated satisfactorily into the institutional system of the Federal Republic. The successful change of the political system, the gaining of freedom and establishment of democracy in the former East Germany, the achievement of parity between East and West, and the development of a common system under the rule of law, common federal structures and municipal self-administration are part of the successful record of East German transformation and German-German integration. However, the advantages of privileged transformation had a flip side: institutions, rules and norms that were elite-controlled and introduced 'from the outside' during the East German transformation process were – and still are – only weakly rooted in the lifeworlds of the citizens of the East German federal states.[57]

Institutional consolidation requires not only that a suitable institutional constellation be elaborated in detail, but also that the contributing actors uphold the rules. In this respect, the entire post-communist EU region still faces a backlog. The justice and administration systems are not yet efficient enough to actually guarantee the democratic standards and human rights that are legally laid out in the respective constitutions. This is the source of another deficit at the institutional level – the gulf between constitutional text and constitutional reality.[58]

Intermediary Consolidation

Political parties and party systems

At the beginning of the period of consolidation, the main line of conflict within the developing party system was the confrontation between supporters of communist dictatorship and reformists. This struggle about the nature of the regime soon gave way to socio-economic conflict pitting the radical market liberalism typical of the early 1990s, represented by conservative or right-wing parties, against state-dominated gradualism, preferred by Social Democratic and (post-)communist parties.[59] In the Baltic states of Estonia, Latvia and Lithuania, however, the main line of conflict is still the ethno-political cleavage between the given titular nation and its Russian-speaking minorities.[60]

The party systems in the post-communist EU region are still in the midst of a lively development period. Confidence in political parties is low; compared to the Netherlands or Austria, it is twice as low in the East of the Federal Republic of Germany and as much as twenty times lower in Latvia (see Figure 12.4). Parties are frequently newly founded, split and fused as well as strategically and programmatically restructured. Meanwhile, the high degree of virulence experienced in the first years of transformation appears to be past. Despite the variety of electoral laws, the eastern EU countries have mostly managed to maintain multi-party systems; bipolar party systems form a minority.[61]

Relatively long-lasting bipolar party systems have developed in the Czech Republic, Hungary and Slovakia. The bipolar party system in Slovakia, however, was destroyed in the wake of the notorious 'Gorilla' affair, a corruption scandal involving the government's party, the Slovakian Democratic and Christian Union (SDKÚ), which consequently achieved only 6 per cent of votes in the 2012 parliamentary elections.[62] Multipolar, highly fragmented multi-party systems have developed

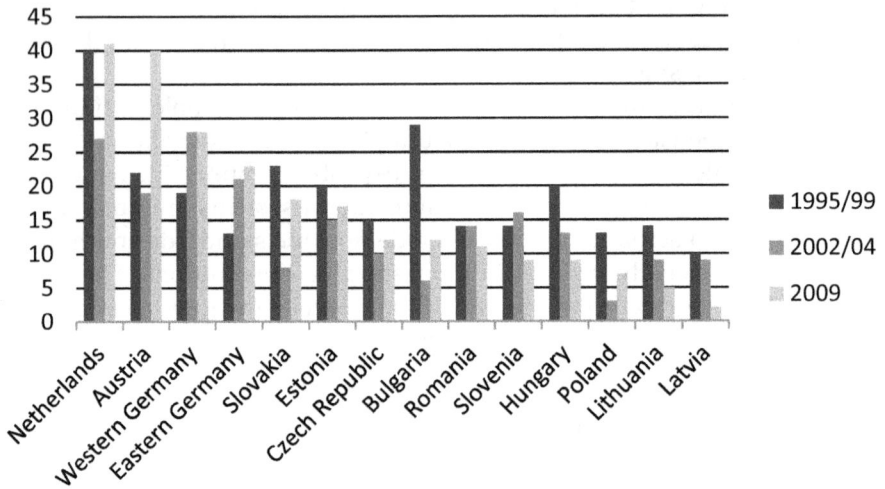

FIGURE 12.4. Confidence in political parties, percentage

Sequence of countries according to figures from 2009; the Netherlands, Austria and western Germany serve as reference countries. Distinguishing marks of the answers were: Very much, quite much trust/not very much, no trust at all.

Sources: 1996/99 = WVS 1995/98 or on reference country Eurobarometer 51 (1999); 2002/04 = Eurobarometer 61 (2004) or on FRG-West and East, Allbus 2002; 2009 = Democracy Index based on Eurobarometer 2009; for Netherlands and Austria, Eurobarometer 71; for FRG-West and East, Allbus 2008. With WVS 1995/98 = four possible answers; with Eurobarometer 51 = two possible answers; with Allbus 2002 = as seven-levelled scale (own calculations – considered to express trust in case of figures from 3.5 to 7).

in Poland, Slovenia and Estonia. Yet despite the marked pluralism of political parties, the party systems can be said to incline towards consolidation.[63] The multipolar party systems in Lithuania, Latvia, Romania and Bulgaria, on the other hand, are still in a troubled period. These party systems are characterized by multifarious renamings, splits and fusions; voting behaviour is immensely volatile. Frequently changing governments are another reflection of the instability of these party systems.[64]

As a rule, political parties in the post-communist EU region are based on low membership numbers. The share of government party members in the overall population in the western Federal Republic, at 10 per thousand, is more than double the 4 per thousand reported for the eastern Federal Republic. Austria's 112-per-thousand share is thirty-seven times higher than the 3 per thousand in the Czech Republic, which originally was culturally related to Austria and had a rich tradition of associations (see Figure 12.5). The parties suffer from lack of participation by citizens

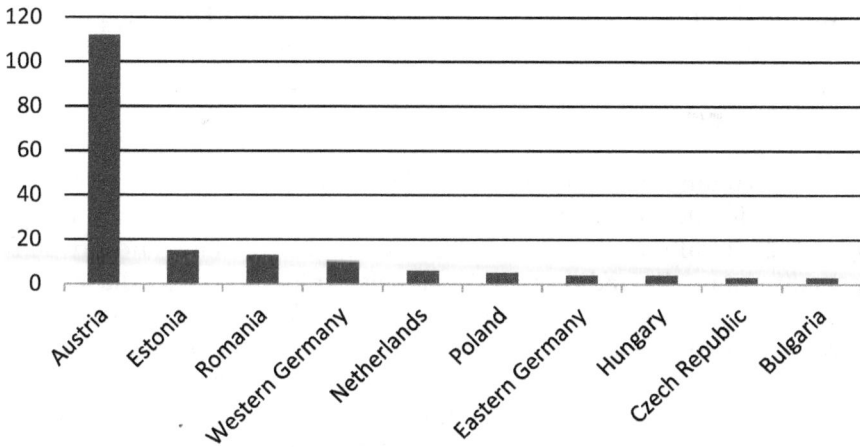

FIGURE 12.5. Share of members of government parties of the total population (per thousand)

Sources: party pages in the respective national language; for Netherlands: Konrad-Adenauer-Stiftung, Berlin/St. Augustin; for FGR-West and East: O. Niedermayer, *Parteimitglieder in Deutschland: Version 2011* (Berlin, 2011). Romania: the more than average number of party members results from one government party, the Democratic Union of Hungarians in Romania, with about 85,000 members, being both an ethnic party and a cultural association.

who, having lived under dictatorship, are mostly depoliticized and distrustful towards political parties, which thus are only loosely rooted in society.[65] Their organizations are consequently grievously out of touch with the desires and interests of the citizens.[66] Accordingly, party leaderships, in their executive and parliamentary offices, make essential decisions with little consideration of the opinions of citizens and convictions of party members. In so doing, the parties easily become vulnerable to political capture by powerful, wealthy interest groups.

Politics and 'business' are often closely interwoven, and cash flow transparency is low.[67] Under conditions of sometimes endemic corruption, economic interest groups transfer enormous sums to political parties to secure the benevolence of current and future government parties, tailor-made laws and public contracts. This happens both legally and, according to several reports, illegally.[68] Some parties are said to have 'a direct interest in staying weak in membership to minimize the internal influence of ordinary party members'; therefore, decisions about candidates and their positions are said to be taken 'among small groups and under the influence of donors'.[69] Monopolization of political parties by financially powerful interest groups ('oligarchs' or 'godfathers') impairs the development of organized political interests, reduces the acceptance of democracy among the population and slows the democratic consolidation of party systems.[70] Estonia, a country with an above-average share of party members, is remarkable in that the 'oligarchs' have no particular influence on politics.[71]

Media

After the communist monopoly on information was broken, the eastern EU countries developed mostly pluralist media systems within a short period. Especially in the early 1990s, the number of state- and privately owned print media, radio and TV channels exploded. The media systems of the Baltic states may be considered particularly progressive. There, freedom of expression and the freedom of press are guaranteed not only legally, by the constitution, but also in practice, by the great variety of media. Thus, the Baltic states achieve top rankings. In fact, Estonia's media system is a pioneer even in worldwide comparison, due to widespread public access to the internet and numerous internet providers (see Figure 12.6).[72]

The duality of media under public law alongside privately owned media tends to increase the independence of reporting, as the privately owned media in the eastern EU countries are mostly in foreign hands. Providers under public law are sometimes regulated and partly controlled.[73] However, Freedom House analyses for the 2002–2011 period indicate that the freedom of the media in Slovakia, Hungary, Bulgaria and Romania is diminished in comparison to others (see Figure 12.6).[74] The Bertelsmann Transformation Index (BTI) report has likewise characterized media freedom in East Central and South East Europe as eroded.[75] Contributing to this situation are the weakness of civil society, political parties' insufficient rootedness in society and the high degree of voter volatility, among other factors. Many governments or party leaderships believe intensive control of the media is a suitable means of winning voters over.[76]

Hungary in particular presents cause for alarm.[77] The FIDESZ party leadership created a new media authority and appointed its staff, who are supposed to regulate the media market while also topically controlling the media, and thus are able to draconically sanction possible 'offences' such as 'unbalanced reporting'. Nine hundred unwelcome public-media journalists have been fired in a wave not unlike a political purge in the period of dictatorship. The many signs of gross violation of the constitutional guarantee of the freedom of media and press have incurred fierce criticism both nationally and internationally. The EU Commission has officially informed Hungary that it believes the new media law is not consistent with EU law.[78] Under pressure from the Organization for Security and Co-operation in Europe (OSCE), EU institutions and EU member states, the Orbán government annulled at least some of the discriminatory regulations in 2011.[79]

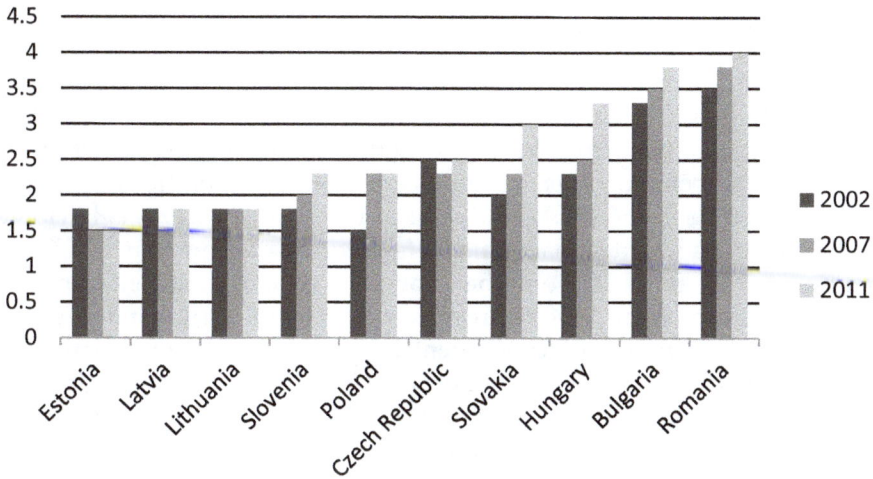

FIGURE 12.6. Independence of media 2002–2011

Sequence of countries according to 2011 figures; 1= highest degree of freedom for media, 7 = lowest degree.

Source: Freedom House. See also M. Brusis, 'Ostmittel- und Südosteuropa: Die demokratische Konsolidierung bleibt aus', in Bertelsmann Stiftung (ed.), *Transformationsindex BTI 2012* (Gütersloh, 2011), 58–66, here 60.

Interest groups

After chaotic beginnings, a mostly structured system of interest representation has taken root in the post-communist EU states. The constitutional guarantees of the freedom of association, right of assembly and right to strike have fostered a broad variety of professional associations, trade unions and citizens' initiatives and increased the capacity to mobilize. Employers' associations and trade unions have gained strength; in fact, trade unions are among the biggest intermediary organizations. The significance of entrepreneurs' associations has also grown. Furthermore, industrial, business and agricultural associations have flourished; likewise, cultural associations and sports clubs as well as various citizens' initiatives have clearly grown in number. But even though legal and tax-related framework conditions are in place to support the existing network of interest groups, citizens' readiness to participate often proves insufficient.

Concerning the role of churches and religious communities, substantial differences between individual eastern EU countries prevail. In Poland, Romania and Slovakia, ties to the different Christian churches are still strong. In the mostly secularized Czech Republic, on the other hand, religion plays a less significant role, although rural residents and older people still have much confidence in religion.[80]

Consolidation of Behaviour: Formal and Informal Actors

To assess the consolidation of behaviour in the post-communist EU, we must distinguish formal from informal political actors. Nevertheless, the consolidation of behaviour in the two groups is interconnected, as close ties between economic interest groups and politics are particularly likely to cause deficits in the consolidation of formal political actors' behaviour. Political parties are often inadequately funded and depend on both official and unofficial funding from the economic sphere; sufficient funding for election campaigns is sometimes crucial to them. Parties and individual party functionaries are consequently highly susceptible to corruption in all fields of the process of political decision-making – the legislative process as well as the work of governments, both of which are strongly oriented to clientelism. All eastern EU countries are characterized by massive (and in Bulgaria and Romania, endemic) corruption that hinders further economic development, compromises both the legitimacy and acceptance of the democratic system, and detracts from the appeal of any given business location.[81] The immense difference between the intensity of corruption in the established democracies of the reference countries (the Netherlands, Austria, Germany[82]) and in the eastern EU countries even tended to grow between 1999 and 2011. None of the eastern EU countries qualitatively improved during that period – on the contrary, the situation has worsened in most, and very much so in some (see Figure 12.7).

As for the behaviour of informal political actors (e.g. the armed forces, financial capital, entrepreneurs), the crucial question is whether they pursue their interests within or outside of the legitimate political system. The army is loyal in every eastern EU country, but the entrepreneurial sector is not infrequently characterized by a tendency to pursue its interests outside the institutional and legal structures of the state. Many enterprises are tempted to advance their interests by illegitimate means such as bribery and clientelism. Particularly in South Eastern Europe, the danger that organized crime poses to young democracies should not be underestimated. The many opportunities that financially powerful interest groups, sometimes even organized crime, have to influence the political process might lead to enduring legal vacuums in the post-communist societies, preventing further consolidation of democracy under the rule of law.[83]

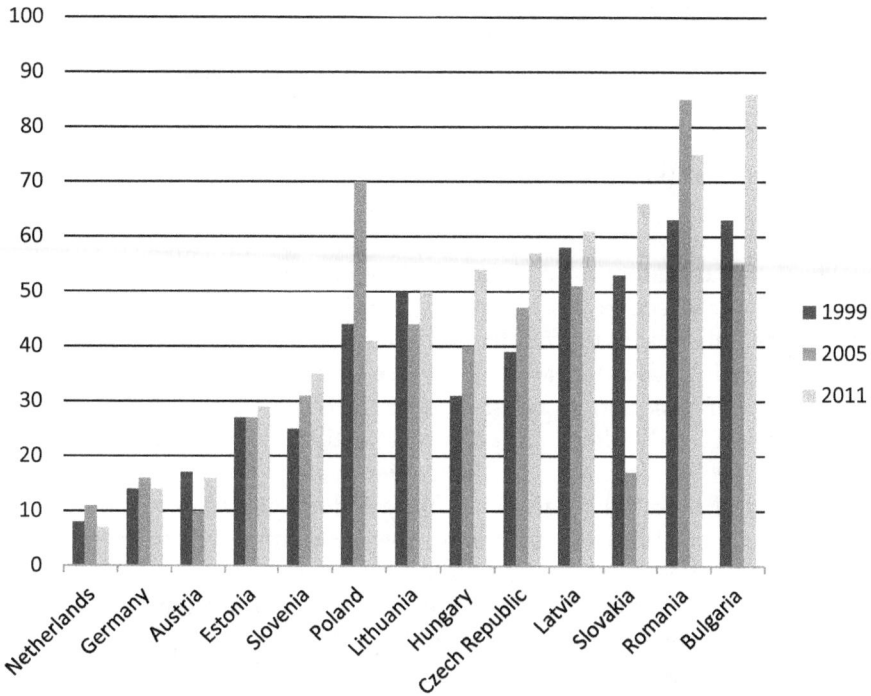

FIGURE 12.7. Ranking in the Corruption Perceptions Index 1999–2011

Netherlands, Germany and Austria as reference countries, sequence of countries according to 2011 figures. In 1999 the CPI evaluated 99 countries; in 2005, 159 countries; in 2011, 183 countries.

Source: Transparency International, Corruption Perceptions Indexes 1999–2011 (http://www.transparency.org).

Economy

Motivation Crisis as a Trigger of System Change

In the 1960s, a new development in the industrial countries was intensified by the oil shocks of the 1970s and 1980s: the world's technologically most advanced countries extended or qualitatively improved their production while stabilizing their consumption of energy and raw materials. That is, the focus of economic development shifted from extensive to intensive factors – economic initiatives, efficiency, innovative thinking. However, this new emphasis in economic development and the resultant increased importance of motivation caused serious setbacks for 'real existing socialism', as the centralized system of planned economy was incapable of moving beyond resource-wasting extensive (i.e. mainly quantitative instead of qualitative) growth. Blocked private initiative, hiring based on ideological criteria rather than performance, nepotism, paternalism and lack of competition resulted in an entirely insufficiently motivated workforce. Systems of planned economy suffered from increasing unproductiveness, lack of technological innovation and outmoded structures of production. The deficient mechanisms of market and money control could not be balanced through central planning because the socialist theory of central planning was utopian.

However, transition to a more efficient economic system was impossible without effective motivation of people. The communist one-party system had always had difficulty stimulating activity, initiative and innovative thinking, for its basic structural elements (state ownership of the means of production, centralized control of society and economy, communist cadre policy) stifled any effective motivation to perform. Thus, the economic failure of the Soviet system was due above all to its structural inability to adjust to the modern global development by turning from the dead end of extensive economic growth to a model of intensive growth. Here the system's immanent dearth of motivation was a crucial obstacle, as the absence of an effective system of incentives would doom such a transition to failure. The wide-ranging economic crisis that had been chronic since the 1970s developed into a creeping erosion of 'real existing socialism', forcing the Soviet leadership to initiate perestroika and thereby becoming a major cause of the turnaround in Eastern Europe.[84]

A Difficult New Beginning

Transition from state-planned economy to free market economy required a difficult, multilevel process of adjustment and reform. The transformation of economic systems in the post-communist EU region entailed a socially painful 'shock treatment' in the form of price liberalization and the abandonment of the tools of central planning, extensive privatization of state property and, at the same time, creation of institutions charged with organizing fair competition in the context of a developing market economy. Negative interactions between still-incomplete economic, legal and political subsystems made the overall transition even more difficult.

Price liberalization and other kinds of 'shock treatment'
Liberalization of state-regulated prices during the transition from planned to market economy was a radical measure. To initiate the market economy process of free pricing, longstanding, socio-politically influenced

fixed prices had to be raised. The centrally fixed prices were frequently much lower than the actual value of goods and services, so in all transition countries price liberalization resulted in soaring prices and even, in several countries, hyperinflation as inflation rates reached several hundred per cent – 585 per cent in Poland in 1990, 334 per cent in Bulgaria in 1991, 210 per cent in Romania in 1992. Recipients of nominally fixed transfer incomes, in particular pensioners, were especially hard hit by this price explosion, which indeed often threatened them with ruin.[85]

Poland was the first country in the dissolving Soviet sphere to introduce a market economy. On 1 January 1990, Finance Minister Leszek Balcerowicz launched a 'shock treatment' that became both legendary and infamous: state regulation of the economy was almost completely abandoned, while the zloty become freely convertible. In 1990, these measures led to a 12 per cent drop in economic growth and the above-mentioned hyperinflation of 585 per cent, which in turn diminished real incomes by almost 25 per cent.[86]

In Estonia in 1992, the democratically elected Isamaaliit government was the first legitimate government to initiate an actual, comprehensive transformation of Estonia's economic system. However, the transition occurred in stages.[87] Latvia's economic transformation also happened in several steps, during which the government prioritized fiscal and political stability over privatization and liberalization.[88] Latvia signed a free trade agreement with its Baltic neighbours in 1993.[89] In Lithuania, the state remained involved in pricing, aiming to socially balance rising prices. Even today the Lithuanian state has the right to intervene in individual sectors such as public transport or the energy market.[90]

The most urgent problem in the former East Germany was mass emigration from East to West after the border was opened in November 1989. The Treaty on the Creation of a Currency, Economic and Social Union, effective as of 1 July 1990, provided that all current payments be switched 1:1 from the GDR mark to the deutschmark. In the course of 1990, the currency union and high wage agreements caused the East-West ratio to rise to more than 5:1.[91] Exploding wages – a product of massive political-social pressure in violation of all economic rules, combined with the GDR's legacy of low productivity – caused industrial collapse throughout eastern Germany and, as a consequence, dramatic job losses. From 1989 to 1993, the number of employees declined by two million (from 7.8 million to 5.8 million),[92] and by mid 1991 the output of East German plants had declined by about a quarter since 1989.[93] Bundesbank president Karl Otto Pöhl, who resigned at that time, went to the heart of the contradiction between economic rationality and political enforceability when he declared the 1:1 introduction of the deutschmark to have been 'an economically disastrous decision. . . . This way, at that time all enterprises went bankrupt at a stroke'. However, 'given the political practice in Germany', a realistic exchange rate 'would not have been implementable. The East German population would not have accepted such a huge pay gap. . . . [Helmut] Kohl as well as the entire political class of the Federal Republic were under immense pressure'.[94]

Price liberalization in the Czech Republic and Slovakia had taken place when they were still Czechoslovakia. One Czechoslovakian particularity was the difference between the (politically advantageous) radical rhetoric of Finance Minister Václav Klaus, who demanded a pure 'market economy without adjectives', and the actual, rather careful and pragmatic way of proceeding. On New Year's Day 1991, a 'shock treatment-like' deregulation of prices took effect, affecting about 85 per cent of all goods. As many had feared, there was indeed inflation, but at 70 per cent it was rather moderate compared to other transition countries.[95] The price shock triggered by Prague, which hit the poorer Slovakian population harder than the Czechs, was one of the causes of the split of Czechoslovakia.[96]

The first shock to the Slovenian economy was the drastic shrinking of the market upon Yugoslavia's dissolution (from 22 million Yugoslav consumers down to two million in Slovenia). Slovenian enterprises, which for decades had sold most of their products on the Yugoslav market, experienced a severe crisis. In 1992, the country's economic output was only two thirds of that of 1988, and inflation and unemployment soared.[97]

Hungary had passed a modern law on competition before the turnaround, initiating competition, making it easier to found enterprises and introducing spontaneous privatization. Economically speaking, it was better prepared for transformation than any other post-communist EU country. However, it was not able to make reasonable use of this advantage. Several attempts at socially balanced modernization ended in failure. At last, when it could no longer even ensure basic macro-economic stability, the government and Finance Minister Lajos Bokros changed course towards the 'shock treatment' propagated by the IMF and World Bank, with the attendant social consequences.[98] Romania, by contrast, was completely unprepared for the transition from planned to market economy. Price liberalization and other radical reforms brought a 30 per cent decline in GDP, hyperinflation and high unemployment.[99]

Privatization
Privatization was at the core of the political transformation from planned to market economy. It affected the structure of the economy, society and politics. The transition countries launched market-controlled, competitive allocation processes by breaking the state monopolies and supporting

the founding of new enterprises. Most state enterprises were privatized by several methods: sale to (often foreign) investors, voucher privatization (distribution of shares among the population), sale to the companies' management. In most countries, privatization was more difficult and took longer than liberalization, as the privatization process was often impeded by irregularities, corruption and misappropriation.

In Estonia, denationalization started as early as 1990, by way of minor privatization. Only Estonian citizens were entitled to participate in the auctions. For major privatization, the privatization enterprise Erastamisettevötte, modelled after the German Treuhand, was founded to purposefully attract foreign investors. In Latvia, privatization laws passed in 1992 allowed for several ways of transforming property: auctions, leasing, transformation into corporations, participation of the population by way of free vouchers[100] or even liquidation. Privatization of small enterprises and restitution of buildings and real estate were the first steps; major privatization followed later.[101] Privatization in Lithuania started with the distribution of vouchers, which helped large parts of the population buy homes or enterprises.[102] Until 1998, the foreign investors so urgently needed for the modernization of Lithuania's economy were scarce because restrictions on the purchase of real estate by foreigners led to investment insecurity.[103] In Poland, privatization followed various models. The privatization of state enterprises was relatively slow, so the initial private sector expansion was due mainly to newly founded enterprises.[104]

As of 1 July 1990 in East Germany, the Treuhandanstalt became the owner of all former *Volkseigene Betriebe* (nationally owned enterprises, which were changed into corporations), and took charge of privatizing almost 15,000 enterprises with about six million employees. About 70 per cent of enterprises could be successfully maintained in either private or public hands. The rest had to be liquidated. This radical political change (due in part to the currency union and wages that were too high because of unavoidable socio-political forces and the great pressure of competition) resulted in transformation costs much higher than the original estimates. Whereas the initial assumption had been that privatization of East German enterprises would bring proceeds of about 600 billion deutschmarks, which would mostly cover the costs of reunification, in the end the Treuhand had a deficit of about 230 billion deutschmarks.[105]

To sell former state property was to buy investors at the same time. In the Czech Republic, foreign direct investments assisted the speedy privatization and modernization of the comprehensive state economy. Smaller companies, most of them in the services sector, were sold to interested parties in the course of 'small privatization'. The big state enterprises were denationalized by way of voucher privatization – for a small fee, all citizens received shares in state enterprises that they could then exchange for shares or securities of the investment companies. The restitution law required a smaller share of state property to be returned to previous owners who had been expropriated by the Communists in 1948. Slovakia, like the Czech Republic, underwent a minor and a major privatization as well as restitution measures. In 1995, however, voucher privatization was ended and replaced by direct sales, which worked to the advantage of the clientele of Vladimír Mečiar's Movement for a Democratic Slovakia (HZDS).[106]

In Slovenia, the government under Janez Drnovšek passed a privatization law that stipulated generous restitution of property (including Church property). Part of the privatization process was the distribution of non-transferable vouchers to citizens, who could then exchange them for shares in enterprises. Some managed to invest these vouchers in successful companies, but many of the vouchers ended up in authorized investment companies (*pooblaščene investicijske družbe*, PID) without much value.

Privatization in Hungary happened in three stages: the time prior to the official system change, the years after the turnaround of 1989/90 and the 'Bokros Packet', and the final wave of privatization from 2002 to 2010. Several scandals and conflicts centred on the privatization of hospitals or individual water suppliers.[107] Romania's privatization began in 1992. Thirty per cent of the shares in each of 6,300-plus state-owned enterprises were transferred to five investment funds that were distributed among citizens. The remaining 70 per cent of shares went to the state-owned investment fund Fondul Proprietatii de Stat, which was supposed to sell 10 to 15 per cent every year. Other enterprises and property were sold directly. The share of employees working in the industrial sector declined from 40 per cent in 1990 to 25 per cent in 1999. Further privatization in the following years often resulted in companies being sold to foreign enterprises.[108]

The Process of Economic Consolidation 1990–2012

The transformation process in the eastern EU states was affected by extremely high inflation rates, surging numbers of unemployed and increased social security benefits for those hit hardest by the process. Political instability, reflected in unstable parliamentary majorities and short-lived governments, slowed the transformation of the legal system and the creation of adequate institutions. Popular trust in democracy and market economy was particularly relevant, as neither democracy nor market economy was likely to be sustainably consolidated without the support of the citizens who had to cope with the new living conditions and values.[109]

In Poland, a heavy recession, high unemployment and declining incomes soon led to widespread disappointment with the market economy. Not until twenty-five years later, in 2005, did real wages reach their 1980 levels.[110] On the other hand, by 1992 Poland had become the first former communist country to record positive rates of GDP growth, which continued in the following years. The economies of the Baltic states clearly grew faster than those in Western Europe (see Figure 12.15) until 2007, but financial crisis thereafter pushed the economies of the 'Baltic Tigers' into serious decline.

In the East German federal states, wages – paid in deutschmarks – rapidly rose to about 80 per cent of the West German level.[111] However, this jump was not commensurate with the increase in productivity and made labour costs much too high, reducing East German companies' competitiveness. West German goods flooded the East German market as the GDR's former export markets in Eastern Europe collapsed. Unfavourable economic factors (currency union, high wage agreements, low productivity, strong pressure of competition, collapse of traditional markets, uncompetitive products) were mutually dependent and reinforcing. Many companies resorted to massive layoffs or bankruptcy; underemployment and unemployment grew rapidly. In 2003, the unemployment rates reached a dramatic 20 per cent, higher than in most other transformation countries.[112] The shock was followed by lengthy, cost-intensive therapy. In the period 1990–2010, transfer payments from western to eastern Germany amounted to about 1.6 trillion euros[113] – more than 96,000 euros per East German citizen[114] or the equivalent of forty budgets of the Czech Republic.[115] Meanwhile the East German federal states developed into an effective business location with a highly modern infrastructure. In May 2012, their unemployment rate was at its lowest since 1989/90; however, it was still almost double that of the West (11 per cent in eastern Germany vs. 6 per cent in western Germany).[116]

The Czech Republic benefited from its central geographic location in Europe, its population's solid education and qualifications, and comparably low wages. Industry grew at an annual rate of 4–10 per cent.[117] At the same time, foreign investors preferred it to most other countries. German enterprises found it the most attractive location in Central and Eastern Europe and invested more there than in the growing markets of Brazil, Russia, China or India.[118] One disadvantage, however, was the Czech crown's fluctuation relative to the euro. Slovakia, which used to be somewhat backward compared to its Czech neighbour, has built a modern economy that has grown enormously (see Figure 12.15). On 1 January 2009, Slovakia became the first country of the former Soviet sphere to introduce the euro. Nonetheless, unemployment there is still notoriously high, and most people are dissatisfied with their living conditions.[119]

The Hungarian economy may be seen as a national economy integrating itself into the international division of labour, with a comparably strong industrial sector and a developing services sector. Risks and disadvantages include its inefficient administration, financial and political instability, excessive taxation, blocked reforms of the social system and a comparatively inflexible labour market. Slovenia, for its part, has well survived both the dissolution of Yugoslavia and the economic transition crisis. Since the system change, its economy has grown at an average annual rate of 4 per cent. In fact, Slovenia has the second-highest average income of all the post-communist EU states, after the former East Germany (see Figure 12.8).

With the dissolution of its centrally administered economy in 1990–92, Romania suffered a severe collapse of production. After a period of recovery from 1993 to 1996, in the 1997–99 period another transformation crisis struck, this time in a context of radical political decision-making. Expanded economic sectors had to be restructured, and loss-making enterprises had to close down. Industrial production sank by more than 20 per cent. In the period from 2000 to 2008, the privatization process intensified in the context of EU accession, and sustainable growth in GDP followed, due particularly to the export business.

Society

Historically Inherited Problems

The communist dictatorships destroyed not only political systems but also economic and legal systems as well as ownership structures. Moreover, forty years of violent rule deformed the moral and ethical values of the pre-totalitarian societies: constant pretence and lying in the public space, as well as bribery, were frequent means of securing one's very existence. People were socialized under conditions of permanent mendacious propaganda. And because the almighty Communist Party was itself the source of the boldest lies, the great majority of the population was highly distrustful of it.

Post-communist societies still exhibit extreme distrust towards political parties, even nearly three decades years after the revolutions; this holds for an astonishing 80 to 98 per cent of citizens.[120] Distrust of political parties – and in this context also of democratic institutions as a whole – is also the reason behind citizens' low willingness to participate. In most cases, they are sceptical about having any power to influence decision-making and

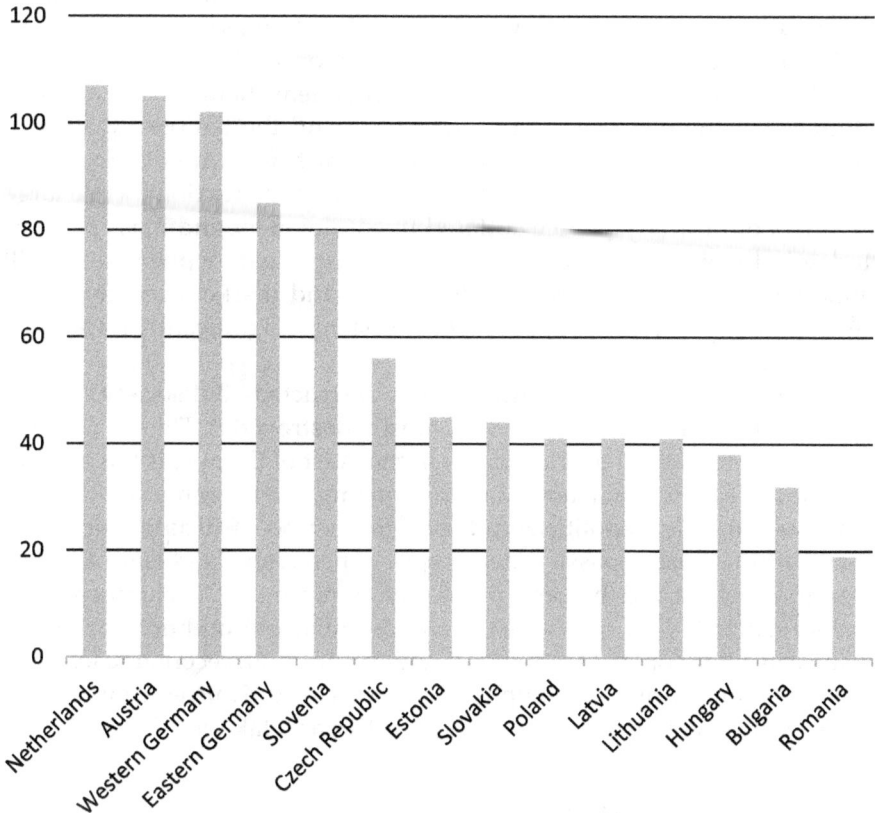

FIGURE 12.8. Average income in 2008 (post-communist EU region, average income as a percentage of the all-German average)

The Netherlands, Austria and western Germany are reference countries.

Sources: 'Medianes Nettoäquivalenzeinkommen in Kaufkraftstandards' (KKS), Index KKS (Deutschland = 100) (http://www.Bpb.de/nachschlagen/zahlen-und-fakten/europa/70628/einkommen); for FRG-West/ East: 'GfK Kaufkraft 2011: Anstieg nach glimpflich verlaufener Krise', 14 December 2010 (http://www. gfk-geomarketing.de/fileadmin/newsletter/pressemitteilung/kaufkraft-deutschland_2011.html; accessed 10 August 2012); own calculations.

are thus politically inactive. Comparison with established EU democracies makes this obvious; for example, voter turnout in the post-communist EU region is permanently clearly lower.[121]

At first, the citizens chafing at communist dictatorship had high expectations of the peaceful revolutions in their countries. But the greater their euphoria during the mass revolts, the deeper their disappointment soon after being confronted with actual democracy and the social consequences of the transition to market economy. Wide parts of the population were battered by the 'shock treatments' entailed in systemic change from planned to market economy. Corruption, already massively widespread in the 'real socialist' *ancien régime*, was further consolidated, reaching completely new dimensions. The side effects of system change – that is, abandonment of the old legal and social norms and the temporary absence of new ones – resulted in social anomie, which for a time allowed the new elites to enrich themselves free of normative restrictions while large numbers of ordinary people suffered unemployment and mass poverty. Today in the post-communist EU region, these negative phenomena still underlie widespread distrust of democracy and market economy. Even almost thirty years later, support for the system is significantly lower than in established democracies.[122]

Furthermore, the communist regimes obstructed civil society's development or, where it already existed, mostly destroyed it. This social class, which had developed over centuries in the West of Europe, is the foundation of both democracy and market economy. Post-communist citizens, who were mostly depoliticized during the period of dictatorship, must shake off their usual passive stereotypes of behaviour and learn to organize themselves and become politically committed. Development of a well-organized, vital civil society is an essential precondition for democratic consolidation.[123] Meanwhile, another enormous, economic learning process is underway as the population begins to cultivate entrepreneurial skills such as willingness to become proactive and take risks.

Sustainable Democratic Potential in East Central Europe

Several factors support the process of political, economic and social consolidation in the East Central European and Baltic EU countries, compared to other post-communist EU states.[124] Relics of pre-totalitarian democratic political culture survive in these societies, and overwhelming majorities of their populations see no alternative to either democracy or market economy. This way of understanding things was extremely important, particularly in the period of disorientation and chaos early in the transition to democracy, as it meant 'the other shore was in sight'. Moreover, the level of economic, social and cultural modernization and the tradition of qualified education that had already been achieved in pre-totalitarian times survived the period of communism to support the market-economic and democratic change. The statehood of all eastern EU countries became more consolidated immediately after the turnaround and has not been questioned by any relevant domestic or foreign political power.

The encouraging prospect of EU accession and the accession process with its demanding accession criteria, including EU membership itself, work as an additional, sustainable consolidation force. These factors – EU accession and consolidated statehood – also definitely support consolidation processes in South Eastern Europe (Romania and Bulgaria).

Consolidation of Civil Society

Political culture, legitimacy, stability
The nature of a country's developing political system hinges on its political culture. In post-communist EU countries that were able to connect to pre-communist traditions of democracy and could refer to certain surviving relics of pre-totalitarian political culture, democracies *in statu nascendi* developed and set off on the road towards consolidation. In those countries whose citizens had no experience of democracy, the post-communist transformation process evolved towards defective democracies or authoritarian regimes.[125]

Constitutional or institutional consolidation may happen smoothly and be largely controlled by the political centre. However, citizens' fundamental convictions about the political system and democratic values cannot simply be quickly changed by ruling elites or imported from elsewhere.[126] On the contrary, gradual change in stereotypes of behaviour and thinking, like the development of civil society, is long term in nature and subject to a variety of influences. Such change is a learning process requiring the participation of citizens, the media, political parties, and legislative, executive and judicial bodies as well as other actors. When a young democracy faces broad-based rejection, its legitimacy is dubious. Yet stability and crisis endurance basically depend on this legitimacy. In the long run, young democracies survive only when their populations fundamentally support them, even in times of severe crisis.[127]

By consolidation of civil society we mean development of a culture of civil society as the sociocultural foundation of democracy.[128] A consolidated civil society is characterized by the population's sustainable support of democracy through their attitudes and values, independently of the current economic and political account balance – that is, civic culture. Another component of civic culture is that citizens are as actively committed as possible to social and political life (civil society).[129]

The populations of the eastern EU countries and eastern German federal states clearly consider democracy the best possible system of government. The overwhelming majority agree with the statements that democracy is the most appropriate system of government and the idea of democracy is good in any case. Despite the overall context of general agreement with democracy, some differences are obvious – such as the greater agreement in the established democracies compared to the post-communist EU region (see Figure 12.9).

But the picture is completely different when it comes to judging democracy *in concreto* (see Figure 12.10). In the established democracies of the reference countries, majorities are satisfied with actual democracy even in times of crisis. In contrast, majorities of the peoples in the post-communist EU region are permanently dissatisfied with the reality of the democracies in their countries.[130]

In the 2009 ranking of countries by their satisfaction with democracy, the eastern part of the Federal Republic had fallen from first (in 1999) to sixth among post-communist EU countries. The situation in five post-communist EU countries must be considered precarious: overwhelming majorities of 80 per cent of citizens have at times been dissatisfied with democracy in these countries. Given such an exorbitant share of dissatisfied citizens, one may question the legitimacy and stability of the system: should a crisis become more severe, can a democracy with such a high share of dissatisfied citizens count on sustainable support from its population? We may assume that aspects of the political culture (e.g. distrust towards everything political, born of the experience of dictatorship) and deep disappointment in the reality of the democratic process account for the very high dissatisfaction figures.[131]

If democracy and its supporters are to persist, an essential precondition is that there exist no bigger groups within the society that favour anti-democratic system alternatives over parliamentary majority democracy. In the research on political culture, acceptance of alternative systems of rule is a particularly telling indicator of how substantial the political support for concrete democratic systems is.[132] In the eastern federal states and the Czech Republic, the level of agreement with anti-democratic system alternatives is about double the figure for the western part of the Federal Republic (a reference country), and in the other eastern EU countries it is even higher (see Figure 12.11).

In the post-communist EU countries, confidence in democratic institutions – another index of agreement with democracy – is frequently low, and distrust is constantly greater than confidence (see Figure 12.12).

In this regard, western and eastern EU countries differ significantly. As in other opinion polls, the figures for eastern Germany differ from those for western Germany but are mostly congruent with the figures for other EU countries in East Central Europe. In Hungary, Poland, Lithuania and Latvia, distrust of parliaments and governments reaches 84 to 94 per cent, and distrust of political parties is expressed by an astounding 91 to 98 per cent of citizens. These figures correspond to these populations' low satisfaction with democracy and indicate a legitimation crisis.

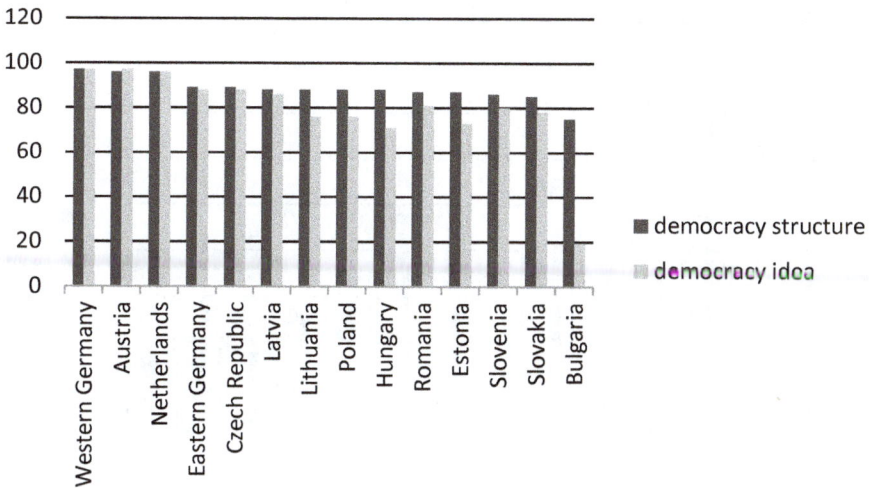

FIGURE 12.9. Agreement with statements about democracy as an idea and system of government

Western Germany, Austria and the Netherlands are reference countries. On democracy as a structure: 'Democracy is the most appropriate system of government'; on democracy as an idea: 'The idea of democracy is good in any case'.

Source: G. Pickel, 'Die subjektive Verankerung der Demokratie in Osteuropa: Die Legitimität der Demokratie in der Bevölkerung als Faktor demokratischer Stabilität und Qualität', in U. Backes, T. Jaskułowski and A. Polese (eds), *Totalitarismus und Transformation: Defizite der Demokratiekonsolidierung in Mittel- und Osteuropa* (Göttingen, 2009), 261–83, here 267, based on WVS 1999/2000.

The Emergence of a Civil Society

The individual country reports in this volume emphasize that citizens' personal commitment to the process of political decision-making is still low, and that on the whole they appear sceptical of their potential to influence politics (see Figure 12.13).

Voter turnout in the eastern EU countries has clearly declined since the founding elections and remains low.[133] As yet, the political parties are only superficially rooted, party-related political participation is low, and democratic parties' recruitment capability is limited. The beneficiaries of the populace's disinclination to participate are the extremist parties on both the left and the right.[134] Meanwhile, compared to the populations of established democracies, the citizenry in post-communist states also exhibit low readiness to participate in intermediary organizations (trade unions, employers' associations and professional associations, citizens' associations, citizens' initiatives, etc.).[135]

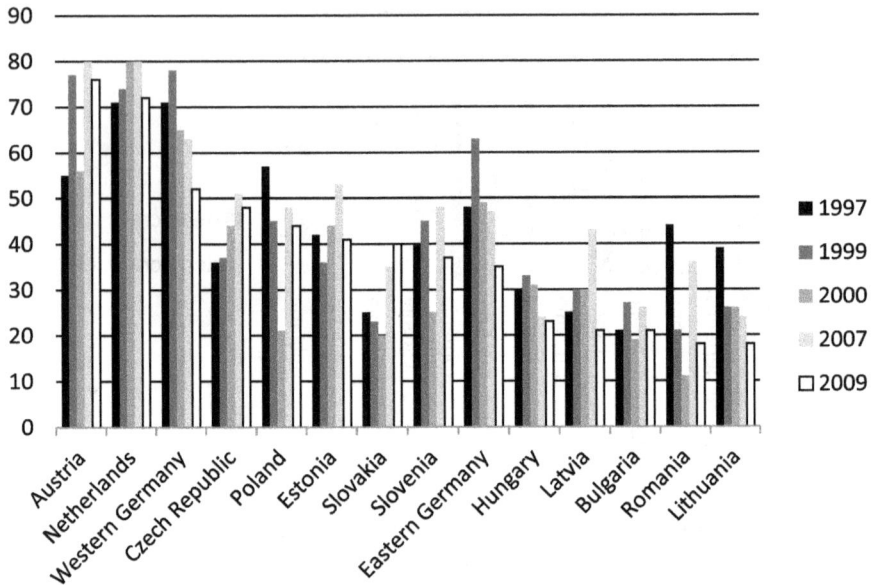

FIGURE 12.10. Satisfaction with actual democracy 1997–2009

Agreement figures in percentages, sequence of countries according to 2009 figures (with one exception each for the Czech Republic, Poland, Estonia and the East German federal states); Austria, the Netherlands and western Germany are reference countries.

State of Consolidation in 2012

The state of a country's society and political culture determines the nature of a newly developing economic and political system.[136] The resulting economic and political processes then mostly decide political developments. The following presentation and analysis of the state of consolidation in 2012 therefore treats society first, followed by economy and then politics.

Society

Social structure, demography

In parallel with the fundamental restructuring and rapid modernization of the economy, changes in the employment structure pushed each eastern EU country towards becoming a services society. The share of those working in industry and agriculture has clearly declined in the course of the transformation. The services sector, on the other hand, boasts high growth rates, mainly in trade but also in many smaller services enterprises. The

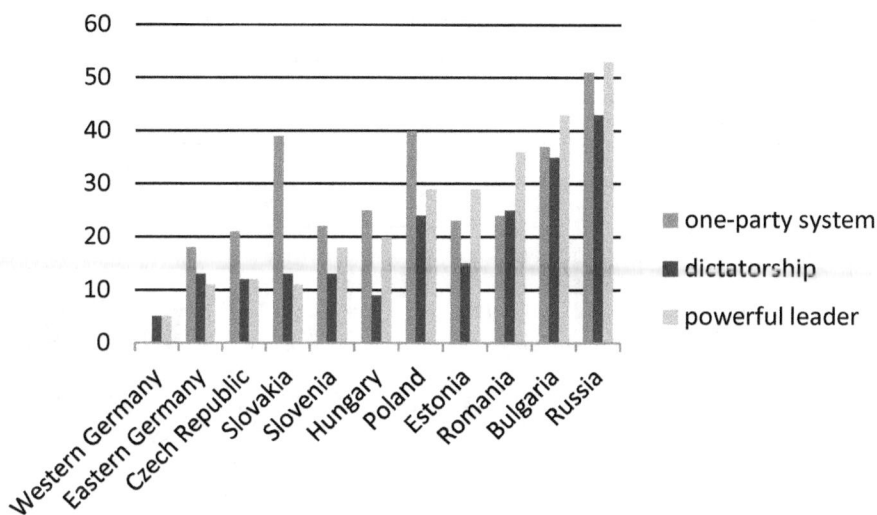

FIGURE 12.11. Agreement with statements about anti-democratic system alternatives in 2000

In percentages; western Germany and Russia are reference countries. One-party-system: 'A multi-party-system is meant to produce chaos. All we need is a one-party-system'; dictatorship: 'Under certain conditions, dictatorship is the best system of government'; strong leader: 'It is best to get rid of the parliament and have a strong leader who will quickly decide about things'.

Sources: see country reports in this volume, in particular Romania and the Czech Republic; see also O. Müller et al., 'Die osteuropäischen Demokratien in der Bevölkerungsmeinung', in G. Pickel et al. (eds), *Osteuropas Bevölkerung auf dem Weg in die Demokratie: Repräsentative Untersuchungen in Ostdeutschland und zehn osteuropäischen Transformationsstaaten* (Wiesbaden, 2006), 155–64, here 164.

number of employees in the state sector radically declined during the privatization process, whereas the number of employees in the private sector has grown massively.

In these countries, the start of the transformation phase came with rocketing unemployment, near total devaluation of savings and drastically declining real incomes as a result of hyperinflation. Joblessness was a new phenomenon, as in 'real socialism' there had officially been full employment. New systems of unemployment benefits and social security had to be established. Further on in the transformation process, income differences between the winners and losers of the process clearly widened. Parts of the population – sensing they would not, even in the long run, benefit from the reform efforts – resisted economic reforms and rejected the market economy. Politically, their strength was evidenced by post-communist parties' election victories and the success of right-wing populist politicians.

High unemployment and low wages, at least in comparison to western EU countries, resulted in massive emigration, particularly of young,

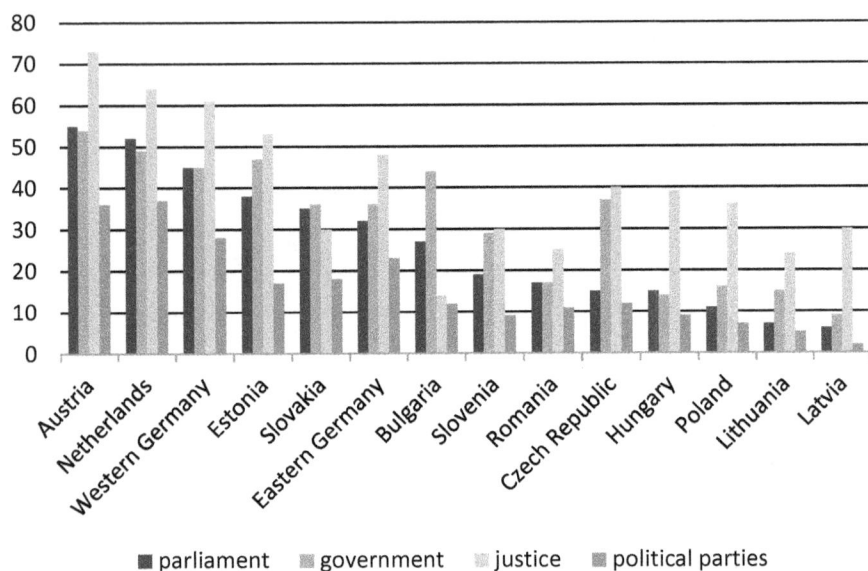

FIGURE 12.12. Confidence in parliament, government, justice and political parties

Sequence of countries according to confidence in parliament, agreement figures in percentages; Austria, the Netherlands and western Germany are reference countries. The wording of the question was 'In general, do you trust/distrust the following institutions?'

Source: Democracy Index based on Eurobarometer Survey 2009. For FRG-West/East, own calculations following Allbus 2008: agreement figures on a seven-point scale (1 = 'no trust at all' up to 7 = 'very great trust'), own calculations from 3.5 on.

qualified and dynamic people, from the East to the West of the EU. In the period from 1990 to 2011, on balance more than 1.7 million people[137] migrated from eastern to western Germany, uninhibited by the language and cultural barriers that citizens of other eastern EU countries faced. Emigrants were mostly qualified people, the majority of them younger women.[138] In the past few years, however, emigration has declined: in 2011 only 5,200 people moved out of the East German federal states on balance.[139] Rural regions are still affected, however: in contrast to urban regions such as Berlin and Potsdam, Leipzig and Dresden as well as the cities of Thuringia, where population rates are stable or even rising, the rural regions of Germany's East stand to lose more than half their inhabitants by 2020.[140]

Other eastern EU countries have also been affected by East-West migration: between 2005 and 2012, the net immigration from eastern to western EU states (not counting inner-German migration) was about 200,000 people per year.[141] Romania's population fell to 21 million in 2010 – almost two million less than the 23 million counted in 1990 – owing to declining

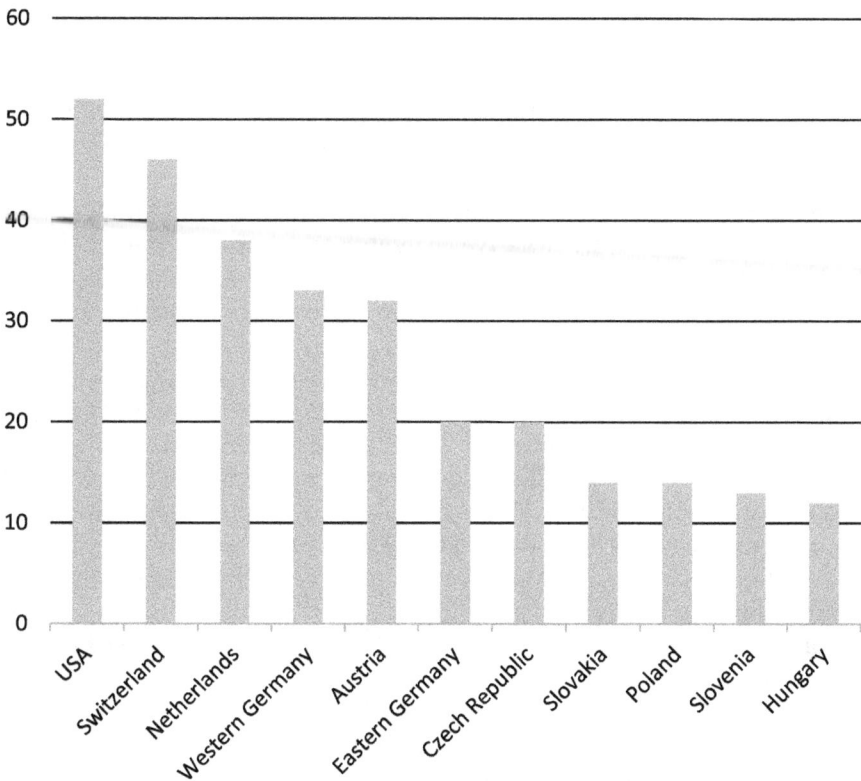

FIGURE 12.13. Perception of one's power to influence politics

Rejection of the statement 'People like me cannot influence the government's actions' in percentages; the United States, Switzerland, the Netherlands, western Germany and Austria are reference countries.

Source: F. Plasser, P. Ulram and H. Waldrauch, *Politischer Kulturwandel in Ost-Mitteleuropa: Theorie und Empirie demokratischer Konsolidierung* (Opladen, 1997), 166.

birth rates coupled with emigration (including the German minority's exodus to the Federal Republic).[142] Lithuania's population declined by about 400,000 people, from 3.7 to 3.3 million, as a result of continuous migration to other countries and declining fertility.[143] Due to the emigrations of hundreds of thousands of young, well-trained Latvians to the older EU states, as well as low birth rates, Latvia also had to cope with a population reduction of about 400,000 people, from 2.7 million to 2.3 million.[144] Hungary too sustained a population decline of some 400,000, from 10.4 million residents in 1989 to ten million in 2010.[145] These population declines had in common the causes of a negative migration balance and low birth rates (the latter are a general phenomenon in Europe).

Emigration from Poland has been particularly massive. When Poland acceded to the EU, Great Britain, Ireland and the Scandinavian states opened their labour markets to Poles, and hundreds of thousands of mostly young Poles seized the chance to pursue new job opportunities in foreign countries. This had the upside of relieving Poland's labour market, but the consequences were ambivalent, for besides the influx of foreign currency remittances saved by the labour migrants and an additional gain in know-how, there were negative economic consequences, such as problematic effects for the already unfavourable demographic development. Furthermore, labour migration disrupted the cohesion of many families, creating 'euro orphans'.[146]

The Czech Republic and Slovakia were less affected by migration, which was hindered by language barriers, lack of a tradition of emigration and rising (though minimally) living standards. Indeed, immigration to the Czech Republic has always on balance outweighed emigration and has even risen significantly (1989: 1,000; 2008: 72,000). The emigration of young, qualified Czechs to the western EU has been more than balanced by immigration from Ukraine, Russia and even other EU countries.[147] During the market economy adaptation crisis, the Czech Republic's population did not decline but grew slightly, from 10.3 million in 1989 to 10.4 million in 2008.[148]

In all countries of the post-communist EU region, 'Western' trends influenced demographic development. Their newly won freedoms and market economies offered previously unknown professional and travel possibilities. Meanwhile, the previously unknown fear of unemployment, alongside new job opportunities and the pressure of competition, pushed family to the back burner, especially in the big cities. Further identifiable causes of significantly declining birth rates include transformation problems, growing social disparities, pessimism regarding the future and tendencies towards social disintegration.[149] On the other hand, the average life expectancy has grown slowly but steadily in all eastern EU countries. Pension schemes have had to adjust to this development in the population structure (i.e. the ageing of society), which has often connected to fundamental political conflicts.[150]

The newly won liberties and growing pressure of competition on the labour market increased young people's motivation to acquire higher education. In all eastern EU countries, the numbers of university graduates have grown considerably, and university systems have been extended and developed. Numbers of private universities, some very diverse in quality, exploded; likewise, the number of state universities grew significantly.[151]

Civil society

People in the transformation countries face a need to change from communist subjects into citizens who think and act independently and are prepared to commit themselves to civic matters. A democracy cannot be considered really consolidated without the active approval of wide parts of the population.[152] The post-communist citizenry must still further internalize this acceptance of democratic values, institutions and processes.[153] For now, in terms of civil society, the consolidation process remains incomplete in the post-communist EU region. Those eastern EU states where an overwhelming majority of citizens – 80 per cent or more – distrust parliament and are dissatisfied with democracy can hardly be called democracies.

On the whole, it seems that citizens' support of democracy is insufficiently sustainable and active. Apart from the formative dictatorship trauma, the main causes of this appear to be the deep rifts carved in the professional and private lives of most citizens during the system transformation, the new threat of unemployment and the rapidly growing social and income disparities after the turnaround.

The specific features of the civil societies in the post-communist EU region are present in the eastern German federal states, where political attitudes and value preferences still differ from those in western Germany. These still extant basic features of political culture, 'as they are similarly found also in other post-communist countries, generally allow for speaking of a post-totalitarian regional special culture', as Wolfgang Rudzio sums up in respect of the differences between the Federal Republic's East and West.[154] According to Wolfgang Ismayr, the weaker support for democracy in the former East Germany is 'an expression of a political culture shaped by the Sozialistische Einheitspartei Deutschlands (SED) state, but partly also a result of personal disappointments after having joined the Federal Republic'.[155]

This relative weakness of civil society is typical of all transition countries. Nevertheless, as is clear from the Freedom House rankings of civil societies' maturity and vitality, the post-communist EU states discussed in this volume number among the top-ranked transformation countries (see Figure 12.14).[156]

Economy

By 2012, the eastern EU countries were able to present themselves as dynamic market economies with open trade and convertible currencies. Slovenia (in 2007), Slovakia (2009) and Estonia (2011) have already joined the EU currency union. The private sector makes up more than two thirds

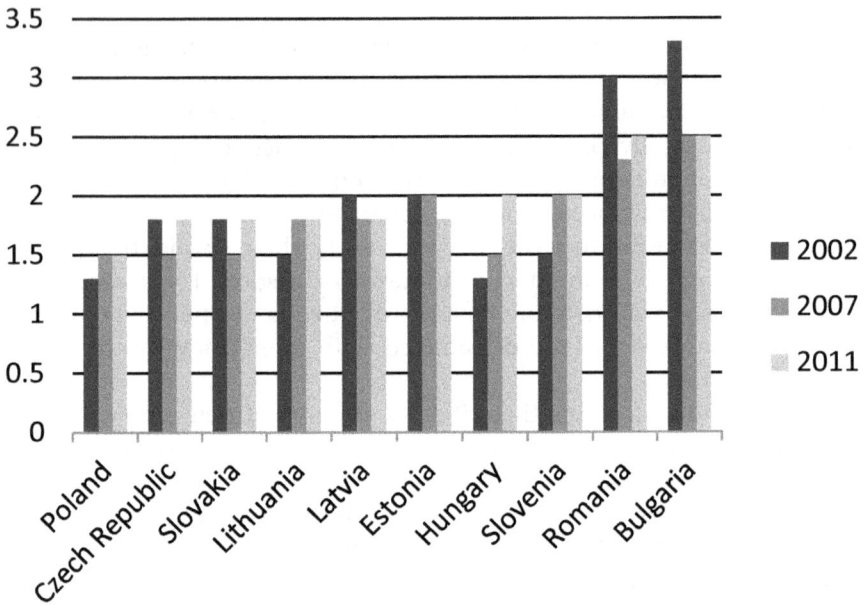

FIGURE 12.14. Consolidation at the level of civil society 2002–2011

1= highest level of democratic progress, 7 = lowest level. Sequence of countries according to 2011 figures, FRG-East not counted. The indicator 'civil society' evaluates the growth of NGOs, their organizational capacities and financial sustainability, and the legal and political environment they work in as well as the development of free trade unions and the participation of interest groups in the political process.

Source: Freedom House, Nations in Transit 2011 (http://www.freedomhouse.org/sites/default/files/inline_images/NIT-2011-Tables.pdf; accessed 27 February 2012).

of all economic activities. The agricultural sector's contribution to GDP has continuously declined in the past few years, but most sites have made the necessary structural adjustments. The services sector has generated dynamic forces, the countries have reoriented trade to world markets, and foreign direct investments, particularly from the western EU region, have risen substantially. In both in the eastern federal states of Germany and all eastern EU countries, EU membership has essentially contributed to economic progress and the above-mentioned far-reaching structural changes. Compared to the initial situation in 1989, fundamentally positive systemic economic change is clear throughout the post-communist EU region. These states have made remarkable progress in liberalizing and stabilizing their economies: per capita GNP, measured in per cent of the EU average, has been rising everywhere – rapidly, in some cases (Slovakia, Estonia, Romania, Bulgaria). At 95 per cent, the East German federal states have almost reached the EU average (see Figure 12.15).

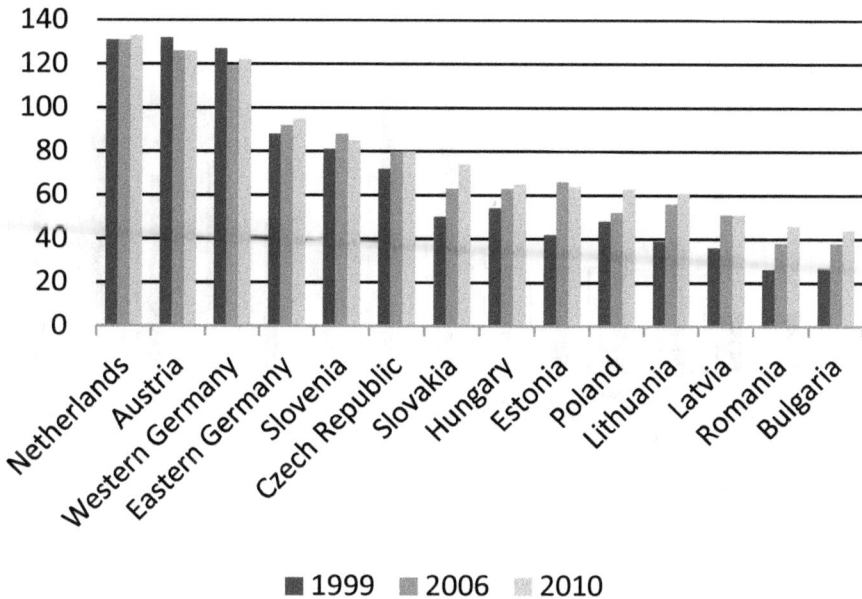

FIGURE 12.15. GDP per capita in per cent of the EU average

Post-communist EU region 1999–2010; the Netherlands, Austria and western Germany are reference countries. In purchasing power standards (PPS), Index (EU-27 = 100).

Sources: http://epp.eurostat.ec.europa.eu/tgm/printTable.do?tab=table&plugin=1&language=de&pco de=tec00114&print-Preview=true (accessed 20 June 2012); for FRG-East/West: http://www.vgrdl.de/ Arbeitskreis_VGR/ergebnisse.asp (accessed 30 June 2012); GDP in prices per working person (national); own calculations.

Nonetheless, the immense social costs of transformation put the reform policies to a difficult test. Above all, the soaring prices that accompanied the liberalization measures and the process of radical privatization had drastic consequences in all transformation countries.

Early on, the system change brought no gains in efficiency because functioning competition did not at once emerge in the process of liberalization of the economy and trade or the introduction of private property rights. The state cannot simply impose a market economy system. Rather, in the area of the economy (just as in politics), the population must undergo a learning process over several years to acquire entrepreneurial skills such as the willingness and ability to think and act independently, uphold legal rules and take initiative and risks.[157] And the middle class – the driving force of dynamic national economies that was extinguished by the communist dictatorships – will have to (re-)acquire the necessary entrepreneurial property, managerial skills and modern know-how over several generations.

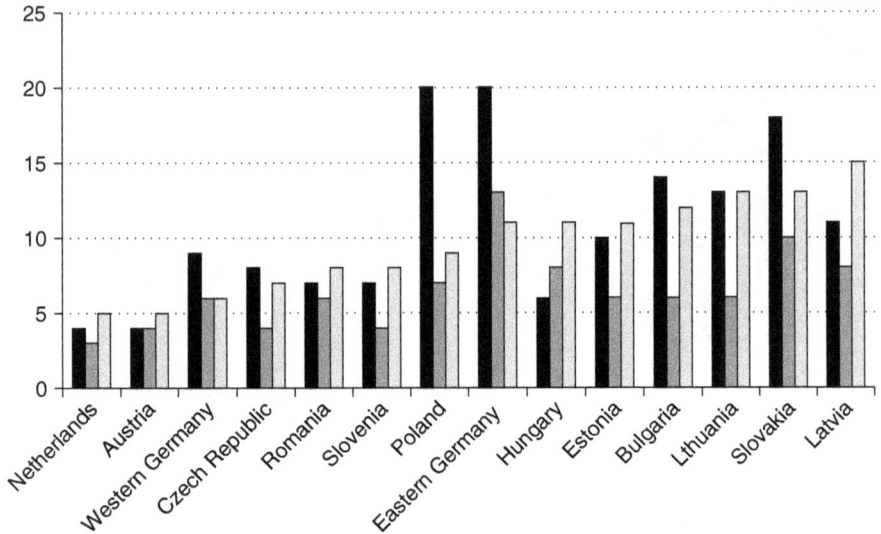

FIGURE 12.16. Unemployment rates 2003–2012

Unemployed as a percentage of the workforce, sequence according to 2012 figures; the Netherlands, Austria and western Germany are reference countries.

Sources: http://wko.at/statistik/eu/europa-arbeitslosenquoten.pdf; http://www.bpb.de/nachschlagen/
zahlen-und-fakten/soziale-situation-in-deutschland/61718/arbeitslose-und-arbeitslosenquote;
Bundesagentur für Arbeit, Monatsbericht Mai 2012 (http://statistik.arbeitsagentur.de/Statischer-Content/
Arbeitsmarktberichte/Monatsbericht-Arbeits-Ausbildungsmarkt-Deutschland/Monatsberichte/
Generische-Publikationen/Monatsbericht-201205.pdf; accessed 11 June 2012).

In the end, the economic upswing can relieve the labour market only bit by bit. Unemployment cannot decline sufficiently even if growth is robust, for enterprises that want to further increase their productivity and be competitive must still reduce the overemployment inherited from planned economy. Unemployment is still particularly high in the Baltic republics, Bulgaria and Slovakia (see Figure 12.16). Although the post-communist EU countries have established functioning systems of unemployment benefits and social security, high unemployment, combined with growing discrepancies in how income and property are distributed among the population, causes social tension – the more so as the revolutionary impetus and excitement over the newly won political and economic liberties are now past.

The transfer payments that balance social hardship burden the post-communist EU countries' budgets and severely constrain their governments financially, while tax revenues still lag behind expectations despite growing domestic demand.[158] Not even the East German federal states have yet succeeded in establishing a dynamic, self-sustaining economic

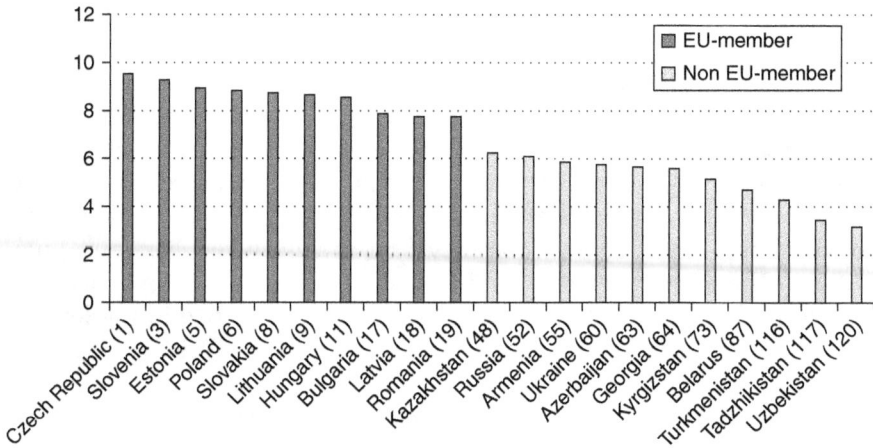

FIGURE 12.17. State of economic transformation

Former Eastern Bloc countries in comparison, BTI 2012; the figures in brackets: sequence of countries according to BTI Ranking Economic Transformation 2012, higher figure = more successful consolidation; BTI scale: 8–10, developed market economies; 7–7.9, functioning market economies; 5–6.9, market economies with functional deficits, 3–4.9, badly functioning market economies; below 3, rudimentary economies.

Source: Transformationsindex BTI 2012, 40 and appendix, results for 'Wirtschaftliche Transformation' (mean evaluations of level of socio-economic development, market system and competition, currency and price stability, private property, social system, performativity of the national economy, sustainability).

path of development: yearly consumption (private consumption, state consumption, investments) is about 30 billion euros higher than production. Thus, they remain structurally dependent on West German streams of financing and goods – but this (the 'transfer trap') cannot be the solution in the long run.[159]

Meanwhile, the 2012 BTI economic transformation rankings characterize most eastern EU countries as 'developed market economies' (see Figure 12.17). The Baltic republics are intensively integrated into the international economy and thus were hit particularly hard by the economic and financial crisis of 2009. Hungary avoided financial collapse only by signing an agreement with the IMF; high budget deficits (80 per cent of GDP) and enormous foreign debt (140 per cent of GDP) still threaten its financial stability. Poland alone managed to not only survive the financial crisis but also gain strength in doing so: even in the crisis year 2009, its GDP registered growth.[160]

Politics

In the course of the transformation process from 1990 to 2012, the stability and efficiency of the new democratic systems increased significantly.[161] The consolidation of their political systems progressed particularly well at the institutional level. Constitutions that accord with the rule of law have been passed, the systematic separation of powers is working, and institutional efficiency, transparency and inclusion are basically guaranteed. The independent constitutional judiciary has shown itself to be key to the juridification of political conflicts. The rise in the level of consolidation has not been steady, but seen in the historical perspective of the transformation of 1990–2012 it is continuous. According to the Freedom House Report 2011, the eastern EU countries are free electoral democracies where human rights are respected.[162] Wolfgang Merkel calls the Eastern European EU countries consolidated democracies, terming Bulgaria, Latvia and Romania 'second group' countries that, with EU assistance, 'may be able to play in the premier league in the coming years'.[163]

The BTI, in its 2012 comparative analysis of 129 transformation countries worldwide, assigned top rankings between No. 1 and No. 16 (BTI Status Index) to the post-communist transformation countries for the state of their market economies and democracies, thus placing them in a small, successful group of twenty-three transformation countries designated 'democracies in consolidation'. The BTI does not evaluate the East German federal states, but other indicators as well as the figures above show that they would doubtless belong in the 'democracies in consolidation' group (Figure 12.19).[164]

When seen in chronological sequence, however, the BTI Index evaluations from 2003 to 2012 do not evince democracy's one-dimensional victory in the post-communist EU region but rather a difficult, sometimes contradictory process. As Figure 12.19 clearly reveals, the overall figures for the Czech Republic, Slovenia and Estonia from 2003 to 2012 basically stayed the same, though at quite a high level.

Poland trended downward for some time but has clearly improved since 2010, not just because of constructive cooperation between President Bronisław Komorowski, in office since 2010, and the Donald Tusk government representing the Citizens' Platform, but also because of the government's greater respect for civil rights compared to its predecessor and, most of all, the party system's increased stability.[165] Bulgaria and Romania, which started out with low figures, have also clearly improved in the past decade. Their gains were most obvious between 2003 and 2008, indicating that the process of EU accession resulted in positive pressure

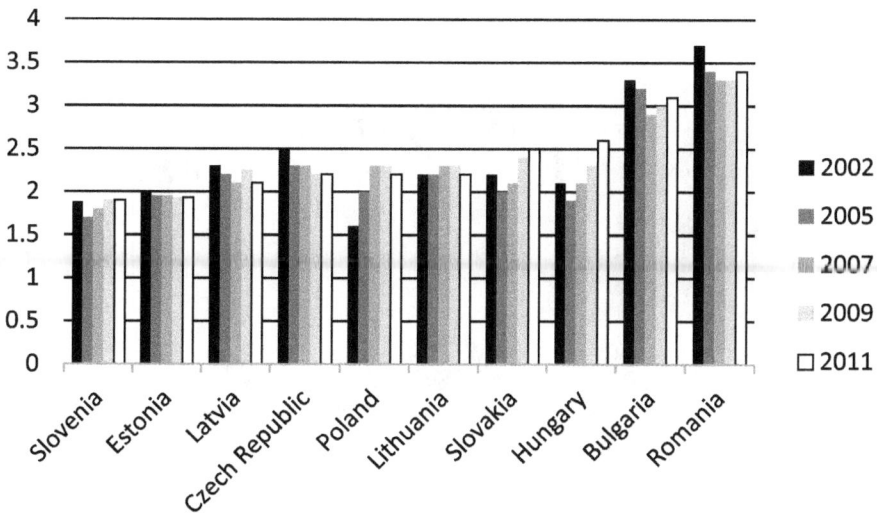

FIGURE 12.18. Level of consolidation of democracies 2002–2012

Sequence of countries according to 2011 figures: 1 = highest level of democratic progress, 7 = lowest level; 1.00–2.99, consolidated democracies; 3.00–3.99, semi-consolidated democracies.

Source: Freedom House, Nations in Transit 2011 (http://www.freedomhouse.org/sites/default/files/inline_images/NIT-2011-Tables.pdf; accessed 27 February 2012).

and consequently mobilization of democratically oriented, pro-European forces.

The overall figures for Slovakia, Lithuania and Latvia, on the other hand, have worsened slightly.[166] The most comprehensive deterioration of democracy figures, however, is observed in Hungary, where Prime Minister Victor Orbán's conservative-populist government and Alliance of Young Democrats (FIDESZ) abused their constitutional majority in the parliament to weaken the control competences of the Constitutional Court, reduce the independence of the central bank and the board for data protection, and restrict the autonomy of NGOs.[167] Hungary's BTI democracy ranking (which does not include economic parameters) slid from No. 4 in 2006 to No. 17 in 2012.[168] The example of Hungary shows that EU membership clearly does not guarantee absolute protection from loss of democratic —quality.[169] However, without the EU's regulation mechanisms and pressure from EU institutions and western EU countries, Hungary's losses in democratic quality would doubtless be more dramatic. The fluctuations in the country assessments of the BTI Index from 2003 to 2012 (Figure 12.19) mostly correspond to the development trends depicted in this volume as well as the assessments and development trends recorded by Freedom House.

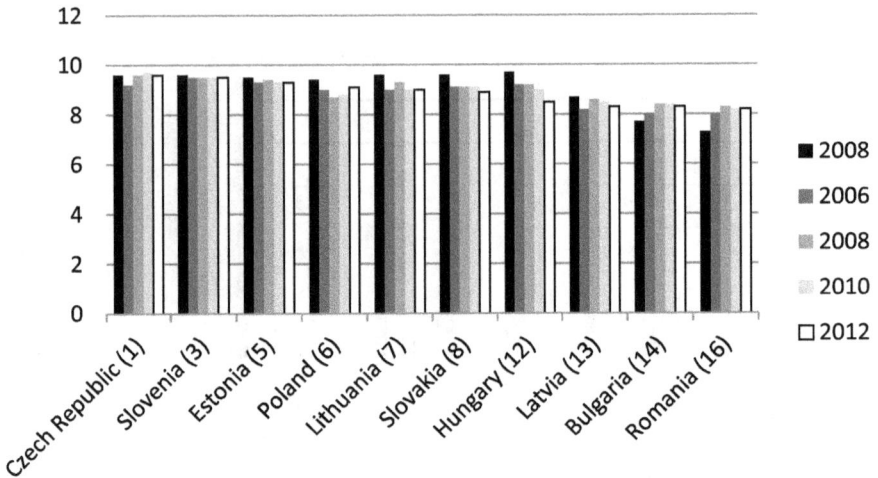

FIGURE 12.19. State of the transformation to market economy and democracy 2003–2012

BTI Status Index, sequence of countries according to 2012 figures; figure in brackets = ranking as a consolidation success. BTI scale: 8–10, consolidating democracies; 6–7.9, defective democracies; 5–5.9, strongly defective democracies; 4–4.9, moderate autocracies; below 4, hardcore autocracies.

Source: Bertelsmann Transformation Index (BTI) 2012, esp. 29 and appendix. The Status Index for each respective year uses the mean of results for the parameters 'political transformation' (statehood, political participation, rule of law, stability of democratic institutions, political and social integration) and 'economic transformation' (level of socio-economic development, market and competition system, currency and price stability, private property, social system, national economic performativity, sustainability).

Society, Economy, Politics: State of Consolidation in Comparison

The post-communist EU region's generally positive figures in the BTI Index and Freedom House rankings should not obscure the fact that these countries are positively assessed only in relation to other transformation countries. When they are compared to the established democracies of the Central European EU, various consolidation deficits are evident at the level of actors, the intermediary level and the fields of political culture and civil society. Figure 12.20 clearly illustrates the significant differences between the reference and the transformation countries.

As could be expected, the most consolidated transformation countries are the East German federal states, followed by Estonia, Slovenia and the Czech Republic. Slovakia, Poland and Hungary are in between, while Bulgaria, Lithuania, Latvia and Romania at the bottom show the highest backlog in meeting demands. The sequence of EU transformation

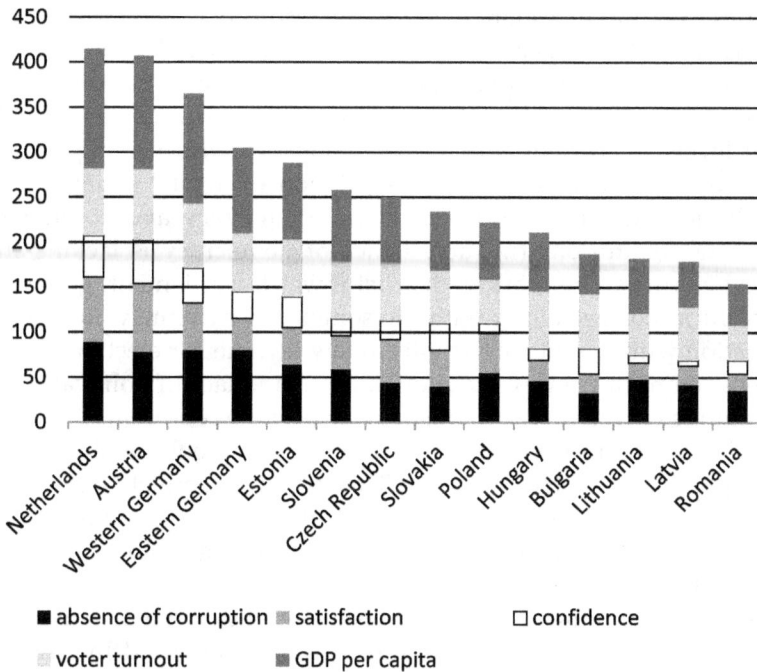

■ absence of corruption   ■ satisfaction   □ confidence

▨ voter turnout   ■ GDP per capita

FIGURE 12.20. From the Eastern Bloc to the EU

Society, economy, politics: state of consolidation 2012 in comparison[a]; higher number = greater consolidation success; the Netherlands, Austria and the West of Germany are reference countries. Indicators of consolidation: absence of corruption[b] for the consolidation of actors' behaviour; satisfaction with actual democracy[c] and confidence in democratic institutions[d] for the consolidation of civil society; election turnout[e] for a committed civil society; GDP per capita[f] as a percentage of the EU average for economic consolidation).

[a]The BTI Index and Freedom House Ranking are reasonably augmented by this diagram, where the depicted indicators of consolidation are not judged subjectively but based exclusively on the identified figures, and because both the eastern German federal states (as a transformation country) and the West of Germany are represented.

[b]CPI figures 2011. Figures go up to 10 for 'very clean', which (multiplied by a factor of 10) is counted as 100 per cent to achieve comparability to other indicators expressed in per cent. *Source:* Transparency International, Corruption Perceptions Index (with only one figure for Germany as a whole), 19 March 2012.

[c]Satisfaction with actual democracy in 2009 in per cent. *Sources:* Eurobarometer surveys; figures for FRG-West and FRG-East: G. Pickel, 'Gerechtigkeit und Politik in der deutschen Bevölkerun: Die Folgen der Wahrnehmung von Gerechtigkeit für die politische Kultur im vereinten Deutschland', unpublished manuscript, 2012.

[d]Trust in parliament, government and political parties 2008/09 in per cent (rounded means for each respective country). *Source:* Democracy Index based on Eurobarometer Survey 2009. For the West and East of Germany: authors' calculations following Allbus 2008, agreement measured on a seven-point scale (1 = no trust at all; 7 = very great trust), where values of 3.5 and higher qualify as 'trust'.

[e]Turnout in the latest parliamentary elections. *Source:* European Election Database (http://www.nsd.uib. no/european_election_database/country; accessed 28 February 2012); for the West and East of Germany: Deutscher Bundestag, 'Aktueller Begriff: Wahlbeteiligung in der Bundesrepublik Deutschland' (Berlin, 2009).

[f]*Source:* see Figure 12.15, figures for 2010.

countries roughly corresponds to both the results of the country reports in this volume and the BTI and Freedom House rankings.[170]

Furthermore, Figure 12.20 expresses correlations between society, economy and politics as well as interdependencies between the individual levels of consolidation. Those countries with the most virulent corruption (i.e. deficits in the consolidation of actors' behaviour) also have the lowest satisfaction with actual democracy and confidence in democratic institutions (i.e. acceptance of democracy is lacking in the political culture). The marked distrust towards parliament, government and political parties, along with the sometimes extremely common dissatisfaction with democracy, results in low turnout for elections (i.e. civil society's commitment is weak). Low turnout and lack of political commitment among citizens work to the detriment of the representative level, in particular the party system: the parties have too few members and are only superficially rooted in society. This in turn negatively affects actors' behaviour: the absence of sufficient control additionally stimulates them to acquire power, influence and material advantages, and supports the further spread of corruption.

Thus we have come full circle. In countries with large democracy deficits and massive corruption, the economy (as measured by per capita GDP) is less efficient, which contributes to the population's distrust of democracy and market economy. As is obvious from these connections, the individual deficits are mutually related and reinforcing. They affect the quality of the democracy and market economy and reduce both economic efficiency and the persistence of democratic systems in the post-communist countries.

Prospects

Societies in the post-communist EU region have been strongly influenced by the forty years of violent communist rule until 1989/90 and the following transformation and radical change. In 1990, Václav Havel described the state of a society that had just been liberated from dictatorship as follows: 'We have become morally ill because we have become used to saying one thing and thinking something else. We have learned to not believe in anything, to be indifferent towards each other, to just care for ourselves'.[171] The first two decades of transformation since the implosion of the communist regimes, which brought insecurities and growth in social disparities along with processes of democratic and economic reform, have not been enough to really cure this illness. The post-communist EU region is still deficient in the social resources of ethos, trust and morality needed for a vital civil society, efficient economy and principled politics. All things considered, the core problem of transformation is mentality change. Mental attitudes, habitual ways of behaviour and the actual quality of market economy and democracy are closely interrelated.

In view of the high, undiminished liability to corruption and sometimes grave violation of rules, the behaviour of the political and economic elites in the eastern EU countries cannot be considered truly consolidated. The citizens distrust the political parties and connect this distrust to their fundamental scepticism towards politics. Those countries whose populations trust political parties and democratic institutions the least also exhibit the greatest dissatisfaction with their democracies. Citizens do not believe their actions can influence actual politics, and they are seldom committed civically. Because sceptical citizenries exercise insufficient control over decision-makers, these are the very countries where corruption is most widespread. Where political parties are only superficially rooted among the population and have few members, the share of swing voters is high, and most party systems are unstable, the consequence is that the governments' average time in office is too short to accomplish anything meaningful.

Thus, the crystallization and consolidation of a responsible, committed civil society and an economic middle class will take several decades. Neither independent thinking and acting nor civic commitment can simply be created: they must unfold and mature, and much indicates that Ralf Dahrendorf was right to predict that 'the realization of civil society' would take two generations or even sixty years.[172]

Concerning the democracy deficits mentioned above, it cannot be ruled out that in some post-communist EU countries the transformation process will temporarily stagnate at the current level of consolidation – with low-quality democracy and limited systemic functionality – or even suffer partial setbacks. This outcome might be reflected in the following complexes of problems:

- continuing domination of politics by financially strong, often shady interest groups (headed by 'godfathers' or 'oligarchs') that directly fund political parties and not infrequently party functionaries in order to benefit from custom-made laws and generous public contracts;
- widespread or even endemic corruption;
- low levels of political participation and confidence in democracy among citizens who are disenchanted with politics;
- a high degree of voter volatility and, as a consequence, unstable party systems;

- comparatively strong right- and left-wing extremist parties and groups;
- inefficient public administration and justice, insufficient law enforcement;
- low levels of public services such as security, education and health systems, science and basic research, traffic and environmental protection;
- limited economic competitiveness resulting from the above-mentioned deficits.

On the other hand, a very positive fact is that for the people in the post-communist EU region, the transition from communist dictatorship to democratic constitutional states and from planned to market economy since 1989/90 has been a great historic achievement. With reason, the eastern EU countries occupy top positions in all international transformation rankings. Earned during the often painful and complicated transformation process towards democracy and market economy as well as the enormous consolidation efforts demanded by the process of EU accession and EU membership, the admirable achievements of the citizens of the eastern EU states become obvious in a comparison with the former Eastern Bloc countries that currently are not EU members (see Figure 12.21).

A comparison of all former Eastern Bloc states shows that the European Union definitely deserved the Nobel Peace Prize it was awarded in 2012 for its successful efforts to promote democratization in the post-communist EU region, among other things. Whereas all independent experts classify the eastern EU countries – without exception – as 'democracies in consolidation', the other former Eastern Bloc countries at best achieve the status of 'defective democracy' (Ukraine). All others are strongly defective democracies or even moderate to hardcore autocracies. The process of EU accession and EU membership certainly played a considerable role in this context. Doubtless also relevant were the remnants of democratic political and cultural traditions in East Central Europe – already existing pre-dictatorship experiences with democracy reinforced and continue to reinforce people's acceptance of democracy.

For the eastern EU countries, the most difficult period is already over. In society, economics and politics, we may generally assume developments are mostly positive. As the transformation process of 1990 to 2012 unfolded, the stability and efficiency of the economic and political systems increased; institutional consolidation in particular made good progress. For the most part, constitutions based on the rule of law and systems of separated powers are increasingly informing political practice. In this context, strong and independent constitutional judiciaries

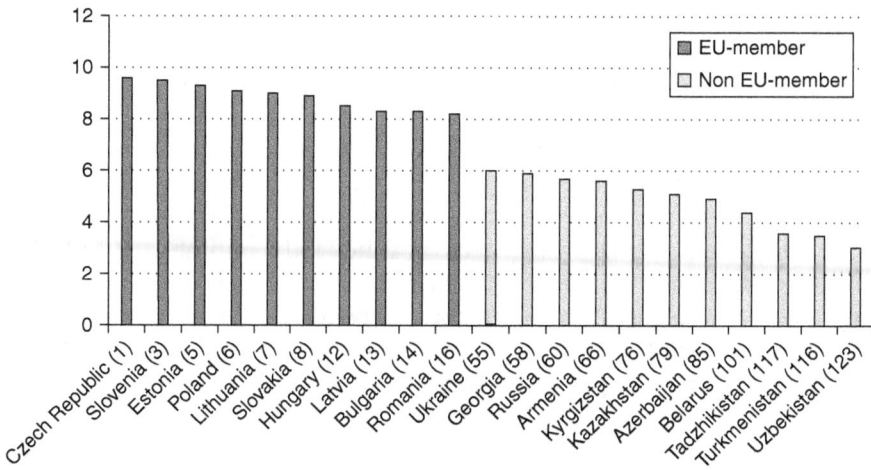

FIGURE 12.21. State of the transformation to market economy and democracy without the former East Germany

Former Eastern Bloc countries in comparison, BTI 2012; figure in brackets = ranking as a consolidation success; BTI evaluation scale: 8–10: consolidating democracies; 6–7.9: defective democracies; 5–5.9: strongly defective democracies; 4–4.9: moderate autocracies; 3.9 and lower: hardcore autocracies.

Source: Bertelsmann Transformation Index (BTI) 2012, esp. 29 and appendix. Status Index for 2012: Mean of the results for the dimensions 'political transformation' (statehood, political participation, rule of law, stability of democratic institutions, political and social integration) and 'economic transformation' (level of socio-economic development, market and competition systems, stability of currency and prices, private property, social system, performativity of the national economy, sustainability).

have proven their worth as an important factor in the juridification of political conflicts and as a means of increasing the constitutionality of political processes. Considering the institutional configurations and political power constellations in the post-communist EU region, the risk of radical de-democratization in a case of severe socio-economic and political crisis appears low (for South East Europe) to very low (for East Central Europe).

In this context, external framework conditions, especially EU and NATO membership, are still vital factors in stabilizing young, fragile democracies. This claim is supported by the diagrams of general international rankings presented above as well as by specific cases of grave violations of the fundamental principles of a democratic constitutional state in Hungary and Romania in 2012, when the EU prevented things from becoming worse. When all is said and done, the strength of democracy and the rule of law in the post-communist space hinges on whether or not the given country is a member of the European Union.

After having completed his studies in history, German philology, social studies and Italian studies, as well as having earned his doctorate (1980), **Günther Heydemann** worked as a member of the scientific staffs of the Universities of Erlangen and Bayreuth as well as of the Deutsches Historisches Institut London. After his habilitation (1991) and interim professorships in Munich and Bonn, he was appointed to the Chair of More Recent and Contemporary History of the University of Leipzig. Since 2009, he has also been Director of the HAIT, and has held visiting professorships and fellowships in Italy, the USA, Russia and Tunisia. His research work focuses on the history of historical science, comparative European history, the dictatorships of the twentieth century as well as the post-socialist transformation processes.

Karel Vodička, Dr of Jurisprudence, born in Aussig, Czechoslovakia, in 1949, went into political exile in the Federal Republic of Germany together with his family. He has undertaken scientific work as a philologist at the HAIT (until 2014) and as a lecturer in the Faculty of Philosophy at Jan-Evangelista-Purkyne University (UJEP) in Ústí nad Labem, Czech Republic. He has published on the history and the political system of the Czech Republic as well as on system transformation in the post-communist EU area. He has authored 126 scientific articles and is the author of sixteen books, most recently *Zündfunke aus Prag: Wie 1989 der Mut zur Freiheit die Geschichte veränderte*, co-authored with Hans-Dietrich Genscher and Petr Pithart (Munich, 2014).

Notes

1. Estonia, Latvia, Lithuania, Poland, Czech Republic, Slovakia, Slovenia, Hungary, Romania, Bulgaria.
2. Such as Austria, the Netherlands and the Federal Republic/West of Germany, which serve as reference countries for this analysis.
3. See 'Transformationsindex BTI 2012: Politische Gestaltung im internationalen Vergleich' (Gütersloh, 2012), 29 and appendix; see also Freedom House, Nations in Transit 2011 (http://www.freedomhouse.org/sites/default/files/inline_images/NIT-2011-Tables.pdf; accessed 27 February 2012).
4. Strongly defective democracies: Georgia, Russia, Armenia, Kyrgyzstan, Kazakhstan; moderate autocracies: Azerbaijan, Belarus; hardcore autocracies: Tajikistan, Turkmenistan, Uzbekistan. Source: Transformation Index BTI 2012, 29 and appendix.
5. See A. Przeworski, 'Spiel mit Einsatz: Demokratisierungsprozesse in Lateinamerika, Osteuropa und anderswo', *Transit* 3 (1991), 190–213, here 190.

6. See K. von Beyme, *Systemwechsel in Osteuropa* (Frankfurt a. M., 1994), 301; W. Merkel, *Systemtransformation: Eine Einführung in die Theorie und Empirie der Transformationsforschung* (Opladen, 1999), 380; C. Offe, *Der Tunnel am Ende des Lichts* (Frankfurt a. M., 1994), 135.

7. W. Merkel, *Systemtransformation: Eine Einführung in die Theorie und Empirie der Transformationsforschung*, 2nd ed. (Wiesbaden, 2010), 111.

8. In Merkel, *Systemtransformation* (2010), 111, the level 'consolidation of behaviour' is limited to informal political actors. This analysis also deals with formal political actors at the level of 'consolidation of behavior', as they are highly relevant to consolidation of the system overall.

9. See Merkel, *Systemtransformation* (2010), 112.

10. See J.J. Linz and A. Stepan, *Problems of Democratic Transition and Consolidation: Southern Europe, South America, and Post-Communist Europe* (Baltimore, 1996), 6; W. Merkel, E. Sandschneider and D. Segert, 'Die Institutionalisierung der Demokratie', in Merkel, Sandschneider and Segert (eds), *Systemwechsel 2* (Opladen, 1996), 10–36, here 21; Merkel, *Systemtransformation* (2010), 113.

11. See W. Ismayr, 'Die politischen Systeme Osteuropas im Vergleich', in W. Ismayr (ed.), *Die politischen Systeme Osteuropas* (Wiesbaden, 2010), 9–78, here 61.

12. See the individual country reports in this volume; see also W. Ismayr, 'Die politischen Systeme Osteuropas im Vergleich', 10–12.

13. See the individual country reports in this volume; see also A. Lorenz, 'Der konstitutionelle Rahmen: Verfassungsgebung und Verfassungsentwicklung', in F. Grotz and F. Müller-Rommel (eds), *Regierungssysteme in Mittel- und Osteuropa* (Wiesbaden, 2011), 47–67, here 51; Ismayr, 'Die politischen Systeme Osteuropas im Vergleich', 10–12.

14. See Dieringer, Hungary, in this volume.

15. H. Gábor, 'Hochproblematisch: Ungarns neues Grundgesetz', *Osteuropa*, 61(12) (2011), 145–66, here 145.

16. See 'Verfassungsreform: EU-Kommission geht gegen Ungarns Rechtsregierung vor', *Spiegel Online*, 17 January 2012 (http://www.spiegel.de/politik/ausland/0,1518,809631,00.html; accessed 25 January 2012).

17. See Gábor, 'Hochproblematisch'; 'Litauen verbietet Unterricht über Homosexualität', *Spiegel Online*, 19 June 2009 (http://www.spiegel.de/politik/ausland/0,1518,809631,00.html; accessed 25 January 2012).

18. See *Frankfurter Allgemeine Zeitung*, 5 January 2013, 1f.; http://www.tagesschau.de/ausland/ungarn400.html (accessed 5 January 2013); A. Renwick, 'Im Interesse der Macht, Ungarns neues Wahlsystem', *Osteuropa* 62(5) (2012), 3–18.

19. See the individual country reports in this volume; see also Ismayr, 'Die politischen Systeme Osteuropas im Vergleich', 28; W. Steffani, 'Zur Unterscheidung parlamentarischer und präsidentieller Regierungssysteme', *Zeitschrift für Parlamentsfragen* 14 (1983), 390–401, here 394; W. Steffani, 'Parlamentarisch-präsidentielle "Mischsysteme"? Bemerkungen zum Stand der Forschung in der Politikwissenschaft', in O. Luchterhandt (ed.), *Neue Regierungssysteme in Osteuropa und der GUS* (Berlin, 2002), 17–66.

20. See T. Beichelt, 'Die Rolle der politischen Institutionen', in U. Backes, T. Jaskułowski and A. Polese (eds), *Totalitarismus und Transformation: Defizite der Demokratiekonsolidierung im Mittel- und Osteuropa* (Göttingen, 2011), 49–62, here 60.

21. This analysis contains a detailed section on the President of the State; see also Ziemer, Poland, in this volume; Ismayr, 'Die politischen Systeme Osteuropas im Vergleich', 28.

22. The president of the Federal Republic of Germany is a special case: the constitution does not explicitly provide him or her with a veto power, but he or she may decline to sign a law to which he or she has raised objections. This competence is similar to a veto power but weaker.
23. See the individual country reports in this volume; see also Ismayr, 'Die politischen Systeme Osteuropas im Vergleich', 24.
24. See Poland in this volume; see also Ismayr, 'Die politischen Systeme Osteuropas im Vergleich', 10.
25. See the individual country reports in this volume; see also Ferdinand Müller-Rommel, 'Regierungen: Binnenstrukturen der Kernexekutiven', in Grotz and Müller-Rommel, *Regierungssysteme in Mittel- und Osteuropa*, 217–34, here 220.
26. See the individual country reports in this volume; see also Grotz and Müller-Rommel, *Regierungssysteme in Mittel- und Osteuropa*, appendix, 321–79, here 370–72; Ismayr, 'Die politischen Systeme Osteuropas im Vergleich', 33.
27. See the individual country reports in this volume; see also Müller-Rommel, 'Regierungen: Binnenstrukturen der Kernexekutiven', 222; Ismayr, 'Die politischen Systeme Osteuropas im Vergleich', 32.
28. See R. Rose, *The Problem of Party Government* (New York, 1974), 398.
29. See the individual country reports in this volume; see also Müller-Rommel, 'Regierungen: Binnenstrukturen der Kernexekutiven', 220.
30. See the individual country reports in this volume; see also K. Vodička, *Das politische System Tschechiens* (Wiesbaden, 2005), 201; Silvia von Steinsdorf, 'Parlamente: Binnenorganisation im Spannungsfeld von Inklusion und Effizienz', in Grotz and Müller-Rommel, *Regierungssysteme in Mittel- und Osteuropa*, 172–93, here 188.
31. See the country reports in this volume; see also F. Müller-Rommel and F. Grotz, 'Die Regierungssysteme der neuen EU-Staaten: institutionelle Konfigurationen und Entwicklungspfade', in Grotz and Müller-Rommel, *Regierungssysteme in Mittel- und Osteuropa*, 303–20, here 311.
32. See Steinsdorf, 'Parlamente', 186.
33. See the country reports in this volume; see also Ismayr, 'Die politischen Systeme Osteuropas im Vergleich', 39; Müller-Rommel and Grotz, 'Die Regierungssysteme der neuen EU-Staaten', 311; Steinsdorf, 'Parlamente', 186–88.
34. See the individual country reports in this volume; see also Merkel, *Systemtransformation* (2010), 119; P. Harfst, 'Wahlsysteme: institutionelle Entwicklung und politische Auswirkungen', in Grotz and Müller-Rommel, *Regierungssysteme in Mittel- und Osteuropa*, 107–26, here 123; D. Nohlen, *Wahlrecht und Parteiensystem* (Opladen, 2007), 239; Ismayr, 'Die politischen Systeme Osteuropas im Vergleich', 51; K. Schmitz, 'Wahl- und Parteiensysteme in Osteuropa: Eine Neubewertung anhand des Konzentrationseffekts', *Zeitschrift für Parlamentsfragen* 37 (2006), 353–76.
35. See D. Bungs, 'Die Rückkehr Estlands, Lettlands und Litauens nach Europa (1989–1999)', in A. Gabanyi and K. Schroeder (eds), *Vom Baltikum zum Schwarzen Meer* (Munich, 2002), 173–96, here 178; Ismayr, 'Die politischen Systeme Osteuropas im Vergleich', 48.
36. See M. Brusis, 'Ostmittel- und Südosteuropa: Die demokratische Konsolidierung bleibt aus', in Bertelsmann Stiftung (ed.),'Transformationsindex BTI 2012', 58–66, here 61.
37. See Ismayr, 'Die politischen Systeme Osteuropas im Vergleich', 48.
38. See 'Ungarn, Verfassungsgericht kippt Orbáns Wahlrechtsreform', *Frankfurter Allgemeine Zeitung*, 5 January 2013, 1f.; Renwick, 'Im Interesse der Macht'.

39. See D. Nohlen and M. Kasapovic, *Wahlsysteme und Systemwechsel in Osteuropa* (Opladen, 1996), 49.
40. See the individual country reports in this volume; see also Harfst, 'Wahlsysteme', 123; Nohlen and Kasapovic, *Wahlsysteme und Systemwechsel in Osteuropa*, 41; Ismayr, 'Die politischen Systeme Osteuropas im Vergleich', 48–49.
41. See the individual country reports in this volume; see also Ismayr, 'Die politischen Systeme Osteuropas im Vergleich', 51.
42. See information in Figure 12.3; see also K. Ziemer, 'Wahlen in postsozialistischen Staaten', in K. Ziemer (ed.), *Wahlen in postsozialistischen Staaten* (Opladen, 2003), 9–28, here 28; K. Vodička and L. Cabada, *Politický systém České republiky* (Prague, 2011), 444.
43. See Brusis, 'Ostmittel- und Südosteuropa' (2012), 61.
44. The Slovak Republic is somewhat of an exception; the 1998 parliamentary elections there were once again a referendum on the nature of the political regime. See K. Vodička, 'Wahlen und Transition in der Slowakei', in Ziemer, *Wahlen in postsozialistischen Staaten*, 255–82, here 274.
45. See Ziemer, 'Wahlen in postsozialistischen Staaten', 26.
46. See figures below in the 'Politics' subsection of the 'State of Consolidation in 2012' section; see also Hungary in this volume (Dieringer).
47. See A. Bozóki, 'Autoritäre Versuchung: Die Krise der ungarischen Demokratie', *Osteuropa* 61(12) (2011), 65–87, here 65; Gábor, 'Hochproblematisch', 145; Renwick, 'Im Interesse der Macht', 16.
48. See G. Brunner, 'Die neue Verfassungsgerichtsbarkeit in Osteuropa', *Zeitschrift für ausländisches Öffentliches Recht und Völkerrecht* 53 (1993), 819–26, here 819; Vodička, *Das politische System Tschechiens*, 220; Herwig Roggemann (ed.), *Die Verfassungen Mittel- und Osteuropas* (Berlin, 1999), 116.
49. See Roggemann, *Die Verfassungen Mittel- und Osteuropas*, 122; Ismayr, 'Die politischen Systeme Osteuropas im Vergleich', 18; Vodička, *Das politische System Tschechiens*, 220.
50. See country reports in this volume; see also Ismayr, 'Die politischen Systeme Osteuropas im Vergleich', 19.
51. See Gábor, 'Hochproblematisch', 149; Brusis, 'Ostmittel- und Südosteuropa' (2012), 60; H. Küpper, 'Mit Mängeln: Ungarns neues Grundgesetz', *Osteuropa* 61(12) (2011), 135–44, here 140 and 144; Bozóki, 'Autoritäre Versuchung', 86.
52. See 'Ungarn. Europäischer Gerichtshof stoppt ungarische Justizreform', *Frankfurter Allgemeine Zeitung*, 6 November 2012.
53. A.U. Gabanyi, 'Politisches Lehrstück', *Osteuropa* 62(9) (2012), 15–36, here 25f; D. Ursprung, 'Machtkampf in Rumänien', *Osteuropa* 62(9) (2012), 3–14, here 11; 'Rumäniens Verfassungsgericht ruft um Hilfe', 7 August 2012 (http://www.swissinfo.ch/ger/rumaeniens-verfassungsgericht-ruft-um-hilfe/33263170; accessed 7 January 2013).
54. See 'Rumänien: EU-Kommission erwartet rasches und eindeutiges Bekenntnis zu Rechtsstaatlichkeit und einer unabhängigen Justiz' (http://europa.eu/rapid/press-release_IP-12-799_de.htm; accessed 5 February 2013); 'Todesdrohungen gegen Rumäniens Richter', 9 August 2012 (http://www.euractiv.de/wahlen-und-macht/artikel/todesdrohungen-gegen-rumaniens-richter-006615; accessed 7 January 2013); G. Westerwelle, 'Wir werden die Entwicklung in Rumänien nicht ignorieren', *Frankfurter Allgemeine Zeitung*, 7 July 2012; Gabanyi, 'Politisches Lehrstück', 25f.
55. See Ursprung, 'Machtkampf in Rumänien', 13.
56. See the country reports in this volume; see also Roggemann, *Die Verfassungen Mittel- und Osteuropas*, 116; Vodička, *Das politische System Tschechiens*, 228.

57. See R. Reißig, 'Von der privilegierten und blockierten zur zukunftsorientierten Transformation', Bundeszentrale für politische Bildung, 19 July 2010 (http://www.bpb.de/apuz/32610/von-der-privilegierten-und-blockierten-zur-zukunftsorientierten-transformation?p=all; accessed 18 September 2012).

58. See the individual country reports in this volume; see also Ismayr, 'Die politischen Systeme Osteuropas im Vergleich', 10.

59. See the individual country reports in this volume; see also Ismayr, 'Die politischen Systeme Osteuropas im Vergleich' (2010), 52; W. Merkel, 'Die Bedeutung von Parteien und Parteiensystemen für die Konsolidierung der Demokratie: ein interregionaler Vergleich', in W. Merkel and E. Sandschneider (eds), *Systemwechsel 3* (Opladen, 1997), 337–67, here 348.

60. See the country reports in this volume; see also Brusis, 'Ostmittel- und Südosteuropa' (2012), 61.

61. See the country reports in this volume; see also Ismayr, 'Die politischen Systeme Osteuropas im Vergleich', 51.

62. See H. Gehring and C. Thane, 'Slowakei vor Regierungswechsel', Konrad-Adenauer-Stiftung, 4 (http://www.kas.de/wf/doc/kas_30433-1522–1–30.pdf; accessed 11 November 2012).

63. See the relevant country reports in this volume; see also Ismayr, 'Die politischen Systeme Osteuropas im Vergleich', 58; A. Reetz, 'Das Baltikum: Stabilität in der Instabilität. Die fünften Parlamente in Estland, Lettland und Litauen', *Zeitschrift für Parlamentsfragen* 42(1) (2011), 96–117, here 114–17.

64. See the relevant country reports in this volume; see also Ismayr, 'Die politischen Systeme Osteuropas im Vergleich', 56; Reetz, 'Das Baltikum', 114–17.

65. See the country reports in this volume, in particular Poland, the Czech Republic, Latvia and Hungary; see also Reetz, 'Das Baltikum', 114–17.

66. See Merkel, *Systemtransformation* (2010), 402.

67. See the country reports in this volume, in particular Poland, Czech Republic, Latvia and Hungary; see also M. Vásárhelyi, 'Angriff auf die Pressefreiheit: Die Medienpolitik der Fidezs-Regierung', *Osteuropa* 61(12) (2011), 157–66, here 159; Vodička and Cabada, *Politický systém České republiky*, 447f.; J. Sopóci, 'Ekonomické záujmové skupiny v slovenskej politike v 90 rokoch', *Politologický časopis* 2 (2001), 166–76, here 174; M. Klíma, 'Výročí televizní manipulace', *Mladá fronta dnes*, 14 March 2003, 8; J. Pehe, 'Vítězství politického šíbrovství', 1 (http://www.pehe.cz/zapisnik/2003/vitezstvi-politickeho-sibrovstvi; accessed 2 October 2010).

68. In Hungary, for example, the sums unofficially transferred to political parties are estimated to be as much as ten times more than their official funding. See Vásárhelyi, 'Angriff auf die Pressefreiheit', 159; see also R. Winkelmann, *Politik und Wirtschaft im Baltikum: Stabilisierung von Demokratie und Marktwirtschaft in Estland, Lettland und Litauen* (Saarbrücken, 2007), 201f.; 'Studie zur Korruption innerhalb des staatlichen Bereichs der EU-Mitgliedsstaaten' (http://www.transparency.de/fileadmin/Regiepdfs/Wissen/Studie%20zur%20Korruption%20innerhalb%20des%20staatlichen%20-Bereichs%20der%20EU-Mitgliedsstaaten.pdf; accessed 11 November 2012).

69. Reetz, 'Das Baltikum', 114.

70. See the country reports in this volume, in particular Latvia, Poland and the Czech Republic; see also Vodička and Cabada, *Politický systém České republiky*, 448.

71. See Estonia in this volume.

72. See the country reports in this volume; see also Freedom House, Nations in Transit 2011.

73. See the country reports in this volume; see also Freedom House, Nations in Transit 2011.

74. See Freedom House, Nations in Transit 2011.

75. See Brusis, 'Ostmittel- und Südosteuropa' (2012), 60.

76. Source: Freedom House, Nations in Transit 2011.

77. See the report on Hungary in this volume; see also Vásárhelyi, 'Angriff auf die Pressefreiheit', 157.

78. See 'Umstrittenes Mediengesetz: EU droht Ungarn mit Verfahren', *Frankfurter Allgemeine Zeitung*, 23 January 2011; Vásárhelyi, 'Angriff auf die Pressefreiheit', 157; Brusis, 'Ostmittel- und Südosteuropa' (2012), 60.

79. See Brusis, 'Ostmittel- und Südosteuropa' (2012), 61.

80. See the relevant country reports in this volume.

81. Source: Transparency International Corruption Perceptions Index 2009 (http://www.transparency.de/Tabellarisches-Ranking.1526.0.html; accessed 25 January 2012).

82. For the Federal Republic of Germany, no data differentiating between East and West are available.

83. See the country reports in this volume; see also Transparency International Corruption Perceptions, Index 2009; Merkel, *Systemtransformation* (2010), 122–24; K. Vodička, 'Political Systems of the Czech and Slovak Republics: A Comparison of Risks and the Consolidation Process', in G. Mesežnikov and O. Gyárfášová (eds), *Slovakia: Ten Years of Independence and a Year of Reforms* (Bratislava, 2004), 27–48, here 41; Sopóci, 'Ekonomické záujmo', 174; Klíma, 'Výročí televizní manipulace'; Pehe, 'Vítězství politického šíbrovství', 1.

84. See K. Vodička, 'Motivationskrise als Auslöser des Systemwechsels in Osteuropa', *Osteuropa* 46(8) (1996), 808–24; S. Kirelli, 'Vom Plan zum Markt: Der wirtschaftliche Transformationsprozess in Ostmitteleuropa', *Der Bürger im Staat* 97(3) (1997), 164–68, here 165; M. Ehrke, 'Das neue Europa: Ökonomie, Politik und Gesellschaft des postkommunistischen Kapitalismus', Friedrich Ebert Stiftung, September 2004, 2 (http://library.fes.de/pdf-files/id/02258.pdf; accessed 24 May 2012).

85. See country reports in this volume, in particular Poland and Estonia; see also M. Dauderstädt, 'Transformation und Integration der Wirtschaft der postkommunistischen Beitrittsländer', *Aus Politik und Zeitgeschichte* 50(5–6) (2004), 15–24, here 15; figures on inflation: http://de.wikipedia.org/wiki/Transformationsökonomie (accessed 11 April 2012).

86. See Poland in this volume; see also Dauderstädt, 'Transformation und Integration', 15.

87. See Estonia in this volume; see also Dauderstädt, 'Transformation und Integration', 15.

88. See Latvia in this volume; see also C. Matthes and U. Wethkamp, 'Aufbruch zur Marktwirtschaft: Lettlands Wirtschaft im ersten Jahr nach der Unabhängigkeit', *Materialien und Dokumente zur Friedens- und Konfliktforschung*, No. 17 (Berlin, 1993), 1f.; K. Schrader and C.F. Laaser, 'Wirtschaft Lettlands', in H. Graf and M. Kerner (eds), *Handbuch Baltikum heute* (Berlin, 1998), 181–210, here 181.

89. See Latvia in this volume; see also Matthes and Wethkamp, 'Aufbruch zur Marktwirtschaft', 5.

90. See Lithuania in this volume; see also U. Böllhoff, *10 Jahre Systemtransformation in den baltischen Staaten: Eine vergleichende empirische Analyse unter besonderer Berücksichtigung länderspezifischer Ausgangsbedingungen und Aspekten zur Integration in die Europäische Union* (Freiburg, 2002), 61.

91. Wages in the GDR were about 7 per cent of the West German level at the beginning of 1990; by the end of that year they had already reached 39 per cent. See M. Fritsch and M. Wyrwich, 'Wirtschaft im Schock', Bundeszentrale für Politische Bildung, 15

November 2010 (http://www.bpb.de/geschichte/deutsche-einheit/lange-wege-der-deut schen-einheit/47101/wirtschaft-im-schock?p=all; accessed 10 October 2012).

92. See ibid.

93. See the GDR in this volume.

94. See 'Karl Otto Pöhl ist überzeugt: "Der Kurs beim Umtausch war verhängnisvoll"', *Die Welt*, 29 August 2004 (http://www.welt.de/print-wams/article115077/Karl-Otto-Poehl-ist-ueberzeugt-Der-Kurs-beim-Umtausch-war-verhaengnisvoll.html; accessed 22 September 2012).

95. See the Czech Republic in this volume; see also J. Kosta, *Die tschechische/tschecho-slowakische Wirtschaft im mehrfachen Wandel* (Münster, 2005), 161f.

96. See K. Vodička, 'Koalitionsabsprache: Wir teilen den Staat!', in R. Kipke and K. Vodička (eds), *Abschied von der Tschechoslowakei* (Cologne, 1993), 77–106, here 106; I. Šujan, 'Wirtschaftliche Folgen der Trennung', in Kipke and Vodička, *Abschied von der Tschechoslowakei*, 153–62, here 162.

97. See Slovenia in this volume.

98. See Hungary in this volume.

99. See Romania in this volume.

100. These were distributed to citizens only, in quantities based on the number of years they had lived in the country. See Matthes and Wethkamp, 'Aufbruch zur Marktwirtschaft', 5.

101. See Latvia in this volume.

102. See S.V. Vardys and W.A. Slaven, 'Lithuania', in W.R. Iwaskiw (ed.), *Estonia, Latvia and Lithuania: Country Studies* (Washington, 1996), 167–242, here 208.

103. See Lithuania in this volume; see also Winkelmann, *Politik und Wirtschaft im Baltikum*, 268.

104. See Poland in this volume.

105. See the GDR in this volume.

106. See the Slovak Republic in this volume; see also G. Mesežnikov, 'Die Slowakei', in Gabanyi and Schroeder, *Vom Baltikum zum Schwarzen Meer*, 339–66, here 350–52.

107. See Hungary in this volume; see also J. Dieringer, *Staatlichkeit im Wandel? Die Regulierung der Sektoren Verkehr, Telekommunikation und Energie im ungarischen Transformationsprozess* (Opladen, 2001).

108. See Romania in this volume. On the Romanian economy, see http://dewikipedia.org/wiki/Wirtschaft_Rumäniens (accessed 4 October 2012).

109. See the section 'Politics' in this chapter; see also G. Pickel, 'Die subjektive Verankerung der Demokratie in Osteuropa: Die Legitimität der Demokratie in der Bevölkerung als Faktor demokratischer Stabilität und Qualität', in Backes, Jaskułowski and Polese, *Totalitarismus und Transformation*, 261–83 here 262; Merkel, *Systemtransformation* (2010), 164; Kirelli, 'Vom Plan zum Markt', 165.

110. See Poland in this volume; see also Mały Rocznik, *Statystyczny 2010*, 610f.

111. Due to the introduction of the deutschmark and high wage agreements, wages rose from 7 per cent to about 80 per cent of the West German level in the course of a few years. See B. Martens, 'Wirtschaftlicher Zusammenbruch und Neuanfang nach 1990', Bundeszentrale für Politische Bildung, 30 March 2010 (http://www.bpb.de/geschichte/deutsche-einheit/lange-wege-der-deutschen-einheit/47133/zusammenbruch; accessed 10 October 2012).

112. See Figure 12.16, Economy; Source: WKO, 'Arbeitslosenquoten' (http://wko.at/statistik/eu/europa-arbeitslosenquoten.pdf); Bundesagentur für Arbeit, 'Monatsbericht May 2012' (http://www.bpb.de/nachschlagen/zahlen-und-fakten/soziale-situation-in-deutschland/61718/arbeitslose-und-arbeitslosenquote; accessed 11 June 2012).

113. Source: 'Die deutsche Einheit kostete 1,6 Billionen Euro', *Frankfurter Allgemeine Zeitung*, 21 August 2009; see also F. Zinsmeister, 'Die Finanzierung der deutschen Einheit: Zum Umgang mit den Schuldlasten der Wiedervereinigung', *Vierteljahrshefte zur Wirtschaftsforschung* 78(2) (2009), 146–60.

114. That is, the 16.64 million GDR citizens in 1989, source: http://www.ddr-wissen.de/wiki/ddr.pl?Bev%F6lkerung (accessed 17 October 2012).

115. In 2010, the Czech Republic had a budget of 40 million euros. Sources: http://www.zeit.de/wirtschaft/2010–03/Aufbau-os-interview/seite-1; http://cs.wikipedia.org/wiki/Státní_rozpočet_České_republiky (accessed 28 October 2012).

116. See 'Jugendarbeitslosigkeit erreicht Tiefstand', *Frankfurter Allgemeine Zeitung*, 1 June 2012, 13.

117. See E15–3 (http://www.e15.cz/financni-data/makroekonomika/?utm_medium=cpc& utm_source=seznam& utm_campaign=prum-mzda; accessed 18 April 2012).

118. See AHK-Umfrage in Tschechien Online, 29 June 2010 (http://www.tschechien-online org/news/17096–tschechien-deutschen-investoren-favorisiert; accessed 20 May 2012).

119. See the Slovak Republic in this volume; see also S. Mau and R. Verwiebe, *Die Sozialstruktur Europas* (Konstanz, 2009), 149; Z. Bútorová and O. Gyárfášová, 'Contemporary Slovakia in Public Opinion', in M. Bútora, G. Mesežnikov and M. Kollár (eds), *Trends in Quality of Democracy: Slovakia 2009* (Bratislava, 2010), 125–55, here 152.

120. See information and figures in the section on political parties.

121. See information and figures in the section 'Elections'.

122. See Figure 12.20; see also M. Ehrke, 'Die Europäische Union und der postkommunistische Raum', *Kompass 2020* (2007), 6 (http://www.fes.de/kompass2020/pdf/postkommunism us.pdf; accessed 7 May 2012); J. Jakobs, *Tücken der Demokratie: Antisystemeinstellungen und ihre Determinanten in sieben postkommunistischen Transformationsländern* (Wiesbaden, 2004); Merkel, *Systemtransformation* (2010), 423.

123. See Pickel, 'Die subjektive Verankerung der Demokratie in Osteuropa'; Jakobs, *Tücken der Demokratie*; Merkel, *Systemtransformation* (2010), 423; Vodička and Cabada, *Politický systém České republiky*, 447; G. Pickel and J. Jacobs, 'Der soziokulturelle Unterbau der neuen Demokratien Osteuropas', in G. Pickel, D. Pollack, O. Müller and J. Jacobs (eds), *Osteuropas Bevölkerung auf dem Weg in die Demokratie: Repräsentative Untersuchungen in Ostdeutschland und zehn osteuropäischen Transformationsstaaten* (Wiesbaden, 2006), 31–52.

124. See M. Brusis, 'Ostmittel- und Südosteuropa', in Bertelsmann Stiftung (ed.), *Transformation Index 2010* (Gütersloh, 2009), 125–43, here 127; W. Merkel, 'Gegen alle Theorie? Die Konsolidierung der Demokratie in Ostmitteleuropa', in Backes, Jaskułowski and Polese, *Totalitarismus und Transformation*, 14–48; S. Kailitz, 'Die kulturelle Prägung macht den Unterschied! Zur Regimeentwicklung postkommunist- ischer Staaten', in C. Vollnhals (ed.), *Jahre des Umbruchs: Friedliche Revolution in der DDR und Transition in Ostmitteleuropa* (Göttingen, 2011), 361–92; Vodička and Cabada, *Politický systém České republiky*, 444.

125. See Figure 12.21; see also 'Transformationsindex BTI 2012, Status Index für das Jahr 2012'. Similar: Freedom House, 'Regions' (http://www.freedomhouse.org/regions/central-and-eastern-europeeurasia); Kailitz, 'Die kulturelle Prägung macht den Unterschied!'; Ismayr, 'Die politischen Systeme Osteuropas im Vergleich', 9f.

126. See Pickel, 'Die subjektive Verankerung der Demokratie in Osteuropa', 261.

127. See Merkel, *Systemtransformation* (2010), 124f.; Pickel, 'Die subjektive Verankerung der Demokratie in Osteuropa', 262.

128. See Merkel, *Systemtransformation* (1999), 146.

129. See Merkel, *Systemtransformation* (2010), 124–25.
130. The wording of the question was 'Are you very satisfied, rather satisfied/not really satisfied, not at all satisfied with the way in which democracy works in your country?' Sources: 1997 = Central and Eastern Europe Eurobarometer 8; figures for Austria and the Netherlands from Eurobarometer 48; for FRG-West and FRG-East from WVS (1996); 1999 = WVS; 2000 = Pickel, 'Die subjektive Verankerung der Demokratie in Osteuropa', 267; figures for Austria and the Netherlands from Eurobarometer 53; 2007/2009 = Eurobarometer surveys; figures for FRG-West and FRG-East from G. Pickel, 'Gerechtigkeit und Politik in der deutschen Bevölkerun: Die Folgen der Wahrnehmung von Gerechtigkeit für die politische Kultur im vereinten Deutschland', unpublished manuscript, 2012.
131. Source: Pickel, 'Die subjektive Verankerung der Demokratie in Osteuropa', 269 (based on PCE 2000).
132. Pickel, 'Die subjektive Verankerung der Demokratie in Osteuropa', 269.
133. See Figure 12.3.
134. See U. Backes, 'Probleme der Demokratiekonsolidierung im östlichen Deutschland'. in G. Besier and K. Stoklosa (eds), *15 Jahre deutsche Einheit: Was ist geworden?* (Berlin, 2007), 41–56, here 49.
135. See Ismayr, 'Die politischen Systeme Osteuropas im Vergleich', 68; Backes, 'Probleme der Demokratiekonsolidierung im östlichen Deutschland', 49; Vodička and Cabada, *Politický systém České republiky*, 251.
136. See Pickel, 'Die subjektive Verankerung der Demokratie in Osteuropa', 261; Kailitz, 'Die kulturelle Prägung macht den Unterschied!'
137. See 'Zukunft Ost: Ende der Ost-West-Abwanderung geschafft?', Migazin, (http://www.migazin.de/2012/09/04/ende-de–ost-west-abwanderung-in-geschafft; accessed 27 November 2012).
138. See, among others, S. Kühntopf and S. Stedtfeld, 'Wenige junge Frauen im ländlichen Raum: Ursachen und Folgen der selektiven Abwanderung in Ostdeutschland', *BiB Working Paper* 3/2012 (http://www.Bibdemografie.de/SharedDocs/Publikationen/DE/Download/BiB_Working_Paper/Geschlechterproportionen.pdf?__blob=publicationFile&v=6; accessed 28 November 2012).
139. See 'Zukunft Ost: Ende der Ost-West-Abwanderung geschafft?'.
140. See the GDR in this volume.
141. See M. Knogler, 'Öffnung der Arbeitsmärkte zum 1. Mai 2011: Positive Effekte überwiegen', Osteuropa Institut Regensburg, Kurzanalysen und Informationen No. 51, April 2011 (http://www.dokumente.ios-regensburg.de/publikationen/info/info-51.pdf; accessed 27 November 2012).
142. See Romania in this volume.
143. See Lithuania in this volume.
144. See Latvia in this volume.
145. See Hungary in this volume.
146. See Poland in this volume.
147. See the Czech Republic in this volume.
148. See ibid.
149. See the Slovak Republic in this volume; see also S. Hradil, *Die Sozialstruktur Deutschlands im internationalen Vergleich* (Wiesbaden, 2006), 53.
150. See the country reports in this volume.
151. See ibid.
152. See Merkel, *Systemtransformation* (1999), 164; Pickel, 'Die subjektive Verankerung der Demokratie in Osteuropa', 262.

153. See Jakobs, *Tücken der Demokratie*; Merkel, *Systemtransformation* (2010), 423; Vodička and Cabada, *Politický systém České republiky*, 447; Pickel and Jacobs, 'Der soziokulturelle Unterbau der neuen Demokratien Osteuropas'; Pickel, 'Die subjektive Verankerung der Demokratie in Osteuropa'.

154. W. Rudzio, *Das politische System der Bundesrepublik Deutschland* (Wiesbaden, 2011), 514; see also F. Schorlemmer, 'Wir haben noch immer eine auseinanderdriftende Gesellschaft', in W. Heitmeyer (ed.), *Deutsch-deutsche Zustände: 20 Jahre nach dem Mauerfall* (Frankfurt a. M., 2009), 311–23.

155. W. Ismayr, 'Das politische System Deutschlands', in W. Ismayr (ed.), *Die politischen Systeme Westeuropas* (Opladen, 1997), 407–44, here 432.

156. See Freedom House, Nations in Transit 2011.

157. See the individual country reports in this volume; see also Kirelli, 'Vom Plan zum Markt', 164–65; Pickel, 'Die subjektive Verankerung der Demokratie in Osteuropa', 262; Merkel, *Systemtransformation* (1999), 164.

158. See country reports in this volume; see also F. Eckert, *Vom Plan zum Markt: Parteipolitik und Privatisierungsprozesse in Osteuropa* (Wiesbaden, 2008), 261; Kirelli, 'Vom Plan zum Markt', 164–65.

159. See Reißig, 'Von der privilegierten und blockierten zur zukunftsorientierten Transformation'.

160. See Brusis, 'Ostmittel- und Südosteuropa' (2012), 62.

161. See the country reports in this volume; see also Ismayr, 'Die politischen Systeme Osteuropas im Vergleich'; Merkel, 'Gegen alle Theorie?'; Kailitz,' Die kulturelle Prägung macht den Unterschied!'

162. Freedom House, 'Freedom in the World 2011' (http://www.freedomhouse.org/template. cfm?page=363& year=2011&country=7594; accessed 24 February 2012).

163. Merkel, 'Gegen alle Theorie?', 37.

164. See 'Transformationsindex BTI 2012', appendix. The BTI 2010 designated the first thirteen transformation countries in the BTI-Ranking Status Index as 'having made much progress'. Bulgaria and Romania, at 14 and 16 respectively, were seen as 'having made progress'.

165. See Poland in this volume; see also Brusis, 'Ostmittel- und Südosteuropa' (2012), 58.

166. However, this is a relative decline, in comparison to other transformation countries, during the first decade of this century. This section's opening statement – that the level of consolidation has tended to increase since 1990 – is not in question.

167. See, e.g., Brusis, 'Ostmittel- und Südosteuropa' (2012), 58.

168. Ibid.

169. Ibid.

170. The exception is Lithuania, which BTI and Freedom House clearly judge more positively. Its downward trend in Figure 12.20 is due to extremely low figures for satisfaction and trust.

171. See K. Vodička, 'Wir sind moralisch krank geworden: Die Neujahransprache des tschechoslowakischen Staatspräsidenten', *Osteuropa* 40(4) (1990), 248–53, here 250.

172. R. Dahrendorf, *Betrachtungen über die Revolution in Europa* (Stuttgart, 1990), 101; see also Merkel, *Systemtransformation* (1999), 164; Kirelli, 'Vom Plan zum Markt', 164–65.

BIBLIOGRAPHY

Ágh, A. 'Bumpy Road Ahead in East Central Europe: Post-Accession Crisis and Social Challenge in ECE', in A. Ágh and A. Ferencz (eds), *Overcoming the EU Crisis: EU Perspectives after the Eastern Enlargement* (Budapest, 2007), 7–35.

Ágh, A. 'The Role of ECE Parliaments in the EU Integration', in A. Ágh (ed.), *Post-Accession in East-Central Europe: The Emergence of the EU 25* (Budapest, 2004), 69–92.

Aidukaite, J. 'Die Entwicklung in der post-sowjetischen Ära: Das litauische Wohlfahrtssystem', in K. Schubert, S. Hegelich and U. Bazanz (eds), *Europäische Wohlfahrtssysteme: Ein Handbuch* (Wiesbaden, 2008), 403–22.

Aidukaite, J. 'The Transformation of Welfare Systems in the Baltic States: Estonia, Latvia and Lithuania', in A. Cerami (ed.), *Post-Communist Welfare Pathways* (Basingstoke, 2009), 96–111.

Akule, D. 'Parliamentary Elections in Latvia: Victory Celebrations Will Be Short as Austerity Measures Should Be Introduced Quickly', *Policy Brief* 27 (October 2010).

Albert, M. *Capitalisme contre capitalisme*. Paris, 1991.

Alexandru, V., A. Moraru and L. Ercuş. *Declinul participării la vot în România: Doar jumătate din participanții la vot din'90 mai sunt astăzi interesați să voteze*. Bucharest, 2009.

Arndt, M. 'Nach den Stasi-Enthüllungen: die bulgarisch orthodoxe Kirche in Staat und Gesellschaft', Konrad-Adenauer-Stiftung. Retrieved 13 February 2013 from http://www.kas.de/wf/doc/kas_6329–1442–1–30.pdf?120329113718.

Aston, C. *Makers of the Modern World: Antonius Piip, Zigfrids Meierovics and Augustinas Voldemaras. The Baltic States*. London, 2010.

Austrevicius, P. 'The Accession of Lithuania to the EU', in G. Vassiliou (ed.), *The Accession Story: The EU from Fifteen to Twenty-Five Countries* (Oxford, 2007), 225–58.

Backes, U. 'Die Linke in der Zerreißprobe: Das "Superwahljahr" 2011 und seine Folgen', in E. Jesse (ed.), *Neue Herausforderungen des politischen Extremismus in Deutschland* (Baden-Baden, 2013), 224–231.

Backes, U. 'Polarisierung aus dem Osten? Linke und rechte Flügelparteien bei der Bundestagswahl 2005', in E. Jesse and R. Sturm (eds), *Bilanz der Bundestagswahl 2005: Voraussetzungen, Ergebnisse, Folgen* (Wiesbaden, 2006), 157–76.

Backes, U. 'Probleme der Demokratiekonsolidierung im östlichen Deutschland', in G. Besier and K. Stoklosa (eds), *15 Jahre deutsche Einheit: Was ist geworden?* (Berlin, 2007), 41–56.

Backes, U. 'Strukturwandel realsozialistischer Autokratien: Vom Totalitarismus zur Transition', in C. Vollnhals (ed.), *Jahre des Umbruchs: Friedliche Revolution in der DDR und Transition in Ostmitteleuropa* (Göttingen, 2011), 141–58.

Backes, U., T. Jaskulowski and A. Polese. *Totalitarismus und Transformation: Defizite der Demokratiekonsolidierung in Mittel- und Osteuropa*. Göttingen, 2009.

Bajomi-Lázár, P. *Romania: A Country Report for the ERC-Funded Project on Media and Democracy in Central and Eastern Europe*. Oxford, 2011.

Bakardjieva, R. 'Der Privatisierungsprozess in Bulgarien: Strategien, Widersprüche und Schlussfolgerungen', Universität Potsdam. Retrieved 13 February 2013 from http://opus.kobv.de/ubp/volltexte/2011/4880/pdf/fiwi-disk_s05.pdf.

Bakke, E., and I. Peters (eds). *20 Years since the Fall of the Berlin Wall: Transitions, State Break-Up and Democratic Politics in Central Europe and Germany*. Cambridge/Berlin, 2011.

Balcerowicz, L. *Socialism, Capitalism and Transformation*. New York, 1995.

Balcytiene, A. 'Lithuanian Media: A Question of Change', in P. Vihalemm (ed.), *Baltic Media in Transition* (Tartu, 2002), 103–34.

Bartošek, K. 'Støední a jiho východní Evropa (Zentral- und Südosteuropa)', in S. Courtois (ed.) *Černá kniha komunismu* (Das Schwarzbuch des Kommunismus) (Prague, 1999), 350–407.

Beck, U. 'Vereinigt und doch zweigeteilt: Zum Stand der deutsch-deutschen Konvergenz auf wirtschaftlichem Gebiet', in K. Bohr and A. Krause (eds), *20 Jahre Deutsche Einheit: Bilanz und Perspektiven*, 2nd ed. (Baden-Baden, 2011), 63–98.

Beichelt, T. 'Die Rolle der politischen Institutionen', in U. Backes, T. Jaskulowski and A. Polese (eds), *Totalitarismus und Transformation: Defizite der Demokratiekonsolidierung im Mittel – und Osteuropa* (Göttingen, 2011), 49–62.

Berend, I.T. *From the Soviet Bloc to the European Union: The Economic and Social Transformation of Central and Eastern Europe since 1973*. Cambridge, 2009.

Besier, G (ed.). *20 Jahre neue Bundesrepublik: Kontinuitäten und Diskontinuitäten*. Berlin, 2012.

Besier, G. 'Das Ost-West-Verhältnis in Deutschland: Ein Volk mit unterschiedlichen Einstellungen, Verhaltensweisen und Kulturen?', in G. Besier and K. Stoklosa (eds), *15 Jahre deutsche Einheit* (Berlin, 2007), 25–39.

Besier, G., and K. Stoklosa (eds). *15 Jahre deutsche Einheit: Was ist geworden?* Berlin, 2007.

Best, H., R. Gebauer, and A. Salheiser (eds). *Elites and Social Change: The Socialist and Post-Socialist Experience*. Hamburg, 2009.

Best, H., and E. Holtmann. 'Die langen Wege der deutschen Einigung: Aufbruch mit vielen Unbekannten', in H. Best and E. Holtmann (eds), *Aufbruch der entsicherten Gesellschaft: Deutschland nach der Wiedervereinigung* (Frankfurt a. M., 2012), 15–29.

Beyer, J., J. Wielgohs and H. Wiesenthal. *Successful Transitions: Political Factors of Socio-Economic Progress in Postsocialist Countries.* Baden-Baden, 2001.

Beyme, K. *Das politische System der Bundesrepublik Deutschland: Eine Einführung.* Wiesbaden, 2010.

Beyme, K.v. *Systemwechsel in Osteuropa.* Frankfurt a. M., 1994.

Bihari, M. *Magyar Politika 1944–2004.* Budapest, 2005.

Blasum, E. 'Tripartism and Industrial Relations in Latvia', in G. Casale (ed.), *Social Dialogue in Central and Eastern Europe* (Budapest, 1999), 202–27.

Bohr, K., and A. Krause (eds). *20 Jahre Deutsche Einheit: Bilanz und Perspektiven*, 2nd ed. Baden-Baden, 2011.

Böick, M. '"Das ist nunmal der freie Markt": Konzeptionen des Marktes beim Wirtschaftsumbau in Ostdeutschland nach 1989'. *Zeithistorische Forschungen* 12 (2015), 448–73.

Böllhoff, U. *10 Jahre Systemtransformation in den baltischen Staaten: Eine vergleichende empirische Analyse unter besonderer Berücksichtigung länderspezifischer Ausgangsbedingungen und Aspekten zur Integration in die Europäische Union.* Freiburg, 2002.

Bongartz, U. 'Lettland: Saeima-Abgeordnete wählen Ex-Banker Andris Bērziņš zum neuen Staatspräsidenten', *Lettische Presseschau*, 2 June 2011. Retrieved 4 April 2012 from http://www.lettische-presseschau.de/politik/lett-land/445–lettland-saeima-abgeordnete-waehlen-ex-banker-andris-brzi-zum-neuen-staatspraesidenten.

Borič, T., and J. Pokorná. 'Die Wirtschaftsverfassung der Tschechischen Republik', in J. Marko, A. Ableitinger et al. (eds), *Revolution und Recht: Systemtransformation und Verfassungsentwicklung in der Tschechischen und Slowakischen Republik* (Frankfurt a. M., 2000), 117–47.

Bos, E., and D. Segert. *Osteuropäische Demokratien als Trendsetter? Parteien und Parteiensysteme nach dem Ende des Übergansjahrzehnts.* Opladen, 2008.

Bozóki, A. 'Autoritäre Versuchung: Die Krise der ungarischen Demokratie'. *Osteuropa* 61(12) (2011), 65–87.

Brahm, H., and J. Deimel. 'Bulgarien', in A. Gabanyi and K. Schroeder (eds), *Vom Baltikum zum Schwarzen Meer* (Munich, 2002), 197–220.

Breuel, B., and M.C. Burda (eds). *Ohne historisches Vorbild: Die Treuhandanstalt 1990 bis 1994. Eine kritische Würdigung.* Berlin, 2005.

Brunner, G. 'Die neue Verfassungsgerichtsbarkeit in Osteuropa'. *Zeitschrift für ausländisches Öffentliches Recht und Völkerrecht* 53 (1993), 819–26.

Brusis, M. 'Ostmittel- und Südosteuropa', in Bertelsmann Stiftung (ed.), *Transformation Index 2010* (Gütersloh, 2009), 125–43.

Brusis, M. 'Ostmittel- und Südosteuropa: Die demokratische Konsolidierung bleibt aus', in Bertelsmann Stiftung (ed.), *Transformationsindex BTI 2012* (Gütersloh, 2011), 58–66.

Budryte, D., and V. Pilinkaite-Sotirovic. 'Lithuania: Progressive Legislation without Popular Support', in B. Rechel (ed.), *Minority Rights in Central and Eastern Europe* (London, 2009), 151–65.

Bundesministerium des Innern (ed.). 'Jahresbericht der Bundesregierung zum Stand der Deutschen Einheit 2010'. Berlin, 2010.

Bundesministerium des Innern (ed.). 'Jahresbericht der Bundesregierung zum Stand der Deutschen Einheit'. Berlin, 2011.

Bundesstelle für Außenhandelsinformation. 'Ostmittel- und Osteuropa im Aufholprozess: Transformation und Wirtschaftslage in Ostmitteleuropa und der GUS 2000/2001'. Berlin, 2001.

Bundesstelle für Außenhandelsinformation. 'Wirtschaftsdaten aktuell: Slowakische Republik'. Cologne, November 1999.

Bungs, D. 'Die Rückkehr Estlands, Lettlands und Litauens nach Europa (1989–1999)', in A. Gabanyi and K. Schroeder (eds), *Vom Baltikum zum Schwarzen Meer* (Munich, 2002), 173–96.

Burger, B., and M. Lenzner. *Estland: Die Entwicklung der Wirtschafts- und Sozialpolitik*, Studie 4, HWWA-Report No. 145. Hamburg, 1994.

Butenschön, M. *Estland, Lettland, Litauen: Das Baltikum auf dem langen Weg in die Freiheit*. Munich, 1992.

Bútora, M., and Z. Bútorová. 'Neznesiteľná ľahkost' rozchodu', in K. Vodička (ed.), *Děle ní Československa: Deset let poté* (Prague, 2003), 69–104.

Bútora, M., et al. 'Foreign Policy: The Year of Anniversaries and Challenges', in M. Bútora, G. Mesežnikov and M. Kollár (eds), *Trends in Quality of Democracy: Slovakia 2009* (Bratislava, 2010), 105–23.

Bútorová, Z., and O. Gyárfášová. 'Contemporary Slovakia in Public Opinion', in M. Bútora, G. Mesežnikov and M. Kollár (eds), *Trends in Quality of Democracy: Slovakia 2009* (Bratislava, 2010), 125–55.

Cândea, S. 'Abandoning a Broken Model of Journalism', *NiemanReports*, 20 April 2011. Retrieved from http://www.nieman.harvard.edu/reports/article/102575/Abandoning-a-Broken-Model-of-Journalism.aspx.

Carey. H. (ed.). *Romania since 1989: Politics, Economics, and Society*. Lanham, MD, 2004.

Červenka, J. 'Demokracie, lidská práva a korupce mezi politiky', CVVM Company Report 2002, 3. Retrieved 15 September 2010 from http://www.cvvm.cas.Cz/upl/zpravy/100110s_pd21004.pdf.

Chichkova, B. *Der Transformationsprozess in Bulgarien: Politische, ökonomische und soziokulturelle Aspekte*. Frankfurt a. M., 2006.

Christova, C., and D. Förger. 'Zur Situation der Medien in Bulgarien', Konrad-Adenauer-Stiftung. Retrieved 15 February 2013 from http://www.kas.de/wf/doc/kas_30139–1522–1–30.pdf?120213153734.

Cornelius, P., and B. Weder. 'Economic Transformation and Income Distribution: Some Evidence from the Baltic Countries', IMF Working Paper 96/14, 1996.

Cramer-Langer, K. *Demokratisierung in der Slowakischen Republik: Entstehung und Entwicklung des Parteiensystems seit 1989*, special ed. Cologne, 1998.

Csaba, L. *The New Political Economy of Emerging Europe*. Budapest, 2005.

CVVM. 'Veøejnost o úspìšnosti ekonomické transformace'. Retrieved 18 September 2010 from http://www.cvvm.cas.cz/upl/zpravy/100497s_ev50622.pdf.

Dahrendorf, R. *Betrachtungen über die Revolution in Europa*. Stuttgart, 1990.

Dahrendorf, R. *Die Krisen der Demokratie: Ein Gespräch*. Munich, 2002.

Dăianu, D. *Transformarea ca proces real: De la comandă la piață*. Bucharest, 1999.

Danckworth, T.-G. 'Estlands Außenpolitik nach dem Beitritt zur Europäischen Union: Handlungsoptionen eines Kleinstaates'. PhD diss., TU Chemnitz 2007.

Dauchert, H. *'Anwalt der Balten' oder Anwalt in eigener Sache? Die deutsche Baltikumpolitik 1991–2004*. Berlin, 2008.

Dauderstädt, M. 'Transformation und Integration der Wirtschaft der postkommunistischen Beitrittsländer'. *Aus Politik und Zeitgeschichte* 43(5–6) (2004), 15–24.

Delhaes, K.v., W. Quaisser and K. Ziemer (eds). *Vom Sozialismus zur Marktwirtschaft: Wandlungsprozesse, Ergebnisse und Perspektiven*. Munich, 2009.

Deutsche Bank Research. 'Währungsreformen in den baltischen Staaten'. *Bulletin – Aktuelle Wirtschafts- und Währungsfragen*, 11 April 1994.

Deutscher Bundestag. 'Aktueller Begriff: Entwicklung der Wahlbeteiligung in der Bundesrepublik Deutschland'. Berlin, 2009.

Deutscher Bundestag. 'Entwicklung der Wahlbeteiligung in der Bundesrepublik Deutschland 2009'. Berlin, 2009.

Dieringer, J. *Das politische System der Republik Ungarn: Entstehung – Entwicklung – Europäisierung*. Opladen, 2009.

Dieringer, J. *Staatlichkeit im Wandel? Die Regulierung der Sektoren Verkehr, Telekommunikation und Energie im ungarischen Transformationsprozess*. Opladen, 2001.

Dieringer, J. 'Transformation der politischen Systeme in Mittel- und Osteuropa nach 1989/1990', in F. Müntefering (ed.), *Der Aufbau Ost im mittelosteuropäischen Vergleich: Eine Bilanz nach 25. Jahren* (Halle (Saale), 2016), 15–27.

Dieringer, J. 'Zwischen Parlamentsvorbehalt und Regierungsdominanz: die wachsende Bedeutung des ungarischen Parlaments im europäischen Integrationsprozess'. *Zeitschrift für Parlamentsfragen* 38(4) (2007), 764–75.

Dieringer, J., P. Laukó and G. Schneider. 'Towards a European Strategy for the Danube Area', in A. Ágh, T. Kaiser and B. Koller (eds), *Europeanization of the Danube Region: The Blue Ribbon Project* (Budapest, 2010), 64–91.

Donskis, L. 'Another Word for Uncertainty: Antisemitism in Modern Lithuania'. *Nordeuropaforum* 1 (2006), 7–26.

Dose, I. 'Nationale Minderheiten im Ostseeraum: Geschichte und Gegenwart, Identität und territoriale Anbindung'. PhD diss., Humboldt-Universität zu Berlin, 2010.

Dragoš, S. 'The Religious Picture of Slovenia: Who Is to Blame?', in M. Drčar-Murko et al. (eds), *Five Minutes of Democracy: The Image of Slovenia after 2004* (Ljubljana, 2004), 309–27.

Dreifelds, J. *Nations in Transit: Latvia 2007*. Retrieved 21 January 2011 from www.freedomhouse.org/inc/content/pubs/nit/inc_country_detail.cfm?page=47&nit=457&year=2008&pf.

Dreifelds, J. *Nations in Transit – Latvia 2008*. Retrieved 21 January 2011 from https://freedomhouse.org/report/nations-transit/2008/latvia.

Dreifelds, J. *Nations in Transit – Latvia 2009*, 307–325. Retrieved 21 January 2011 from https://freedomhouse.org/report/nations-transit/2009/latvia.

Dreifelds, J. *Nations in Transit – Latvia 2010*. Retrieved 21 January 2011 from https://freedomhouse.org/report/nations-transit/2010/latvia.

Eamets, R. 'Labour Market and Employment Issues in Transition Economies: The Case of Estonia'. *Communist Economies and Economic Transformation* 6(1) (1994), 55–73.

Eckart, K., and E. Jesse (eds). *Das wieder vereinigte Deutschland: Eine erweiterte oder eine neue Bundesrepublik?* Berlin, 1999.

Eckert, F. *Vom Plan zum Markt: Parteipolitik und Privatisierungsprozesse in Osteuropa*. Wiesbaden, 2008.

Eerma, D., and J. Sepp, 'Estonia in Transition under the Restrictions of European Institutional Competition', *Ordnungspolitische Diskurse* (2009). Retrieved 7 May 2012 from http://www.ordnungspolitisches-portal.com/Diskurse/ Diskurse_2009-02.pdf.

Eesti Erastamisagentuur (Estonian Privatization Agency). *Privatization in Estonia*. Tallinn, 1994.

Eesti Pank (Bank of Estonia), 'Estonian Kroon – Finance Economy' (June 1993).

Eesti Pank (Bank of Estonia), 'Law on the Central Bank of the Republic of Estonia', Version 18 (May 1993), English translation, manuscript with no year given.

Eesti Riiklik Arengukava, *European Union – Structural Funds*. Tallinn, no year given.

Ehrke, M. 'Die Europäische Union und der postkommunistische Raum'. *Kompass 2020* (2007). Retrieved 7 May 2012 from http://www.fes.de/kompass2020/pdf/ postkommunismus.pdf.

Ehrke, M. 'Das neue Europa: Ökonomie, Politik und Gesellschaft des post-kommunistischen Kapitalismus', Friedrich Ebert Stiftung, September 2004. Retrieved 24 May 2012 from http://library.fes.de/pdf-files/id/02258.pdf.

Ekiert, G., and S.E. Hanson (eds). *Capitalism and Democracy in Central and Eastern Europe: Assessing the Legacy of Communist Rule*. Cambridge, 2003.

Enache, M., and M. Constantinescu. *Renaşterea parlamentarismului în România*. Iaşi, 2001.

Ennuste, Ü., and L. Wilder. *Essays in Estonian Transformation Economics*. Tallinn, 2003.

Europäische Kommission. 'Agenda 2000. Eine stärkere und erweiterte Union'. *Bulletin der Europäischen Union*, Beilage 5/97, 46. Luxemburg, 1997.

Europäische Kommission. 'Stellungnahme der Kommission zum Antrag der Slowakei auf Beitritt zur Europäischen Union'. *Bulletin der Europäischen Union*, Beilage 9/97, 17. Luxemburg, 1997.

Falter, J.W., et al. *Sind wir ein Volk?* Munich, 2006.

Feest, D. *Zwangskollektivierung im Baltikum: Die Sowjetisierung des estnischen Dorfes 1944–1953*. Cologne and Vienna 2007.

Fink-Hafner, D. 'Slovenia since 1989', in S.P. Ramet (ed.), *Central and Southeast European Politics since 1989* (Cambridge, 2010), 246–57.

Fischer, M. 'The New Leaders and the Opposition', in D. Nelson (ed.), *Romania after Tyranny* (Boulder, 1992), 45–65.

Frensch, R. 'Von der Plan- zur Marktwirtschaft: Die ökonomische Umgestaltung Mittelosteuropas nach dem Ende des Kommunismus', in F. Müntefering (ed.), *Der Aufbau Ost im mittelosteuropäischen Vergleich: Eine Bilanz nach 25 Jahren* (Halle (Saale), 2016), 50–72.

Freytag, A. 'Einige Anmerkungen zur Wahl der Reservewährung eines Currency Boards'. *Zeitschrift für Wirtschaftspolitik* 47(1) (1998), 3–19.

Fritsch, M., and M. Wyrwich. 'Wirtschaft im Schock', Bundeszentrale für Politische Bildung, 15 November 2010. Retrieved 10 October 2012 from http://www.bpb.de/geschichte/deutsche-einheit/lange-wege-der-deutschen-einheit/47101/wirtschaft-im-schock?p=all.

Fritz, V. *State-Building: A Comparative Study of Ukraine, Lithuania, Belarus, and Russia*. Budapest, 2007.

Gabanyi, A.U. 'Politisches Lehrstück'. *Osteuropa* 62(9) (2012), 15–36.

Gabanyi, A.U., and K. Schroeder. *Vom Baltikum zum Schwarzen Meer: Transformation im östlichen Europa*. Munich, 2002.

Gábor, H. 'Hochproblematisch: Ungarns neues Grundgesetz'. *Osteuropa* 61(12) (2011), 145–66.

Gabriel, O.W. 'Bürger und Demokratie im vereinigten Deutschland'. *Politische Vierteljahreszeitschrift* 48(3) (2007), 540–52.

Gabriel, O.W. 'Politische Einstellungen und politische Kultur', in O.W. Gabriel and E. Holtmann (eds), *Handbuch politisches System der Bundesrepublik Deutschland*, 3rd ed. (Munich, 2005), 459–522.

Gabriel, O.W. 'Politische Einstellungen und politische Kultur', in O.W. Gabriel and S. Kropp (eds), *Die EU-Staaten im Vergleich: Strukturen, Prozesse, Politikinhalte*, 3rd ed. (Wiesbaden, 2008), 207.

Gabriel, O.W. 'Wächst zusammen, was zusammen gehört?', in O.W. Gabriel, J.W. Falter and H. Rattinger (eds), *Wächst zusammen, was zusammen gehört?* (Baden-Baden, 2005), 385–420.

Gabriel, O.W., J.W. Falter and H. Rattinger (eds). *Wächst zusammen, was zusammengehört? Stabilität und Wandel politischer Einstellungen im wieder vereinigten Deutschland*. Baden-Baden, 2005.

Gál, F. 'Rozpad Československa v politickej perspektíve', in K. Vodička (ed.), *Děle ní Československa: Deset let poté* (Prague, 2003), 105–18.

Galbreath, D.J. 'European Integration through Democratic Conditionality: Latvia in the Context of Minority Rights'. *Journal of Contemporary European Studies* 14(1) (2006), 69–87.

Galbreath, D.J., and D. Auers. 'Green, Black and Brown: Uncovering Latvia's Environmental Politics'. *Journal of Baltic Studies* 40(3) (2009), 333–48.

Gardó, S. 'Rumänien: Wirtschaft in Transformation', in T. Kahl, M. Metzeltin and M. Ungureanu (eds), *Rumänien* (Vienna, 2006), 655–92.

Garleff, M. *Die baltischen Länder: Estland, Lettland, Litauen vom Mittelalter bis zur Gegenwart*. Regensburg, 2001.

Gatzweiler, H.-H., and C. Schlömer, 'Zur Bedeutung von Wanderungen für die Raum- und Stadtentwicklung', *Informationen zur Raumentwicklung* 3/4 (2008), 245–260.

Gehring, H., and A. Pešková. *Wahlhandbuch Slowakei 2010*. Bratislava, 2010.

Gehring, H., and C. Thane. 'Slowakei vor Regierungswechsel', Konrad-Adenauer-Stiftung. Retrieved 11 November 2012 from http://www.kas.de/wf/doc/kas_30433–1522–1–30.pdf.

Geißler, R. *Die Sozialstruktur Deutschlands: Zur gesellschaftlichen Entwicklung mit einer Bilanz zur Vereinigung*, 6th ed. Wiesbaden, 2011.

Georgiev, I. 'Wahlen im postsozialistischen Bulgarien: Mittel für politisches Krisenmanagement?', in K. Ziemer (ed.), *Wahlen in postsozialistischen Staaten* (Opladen, 2003), 57–78.

Germany Trade & Invest. 'Energiewirtschaft 2008/09: Slowakische Republik'. Cologne, 2010.

Germany Trade & Invest. 'Wirtschaftsdaten kompakt: Slowakische Republik'. Cologne, November 2009.

Germany Trade & Invest. 'Wirtschaftstrends Slowakische Republik: Jahreswechsel 2009/10'. Cologne, 2009.

Ghețău, V. 'Impactul evoluțiilor demografice asupra structurii profesionale', in S. României (ed.), *Reprofesionalizarea României II: Raport al Institutului de Proiecte pentru Inovație și Dezvoltare (IPID)* (Bucharest, 2009), 63–66.

Gjuzelev, B. 'Die Minderheiten in Bulgarien unter Berücksichtigung der letzten Volksbefragung vom Dezember 1992'. *Südosteuropa* 43(6–7) (1994), 361–73.

Glismann, H.H., and K. Schrader. 'Privatisierung staatlichen Eigentums in den mittel- und osteuropäischen Ländern: Eine kritische Analyse', Kiel Working Paper No. 573, Kiel Institute for the World Economy 1993. Retrieved 13 February 2013 from http://www.econstor.eu/bitstream/10419/640/1/04301237X.pdf.

Gnauck, G. '20 Jahre nach "Sowjet-Besatzung" siegt ein Russe', *Die Welt*, 19 September 2011.

Golinowska, S. 'The National Model of the Welfare State in Poland: Tradition and Changes', in S. Golinowska, P. Hengstenberg and M. ̄ukowski (eds), *Diversity and Commonality in European Social Policies: The Forging of a European Social Model* (Warsaw, 2009), 213–60.

Golob, J. (ed.). *Žrtve vojne in revolucije*. Ljubljana, 2005. Unpublished manuscript.

Götz, N., G. Hanne and E.-C. Onken. 'Ethnopolitik', in H. Graf and M. Kerner (eds), *Handbuch Baltikum heute* (Berlin, 1998), 299–334.

Gough, R. *A Good Comrade*. London, 2006.

Graf, H. 'Massenmedien', in H. Graf and M. Kerner (eds), *Handbuch Baltikum heute* (Berlin, 1998), 335–67.

Großbölting, T., R. Kollmorgen, S. Möbius and R. Schmidt, *Das Ende des Kommunismus: Die Überwindung der Diktaturen in Europa und ihre Folgen*. Essen, 2010.

Grotz, F., and F. Müller-Rommel. *Regierungssysteme in Mittel- und Osteuropa: Die neuen EU-Staaten im Vergleich.* Wiesbaden, 2011.

Gruber, D. *Zuhause in Estland? Eine Untersuchung zur sozialen Integration ethnischer Russen an der Außengrenze der Europäischen Union.* Berlin, 2008.

Grundey, D. 'Media Business in the Baltic States: A Comparative Analysis of Lithuania, Latvia and Estonia'. *Transformations in Business & Economics* 7(1) (2008), 104–36.

Gyárfášová, O., and M. Velšic. 'Public Opinion', in G. Mesežnikov, M. Kollár and T. Nicholson (eds), *Slovakia 2002: A Global Report on the State of Society* (Bratislava, 2003), 219–46.

Haerpfer, C.W. 'Post-Communist Europe and Post-Soviet Russia', in C.W. Haerpfer et al. (eds), *Democratization* (Oxford, 2009), 309–20.

Hannula, H., S. Radosevic and N.v. Tunzelmann (eds). *Estonia, the New EU Economy: Building a Baltic Miracle.* Aldershot, 2006.

Hansen, M. 'Eine spektakuläre Geschichte von Boom und Pleite: Ein Blick aus Riga', in M. Ehrke (ed.), *Die globale Krise an der europäischen Peripherie: Ein Blick aus Zentral- und Südosteuropa*, Internationale Politikanalyse der Friedrich-Ebert-Stiftung (Berlin, 2009), 7–9.

Hanssen-Decker, U. *Von Madrid nach Göteborg: Schweden und der EU-Beitritt Estlands, Lettlands und Litauens 1995–2001.* Frankfurt a. M., 2008.

Hansson, A. 'Transforming an Economy while Building a Nation: The Case of Estonia', WIDER (World Institute for Development Economics Research), Working Paper No. 113, 1993.

Harcsa, I., G. Papp and G. Vukovich. 'Magyarország a társadalmi jelzőszámok tükrében', in T. Kolosi, I. Tóth and G. Vukovich (eds), *Társadalmi Riport 2006* (Budapest, 2006), 435–66.

Harfst, P. 'Wahlsysteme: institutionelle Entwicklung und politische Auswirkungen', in F. Grotz and F. Müller-Rommel (eds), *Regierungssysteme in Mittel- und Osteuropa* (Wiesbaden, 2011), 107–26.

Harfst, P. *Wahlsystemwandel in Mittelosteuropa: Strategisches Design einer politischen Institution.* Wiesbaden, 2007.

Hartleb, F. 'Parteien in den alten Bundesländern seit 1990', in E. Jesse and E. Klein (eds), *Das Parteienspektrum im wieder vereinigten Deutschland* (Berlin, 2007), 65–83.

Hartung, G. *Neue Staaten – neue Gewerkschaften? Die Gewerkschaften in Litauen, Lettland und Estland Anfang der 90er Jahre.* Leipzig, 1994.

Heitmeyer, W. (ed.). *Deutsch-deutsche Zustände: 20 Jahre nach dem Mauerfall.* Bonn, 2009.

Heitmeyer, W. 'Leben wir noch immer in zwei Gesellschaften? 20 Jahre Vereinigungsprozess und die Situation Gruppenbezogener Menschenfeindlichkeit', in H. Heitmeyer (ed.), *Deutsch-deutsche Zustände: 20 Jahre nach dem Mauerfall* (Bonn, 2009), 13–49.

Herfert, G. 'Regionale Polarisierung der demographischen Entwicklung in Ostdeutschland: Gleichwertigkeit der Lebensverhältnisse?' *Raumforschung und Raumordnung* 5 (2007), 435–55.

Heydemann, G. 'Die Revolution nach der Revolution. Die wirtschaftliche und soziale Transformation in Sachsen im Kontext des vereinten Deutschlands seit 1989/90: Erfolge und Probleme', in K. Hermann (ed.), *Sachsen seit der Friedlichen Revolution: Tradition, Wandel, Perspektiven* (Dresden, 2010), 249–66.

Heydemann, G., and K. Vodička. *Vom Ostblock zur EU: Systemtransformationen 1990–2012 im Vergleich*. Göttingen, 2013.

Hinrichs, W., and R. Neuenburg. 'Unterschiedliche Demokratiezufriedenheit in West- und Ostdeutschland'. *Deutschland Archiv* 38(3) (2005), 393–401.

Hirschmann, A.O. 'Abwanderung, Widerspruch und das Schicksal der Deutschen Demokratischen Republik'. *Leviathan* 20 (1992), 330–58.

Holländer, P. 'Die Gerichtsbarkeit in der Tschechischen Republik', in M. Joseph et al. (eds), *Revolution und Recht: Systemtransformation und Verfassungsentwicklung in der Tschechischen und Slowakischen Republik* (Frankfurt a. M., 2000), 87–115.

Hollstein, A. 'Das Verhältnis von Parlament, Staatspräsident und Regierung in der Republik Litauen', in B. Meissner, D.A. Loeber and C. Hasselblatt (eds), *Der Aufbau einer freiheitlich-demokratischen Ordnung in den baltischen Staaten: Staat-Wirtschaft-Gesellschaft* (Hamburg, 1995), 105–15.

Höpken, W. 'Bulgarien', in W. Weidenfeld (ed.), *Demokratie und Marktwirtschaft in Osteuropa* (Gütersloh, 1995), 195–212.

Horáková, N. 'Uplatňování demokratických práv občanů a hodnocení politického systému u nás', CVVM Company Report 2004. Retrieved 6 September 2010 from http://www.cvvm.cas.cz/upl/zpravy/100322s_pd40216.pdf.

Horváth, Z., and B. Ódor (eds). *Magyar EU-elnökség 2011*. Budapest, 2010.

Hradil, S. *Die Sozialstruktur Deutschlands im internationalen Vergleich*. Wiesbaden, 2006.

Hren, B. 'Konec mita o Sloveniji kot zmagovalki tranzicije'. *Dnevnik*, 23 April 2011.

Hren, B. 'Slovenija je po dohodkovni (ne)enakosti še v socializmu'. *Dnevnik*, 12 March 2011.

Hrvatin, S. 'Media Liberalism', in S.P. Ramet and D. Fink-Hafner (eds), *Democratic Transition in Slovenia: Value Transformation, Education and Media* (Richmond, 2006), 168–84.

Hrvatin, S., L.J. Kučić and B. Petković. 'Medijsko lastništvo: Vpliv lastništva na neodvisnost in pluralizem medijev v Sloveniji in drugih post-socialističnih evropskih državah'. The Peace Institute, Ljubljana 2004. Retrieved from http://mediawatch.mirovni-institut.si/edicija/seznam/15/mediawatch15.pdf.

Huber, M. *Moskau, 11. März 1985: Die Auflösung des sowjetischen Imperiums*. Munich, 2002.

Hudalla, A. *Der Beitritt der Tschechischen Republik zur Europäischen Union*. Münster, 1996.

Huntington, S.P. *The Third Wave: Democratization in the Late Twentieth Century*. London, 1990.

Ikstens, J. 'Latvia'. *European Journal of Political Research* 48 (2009), 1015–21.

Ionete, C. *Criza de sistem a economiei de comandă şi etapa sa explozivă*. Bucharest, 1993.

Ismayr, W. 'Das politische System Deutschlands', in W. Ismayr (ed.), *Die politischen Systeme Westeuropas* (Wiesbaden, 2009), 515–65.

Ismayr, W. *Die politischen Systeme Osteuropas*. Wiesbaden, 2010.

Ismayr, W. 'Die politischen Systeme Osteuropas im Vergleich', in W. Ismayr (ed.), *Die politischen Systeme Osteuropas* (Opladen, 2004), 9—69.

Ismayr, W. 'Die politischen Systeme Osteuropas im Vergleich', in W. Ismayr (ed.), *Die politischen Systeme Osteuropas*, 3rd ed. (Wiesbaden, 2010), 9–78.

Jakobs, J. *Tücken der Demokratie: Antisystemeinstellungen und ihre Determinanten in sieben postkommunistischen Transformationsländern*. Wiesbaden, 2004.

Jesse, E. 'Bundestags-, Landtags- und Europawahlen in den neuen Bundesländern seit 1990'. *Deutschland Archiv* 42(6) (2009), 965–72.

Jesse, E. 'Die demokratische Konsolidierung der neuen Bundesländer', in C. Vollnhals (ed.), *Die friedliche Revolution in der DDR 1989/90: Transition im ostmitteleuropäischen Vergleich* (Göttingen, 2011), 345–360.

Jesse, E. 'Parteien und Parteiensystem in den neuen Bundesländern', in V. Kronenberg and T. Mayer (eds), *Volksparteien: Konzepte, Konkurrenzen und Konstellationen, Erfolgsmodell für die Zukunft?* (Freiburg, 2009), 291–303.

Jesse, E. 'Parteiensystem im Wandel? Das deutsche Parteiensystem vor und nach der Bundestagswahl 2005', in U. Backes, A. Gallus and E. Jesse (eds), *Demokratie in Deutschland: Diagnosen und Analysen* (Cologne, 2008), 294–316.

Jesse, E., and E. Klein (eds). *Das Parteienspektrum im wieder vereinigten Deutschland*. Berlin, 2007.

Jesse, E., and J.P. Lang. *DIE LINKE: Der smarte Extremismus einer deutschen Partei*. Munich, 2008.

Jesse, E., and E. Sandschneider (eds). *Neues Deutschland: Eine Bilanz der deutschen Wiedervereinigung*. Baden-Baden, 2008.

Jesse, E., and R. Sturm. 'An den Grenzen des traditionellen Parteienwettbewerbs? Ein Ausblick auf das Wahljahr 2013', in E. Jesse and R. Sturm (eds), *'Superwahljahr' 2011 und die Folgen* (Baden-Baden, 2012), 435–51.

Jonsson, A. 'Changing Concepts of Rights in Post-Communist Societies', in S.P. Ramet and D. Fink-Hafner (eds), *Democratic Transition in Slovenia: Value Transformation, Education and Media* (Richmond, 2006), 89–97.

Jordan, P., and T. Kahl. 'Ethnische Struktur', in T. Kahl, M. Metzeltin and M. Ungureanu (eds), *Rumänien* (Vienna, 2006), 63–87.

Kailitz, S. 'Die kulturelle Prägung macht den Unterschied! Zur Regimeentwicklung postkommunistischer Staaten', in C. Vollnhals (ed.), *Jahre des Umbruchs: Friedliche Revolution in der DDR und Transition in Ostmitteleuropa* (Göttingen, 2011), 361–92.

Kala, A. 'Foreign Trade', in Estonian Academy of Sciences and Institute of Economics (eds), *Transforming the Estonian Economy* (Tallinn, 1995), 280–308.

Kallas, S. 'Estonia and the European Union'. *European Business Journal* 8 (1996), 13–20.

Kalvas, F., and T. Kostelecký. 'Hodnocení současného vývoje v České republice veřejností', in G. Mesežnikov (ed.), Povolebné Slovensko (Bratislava, 2003), 43–54.

Kämpfe, M. 'EU-Strukturfonds: Aufstockung der Mittel nach jüngster Erweiterung zu erwarten'. Wirtschaft im Wandel 7 (2004), 209–13.

Kämpfer, S. 'Regionale Ungleichheiten in der Tschechischen und Slowakischen Republik im Zuge des Erweiterungsprozesses der Europäischen Union: Eine empirische Untersuchung im Zeitraum von 1998 bis 2003'. Soziale Welt 59 (2008), 351–71.

Kasekamp, A. A History of the Baltic States. Basingstoke, 2010.

Keane, J. The Life and Death of Democracy. London, 2009.

Kehris, I.B. 'Citizenship, Participation and Representation', in N. Muižnieks (ed.), How Integrated Is Latvian Society? An Audit of Achievements, Failures and Challenges (Riga, 2010), 93–122.

Kein, A., and V. Tali. 'The Process of Ownership Reform and Privatization', in Estonian Academy of Sciences and Institute of Economics (eds), Transforming the Estonian Economy (Tallinn, 1995), 140–68.

Kerner, M., and A. Reetz. 'Parteiensysteme in den baltischen Staaten'. Der Bürger im Staat 54(2) (2004), 120–25.

Kiaupa, Z., A. Mäesalu, et al. Geschichte des Baltikums. Tallinn, 1999.

Kießling, A. Politische Kultur und Parteien im vereinten Deutschland. Munich, 1999.

Kilvits, K. Industrial Restructuring in Estonia, Estonian Academy of Science, Preprint 43. Tallinn, 1995.

Kipke, R. 'Das politische System der Slowakei', in W. Ismayr (ed.), Die politischen Systeme Osteuropas, 3rd ed. (Wiesbaden, 2010), 317–56.

Kirelli, S. 'Vom Plan zum Markt: Der wirtschaftliche Transformationsprozess in Ostmitteleuropa'. Der Bürger im Staat 97(3) (1997), 164–68.

Klein, A.M. 'Eine unheilige Allianz'. KAS Länderbericht Lettland, 16 June 2010.

Klein, A.M. 'Kommunalwahl in Lettland'. KAS Länderbericht Lettland, 7 June 2010.

Klein, A.M. 'Lettlands Parlament wählt neues Staatsoberhaupt'. KAS Länderbericht Lettland, 6 March 2011.

Klein, A.M. 'Lettland reloaded: die Parteien versuchen, den Geist von 1991 zu beleben'. KAS Auslandsinformationen 1 (2011), 76–90.

Klein, A.M. 'Partei ohne Volk'.: KAS Länderbericht Lettland, 20 July 2011.

Klein, A.M. 'Saeima bestätigt Mitte-Rechts-Regierung'. KAS Länderbericht Lettland, 31 October 2011.

Klíma, M. 'Klientelistická strana', Mladá fronta dnes, 7 April 2003, 8.

Klíma, M. 'Výročí televizní manipulace', Mladá fronta dnes, 14 March 2003, 8.

Knogler, M. 'Öffnung der Arbeitsmärkte zum 1. Mai 2011: Positive Effekte überwiegen', Osteuropa Institut Regensburg, Kurzanalysen und Informationen No. 51 (April 2011). Retrieved 27 November 2012 from http://www.dokumente.ios-regensburg.de/publikationen/info/info-51.pdf.

Kommission der Europäischen Gemeinschaften. Regional Policy – Info regio, no year given. Retrieved 28 November 2012 from http://ec.europa.eu/regional_policy/country/gateway/estonia_en.cfm?gw_ide=1719&lg=en.

Kommission der Europäischen Gemeinschaften. *Stellungnahme der Kommission zum Antrag Estlands auf Beitritt zur Europäischen Union*, KOM (97) 2006. Brussels, 1997.

König, H. 'Das deutschsowjetische Vertragswerk von 1939 und seine geheimen Zusatzprotokolle: Eine Dokumentation'. *Osteuropa* 39(5) (1989), 413–58.

Kornai, J. *The Socialist System: The Political Economy of Communism*. Oxford, 1992.

Körösényi, A. 'Gyurcsány-vezér: A magyar politika "prezidencializálódása"', in P. Sándor, L. Vass and A. Tolnai (eds), *Magyarország politikai évkönyve 2006* (Budapest, 2006), 141–49.

Körösényi, A., C. Tóth and G. Török. *A Magyar politikai rendszer*. Budapest, 2003.

Kosta, J. *Die tschechische/tschechoslowakische Wirtschaft im mehrfachen Wandel*. Münster, 2005.

Kowalski, S. 'Konstrukcja i dekonstrukcja III RP: Symetrie i asymetrie', in M. Czyżewski, S. Kowalski and T. Tabako (eds), *Retoryka i polityka: Dwudziestolecie polskiej transformacji* (Warsaw, 2010), 47–81.

Kraatz, S., and S.v. Steinsdorff. *Parlamente und Systemtransformation im postsozialistischen Europa*. Opladen, 2002.

Krašovec, T. 'Deset let gospodarskega razvoja v samostojni Sloveniji'. The Managers' Association of Slovenia, Ljubljana 2001. Retrieved from http://www.uradni-list.si/1/objava.jsp?urlid=200596&stevilka=4191.

Krivý, V. 'Citizens' Value Orientations', in Z. Bútorová (ed.), *Democracy and Discontent in Slovakia: A Public Opinion Profile of a Country in Transition* (Bratislava, 1998), 37–49.

Krivý, V. 'Súvislosti hodno tenia činnosti vlády SR verejnosťou', in G. Mesežnikov (ed.), *Povolebné Slovensko* (Bratislava, 2003), 21–41.

Krivý, V., and I. Radičová. 'Atmosféra dovery a atmosféra nedovery?'. *Sociologické aktuality* 2 (1992), 1–5.

Kröhnert S., F. Medicus and R. Klingholz. *Die demografische Lage der Nation: Wie zukunftsfähig sind Deutschlands Regionen? Daten, Fakten, Analysen*. Munich, 2006.

Krumm, K. 'Aufbau der Zivilgesellschaft in Ostmitteleuropa', in F. Müntefering (ed.), *Der Aufbau Ost im mittelosteuropäischen Vergleich: Eine Bilanz nach 25 Jahren* (Halle (Saale), 2016), 92–105.

Krupavicius, A. 'Semi-presidentialism in Lithuania: Origins, Development, Challenges', in R. Elgie and S. Moestrup (eds), *Semi-presidentialism in Central and Eastern Europe* (Manchester, 2008), 65–84.

Kubátová, J. 'Názory české veřejnosti na ekonomickou transformaci a její sociální důsledky v období 1989–1998'. Retrieved 28 November 2012 from http://publib.upol.cz/~obd/fulltext/Politologica1/Politologica4.pdf.

Kubis, A., and L. Schneider. '"Sag mir, wo die Mädchen sind. . .": Regionale Analyse des Wanderungsverhaltens junger Frauen'. *Wirtschaft im Wandel* 13(8) (2007), 298–307.

Kučera, R. 'Making Standards Work: Semantics of Economic Reform in Czechoslovakia 1985–1992'. *Zeithistorische Forschungen* 12 (2015), 427–47.

Kühntopf, S., and S. Stedtfeld. 'Wenige junge Frauen im ländlichen Raum: Ursachen und Folgen der selektiven Abwanderung in Ostdeutschland'.

BiB Working Paper 3/2012. Retrieved 28 November 2012 from http://www. Bibdemografie.de/SharedDocs/Publikationen/DE/Download/BiB_Working_ Paper/Geschlechterproportionen.pdf?__blob=publicationFile&v=6.

Küpper, H. 'Mit Mängeln: Ungarns neues Grundgesetz'. *Osteuropa* 61(12) (2011), 135–44.

Kwasowski, M., and S. Zaleski. 2009. 'Die Landwirtschaft in Polen fünf Jahre nach dem Beitritt zur Europäischen Union'. *Polen-Analysen* 51 (5 May 2009). Retrieved 3 February 2011 from http://www.laender-analysen.de/polen/pdf/ PolenAnalysen51.pdf.

Laar, M. *Das estnische Wirtschaftswunder*. Tallinn, 2002.

Laar, M. *The Power of Freedom: Central and Eastern Europe after 1945*. Brussels, 2010.

Laaser, C.-F. 'Knocking on the Door: The Baltic Rim Transition Countries Ready for Europe?', in L. Hedegaard et al. (eds), *The NEBI Yearbook: North European and Baltic Sea Integration*, 5th ed. (Berlin, 2003), 21–45.

Laaser, C.-F., and K. Schrader. 'Die baltischen Staaten in der europäischen Arbeitsteilung'. *Der Bürger im Staat* 54(2) (2004), 141–46.

Lane, T. 'Lithuania: Stepping Westwards', in D.J. Smith and A. Pabriks (eds), *The Baltic States Estonia, Latvia and Lithuania* (London, 2002), 209–238.

Lang, K.-O. 'Populism in "Old" and "New" Europe: Trends and Implications', in M. Bútora, O. Gyárfášová, G. Mesežnikov and T.W. Skladony (eds), *Democracy and Populism in Central Europe: The Visegrad Elections and Their Aftermath* (Bratislava, 2007), 125–40.

Lauristin, M. *Estonia's Transition to the EU: Twenty Years On*. London, 2010.

Lauristin, M., and P. Vihalemm. 'The Transformation of Estonian Society and Media: 1987–2001', in P. Vihalemm (ed.), *Baltic Media in Transition* (Tartu, 2002), 17–63.

Leinsalu, M. *Troubled Transitions: Social Variation and Long-Term Trends in Health and Mortality in Estonia*. Stockholm, 2004.

Lemke, J. 'Zwölf Jahre, zwölf Regierungen: Akteure, Ereignisse, Spezifika der litauischen Politik', *Osteuropa* 52(9/10) (2002), 1236–48.

Leping, K. *Ethnic Wage Gap and Political Break-ups: Estonia During Political and Economic Transition*. Tartu, 2007.

Leppik, L. *Transformation of the Estonian Pension System: Policy Choices and Policy Outcomes*. Tallinn, 2006.

Leppik, L., and G. Männik. 'Transformation of Old-Age Security in Estonia', in W. Schmähl and S. Horstmann (eds), *Transformation of Pension Systems in Central and Eastern Europe* (Cheltenham, 2002), 89–124.

Levits, E. 'Lettland unter der Sowjetherrschaft und auf dem Wege zur Unabhängigkeit', in B. Meissner (ed.), *Die Baltischen Nationen Estland, Lettland, Litauen*, 2nd ed. (Cologne, 1991), 139–222.

Lieven, A. *The Baltic Revolution: Estonia, Latvia, Lithuania and the Path to Independence*. New Haven, CT, 1999.

Lijphart, A. *Modele ale democraţiei*. Iaşi, 2000.

Linz, J.J., and A. Stepan. *Problems of Democratic Transition and Consolidation: Southern Europe, South America, and Post-Communist Europe*. Baltimore, MD, 1996.

Lipset, S., and S. Rokkan. 'Cleavages Structures, Party Systems and Voter Alignments: Introduction', in S. Lipset and S. Rokkan (eds), *Party Systems and Voter Alignments: Cross-National Perspectives* (New York, 1967), 1–64.

Lopourová, V. 'Koncept korupce v českém transformačním kontextu'. *Politologický Časopis* 11(4) (2004), 354–69.

Lorenčič, A. 'Tranzicija slovenskega gospodarstva v letih 1990–2004'. PhD diss., Department of History, Faculty of Arts in Ljubljana, 2010.

Lorenz, A. 'Der konstitutionelle Rahmen: Verfassungsgebung und Verfassungsentwicklung', in F. Grotz and F. Müller-Rommel (eds), *Regierungssysteme in Mittel- und Osteuropa* (Wiesbaden, 2011), 47–67.

Lorenz, A. (ed.). *Ostdeutschland und die Sozialwissenschaften: Bilanz und Perspektiven 20 Jahre nach der Wiedervereinigung.* Opladen, 2011.

Löw, K. (ed.). *Zehn Jahre deutsche Einheit.* Berlin, 2001.

Ludwig, U. 'Licht und Schatten nach 15 Jahren wirtschaftlicher Transformation in Ostdeutschland'. *Deutschland Archiv* 38(3) (2005), 410–16.

Lugus, O. *Transforming the Estonian Economy.* International Center for Economic Growth, Tallinn, 1995.

Lukosiunas, M., and V. Bartasevicius. 'Lithuania: Reshaping the Media and Society', in S. Hoyer, E. Lauk and P. Vihalemm (eds), *Towards a Civic Society: The Baltic Media's Long Road to Freedom. Perspectives on History, Ethnicity and Journalism* (Tartu, 1993), 253–61.

Machonin, P., and K. Müller. 'Problémy a perspektivy modernizace a sociální soudržnosti', in M. Tuček et al. (eds), *Dynamika české společnosti* (Prague, 2003), 392–413.

Machonin, P., and M. Tuček. *Česká společnost v transformaci.* Prague, 1996.

Machonin, P., and M. Tuček. 'Proměnysociálních nerov ností', in M. Tuček et al. (eds), *Dynamika české společnosti* (Prague, 2003), 197–223.

Maćków, J. *Autoritarismus in Mittel und Osteuropa.* Wiesbaden, 2009.

Maæków, J. *Am Rande Europas? Nation, Zivilgesellschaft und außenpolitische Integration in Belarus, Litauen, Polen, Russland und der Ukraine.* Freiburg, 2004.

Maćków, J. *Totalitarismus und danach: Einführung in den Kommunismus und die postkommunistische Systemtransformation.* Baden-Baden, 2005.

Maćków, J. 'Der Wandel des kommunistischen Totalitarismus und die post-kommunistische Systemtransformation: Periodisierung, Problematik und Begriffe'. *Zeitschrift für Politikwissenschaft* 9(4) (1999), 1347–80.

Mai, R. 'Die altersselektive Abwanderung aus Ostdeutschland'. *Raumforschung und Raumordnung* 5 (2006), 355–69.

Maliszewski, M. 'Fernsehen und Rundfunk in Polen: Marktentwicklung und politische Einbettung', *Polen-Analysen* 6 (6 February 2007). Retrieved 3 February 2011 from http://www.laender-analysen.de/polen/pdf/ PolenAnalysen06.pdf.

Mansfeldová, Z. 'Das tschechische Parlament in Zeichen allmählicher Stabilisierung', in S. Kraatz and S. von Steinsdorff (eds), *Parlamente und Systemtransformation im postsozialistischen Europa* (Opladen, 2002), 111–25.

Mansfeldová, Z. 'Zivilgesellschaft in der Tschechischen und Slowakischen Republik'. *Aus Politik und Zeitgeschichte* 48(6–7) (1998), 13–19.

Mareš, M. 'Rechtsextremistische Parteien in Ostdeutschland, Tschechien, Polen und Russland', in U. Backes, T. Jaskulowski and A. Polese (eds), *Totalitarismus und Transformation: Defizite der Demokratiekonsolidierung in Mittel- und Osteuropa* (Göttingen, 2011), 112–123.

Martens, B. 'Wirtschaftlicher Zusammenbruch und Neuanfang nach 1990', Bundeszentrale für Politische Bildung, 30 March 2010. Retrieved 10 October 2012 from http://www.bpb.de/geschichte/deutsche-einheit/lange-wege-der-deutschen-einheit/47133/zusammenbruch.

Martens, M. 'Armut und Abwanderung: Exodus aus Bulgarien'. *Frankfurter Allgemeine Zeitung*, 18 February 2013. Retrieved 18 February 2013 from http://www.faz.net/aktuell/politik/ausland/europa/armut-und-abwanderung-exodus-aus-bulgarien-12085240.html.

Matějka, O. 'Inwieweit beeinflusst die Auseinandersetzung mit der Vergangenheit die Entwicklung in Deutschland und Europa heute?', in F. Müntefering (ed.), *Der Aufbau Ost im mittelosteuropäischen Vergleich: Eine Bilanz nach 25 Jahren* (Halle (Saale), 2016), 125–35.

Matthes, C., and U. Wethkamp. 'Aufbruch zur Marktwirtschaft: Lettlands Wirtschaft im ersten Jahr nach der Unabhängigkeit'. *Materialien und Dokumente zur Friedens- und Konfliktforschung*, No. 17 (Berlin, 1993), 1f.

Matthes, C.-Y. 'Die Herausbildung des Parteiensystems in Lettland seit Beginn der Perestroika', in Freie Universität Berlin (ed.), *Berichte der Berliner Interuniversitären Arbeitsgruppe Baltische Staaten* (Berlin, 1996), 42.

Matthes, C.-Y. 'Politisches und Rechtssystem Lettlands', in H. Graf and M. Kerner (eds), *Handbuch Baltikum heute* (Berlin, 1998), 49–88.

Matthes, C.-Y., M. Kacinskiene, F. Rajevska ad A. Toots, 'Rentenreform im Baltikum: Neue Modelle im Praxistest'. *Osteuropa* 57(7) (2007), 47–56.

Mau, S., and R. Verwiebe. *Die Sozialstruktur Europas*. Konstanz, 2009.

Mauritz, M. *Tschechien*. Regensburg, 2002.

Merkel, W. 'Die Bedeutung von Parteien und Parteiensystemen für die Konsolidierung der Demokratie: ein interregionaler Vergleich', in W. Merkel and E. Sandschneider (eds), *Systemwechsel 3* (Opladen, 1997), 337–67.

Merkel, W. 'Gegen alle Theorie? Die Konsolidierung der Demokratie in Ostmitteleuropa'. *Politische Vierteljahresschrift* 48 (2007), 413–33.

Merkel, W. 'Gegen alle Theorie? Die Konsolidierung der Demokratie in Ostmitteleuropa', in U. Backes et al. (eds), *Totalitarismus und Transformation* (Göttingen, 2009), 14–48.

Merkel, W. 'Gegen alle Theorie? Die Konsolidierung der Demokratie in Ostmitteleuropa', in K.H. Schrenk and M. Soldner (eds), *Analyse demokratischer Regierungssysteme* (Wiesbaden, 2010), 545–62.

Merkel, W. *Systemtransformation: Eine Einführung in die Theorie und Empirie der Transformationsforschung*. Opladen, 1999.

Merkel, W. *Systemtransformation: Eine Einführung in die Theorie und Empirie der Transformationsforschung*, 2nd ed. Wiesbaden, 2010.

Merkel, W., H. Puhle, et al. *Defekte Demokratie: Vol. 2 Regionalanalysen*. Wiesbaden, 2006.

Merkel, W., E. Sandschneider and D. Segert. 'Die Institutionalisierung der Demokratie', in W. Merkel, E. Sandschneider and D. Segert (eds), *Systemwechsel 2* (Opladen, 1996), 10–36.

Merkel, W., et al. *Defekte Demokratien, Vol. 2: Defekte Demokratien in Osteuropa, Ostasien und Lateinamerika*. Wiesbaden, 2006.

Mertelsmann, O. (ed.). *Der stalinistische Umbau in Estland: Von der Markt- zur Kommandowirtschaft*. Hamburg, 2006.

Mesežnikov, G. 'Die Slowakei', in A.U. Gabanyi and K. Schroeder (eds), *Vom Baltikum zum Schwarzen Meer: Transformation im östlichen Europa* (Munich, 2002), 339–66.

Mesežnikov, G., P. Učeň and S. Szomolányi. 'Democratic Institutions and the Rule of Law', in M. Bútora, G. Mesežnikov and M. Kollár (eds), *Trends in Quality of Democracy: Slovakia 2009* (Bratislava, 2010), 15–39.

Meurs, W.v. 'Der Weg der baltischen Staaten in die EU'. *Der Bürger im Staat: Die baltischen Staaten* 54(2) (2004), 134–40.

Mihai, S. 'Rumänien und Bulgarien: Hoffen auf Europa'. *Aus Politik und Zeitgeschichte* 63(6–7) (2013), 42–46.

Ministry of Social Affairs. *Health, Labour and Social Life in Estonia 2000–2008*. Tallinn, 2009.

Misiunas, R., and R. Taagepera. *The Baltic States: Years of Dependence 1940–1990*, 2nd ed. London, 2006.

Moshes, A. 'Overcoming Unfriendly Stability: Russian-Latvian Relations at the End of the 1990s', in *Programme of the Northern Dimension of the CSFP*, Vol. 4 (Helsinki, 1999), 16–23.

Motiejunaite, A. 'Female Employment in Lithuania: Testing Three Popular Explanations'. *Journal of Baltic Studies* 41(2) (2010), 237–58.

Možný, I. *Česká společnost: Nejdůležitější fakta o kvalitě našeho života*. Prague, 2002.

Muižnieks, N. (ed.), *Latvian-Russian Relations: Domestic and International Dimensions*. Riga, 2006.

Muižnieks, N. *Russians in Latvia: History, Current Status and Prospects 2004*. Retrieved 25 January 2011 from www.mfa.gov.lv/en/policy/4641/Muiznieks/print=on.

Müller, O., et al. 'Die osteuropäischen Demokratien in der Bevölkerungsmeinung', in G. Pickel et al. (eds), *Osteuropas Bevölkerung auf dem Weg in die Demokratie: Repräsentative Untersuchungen in Ostdeutschland und zehn osteuropäischen Transformationsstaaten* (Wiesbaden, 2006), 155–64.

Müller-Rommel, F. 'Regierungen: Binnenstrukturen der Kernexekutiven', in F. Grotz and F. Müller-Rommel (eds), *Regierungssysteme in Mittel- und Osteuropa* (Wiesbaden, 2011), 217–34.

Müller-Rommel, F., and F. Grotz. 'Die Regierungssysteme der neuen EU-Staaten: institutionelle Konfigurationen und Entwicklungspfade', in F. Grotz and F. Müller-Rommel (eds), *Regierungssysteme in Mittel- und Osteuropa*, (Wiesbaden, 2011), 303–20.

Münch, I.v., and G. Hoog. 'Auflösung des tschechoslowakischen Staates aus völkerrechtlicher Sicht', in R. Kipke and K. Vodièka (eds), *Abschied von der Tschechoslowakei* (Cologne, 1993), 163–79.

Münch, I.v., and G. Hoog. 'Zánik èeskoslovenského státu z mezinárodnìprávního hlediska', in K. Vodièka (ed.), *Děle ní Československa: Deset let poté* (Prague, 2003), 131–53.

Mungiu-Pippidi, A. *Politica după communism: Structură, cultură şi psihologie politică*. Bucharest, 2002.

Müntefering, F. *Der Aufbau Ost im mittelosteuropäischen Vergleich: Eine Bilanz nach 25 Jahren*. Halle (Saale), 2016.

Murgescu, B. (ed.). *History of the Romanian Court of Accounts (1864–2004)*. Bucharest, 2005.

Murgescu, B. *România şi Europa: Acumularea decalajelor economice (1500–2010)*. Iaşi, 2010.

Mzavanadze, N. 'Sustainable Development in Lithuania: Between the Government Agenda and the Undiscovered Civil Society'. *Journal of Baltic Studies* 40(3) (2009), 397–414.

Neller, K. *DDR Nostalgie*. Wiesbaden, 2006.

Niedermayer, O. *Parteimitglieder in Deutschland: Version 2011*. Berlin, 2011.

Noelle, E. 'Geteilte Freude', *Frankfurter Allgemeine Zeitung*, 27 November 2002.

Nohlen, D. *Wahlrecht und Parteiensystem*. Opladen, 2007.

Nohlen, D., and M. Kasapovic. *Wahlsysteme und Systemwandel in Osteuropa*. Opladen, 1996.

North, D., J. Wallis and B. Weingast. *Violence and Social Orders: A Conceptual Framework for Interpreting Recorded Human History*. Cambridge, 2009.

Nugaraite, A. 'Lithuania', in S. Huber (ed.), *Media Markets in Central and Eastern Europe: An Analysis on Media Ownership in Bulgaria, Czech Republic, Estonia, Hungary, Latvia, Lithuania, Poland, Romania, Slovakia and Slovenia* (Vienna, 2006), 55–58.

Oberender, P. *Osterweiterung der EU und Transformation als Herausforderungen: Zur Situation in Rußland und Estland*. Bayreuth, 2001.

OECD. *Investitionsführer Estland*, ed. Zentrum für Zusammenarbeit mit den Reformländern der OECD. Paris, 1997.

Offe, C. *Der Tunnel am Ende des Lichts*. Frankfurt a. M., 1994.

Onken, E.-C. *Demokratisierung der Geschichte in Lettland: Staatsbürgerliches Bewusstsein und Geschichtspolitik im ersten Jahrzehnt der Unabhängigkeit*. Hamburg, 2003.

Oplatka, A. *Der eiserne Vorhang reißt*. Zürich, 1990.

Oppenländer, K.H. (ed.). *Wiedervereinigung nach sechs Jahren: Erfolge, Defizite, Zukunftsperspektiven im Transformationsprozess*. Berlin, 1997.

Oppong, M. 'Was kostet die Deutsche Einheit?' *Freiraum* 7 (2005), 14.

Orszulik, A. *Czas przełomu: Notatki z rozmów z władzami PRL w latach 1981–1989*. Warsaw/Z¹bki, 2006.

Osteuropa-Institut München. 'Den Transformationsschritt messen: Die staatliche Einflußnahme auf die Wirtschaftstätigkeit in ausgewählten Transformationsstaaten, Gutachten, erstellt im Auftrag des Bundesministeriums für Wirtschaft'. Munich, 1997.

Paas, T. 'Estonia: A Small Open Economy'. *EMERGO* 4(2) (1997), 37–53.

Pajuste, A.A. 'Entwicklung des Steuersystems in Estland', in W. Wacker (ed.), *Europäisierung des Steuerrechts und steuerliche Entwicklung in Osteuropa* (Göttingen, 1997), 75–83.

Palang, H., and A. Printsmann. 'From Totalitarian to Democratic Landscapes: The Transition in Estonia', in J. Primdahl and S. Swaffield (eds), *Globalisation and Agricultural Landscapes* (Cambridge, 2010), 169–84.

Pänke, J., and I. Samson. 'Zwischen Wirtschaftswunder und Extremismus: Schatten auf der slowakischen Euro-Euphorie?' *DGAPanalyse* 2 (2009), 9f.

Paqué, K.-H. *Die Bilanz: Eine wirtschaftliche Analyse der Deutschen Einheit*. Munich, 2009.

Paschke, U.K. (ed.). *Holle Universalgeschichte*. Erlangen, 1991.

Pasti, V. *The Challenges of Transition: Romania in Transition*. Boulder, CO, 1997.

Pçtersone, K. 'Latvia: The Hot Month of February', *Baltic Review*, 14 February 2012. Retrieved 2 April 2012 from http://baltic-review.com/2012/02/latvia-the-hot-month-of-february/.

Pickel, G. 'Gerechtigkeit und Politik in der deutschen Bevölkerung: Die Folgen der Wahrnehmung von Gerechtigkeit für die politische Kultur im vereinten Deutschland'. Unpublished manuscript, 2012.

Pickel, G. 'Die subjektive Verankerung der Demokratie in Osteuropa: Die Legitimität der Demokratie in der Bevölkerung als Faktor demokratischer Stabilität und Qualität', in U. Backes, T. Jaskułowski and A. Polese (eds), *Totalitarismus und Transformation: Defizite der Demokratiekonsolidierung in Mittel- und Osteuropa* (Göttingen, 2009), 261–83.

Pickel, G., and J. Jacobs. 'Einstellungen zur Demokratie und zur Gewährleistung von Rechten und Freiheiten in den jungen Demokratien Mittel- und Osteuropas'. Frankfurter Institut für Transformationsstudien, 2001, *Studie No. 9/01*. Frankfurt (Oder), 2001.

Pickel. G., and J. Jacobs. 'Der soziokulturelle Unterbau der neuen Demokratien Osteuropas', in G. Pickel, D. Pollack, J. Jacobs and O. Müller (eds), *Osteuropas Bevölkerung auf dem Weg in die Demokratie: Repräsentative Untersuchungen in Ostdeutschland und zehn osteuropäischen Transformationsstaaten* (Wiesbaden, 2006), 31–52.

Pickel, G., and S. Pickel. *Demokratisierung im internationalen Vergleich: Neue Erkenntnisse und Perspektiven*. Wiesbaden, 2006.

Pickel, G., et al. *Osteuropas Bevölkerung auf dem Weg in die Demokratie: Politische Kultur in den neuen Demokratien Europas*. Wiesbaden, 2006.

Pithart, P. 'Konec dobrý, všechno dobré?', in K. Vodička (ed.), *Dělení Československa: Deset let poté* (Prague, 2003), 317–21.

Plakans, A. 'Latvia: Normality and Disappointment'. *East European Politics and Society* 24(4) (2010), 518–25.

Plasser, F., P. Ulram and H. Waldrauch. *Politischer Kulturwandel in Ost- und Mitteleuropa: Theorie und Empirie demokratischer Konsolidierung*. Opladen, 1997.

Poledna, R. *Sint ut sunt: Aut non sunt? Transfo mări sociale la saşii ardeleni după 1945: O analiză sociologică din perspectivă sistemică*. Cluj-Napoca, 2001.

Polián, M. 'Die Verwaltungsgerichtsbarkeit in Tschechien', in B. Wieser and A. Stolz (eds), *Vergleichen des Verwaltungsrecht in Ostmitteleuropa* (Vienna, 2004), 459–89.

Pollack, D., and J. Wielgohs. *Dissent and Opposition in Communist Eastern Europe: Origins of Civil Society and Democratic Transition*. Aldershot, 2004.

Preda, C., and S. Soare. *Regimul: partidele şi sistem ul politic din România*. Bucharest, 2008.

Pregelj, L.P., A. Gabrič and B. Repe. *The Repluralization of Slovenia in the 1980s: New Revelations from Archival Records*. Seattle, 2000.

Pridham, G. 'The International Context of Democratic Consolidation: Southern Europe in Comparative Perspective', in R. Gunther, N.P. Diamandouros and H.-P. Puhle (eds), *The Politics of Democratic Consolidation: Southern Europe in Comparative Perspective* (Baltimore, MD, 1995), 166–203.

Pridham, G. 'Securing the Only Game in Town: The EU's Political Conditionality and Democratic Consolidation in Post-Soviet Latvia'. *Europe-Asia Studies* 61(1) (2009), 51–84.

Przeworski, A. 'Some Problems in the Study of the Transition to Democracy', in G. O'Donnell, P.C. Schmitter and L. Whitehead (eds), *Transitions from Authoritarian Rule: Comparative Perspectives* (Baltimore, MD, 1986), 47–63.

Przeworski, A. 'Spiel mit Einsatz: Demokratisierungsprozesse in Lateinamerika, Osteuropa und anderswo'. *Transit* 3 (1991), 190–213.

Purju, A. 'Voucher Privatisation in Estonia'. *Communist Economies and Economic Transformation* 7(3) (1995), 385–408.

Ragnitz, J. 'Wohl und Wehe von 20 Jahren Wirtschaftspolitik: Ostdeutschland als Beispiel für die Grenzen wirtschaftspolitischer Interventionen', in A. Lorenz (ed.), *Ostdeutschland und die Sozialwissenschaften: Bilanz und Perspektiven 20 Jahre nach der Wiedervereinigung* (Opladen, 2011), 153–68.

Ragnitz, J., and L. Schneider. 'Demographische Entwicklung und ihre ökonomischen Folgen'. *Wirtschaft im Wandel* 13(6) (2007), 195–202.

Rajevska, F. 'Vom Sozialstaat zum Wohlfahrtsmix: Das lettische Wohlfahrtssystem nach Wiedererlangung der Unabhängigkeit', in K. Schubert, S. Hegelich and U. Bazant (eds), *Europäische Wohlfahrtssysteme: Ein Handbuch* (Wiesbaden, 2007), 423–42.

Ramonaite, A. 'The Development of the Lithuanian Party System: From Stability to Perturbation', in S. Jungerstam-Mulders (ed.), *Post-Communist EU Member States: Parties and Party Systems* (Aldershot, 2006), 69–90.

Rattinger, H., et al. *Zwischen Langeweile und Extremen: die Bundestagswahl 2009*. Baden-Baden, 2011.

Rauch, G.v. *Geschichte der baltischen Staaten*, 2nd ed. Munich, 1986.

Rauch, G.v. *Geschichte der baltischen Staaten*, 3rd ed. Munich, 1990.

Raudjärv, M. 'Wirtschaftspolitsche Ziele und marktwirtschaftliche Transformation in Estland', *Wirtschaftswissenschaftliche Diskussionspapiere* 4 (2004).

Reetz, A. 'Das Baltikum: Stabilität in der Instabilität. Die fünften Parlamente in Estland, Lettland und Litauen'. *Zeitschrift für Parlamentsfragen* 42(1) (2011), 96–117.

Reetz, A. *Die Entwicklung der Parteiensysteme in den baltischen Staaten: Vom Beginn des Mehrparteiensystems 1988 bis zu den dritten Wahlen.* Wittenbach, 2004.

Reiljan, J. 'Vergrößerung der regionalen Disparitäten der Wirtschaftsentwicklung Estlands', *Ordnungspolitischer Diskurs* No. 2010–3 (2010), 10. Retrieved from http://www.ordnungspolitisches-portal.de /05_02_OPO_Diskurse_2010–03. pdf.

Reiljan, J. 'Die wirtschaftspolitischen Probleme des selbständigen Estland'. *Deutsche Studien* 29(116) (1991), 371–89.

Reißig, R. 'Von der privilegierten und blockierten zur zukunftsorientierten Transformation', Bundeszentrale für Politische Bildung, 19 July 2010. Retrieved 18 September 2012 from http://www.bpb.de/apuz/32610/ von-der-privilegierten-und-blockierten-zur-zukunftsorientierten-transformation?p=all.

Renwick, A. 'Im Interesse der Macht, Ungarns neues Wahlsystem'. *Osteuropa* 62(5) (2012), 3–18.

Repe, B. *Jutri je nov dan: Slovenci in razpad Jugoslavije.* Ljubljana, 2004.

Richter, M. 'Doppelte Demokratisierung und deutsche Einheit'. *Aus Politik und Zeitgeschichte* 60(11) (2010), 20–26.

Riedel, S. 'Das politische System Bulgariens', in W. Ismayr (ed.), *Die politischen Systeme Osteuropas* (Wiesbaden, 2010), 677–728.

Rimantas, V. 'Political Rebirth in Lithuania, 1990–1991: Events and Problems'. *Journal of Baltic Studies* 25(2) (1994), 183–188.

Risberg, A., and A. Ainamo. 'Expansion of the Nordic Business Press: Äripäev in Estonia as a Carrier of Western Discourses', in P. Kjaer and T. Slaatta (eds), *Mediating Business: The Expansion of Business Journalism* (Copenhagen, 2007), 101–28.

Ritter, G.A. 'Die deutsche Wiedervereinigung'. *Historische Zeitschrift* 286 (2008), 289–339.

Ritter, G.A. *Wir sind das Volk! Wir sind ein Volk! Geschichte der deutschen Einigung.* Munich, 2009.

Rizman, R.M. *Uncertain Path: Democratic Transition and Consolidation in Slovenia.* Texas, 2006.

Rödder, A. *Deutschland einig Vaterland: Die Geschichte der Wiedervereinigung.* Munich, 2009.

Rode, C. 2008. 'Die aktuelle Situation der Gewerkschaften in Polen'. *Polen-Analysen* 36 (1 July 2008). Retrieved 3 February 2011 from www.laender-analy sen.de/polen/pdf/PolenAnalysen36.pdf.

Roggemann, H. (ed.). *Die Verfassungen Mittel- und Osteuropas.* Berlin, 1999.

Roos, S.R. 'EU-Erweiterung: Wachhund und Kooperationspartner'. *Entwicklung und Zusammenarbeit*, 24 February 2010. Retrieved 2 February 2013 from http:// www.dandc.eu/de/article/zivilgesellschaftliche-organisationen-kaempfen-rumaenien-und-bulgarien-fuer.

Rose, R. 'Learning to Support New Regimes in Eastern Europe', in L. Diamond and M.F. Plattner (eds), *How People View Democracy* (Baltimore, MD, 2008), 45–58.

Rose, R. *The Problem of Party Government*. New York, 1974.

Rosůlek, P. 'Bulharsko: Monokameralismus se silným postavením premiéra', in L. Cabada (ed.), *Nové demokracie střední a východní Evropy* (Prague, 2008), 181–98.

Rothacher, A. 'Estland: Wirtschaft und Politik in der reinen Marktwirtschaft'. *KAS-Auslandsinformation*, No. 01/97 (1997), 94–101.

Rozenvalds, J. 'Ethnos und Demos. Die Parlamentswahlen in Lettland 2011'. *Osteuropa* 61(11) (2011), 43–54.

Rudzio, W. *Das politische System der Bundesrepublik Deutschland*. Wiesbaden, 2011.

Rus, V., and N. Toš. *Vrednote Slovencev in Evropejcev: Analiza vrednostnih orientacij Slovencev ob koncu stoletja. Dokument Slovenskega javnega mnenja*. Ljubljana, 2005.

Sandschneider, E. *Stabilität und Transformation politischer Systeme: Stand und Perspektiven politikwissenschaftlicher Transformationsforschung*. Opladen, 1995.

Sarnet, V. 'Economic Transition in Estonia – 1996', in A. Böhm (ed.), *Economic Transition Report 1996* (Ljubljana, 1996), 113–131.

Schmid, K. 'Die Slowakische Republik seit dem 1. Januar 1993: Verfassung und Verfassungsleben', in M. Hofmann and H. Küpper (eds), *Kontinuität und Neubeginn: Staat und Recht in Europa zu Beginn des 21. Jahrhunderts* (Baden-Baden, 2001), 368–83.

Schmidt, A. *Geschichte des Baltikums: Von den alten Göttern bis zur Gegenwart*. Munich, 1992.

Schmidt, H. *Auf dem Weg zur deutschen Einheit. Bilanz und Ausblick*. Reinbek b. Hamburg, 2005.

Schmidt, H. 'Methodenfragen der Privatisierung, dargestellt am Beispiel Estland', in Ludwig-Erhard-Stiftung (ed.), *Soziale Marktwirtschaft als historische Weichenstellung* (Bonn, 1996), 523–57.

Schmidt, T. *Die Außenpolitik der baltischen Staaten im Spannungsfeld zwischen Ost und West*. Opladen, 2003.

Schmidt, T. 'Die lettische Saeima zwischen Kontinuität und Wandel', in S. Kraatz and S.v. Steinsdorff (eds), *Parlamente und Systemtransformation im postsozialistischen Europa* (Opladen, 2002), 221–45.

Schmidt, T. 'Das politische System Lettlands', in W. Ismayr (ed.), *Die politischen Systeme Osteuropas*, 3rd ed. (Wiesbaden, 2010), 123–70.

Schmidt-Schweizer, A. 'Der Kádárismus – das "lange Nachspiel" des ungarischen Volksaufstandes', in R. Kipke (ed.), *Ungarn 1956: Zur Geschichte einer gescheiterten Volkserhebung* (Wiesbaden, 2006), 161–87.

Schmitt, R. *Kleines Handbuch Bulgarien*. Rostock, 2012.

Schmitz, K. 'Wahl- und Parteiensysteme in Osteuropa: Eine Neubewertung anhand des Konzentrationseffekts'. *Zeitschrift für Parlamentsfragen* 37 (2006), 353–76.

Schorlemmer, F. 'Wir haben noch immer eine auseinanderdriftende Gesellschaft', in W. Heitmeyer (ed.), *Deutsch-deutsche Zustände: 20 Jahre nach dem Mauerfall* (Frankfurt a. M., 2009), 311–23.

Schrader, K. *Estland auf dem Weg zur Marktwirtschaft: Eine Zwischenbilanz.* Kiel, 1994.

Schrader, K. 'Integration of the Baltic States with Europe', in L. Orlowski and D. Salvatore (eds), *Trade and Payments in Central and Eastern Europe's Transforming Economies* (London, 1997), 330–45.

Schrader, K., and C.-F. Laaser. 'Die baltischen Staaten auf dem Weg nach Europa: Lehren aus der Süderweiterung der EG', in H. Siebert (ed.), *Kieler Studien*, Vol. 264 (Tübingen, 1994), 88–112.

Schrader, K., and C.-F. Laaser. *Der Transformationsprozess in den baltischen Staaten: Ordnungspolitische Fortschritte und strukturelle Anpassungsprozesse.* Kieler Arbeitspapiere No. 783 (1997).

Schrader, K., and C.F. Laaser. 'Wirtschaft Lettlands', in H. Graf and M. Kerner (eds), *Handbuch Baltikum heute* (Berlin, 1998), 181–210.

Schrader, K., and C.-F. Laaser. 'Wirtschaft Litauens', in H. Graf and M. Kerner (eds), *Handbuch: Baltikum heute* (Berlin, 1998), 151–79.

Schuller, K. 'Gegen Russisch als Staatssprache', *Frankfurter Allgemeine Zeitung*, 19 February 2012.

Schumacher, T. *Transformation und wirtschaftliche Selbstverwaltung: Das Beispiel Estland.* Frankfurt a. M., 1997.

Seliger, B. 'Integration of the Baltic States in the European Union in the Light of the Theory of Institutional Competition'. *Communist Economies and Economic Transformation* 10(1) (1998), 95–109.

Sepp, J. 'Estland – eine ordnungspolitische Erfolgsgeschichte?', in B. Seliger, J. Sepp and R. Wrobel (eds), *Das Konzept der Sozialen Marktwirtschaft und seine Anwendung: Deutschland im internationalen Vergleich* (Frankfurt a. M., 2009), 143–61.

Sepp, J., and R. Wrobel. 'Besonderheiten der Wettbewerbspolitik in einem Transformationsland: Die Entwicklung der Wettbewerbsordnung in Estland als Beispiel'. *Wirtschaft und Wettbewerb* 1 (2000), 26–44.

Sepp, J., and R. Wrobel. 'Das Steuersystem in Estland im Spannungsfeld zwischen Transformationserfordernissen und EU-Harmonisierung', in R. Hasse, K.-E. Schenk and A.W.v. Czege (eds), *Europa zwischen Wettbewerb und Harmonisierung* (Baden-Baden, 2002), 69–75.

Siani-Davies, P. *The Romanian Revolution of December 1989.* Ithaca, 2005.

Šilde, A. 'Die Entwicklung der Republik Lettland', in B. Meissner (ed.), *Die Baltischen Nationen Estland, Lettland, Litauen*, 2nd ed. (Cologne, 1991), 63–74.

Simion, C., A. Gheorghe and I. Comănescu. *Cartea albă a presei III: Probleme economice ale presei.* Bucharest, 2007.

Snyder, T. *The Reconstruction of Nations: Poland, Ukraine, Lithuania, Belarus 1569–1999.* New Haven, CT, 2003.

Sommer, R. *Estlands Weg in die Informationsgesellschaft: ökonomische, soziale, politische und kulturelle Faktoren.* Saarbrücken, 2007.

Sopóci, J. 'Ekonomické záujmové skupiny v slovenskej politike v 90 rokoch'. *Politologický časopis* 2 (2001), 166–76.

Sõrg, M. 'Estonian Strategies in the Reconstruction of Ist Monetary System', in D.E. Fair and R. Raymond (eds), *The Competitiveness of Financial Institutions and Centres in Europe* (Dordrecht, 1994), 171–82.

Sozialwissenschaftliches Forschungszentrum (ed.). *Sozialreport 2008*. Berlin, 2008.

Stan, L., and L. Turcescu. *Religion and Politics in Post-Communist Romania*. Oxford, 2007.

Statistisches Amt der Europäischen Gemeinschaften. 'Europa in Zahlen: Eurostat Jahrbuch 2009'. Luxemburg, 2009.

Steen, A. 'The Baltic Elites after the Challenge of the Regime', in H. Best and U. Becker (eds), *Elites in Transition: Elite Research in Central and Eastern Europe* (Opladen, 1997), 152–171.

Štefančík, R. *Christlich-demokratische Parteien in der Slowakei*. Trnava, 2008.

Steffani, W. 'Parlamentarisch-präsidentielle "Mischsysteme"? Bemerkungen zum Stand der Forschung in der Politikwissenschaft', in O. Luchterhandt (ed.), *Neue Regierungssysteme in Osteuropa und der GUS* (Berlin, 2002), 17–66.

Steffani, W. 'Zur Unterscheidung parlamentarischer und präsidentieller Regierungssysteme'. *Zeitschrift für Parlamentsfragen* 14 (1983), 390–401.

Stegherr, M., and K. Liesem. *Die Medien in Osteuropa: Mediensysteme im Transformationsprozess*. Wiesbaden, 2010.

Steier, S. 'Bildungspolitik und Bildungssystem', in D. Bingen and K. Ruchniewicz (eds), *Länderbericht Polen* (Bonn, 2009), 477–95.

Stein, E. *Česko-Slovensko. Konflikt – roztržka – rozpad*. Prague, 2000.

Steinsdorf, S.v. 'Parlamente: Binnenorganisation im Spannungsfeld von Inklusion und Effizienz', in F. Grotz and F. Müller-Rommel (eds), *Regierungssysteme in Mittel- und Osteuropa* (Wiesbaden, 2011), 172–93.

Stolz, A. 'Die Verwaltungsorganisation im Vergleich', in B. Wieser and A. Stolz (eds), *Vergleichen des Verwaltungsrecht in Ostmitteleuropa* (Vienna, 2004), 159–95.

Šujan, I. 'Hospodár ske a sociálne dosledky èesko-slo venského rozchodu', in K. Vodièka (ed.), *Děle ní Československa: Deset let poté* (Prague, 2003), 119–28.

Šujan, I. 'Wirtschaftliche Folgen der Trennung', in R. Kipke and K. Vodička (eds), *Abschied von der Tschechoslowakei* (Cologne, 1993), 153–62.

Sum, P., and G. Bădescu. 'An Evaluation of Six Forms of Political Participation', in H. Carey (ed.), *Romania since 1989* (Lanham, MD, 2004), 179–94.

Szabó, M. 'Die Zivilgesellschaft in Ungarn: Zwischen EU-Beitritt und globalen Herausforderungen', in J. Dieringer and S. Okruch (eds), *Von der Idee zum Konvent: Eine interdisziplinäre Betrachtung des europäischen Integrationsprozesses* (Budapest, 2004), 81–98.

Szalai, W. 'Sieben Anmerkungen', in C. John and K. Schimmel (eds), *GrenzFall Einheit: Zwischenberichte aus Sachsen* (Leipzig, 2005), 35–41.

Szylko-Skoczny, M. 'Arbeitsmarktlage und Arbeitsmarktpolitik', in D. Bingen and K. Ruchniewicz (eds), *Länderbericht Polen* (Bonn, 2009), 294–308.

Taube, C. *Constitutionalism in Estonia, Latvia and Lithuania: A Study in Comparative Constitutional Law*. Uppsala, 2001.

Tauber, J. 'Litauen', in W. Weidenfeld (ed.), *Den Wandel gestalten: Strategien der Transformation'*, Vol. 2: *Dokumentation der internationalen Recherche* (Gütersloh, 2001), 110–38.

Tauber, J. 'Das politische System Litauens', in W. Ismayr (ed.), *Die politischen Systeme Osteuropas*, 3rd ed. (Wiesbaden, 2010), 171–208.

Thüringischen Ministerium für Wirtschaft (ed.). 'Arbeit und Technologie, Zukunft Ost. Analysen, Trends, Handlungsempfehlungen'. Roland Berger Strategy Consultants, August 2012. Retrieved 8 October 2012 from http://www.thueringen.de/imperia/md/con-tent/tmwta/zukunft_ost.pdf.

Tiemann, G., and D. Jahn. 'Koalitionen in den baltischen Staaten: Lehrstücke für die Bedeutung funktionierender Parteien', in S. Kropp, S.S. Schüttemeyer and R. Sturm (eds), *Koalitionen in West- und Osteuropa* (Opladen, 2002), 271–300.

Toming, K. 'The Price Impact of Adopting the Common Agricultural Policy in Estonia: Estimated versus Actual Effects', Universiti of Tartu/Faculty of Economics and Business Administration Working Paper No. 45/2006.

Toš, N., and K.H. Müller (eds). *Political Faces of Slovenia: Political Orientation and Values at the End of the Century*. Vienna, 2005.

Tuchscheerer, H. *20 Jahre vereinigtes Deutschland: Eine "neue" oder "erweiterte" Bundesrepublik"?* Baden-Baden, 2010.

Tvarůžková, L. 'Jak zachránit Kavčí hory'. *Týden* 16 (2003), 40–44.

Uhlin, A. *Post-Soviet Civil Society: Democratization in Russia and the Baltic States*. London, 2006.

United Nations Development Programme. 'UNDP-Bericht: Únik z pasce závislosti. Rómovia v strednej a východnej Európe'. Bratislava, 2003.

Ursprung, D. 'Machtkampf in Rumänien'. *Osteuropa* 62(9) (2012), 3–14.

Vardys, S.V., and W.A. Slaven. 'Lithuania', in W.R. Iwaskiw (ed.), *Estonia, Latvia and Lithuania: Country Studies* (Washington, 1996), 167–242.

Vásárhelyi, M. 'Angriff auf die Pressefreiheit: Die Medienpolitik der Fidesz-Regierung'. *Osteuropa* 61(12) (2011), 157–66.

Veen, H.-J. *Alte Eliten in jungen Demokratien? Wechsel, Wandel und Kontinuität in Mittel- und Osteuropa*. Cologne/Weimar/Vienna, 2004.

Verebélyi, I. 'A magyar közigazgatás modernizációja', in S. Kurtán, P. Sándor and L. Vass (eds), *Magyarország politikai évkönyve* (Budapest, 1993), 80–86.

Vitsur, E. 'Investment Policy and Development of Foreign Investments', in Estonian Academy of Sciences and Institute of Economics (eds), *Transforming the Estonian Economy* (Tallinn, 1995), 208–25.

Vodička, K. '25 Jahre Systemtransformation in Mittelosteuropa: eine Bilanz', in F. Müntefering (ed.), *Der Aufbau Ost im mittelosteuropäischen Vergleich: Eine Bilanz nach 25 Jahren* (Halle (Saale), 2016), 156–93.

Vodička, K. 'Einmal Verlierer, immer Verlierer? Zur Situation der Roma in der Slowakei'. *Blätter für deutsche und internationale Politik* 48(6) (2003), 724–30.

Vodička, K. 'Koalitionsabsprache: Wir teilen den Staat!', in R. Kipke and K. Vodička (eds), *Abschied von der Tschechoslowake* (Cologne, 1993), 77–106.

Vodička, K. 'Motivationskrise als Auslöser des Systemwechsels in Osteuropa'. *Osteuropa* 46(8) (1996), 808–24.

Vodička, K. 'Na nebezpečné české stezce: Demokracie v Česku'. *Ekonom* 1 (2010), 36f.

Vodička, K. 'Political Systems of the Czech and Slovak Republics: A Comparison of Risks and the Consolidation Process', in G. Mesežnikov and Olga Gyárfášová (eds), *Slovakia: Ten Years of Independence and a Year of Reforms* (Bratislava, 2004), 27–48.

Vodička, K. *Das politische System Tschechiens*. Wiesbaden, 2005.

Vodička, K. 'Das politische System Tschechiens', in W. Ismayr (ed.), *Die politischen Systeme Osteuropas* (Wiesbaden, 2010), 275–315.

Vodička, K. *Politisches System Tschechiens*. Münster, 1996.

Vodička, K. 'Příčiny rozdělení: shrnující analýza po deseti letech', in K. Vodička (ed.), *Děle ní Československa: Deset let poté* (Prague, 2003), 205–64.

Vodička, K. 'Risikofaktoren im Konsolidierungsprozess der Slowakei'. *Europäische Rundschau* 29(4) (2001), 43–52.

Vodička, K. 'Die Roma in der Slowakei: Stolperstein auf dem Weg in die EU?'. *Osteuropa* 51(7) (2001), 832–46.

Vodička, K. 'Wahlen und Transition in der Slowakei', in K. Ziemer (ed.), *Wahlen in postsozialistischen Staaten* (Opladen, 2003), 255–82.

Vodička, K. 'Wir sind moralisch krank geworden: Die Neujahransprache des tschechoslowakischen Staatspräsidenten'. *Osteuropa* 40(4) (1990), 248–53.

Vodička, K., and L. Cabada. *Politický systém České republiky*. Prague, 2011.

Vodička, K., and G. Heydemann. 'Postkommunistischer EU-Raum: Konsolidierungsstand und Perspektiven', in G. Heydemann and K. Vodička (eds), *Vom Ostblock zur EU: Systemtransformationen 1990–2012 im Vergleich* (Göttingen, 2013), 319–80.

Völkl, K. 'Fest verankert oder ohne Halt? Die Unterstützung der Demokratie im vereinigten Deutschland', in O.W. Gabriel, J.W. Falter and H. Rattinger (eds), *Wächst zusammen, was zusammengehört? Stabilität und Wandel politischer Einstellungen im wiedervereinigten Deutschland* (Baden-Baden, 2005), 249–84.

Vollnhals, C (ed.). *Jahre des Umbruchs: Friedliche Revolution in der DDR und Transition in Ostmitteleuropa*. Göttingen, 2011.

Volze, A. 'Zur Devisenverschuldung der DDR: Entstehung, Bewältigung und Folgen', in E. Kuhrt (ed.), *Die Endzeit der DDR-Wirtschaft: Analysen zur Wirtschafts-, Sozial- und Umweltpolitik* (Opladen, 1999), 151–83.

Vorländer, H. (ed.). 'Pathos und Ernüchterung: Über den Zusammenhang von Revolution und demokratischer Neugründung', in H. Vorländer (ed.), *Revolution und demokratische Neugründung* (Dresden, 2011), 15–30.

Vorländer, H. *Revolution und demokratische Neugründung*. Dresden, 2011.

Wasilewski, J. 'Formowanie siê nowej struktury spo³ecznej', in J. Wasilewskiego (ed.), *Współczesne społeczeństwo polskie: Dynamika zmian* (Warsaw, 2006), 47–102.

Weil, F. *Herrschaftsanspruch und soziale Wirklichkeit: Zwei sächsische Betriebe in der DDR während der Honecker-Ära*. Cologne, 2000.

Weßels, B., and A. Wagner. 'Regionale Differenzierung des Wahlverhaltens', in H. Rattinger et al. (eds), *Zwischen Langeweile und Extremen: Die Bundestagswahl 2009, Wahlen in Deutschland*, Vol. 1 (Baden-Baden, 2011), 119–30.

Westerwelle, G. 'Wir werden die Entwicklung in Rumänien nicht ignorieren', *Frankfurter Allgemeine Zeitung*, 7 July 2012.

Widmaier, U., A. Gawrich and U. Becker. *Regierungssysteme Zentral- und Osteuropas: Ein einführendes Lehrbuch*. Opladen, 1999.

Wilkin, J. 'Rozpad i instytucjonalizacja ładu społeczno: ekonomicznego w Polsce: przypadek transformacji postsocjalistycznej', in *Więzi społeczne i przemiany gospodarcze. Polska i inne kraje europejskie: Zbiór esejów na jubileusz profesor Zofii Moreckiej* (Warsaw, 2009), 64–74.

Winkelmann, R. *Politik und Wirtschaft im Baltikum: Stabilisierung von Demokratie und Marktwirtschaft in Estland, Lettland und Litauen*. Saarbrücken, 2007.

Wolff, R. 'Historischer Sieg für Linksbündnis', *Die Tageszeitung*, 18 September 2011.

Wrobel, R. 'Die Bedeutung der Institutionen: Transformation für die EU-Integration der drei baltischen Staaten', in Tallinner Technische Universität and Tartuer Universität (eds), *Aktuaalsed Majanduspoliitika Küsimused Euroopa Liidu Riikides Ja Eesti Vabariigis*, Vol. 2 (Tallinn, 1996), 393–403.

Wrobel, R. 'Culture and Economic Transformation: "Economic Style" in Europe, Russia and China', in M. Jovanovic, L. Dalgon and B. Seliger (eds), *System Transformation in Comparative Perspective: Affinity and Diversity in Institutional, Structural and Cultural Patterns* (Berlin, 2007), 163–85.

Wrobel, R. *Estland und Europa: Die Bedeutung des Systemwettbewerbs für die Evolution und Transformation von Wirtschaftssystemen*. Tartu, 2000.

Wrobel, R. 'Local Administration Reform in Estonia: Alternatives from an Economic Point of View'. *Post-Communist Economies* 15(2) (2003), 277–95.

Wrobel, R. 'Die ökonomische Transformation Estlands: Ein Beispiel endogenen Wandels', in M. Brunn, F. Ettrich et al. (eds), *Transformation und Europäisierung: Eigenarten und (Inter-) Dependenzen von postsozialistischem Wandel und Europäischer Integration* (Münster, 2010), 201–21.

Wrobel, R. 'Die Osterweiterung des europäischen Leviathan: Der Integrationsprozeß des marktwirtschaftlichen Musterknaben Estland in die wohlfahrtsstaatliche EU'. *Liberal – Vierteljahreshefte für Politik und Kultur* 41(4) (1999), 66–70.

Wrobel, R. 'Umstrittene Standortpolitiken in Europa: Estland und Irland im Vergleich', in Tallinner Technische Universität and Tartuer Universität (eds), *Sammelband zur XIII. wirtschaftspolitischen Konferenz* (Tartu, 2005), 346–54.

Zamfir, C. (ed.). *Raport social al ICCV 2010. România: răspunsuri la criză*. Bucharest, 2011.

Zgaga, B. 'Good Evening and Good Night', in M. Drčar-Murko et al. (eds), *Five Minutes of Democracy: The Image of Slovenia after 2004* (Ljubljana, 2004), 213–46.

Ziemer, K. 'Auf dem Weg zum Systemwandel in Polen (II)'. *Osteuropa* 39(11/12) (1989), 957–80.

K. Ziemer, *Das politische System Polens: Eine Einführung* Wiesbaden, 2013.

Ziemer, K. 'Nachbar Polen heute: Bevölkerung, Sozialstruktur, Politik', in W. Keim (ed.), *Vom Erinnern zum Verstehen: Pädagogische Perspektiven deutsch-polnischer Verständigung* (Berlin, 2003), 127–44.

Ziemer, K. 'Wahlen in postsozialistischen Staaten', in K. Ziemer (ed.), *Wahlen in postsozialistischen Staaten* (Opladen, 2003), 9–28.

Ziemer, K., and C.-Y. Matthes. 'Das politische System Polens', in W. Ismayr (ed.), *Die politischen Systeme Osteuropas*, 3rd ed. (Opladen, 2010), 209–73.

Zinsmeister, F. 'Die Finanzierung der deutschen Einheit: Zum Umgang mit den Schuldlasten der Wiedervereinigung'. *Vierteljahreshefte zur Wirtschaftsforschung* 78(2) (2009), 146–60.

Zoll, A., M. Safjan and J. Stêpień. 2009. 'Oœwiadczenie by³ych Prezesów Trybuna³u Konstytucyjnego'. *Gazeta Wyborcza*, 5 February 2009. Retrieved 3 February 2011 from http://wyborcza.pl/1,76842,6237771,Oswiadczenie_bylych_Prezesow_Trybunalu_Konstytucyjnego.html.

INDEX

Studies in Contemporary European History

Editors:

Konrad Jarausch, Lurcy Professor of European Civilization, University of North Carolina, Chapel Hill, and a Director of the Zentrum für Zeithistorische Studien, Potsdam, Germany

Henry Rousso, Senior Research Fellow at the Institut d'histoire du temps présent (Centre national de la recherche scientifique, Paris)

www.ingramcontent.com/pod-product-compliance
Lightning Source LLC
Chambersburg PA
CBHW070900030426
42336CB00014BA/2264